Mathematics
UNLIMITED

HBJ **Harcourt Brace Jovanovich, Inc.**

Holt, Rinehart and Winston, Inc.

Orlando · Austin · San Diego · Chicago · Dallas · Toronto

AUTHORS

Francis "Skip" Fennell
Associate Professor of Education
Western Maryland College
Westminster, Maryland

Robert E. Reys
Professor of Mathematics Education
University of Missouri
Columbia, Missouri

Barbara J. Reys
Assistant Professor of Curriculum
and Instruction
University of Missouri, Columbia, Missouri
Formerly Junior High Mathematics Teacher
Oakland Junior High, Columbia, Missouri

Arnold W. Webb
Senior Research Associate
Research for Better Schools
Philadelphia, Pennsylvania
Formerly Asst. Commissioner of Education
New Jersey State Education Department

Copyright © 1991 by Holt, Rinehart and Winston, Inc.

All rights reserved. No part of this publication may be reproduced or transmitted in any form or by any means, electronic or mechanical, including photocopy, recording, or any information storage and retrieval system, without permission in writing from the publisher.

Requests for permission to make copies of any part of the work should be mailed to: Permissions Department, Holt, Rinehart and Winston, Inc., 8th Floor, Orlando, Florida 32887

Material from earlier editions copyright © 1988, 1987 by Holt, Rinehart and Winston, Inc. All rights reserved.

ILLUSTRATION

Anthony Accardo: pp. 56, 57, 82, 280, 281 • Bob Aiese: pp. 168, 169 • Beth Baum: pp. 250, 254, 255, 331, 332, 333, 343 • Ron Becker: pp. 71, 305 • Robin Brickman: pp. 246-247, 260, 460 • Brad Clark: pp. 14, 108, 130, 131, 418 • Laura Cornell: pp. 22, 23 • Jack Davis: p. 193 • Jack Freas: pp. 44, 45, 200 • Mark Giglio: pp. 166, 167 • Deirdre Newman Griffin: p. 18 • Meryl Henderson: p. 182 • Debora Kaplan: p. 242 • Linda Miyamoto: pp. 4, 5, 90, 100, 101, 113, 132, 133, 134, 210, 220, 221, 328 • Jim Owens: pp. 230, 272, 346, 460 • Rosanne Percivalle: pp. 30, 142, 187, 209, 226 • Tom Powers: pp. 52, 53, 120, 121, 148, 149, 176, 216, 217, 316, 336, 347, 412, 420, 454, 455 • David Reinbold: p. 46 • Beverly Rich: p. 272 • Claudia Sargent: pp. 70, 156, 273, 338, 366, 382, 383, 389, 426 • Joel Snyder: pp. 310, 460 • Krystyna Stasiak: pp. 104, 105 • Jane Sterrett: pp. 258, 259, 440 • Arthur Thompson: pp. 431, 461 • Debbie Tilley: pp. 106, 107, 295 • Vantage Art Inc.: p. 245 • Nina Wallace: pp. 58, 59, 174, 322, 438 • Debora Whitehouse: pp. 89, 124, 125, 138, 188, 206, 207, 254, 255, 325, 384, 398, 446, 447 • Nina Winter: pp. 134, 152, 153, 284, 344 • Paul Yalowitz: pp. 28, 29, 35, 231, 246, 247, 260, 261 • Mark Yankus: pp. 6, 7 • M. O'Reilly: pp. H212, H215, H227. **Chapter Opener Illustrations:** Joe Lapinsky: pp. 1, 41, 79, 119, 165, 199, 239, 279, 313, 353, 397, 437. **Cover Illustration:** Jeannette Adams.

PHOTOGRAPHY

Animals, Animals/Richard Kollar: p. 54; Patti Murray: pp. 136, 137 • AP/World Wide Photos: p. 374 • Art Resource: p. 110 • David Bartruff: p. 404 • Black Star/Andy Levin: p. 378; Steve Northrup: p. 13; Doug Wilson: p. 12 • R. J. Dufour, Rice University, courtesy Hansen Planetarium, Salt Lake City: p. 85 • Earth Scenes/Charles Palek: p. 270 top • Focus West/John Biever: p. 344; Lee Mason: p. 48 • Granger Collection: p. 102 • Michal Heron: pp. 128, 141, 228, 262, 326-327 • HRW Photo/Richard Haynes: pp. 84, 170, 330, 342; William Hubbell: p. 150 • Image Bank/John Banagan: p. 24; A. Broccaccio: p. 372; Louis Castaneda: p. 62; Gary Cralle: p. 9; Arthur d'Arazien: p. 386; Geoffrey Gove: p. 144; D. W. Hamilton: p. 190; Terry Madison: p. 127; David Miser: p. 443; O'Rourke: p. 184 • Lawrence Migdale 1983: p. 76 • Museum of Modern Art (Gift of Robert W. deForest, 1925): p. 154 • Odyssey Productions/Walter Frerck: p. 68 • Omni-Photo Communications, Inc./Ken Karp: pp. 18-19, 20-21, 60-61, 94-95, 96, 146-147, 186, 204, 224-225, 286-287, 358-359, 376-377, 452-453; John Lei: pp. 98, 120-121, 122-123, 138-139, 282-283, 298, 338, 444-445 • Photo Researchers/Russ Kinne: p. 2; Helen Marcus: pp. 290-291; Tom McHugh: p. 372; Gerard Vandystadt: p. 181; Daniel Zirinsky 1981: p. 173 • Rainbow/Linda K. Moore: p. 414; Bill Pierce: p. 102 • Shostal Associates: p. 33 • Sports Illustrated/Neil Leifer: p. 314 • Stock Market/Mark Ferri: p. 222; Kasz Macaig: p. 47; Ted Mahve: p. 378; Louis Portnoy: p. 68; Robert Semenuik: pp. 27, 406; Christopher Springmann: p. 288 • Woodfin Camp & Associates/Craig Aurness: pp. 296-297; Jonathan Blair: p. 86; Jim Brandenburg: p. 16; David Cupp: p. 270 bottom; Dick Durrance: p. 386; Timothy Eagan: p. 215; George Hall: pp. 302, 458; Michal Heron; pp. 32, 172, 212, 236; Roland & Sabrina Michaud: p. 108 • Mike Yamashita: p. 428 • Leo de Wys/E. Johnson: p. 269; Richard Laird: p. 50. Page H207, Steve Satushek/The Image Bank; H208, HBJ Photo/Earl Kogler; H209, HBJ Photo/Earl Kogler; H210, Roy Morsch/The Stock Market; H211, Mary Kate Denny/PhotoEdit; H214, Robert Everts/ Tony Stone Worldwide; H216, Eric Hayman/Tony Stone Worldwide; H218, HBJ Photo/Earl Kogler; H219, John V.A.F. Neal/Photo Researchers; H220, Tony Freeman/PhotoEdit; H221, Maurits Cornelis Escher, DEPTH, 1955/Art Resource; H222, Tony Freeman/PhotoEdit; H224, HBJ Photo/Earl Kogler; H225, HBJ Photo/Earl Kogler; H230, Jeffry W. Myers/The Stock Market.

Printed in the United States of America

ISBN 0-15-351569-4

CONTENTS

FRACTIONS

MEASUREMENT

RATIO, PROPORTION, PERCENT

7 INTEGERS, RATIONALS, REALS

8 EQUATIONS AND INEQUALITIES
One Variable

9 STATISTICS AND PROBABILITY

GEOMETRY

PERIMETER, AREA, VOLUME

EQUATIONS AND INEQUALITIES
Two Variables

STUDENT HANDBOOK

Between the summer solstice and the winter solstice, the days become progressively shorter, and the nights become progressively longer. What would you need to know to determine how much shorter your days will be in a week? in a month? Where would you find the information you need to answer the question?

1 ADDITION AND SUBTRACTION
Whole Numbers and Decimals

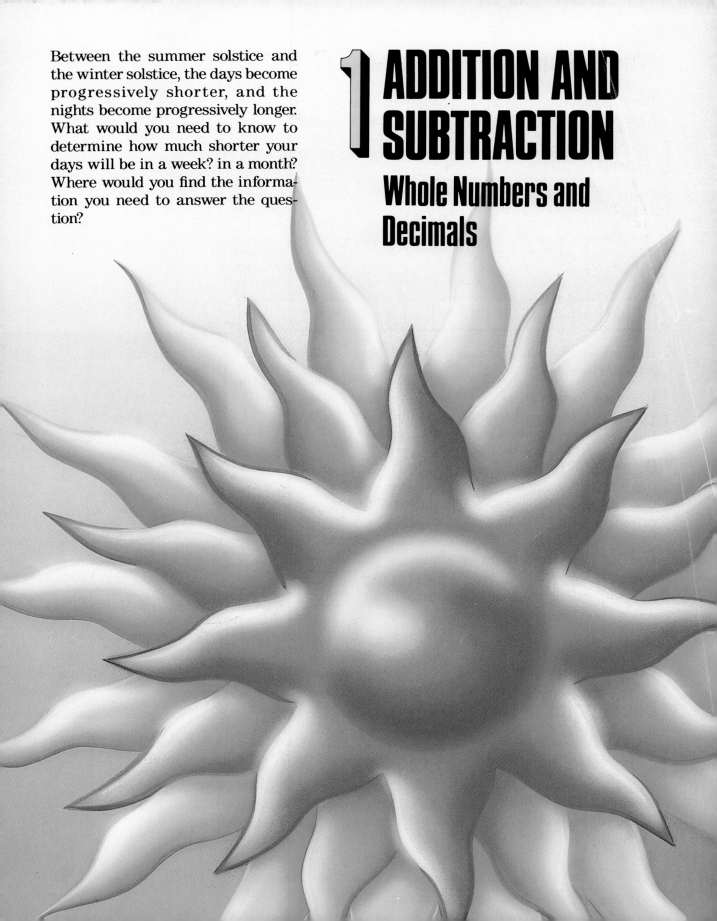

Whole-Number Place Value

A. The distance that light travels per year is 5,878,496,538,000 miles. How do you read this number?

PERIODS	Trillions			Billions			Millions			Thousands			Ones		
	hundred trillions	ten trillions	trillions	hundred billions	ten billions	billions	hundred millions	ten millions	millions	hundred thousands	ten thousands	thousands	hundreds	tens	ones
			5	8	7	8	4	9	6	5	3	8	0	0	0

Numbers have **commas** that separate every 3 digits into **periods**.

Standard form: 5,878,496,538,000
Short word name: 5 trillion, 878 billion, 496 million, 538 thousand

B. The 6 in the number 362,841,095,002,732 is in the ten trillions place. The **value** of the 6 is $6 \times 10,000,000,000,000$; or 60,000,000,000,000; or 60 trillion.

C. The **expanded form** of a number shows its value.
3,060,002,560 =
   3,000,000,000 + 60,000,000 + 2,000 + 500 + 60

Checkpoint   Write the letter of the correct answer.

1. Find the value of the 8 in 735,680,004,132.

   a. 80 thousand
   b. 8 million
   c. 80 million
   d. 80 billion

2. Write the number in standard form for 72 trillion, 900 million, 3.

   a. 72,900,000,003
   b. 72,000,900,000,003
   c. 72,000,000,900,003
   d. 72,000,090,000,003

Write in standard form.

1. 6 million, 200 thousand, 78
2. 300 million, 90 thousand, 800
3. 71 trillion, 8 billion
4. 245 trillion, 9 million, 106
5. 304 billion, 29 thousand, 5
6. 9 billion, 732 million

Write the short word name.

7. 4,360,000
8. 28,000,004
9. 51,000,000,070
10. 80,004,000
11. 913,000,600,000
12. 7,060,000,002,000

Write the place and the value of the underlined digit.

13. 8,613,4<u>9</u>2
14. <u>6</u>3,184,297,351
15. 72,1<u>8</u>4,005
16. 9<u>4</u>9,524,625
17. 6,51<u>9</u>,793,150,603
18. 7,237,<u>7</u>52,342

Write each number in standard form.

19. 80,000,000 + 7,000,000 + 6,000 + 50 + 3

20. 9,000,000,000 + 40,000,000 + 6,000,000 + 2,000 + 80

21. 400,000,000 + 2,000,000 + 700

Write each number in expanded form.

22. 50,063
23. 7,000,420
24. 82,005,032
25. 6,000,705,600

Solve.

26. The average rainfall in the United States is 4 trillion, 300 billion gallons per day. Write this number in standard form.

27. There are about 512,700,000,000 tons of iron ore mined in the world each year. Give the short word name for this number.

CHALLENGE   Patterns, Relations, and Functions

Write the letter of the correct answer.

Which figure comes next in this sequence?

a.  b.   c.

Comparing and Ordering Whole Numbers

A. The Caribbean Sea covers 971,400 square miles.
The Mediterranean Sea covers 969,100 square miles.
Which sea is larger?

To compare two numbers, begin by lining up the digits.
Then compare digits, beginning at the left.

971,400   9 hundred = 9 hundred
               thousand   thousand

969,100   7 ten thousand > 6 ten thousand

So, 971,400 > 969,100; or 969,100 < 971,400.

> means "is greater than."
< means "is less than."

The Caribbean Sea is larger than the Mediterranean Sea.

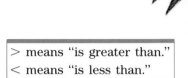

B. Order 6,129; 21,434; 20,989; and 21,344 from the
least to the greatest.

Compare to find the least.	Compare to find the next least.	Compare to find the greatest.
6,129 — 6,129 has no ten thousands. 21,434 20,989 21,344	20,989 < 21,434 20,989 < 21,344	21,434 > 21,344
6,129 is the least.	20,989 is the next greatest.	21,434 is the greatest.

The order from the least to the greatest is 6,129;
20,989; 21,344; 21,434.

Numbers can also be ordered from the greatest to the
least. Order 74,349; 72,989; 7,861; and 74,536 from the
greatest to the least.

Compare to find the greatest.	Compare to find the next greatest.	Compare to find the least.
74,536 > 74,349	74,349 > 72,989	72,989 > 7,861

The order from the greatest to the least is 74,536;
74,349; 72,989; 7,861.

Compare. Write >, <, or = for ●.

1. 65,286 ● 67,286

2. 131,842 ● 113,842

3. 8,505,403 ● 8,505,304

4. 50,456,100 ● 50,465,100

5. 684 million ● 684,000,000

6. 27,684 ● 26,784

7. 312,666 ● 322,666

8. 46,012 ● 46,102

9. 22 million ● 220,000,000

10. 76,433,334 ● 76,343,334

Order the numbers from the least to the greatest.

11. 854; 8,540; 850; 8,545

12. 43,196; 43,169; 43,691; 43,619

13. 5,781; 5,871; 5,718; 5,817

14. 221,894; 212,894; 212,948; 212,849

15. 332; 322; 3,323; 3,233

16. 76,676; 76,766; 77,677; 76,677

Order the numbers from the greatest to the least.

17. 1,623; 163; 1,263; 1,632

18. 934; 9,343; 9,433; 943

19. 6,892; 6,982; 69,829; 698

20. 823,324; 822,334; 84,264; 832,322

21. 465; 4,656; 456; 6,545

22. 1,423; 1,344; 1,432; 14,243

Solve. For Problem 24, use the Infobank.

23. The diameter of Earth at the equator is 7,926 mi. The diameter from pole to pole is 7,899 mi. Which diameter is larger?

24. Use the information on page 473 to solve. List the world's five longest rivers and their lengths, in miles, in order from the longest to the shortest.

FOCUS: REASONING

What is the place-value name of the 6 in the number?

$$236,452,198,000,000,000,000,000$$

sextillions quintillions quadrillions trillions

The value of the 6 is 6 *sextillion*.

Give the place-value name of the underlined digit.

1. 32,760,466,378,452,906

2. 746,921,000,000,000,000,000

Addition and Subtraction

A. Addition is **commutative.** In addition, the *order* of the addends does not change the sum.

$$42 + 830 = 830 + 42$$

For any numbers a and b,
$a + b = b + a$.

Subtraction is **not commutative.** In subtraction, the order of the numbers may change the difference.

$$13 - 6 \overset{?}{=} 6 - 13$$
$$7 \neq 6 - 13$$

> $\neq$ means "is not equal to."

B. Addition is **associative.** In addition, the *grouping* of the addends does not change the sum.

$$94 + (17 + 42) = (94 + 17) + 42$$

For any numbers a, b, and c,
$a + (b + c) = (a + b) + c$.

Subtraction is **not associative.** In subtraction, the grouping of the numbers may change the difference.

$$29 - (14 - 7) \overset{?}{=} (29 - 14) - 7$$
$$29 - 7 \overset{?}{=} 15 - 7$$
$$22 \neq 8$$

C. Zero is the **identity element** for addition. The sum of a number and zero is the number.

$$7 + 0 = 7 \qquad 0 + 16 = 16$$

For any number a,
$a + 0 = a \qquad 0 + a = a$.

The difference when zero is subtracted from a number is the number.

$$67 - 0 = 67$$

For any number a, $a - 0 = a$.

D. When a number is subtracted from itself, the difference is zero.

$$89 - 89 = 0$$

For any number a, $a - a = 0$.

E. Addition and subtraction are **inverse operations.** They undo each other.

$$37 - 12 = 25 \longleftrightarrow 25 + 12 = 37$$

For any numbers a, b, and c,

if $c - b = a$, then $a + b = c$.

Math Reasoning, page H207

Complete.

1. $135 + 26 = 26 + \blacksquare$

2. $4{,}531 - 4{,}531 = \blacksquare$

3. $(8 + 13) + 62 = 8 + (\blacksquare + 62)$

4. $0 + 92 = \blacksquare$

5. $531 - 0 = \blacksquare$

6. $17 - 9 = 9 - \blacksquare$

7. $3{,}723 + 1{,}405 = \blacksquare + 3{,}723$

8. $(9 - 2) - 3 = 9 - (\blacksquare - 3)$

9. $8{,}732 + (18 + 1) = (\blacksquare + 18) + 1$

10. $\blacksquare - 50 = 50 - 35$

11. $7{,}651 - \blacksquare = 0$

12. $(10 - 9) - 1 = \blacksquare - (9 - 1)$

13. $117 + \blacksquare = 117$

14. $65 - \blacksquare = 65$

15. $124 + 282 - \blacksquare = 282$

16. $14 + 31 - 14 = \blacksquare$

17. $78 - 35 = 43$
$43 + \blacksquare = 78$

18. $199 + 26 = 225$
$225 - 199 = \blacksquare$

19. $\blacksquare - 0 = a$

20. $b + a = a + \blacksquare$

21. $c - \blacksquare = 0$

22. $a + (b + c) = (a + \blacksquare) + c$

23. $a + b - a = \blacksquare$

24. $x + 0 = \blacksquare$

CHALLENGE

In one large office, 9 editors are arranged as shown.
Copy the figure and draw only 2 more squares to give
each editor a separate office.

Rounding Whole Numbers

A. The greatest ocean depths are found in long, narrow crevices called *trenches*. The Tonga Trench in the Pacific Ocean reaches a depth of 10,882 meters. Round this number to the nearest thousand meters.

10,882 is between 10,000 and 11,000.
10,882 is closer to 11,000.
So, 10,882 rounds to 11,000.

The Tonga Trench is about 11,000 meters in depth.

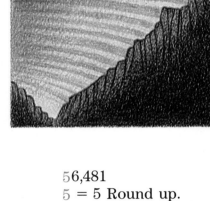

B. You can also round by using the digit to the right of the place to which you are rounding.

Round 365,747; 641,057; and 56,481 to the nearest hundred thousand.

365,747	641,057	56,481
6 > 5 So, round up.	4 < 5 Round down.	5 = 5 Round up.
365,747 $\longrightarrow$ 400,000	641,057 $\longrightarrow$ 600,000	56,481 $\longrightarrow$ 100,000

Round to the nearest ten thousand.

1. 12,482   **2.** 85,555   **3.** 310,942   **4.** 7,037

5. 16,051   **6.** 279,679   **7.** 41,589   **8.** 99,843

Round to the nearest hundred thousand.

9. 327,438   **10.** 5,482,525   **11.** 86,397   **12.** 807,831

13. 987,123   **14.** 196,001   **15.** 7,211,999   ★**16.** 12,889

Round to the nearest million.

17. 6,181,313   **18.** 18,901,010   **19.** 327,039,999

20. 780,410   **21.** 3,822,321   ★**22.** 97,814

PROBLEM SOLVING
Estimation

Sometimes you have to estimate to solve a problem.

Zach and Byron are planning a camping trip. They want to spend 2 nights and 2 days camping. They will decide which park they will go to after they decide how much money they can afford to spend on bus fare. They must make campsite reservations 2 weeks in advance. Here is some information:

- To rent a tent costs from $10 to $15 per night.

- Food will cost from $3 to $5 per day for each.

- By the day the trip begins, Zach will have earned $30 to $40 doing yard work.

- By the day the trip begins, Byron will have earned $25 to $45 from baby-sitting.

- Zach has already saved $5, and Byron has $8.

BUS FARES	
(round trip, per person)	
Grey Forest Park	$8.40
Sumac Point	$9.10
Eagle's Neck Park	$15.55
Ropa Canyon	$23.25

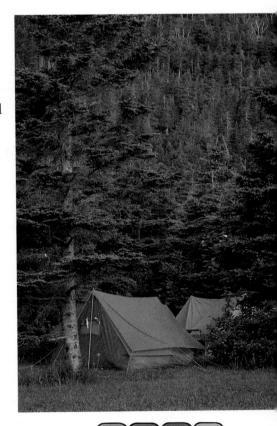

Answer each question to help Zach and Byron make their plans. You may have to go back to the plan and revise the numbers as you work.

1. How much money will Zach and Byron have by the time the trip begins?

2. About how much should they plan to spend to rent a tent?

3. How much should they plan to spend for food?

4. How much money will they have for bus fare?

5. At which park do you think Zach and Byron should make reservations? Explain.

Estimating Sums of Whole Numbers

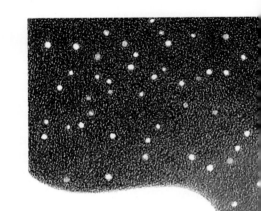

A. Astronomers estimate that 12,242 meteorites fall into the oceans annually. Another 448 meteorites fall on the United States, and 6,300 fall over the landmass of the rest of Earth. About how many meteorites hit Earth annually?

Since the data are not exact, an exact answer is not necessary. Find the sum by using front-end estimation or by rounding.

<table>
<tr><td>

Using front-end estimation

$\left.\begin{array}{r} 12,242 \\ 448 \\ 6,300 \end{array}\right\}$ about 1,000

Add the lead digits.
12 + 6 = 18. Use 18,000.

Adjust the sum.
18,000 + 1,000 = 19,000

Estimate: 19,000

</td><td>

This number is insignificant.

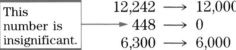

Rounding to the nearest thousand

12,242 $\longrightarrow$ 12,000
448 $\longrightarrow$ 0
6,300 $\longrightarrow$ 6,000

Add the rounded numbers.
12,000 + 0 + 6,000 = 18,000

Estimate: 18,000

</td></tr>
</table>

Both 18,000 and 19,000 are good estimates of the number of meteorites that hit Earth annually.

B. You can also estimate sums of money. Estimate the total cost of the items on the sales receipt.

	Front end	**Rounding**
$8.98	$8.98 $\longrightarrow$ about $1	$8.98 $\longrightarrow$ $9
4.89	4.89 $\Big\}$ about $1	4.89 $\longrightarrow$ 5
0.15	0.15	0.15 $\longrightarrow$ 0
9.49	9.49 $\Big\}$ about $1	9.49 $\longrightarrow$ 9
6.44	6.44	6.44 $\longrightarrow$ 6
0.07	0.07	0.07 $\longrightarrow$ 0

Front end:
Add the lead digits: $27
Adjust: $27 + $3
Estimate: $30

Rounding:
Add: $29
Estimate: $29.00

Both $29 and $30 are reasonable estimates.

Estimate the sum.

1.
```
  4,325
  9,683
  5,085
+ 3,897
```

2.
```
  50,476
  47,295
  77,850
+ 14,948
```

3.
```
 $92.16
  45.27
   1.59
+ 78.62
```

4.
```
 682,345
 950,265
 642,817
+ 17,294
```

5. $179.85 + $49.65 + $87.93

6. 72,895 + 57,623 + 136 + 2,571

7. $4.36 + $5.98 + $6.65 + $0.89 + $0.32 + $7.56

Estimate. Write > or < for ●.

8. 4,536 + 6,274 + 5,327 ● 15,000

9. 6,275 + 2,895 + 9,879 ● 20,000

10. 8,886 + 3,127 + 8,527 ● 19,000

11. 5,187 + 278 + 5,246 ● 10,000

12. 45,265 + 87,867 + 96,845 ● 250,000

13. 89,247 + 7,534 + 71,650 ● 160,000

14. 562,754 + 695,375 + 87,295 + 43,876 ● 1,500,000

15. 4,417,569 + 9,743,417 + 7,195,265 + 3,499,999 ● 21,400,000

16. 1,123,754 + 4,256,295 + 172,546 + 1,075,286 ● 7,000,000

Choose the letter of the best estimate for the sum.

17. 361,287 + 4,635 + 136,830 + 99,375

18. 173,285 + 126,501 + 194,126 + 11,950

19. 370,920 + 7,875 + 341,623 + 9,221

20. 92,250 + 121,476 + 192,565

21. 121,292 + 326,275 + 317,754 + 43,329

a. 400,000

b. 500,000

c. 600,000

d. 700,000

e. 800,000

Solve.

22. The diameter of planet Saturn is approximately equal to those of Earth, Mars, Uranus, and Neptune combined. Use the data in the table to estimate the diameter of Saturn.

23. Use the data in the table at the right to write and solve a word problem.

Planet	Average Diameter (km)
Mercury	4,880
Venus	12,100
Earth	12,756
Mars	6,785
Jupiter	142,800
Saturn	
Uranus	51,800
Neptune	49,500
Pluto	3,000 ?

Estimating Differences of Whole Numbers

One estimate indicates that 2,857,000 megawatts of water power are available in the world. Of this supply of potential energy, only about 249,000 megawatts are used. About how many megawatts of water power are not used?

Estimate 2,857,000 − 249,000.

Using front-end estimation

2,857,000
− 249,000

> Look at the smaller number to find the number of lead digits.

Subtract the lead digits. 28 − 2 = 26. Use 2,600,000.

Adjust the difference. 57,000 > 49,000. So, the
  difference is greater than 2,600,000. Adjust up.
Estimate: More than 2,600,000, or 2,600,000$^+$.

Rounding to the largest place

2,857,000 $\longrightarrow$ 3,000,000
− 249,000 $\longrightarrow$ 0

Subtract the rounded numbers.
  3,000,000 − 0 = 3,000,000
Estimate: 3,000,000

Rounding to the nearest hundred thousand

2,857,000 $\longrightarrow$ 2,900,000
− 249,000 $\longrightarrow$ 200,000

Subtract the rounded numbers.
  2,900,000 − 200,000 = 2,700,000
Estimate: 2,700,000

An estimate of 3,000,000 megawatts is not reasonable, in this case, because there are less than 2,857,000 megawatts available. Either 2,600,000$^+$ or 2,700,000 megawatts is a good estimate for the amount of potential water power that is not used.

Another example:
Estimate $5,726.35 − $2,834.29.

Front-end
  $5,726.35
− 2,834.29

Subtract lead digits. $3,000
Adjust: Since $726.35 < $834.29,
  adjust down.
Estimate: $3,000$^-$

Rounding to the nearest thousand
  $5,726.35 $\longrightarrow$ $6,000
− 2,834.29 $\longrightarrow$ 3,000

Subtract: $3,000
Estimate: $3,000

Both $3,000$^-$ and $3,000 are reasonable estimates.

Estimate the difference.

1. 6,823
   − 4,454

2. 53,916
   − 28,476

3. 269,706
   − 178,295

4. 8,929,545
   − 5,876,398

5. 4,728
   − 934

6. 26,799
   − 6,893

7. 387,562
   − 96,753

8. 7,645,213
   − 843,524

9. $532.23 − $75.00

10. $6,549.92 − $448.39

11. 92,835,493 − 4,679,821

12. 239,586,722 − 89,685,736

Estimate. Write > or < for ●.

13. 4,023 − 1,289 ● 4,000

14. 9,765 − 3,856 ● 7,000

15. 11,825 − 7,763 ● 3,000

16. 28,378 − 9,243 ● 18,000

17. 73,757 − 28,655 ● 50,000

18. 247,123 − 105,322 ● 100,000

19. 596,338 − 298,317 ● 400,000

20. 746,879 − 39,798 ● 710,000

21. $829.95 − $35.68 ● $780.00

22. $3,411.27 − $825.39 ● $2,700.00

23. North America uses about 76,000 megawatts of water power. This continent has 313,000 megawatts of water power available. Estimate the amount of potential water power that is not used.

24. The Grand Coulee Dam in Washington State has a rated capacity of 6,430 megawatts. Its ultimate capacity is over 10,000 megawatts. About how much additional water power should the Grand Coulee Dam eventually generate?

FOCUS: REASONING

A plumber, a teacher, and a pilot live in three adjoining houses. The brick house is just to the left of the log cabin. The plumber recently moved from the house on the left. The pilot lives next door to the teacher. The teacher lives in the stucco house. Who lives in the log cabin? (HINT: Draw a picture or act it out.)

For additional activities, see *Connecting Math Ideas*, page 469.

Adding and Subtracting Whole Numbers

A. Marjorie climbed a mountain in four days. The table lists how far she climbed each day. How far did she climb in all?

Add 3,268 + 2,849 + 674 + 1,934.

Day 1	3,268 ft
Day 2	2,849 ft
Day 3	674 ft
Day 4	1,934 ft

Estimate the sum before you compute.

$$
\begin{array}{rcl}
3,268 & \longrightarrow & 3,000 \\
2,849 & \longrightarrow & 3,000 \\
674 & \longrightarrow & 1,000 \\
+\,1,934 & \longrightarrow & +\,2,000 \\
\hline
 & & 9,000
\end{array}
$$

Add. Regroup if necessary.

$$
\begin{array}{r}
\overset{2\ \ 22}{} \\
3,268 \\
2,849 \\
674 \\
+\,1,934 \\
\hline
8,725
\end{array}
$$

The answer is reasonable.

Marjorie climbed 8,725 ft.

B. You can use addition to check your answer when you subtract.

Find the difference between 15,006 and 8,898.

$$
\begin{array}{r}
15,006 \\
-\ \ 8,898 \\
\hline
6,108
\end{array}
$$

Check: 6,108 + 8,898 = 15,006

Find $4,209.10 − $2,110.08.

$$
\begin{array}{r}
\$4,209.10 \\
-\ \ 2,110.08 \\
\hline
\$2,099.02
\end{array}
$$

Check: $2,099.02 + $2,110.08 = $4,209.10

Checkpoint   Write the letter of the correct answer.

Add or subtract.

1.   53,689
    + 1,492

a. 52,197
b. 55,181
c. 54,071
d. 54,181

2. $494,932.74
    + 16,779.87

a. $478,152.87
b. $500,602.51
c. $511,712.61
d. $400,601.51

3. $845.42
    − 468.95

a. $376.47
b. $423.53
c. $487.57
d. $1,314.37

4.   1,400,603
    − 847,986

a. 2,248,589
b. 552,617
c. 647,383
d. 663,727

Add.

1. 3,482
+ 1,516

2. 58,142
+ 17,964

3. 384,068
+ 615,846

4. $31,348.76
+ 84,596.72

5. 679,483
+ 92,998

6. 8,167
398
+ 1,462

7. 58,672
1,495
+ 37,152

8. $ 6.74
19.87
+ 356.72

9. 34,645
8,997
743
+ 36,482

10. 748,963
742
68,149
+ 436,157

Subtract.

11. 8,846
− 3,415

12. 45,632
− 14,836

13. 446,312
− 24,101

14. $300.07
− 59.19

15. 8,000,007
− 612,349

Add or subtract.

16. 6,789,123 + 4,713,893

17. $6,740.00 − $367.43

18. $643,498 − $41,739

19. 137,982 + 7,821 + 83 + 999

20. 31,462 − 1,847 + 298

21. 77,334 + 1,298 − 53,186

22. 382 billion
+ 179 billion

23. 752 billion
− 359 billion

24. 936 trillion
− 354 trillion

Find the missing digits.

★25. ■■,■■■■
− 26,784
64,871

★26. 69■,984
− ■■6,■■■
486,548

★27. 631,427
843,968
+ ■■■,■■■
2,389,563

★28. 5,632
■,■■■
+ 7,194
18,793

Solve.

29. One of China's highest mountains, Muztagh Ata, is 7,546 m high. The highest mountain in Pakistan, K–2, is 1,204 m higher. How high is K–2?

30. Look up the altitudes of five other mountains. Draw a table that displays them in order from the greatest elevation to the least elevation.

31. The highest mountain in the world is Mount Everest, at 29,028 ft. The highest mountain in the United States is Mount McKinley, at 20,320 ft. How much higher is Mount Everest?

★32. Mr. Martin bought a camp stove for $39.75, a lantern for $19.92, and a cookware set for $22.84. If the sales tax was $5.78 and he gave the cashier a 100-dollar bill, how much change did he receive?

PROBLEM SOLVING
4-Step Plan

The key to solving any problem is to proceed in a logical and organized manner. The following 4-step plan will help you to do this. Be sure to complete each step before going on to the next one.

How many acres larger is Yosemite National Park than Sequoia National Park?

OLDEST NATIONAL PARKS

Park	Year	Area (acres)
Yellowstone	1872	2,219,785
Kings Canyon	1890	461,901
Sequoia	1890	402,482
Yosemite	1890	761,170

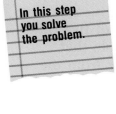

In this step you get ready to solve the problem.

1. QUESTIONS
Read the problem. Do you understand the *question* being asked? Do you know the vocabulary? Do you have all the information you need? To help you understand the question restate it in your own words.

Find the difference between the areas of the two parks.

In this step you plan your solution.

2. TOOLS
Choose the *tools* you will need to solve the problem. Tools are operations like addition and multiplication, strategies like estimating and finding patterns, and resources like graphs and reference books.

Find the needed information in the table. Use subtraction to find the difference.

In this step you solve the problem.

3. SOLUTIONS
Find the *solution* by applying the tools you have chosen. Use the table to find the areas of Sequoia and Yosemite national parks. Then subtract the areas to find the difference.

```
  761,170←Yosemite
− 402,482←Sequoia
  358,688
```
Yosemite is 358,688 acres larger.

In this step you check your answer.

4. CHECKS
Check your solution. Does it answer the question? Is it reasonable? Can you solve the problem in a different way to double-check your solution?

Use addition to check.
```
  358,688
+ 402,482
  761,170
```

Solve each of the following by following the 4-step plan.

- State the problem in your own words.
- Tell which tool you will use to solve the problem.
- Solve the problem.
- Check your solution.

1. The newest national park, Great Basin in Nevada, was established in 1986. How much older than Great Basin is Yellowstone National Park?

2. What is the combined area of the four oldest national parks?

3. The lowest point in Yosemite has an elevation of 610 meters above sea level. How high above that point is the summit of Yosemite's highest mountain, at 3,960 meters above sea level?

4. What is larger, Yellowstone National Park or the combined areas of Kings Canyon, Sequoia, and Yosemite National Parks?

5. The National Park Service manages 68,234,091 acres of federal land. The U.S. Forest Service manages 189,407,924 acres of land. How much larger is the Forest Service's acreage than that of the Park Service?

6. Yosemite Falls, the tallest waterfall in the United States, is in Yosemite National Park. It falls in three stages of 1,430 feet, 320 feet, and 675 feet. Find the height of the falls from top to bottom.

7. The world's tallest sequoia tree is in Sequoia National Park. It is 275 feet tall. The world's tallest Douglas fir tree in Olympic National Park is 221 feet tall. About how much taller is the tallest sequoia tree than the tallest Douglas fir tree?

8. Mount Whitney in Sequoia National Park is the highest point in the continental United States. It is 14,494 feet above sea level. Just 60 miles away in Death Valley is the lowest point, 282 feet below sea level. How high above the lowest point is the summit of Mount Whitney?

9. Acadia National Park was established 44 years after Yellowstone National Park. Redwood National Park was established 52 years after Acadia. In what year was Redwood National Park established?

10. The largest national park, Wrangell–St. Elias, has an area 6,725,215 acres larger than the area of Yellowstone National Park. By how much does its area exceed that of Yosemite National Park?

Decimal Place Value

Scientists use **atomic weight** to describe the weight of elements. The atomic weight of aluminum is 26.9815. How do you read this number? The number 26.9815 is a decimal. The place-value chart can be extended to decimals.

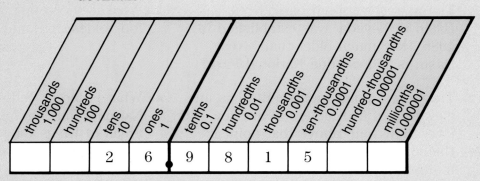

thousands 1,000	hundreds 100	tens 10	ones 1	tenths 0.1	hundredths 0.01	thousandths 0.001	ten-thousandths 0.0001	hundred-thousandths 0.00001	millionths 0.000001
		2	6	9	8	1	5		

Read: twenty-six **and** nine thousand eight hundred fifteen ten-thousandths. This is the word name for the number 26.9815.

The 4 in 2.103462 appears in the ten-thousandths place. The value of the 4 is 4 ten-thousandths, or 0.0004.

You can write zeros to the right of any decimal without affecting the value.

$$5.75 = 5.750 = 5.7500 \text{ and } 25 = 25.0 = 25.00$$

The expanded form of 42.097 is $40 + 2 + 0.09 + 0.007$.

Al

Aluminum is used in airplane construction because it is lightweight.

Checkpoint Write the letter of the correct answer.

1. Choose the decimal for sixteen ten-thousandths.

   a. 0.00016   **b.** 0.0016
   c. 0.016   **d.** 16,000

2. What is the value of 8 in 1.038793?

   a. thousandths   **b.** 8 thousandths
   c. 8 hundredths   **d.** 8

Fe

Iron occurs in the body in the red blood cells.

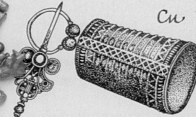

Cu

Because of its beautiful color, Copper is used in ornaments & art work.

Write the decimal.

1. six hundred fifty-five thousandths

2. one and nine hundred-thousandths

3. thirty-five millionths

4. two hundred seven thousandths

5. three thousand eight hundred sixty-one hundred-thousandths

Write the word name.

6. 8.543 **7.** 1.000009 **8.** 0.0493 **9.** 1.00163 **10.** 7.03541

Write the value of the underlined digit.

11. 6.05<u>3</u> **12.** 7.135<u>6</u>2 **13.** 0.15976<u>3</u> **14.** 3.4352<u>17</u>

Write the decimal.

15. 0.04 + 0.005 + 0.0006

16. 4 + 0.3 + 0.05

17. 0.8 + 0.009

18. 7 + 0.3 + 0.04 + 0.00007

19. 30 + 5 + 0.05 + 0.007 + 0.00006 + 0.000003

Solve.

20. The atomic weight of argon is 39 + 0.9 + 0.04 + 0.008. Write this as a decimal.

21. Tellurium was discovered in 1782. Nobelium was discovered in 1957. How many years elapsed between these two discoveries?

22. Find the atomic weight in decimals for four other elements, and write the word name for each weight.

★23. The atomic weight of aluminum is 26.9815. Write this in expanded form using the word name.

MIDCHAPTER REVIEW

Write the place and the value of the underlined digit.

1. 75<u>2</u>,321 **2.** 61,356,9<u>0</u>8 **3.** 0.001<u>4</u> **4.** 17.9<u>3</u>28

Add or subtract.

5.	3,154	**6.**	19,547	**7.**	$342.09	**8.**	796,942	**9.**	4,628,049
	+ 4,521		+ 60,428		+ 65.34		+ 81,064		+ 7,247,361

10.	6,236	**11.**	76,581	**12.**	$565.03	**13.**	854,926	**14.**	6,477,005
	− 4,024		− 24,377		− 248.27		− 78,399		− 6,249,183

Comparing and Ordering Decimals

A. The **specific gravity** of a mineral is found by comparing the weight of a mineral with the weight of an equal volume of water. The specific gravity of calcite is 2.71. The specific gravity of graphite is 2.3. Which mineral has the greater specific gravity?

To compare decimals, align the decimal points. Compare as you would with whole numbers.

2.71   2 = 2   So, 2.71 > 2.3.
2.3   7 > 3

Calcite has the greater specific gravity.

B. Order these decimals from the greatest to the least: 3.04, 3.1, 3.153, 3.0438.

To order decimals, line up the decimal points and compare digits from the left to the right. Write zeros if needed to line up the decimal points.

Compare to find the greatest.

3.0400
3.1000 ⎤
3.1530 ⎦ 3.1530 > 3.100
3.0438

3.153 is the greatest.

Compare to find the next greatest.

3.1000 > 3.0400

3.1000 > 3.0438

3.100 is the next greatest.

Compare to find the least.

3.0438 > 3.0400

The order from the greatest to the least is: 3.153, 3.1, 3.0438, 3.04.

C. Order these decimals from the least to the greatest: 5.110, 5.001, 5.10, 5.01.

Compare to find the least.

5.001 < 5.010

Compare to find the next greatest.

5.01 < 5.10

Compare to find the greatest.

5.100 < 5.110

The order from the least to the greatest is: 5.001, 5.01, 5.10, 5.110.

Compare. Write >, <, or = for ●.

1. 0.43 ● 0.5
2. 3.014 ● 3.1
3. 3.004 ● 3.04
4. 0.6321 ● 0.6312
5. 9.1506 ● 9.15060
6. 0.304 ● 0.3040
7. 0.13642 ● 0.136
8. 3.21 ● 3.2047
9. 6.047 ● 6.0470
10. 1.137624 ● 1.137642
11. 0.678 ● 0.678000
12. 0.531 ● 0.541362

Order the decimals from the greatest to the least.

13. 0.156, 0.1036, 0.019, 0.091
14. 9.006, 9.0008, 9.0043, 9.0062
15. 0.41283, 0.4168, 0.0431, 0.04
16. 6.39, 6.0342, 6.37, 6.03842
17. 0.074, 0.0704, 0.7044, 0.0074
18. 22.01, 202.1, 22.10, 221.0

Order the decimals from the least to the greatest.

19. 4.0362, 4.3182, 4.03
20. 0.148, 0.0148, 0.1483
21. 0.8, 0.81362, 0.8163
22. 3.144263, 3.15, 3.14436, 3.1582
23. 7.813, 7.8131, 7.1831, 7.0831
24. 0.732, 0.731, 0.7031, 0.7321

Solve. For Problem 26, use the Infobank.

25. Each year, Australia produces 0.168 million tons of lead ore. Mexico produces 0.162 million tons. Which country produces more lead ore?

26. Use the information on page 473 to solve. Order the four minerals from the one with the least specific gravity to the one with the greatest.

27. The melting point of antimony is 630.74°C, the melting point of germanium is 937.4°C, and the melting point of iodine is 113.5°C. Which mineral has the lowest melting point and which has the highest?

ANOTHER LOOK

Round to the nearest hundred.

1. 671
2. 308
3. 767
4. 941
5. 483
6. 650

Round to the nearest million.

7. 6,217,904
8. 27,415,198
9. 54,521,091
10. 45,500,554

Rounding Decimals

A. You can use a number line to help you round a decimal.

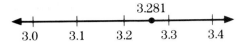

3.281 is between 3.2 and 3.3.
3.281 is nearer to 3.3.

So, rounded to the nearest tenth, 3.281 is 3.3.

B. To round decimals, look at the digit to the right of the rounding place. If the digit is 5 or more, round up. If the digit is less than 5, round down.

Round 57.9129 to the nearest hundredth.
   57.9129   2 < 5   So, round down to 57.91.

Rounded to the nearest hundredth, 57.9129 is 57.91.

C. Round $8.479 to the nearest cent.

Rounding to the nearest cent is the same as rounding to the nearest hundredth.

$8.479 rounded to the nearest cent is $8.48.
$8.479 rounded to the nearest ten cents is $8.50.

Checkpoint Write the letter of the correct answer.

1. Round 3.2345 to the nearest thousandth.

a. 3.23   **b.** 3.2   **c.** 3.234   **d.** 3.235

2. Round $0.39832 to the nearest cent.

a. $0.30   **b.** $0.39   **c.** $0.40   **d.** $0.41

3. Round 0.00834 to the nearest ten-thousandth.

a. 0.008   **b.** 0.01   **c.** 0.0084   **d.** 0.0083

Round to the nearest whole number.

1. 0.478   **2.** 136.8   **3.** 4.5455   **4.** 0.864

Round to the nearest tenth or to the nearest 10 cents.

5. 7.145   **6.** $0.5692   **7.** 8.3512   **8.** $9.46052

Round to the nearest hundredth or to the nearest cent.

9. $4.285   **10.** 0.01562   **11.** 6.8995   **12.** $13.899

Round to the nearest thousandth.

13. 0.00562   **14.** 0.41899   **15.** 4.27459   **16.** 0.78105   **17.** 2.35363

Round to the nearest ten-thousandth.

18. 1.44883   **19.** 0.96455   **20.** 6.83114   **21.** 6.04593   **22.** 72.998333

Round to the nearest hundred-thousandth.

23. 0.007359   **24.** 42.614212   **25.** 0.593004   **26.** 0.000941

Solve.

27. The measurement used for water depth in Norway is called a **farn.** Converted to feet, this is 6.176 ft. Round this number to the nearest hundredth.

28. The **vadem** is the unit used to measure water depth in the Netherlands. Converted to feet, this is 5.905 ft. Round this number to the nearest hundredth.

29. The highest waterfall in the world is Angel Falls in Venezuela, at 3,212 ft. The highest waterfall in the United States is Ribbon Falls, at 1,612 ft. How much higher is Angel Falls than Ribbon Falls?

NUMBER SENSE

0.01	0.5027
0.4537	0.49
0.02	0.113
0.976	0.9537
	0.9

When estimating with decimals, the important digits are right after the decimal point. The other digits are for precision.

Each number in the box is between 0 and 1. Find the three decimals

1. closest to 1.   **2.** closest to 0.5.   **3.** closest to 0.

PROBLEM SOLVING
Using Outside Sources, Including the Infobank

Sometimes the information you need to solve a problem is not given in the problem itself. You can often go to books, magazines, newspapers, Infobanks, or other data sources to find the information you need.

> At a restaurant, Dr. Carter can choose peas or broccoli as a side dish. If each serving is 1 cup, which vegetable will provide her with more protein?

You could answer this question if you knew how much protein was contained in 1 cup of each vegetable. Here are the steps you should take to find the information you need.

1. Find a source that might have the information you need. To answer this question, you might use an almanac, an encyclopedia, or a book about health and nutrition.

2. To find the page you need, look in the table of contents or in the index.

3. If the source does not have the information, try another source.

To answer the question, you must know how much protein a cup of each vegetable contains. Look at the Infobank on page 473 to find the information you need.

When you have the information, answer the question.

There are 8.6 grams of protein in a cup of peas.
There are 4.8 grams of protein in a cup of broccoli.
3.8 more grams in 1 cup of peas

$8.6 > 4.8$

Dr. Carter will receive more grams of protein if she orders peas.

Would you need a reference source to answer each question? Write *yes* or *no*.

1. In a hospital kitchen, the cook prepares two 1-cup servings of corn and three 1-cup servings of okra. What is the total amount of carbohydrates contained in these servings?

2. Dana has 1 cup of celery and 1 cup of peas. Peas contain 8.6 grams of protein per cup, and celery contains 1.2 grams. How much protein does Dana have?

Solve each problem. Use the Infobank on pages 473–478 if you need additional information.

3. Earl is visiting Australia. He rented a car and drove from Sydney to Dubbo and then to Orange. How many kilometers did he drive?

4. The Nile River is the longest river in the world. The Yangtze is 578 miles shorter. How long is the Yangtze River?

5. The Gateway Arch in St. Louis is the tallest monument built in the United States. How much shorter is it than the tallest office building with mast in the United States?

6. Eleni buys one pound of fiber rush. She needs 135 feet for a basket she plans to weave and 85 feet for the lid. Will she have enough fiber rush?

7. Which mineral has the greatest specific gravity: magnesite, olivine, graphite, or barite?

8. Wilt Chamberlain scored 2,649 points in 1966. How many more points did he score in 1962?

9. The city of Geneva was originally settled by soldiers from the Roman Empire. How many years passed between the founding of Rome and the founding of Geneva?

10. Ferdinand's minimum daily requirement of protein is 40 grams. His intake so far today has been 10 grams at breakfast and 14 grams at lunch. If he has a serving of Heidi's Hearty Chicken Noodle Soup for dinner, will he meet his minimum requirement?

11. Nina made a special salad for her friends. The salad consisted of broccoli, celery, cauliflower and green beans. Compare and order the vegetables, from the least to the greatest, by the amount of protein.

12. Dave drove from Coolgardie to Port Augusta in 2 days. Mike drove from Nullarbor to Dubbo in 2 days. Who drove the most kilometers in 2 days? How many more kilometers did he drive?

Estimating Sums and Differences of Decimals

A. On Friday, it rained 2.6 inches in Yennemsville. On Saturday, it rained 2.4 inches, and on Sunday, it rained 1.7 inches. On Monday only 0.29 inches of rain fell. Did it rain more than the record of 6 inches in four days in Yennemsville?

You can answer the question without using exact computation. Estimate $2.6 + 2.4 + 1.7 + 0.29$.

Using front-end estimation

Add the whole numbers.
$$2 + 2 + 1 + 0 = 5$$

Adjust the sum.
$$\underbrace{0.6 + 0.4}_{1} + \underbrace{0.7 + 0.29}_{\text{about } 1}$$
$$5 + 1 + 1 = 7$$

Estimate: 7
$$2.6 + 2.4 + 1.7 + 0.29 > 6$$

Rounding to the nearest whole number

Add: $2.6 + 2.4 + 1.7 + 0.29$
$$3 + 2 + 2 + 0 = 7$$

Yes, it rained more than the record of 6 inches in a four-day period.

B. Estimate $3.2195 - 2.7208$.

Using front-end estimation

Subtract the whole numbers.
$$3 - 2 = 1$$

Adjust the difference.
$0.2195 < 0.7208$. Adjust down.

Estimate: 1^-

Rounding to the nearest whole number

Subtract: $3 - 3 = 0$ ← You need a more exact estimate.

Rounding to the nearest tenth
$$3.2 - 2.7 = 0.5$$

Estimate: 0.5

Other examples:
Estimate $\$14.95 + \$6.53$.

Front end
Add the whole numbers. $\$14 + \$6 = \$20$
Adjust: $\$20 + \$1.50$
Estimate: $\$21.50$

Rounding
Add: $\$15 + \$7 = \$22$, or
$\$15.00 + \$6.50 = \$21.50$
Estimate: $\$22.00$ or $\$21.50$

Estimate $\$95.60 - \$45.75$.
Front end $9 - 4 = 5 \longrightarrow \$50$. Since $\$0.60 < \$0.75$, adjust down. Estimate: $\$50.00^-$
Rounding $\$96 - \$46 = \$50$, or $\$100 - \$50 = \$50$. Estimate: $\$50.00$

Estimate the sum.

1.
```
  4.17
  3.82
+ 1.49
```

2.
```
  15.27
  2.352
+ 1.3296
```

3.
```
  0.527
  0.075
  0.38
+ 2.9
```

4.
```
  485.79
    3.25
    4.98
+   2.175
```

5. $5.98 + $0.25 + $0.35 + $0.49

6. 29.5 + 10.36 + 12.217

Estimate the difference.

7.
```
  $56.27
-  43.35
```

8.
```
  $46.95
-  12.78
```

9.
```
  485.2
-  13.54
```

10.
```
  7.892
- 4.7
```

11. 0.3652 − 0.091286

12. 9.74 − 2.195

13. 12.0534 − 1.17

Estimate. Write > or < for ●.

14. 0.0271 + 0.9 + 0.15 ● 1

15. 0.0594 + 0.00087 ● 0.1

16. 4.87 + 4.96 + 3.25 ● 14

17. 38.8 + 9.887 + 9.789 ● 57

18. $24.95 + $19.85 ● $46.00

19. $7.98 + $0.88 + $0.75 ● $9.00

20. 5.27 − 1.19 ● 3

21. 8.327 − 5.64 ● 3

22. 1.475 − 0.39 ● 1

23. 0.815 − 0.0527 ● 0.5

24. 0.09 − 0.0856 ● 0.01

25. $30.65 − $14.89 ● $25.00

Estimate to solve.

26. On Tuesday, barometric pressure in Yennemsville measured 29.35 in. On Wednesday, it soared to 30.23 in. Was the change in barometric pressure greater than 1 in.?

27. In Yennemsville, normal precipitation in the month of December is 5.7 inches. In January, precipitation drops to 3.4 inches. In February, 3.2 inches of rain fall. Normal precipitation for those months is 14.4 inches in New Orleans, Louisiana. Is there more or less precipitation in Yennemsville?

Adding Decimals

The average monthly snowfall in White Falls for December, January, and February is listed in the chart at the right. What is the total snowfall for these three months?

To add decimals, line up the decimal points, add as for whole numbers, and place the decimal point in the sum.

Month	Average snowfall
December	7.35 cm
January	10.31 cm
February	5.48 cm

Estimate the sum before you compute.

$$
\begin{array}{rcl}
7.35 & \longrightarrow & 7 \\
10.31 & \longrightarrow & 10 \\
+\ 5.48 & \longrightarrow & +\ 5 \\
\hline
& & 22
\end{array}
$$

Add. Regroup if necessary.

$$
\begin{array}{r}
\overset{1\ 1\ \ \ 1}{\ 7.35} \\
10.31 \\
+\ \ \ 5.48 \\
\hline
23.14
\end{array}
$$

The total snowfall for these three months is 23.14 cm.

The answer is reasonably close to the estimate.

Other examples:

Add 13 + 1.643 + 0.09 + 3.1006.

Write zeros in the remaining places to line up decimal places.

$$
\begin{array}{r}
13.0000 \\
1.6430 \\
0.0900 \\
+\ \ 3.1006 \\
\hline
17.8336
\end{array}
$$

Write zeros as needed to line up the decimal places.

Add $14.29 + $3.17.

$$
\begin{array}{r}
\$14.29 \\
+\ \ \ 3.17 \\
\hline
\$17.46
\end{array}
$$

Checkpoint Write the letter of the correct answer.

Add.

1. 0.092 + 2.314 + 3.185

a. 5.591　　**b.** 6.419　　**c.** 14.699　　**d.** 5591

2. 0.48 + 1.9 + 0.005 + 2

a. 0.74　　**b.** 01.585　　**c.** 4.385　　**d.** 4385

3. 13.6 + 0.08 + 6 + 0.1945

a. 14.4745　　**b.** 19.8745　　**c.** 20.5945　　**d.** 198745

Math Reasoning, page H208

Add.

1.   0.62
  + 0.27

2.   4.59
  + 3.34

3.   65.721
 + 28.248

4.   307.924
 + 738.018

5. $18,951.36
 + 55,008.29

6.   6.43
  + 8.912

7.   38.924
  + 6.08

8.   74.21
 + 808.4627

9.   7,412.6
 +   99.439

10. $ 890.08
 + 4,267.33

11.   0.361
   6.452
 + 0.009

12.   35.84
  77.6
 + 142.096

13.   4.5236
  87
 + 3.6115

14.   3.426
  9.211
  0.904
 + 0.270

15.   96.824
  3.57
  66.9
 + 458.023

16.   11,740
 +   692.35

17. $ 32.45
  719.80
 +   6.34

18. $3,430.88
  800.91
  56.03
 + 4,620.74

19.   0.0054
  0.02
  0.6977
 + 44.36

20. 46,512.3
  8.4
  4,280
 + 27,095.9

21. 67 + 754.8 + 122.094

22. $768.40 + $7.11 + $0.68 + $12.47

23. $42.50 + $9,737 + $64.27

24. 82,926 + 54.85 + 36.7

25. 0.0239 + 12.3047 + 8.4009

26. $31.40 + $0.08 + $779.66 + $11.54

Solve.

27. In Perdale, there was a four-day snowstorm. The following daily snow accumulations resulted: 13.25 cm, 14.8 cm, 11.64 cm, and 9.74 cm. How much snow accumulated?

28. The lowest barometer reading for one day was 756.41 mm. The highest reading for the same day was 2.29 mm more. What was the highest reading for the day?

29. A hailstone measures 5.34 cm in diameter. Another one measures 3.28 cm in diameter. Round these figures to the nearest centimeter.

30. Look in your local newspaper for precipitation figures, and find the total precipitation for one week.

ANOTHER LOOK

Write the decimal that has the greatest value.

1. 4.15, 4.296, 4.612

2. 16.81, 16.9, 16.777

3. 843.04, 840.43, 843.039

4. 0.3027, 0.0336, 0.3035

Subtracting Decimals

Astronomers use a unit of measure called an **astronomical unit (AU)** to describe the distance of a planet from the sun. The chart lists the distances from the sun to some planets. How much farther away from the sun is Venus than Mercury?

Planet	Distance from Sun (Astronomical units)
Mercury	0.387
Venus	0.723
Mars	1.523
Uranus	19.247
Pluto	39.641

To subtract decimals, line up the decimal points, subtract as for whole numbers, and place the decimal point in the difference. Check by adding.

$$
\begin{array}{r}
\scriptstyle 11 \\
\scriptstyle 6\ \cancel{1}\ 13 \\
0.7\,2\,3 \\
-\ 0.3\,8\,7 \\
\hline
0.3\,3\,6
\end{array}
$$

Add to check.

$$
\begin{array}{r}
0.336 \\
+\ 0.387 \\
\hline
0.723
\end{array}
$$

Venus is 0.336 astronomical units farther away.

Other examples:

Subtract 7.34 − 3.1986.

$$
\begin{array}{r}
\scriptstyle 13\ 9 \\
\scriptstyle 2\ 3\ \cancel{10}\,10 \\
7.3\,4\,\cancel{0}\,\cancel{0} \\
-\ 3.1\,9\,8\,6 \\
\hline
4.1\,4\,1\,4
\end{array}
$$

Write zeros as needed.

Check by estimating.

$$
\begin{array}{r@{}l}
7.34 & \longrightarrow\quad 7 \\
-\ 3.1986 & \longrightarrow\ -\ 3 \\
\hline
& \qquad\ 4
\end{array}
$$

Subtract $53.84 − $31.78.

$$
\begin{array}{r}
\$53.84 \\
-\ \ 31.78 \\
\hline
\$22.06
\end{array}
$$

Checkpoint Write the letter of the correct answer.

Subtract.

1. 0.863 − 0.065   **a.** 0.808   **b.** 798   **c.** 0.928   **d.** 0.798

2. 5.039 − 0.002432   **a.** 5.037568   **b.** 4.7962   **c.** 5.036568   **d.** 5.041432

3. 16 − 3.482   **a.** 12.518   **b.** 13.482   **c.** 13.518   **d.** 12.628

Subtract.

1. 57.7
 − 16.2

2. 84.32
 − 21.28

3. 643.49
 − 128.64

4. 0.842
 − 0.638

5. 7.4291
 − 3.7461

6. 0.476
 − 0.32

7. 0.9611
 − 0.472

8. 0.3074
 − 0.024

9. 0.53
 − 0.498

10. 0.8004
 − 0.239

11. 41.53
 − 33.4

12. $437.92
 − 8.26

13. $7,196
 − 320.62

14. 18.548
 − 9.4726

15. 3,410.065
 − 98.47

16. $486.54 − $329.80

17. 6,840 − 329.781

18. 270.006 − 41.293

19. 671 − 456.082

20. 0.294 − 0.2507

21. $816 − $747.28

22. 100.849 − 3.4082

23. 1.001826 − 0.000099

Solve.

24. Mercury is the closest planet to the sun, and Pluto is the most distant. How much farther away is Pluto? Use the chart on the previous page.

25. The density of Saturn is 0.619. The density of Jupiter is 0.631 more than Saturn. What is the density of Jupiter?

26. *Eccentricity* defines the shape of the orbit of a planet. The eccentricity of Mars is 0.093379, and the eccentricity of Venus is 0.006787. What is the difference between their eccentricities?

★27. Use the chart on the previous page to solve. Which planet is closer to Venus: Mercury or Mars? How much closer?

NUMBER SENSE

The decimal point in each number is missing. Insert the decimal point to make the number reasonable.

1. Gerry gets $475 per hour for mowing lawns.

2. The deposit is $10 on each soda bottle.

3. It took 1112 gallons of fuel to fill the car's fuel tank.

4. Carlo weighed 1236 pounds on his 13th birthday.

PROBLEM SOLVING
Using a Graph

A double-bar graph makes it easy to compare two sets of information that are related to each other.

Use the double-bar graph below to answer this question: Which city has the greatest range in precipitation between February and August?

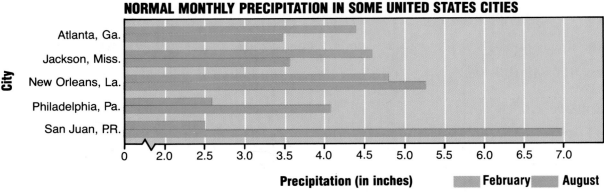

NORMAL MONTHLY PRECIPITATION IN SOME UNITED STATES CITIES

City: Atlanta, Ga. / Jackson, Miss. / New Orleans, La. / Philadelphia, Pa. / San Juan, P.R.

Precipitation (in inches): 0, 2.0, 2.5, 3.0, 3.5, 4.0, 4.5, 5.0, 5.5, 6.0, 6.5, 7.0

■ February ■ August

- The title tells you that this double-bar graph compares the amount of precipitation for February and August in some United States cities.

- The vertical axis is the line at the left. The horizontal axis is the line at the bottom. The scale along the horizontal axis shows you the amounts of precipitation in inches. The label along the vertical axis shows you the names of the cities.

- The legend tells you that the aqua bar represents the month of February and the orange bar represents the month of August.

  By comparing the two bars for each city, you can see that San Juan, Puerto Rico, has the greatest range in precipitation (2.5 inches and 7.0 inches).

Use the double-bar graph on page 32 to answer each question. Write the letter of the correct answer.

1. Which city has the greatest amount of precipitation in February?

   a. Jackson
   b. New Orleans
   c. San Juan

2. Which city has a range in precipitation of 1.5 inches?

   a. Atlanta
   b. New Orleans
   c. Philadelphia

Solve if possible.

3. Which cities are drier in August than in February?

4. Which city is the driest during the month of February?

5. Which city has the smallest range in precipitation between February and August?

6. Suppose that, for reasons of health, you needed to live in a city that has dry summers. Which two cities would probably provide the best conditions?

7. Which two cities are closest to each other in the amount of precipitation that falls in February and August?

8. Which cities are wetter in August than in February?

9. Which two cities have a range in precipitation of about 1 inch?

10. What is the normal amount of precipitation in Atlanta during August?

11. Which city has the greatest total amount of precipitation for February and August combined?

★12. How much of the precipitation in February in Philadelphia falls as snow?

CALCULATOR

When you work with decimals on your calculator, be sure to estimate your answer first. It is easy to press the wrong key or to press an extra 0.

Add: 90.2305 + 35.1902 = ■.

Your estimate should be about 125. If your computed answer is not close to the estimate, work the problem again. The correct answer is 125.4207.

Sometimes it is difficult to compute with very large numbers. Enter this number on your calculator: 872.910289. Does the number appear as you entered it? Most calculators display only eight digits.

Add: 872.910289 + 310.190004 = ■.

To do a problem like this, you should break up both numbers into two or more parts and add the parts separately. Then add the answers without the calculator.

```
   872.910289
+  310.190004
```
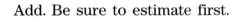
      1.100293 ⟵ Add the decimal parts.
  1182   ⟵ Add the whole number parts.
1,183.100293 ⟵ Find the sum.

Add. Be sure to estimate first.

1. 473.131262 + 120.970201	**2.** 445.597211 + 604.300113	**3.** 878.751081 + 389.512446	**4.** 29.6177137 + 10.6121598
5. 417,339,978 + 176,108,415	**6.** 600,036,275 + 293,002,004	**7.** 771,441,651 + 13,992,013	**8.** 896,458,231 + 724,827,001
9. 741,986,754 528,459,878 + 287,219,326	**10.** 845,796,782 147,265,821 + 96,487,099	**11.** 9,437,821,891 328,946,721 + 79,480,429	**12.** 2,712,894,875 3,643,754,921 + 6,789,163,587

GROUP PROJECT

The Inn on the Mountain

The problem: You have a 22-year-old cousin who works in a tourist shop at the foot of a beautiful mountain. She sells paintings of the mountain to visitors. She tells you that her dream is to own and operate a small inn called Hikers' Hut, which is perched on the top of the mountain. She wants to serve those hikers who are hearty enough to arrive there. She says it will take her a year to earn enough money to buy the inn. In response to your questions, she gives you the information provided below. Consider this information, and determine whether her estimate is correct. If it isn't, find out when she will be able to buy Hikers' Hut.

Key Facts

- Hikers' Hut costs $27,550.

- She is paid $23.50 for each painting that she sells.

- She sells an average of 5 paintings each day.

- The tourist shop is open from Monday to Friday.

- Each month that she works at the shop, she spends $75 for rent, $175 for food, and $50 for other expenses.

- She works on her family's farm for 2 months of the year.

CHAPTER TEST

Write each number using short word names and in expanded form. (pages 2–3 and 18–19)

1. 621,472

2. 7,946,000,310

3. 40,000,000,309,436

4. 0.124

5. 4.500092

6. 91.003906

Write each number in standard form. (pages 2–3 and 18–19)

7. 36 trillion, 519 million, 137

8. 374 trillion, 9 billion, 7 thousand

9. 500,000,000 + 50,000,000 + 8,000,000 + 700 + 3

10. 10,000,000,000 + 400,000,000 + 30,000 + 2,000 + 40

11. seven hundred fourteen thousand twenty-six millionths

12. 0.4 + 0.03 + 0.007 + 0.00008

13. 20 + 9 + 0.6 + 0.0008 + 0.00004 + 0.000005

Write the value of the underlined digit. (pages 2–3 and 18–19)

14. 204,3<u>1</u>3,940,600

15. 4.90372<u>4</u>

Compare. Use >, <, or = for ●. (pages 4–5 and 20–21)

16. 9,581,243 ● 9,581,423

17. $461,210.93 ● $461,201.96

18. 428.0694 ● 428.049

19. 0.06238 ● 0.062381

Order from the greatest to the least. (pages 4–5 and 20–21)

20. 903,582; 930,582; 903,852

21. 7.4921; 4.9217; 7.44902; 4.9172

Order from the least to the greatest. (pages 4–5 and 20–21)

22. 89,465; 88,465; 89,456; 89,564

23. $2,174.05; $2,175.40; $2,157.54

Round to the nearest hundred million. (page 8)

24. 2,874,207,430,608.5

25. 459,968,004,897

Round to the nearest ten-thousandth. (pages 22–23)

26. 0.87655

27. 1.000643

Round to the nearest ten cents. (pages 22–23)

28. $523.62

29. $1,434.96

Estimate the sum or the difference. (pages 10–13 and 26–27)

30. 2,428,784 + 432 + 572,678

31. 672,087 − 547,491

32. 5.26 + 3.81 + 19.56

33. 6.93 − 4.32

Add or subtract. (pages 14–15 and 28–31)

34. $5,678.32 + $403.82

35. 204.07 − 5.072

36. 49 + 872.3 + 86,870.04 − 0.861

37. 642,811 + 7,410,000 + 3.42 − 11.1

Use the double-bar graph to solve. (pages 32–33)

38. Would you expect 1982 energy production to be greater than or less than 65 quadrillion Btu?

39. What trend can you see in United States energy imports?

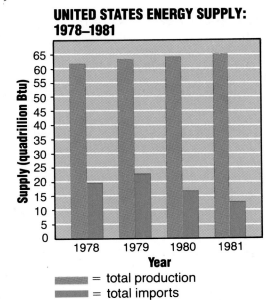

UNITED STATES ENERGY SUPPLY: 1978–1981

BONUS

Use the double-bar graph to solve.

In which year was the difference between production and import of energy the least? the greatest? Estimate the difference for each of these years.

RETEACHING

To add or subtract decimals, line up the decimal points vertically. Then add or subtract each column as you would for whole numbers. Place the decimal point in the answer directly under the decimal points in the numbers being combined.

Add 0.06 + 1.235 + 46 + 0.078.

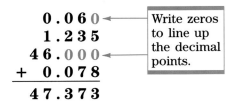

```
  0.060
  1.235
 46.000
+ 0.078
--------
 47.373
```
Write zeros to line up the decimal points.

Subtract $20 − $6.38.

```
$20.00
− 6.38
-------
$13.62
```
Write zeros.

Perform the indicated operation.

1.
```
  325.04
  182.76
  225.35
+ 490.27
```

2.
```
  8.3502
 10
  1.253
+ 6.4796
```

3.
```
 7.0542
 0.87
 8.543
+ 1
```

4.
```
 263.12
  13.05
   8.6573
+ 69
```

5. 0.47 + 0.1786

6. $0.24 + $0.87

7. 0.014 + 16 + 13.082

8. 0.63 + 1.574 + 0.9738

9. 43.2 + 0.136 + 6

10. 1.007 + 0.08 + 10.074 + 7

11. 231 + 0.8711 + 2.327 + 22.43

12. 0.008 + 0.1 + 100 + 14 + 1.047

13.
```
  0.4684
− 0.1679
```

14.
```
  0.6492
− 0.4975
```

15.
```
$175.27
− 93.49
```

16.
```
 4.3
− 0.372
```

17.
```
5,986.2
−  49.379
```

18.
```
$473
−   9.88
```

19.
```
6,342.98
−    6.399
```

20.
```
0.368
− 0.0867
```

21. 0.16 − 0.07

22. $16 − $1.49

23. 3.73 − 1.965

24. 8 − 1.742

25. 21 − 0.409

26. 151 − 0.909

27.
```
  965.06
    1.327
   14
    0.2
+ 103.51
```

28.
```
692.04
−  0.334
```

29.
```
1,000.04
    9.072
   64
    0.76
+   5.001
```

30.
```
4,679.13
−  62.0197
```

ENRICHMENT

Ancient Number Systems

Egyptian							
	1	10	100	1,000	10,000	100,000	1,000,000

The Egyptian number system is called *additive* because the value of a number is found by adding together the values of the symbols for that number.

= 21,308

The Babylonian number system was based on the number 60 instead of the number 10. Because the Babylonians had only two symbols, place value is also important. A "10" symbol in the first (ones) place has a value of 10, but in the second (sixties) place, the same symbol has a value of 10 sixties, or 600.

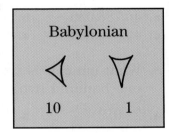

Babylonian

10   1

Third place	Second place	First place

11 thirty-six hundreds   22 sixties   33 ones
$11 \times 3,600$ + 22×60 + 33×1 = 40,953

Roman	I	V	X	L	C	D	M
	1	5	10	50	100	500	1,000

The Roman number system is both additive and subtractive. If a symbol has a value greater than or equal to the value of the symbol to its right, then add. If the symbol has a lesser value, then subtract it from the symbol to its right.

MCMLXXXIV = 1,984

Write each number in Egyptian, Babylonian, and Roman numerals.
For additional activities, see *Connecting Math Ideas,* page 469.

1. 14   **2.** 683   **3.** 4,342

CUMULATIVE REVIEW

Write the letter of the correct answer.

1. What number is 432 trillion, 682?

   a. 432,006,082
   b. 432,682,000
   c. 432,000,000,000,682
   d. not given

2. Round 40,785,924 to the nearest ten thousand.

   a. 40,786,000   b. 40,790,000
   c. 40,800,000   d. not given

3. What number is twenty-eight and one hundred two thousandths?

   a. 28.012   b. 28.102
   c. 28,120   d. not given

4. Estimate 9,129 + 25,681 + 34,827.

   a. 60,000   b. 70,000
   c. 80,000   d. 100,000

5. 48,627,061 − 957,399

   a. 47,669,662   b. 48,679,672
   c. 48,779,772   d. not given

6. What number is fifty-two millionths?

   a. 0.0052   b. 0.00052
   c. 0.000052   d. not given

7. Round $84,976.47 to the nearest dollar.

   a. $84,976   b. $84,976.50
   c. $84,977   d. not given

8. Estimate 111.57 − 0.653.

   a. 100^- b. 112^+
   c. 110   d. 100

9. What number is five trillion, four billion, seven?

   a. 5,004,000,007
   b. 5,000,400,000,007
   c. 5,400,000,000,007
   d. not given

10. 15 − 9.9009

    a. 5.0991   b. 5.1091
    c. 6.1001   d. not given

G. COMPANY CAR SALES

Model	This year	Last year
Streak	43,331	50,504
Wave	53,642	39,721
Boreas	51,724	49,837

11. Use the table to find the total number of cars sold this year.

    a. 147,687   b. 147,697
    c. 148,697   d. not given

12. Use the table to estimate how many more Streaks were sold than Waves last year.

    a. 10,000   b. 11,000
    c. 12,000   d. not given

If you could choose the vacation of your dreams, where would you go? You have one week in which to travel on your dream vacation. Decide where you want to go and what you want to do on your trip. Plan and write a budget for the week.

2 MULTIPLICATION AND DIVISION
Whole Numbers and Decimals

Multiplication and Division

A. Multiplication is **commutative**. The *order* of the factors does not change the product.

$5 \times 7 = 7 \times 5$
For any numbers a and b,
$a \times b = b \times a$.

B. Multiplication is **associative**. The *grouping* of the factors does not change the product.

$(6 \times 3) \times 2 = 6 \times (3 \times 2)$
For any numbers a, b, and c,
$(a \times b) \times c = a \times (b \times c)$.

C. Multiplication is **distributive** over addition. To multiply a sum by a number, you can multiply each addend by the number and then add the products.

$3 \times (5 + 4) = (3 \times 5) + (3 \times 4)$
For any numbers a, b, and c,
$a \times (b + c) = (a \times b) + (a \times c)$.

D. Here are some important facts about 0 and 1.

The product of a number and 1 is the number. For multiplication, 1 is the **identity element.**

$9 \times 1 = 9 \qquad 1 \times 16 = 16$
For any number a,
$a \times 1 = a$ and $1 \times a = a$.

The product of a number and 0 is 0.

$8 \times 0 = 0 \qquad 0 \times 17 = 0$
For any number a,
$a \times 0 = 0$ and $0 \times a = 0$.

If a number other than 0 is divided by itself, the quotient is 1.

$28 \div 28 = 1$
For any number a, if $a \neq 0$, $a \div a = 1$.

If a number is divided by 1, the quotient is that number.

$7 \div 1 = 7$
For any number a, $a \div 1 = a$.

If 0 is divided by any number other than 0, the quotient is 0.

$0 \div 5 = 0 \qquad 0 \div 29 = 0$
For any number a, if $a \neq 0$, $0 \div a = 0$.

You cannot divide by 0. The quotient is undefined.

$8 \div 0$ is undefined because no number n makes $n \times 0 = 8$ true.

E. Multiplication and division are **inverse** operations. They undo each other.

$24 \times 2 = 48 \qquad 56 \div 7 = 8$
$48 \div 2 = 24 \qquad 8 \times 7 = 56$

Name the property shown.

1. $37 \times 43 = 43 \times 37$

2. $(7 \times 9) \times 2 = 7 \times (9 \times 2)$

3. $59 \times 1 = 59$

4. $15 \times (3 + 7) = 15 \times 3 + 15 \times 7$

5. $4 \times (12 \times 11) = (4 \times 12) \times 11$

6. $72 \times 83 = 83 \times 72$

Find n.

7. $0 \times 9 = n$

8. $8 \div 8 = n$

9. $843 \div 1 = n$

10. $6 \times (2 + 8) = 6 \times 2 + 6 \times n$

11. $246 \times 0 = n$

12. $3,142 \times 1 = n$

13. $75 \times n = 75$

14. $93 \div n = 1$

15. $45 \times n = 0$

16. $72 \times 94 = 94 \times n$

17. $14 \div 1 = n$

18. $9 \times (7 + 2) = n \times 7 + 9 \times 2$

19. $(21 \times 2) \times 9 = n \times (2 \times 9)$

20. $143 \times 79 = 79 \times n$

21. $184 \div 2 = 92$
$92 \times n = 184$

22. $18 \times n = 36$
$36 \div 2 = 18$

Use the properties to compute.

23. $6 \times (12 + 13)$

24. $(52 \times 7) + (52 \times 3)$

25. $(8 \times 1) \times 3$

26. $\frac{1}{2} \times (16 + 24)$

Solve.

27. Does $24 \div 8 = 8 \div 24$?

Is division commutative?
Explain.

★28. Does $(48 \div 24) \div 6 = 48 \div (24 \div 6)$?

Is division associative?
Explain.

★29. Does $(12 + 9) \div 3 = (12 \div 3) + (9 \div 3)$?

Is it true that for any numbers a, b, and c,
$(a + b) \div c = (a \div c) + (b \div c)$?

★30. Does $5 \times (10 - 1) = (5 \times 10) - (5 \times 1)$?

Is it true that for any numbers a, b, and c,
$a \times (b - c) = (a \times b) - (a \times c)$?

Multiplying and Dividing by Multiples of 10

A. Powers of 10 are numbers such as 10; 100; and 1,000.

Look at this pattern.

$$10 \times 47 = 470$$
$$100 \times 47 = 4,700$$
$$1,000 \times 47 = 47,000$$

Look at these examples.

$$2 \times 30 = 60 \qquad\qquad 40 \times 5 = 200$$
$$20 \times 30 = 600 \qquad\qquad 40 \times 50 = 2,000$$
$$200 \times 30 = 6,000 \qquad\qquad 40 \times 500 = 20,000$$
$$2,000 \times 30 = 60,000 \qquad\qquad 40 \times 5,000 = 200,000$$

Multiply the two numbers without the zeros. Then write as many zeros as there are in the two factors.

B. To divide by a power of 10, you can change to an easier problem. Use patterns to help you.

$$50 \div 10 = 5 \qquad 300 \div 100 = 3 \qquad 7,000 \div 1,000 = 7$$
$$470 \div 10 = 47 \qquad 2,900 \div 100 = 29 \qquad 80,000 \div 1,000 = 80$$
$$6,000 \div 10 = 600 \qquad 64,000 \div 100 = 640 \qquad 120,000 \div 1,000 = 120$$

Other examples:

$$60 \div 30 = 2 \qquad\qquad \text{Think: } 6 \div 3 = 2.$$
$$24,000 \div 800 = 30 \qquad\qquad \text{Think: } 240 \div 8 = 30.$$
$$35,000 \div 5,000 = 7 \qquad\qquad \text{Think: } 35 \div 5 = 7.$$
$$\$200,000 \div 4,000 = \$50 \qquad\qquad \text{Think: } 200 \div 4 = 50.$$

To simplify a division problem, you can remove the same number of zeros from the dividend and the divisor.

Checkpoint Write the letter of the correct answer.

Multiply or divide.

1. 38×100 **a.** 380   **b.** 3,800   **c.** 38,000   **d.** 380,000

2. $6,400 \div 100$ **a.** 64   **b.** 640   **c.** 64,000   **d.** 640,000

3. $3,000 \times 70$ **a.** 43   **b.** 10,000   **c.** 210,000   **d.** 2,100,000

Find the product.

1. 8×10
2. 13×10
3. 10×870
4. $4{,}120 \times 10$

5. 100×5
6. $100 \times \$20$
7. 760×100
8. $1{,}430 \times 100$

9. $9 \times 1{,}000$
10. $1{,}000 \times 25$
11. $508 \times 1{,}000$
12. $1{,}000 \times \$3{,}300$

13. 6×60
14. 300×80
15. $7{,}000 \times \$50$
16. $600 \times 9{,}000$

Find the quotient.

17. $10\overline{)90}$
18. $10\overline{)\$600}$
19. $10\overline{)2{,}000}$
20. $10\overline{)10{,}100}$

21. $4{,}000 \div 100$
22. $8{,}500 \div 100$
23. $\$13{,}300 \div 100$
24. $27{,}000 \div 100$

25. $\dfrac{\$34{,}000}{1{,}000}$
26. $\dfrac{77{,}000}{1{,}000}$
27. $\dfrac{245{,}000}{1{,}000}$
28. $\dfrac{407{,}000}{1{,}000}$

29. $400 \div 20$
30. $16{,}000 \div 400$
31. $\$90{,}000 \div 3{,}000$
32. $640{,}000 \div 8{,}000$

Solve.

33. Arthur rents out his fishing boat for $50 per day. If he rented it out 20 days last summer, how much money did he earn?

34. Amy water-skied for a total of 20 hours. If she skied for the same number of hours on each of 10 days, for how many hours did she ski each day?

35. Plan a vacation day for yourself, and schedule the amount of time for each activity. If you were to follow the same schedule for 20 days, how much time would you spend on each activity?

36. A corporate plane is flying at an average speed of 120 mph. At that rate, how far would it fly in 1 min? If it did not need refueling, how far could it fly in 10 h?

ANOTHER LOOK

Add or subtract.

1. $3.9 + 2.2$
2. $0.43 + 2.07$
3. $0.08 + 1.12$
4. $6.39 + 3.61$

5. $6.2 - 1.5$
6. $8.27 + 4.9$
7. $4.2 + 0.39$
8. $5.06 - 4.4$

9. $0.694 + 5.72$
10. $0.902 - 0.41$
11. $9.1 + 0.944$
12. $1.083 - 0.397$

Estimating Products and Quotients of Whole Numbers

A. The Martin family plans a 28-day camping trip along New York State's Seaway Trail. They budget about $75.00 a day for their trip. About how much money do they plan to spend?

The amount of money they will spend will vary somewhat from day to day. So it is reasonable to estimate the product.

Round each factor to its largest place.   Multiply.
$28 \times \$75 \longrightarrow 30 \times \$80$ $30 \times \$80 = \$2,400$

The Martins plan to spend about $2,400. Since both factors were rounded up, this is an overestimate. The estimated product is $\$2,400^-$.

Other examples:

$\$523.85 \longrightarrow$	$\$500$	Both factors
$\times \quad 32 \longrightarrow$	$\times \quad 30$	were rounded down.
	$\$15,000^+$	

$4,353 \longrightarrow$	$4,000$	One factor
$\times \quad 897 \longrightarrow$	$\times \quad 900$	is rounded up, and one factor
	$3,600,000$	is rounded down.

B. You can also adjust when you estimate quotients.
Estimate $25,850 \div 15$.
Decide on the number of digits in the quotient.

Think: $15\overline{)25}$. Write 1.   Write zeros for the other digits.

$$\overset{1\;---}{15\overline{)25,850}}$$ $15\overline{)25,850} \longrightarrow 1,000$

Because $15 \times 1,000$ is 15,000, the estimate is an underestimate. Adjust by writing it as $1,000^+$.

C. Sometimes it is easier to divide with numbers that are close to the divisor and the dividend. Look for numbers that divide with a remainder of 0. These are called **compatible numbers.**

Estimate $\$47.91 \div 23$.
Think: $\$46 \div 23 = \$2$ or $\$40 \div 20 = \$2$

$\$47.91 \div 23$ is about $2.

Estimate the product.

1. 6×49 **2.** 8×74 **3.** $7 \times \$13.26$ **4.** $5 \times 3{,}697$

5. 32×84 **6.** 56×326 **7.** $48 \times \$3.23$ **8.** $683 \times \$8.71$

9. $876 \times 5{,}432$ **10.** $2{,}463 \times 6{,}879$ **11.** $6{,}345 \times \$18.57$ **12.** $7{,}689 \times 8{,}342$

Estimate. Write $>$ or $<$ for ●.

13. $6{,}289 \times 72$ ● $420{,}000$ **14.** 38×491 ● $12{,}000$

15. $30 \times \$49.75$ ● $\$1{,}500$ **16.** $63 \times 4{,}856$ ● $250{,}000$

17. $283 \times 46{,}328$ ● $8{,}000{,}000$ **18.** $6{,}985 \times 9{,}498$ ● $54{,}000{,}000$

Estimate the quotient.

19. $63\overline{)37{,}867}$ **20.** $58\overline{)46{,}789}$ **21.** $32\overline{)568{,}345}$ **22.** $49\overline{)\$285.73}$

23. $284\overline{)34{,}556}$ **24.** $793\overline{)94{,}587}$ **25.** $967\overline{)456{,}983}$ **26.** $653\overline{)\$482.65}$

27. $8{,}452\overline{)234{,}673}$ **28.** $5{,}793\overline{)3{,}876{,}452}$ **29.** $3{,}456\overline{)165{,}679}$ **30.** $4{,}683\overline{)\$3{,}432.80}$

Solve.

31. As part of their trip, the Martins camp at the nation's oldest state park, Niagara Reservation. They see Niagara Falls at night and learn that the amount of water flowing over the falls is about 350,000 gallons per second. About how many gallons is that in 2 minutes?

32. Mrs. Martin's friends have given her money to buy them T-shirts that say, "I Didn't Go Over the Falls in a Barrel, But I Had a Barrel of Fun." She buys 11 shirts that cost a total of $129.75. About how much does each shirt cost?

PROBLEM SOLVING
Identifying Extra/Needed Information

> The *Tour de France* bicycle race covers about
> 2,500 miles. More than 100 cyclists compete
> annually. The Tour of Somerville in the United
> States covers 50 miles. In 1976, a group of bikers
> led 10,000 other bikers along the trail. How many
> bikers were there in each leader's group?

A problem may not contain enough information for
you to solve it. Sometimes you can supply the
information you need. You may also find problems that
contain extra information. You have to focus on only
the information you need. Follow these steps.

1. Study the question.

How many bikers were there in each leader's
group?

2. List the facts. Cross out the facts that won't
help you.

a. The *Tour de France* is 2,500 miles long.
b. The Tour of Somerville is 50 miles long.
c. More than 100 cyclists compete annually in the
Tour de France.
d. A total of 10,000 bikers were led in the Tour of
Somerville in 1976.
e. Some bikers led groups of other bikers.
Cross out *a, b,* and *c.*

3. List the facts you need that were not stated in
the problem.

the number of leaders

4. Study the facts you have. If you have all the
information you need, or if you know where to
find it, solve the problem. If not, write *There is
not enough information.*

There is not enough information to solve this problem.

Write the letter of the sentence that describes the problem.

1. Almost 100,000 bike riders are members of the League of American Cyclists. They are among the 75 million cyclists in the United States. If 10,000 cyclists live in Pennsylvania, how many live in other states?

   a. There is not enough information to solve the problem.

   b. There is more information than you need to solve the problem.

2. The bicycle was introduced in the United States in 1866. By 1897, about 4 million Americans were riding bikes. What was the bike-riding population of California?

   a. There is not enough information to solve the problem.

   b. There is more information than you need to solve the problem.

Solve if possible. Identify any needed information.

3. The bicycle was invented in 1790. In 1896, cycling became an official event of the Olympic Games. In how many Olympics has cycling been an event? (HINT: There were no Olympics in 1916, 1940, and 1944.)

4. In 1983, Laurent Fignon won the *Tour de France* in a little more than 105 hours. The race was 2,315 miles long. How much faster was his average mile-per-hour speed than the average speed of the racer who finished second?

5. In 1980, people in the United States bought about 7 million bicycles made in their country. They also bought about 2 million imported bicycles. The average foreign-made bike sold for $200. About how much did those people spend on bikes that year?

6. A bike shop sells rebuilt 3-speed bikes for $77.50 each. On Monday, 4 people bought rebuilt bikes and 2 people bought new bikes. How much money did the shop receive that day?

7. A biker took a 4-day tour. He biked 35 miles per day. How many miles did he travel?

8. A cross-country bike trail covers 4,300 miles. It passes through or near 28 national parks in 10 states. Oregon has 6 of these parks, Idaho has 3, and Montana has 4. How many parks in other states does the trail pass through or near?

Multiplying Whole Numbers

Rita is a flight attendant. In the first 10 weeks of the year, she traveled an average of 7,185 miles each week. At that rate, if she works 48 weeks per year, how many miles would she travel per year?

Multiply 48 × 7,185 to find the number of miles.

You can estimate to see whether your answer is reasonable.

$$
\begin{array}{r}
7{,}185 \\
\times \quad 48 \\
\end{array}
\longrightarrow
\begin{array}{r}
7{,}000 \\
\times \quad 50 \\
\hline
350{,}000 \\
\end{array}
\qquad
\begin{array}{r}
7{,}185 \\
\times \quad 48 \\
\hline
57\ 480 \\
287\ 400 \\
\hline
344{,}880 \\
\end{array}
$$

Rita travels 344,880 miles per year. The answer is reasonably close to 350,000.

Other examples:

$$
\begin{array}{r}
529 \\
\times\ 476 \\
\hline
3\ 174 \\
37\ 030 \\
211\ 600 \\
\hline
251{,}804 \\
\end{array}
$$

You can omit these zeros.

$$
\begin{array}{r}
5{,}218 \\
\times\quad 306 \\
\hline
31\ 308 \\
1\ 565\ 40 \\
\hline
1{,}596{,}708 \\
\end{array}
$$

Write a zero in the tens place and continue to multiply.

$$
\begin{array}{r}
\$49.65 \\
\times\quad 27 \\
\hline
347\ 55 \\
993\ 0 \\
\hline
\$1{,}340.55 \\
\end{array}
$$

4 × 223 million = 892 million   13 × 57 billion = 741 billion

Checkpoint Write the letter of the correct answer.

Multiply.

1. 25 × $4,863

a. $34,041   b. $106,265
c. $121,575   d. $133,815

2. 208 × 7,234

a. 72,340   b. 202,552
c. 1,504,672   d. 1,535,682

Multiply.

1. 324 × 2	2. 3,225 × 3	3. 7,050 × 9	4. 32,156 × 4	5. $4,360.75 × 7
6. 43 × 27	7. 139 × 62	8. 9,062 × 83	9. $135.22 × 74	10. 761,470 × 14
11. 231 × 145	12. 704 × 352	13. $1,643 × 229	14. $137.06 × 355	15. 8,937 × 525

16.   27 million
× 3

17.   462 billion
× 45

18.   64 billion
× 326

19.   821 trillion
× 249

20. $74 \times 2,305$

21. $81,432 \times 6$

22. $32 \times 14,477$

23. $124,872 \times 4$

24. $43 \times 333,111$

25. $426 \times 75,193$

Solve.

26. Elroy drove an average of 17,740 miles each summer for the last 14 years. What is the total number of miles he drove during the summers?

27. A Boeing 727 seats 147 passengers, and a Boeing 757 seats 185 passengers. How many more passengers does the 757 seat?

28. Mr. Sorkin made 8 round-trip business flights across the United States last year. It is 2,572 air miles each way. How many air miles did he fly last year?

★29. A train from New York to Boston travels 75 mph for 2 h. Then, because of signal problems, it slows to 35 mph for the rest of the trip. If the trip takes 4 h, how many miles does the train travel?

NUMBER SENSE

Find an easy way to compute mentally.

Example: $9 \times \overset{10}{5 \times 8} \times 2 = 720$

$\underset{72}{\qquad}$

1. $13 \times 5 \times 2$

2. $2 \times 58 \times 50$

3. $8 \times 9 \times 5$

4. $6 \times 4 \times 1 \times 5$

5. $2 \times 7 \times 9 \times 5$

6. $5 \times 10 \times 8 \times 2$

7. $10 \times 3 \times 50 \times 1$

8. $10 \times 5 \times 4 \times 4 \times 2$

9. $4 \times 10 \times 3 \times 2 \times 5$

Dividing Whole Numbers

There were 2,208 passengers on a recent crossing of the *Queen Elizabeth II* (*QE2*). The list of passengers was printed on computer paper, with 53 names on each sheet. How many full sheets were there? How many names were there on the sheet that was not full?

Divide $53\overline{)2,208}$.

Divide the thousands.   Think: $53\overline{)2}$.   Not enough thousands.
Divide the hundreds.   Think: $53\overline{)22}$.   Not enough hundreds.

Divide the tens.
Think: $53\overline{)220}$, or $5\overline{)22}$.
Estimate 4.

$$
\begin{array}{r}
4 \\
53\overline{)2,208} \\
2\ 12 \\
\hline
8
\end{array}
$$
Multiply.
Subtract and compare.

Divide the ones.
Think: $53\overline{)88}$, or $5\overline{)8}$.
Estimate 1.

$$
\begin{array}{r}
41\ \text{R}35 \\
53\overline{)2,208} \\
2\ 12\downarrow \\
\hline
88 \\
53 \\
\hline
35
\end{array}
$$
Multiply.
Subtract and compare.

Check.

$$
\begin{array}{r}
41 \quad \leftarrow \text{quotient} \\
\times\ 53 \quad \leftarrow \text{divisor} \\
\hline
123 \\
2\ 05 \\
\hline
2,173 \\
+\quad 35 \quad \leftarrow \text{remainder} \\
\hline
2,208 \quad \leftarrow \text{dividend}
\end{array}
$$

There were 41 full sheets and 1 sheet with 35 names on it.

Other examples:

$5,931 \div 9$

$$
\begin{array}{r}
659 \\
9\overline{)5,931} \\
5\ 4 \\
\hline
53 \\
53 \\
\hline
45 \\
45 \\
\hline
81 \\
81 \\
\hline
0
\end{array}
$$

$26,879 \div 215$

$$
\begin{array}{r}
125\ \text{R}4 \\
215\overline{)26,879} \\
21\ 5 \\
\hline
5\ 37 \\
4\ 30 \\
\hline
1\ 079 \\
1\ 075 \\
\hline
4
\end{array}
$$

$\dfrac{3,635}{12}$

$$
\begin{array}{r}
302\ \text{R}11 \\
12\overline{)3,635} \\
3\ 6 \\
\hline
35 \\
24 \\
\hline
11
\end{array}
$$

$\$42,084 \div 7$

$$
\begin{array}{r}
\$6,012 \\
7\overline{)\$42,084} \\
42 \\
\hline
08 \\
7 \\
\hline
14 \\
14 \\
\hline
0
\end{array}
$$

Math Reasoning, page H209

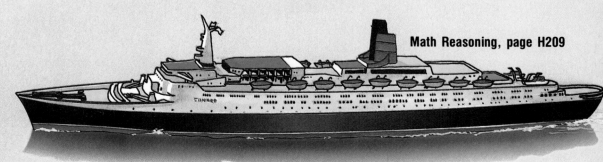

52

Divide

1. $6\overline{)48}$ 2. $8\overline{)720}$ 3. $7\overline{)143}$ 4. $9\overline{)355}$

5. $24\overline{)459}$ 6. $38\overline{)789}$ 7. $45\overline{)3,095}$ 8. $77\overline{)\$8,316}$

9. $196\overline{)5,481}$ 10. $590\overline{)19,663}$ 11. $837\overline{)67,514}$ 12. $426\overline{)130,782}$

13. $292 \div 4$ 14. $1,587 \div 3$ 15. $3,644 \div 7$ 16. $1,932 \div 4$

17. $8,049 \div 46$ 18. $78,492 \div 93$ 19. $120,223 \div 57$ 20. $13,728 \div 15$

21. $\$10,584 \div 108$ 22. $136,412 \div 576$ 23. $205,833 \div 670$ 24. $\$927,827 \div 393$

25. $\dfrac{763}{7}$ 26. $\dfrac{4,196}{5}$ 27. $\dfrac{32,940}{9}$ 28. $\dfrac{6,421}{6}$

29. $\dfrac{75,126}{31}$ 30. $\dfrac{105,600}{88}$ 31. $\dfrac{50,370}{34}$ 32. $\dfrac{723,946}{21}$

33. $\dfrac{262,685}{658}$ 34. $\dfrac{\$1,906,000}{479}$ 35. $\dfrac{2,412,954}{318}$ 36. $\dfrac{9,918,740}{996}$

Solve.

37. If the *QE2* travels at a speed of 32 nautical miles per hour, how many hours will it take to travel 2,752 nautical miles?

38. A group of 16 people chartered a boat at a cost of $24,288 for a week. How much did it cost per person?

39. The cruise ship *South Seas* leaves Los Angeles with 1,263 passengers on board. If another 1,548 passengers board in Panama, how many passengers are there on board?

★40. Two advertisements for Scandinavian cruises list different rates. The first rate is $7,450 for 18 days. The second rate is $5,800 for 14 days. Which cruise costs less per day?

MIDCHAPTER REVIEW

Name the property.

1. $76 \times 1 = 76$

2. $5 \times (6 + 12) = (5 \times 6) + (5 \times 12)$

3. $13 \times (3 \times 78) = (13 \times 3) \times 78$

4. $123 \times 87 = 87 \times 123$

Find the product or the quotient.

5. 70×400 6. 200×600 7. $\$4,673 \times 6$ 8. $\$456.43 \times 74$

9. $50,200 \div 100$ 10. $4,500 \div 90$ 11. $900\overline{)\$8,100}$ 12. $70\overline{)\$49,000}$

PROBLEM SOLVING
Estimation

Sometimes you can solve a problem by estimating. In many cases, you must decide whether you should **overestimate** or **underestimate.**

> Samantha is planning to drive to a park about 100 miles away. Her car is almost out of gas. She remembers that gas costs $1.39 per gallon. Her car travels about 25 miles per gallon. How much money will Samantha have to pay for gas? Samantha decides to estimate.

When estimating to find out whether you have enough money, is it usually better to overestimate or to underestimate costs? Samantha overestimates to be sure that she will have enough money.

When estimating how much gasoline she will need, should she round her gas mileage up or down? She rounds down to be sure that she won't use more gas than she has planned to use.

$$25 \rightarrow 20$$

Samantha realizes that since the park is about 100 miles away, the total number of miles for the round trip is about 200 miles. Samantha divides the number of miles by the 20 miles per gallon.

$$200 \div 20 = 10$$

Samantha estimates that she will need about 10 gallons of gas for the round trip. She overestimates the cost per gallon as $1.50 to be on the safe side. She multiplies her estimate of the number of gallons by the estimated price per gallon.

$$10 \times \$1.50 = \$15$$

Samantha decides to take at least $15 to pay for gas.

If you were going to estimate to solve, which amounts in the problems should be overestimated or underestimated? Write the letter of the correct answer.

1. Bobby must be home to meet Claude, who is driving 272 miles to visit him. If Claude leaves at 11:10 A.M. and averages 53 miles per hour, at what time should Bobby plan to be home?

a. Overestimate the number of miles and underestimate the rate of speed.
b. Underestimate the number of miles and overestimate the rate of speed.
c. Underestimate both the number of miles and the rate of speed.

2. Al's car is almost out of gas. He must drive 72 miles to his home. The car travels 33 miles per gallon. How much gas should he buy?

a. Overestimate the miles per gallon and underestimate the number of miles.
b. Overestimate both the miles per gallon and the number of miles.
c. Underestimate the miles per gallon and overestimate the number of miles.

Solve by estimation.

3. Travis has $10. He wants to take a taxi across town. Taxis charge $2.22 for the first mile and $1.46 for each additional mile. His destination is 5 miles away. Does Travis have enough money for a taxi?

4. Shelly has $50 to spend on a whale-watch cruise for herself and her sister. Tickets cost $11.60 each, and lunch costs $4.85 per person. Will she have enough money left to buy an $18.99 pair of binoculars?

5. Shelly and her sister are taking the 12:35 P.M. train. They can walk to the train station in about 22 minutes. They plan to allow 20 minutes to buy their tickets and board the train. At what time should they leave their house?

6. Shelly's sister is paying for the transportation. Round-trip train tickets cost $12.75 per person. A taxi from the train to the harbor costs $5.50. How much will round-trip transportation cost?

7. At a cafeteria, prices for adults average about $3.60 for main courses and $0.90 for side dishes. Children's portions are half price. If a family of 2 adults and 2 children each have a main dish and 2 side dishes, how much will the meal cost in all?

Decimals and Powers of 10

A. Tara was motorcycling cross-country. At the end of the first day, she had traveled 285.4 miles. If she maintains this rate, how many miles can she travel in 10 days?

To multiply a decimal by a power of 10, move the decimal point one place to the right for each zero in the factor.

Look at the pattern.

$$10 \times 285.4 = 2\,8\,5\,4. \qquad = 2{,}854 \qquad \text{one place to the right}$$
$$100 \times 285.4 = 2\,8\,5\,4\,0. \qquad = 28{,}540 \qquad \text{two places}$$
$$1{,}000 \times 285.4 = 2\,8\,5\,4\,0\,0. = 285{,}400 \qquad \text{three places}$$

Tara can travel 2,854 miles in 10 days.

B. Divide 57.24 by 1,000.

To divide a decimal by a power of 10, move the decimal point one place to the left for each zero in the divisor. Write extra zeros if necessary.

Look at the pattern.

$$57.24 \div 10 = 5\,7.2\,4 \qquad = 5.724 \qquad \text{one place to the left}$$
$$57.24 \div 100 = 0\,5\,7.2\,4 \qquad = 0.5724 \qquad \text{two places}$$
$$57.24 \div 1{,}000 = 0\,0\,5\,7.2\,4 = 0.05724 \qquad \text{three places}$$

Checkpoint   Write the letter of the correct answer.

Compute.

1. 83.75×100 **a.** 0.8375   **b.** 83.7500   **c.** 8,375   **d.** 837,500

2. $6.8 \times 1{,}000$ **a.** 0.0068   **b.** 6.8000   **c.** 6,800   **d.** 6,800,000

3. $7.1 \div 10$ **a.** 0.071   **b.** 0.71   **c.** 07.1   **d.** 71

4. $3.05 \div 1{,}000$ **a.** 0.000305   **b.** 0.00305   **c.** 0003.05   **d.** 3,050

Find the product.

1. 10×7.3
2. 10×64.85
3. 151.32×10
4. 0.45×100
5. 100×2.634
6. 34.219×100
7. $1,000 \times 0.164$
8. $39.7 \times 1,000$
9. $1,000 \times 412.635$
10. 100×58.951
11. $1,000 \times 8,762.48$
12. 110.06×100
13. 0.54×10
14. $1,000 \times 0.0087$
15. $10 \times 6,459.08$

Find the quotient.

16. $10\overline{)3.7}$
17. $10\overline{)62.4}$
18. $10\overline{)521.57}$
19. $100\overline{)0.023}$
20. $100\overline{)784.91}$
21. $100\overline{)2,153.6}$
22. $33.26 \div 1,000$
23. $574.394 \div 1,000$
24. $8,017.96 \div 1,000$
25. $8.653 \div 10$
26. $89.53 \div 10$
27. $787.217 \div 10$
28. $\frac{90.063}{100}$
29. $\frac{1,759.32}{100}$
30. $\frac{41,085.7}{100}$
31. $\frac{748.85}{1,000}$
32. $\frac{2,196.57}{1,000}$
33. $\frac{57,430.08}{1,000}$

Solve.

34. During a 10-day raft trip, Tara spent a total of 110.5 hours onshore. On average, about how many hours a day did Tara spend onshore?

35. In order to join the White-Water Explorer's Club, Lucian had to spend 100 h rafting on the river. If his average speed was 8.45 km/h, how many kilometers did he travel?

36. In a 1-km race, 4 rafts finished with times of 5.6 min, 8.4 min, 6.5 min, and 5.8 min. What was the difference in time between the fastest raft and the slowest raft?

★37. One team's finishing time in a 100-km white-water marathon was 638.25 min. They finished the last kilometer in 5.73 min. How much faster than their average speed was their speed in the last kilometer?

CHALLENGE

If you can recycle 4 aluminum cans into 1 can, into how many cans can you recycle 16 cans?

Classwork/Homework, page H24

Estimating Products of Decimals

A. The average household in the United States has the television set on for 46.4 hours a week. For about how many hours is the television set on during a year?

The amount of time the television is on varies for each week. It is reasonable to estimate the product.

Think: there are 52 weeks in a year.

Round each factor. Then multiply.

$$52 \times 46.4$$
$$\downarrow \qquad \downarrow$$
$$50 \times 46 = 2{,}300$$

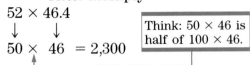

Think: 50×46 is half of 100×46.

The television set is on for about 2,300 hours during a year.

B. You can estimate products of decimals by rounding each number to its largest place.

Estimate 6.18×6.172.
$$\downarrow \qquad \downarrow$$
$$6 \times 6 = 36$$

Since both numbers are rounded down, 36 is an underestimate. The adjusted estimate is 36^{+}.

C. When you multiply with decimals, look for factors that are close to 1 or close to $\frac{1}{2}$.

Estimate 0.923×3.7.
0.923×3.7
$$\downarrow \qquad \downarrow$$
$$1 \times 3.7 = 3.7$$

The product is 3.7^{-}, or slightly less than 3.7.

Estimate 0.5223×0.72.
0.5223×0.72
$$\downarrow \qquad \downarrow$$
$$\frac{1}{2} \times 0.72 = 0.36$$

The product is 0.36^{+}, or slightly greater than 0.36.

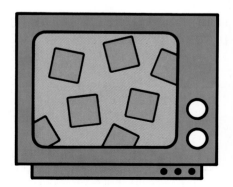

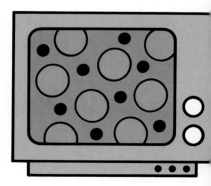

Estimate by rounding.

1. 26×4.57
2. 714×6.82
3. 32.5×28
4. 0.81×857

5. 7×23.8
6. 0.04×92
7. 317×0.86
8. 61.6×18

9. 4.8×6.8
10. 17.8×0.4
11. 39.2×0.13
12. 2.88×8.8

13. 0.056×3.9
14. 507.4×6.7
15. 0.009×8.98
16. 2.003×16.6

17. 89×0.046
18. 313.2×1.9
19. 14.9×0.06
20. 0.08×0.37

In each exercise below, the decimal point has been left out of the product. Estimate to write the correct product.

21. $6.72 \times 8.4 = 56448$
22. $6.69 \times 2.2 = 14718$

23. $4.87 \times 0.521 = 253727$
24. $0.71 \times 0.513 = 36423$

25. $12.1 \times 2.8 = 3388$
26. $37.6 \times 0.007 = 2632$

27. $0.91 \times 68 = 6188$
28. $0.601 \times 28.61 = 1719461$

Estimate. Look for numbers close to 1 or $\frac{1}{2}$.

29. 0.91×6.01
30. 1.07×88
31. 0.509×88.9

32. 22.2×0.46
33. 1.4×65
34. 0.02×0.94

35. 617×0.52
36. 0.86×328.7
37. 0.037×0.591

Solve.

38. A Nielsen rating point represents 849,000 television households. One evening, a popular TV program had a rating of 18.6. Estimate the number of households watching the program.

★39. A solid-state color TV uses an average of 305 kilowatt hours of electricity per year. If a kilowatt of electricity costs 12.3 cents, estimate the yearly cost to operate the TV.

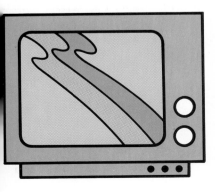
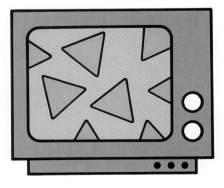
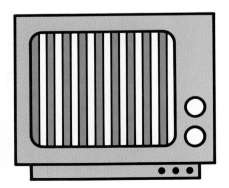

Multiplying Decimals

While visiting London, Karen purchased 15.5 gallons of gasoline for her rented car. The gasoline cost 1.72 pounds sterling (£) per gallon. How much did she spend for gasoline?

Multiply 1.72 by 15.5.

First, estimate the product. $2 \times 16 = 32$

$$
\begin{array}{r}
1.7\ 2 \quad \leftarrow \textbf{two places} \\
\times\ 1\ 5.5 \quad \leftarrow \textbf{one place} \\
\hline
8\ 6\ 0 \\
8\ 6\ 0 \\
1\ 7\ 2 \\
\hline
2\ 6.6\ 6\ 0 \quad \leftarrow \textbf{three places}
\end{array}
$$

Karen spent £26.66 for gasoline. The answer is reasonably close to £32.

Other examples:

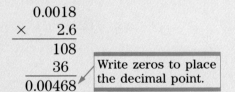

$$
\begin{array}{r}
0.0018 \\
\times\quad 2.6 \\
\hline
108 \\
36 \\
\hline
0.00468
\end{array}
$$

Write zeros to place the decimal point.

$$
\begin{array}{r}
\$3.72 \\
\times\quad 5.8 \\
\hline
2\ 976 \\
18\ 60 \\
\hline
\$21.576 \longrightarrow \$21.58
\end{array}
$$

to the nearest cent

Checkpoint   Write the letter of the correct answer.

Multiply.

1. $\$36.45 \times 7$ **a.** $25.515   **b.** $255.15   **c.** $2,551.50   **d.** $25,515

2. 0.63×2.7 **a.** 0.243   **b.** 1.701   **c.** 17.01   **d.** 170.1

3. 30.0019×0.06 **a.** 0.0114   **b.** 1.800114   **c.** 180.0114   **d.** 18,001.14

4. $5.12 \times 0.4 \times 0.3$ **a.** 0.1536   **b.** 0.6144   **c.** 61.44   **d.** 6,144

Math Reasoning, page H209

Multiply.

1.	3.5 × 6	**2.**	12.59 × 0.8	**3.**	605.14 × 0.3	**4.**	0.1034 × 9
5.	0.471 × 0.32	**6.**	2.75 × 72	**7.**	483.96 × 3.7	**8.**	0.0025 × 7.8
9.	52 × 3.64	**10.**	740.03 × 0.0468	**11.**	22,954.2 × 39.7	**12.**	160.528 × 324

Multiply. Round the product to the nearest cent when necessary.

13.	$37.54 × 32	**14.**	$8.63 × 4.9	**15.**	$71.09 × 0.7	**16.**	$452.20 × 1.87
17.	$63.38 × 0.008	**18.**	$2,196.47 × 47.6	**19.**	$4,193.51 × 0.0029	**20.**	$76,640.07 × 0.438

21. 0.799 × 783.02   **22.** 5,143.2 × 0.00386   **23.** 55.9234 × 0.4

24. 8,912.83 × 0.56   **25.** 36.4 × 91.57   **26.** 0.00462 × 878

27. 3.6 × 3 × 0.42   **28.** 0.152 × 82,510 × 6.9

Solve. For Problem 29, use the Infobank.

29. Use the information on page 473 to solve. A teen group is going on a 4-week sight-seeing trip around the United States. If they rent one 47-passenger bus and two vans, what is the total cost of the trip?

30. Edward paid £3.40 for a visit to Madame Tussaud's wax museum, £3.50 to go to a movie, and £4.20 to go to a concert. How much did this entertainment cost him?

ANOTHER LOOK

Solve.

1. Tanya visits 47 cities. If she spends an average of 3 days in each city, how long will her trip take?

2. Bob planned a budget for his 6-week trip. If he budgeted $150 a week for hotels, how much has he budgeted for hotels for the trip?

PROBLEM SOLVING
Choosing the Operation

You can find hints in a problem that will help you choose the best operation to use to solve it.

Don and his family plan to travel by train to several countries in Europe. To save money, Don buys 6 special passes that allow them to travel anywhere they want for a month. Each pass costs $256.45. How much did Don spend on the passes?

Hints:

If you know	and you want to find	you can
• the number in two or more sets	the total number	add.
• the number in one set • the number taken away	the number that is left	subtract.
• the number in two sets	how much larger one set is than the other	subtract to compare.
• the number in one set • the number in part of the set	the number in the remaining part of the set	subtract.
• the number in each set is the same • the number in each set • the number of sets	the total number	multiply.

You could add to find the total number, but it would be easier to multiply.

the number of sets   the number in each set   the total number
$$6 \quad \times \quad \$256.45 \quad = \quad \$1{,}538.70$$

Don spent $1,538.70 on the passes.

Write the letter of the operation you would use to solve each problem.

1. Roberta's excursion boat carried 87 passengers on the first trip. On the second trip, there were 90 passengers, and on the last trip, there were 107 passengers. How many passengers did the boat carry on the three trips?

   a. addition
   b. subtraction
   c. multiplication

2. The Sea Watch restaurant sells a fish dinner for $7.50. If the cost of preparing the dinner is $3.83, how much of the price is not part of the cost of the dinner?

   a. addition
   b. subtraction
   c. multiplication

Solve.

3. One airline carried 2,346,205 passengers in a year. Another airline carried 846,989 fewer passengers than the first airline. How many passengers did the second airline carry?

4. Anita exchanged $425.00 of her $875.32 of spending money for francs. How much money in United States currency did she have left?

5. The Gomez family visited a park that had 5,824 acres. Then they visited another park that had 455,312 more acres than the first park. How large was the second park?

★6. At a recreation park, the admission charge is $4.25 for adults and $2.25 for children. Ms. Brown paid for 1 adult and 2 children. She gave the ticket seller a $20 bill. How much change did she receive?

★7. An airline agent checked a bag that weighed 35 pounds, another that weighed 4.5 pounds less than the first, another that weighed 13 pounds less than the second, and a fourth that weighed 7.5 pounds more than the first. How many pounds of baggage did the agent check?

★8. In 1984, Chicago's O'Hare Airport had 671,742 takeoffs and landings. This was 28,576 fewer than the San Francisco and Anchorage airports combined. If the Anchorage Airport had 335,509 takeoffs and landings, how many did the San Francisco Airport have?

Dividing Decimals by Whole Numbers

A. Steve went on a 21-day bicycle trip.
He traveled 520.8 miles. How many
miles per day did he average?

Divide 520.8 by 21.

To divide a decimal by a whole number,
place the decimal point in the quotient
above the decimal point in the dividend.
Then divide as you would with whole
numbers.

Steve averaged 24.8 miles per day.

```
      24.8
  21)520.8
      42
      100
       84
      16 8
      16 8
         0
```

Estimate to check.

$20 \times 25 = 500$
500 is close to 520.8
So, 24.8 is a reasonable
answer.

B. Sometimes you round quotients.
Money is usually rounded to the
nearest cent.

Divide 0.2352 by 24
and round to the
nearest thousandth.

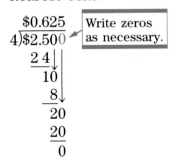

```
    0.0098  ←  Sometimes
24)0.2352      you need to
   216          write extra
   192          zeros.
   192
     0
```

0.0098 ⟶ 0.010

Divide $2.50 by 4
and round to the
nearest cent.

```
   $0.625  ←  Write zeros
4)$2.500      as necessary.
  2 4
   10
    8
   20
   20
    0
```

$0.625 ⟶ $0.63

Divide 407.55 by 325
and round to the
nearest hundredth.

```
      1.254
325)407.550
    325
     82 5
     65 0
     17 55
     16 25
      1 300
      1 300
          0
```

1.254 ⟶ 1.25

Checkpoint Write the letter of the correct answer.

Divide.

1. $1.564 \div 34$

  a. 0.0046   **b.** 0.046   **c.** 0.46   **d.** 46

Round to the nearest cent.

2. 8)$17.33

  a. $2.16   **b.** $2.17   **c.** $21.70   **d.** 217

Divide.

1. 6)22.8   **2.** 9)210.6   **3.** 7)5.67   **4.** 8)$2.16

5. 13)50.7   **6.** 33)$5.61   **7.** 64)0.768   **8.** 28)7.812

9. 231)1,062.6   **10.** 147)79.674   **11.** 734)$29.36   **12.** 518)86.3506

13. $44.5 \div 5$ **14.** $0.552 \div 8$ **15.** $149.8 \div 4$ **16.** $\$19.71 \div 9$

17. $3.901 \div 83$ **18.** $9.2512 \div 59$ **19.** $4.3418 \div 34$ **20.** $0.864 \div 72$

21. $\frac{4.5}{36}$ **22.** $\frac{3.486}{83}$ **23.** $\frac{\$48.60}{72}$ **24.** $\frac{59.644}{52}$

25. $\frac{149.144}{412}$ **26.** $\frac{29.825}{125}$ **27.** $\frac{437.1312}{561}$ **28.** $\frac{\$4,923.63}{681}$

Divide. Round each quotient to the nearest tenth.

29. 6)14.04   **30.** 27)172.26   **31.** 91)58.24   **32.** 337)19,680.8

Divide. Round each quotient to the nearest cent or the nearest hundredth.

33. $37.583 \div 7$ **34.** $\$8.70 \div 4$ **35.** $\$48.60 \div 72$ **36.** $21.033 \div 246$

Divide. Round each quotient to the nearest thousandth.

37. $\frac{2.4682}{7}$ **38.** $\frac{12.4868}{53}$ **39.** $\frac{4.4791}{47}$ **40.** $\frac{589.2045}{459}$

Solve.

41. On a trip, 15 teenagers stopped to visit a museum and paid a total of $56.25 for admission. If they all paid the same amount, how much was each admission?

42. The longest tandem bicycle ever built is 803 in. long. What is its length to the nearest tenth of a foot?

NUMBER SENSE

You can use short division when the divisor is less than 10. Multiply and subtract mentally. Write each remainder beside the next digit as shown.

$$2 \ ,2 \ 4 \ 9$$
$$7)15^1,7^34^63$$

Use short division to find the quotient.

1. 4)3,384   **2.** 9)2,212.2   **3.** 6)2,522.46   **4.** 8)829.344

Dividing Decimals by Decimals

Marina drove 206.4 miles during the weekend. Her car used 9.6 gallons of gas. What was the rate of fuel usage in miles per gallon?

Divide 9.6)206.4.

When the divisor is a decimal, multiply both the divisor and the dividend by the smallest power of 10 that will make the divisor a whole number. Place the decimal point in the quotient, and divide as you would with whole numbers.

The rate was 21.5 miles per gallon.

Multiply by 10.	Check.

```
         2 1.5              21.5
9.6)2 0 6.4,0            ×  9.6
    1 9 2                  1290
    1 4 4                  1935
      9 6               206.40
      4 8 0
      4 8 0
          0
```

Other examples:

```
        $ 2.4 0
9.7 5)$2 3.4 0,0 0
      1 9 5 0
      3 9 0 0
      3 9 0 0
            0
```

```
          7.2 5
3.6 2 4)2 6 2 7.4 0 0
        2 5 3 6 8
          9 0 6 0
          7 2 4 8
          1 8 1 2 0
          1 8 1 2 0
                  0
```

Find $\dfrac{0.02310}{4.2}$, rounded to the nearest thousandth.

```
        0.0 0 5 5
4.2)0.0 2 3 1 0
      2 1 0
      2 1 0
      2 1 0
          0
```

$0.0055 \longrightarrow 0.006$

Checkpoint Write the letter of the correct answer.

Divide.

1. 3.6)10.08　　　**a.** 0.028　　**b.** 0.28　　**c.** 2.8　　**d.** 28

2. 0.018)72　　　**a.** 0.004　　**b.** 4　　**c.** 400　　**d.** 4,000

3. 0.24)0.0216　　**a.** 0.000009　　**b.** 0.0009　　**c.** 0.09　　**d.** 0.9

4. Round 0.0887 ÷ 0.033 to the nearest tenth.

a. 2.68　　**b.** 2.6　　**c.** 2.69　　**d.** 2.7

Divide.

1. $0.7\overline{)4.9}$
2. $0.6\overline{)0.0228}$
3. $8\overline{)1.68}$
4. $0.04\overline{)14.676}$

5. $9.2\overline{)\$3.22}$
6. $0.074\overline{)0.0259}$
7. $7.5\overline{)\$2.70}$
8. $4.8\overline{)96}$

9. $2.4 \div 0.12$
10. $\$1.47 \div 0.35$
11. $10.5 \div 0.0015$
12. $2.83668 \div 9.21$

13. $1.71 \div 0.0342$
14. $132.3472 \div 457$
15. $20.9588 \div 6.04$
16. $711.5435 \div 0.0863$

17. $\frac{0.02304}{0.64}$
18. $\frac{91}{0.13}$
19. $\frac{0.46113}{5.7}$
20. $\frac{29.659}{31.22}$

21. $\frac{32.9346}{42.8}$
22. $\frac{4.998}{850}$
23. $\frac{0.002872}{0.0718}$
24. $\frac{71.4974}{1.07}$

Divide. Round each quotient to the nearest tenth.

25. $0.6\overline{)0.7}$
26. $3.6\overline{)1.45}$
27. $0.09\overline{)2.75}$
28. $0.0458\overline{)2.823}$

Divide. Round each quotient to the nearest hundredth
or the nearest cent.

29. $0.426 \div 0.8$
30. $\$2.96 \div 7.3$
31. $\$0.74 \div 0.0632$
32. $5.13216 \div 3.52$

Divide. Round each quotient to the nearest thousandth.

33. $\frac{0.2741}{7}$
34. $\frac{1.7}{0.42}$
35. $\frac{1.0463}{0.53}$
36. $\frac{0.381}{10.4}$

Solve. For Problem 39, use the Infobank.

37. Natalie drove her car 178.3 miles. If her car gets about 19.5 miles to the gallon, about how many gallons of gas did Natalie use on this trip? Round the answer to the nearest gallon.

38. Jason used 3.6 gallons of gas to drive his economy car 138.7 miles. At what rate in miles per gallon, rounded to the nearest tenth, did his car use gas?

39. Use the information on page 473 to solve. A group of 69 people from Chicago want to take a week long trip to Washington, D.C. According to the rental rates, how much would it cost each person to travel the cheapest way to Washington, D.C. by bus?

★40. A speedboat's gas-consumption rate is measured in gallons per hour. The speedboat *Silvershark* uses 18.9 gallons in 2.25 hours. At what rate does the *Silvershark* use gas? If there are 6.3 gallons left in the tank, for how many more hours will the *Silvershark* run?

PROBLEM SOLVING
Solving Multi-step Problems/Making a Plan

You may need to use more than one step to solve a problem. Before you can answer the question that is asked, you may have to find some facts that are not stated. You can use the numbers that are given to find the numbers that you need. Making a plan can help you solve such a problem.

The Smiths are going on a trip for 4 days. While they are away, a neighbor will feed their 8 parrots. Each parrot eats about 3 bags of birdseed per day. Birdseed is packaged 16 bags to a box. How many boxes of birdseed will be needed for 4 days?

Needed data: bags of birdseed eaten each day
bags of birdseed needed for 4 days

Plan

Step 1: Find the number of bags of birdseed eaten by the 8 parrots each day.

Step 2: Find the number of bags of birdseed needed for 4 days.

Step 3: Find the number of boxes of birdseed needed.

> *Work backward* to find the total number of boxes.

Step 1:
number of bags = number of bags × number of
 per day per parrot parrots
 n = 3 bags × 8 parrots; So $n = 24$.

Step 2:
bags needed = bags per day × number of days
 for 4 days
 x = 24 bags × 4 days; So $x = 96$.

Step 3:
boxes needed = bags needed ÷ number of bags per box
 for 4 days
 y = 96 bags ÷ 16 bags per box
 y = 6

So, 6 boxes of birdseed will be needed for 4 days.

Complete the plan for each problem by writing the missing steps.

1. Each of the 27 members of the Wilderness Club carries a 30-pound backpack on a camping trip. If nonfood items make up 20 pounds of each person's backpack, what is the total weight of the food supplies carried by all the club members?

   ___ 1. Find the amount of food carried by each person.

   ___ 2.

2. A camping store stocks 1,000 kerosene lanterns of various sizes. One of every 10 lanterns is large. The store sells large lanterns for $50 each. How much money does the store take in if it sells every large lantern in its stock?

   ___ 1. Find the number of large lanterns that the store has in stock.

   ___ 2.

Make a plan for each problem. Solve. For some problems, you may find it helpful to work backward.

3. In the last 12 days, 2,400 people have taken the Royal Gorge Ranch raft trip through the rapids. The ranch used 25 rafts each day. On the average, how many people rode in each raft each day?

4. The Thunderama Roller Coaster has 12 cars. Each car holds 5 people. The roller coaster completes 6 rides per hour, 12 hours per day. How many people can ride the Thunderama in a day?

5. An airport checks in an average of 1,500 passengers per hour. Each passenger checks an average of 30 pounds of baggage. How many pounds of baggage are handled in one day?

6. Gail bought a backpack that cost $58.00. The sales tax on $58.00 amounted to $4.35. Gail gave the salesclerk four $20 bills. How much change did Gail receive?

7. A bus goes from the airport to the center of the city and back. The fare is $2.55 each way. The bus can hold 28 passengers. On holidays, the bus is always full. How much money is collected in total fares for 3 round trips on a holiday?

★8. Mr. and Mrs. Coe plan to spend $1,200 for a 10-day trip. It will cost them $47 per day to rent a van. They will spend 2 nights in a hotel that charges $50 per night and the rest of the time at a campsite that charges $2.00 per night. They plan to spend $30 per day for food. How much will they have available to spend per day on other items?

MATH COMMUNICATION

Fields as varied as business, science, and recreational handicrafts have their own special vocabularies. Read this paragraph.

When using a pattern to cut a waistcoat in corduroy, lay the pattern with the grain so that the nap will run upward. Cut notches and mark darts, buttonholes, and pockets before removing pattern pieces. When attaching facings, ease underarm and neckline on garment. Trim seam allowances and selveges; then bind seams.

If you were a tailor working with napped fabric, you would know what these words mean. When you work with mathematics, you need to know the meanings of special words and phrases.

Match the word or the phrase with its meaning.

1. Commutative Properties

2. Associative Properties

3. Identity element for addition

4. inverse operations

5. digit

6. Distributive Property

a. a whole number from 0 through 9

b. To multiply a sum by a number, you can multiply each addend by the number and then add the products.

c. two operations that undo each other, such as addition and subtraction

d. 0: when zero is added to a number, the answer is the same as the original number.

e. The grouping of addends or factors does not change the sum or the product.

f. The order of addends or factors does not change the sum or the product.

Name the property or properties that each example illustrates.

7. $(13 \times 4) \times 6 = 13 \times (4 \times 6)$

8. $(7 \times 13) + (7 \times 14) = 7 \times (13 + 14)$

9. $25 \times 780 = 780 \times 25$

10. $2(10 + 7) = 2 \times 10 + 2 \times 7$

GROUP PROJECT

Not Just Hamburgers

The problem: You are visiting some friends in Japan. Your parents want you to take your two hosts out to dinner. They have sent you $60 in United States currency for the entire meal. Since you are treating, your hosts ask you to order the meal. Using the menu below, figure out what to order that will not cost more than $80, and add up the bill. 140 yen (¥) equals $1.

KYOTO GARDENS RESTAURANT

Salads

Bean Sprout Salad	¥275
Green Salad	¥275

Side Orders

Tempura—fried shrimp and vegetables	¥900
Spring Roll	¥275
Kara-Age—Japanese-style chicken wings	¥510

Noodles and Rice

Fried Rice	¥425
Yakisoba—Japanese noodles	¥425

Entrees

Chicken Teriyaki	¥1,015
Beef Teriyaki	¥1,070
Tempura Dinner	¥1,300
Sukiyaki—sliced beef and vegetables	¥1,015
Sushi—raw fillets of fish on rice	¥960

Beverages

Calpico—Japanese Soft Drink	¥150
American Soft Drinks	¥150
Tea	¥100

CHAPTER TEST

Multiply or divide. (pages 44–45, 50–53, 56–57, 60–61, and 64–67)

1. 326
  × 8

2. 7,184
  × 6

3. 539
  × 27

4. 4,572
  × 86

5. 52,006
  × 329

6. 2,782
  × 5,014

7. 131
  × 258

8. 7,904
  × 176

9. 28,917
  × 843

10. $109.52 × 634

11. 24)3,168

12. 273)$1,646.19

13. 434,561 ÷ 702

14. 6,792 ÷ 10

15. 13 × 200

16. 28.72596 × 1,000

17. 6.24 ÷ 10

18. 36.518 ÷ 10

19. 7.001408 ÷ 1,000

20. 328.741 ÷ 100

21. 0.723 ÷ 100

22. $\frac{3.21}{100}$

23. $\frac{7.954}{100}$

24. $\frac{36.5107}{1,000}$

25. $\frac{0.07}{1,000}$

26. 4.92
  × 78

27. 0.643
  × 246

28. 12.52
  × 0.731

29. 4.926
  × 3.141

30. 0.17692
  × 3.4

31. 0.0824
  × 309

32. 9.54
  × 2.7

33. 32.794
  × 0.015

34. 43)149.64

35. 319)4.147

36. 1.9)15.58

37. 2.015)0.058435

38. 0.078)0.500838

39. 4.00027)772.852164

Estimate the product or the quotient. (pages 46–47 and 58–59)

40. 54 × 76

41. 3,872 × 9,405

42. 0.038 × 0.472

43. 12.762 × 0.00839

44. 24)2,897

45. 214,272 ÷ 186

Identify any extra or needed information. Solve if possible. (pages 48–49)

46. Lily is changing her American dollars to francs. She has $128. If there are 6 francs to the dollar, how much is 1 franc worth?

47. Lucian is visiting Venice. After a trip to St. Mark's Square, he tips the gondolier $3. About how many Italian lire is this?

Write the letter of the operation you would use to solve the problem. (pages 62–63)

48. Daryl made a bicycle trip across his state. On the first day he rode 83 miles, 97 miles on the second day, 70 miles on the third day, 102 miles on the fourth day, and 56 miles on the fifth day. How many total miles did he travel?

  a. addition   **b.** subtraction   **c.** multiplication

Solve. (pages 68–69)

49. Lucian spends 3 days in Venice, 5 days in Rome, 9 days in Florence, 2 days in Trieste, and 7 days in Naples. He also spends time in Milan and returns home from there. If his entire trip is 30 days and he leaves Milan on August 31, on what day did he arrive in Milan?

BONUS

Solve.

Rita's skiing trip was planned for 6 days and 5 nights. Transportation to the ski resort cost $55.70 and her ski lodge cost $35.00 per night. If she had a budget of $620.00, how much would she have left to spend each day for food and entertainment after she paid for transportation and lodging?

RETEACHING

To divide a decimal by a decimal, multiply the divisor and the dividend by the power of 10 that will make the divisor a whole number. Then divide as you would with whole numbers.

Divide $0.12\overline{)0.612}$.

Multiply by 100 (move each decimal point two places to the right).

Place the decimal point in the quotient above the decimal point in the dividend.

Divide as with whole numbers.

$$0.12\overline{)0.6\,1\,2} \qquad 12\overline{)6\,1\,\overset{\cdot}{1}\,2}$$

$$\begin{array}{r} 5\,.\,1 \\ 12\overline{)6\,1\,.\,2} \\ 6\,0 \\ \hline 1\ 2 \\ 1\ 2 \\ \hline 0 \end{array}$$

Divide 45 by 16 1. Round to the nearest hundredth.

$$16.1\overline{)45.0\overset{\uparrow}{}}$$

$$\begin{array}{r} 2.795 \rightarrow 2.80 \\ 161\overline{)450.000} \\ 322 \\ \hline 128\ 0 \\ 112\ 7 \\ \hline 15\ 30 \\ 14\ 49 \\ \hline 810 \\ 805 \\ \hline 5 \end{array}$$

Multiply by 10 (move each decimal point one place to the right). Place the decimal point in the quotient. Write zeros where necessary.

Divide to one place more (thousandths) than the place to which you are rounding.

Divide.

1. $\$0.50\overline{)\$88.50}$ **2.** $0.3\overline{)62.628}$ **3.** $19.6\overline{)82.32}$ **4.** $0.57\overline{)368.79}$

5. $0.36\overline{)0.96156}$ **6.** $0.035\overline{)0.1365}$ **7.** $0.105\overline{)2,452.38}$ **8.** $0.263\overline{)789}$

Find each quotient to the nearest tenth.

9. $1.15\overline{)825}$ **10.** $0.061\overline{)14}$ **11.** $25.4\overline{)82.25}$ **12.** $0.342\overline{)1}$

Find each quotient to the nearest hundredth.

13. $\$0.49\overline{)\$10.43}$ **14.** $1.8\overline{)44.2}$ **15.** $0.079\overline{)197}$ **16.** $\$0.03\overline{)\$4}$

ENRICHMENT

Number Sequences

A set of numbers written in a particular order is called a **sequence.** Each number in the sequence is called a **term.** There are seven terms in the following sequence.

$$2, 5, 8, 11, 14, 17, 20$$

If a pattern is obvious, all the terms do not have to be written. Instead, you can use the symbol ". . . ," which means, "and so on."

$$2, 5, 8, \ldots , 20$$

Since the first three terms differ by 3, it is easy to determine that 11, 14, and 17 are the unwritten terms of the sequence.

If a sequence never stops, it is **infinite** and can be written with the "and so on" symbol at the end.

$$1, 3, 5, 7, 9, \ldots$$

Sequences can be formed by using any of the arithmetic operations.

1, 2, 4, 7, 11, 16, . . .
(+1) (+2) (+3) (+4) (+5)

57, 52, 47, 42, 37, . . .
(−5) (−5) (−5) (−5)

5, 15, 45, 135, 405, . . .
(×3) (×3) (×3) (×3)

720, 144, 36, 12, 6, 6.
(÷5) (÷4) (÷3) (÷2) (÷1)

Find the pattern. Write the next three terms in each sequence.

1. 6, 12, 18, . . .

2. 7, 28, 112, . . .

3. 112, 109, 105, 100, . . .

4. 896, 448, 224, . . .

5. 1, 4, 9, 16, . . .

6. 3, 3, 6, 18, 72, . . .

7. 6,561, 2,187, 729, . . .

8. 1, 8, 27, 64, . . .

9. 1, 1, 2, 3, 5, 8, 13, . . .

10. 5, 5, 10, 15, 25, 40, . . .

11. 1, 9, 33, 105, 321, . . .

12. 1, 6, 4, 9, 7, 12, 10, 15, . . .

14. 16.2, 8.1, 4.05, . . .

13. $\frac{1}{2}, \frac{3}{3}, \frac{5}{4}, \frac{7}{5}, \frac{9}{6}, \ldots$

For additional activities, see *Connecting Math Ideas*, page 469.

TECHNOLOGY

You can use the IF . . . THEN statement in BASIC to compare two numbers or variables.

1. Write the symbol or symbols that will make each statement true.

IF B ● 10 THEN PRINT "B IS LESS THAN 10"
IF B ● 10 THEN PRINT "B IS LESS THAN OR EQUAL TO 10"
IF B ● 10 THEN PRINT "B IS NOT EQUAL TO 10"
IF B ● 10 THEN PRINT "B IS GREATER THAN 10"
IF B ● 10 THEN PRINT "B IS GREATER THAN OR EQUAL TO 10"

You can use the GOTO statement to send the program to another line.

The GOTO statement tells the computer which line to do next. It can tell the computer to jump forward and skip lines or to jump back to a previous line.

2. What does this program print when you RUN it?

```
10 PRINT "THE DOG IS"
20 GOTO 40
30 PRINT "NOT"
40 PRINT "A POODLE"
```

You can use the GOTO statement with the IF . . . THEN statement. Here is a program that asks for two numbers, and then subtracts the numbers and tells you the difference. In this program, B must be less than A.

```
10 PRINT "TYPE A NUMBER"
20 INPUT A
30 PRINT "TYPE A NUMBER SMALLER THAN" A
40 INPUT B
50 IF B > A THEN GOTO 30
60 LET C = A − B
70 PRINT "THE DIFFERENCE BETWEEN" A
"AND" B "IS" C
```

3. Rewrite the program so that it asks for two numbers and prints the quotient of the first divided by the second. Be sure that the second number is not zero.

Here is a program that asks for two numbers and their product. Notice that you can put two statements on one line by using a colon.

```
10 PRINT "TYPE A NUMBER": INPUT I
20 PRINT "TYPE ANOTHER NUMBER": INPUT J
30 LET K = I * J
40 PRINT "WHAT IS THE PRODUCT OF" I "AND" J: INPUT N
50 IF N = K THEN GOTO 90
60 PRINT "THAT'S NOT RIGHT"
70 PRINT "TRY AGAIN"
80 GOTO 40
90 PRINT "GOOD WORK"
```

4. If you ran this program, typed in 8 and 20, and then typed 170, what would the computer print?

5. Finish this program. It asks for two numbers and their product. It tests whether your answer is too great, too small, or correct. If your answer is too great or too small, the program goes back and has you try again.

```
10 PRINT "TYPE A NUMBER ";: INPUT I
20 PRINT "TYPE ANOTHER NUMBER ";: INPUT J
30 LET K = I * J
40 PRINT "WHAT IS THE PRODUCT OF" I "AND" J: INPUT N
50 IF N = K THEN GOTO 130
60 IF N > K THEN GOTO _____
70 PRINT "_____"
80 PRINT "TRY AGAIN"
90 GOTO _____
100 PRINT "TOO GREAT"
110 PRINT "TRY AGAIN"
120 GOTO _____
130 PRINT "GOOD WORK"
```

CUMULATIVE REVIEW

Write the letter of the correct answer.

1. Estimate 85,835 − 26,751.

a. 20,000   b. 59,000
c. 79,000   d. 81,000

2. 49,719 + 163,321 + 2,472,857 + 64,099

a. 2,538,877   b. 2,638,996
c. 2,749,997   d. not given

3. Estimate 9.341 + 28.6962 + 0.8542.

a. 30   b. 45
c. 39   d. 50

4. 342 − 43.091

a. 298.019   b. 298.909
c. 299.091   d. not given

5. Order from the greatest to the least: 4.0134, 4.0143, 40.1343.

a. 4.0134, 4.0143, 40.1343
b. 40.1343, 4.0134, 4.0143
c. 40.1343, 4.0143, 4.0134
d. not given

6. $6,006.93 − $17.89

a. $5,098.04   b. $5,989.04
c. $5,999.14   d. not given

7. 9.0894 − 0.32908

a. 8.75996   b. 8.76006
c. 9.75996   d. not given

8. 8.932 + 89.32 + 809.2 + 3.9824

a. 65.780   b. 908.4344
c. 947.276   d. not given

9. Round 7,343.02456 to the nearest thousandth.

a. 8,000   b. 7,343.02
c. 7,343.025   d. not given

10. Compare 6,987,521  6,985,721.

a. >   b. <
c. =   d. not given

11. What number is 7,000,000 + 40,000 + 4,000 + 7?

a. 7,447   b. 7,404,007
c. 7,044,007   d. not given

12. Use the bar graph to find the food that showed the greatest gain in consumption from 1959 to 1981.

a. eggs   b. poultry
c. cheese   d. not given

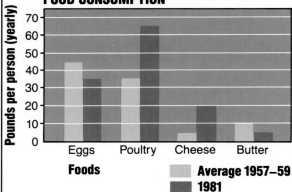

FOOD CONSUMPTION

Pounds per person (yearly)

Foods: Eggs, Poultry, Cheese, Butter

Average 1957–59
1981

13. Use the bar graph to find the food that was consumed the least from 1957 to 1959.

a. eggs   b. cheese
c. butter   d. not given

Do you think that there is a prime number that is larger than every other prime number? Mathematicians have answered this question by using logic. Find out whether you can discover a prime number that is greater than 1,000. Do you think that there is a greatest prime? How could you prove your answer?

3 NUMBER THEORY, EXPRESSIONS AND EQUATIONS

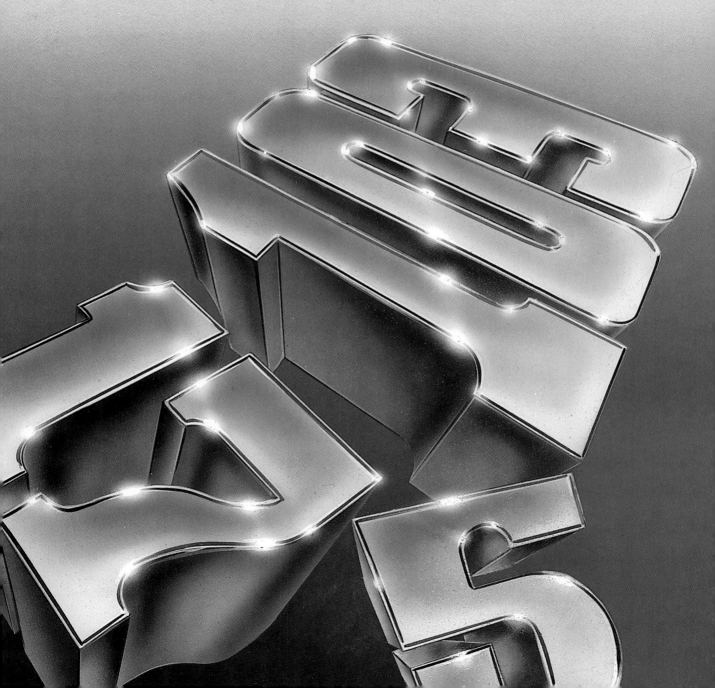

Divisibility

If a number is divided by another number and the remainder is zero, the first number is **divisible** by the other number.

A whole number is divisible by

2	if the number ends in 2, 4, 6, 8, or 0.
	A number that is divisible by 2 is called an **even number.** All other numbers are **odd numbers.**
3	if the sum of its digits is divisible by 3.
	$651 \rightarrow 6 + 5 + 1 = 12 \rightarrow 12 \div 3 = 4$
4	if the number formed by the last two digits is divisible by 4.
	$536 \rightarrow 36 \div 4 = 9 \qquad 536$ is divisible by 4.
5	if the number ends in 0 or 5.
	9,865 is divisible by 5, because it ends in 5.
6	if the number is divisible by 2 and by 3.
	114 ends in 4. $\qquad 114 \rightarrow 1 + 1 + 4 = 6 \rightarrow 6 \div 3 = 2$ 114 is divisible by 2 and by 3. So, it is divisible by 6.
8	if the number formed by the last three digits is divisible by 8.
	$9,208 \rightarrow 208 \div 8 = 26$
9	if the sum of the digits is divisible by 9.
	$3,654 \rightarrow 3 + 6 + 5 + 4 = 18 \rightarrow 18 \div 9 = 2$
10	if the ones digit is 0, as in 40; 170; and 5,630.

Is 87,624 divisible by 6?

Since 4 is in the ones place, 87,624 is divisible by 2.
Since $8 + 7 + 6 + 2 + 4 = 27$, and 27 is divisible by 3, 87,624 is divisible by 3. So, 87,624 is divisible by 6, because it is divisible by 2 and by 3.

Write *yes* or *no*.

Is the number divisible by 2?

1. 189   **2.** 83   **3.** 254   **4.** 5,050   **5.** 5,095

Is the number divisible by 3?

6. 424   **7.** 120   **8.** 5,424   **9.** 35,183   **10.** 3,393

Is the number divisible by 4?

11. 2,460   **12.** 1,786   **13.** 18,604   **14.** 2,004   **15.** 21,000

Is the number divisible by 5?

16. 255   **17.** 112   **18.** 4,024   **19.** 21,005   **20.** 10,002

Is the number divisible by 6?

21. 324   **22.** 892   **23.** 7,166   **24.** 10,813   **25.** 10,950

Is the number divisible by 3? by 9? by 10?

26. 1,944   **27.** 2,072   **28.** 32,136   **29.** 11,118   **30.** 39,006

31. 2,005   **32.** 3,250   **33.** 4,000   **34.** 10,010   **35.** 25,155

Solve.

36. Use divisibility rules to write $\frac{4,212}{7,920}$ in simplest form.

37. Use divisibility rules to write $\frac{1,728}{10,368}$ in simplest form.

38. Write a number that is divisible by 2, 3, 4, and 5.

39. Write a divisibility test to show when a number is divisible by 12.

NUMBER SENSE

It is easy to multiply by 10, 100, and 1,000. You can use them to estimate quickly.

Example: $9.67 × 15
Since $9.67 is close to $10, estimate $10 × 15 = $150.

Estimate. Use 10, 100, and 1,000 where possible.

1. 47 × 96   **2.** 45 × $9.77   **3.** 356 × 981

4. 19 × $102.53   **5.** 1,037 × 826   **6.** 98 × 4,753

Powers and Roots

A. What is the value of 2^5?

In the expression 2^5, 5 is called the **exponent** and 2 is called the **base.**

$$2^{5 \leftarrow \text{exponent}} = \underbrace{2 \times 2 \times 2 \times 2 \times 2}_{\text{5 factors}} = 32$$
$$\text{base} \rightarrow$$

An exponent shows how many times a number or base is used as a factor. So, $2^5 = 32$.

32 is said to be a **power** of 2.

To find the value of the expression 4^2, use the base 4 as a factor 2 times.

$$4^2 = 4 \times 4 = 16$$

Zero can be used as an exponent.

$$8^0 = 1 \qquad 25^0 = 1 \qquad 162^0 = 1$$

Any number multiplied by itself is called the **square of the number.**

Since $4^2 = 16$, you can say that the **square root** of 16 is 4, or $\sqrt{16} = 4$.

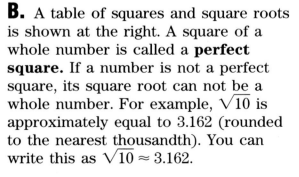

B. A table of squares and square roots is shown at the right. A square of a whole number is called a **perfect square.** If a number is not a perfect square, its square root can not be a whole number. For example, $\sqrt{10}$ is approximately equal to 3.162 (rounded to the nearest thousandth). You can write this as $\sqrt{10} \approx 3.162$.

Number	Square	Square root
1	1	1
2	4	1.414
3	9	1.732
4	16	2
5	25	2.236
6	36	2.449
7	49	2.646
8	64	2.828
9	81	3
10	100	3.162

Write as a product of factors and evaluate.

1. 5^2 **2.** 1^3 **3.** 7^4 **4.** 8^1

5. 2^3 **6.** 9^5 **7.** 6^4 **8.** 10^4

Rewrite and evaluate each. Use exponents.

9. 3×3 **10.** $5 \times 5 \times 5 \times 5$ **11.** $14 \times 14 \times 14$

12. $2 \times 2 \times 2$ **13.** $5 \times 5 \times 5 \times 5 \times 5$ **14.** 10×10

15. $10 \times 10 \times 10 \times 10$ **16.** $6 \times 6 \times 6 \times 6 \times 6$ **17.** $2 \times 2 \times 3 \times 3$

Find the square root. Use the table.

18. $\sqrt{1}$ **19.** $\sqrt{25}$

20. $\sqrt{64}$ **21.** $\sqrt{81}$

22. $\sqrt{49}$ **23.** $\sqrt{144}$

24. $\sqrt{36}$ **25.** $\sqrt{4}$

26. $\sqrt{100}$ **27.** $\sqrt{121}$

28. $\sqrt{400}$ **29.** $\sqrt{225}$

30. $\sqrt{45}$ **31.** $\sqrt{19}$

32. $\sqrt{37}$ **33.** $\sqrt{22}$

34. $\sqrt{46}$ **35.** $\sqrt{13}$

★**36.** $\sqrt{1.44}$ ★**37.** $\sqrt{9.61}$

★**38.** $\sqrt{21.16}$

n	n^2	$\sqrt{n}$	n	n^2	$\sqrt{n}$
1	1	1.000	26	676	5.099
2	4	1.414	27	729	5.196
3	9	1.732	28	784	5.292
4	16	2.000	29	841	5.385
5	25	2.236	30	900	5.477
6	36	2.449	31	961	5.568
7	49	2.646	32	1,024	5.657
8	64	2.828	33	1,089	5.745
9	81	3.000	34	1,156	5.831
10	100	3.162	35	1,225	5.916
11	121	3.317	36	1,296	6.000
12	144	3.464	37	1,369	6.083
13	169	3.606	38	1,444	6.164
14	196	3.742	39	1,521	6.245
15	225	3.873	40	1,600	6.325
16	256	4.000	41	1,681	6.403
17	289	4.123	42	1,764	6.481
18	324	4.243	43	1,849	6.557
19	361	4.359	44	1,936	6.633
20	400	4.472	45	2,025	6.708
21	441	4.583	46	2,116	6.782
22	484	4.690	47	2,209	6.856
23	529	4.796	48	2,304	6.928
24	576	4.899	49	2,401	7.000
25	625	5.000	50	2,500	7.071

39. Use the information in the Infobank on page 474 to find the cube root of 729.

CALCULATOR

You can use the trial-and-error method to estimate square roots on a calculator.

$\sqrt{12}$ is between $\sqrt{9}$ and $\sqrt{16}$. $\sqrt{12}$ is between 3 and 4.

Try 3.4. $3.4 \times 3.4 = 11.56$ Try 3.5. $3.5 \times 3.5 = 12.25$

3.5 is the better estimate.

Find the square root on a calculator. Round to the nearest tenth.

1. $\sqrt{17}$ **2.** $\sqrt{56}$ **3.** $\sqrt{72}$ **4.** $\sqrt{88}$ **5.** $\sqrt{112}$ **6.** $\sqrt{473}$

Scientific Notation

A. It is often difficult to compute with very large numbers. Some numbers are even too large for your calculator.

- How many digits will your calculator display? Find out by entering the digits 1, 2, 3, 4, ... until the display is full.

- What number does your display show? Using pencil and paper, multiply that number by 10.

- Now do this multiplication on your calculator.

- Compare your display with those on your classmates' calculators. Did anyone get a result that is different from yours? How does your display compare to your answer on paper?

- Did any of the calculators display a decimal between 1 and 10 for the product? If so, could you multiply this number by a power of 10 to get the actual product?

Thinking as a Team

Very large numbers are often written in a shorthand called **scientific notation.** This notation uses a decimal multiplied by a power of 10. The decimal is always greater than or equal to 1 but is less than 10.

In scientific notation the number 40,000,000 is written 4×10^7. 45,000,000 is written 4.5×10^7. How would you write 75,000 in scientific notation?

1. What is a quick way to multiply a decimal by a power of ten?

2. How would you write 5.01×10^5 in standard form?

3. How would you write 28,500,000 in scientific notation?

4. How would you write 12,140 in scientific notation?

5. How would you write a power of 10 in scientific notation?

B. A light-year is the distance light travels in one year. Light travels at the rate of approximately 186,000 miles per second. About how many miles in length is a light-year?

Working as a Team

1. About how many seconds are there in a year? How would you write this number in scientific notation? How would you write the speed of light in scientific notation?

2. How could you use your calculator to find the number of miles in a light-year?

3. When you multiply two numbers written in scientific notation, which part is easier to multiply first? What relationship do you see between the exponents in the factors and the exponent in the product?

4. Try multiplying other numbers using scientific notation to see whether this relationship is always true.

5. How does scientific notation help you to multiply large numbers?

The average distance from the Sun to Earth is about 93,000,000 miles. How could you use scientific notation and a calculator to find the number of seconds it takes for light from the Sun to reach Earth? What relationship do you see among the exponents of the numbers in this calculation?

Find the volume of a cube whose edge is 2.1×10^3 cm long. Write your answer in scientific notation.

In which other fields of science might you use scientific notation to express large numbers? Find some examples to share with your classmates.

PROBLEM SOLVING
Checking for a Reasonable Answer

Some errors in arithmetic can lead to answers that are far from the correct answer. When you solve a problem, think about the reasonableness of the answer. Is it much too great? Is it much too small? You can often spot a wrong answer just by thinking about whether it is reasonable.

A newly published book on mathematics and architecture sells for $28.95. Library purchases for the first month were reported to be 4,468 copies. What was the total amount paid for those copies?

  a. $120,000   **b.** $1,200   **c.** $1,200,000

Without computing the exact answer, try to find a reasonable estimate. You can see that choice *b* is much too small and choice *c* is much too large. The most reasonable answer to the problem is choice *a*, or $120,000.

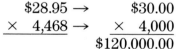

$$\begin{array}{rcr} \$28.95 & \rightarrow & \$30.00 \\ \times\quad 4,468 & \rightarrow & \times\quad 4,000 \\ \hline & & \$120,000.00 \end{array}$$

Read each problem. Without computing the exact answer, write the letter of the most reasonable answer.

1. Each chapter of the book is illustrated with 83 engravings of buildings. If the book has twenty-five chapters, how many engravings are there in the book?

   a. 200 engravings
   b. 2,000 engravings
   c. 20,000 engravings

2. One bookstore ordered 762 books. If the total cost of the order, including shipping charges, was $23,926.80, what was the total cost per book?

   a. $3.10
   b. $30.00
   c. $310.00

Read each problem. Without computing the exact answer, write the letter of the most reasonable answer.

3. An illustration of a square Roman courtyard showed that there were 6,875 tiles on one edge of the floor. About how many tiles were there in the courtyard floor?

a. 49,000
b. 4,900,000
c. 49,000,000

4. In building a scale model of a Babylonian building, Janice used materials worth $2.75. Rachel spent 23 times as much on her model of the Roman Forum. About how much did Rachel spend?

a. about $30
b. about $40
c. about $65

5. Members of the Mideastern High School archeology club built a *diorama* of ancient Babylon. The original plans called for the total number of trees, bushes, and plants to be 14 times the number of buildings. If 896 buildings were planned, how many trees, bushes, and plants would there have been?

a. 8,000
b. 14,000
c. 100,000

6. The practice of cubing a number goes back at least as far as the tenth century. More recently, Manny was estimating cube roots in a math contest. The contest's deciding question was $\sqrt[3]{27,000}$. What answer should Manny have given?

a. 30
b. 130
c. 3,000

7. Louise wanted to determine the distance from Mercury to Earth. If Mercury is 36,000,000 miles from the sun, and Earth is 93,000,000 miles from the sun, which is the most reasonable estimate of their distance from each other?

a. 5×10^7
b. 5×10^8
c. 5×10^6

★8. In around 580 B.C., Pythagoras used an equation to find the length of the longest side of a right triangle. Use the equation $c = \sqrt{a^2 + b^2}$. If a is 3 m and b is 4 m, how long is c?

a. 0.5 m
b. 5 m
c. 50 m

Factors, Primes, and Composites

A. In about 300 B.C., the Greek mathematician Euclid used the notion of factors to develop a theorem relating prime numbers to factorization.

A **factor** is any number used in multiplication to produce a product.

A **prime number** is any number greater than 1 whose only factors are itself and 1.

Is 7 a prime number?

Since the only factors of 7 are 7 and 1, 7 is a prime number.

Some other prime numbers are 2, 3, 5, 11, and 13.

B. A number greater than 1 that has more than two factors is called a **composite number.**

Is 12 a prime number or a composite number?

To find the factors of 12, write 12 as the product of different pairs of numbers.

$$12 = 1 \times 12 \qquad 12 = 2 \times 6 \qquad 12 = 3 \times 4$$

The factors of 12 are 1, 2, 3, 4, 6, and 12.

So, 12 is a composite number because it has factors other than itself and 1.

C. The number 1 is neither prime nor composite, and occasionally is called **unity.** The smallest prime number is 2.

Checkpoint Write the letter of the correct answer.

1. A factor of 24 is ■.   **a.** 6   **b.** 48   **c.** 7   **d.** 96

2. A prime number is ■.   **a.** 2   **b.** 9   **c.** 51   **d.** 25

3. A composite number is ■.   **a.** 5   **b.** 17   **c.** 23   **d.** 57

Math Reasoning, page H211

Find all the factors of each number.

1. 10
2. 14
3. 15
4. 18
5. 19
6. 24
7. 27
8. 33
9. 38
10. 45
11. 40
12. 55
13. 60
14. 75
15. 85

Write *prime* or *composite*.

16. 7
17. 10
18. 14
19. 19
20. 63
21. 29
22. 11
23. 5
24. 4
25. 9
26. 55
27. 60
28. 81
29. 71
30. 15
31. 27
32. 91
33. 87
34. 53
35. 39
36. 58
37. 77
38. 82
39. 90
40. 45

Solve.

41. The **Sieve of Eratosthenes** is a method for finding primes by sifting out composite numbers. To start the sieve, copy the list of numbers and continue to 200. Cross out 1 because it is not prime.

    Circle 2 and cross out all numbers that have 2 as a factor.

    Circle 3 and cross out all numbers that have 3 as a factor.

    Continue in this manner, circling the next prime number and crossing out all numbers that have the circled number as a factor. The remaining numbers should be the prime numbers from 1 to 200.

    How many primes are there?

42. Every even number can be written as the sum of two prime numbers. The number 40 is the sum of 37 + 3. What are the other ways to write 40 as the sum of two prime numbers?

SIEVE OF ERATOSTHENES

1 2 3 4 5 6 7 8 9 10
11 12 13 14 15 16 17 18 19 20
21 22 23 24 25 26 27 28 29 30
31 32 33 34 35 36 37 38 39 40

ANOTHER LOOK

Divide.

1. $5.95 ÷ 35
2. $18.63 ÷ 81
3. $229.50 ÷ 450
4. $428.17 ÷ 911

Prime Factorization

A. Prime numbers are helpful in factoring because each composite number can be written as the product of prime numbers. This is called the **prime factorization** of the number.

A **factor tree** can be used to find the prime factorization of 120. Begin by choosing any two numbers whose product is 120. Continue until every "branch" ends with a prime factor.

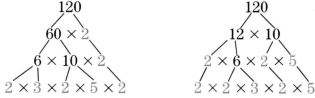 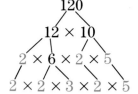

The prime factorization of 120 is $2 \times 3 \times 2 \times 5 \times 2$, or $2 \times 2 \times 3 \times 2 \times 5$. The prime factorization is the same, just the order of the factors is different.

If a factor appears more than once, use exponents to show how many times the factor is used. Write the factors in order. The prime factorization of 120 is $2^3 \times 3 \times 5$.

B. You can also find the prime factorization by using division. Divide by prime numbers in order until the quotient is 1. Use divisibility rules to help you.

$$
\begin{array}{r|r}
2 & 30 \\ \hline
3 & 15 \\ \hline
5 & 5 \\ \hline
 & 1
\end{array}
$$

$$
\begin{array}{r|l}
3 & 231 \leftarrow \text{not divisible by 2} \\ \hline
7 & 77 \leftarrow \text{not divisible by 5} \\ \hline
11 & 11 \\ \hline
 & 1
\end{array}
$$

The prime factorization of 30 is $2 \times 3 \times 5$.

The prime factorization of 231 is $3 \times 7 \times 11$.

Find the prime factorization of each number. Use factor trees. Use exponents to write the answer.

1. 12	**2.** 40	**3.** 54	**4.** 160	**5.** 128
6. 333	**7.** 108	**8.** 300	**9.** 220	**10.** 480
11. 900	**12.** 750	**13.** 960	**14.** 620	**15.** 824
16. 1,260	**17.** 1,402	**18.** 1,521	**19.** 2,025	**20.** 2,431

Write the prime factorization of each number. Use exponents.

21. 9	**22.** 20	**23.** 27	**24.** 64	**25.** 35
26. 80	**27.** 75	**28.** 94	**29.** 135	**30.** 150
31. 180	**32.** 48	**33.** 335	**34.** 425	**35.** 111
36. 240	**37.** 2,750	**38.** 1,960	**39.** 5,184	**40.** 11,475

Write the number for each prime factorization.

41. $2 \times 3 \times 5$

42. $2^2 \times 3 \times 5$

43. $3 \times 5 \times 7^2$

44. $5^2 \times 7 \times 11$

45. $2^4 \times 3^2 \times 5$

46. $11 \times 13 \times 17$

Solve.

47. Which prime factors do 24 and 80 share?

48. List the shared prime factors of 36 and 144.

49. Find the prime factors of 31 and 53. How many factors do they have in common?

★50. What is the smallest number that has six different primes in its prime factorization?

CHALLENGE

Use the Infobank on page 474 to solve. Write the cube roots and break the code.

"What is the most difficult thing to do on a long trip?"

$\sqrt[3]{125}$ $\sqrt[3]{512}$ $\sqrt[3]{343}$ $\sqrt[3]{27}$

$\sqrt[3]{343}$ $\sqrt[3]{64}$ $\sqrt[3]{343}$ $\sqrt[3]{729}$ $\sqrt[3]{216}$

$3 = Y$
$4 = W$
$5 = S$
$6 = E$
$7 = A$
$8 = T$
$9 = K$

Greatest Common Factor (GCF)

A. The rule for finding the **greatest common factor (GCF)** of a set of numbers was probably first used by Boethius, who lived around A.D. 510.

What is the GCF of 12 and 18?

To find the GCF of two numbers, list all the factors of each number.

Then circle the common factors. The GCF is the largest common factor.

Factors of 12: ①, ②, ③, 4 , ⑥, 12

Factors of 18: ①, ②, ③, ⑥, 9 , 18

Common factors: ①, ②, ③, ⑥

GCF: 6

B. Another way to find the GCF is to use prime factorization. To find the GCF of 54, 90, and 126, use exponents to write the prime factorization for each.

Prime factorization of 54: 2×3^3

Prime factorization of 90: $2 \times 3^2 \times 5$

Prime factorization of 126: $2 \times 3^2 \times 7$

Product of common prime factors: 2×3^2

GCF: 18

C. Numbers are called **relatively prime** when their only common factor is 1.

To find the GCF of 8 and 15, factor.

Factors of 8: ①, 2 , 4 , 8

Factors of 15: ①, 3 , 5 , 15

The GCF of 8 and 15 is 1. The numbers are relatively prime.

List the factors to find the GCF.

1. 27, 81   **2.** 77, 28   **3.** 9, 50   **4.** 10, 48

5. 41, 25   **6.** 12, 20   **7.** 20, 35   **8.** 12, 42

9. 26, 31, 39   **10.** 15, 33, 54   **11.** 17, 23, 46   **12.** 64, 48, 26

Use prime factorization to find the GCF. Use exponents and evaluate.

13. 14, 35   **14.** 12, 60   **15.** 11, 55   **16.** 15, 40

17. 18, 63   **18.** 16, 52   **19.** 25, 90   **20.** 10, 125

21. 27, 63, 45   **22.** 32, 40, 58   **23.** 16, 24, 80   **24.** 31, 50, 75

25. 8, 100   **26.** 27, 75, 120   **27.** 24, 42, 54   **28.** 360, 756

29. 45, 370, 590   **30.** 56, 420   **31.** 21; 1,087; 3,842   **32.** 204; 3,897

Solve.

33. If the GCF of three numbers is 45, what is the smallest that any of the three numbers could be?

34. If the GCF of two numbers is 36, what are some of the prime factors of each number?

CHALLENGE

The Greek mathematician Euclid discovered an easy way to find the GCF of two numbers.
To find the GCF of 42 and 312

1. Divide the larger number by the smaller.

$$\begin{array}{r} 7 \\ 42\overline{)312} \\ \underline{294} \end{array}$$

2. Divide the previous divisor by the remainder. Repeat until the remainder is 0.

$$\begin{array}{r} 2 \\ 18\overline{)42} \\ \underline{36} \end{array}$$

3. The last divisor is the GCF.

$$\begin{array}{r} 3 \\ 6\overline{)18} \rightarrow 6 \text{ is the GCF.} \\ \underline{18} \\ 0 \end{array}$$

Use Euclid's method to find the GCF of these numbers.

a. 36, 78   **b.** 91, 669   **c.** 146, 722

Least Common Multiple

A. A **multiple** of a number is any product that has the number as a factor.

To find the smallest or the **least common multiple (LCM)** of two numbers, list some of the multiples of each number.

What is the LCM of 6 and 15?

Multiples of 6: 0, 6, 12, 18, 24, 30, 36, 42, 48, 54, 60, . . .

Multiples of 15: 0, 15, 30, 45, 60, 75, . . .

Common multiples: 0, 30, 60, . . .

The smallest nonzero multiple, 30, is the LCM of 6 and 15.

B. Another way to find the LCM of two or more numbers is to use prime factorization.

Find the LCM of 6, 15, and 28.

Prime factorization of 6: $2 \times \text{\textcircled{3}}$

Prime factorization of 15: $3 \times \text{\textcircled{5}}$

Prime factorization of 28: $\text{\textcircled{$2^2$}} \times \text{\textcircled{7}}$

Different prime factors: 2, 3, 5, 7

Circle the highest power of each prime factor. The LCM is the product of the highest power of each of the different prime factors.

LCM: $2^2 \times 3 \times 5 \times 7$, or 420.

Checkpoint Write the letter of the correct answer.

1. A common multiple of 6 and 12 is ■.

   a. 2   **b.** 3   **c.** 6   **d.** 24

2. The LCM of 9 and 15 is ■.

   a. 3   **b.** 15   **c.** 45   **d.** 135

List the first five nonzero multiples of each number.

1. 2   **2.** 3   **3.** 5   **4.** 6

5. 7   **6.** 9   **7.** 11   **8.** 12

9. 20   **10.** 25   **11.** 100   **12.** 500

List multiples to find the LCM.

13. 24, 30   **14.** 6, 12   **15.** 6, 9   **16.** 3, 5

17. 8, 20   **18.** 6, 27   **19.** 10, 12   **20.** 12, 16

21. 4, 30   **22.** 17, 3   **23.** 10, 25, 20   **24.** 15, 60, 90

Use prime factorizations to find the LCM.

25. 30, 70   **26.** 16, 200   **27.** 36, 54   **28.** 12, 34

29. 15, 50   **30.** 42, 84   **31.** 24, 60   **32.** 45, 54

33. 14, 27, 35   **34.** 25, 42, 45   **35.** 6, 15, 150   **36.** 32, 63, 144

MIDCHAPTER REVIEW

1. Is 42,926 divisible by 3? by 4? by 8?

2. Is 3,970,615 divisible by 2? by 3? by 5?

3. Indicate whether the number is prime or composite: 127; 91.

Evaluate.

4. 7^2 **5.** 5^3 **6.** 3^4 **7.** 6^4 **8.** 8^5 **9.** 9^7

Find the square root. Use the table on page 83.

10. $\sqrt{169}$ **11.** $\sqrt{289}$ **12.** $\sqrt{1,296}$ **13.** $\sqrt{26}$ **14.** $\sqrt{38}$

Write in scientific notation.

15. 1,800   **16.** 96,320   **17.** 4,001,900   **18.** 327,000,000

Use prime factorization to find the GCF and the LCM.

19. 16, 56   **20.** 112, 220   **21.** 786; 1,116   **22.** 2,375; 1,775

PROBLEM SOLVING
Using a Table

Sometimes you can use a *rate* table to find the information you need to solve a problem.

UNITED STATES POSTAGE RATES (1988)

Weight	Rate
Letters—first class, within the United States	
1–11 oz	$0.25 for the first ounce and $0.20 for each additional ounce or fraction of an ounce.
Letters—first class to Mexico	
1–12 oz	$0.25 for the first ounce and $0.20 for each additional ounce or fraction of an ounce.
Letters—surface mail to countries other than Canada and Mexico	
1–8 oz	$0.40 for the first ounce and $0.23 for each additional ounce or fraction of an ounce.

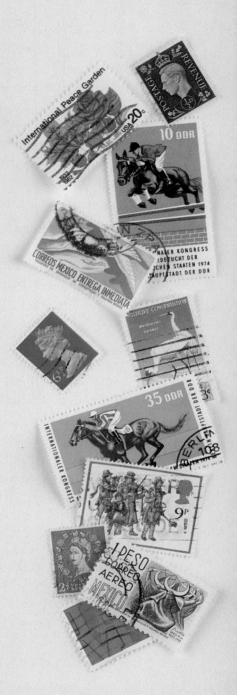

Ben lives in New Hampshire. One day, he went to the post office to mail some letters. He mailed one letter to a friend in Arizona. The letter weighted 2.3 ounces. Ben mailed a second letter to a friend in Mexico. It weighed 5.6 ounces. Finally, he mailed a letter and some photos to a friend in West Germany. That letter weighed 7.4 ounces, and Ben sent it by surface mail. How much postage did Ben buy for each letter?

To find the amount of postage that Ben bought, use the postage-rate table above. A letter that weighs 2.3 ounces, mailed first class within the United States, costs $0.65 ($0.25 + $0.20 + $0.20). A letter that weighs 5.6 ounces, sent first class to Mexico, costs $1.25. A letter that weighs 7.4 ounces, sent by surface mail to West Germany, costs $2.01.

Use the table on page 96 and the table at the right to solve.

1. Freddie mailed thank-you notes. He sent 15 one-ounce notes first class to addresses in the United States. How much postage did he pay?

2. Faye wants to send a gift to her aunt in Great Britain, the rate for which is in Rate Group C. How much will it cost her to send a 2-lb 7-oz package air parcel post?

3. Felice has to send a package air parcel post from her company in the United States to Japan. The rate is listed in Rate Group E. The package weighs 5 pounds 14 ounces. How much postage will be required?

4. Geoffrey paid $15.15 to mail a small package air parcel post to his cousin in Peru, as calculated in Rate Group B. About how much did the package weigh?

5. Cindy mailed letters by surface mail to Greenland, Ethiopia, and Australia. The letter to Ethiopia weighed 1.3 times as much as the letter to Greenland, and the letter to Greenland weighed 1.75 times as much as the letter to Australia. If the letter to Australia weighed 2.6 ounces, how much did Cindy spend on postage in order to mail the three letters?

UNITED STATES AIR PARCEL POST RATES (1988)

Weight not more than	Rate Group				
	A	**B**	**C**	**D**	**E**
1 lb	$5.50	$7.15	$8.70	$10.30	$11.95
2	8.30	11.15	13.50	16.10	18.75
3	11.10	15.15	18.30	21.90	25.55
4	13.90	19.15	23.10	27.70	32.35
5	16.70	23.15	27.90	33.50	39.15
6	18.70	26.15	31.90	38.50	45.15
7	20.70	29.15	35.90	43.50	51.15
8	22.70	32.15	39.90	48.50	57.15
9	24.70	35.15	43.90	53.50	63.15
10	26.70	38.15	47.90	58.50	69.15
11	28.70	41.15	51.90	63.50	75.15
12	30.70	44.15	55.90	68.50	81.15
13	32.70	47.15	59.90	73.50	87.15
14	34.70	50.15	63.90	78.50	93.15
15	36.70	53.15	67.90	83.50	99.15
16	38.70	56.15	71.90	88.50	105.15
17	40.70	59.15	75.90	93.50	111.15
18	42.70	62.15	79.90	98.50	117.15
19	44.70	65.15	83.90	103.50	123.15
20	46.70	68.15	87.90	108.50	129.15
21	48.70	71.15	91.90	113.50	135.15
22	50.70	74.15	95.90	118.50	141.15
Each additional 1 lb or fraction of 1 lb	2.00	3.00	4.00	5.00	6.00

6. Henry has a letter that he wants to send to Mexico. The letter weighs 1.1 ounces. Before he seals the envelope, Henry decides to add 4 magazine clippings. Each clipping weighs 0.25 ounces, Henry gives the postal clerk a $1 bill. How much change does he receive?

Order of Operations

A. What is $15 + 3 \times 5 - 2$ simplified?

Without rules for simplifying an expression, $15 + 3 \times 5 - 2$ might yield three different answers.

$15 + 3 \times 5 - 2$	$15 + 3 \times 5 - 2$	$15 + 3 \times 5 - 2$
$18 \times 5 - 2$	$15 + 15 \quad -2$	$18 \times 5 - 2$
$90 - 2$	$30 - 2$	18×3
$88?$	$28?$	$54?$

To avoid this problem, you can use these rules that specify the order for carrying out the operations.

Rules for the Order of Operations
1. Multiply as indicated by exponents.
2. Multiply and divide from left to right in order.
3. Add and subtract from left to right in order.
4. If parentheses are used, simplify within the parentheses first. Use rules 1 through 3.

By following the rules, you can see that $15 + 3 \times 5 - 2 = 28$.

B. Simplify $3 \cdot 4 + (5^2 + 4 \cdot 2) - 9.82$.

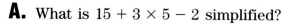
$\cdot$ means multiply.

$$
\begin{aligned}
3 \cdot 4 + (5^2 + 4 \cdot 2) - 9.82 &= 3 \cdot 4 + (25 + 4 \cdot 2) - 9.82 \\
&= 3 \cdot 4 + (25 + 8) - 9.82 \\
&= 3 \cdot 4 + 33 - 9.82 \\
&= 12 + 33 - 9.82 \\
&= 35.18
\end{aligned}
$$

C. Many calculators do not follow the rules for order of operations. For example, if you use a calculator to find the value of $6 + 4 \times 3$, you may get the answer 30, which is not correct.

To get the correct answer, rewrite the expression in the order that the operations should be performed.

$6 + 4 \times 3 = 4 \times 3 + 6 = 18$

Math Reasoning, page H212

Simplify.

1. $4 + 3 \cdot 2$ **2.** $9 + 6 \div 3$ **3.** $14 \div 2 - 2$

4. $11 - 7 + 3$ **5.** $7 + 5 - 3$ **6.** $15 \div 3 + 6$

7. $14 + 4 - 18 \div 3$ **8.** $50 \cdot 4 \div 5 + 6 - 6$ **9.** $14 + 2 \cdot 5$

10. $8 \cdot 3 - 7$ **11.** $82 + 2 \cdot 10$ **12.** $6 \cdot 9 \div 3$

13. $15 \cdot (14 - 2)$ **14.** $18 - (12 - 3)$ **15.** $13 - 3^2$

16. $15 + 8^2$ **17.** $(3 + 6)^2$ **18.** $(10 - 2)^2$

19. $3 + 6^2$ **20.** $10 - 2^2$ **21.** $80 - 8 \cdot (13 - 9)$

22. $19 + (7 + 4)^3$ **23.** $84 - (16 - 8)^2$ **24.** $18 + 7 \cdot (32 - 6)$

Use parentheses to make each answer true.

25. $9 - 3 + 2 = 4$ **26.** $1.8 - 0.8 \cdot 7 = 7$

27. $4 \cdot 5 - 3 \cdot 5 = 5$ **28.** $3 + 2 \cdot 6 \div 6 = 5$

29. $15 \div 5 + 2 = 5$ **30.** $10 + 15 \div 5 = 5$

31. $7 \cdot 3 - 3 \div 3 = 0$ **32.** $2.9 + 1.1 \cdot 5 = 20$

Write each expression so that a calculator may be used to simplify the expression. Then simplify.

33. $8 + 5 \times 5$ **34.** $18 + 6 \div 2$ **35.** $12 \times (14 - 5)$

36. $7.2 \times (3.4 + 1.2)$ **37.** $18 + 4^2$ **38.** $90 + 2^2 \times 5$

Write each expression and then simplify it.

39. Add the product of 3 and 2 to 4 squared; then subtract 1.

40. Multiply the difference between 4 squared and 2 squared by 3 squared.

41. What is the value of 2.5 multiplied by 5?

42. Multiply the value of 3 squared minus the product of 2 and 4 by 4.

CHOOSING THE METHOD

Decide which method you would use to compute each exercise: mental math, calculator, or paper and pencil. Explain your answer.

1. $80,000 \div 40$ **2.** $7,452 \div 12$ **3.** $12\overline{)60,000}$

4. $360 \div 0.95$ **5.** $36\overline{)5,000}$ **6.** $89.5 \div 0.01$

Equations

A. Solve $x + 3 = 9$.

Equations such as the one above were used by the Egyptians as long ago as 1700 B.C.

$6 < 9$	$5 + 3 = 8$	$11 + 2 > 7.6$	$13 + 1 \neq 12$	$y - 4 = 10$

All of the above are number sentences because they show the relationship between numbers, but only $5 + 3 = 8$ and $y - 4 = 10$ are **equations.** Equations show **equality.**

The letters in $x + 3 = 9$ and $y - 4 = 10$ are **variables.** They replace numbers. A number sentence that contains a variable is an **algebraic sentence.**

To solve $x + 3 = 9$, substitute members of the replacement set $\{4,5,6\}$ for the variable. Find the replacement that makes $x + 3 = 9$ a true statement.

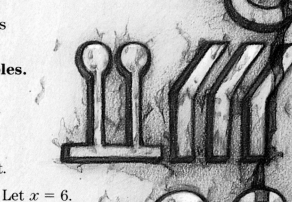

Let $x = 4$.

$x + 3 = 9$
$4 + 3 \overset{?}{=} 9$
$7 \neq 9$

4 *is not* a solution.

Let $x = 5$.

$x + 3 = 9$
$5 + 3 \overset{?}{=} 9$
$8 \neq 9$

5 *is not* a solution.

Let $x = 6$.

$x + 3 = 9$
$6 + 3 \overset{?}{=} 9$
$9 = 9$

6 *is* a solution.

Equations of this type have exactly one solution. So, 6 is the solution of $x + 3 = 9$.

B. Use the replacement set $\{0,1,2,3,4,5,6,7,8,9,10\}$ to solve.

$n + 3.4 = 8.4$

$5 + 3.4 \overset{?}{=} 8.4$

$8.4 = 8.4$

5 is the solution.

$7b = 21$

$7 \cdot 3 \overset{?}{=} 21$

$21 = 21$

3 is the solution.

> 7b means
> $7 \cdot b$.

$\frac{k}{4} = 6$

$\frac{24}{4} \overset{?}{=} 6$

$6 = 6$

24 *is not* a value in the given replacement set.

So, there is no solution in the replacement set.

Write *true* if the replacement value is a solution.
Write *false* if it is not.

1. $x + 4 = 9$, if $x = 5$

2. $3 + y = 7$, if $y = 3$

3. $y - 3 = 5$, if $y = 9$

4. $8 - y = 2$, if $y = 6$

5. $7x = 21$, if $x = 4$

6. $15x = 45$, if $x = 3$

7. $y + 7 = 8.5$, if $y = 2.5$

8. $\frac{20}{x} = 4$, if $x = 6$

9. $\frac{w}{3} = 4$, if $w = 12$

10. $3.8 + z = 8$, if $z = 4.2$

Use the replacement set {0,1,2,3,4,5,6,7,8, . . .} to find
the solution. If there is no solution in the replacement
set, write *none*.

11. $x + 5.4 = 9.4$

12. $x + 1 = 19$

13. $x + 3.5 = 8.5$

14. $22 + x = 30$

15. $x + 0 = 3$

16. $x - 9 = 12$

17. $x - 3.5 = 6.5$

18. $5 - x = 3$

19. $x - 9 = 9$

20. $x - 0 = 15$

21. $4x = 20$

22. $2x = 16$

23. $4x = 15$

24. $6x = 18$

25. $3x = 21$

26. $\frac{x}{6} = 4$

27. $\frac{x}{2} = 10$

28. $\frac{12}{x} = 3$

29. $\frac{x}{5} = 20$

30. $\frac{x}{4} = 12$

31. $41 = 9 + x$

32. $84 + h = 350$

33. $106 = 125 - z$

34. $4.8a = 19.2$

★35. $\frac{118.5}{m} = 39.5$

★36. $\frac{w}{1.2} = 12$

★37. $\frac{1,000}{n} = 100$

Solve.

38. Does the replacement set {2,3,4}
include the solution to
$3 \cdot 4(x + 2^2) \div 6 = 0$?

39. If xx was written instead of x^2,
what would the solution to $xx = 64$
be?

ANOTHER LOOK

Subtract.

1. $7 - 2.65$

2. $12 - 6.312$

3. $96 - 18.769$

4. $13.21 - 9$

5. $46.098 - 7$

6. $22.36 - 20.84$

PROBLEM SOLVING
Choosing the Operation

When you are trying to decide how to solve a problem, you can look at the wording and at the question that is asked for hints. You can use these hints to choose the best operation to use to solve the problem.

> Pythagoras was a famous Greek mathematician who taught his classes while walking through the countryside. One year, he had 187 students. He grouped them into 11 classes. Each class had the same number of students in it. How many students were there in each class?

Hints:

If you know	and you want to find	you can
• the number in each set is the same • the number in each set • the total number	the number of sets	divide.
• the number in each set is the same • the total number • the number of sets	the number in each set	divide.

Once you have chosen the best operation, you can solve the problem.

			the number
the total number		the number of sets	in each set
187	÷	11	=	17

There were 17 students in each class.

Write the letter of the operation you would use to solve each problem.

1. A mechanical device invented in the nineteenth century could draw 3 pictures per hour. It was called the Green Lady. How many pictures could the Green Lady draw in 5 hours?

   a. addition
   b. subtraction
   c. multiplication
   d. division

2. A computer called the Imagix can draw 17 pictures per minute. How long would it take the Imagix to draw 289 pictures?

   a. addition
   b. subtraction
   c. multiplication
   d. division

Solve.

3. Jerzy has a colossal abacus that has 52 columns. Each column is 2.5 inches wide. How wide are all the columns together?

4. One abacus has 30 columns of 5 beads each. A second abacus has 15 columns of 6 beads each. How many more beads does the first abacus have than the second?

5. In 1642, Blaise Pascal built the first mechanical counting machine. The first machine that could do all four mathematical operations was built 178 years later. In which year was the second machine built?

6. Charles Babbage invented an early computer called the Analytical Engine. The machine had 50 counter wheels that could store 1,000 figures each. How many figures could the entire machine store?

7. The first United States census to be tallied by computer took place in 1890. The idea for the computer was based on the Jacquard fabric loom, which was invented 83 years before the 1890 census. When was the Jacquard loom invented?

★8. Barbara Schwartz is word processing a 196-page report on the history of computers. She is storing the report on disks that hold about 90 pages. How many disks will she need?

★9. The Mark I could perform 50 operations per second. ENIAC could perform 50,000 operations in 10 seconds. How many times faster was ENIAC than the Mark I?

★10. When ENIAC was built, it was estimated that it would take 100 engineers 1 year to do a calculation that ENIAC could perform in 2 hours. How many years would it have taken 10 engineers to do a problem that took ENIAC 1 hour?

Solving Equations (+ and −)

A. It is believed that the earliest methods of solving equations involved testing replacements. Later, however, Arab mathematicians began to use methods that were more convenient than the trial-and-error method.

Because addition and subtraction are inverse operations, one can be used to undo the other.

If you add or subtract the same number on both sides of an equation, the resulting equation has the same solution.

To find the solution of $x + 18 = 54$, subtract 18 from both sides of the equation.

$$x + 18 = 54$$
$$x + 18 - 18 = 54 - 18$$
$$x = 36$$

To check, let $x = 36$.
$$36 + 18 \overset{?}{=} 54$$
$$54 = 54 ✔$$

So, $x = 36$.

B. To find the solution of $y - 1.5 = 3.5$, add 1.5 to both sides of the equation.

$$y - 1.5 = 3.5$$
$$y - 1.5 + 1.5 = 3.5 + 1.5$$
$$y = 5$$

To check, let $y = 5$.
$$5 - 1.5 \overset{?}{=} 3.5$$
$$3.5 = 3.5 ✔$$

The solution is 5.

Checkpoint Write the letter of the correct answer.

1. The next step in the solution of $y - 3 = 5$ is ▧.

a. $y - 3 + 5 = 5$ **b.** $y - 3 = 5 + 3$ **c.** $y - 3 + 3 = 5 + 3$

2. The next step in the solution of $x + 3 = 10$ is ▧.

a. $x + 3 - 3 = 10 - 10$ **b.** $x + 3 - 3 = 10 - 3$ **c.** $x + 3 - 10 = 10 - 3$

3. The solution of $500 + x = 750$ is ▧.

a. $x = 1,250$ **b.** $x = 750$ **c.** $x = 250$

Solve each equation.

1. $x - 12 = 68$

2. $b - 27 = 41$

3. $c - 2.4 = 6.7$

4. $y - 15 = 32$

5. $w + 805 = 904$

6. $r - 9 = 5$

7. $x - 6 = 34$

8. $t - 14.4 = 16.9$

9. $9 + y = 84$

10. $m + 112 = 146$

11. $t - 92 = 109$

12. $t + 81.6 = 110.5$

13. $c - 81 = 53$

14. $c + 57.9 = 84.2$

15. $d - 2.3 = 1.7$

16. $x - 5.5 = 7$

17. $s + 4.6 = 9.7$

18. $t + 23.4 = 42.3$

19. $y - 7 = 15$

20. $d + 12.8 = 19.7$

21. $r + 12 = 78$

22. $y - 11.2 = 74$

23. $15 + s = 84$

24. $t - 19 = 143$

25. $y + 9.5 = 20$

26. $a + 7.3 = 15.2$

27. $x + 1.6 = 5.8$

28. $n + 3.7 = 10.3$

29. $t - 32.9 = 73.8$

★30. $c + (6.2 + 3.9) = 25.5$

★31. $n + 3.7 + 6.9 = 15$

★32. $m - 2.4 - 3 = 10$

★33. $(9.5 + 0.8) + m = 15.7$

FOCUS: REASONING

The geometry that you are familiar with was developed by Euclid 2,000 years ago. In the 1830's, three European mathematicians—the German, Karl Gauss; the Russian, Nikolai Lobachevsky; and the Hungarian, Janos Bolyai—all published works challenging Euclidean geometry.

Many of Europe's top students traveled to study with at least one of these three mathematicians. Of a sample group of 30, 12 studied with Gauss and 9 with Lobachevsky. Of Gauss's students, $\frac{1}{3}$ also studied with Lobachevsky, and another $\frac{1}{3}$ also studied with Bolyai. Of Lobachevsky's students, $\frac{2}{3}$ also studied with Bolyai. 3 students studied with all of them, and 4 students studied with none of them. Use the Venn diagram at the right to find how many studied with Bolyai.

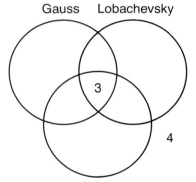

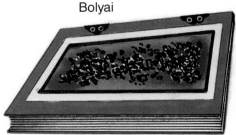

Solving Equations ($\times$ and $\div$)

A. Since the multiplication symbol $\times$ can become confused with the variable x, either $\cdot$ or no symbol at all is used in equations to mean multiplication.

12 times r can be written $12 \cdot r$ or $12r$.

Since multiplication and division are inverse operations, one can be used to undo the other. If you multiply or divide both sides of an equation by the same number (except 0) the resulting equation has the same solution.

To solve $12r = 132$, divide both sides of the equation by 12.

$$12r = 132 \qquad \text{To check, let } r = 11.$$
$$\frac{12r}{12} = \frac{132}{12} \qquad 12 \cdot 11 \overset{?}{=} 132$$
$$r = 11 \qquad\qquad 132 = 132 \; \blacktriangleright$$

So, $r = 11$.

B. To solve $\frac{y}{9} = 43$, multiply both sides by 9.

$$\frac{y}{9} = 43 \qquad \text{To check, let } y = 387.$$
$$9 \cdot \frac{y}{9} = 9 \cdot 43 \qquad \frac{387}{9} \overset{?}{=} 43$$
$$y = 387 \qquad\qquad 43 = 43 \; \blacktriangleright$$

The solution is 387.

Checkpoint Write the letter of the correct answer.

1. If $12y = 36$, then $y = \blacksquare$.

  a. $\frac{1}{3}$ **b.** 3   **c.** 24   **d.** 432

2. If $\frac{x}{4} = 32$, then $x = \blacksquare$.

  a. $\frac{1}{8}$ **b.** 28   **c.** 8   **d.** 128

Math Reasoning, page H212

Solve.

1. $8k = 64$

2. $5m = 90$

3. $2.5c = 10$

4. $8t = 296$

5. $1.4z = 4.2$

6. $0.3k = 42.3$

7. $12m = 156$

8. $6m = 774$

9. $15j = 285$

10. $4x = 196$

11. $4.5p = 288$

12. $4.3t = 8.6$

13. $0.4c = 0.36$

14. $4m = 232$

15. $3.6y = 10.8$

16. $5g = 175$

17. $\frac{a}{6} = 18$

18. $\frac{y}{27} = 5$

19. $\frac{y}{1.5} = 15$

20. $\frac{w}{25} = 7$

21. $\frac{p}{2} = 13$

22. $\frac{s}{0.8} = 3.4$

23. $\frac{c}{80} = 7$

24. $\frac{c}{16} = 20$

25. $\frac{n}{0.5} = 12$

26. $\frac{n}{11} = 10$

27. $\frac{x}{3.3} = 30$

28. $\frac{b}{0.3} = 30$

29. $\frac{t}{4} = 2.1$

30. $\frac{c}{20} = 0.5$

31. $\frac{m}{18} = 7$

32. $\frac{y}{2} = 256$

★33. $\frac{y}{7} = 56 - 49$

CHALLENGE

1. Harvey has a son whose age, raised to the fourth power, is the same as the son's age times 27. How old is Harvey's son?

2. Harvey also has two daughters. Sarah is four times as old as Andrea. Sarah's age raised to the third power is equal to Andrea's age raised to the ninth power. How old are Harvey's daughters?

3. Harvey's mother's birthday is next week. Her present age can be expressed as $a^b \cdot b^a$, where a and b are both single-digit prime factors. How old will Harvey's mother be on her upcoming birthday?

4. Harvey is 5 years older than his wife. The second digit in his wife's age is 2 more than the first digit in her age and 1 more than the first digit in Harvey's age. The sum of the digits in her age is twice the sum of the digits in Harvey's age. How old are Harvey and his wife?

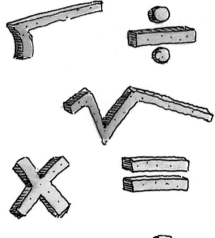

Solving Two-Step Equations

A. Solving equations is part of *algebra*, a word that comes from two Arab words that mean "opposition" and "restoration." Opposite operations undo equal terms on one side of an equation and restore them on the other side.

To solve $3x + 4.6 = 19.6$, first subtract 4.6 from both sides of the equation; next divide both sides by 3.

$$3x + 4.6 = 19.6$$
$$3x + 4.6 - 4.6 = 19.6 - 4.6$$
$$3x = 15$$
$$\frac{3x}{3} = \frac{15}{3}$$
$$x = 5.$$

To check, let $x = 5$.
$$3 \cdot 5 + 4.6 \stackrel{?}{=} 19.6$$
$$15 + 4.6 \stackrel{?}{=} 19.6$$
$$19.6 = 19.6 \; ✔$$

B. To solve $\frac{r}{5} - 9 = 11$, first add 9 to both sides of the equation; next multiply both sides by 5.

$$\frac{r}{5} - 9 = 11$$
$$\frac{r}{5} - 9 + 9 = 11 + 9$$
$$\frac{r}{5} = 20$$
$$\frac{r}{5} \cdot 5 = 20 \cdot 5$$
$$r = 100$$

To check, let $r = 100$.
$$\frac{100}{5} - 9 \stackrel{?}{=} 11$$
$$20 - 9 \stackrel{?}{=} 11$$
$$11 = 11 \; ✔$$

Checkpoint Write the letter of the correct answer.

1. The solution of $2x + 8 = 20$ is $x = $ ■.

a. 6　　**b.** 2　　**c.** 24　　**d.** 56

2. The solution of $\frac{t}{2} - 14 = 14$ is $t = $ ■.

a. 0　　**b.** 42　　**c.** 14　　**d.** 56

Solve. For additional activities, see *Connecting Math Ideas,* page 470.

1. $7n - 12 = 16$

2. $9d - 27 = 36$

3. $\frac{m}{4} + 6 = 30$

4. $\frac{y}{5} - 9 = 11$

5. $\frac{s}{3} - 15 = 15$

6. $9x + 5 = 77$

7. $\frac{x}{4} - 3 = 1$

8. $\frac{x}{5} + 9 = 14$

9. $4v + 5 = 37$

10. $9d - 9 = 9$

11. $\frac{x}{7} + 4 = 10$

12. $5m - 4 = 26$

13. $6z + 3 = 69$

14. $2a + 9 = 17$

15. $\frac{h}{5} + 8 = 15$

16. $\frac{r}{9} - 4 = 7$

17. $2k - 6 = 8$

18. $4a + 8 = 32$

19. $7w - 9 = 12$

20. $2a - 19 = 31$

21. $\frac{n}{6} + 8 = 12$

22. $4j + 7 = 31$

23. $\frac{h}{8} + 10 = 14$

24. $\frac{t}{5} - 7 = 13$

25. $7f - 1 = 27$

26. $\frac{g}{7} - 3 = 2$

27. $9c - 4 = 41$

28. $3n - 3 = 15$

29. $\frac{s}{9} - 2 = 3$

30. $\frac{y}{10} + 4 = 16$

31. $4k - 6 = 34$

32. $\frac{m}{2} - 5 = 15$

33. $3y - 11 = 25$

34. $0.5n + 3 = 8.5$

35. $24.1 + 6x = 38.5$

36. $3.5 + 2x = 13.5$

37. $\frac{y}{3.5} + 15 = 17$

38. $2a - 23 = 40$

39. $3y - 22 = 32$

CHALLENGE Patterns, Relations, and Functions

You can use the pattern to find products of numbers that are nearly equal.

$7^2 = 7 \times 7 = 49$	$8^2 = 8 \times 8 = 64$	$9^2 = 9 \times 9 = 81$
$8 \times 6 = 48$	$9 \times 7 = 63$	$10 \times 8 = 80$
$9 \times 5 = 45$	$10 \times 6 = 60$	$11 \times 7 = 77$
$10 \times 4 = 40$	$11 \times 5 = 55$	$12 \times 6 = 72$

Does this pattern hold for all squares?

Use the pattern to find the following products.

1. 101×99

2. 102×98

3. 103×97

4. 201×199

5. 202×198

6. 203×197

7. See if you can extend the pattern to find 204×196.

PROBLEM SOLVING
Writing an Equation

Many word problems can be solved by writing the problem in the form of an equation. When writing an equation, be sure that you state the facts in the problem correctly.

A basic unit of weight in ancient Babylon was called a *mina*. A Babylonian farmer had two piles of grain to sell. The first pile of grain weighed 15 minas, which was 3 more than 4 times the weight of the second pile of grain. What was the weight of the second pile of grain?

1. List what you know and what you need to find.

Know

- The first pile of grain weighed 15 minas.
- The first pile of grain weighed 3 more than 4 times the second pile of grain.

Find

- the weight of the second pile of grain

2. Think about how you can use the given information to form an equation. Use a variable to represent the number you need to find.
Let n = the weight of the second pile of grain.

weight of the first pile of grain	was	3	more than	4 times the weight of the second pile of grain
↓	↓	↓	↓	↓
15	=	3	+	$4n$

Think: You can rewrite the equation as $4n + 3 = 15$.

3. Solve the equation, and write the answer.

$$4n + 3 = 15$$
$$4n + 3 - 3 = 15 - 3$$
$$4n = 12$$
$$\frac{4n}{4} = \frac{12}{4}$$
$$n = 3$$

The second pile of grain weighed 3 minas.

Write the letter of the correct equation.

1. In the 1700's, the United States foot was divided into 1,000 parts. This foot was 33 parts longer than the Roman foot. How many parts long was the Roman foot?

   a. $18 + n = 1,000$
   b. $n + 33 = 1,000$
   c. $n - 33 = 1,000$

2. The Venice foot was used in some cities in Italy. This foot was 62 parts longer than 1.1 times the United States foot. How many parts long was the Venice foot?

   a. $\frac{n}{1.1} + 62 = 1,000$
   b. $1.1n + 62 = 1,000$
   c. $n - 62 = 1.1 \times 1,000$

Write an equation, and solve.

3. The Antwerp foot was used in Belgium. It was 54 parts shorter than the 1,000-part American foot. How many parts long was the Antwerp foot?

4. A Babylonian farmer had two bags of dried peas. One bag weighed 35 *shekels*, which was 5 more than twice the weight of the other bag. How much did the other bag weigh?

5. In ancient Rome, an *amphora* was a unit of liquid measure. A container holding 12 amphora of olive oil holds 2 amphora more than $\frac{1}{3}$ as much as a second container. How many amphora of olive oil does the second container hold?

6. A Roman merchant had 2 containers of honey. The first container held 52 amphora. This amount was 8 less than 3 times the amount of honey in the second container. How many amphora of honey did the second container hold?

7. In a Babylonian market, a farmer sold 2 piles of vegetables. The first pile of vegetables weighed 12 minas, which was 6 minas less than 0.75 times the weight of the second pile of vegetables. What was the weight of the second pile of vegetables?

★8. In about A.D. 1400, the English foot measured 13.2 inches. The United States *pole* measures 23.76 inches longer than the square of the number of inches in the old English foot. How many inches are there in a United States pole?

CALCULATOR

When you multiply two 1-digit numbers, how many digits can there be in the answer? This answer is obvious: the smallest such product is $0 \times 0 = 0$ and the largest product is $9 \times 9 = 81$. So, there must be 1 or 2 digits in the product of two 1-digit numbers.

Use your calculator (and your problem-solving skills) to complete this chart.

Number of Digits in the First Factor	Number of Digits in the Second Factor	Smallest Product	Number of Digits in Smallest Product	Largest Product	Number of Digits in Largest Product
1	1	$0 \times 0 = 0$	1	$9 \times 9 = 81$	2
2	2	$10 \times 10 = 100$	3	$99 \times 99 = 9{,}801$	4
3	3	1. ▩	2. ▩	3. ▩	4. ▩
4	4	5. ▩	6. ▩	7. ▩	8. ▩
5	5	★9. ▩	★10. ▩	★11. ▩	★12. ▩
6	6	★13. ▩	★14. ▩	★15. ▩	★16. ▩
7	7	★17. ▩	★18. ▩	★19. ▩	★20. ▩
2	3	21. $10 \times 100 =$ ▩	22. ▩	23. $99 \times 999 =$ ▩	24. ▩
2	4	25. ▩	26. ▩	27. ▩	28. ▩
2	5	29. ▩	30. ▩	31. ▩	32. ▩
3	4	33. ▩	34. ▩	35. ▩	36. ▩
3	5	37. ▩	38. ▩	39. ▩	40. ▩
4	7	★41. ▩	★42. ▩	★43. ▩	★44. ▩

45. Using an 8-digit calculator, what is the largest whole number that can be multiplied by itself and correctly displayed?

GROUP PROJECT

Setting Your Own Standards

The problem: How would you measure the weight of objects if you didn't use pounds or ounces? Many ancient measurement systems used a physical object, such as a kernel of corn, as a standard. For example, if 250 corn kernels equaled one pound, a 47-pound dog would weigh 11,750 kernels of corn in an ancient measuring system. What objects would you use as standards for measurement? Consider the key questions, and invent your own system of weights based on one object or several objects. Then find the weight of your object(s) in pounds or ounces. Make a chart like the one below, and calculate the weight of each item by using your new system of weights.

Key Questions

- Will you use one kind of object as a measurement of everything?

- How efficiently will your object(s) measure very heavy items? very light items?

- How easy to handle will large quantities of your object(s) be?

Item	Customary weight	New system
Can of soup	■	■
Blue whale	■	■
Pizza	■	■
Typewriter	■	■
Toaster	■	■
Toast	■	■
Potato	■	■

CHAPTER TEST

Write whether each number is divisible by 2, 3, 4, 5, 6, 8, 9, 10, or none of these numbers. (pages 80–81)

1. 699

2. 3,168

3. 4,217

Find the square root. (pages 82–83)

4. $\sqrt{16}$

5. $\sqrt{25}$

6. $\sqrt{36}$

Write in scientific notation. (pages 84–85)

7. 480,000

8. 3,215,700

9. 619,720

Write in standard form. (pages 84–85)

10. 3.24×10^3

11. 5.4321×10^6

Write the prime factorization for each number. Use exponents. (pages 90–91)

12. 54

13. 48

14. 525

Find the GCF. (pages 92–93)

15. 14 and 82

16. 25, 50, 75

Find the LCM. (pages 94–95)

17. 7 and 9

18. 4, 9, and 12

Simplify. (pages 98–99)

19. $2(7 + 8) \div (9 - 4)$

20. $(36 \div 3^2 + 3) \times (18 - 12)$

Solve. (pages 100–101 and 104–107)

21. $x + 18 = 42$

22. $a - 9.2 = 4.6$

23. $7y = 56$

24. $\frac{b}{2} = 8.7$

Solve. (pages 108–109)

25. $4n - 25 = 23$

26. $\frac{c}{2.1} + 8 = 13$

27. $7m + 6.5 = 41.5$

28. $\frac{d}{5} - 14 = 2$

Solve. (pages 86–87 and 110–111)

29. The area a yoke of oxen could plow in one day was called an *acre*. It is 43,560 square feet. There are 9 square feet in 1 square yard. How many square yards are there in 1 acre?

30. It took Margaret 17.5 minutes to walk to school. It took Julie 7.3 minutes less. Find how long it took Julie to get to school.

31. A *carat* weighs 200 milligrams, or 3.085 grains troy. How many milligrams does a 24.5-carat stone weigh? How many grains troy does it weigh?

32. Find the prime factors of 312. Then find the prime factors of 520. Use your first answer to see if your second answer is reasonable.

Use the table below to solve. (pages 96–97)

COST OF ELECTRICITY (PER KWH)

	First 250 kwh	Additional kwh
June 1 to September 30	13.28¢	14.26¢
October 1 to May 31	13.28¢	12.41¢

33. The DeFiore household uses 415 kwh of electricity during the month of August. Find the cost of this electricity to the nearest cent.

BONUS

Solve.

The Babylonian *mina* was shaped like a duck and weighed about 640 grams. A swan weighed 30 mina. If you had 70 minas, how many grams would they weigh, and how many swans could you balance on a scale?

RETEACHING

When an expression contains several operations, simplify it in the following order.

1. Simplify powers and roots.

2. If parentheses are used, evaluate the expressions enclosed in parentheses first, and use the order outlined below.

3. Perform multiplications and divisions from left to right.

4. Perform additions and subtractions from left to right.

Simplify $(3^2 \cdot 5) \div (1 + 2^3) + (6 - 3)$.

$$(3^2 \cdot 5) \div (1 + 2^3) + (6 - 3) = (9 \cdot 5) \div (1 + 8) + (6 - 3)$$
$$= 45 \div 9 + 3$$
$$= 5 + 3$$
$$= 8$$

Simplify each expression.

1. $5 + 6 \cdot 2$

2. $9 + 6 - 5$

3. $18 \div 6 + 2$

4. $12 \div 2 - 3$

5. $3 \cdot (5 + 4)$

6. $(3 + 5) \cdot 7$

7. $8 \cdot (30 \div 5)$

8. $3 \cdot 4 \cdot (7 + 5)$

9. $30 + 20 \div 4$

10. $60 \div (12 + 3)$

11. $3 \cdot (4 + 5) \div 9$

12. $8 \cdot (4 - 1) \div 6$

13. $7 + 3 \cdot 2 + 16$

14. $40 \div (8 - 4) + 5$

15. $(5 + 6) \div (12 - 1)$

16. $4^3 \div 4 + 4 - 4$

17. $3 + (1 + 2)^2$

18. $(9 + 5) \div (2 + 5)$

19. $3^2 \div 1 + (3 + 6)$

20. $2 + 2^2 - 2$

21. $10 + 6^2$

22. $(19 - 4^2)$

23. $(13 - 4)^2$

24. $86 - 8 \cdot (4 + 6)$

Use parentheses to make each answer true.

25. $4 + 6 \div 2 = 5$

26. $9 - 6 \cdot 5 = 15$

27. $14 \div 9 - 2 = 2$

28. $36 \div 3 + 6 = 4$

29. $2 \cdot 9 \div 3 + 3 = 3$

30. $12 + 6 \cdot 3 + 3 = 108$

ENRICHMENT

Expressions as Rules

Since a **sequence** is a set of numbers written in a particular order, the relationship between a term and its position in the sequence can be expressed as a **rule** for the sequence.

For the sequence 15, 30, 45, 60, 75, . . .

the value of the term is $\quad$ 15, 30, 45, 60, 75, . . .

the number of each term is $\ $ 1, $\ $ 2, $\ $ 3, $\ $ 3, $\ $ 4, . . .

The relationship between the number of each term (n) and the value of the term can be expressed as the rule $15n$.

The value of the sixth term would therefore be

$$15 \cdot 6 = 90.$$

Given the rule for a sequence, it is possible to calculate any term of the sequence independently of the others.

Use the rule $3n + 4$ to find the first three terms and the tenth term of the sequence.

$3 \cdot 1 + 4 = 7$
$3 \cdot 2 + 4 = 10$
$3 \cdot 3 + 4 = 13$
$3 \cdot 10 + 4 = 34$

The first three terms of the sequence are 7, 10, and 13. The tenth term is 34.

Write the rule for each sequence.

1. 7, 12, 17, 22, . . .

2. 4; 16; 64; 256; 1,024; . . .

3. 1, 4, 9, 16, . . .

4. 4, $\frac{5}{2}$, 2, $\frac{7}{4}$, $\frac{8}{5}$, . . .

Use each rule to find the first five terms and the thirtieth term.

5. $7n - 4$

6. n^3

7. $\frac{3}{n}$

8. $\left(\frac{1}{n+1}\right)^2$

CUMULATIVE REVIEW

Write the letter of the correct answer.

1. Estimate $324\overline{)9,572}$.

a. 3   **b.** 30
c. 300   **d.** 3,000

2. $5,000 \div 100$

a. 5   **b.** 50
c. 500   **d.** not given

3. Estimate $9,324 \times 5,711$.

a. 53,000   **b.** 540,000
c. 54,000,000   **d.** 5,400,000

4. $40,724 \times 296$

a. 11,943,204   **b.** 12,054,304
c. 12,054,414   **d.** not given

5. $7,008 \div 213$

a. 22 R192   **b.** 32
c. 32 R192   **d.** not given

6. 0.09872×59

a. 0.482338   **b.** 5.71448
c. 5.82448   **d.** not given

7. What number is 921 million, 123 thousand?

a. 921,123   **b.** 921,100,023
c. 921,123,000   **d.** not given

8. Estimate $89,456 + 98,546$.

a. 19,000   **b.** 100,000
c. 190,000   **d.** 2,000,000

9. $19.40701 - 1.94072$

a. 17.46629   **b.** 18.54773
c. 18.56739   **d.** not given

10. Round to thousandths and subtract: $5.80992 - 2.93427$.

a. 2.874   **b.** 2.876
c. 3.744   **d.** not given

11. $6,750,042 + 7,439,968 + 318,765$

a. 13,497,645   **b.** 13,871,245
c. 14,190,010   **d.** not given

12. $721.0409 + 16.939 + 72.104$

a. 729.9452   **b.** 810.0839
c. 1,611.6709   **d.** not given

13. James rented a store for 2 years for $13,380 per year. How much was his monthly rent?

a. $1,115   **b.** $13,380
c. $26,760   **d.** not given

14. Irene bought 7 sweaters at $15.50 each and sold them for $5 more each. Find the amount she charged for all the sweaters.

a. $73.50   **b.** $108.50
c. $143.50   **d.** not given

Which American handicrafts are you familiar with? Do you know anyone who enjoys whittling, making pottery, basket weaving, leather tooling, or quilting? Most craftspeople use mathematics when they design their crafts. Choose a craft. Which math skills might you need?

4 FRACTIONS

Equivalent Fractions

A. A fraction can be used to represent part of a whole or part of a set.

Equivalent fractions name the same number but use different terms. The fractions $\frac{1}{2}$, $\frac{2}{4}$, and $\frac{4}{8}$ are equivalent fractions.

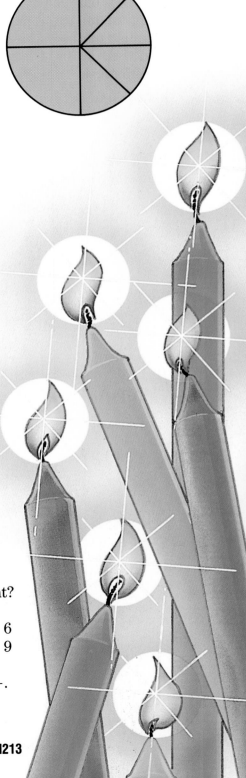

B. To find an equivalent fraction, you can multiply or divide the numerator and the denominator of a fraction by the same number.

numerator $\longrightarrow$
denominator $\longrightarrow$

$$\frac{2}{3} = \frac{2 \times 2}{3 \times 2} = \frac{4}{6} \qquad \frac{6}{12} = \frac{6 \div 6}{12 \div 6} = \frac{1}{2}$$

$$\frac{2}{3} = \frac{2 \times 3}{3 \times 3} = \frac{6}{9} \qquad \frac{6}{12} = \frac{6 \div 2}{12 \div 2} = \frac{3}{6}$$

A fraction is in simplest form if the **greatest common factor (GCF)** of the numerator and the denominator is 1.

To write a fraction in simplest form, divide the numerator and the denominator by the GCF.

Write $\frac{15}{21}$ in simplest form.

$$\frac{15}{21} = \frac{15 \div 3}{21 \div 3} = \frac{5}{7}$$

Think:
The GCF of 15 and 21 is 3.

C. To find the missing term in $\frac{2}{3} = \frac{n}{12}$

Think: $3 \times \blacksquare = 12$. $3 \times 4 = 12$

Multiply 2 by 4. $\frac{2}{3} = \frac{2 \times 4}{3 \times 4} = \frac{8}{12}$ $\qquad$ So, $n = 8$.

D. Use cross products to find whether two fractions are equivalent.

Are $\frac{3}{5}$ and $\frac{12}{20}$ equivalent? $\qquad\qquad$ Are $\frac{2}{9}$ and $\frac{1}{3}$ equivalent?

$$3 \times 20 = 60 \qquad\qquad\qquad 2 \times 3 = 6$$
$$5 \times 12 = 60 \qquad\qquad\qquad 9 \times 1 = 9$$

Yes, since $60 = 60$, $\frac{3}{5} = \frac{12}{20}$. $\qquad$ No, since $9 \neq 6$, $\frac{2}{9} \neq \frac{1}{3}$.

Math Reasoning, page H213

Write two equivalent fractions for each.

1. $\frac{3}{4}$ **2.** $\frac{1}{5}$ **3.** $\frac{2}{7}$ **4.** $\frac{3}{8}$ **5.** $\frac{4}{9}$

Write the fraction in simplest form.

6. $\frac{8}{12}$ **7.** $\frac{14}{21}$ **8.** $\frac{15}{20}$ **9.** $\frac{9}{10}$ **10.** $\frac{55}{80}$

Find the missing term.

11. $\frac{1}{4} = \frac{n}{12}$ **12.** $\frac{2}{3} = \frac{n}{15}$ **13.** $\frac{5}{9} = \frac{n}{27}$ **14.** $\frac{1}{3} = \frac{n}{18}$ **15.** $\frac{5}{6} = \frac{n}{30}$

16. $\frac{2}{7} = \frac{n}{21}$ **17.** $\frac{1}{10} = \frac{n}{100}$ **18.** $\frac{3}{8} = \frac{n}{32}$ **19.** $\frac{3}{2} = \frac{n}{24}$ **20.** $\frac{5}{1} = \frac{n}{4}$

21. $\frac{6}{7} = \frac{18}{n}$ **22.** $\frac{1}{5} = \frac{25}{n}$ **23.** $\frac{2}{3} = \frac{16}{n}$ **24.** $\frac{5}{9} = \frac{30}{n}$ **25.** $\frac{2}{7} = \frac{18}{n}$

26. $\frac{5}{4} = \frac{35}{n}$ **27.** $\frac{3}{4} = \frac{18}{n}$ **28.** $\frac{1}{2} = \frac{49}{n}$ **29.** $\frac{6}{8} = \frac{36}{n}$ **30.** $\frac{5}{6} = \frac{20}{n}$

31. $\frac{4}{5} = \frac{n}{15}$ **32.** $\frac{8}{1} = \frac{48}{n}$ **33.** $\frac{2}{3} = \frac{6}{n}$ **34.** $\frac{3}{5} = \frac{n}{15}$ **35.** $\frac{5}{9} = \frac{n}{36}$

Use cross products to write $=$ or $\neq$ for the ●.

36. $\frac{3}{4}$ ● $\frac{12}{16}$ **37.** $\frac{5}{6}$ ● $\frac{7}{9}$ **38.** $\frac{5}{8}$ ● $\frac{12}{16}$ **39.** $\frac{9}{15}$ ● $\frac{3}{5}$ **40.** $\frac{1}{6}$ ● $\frac{1}{3}$

Solve.

41. A class made wax candles for a history project. That day, 4 of the 28 students in the class were absent. What fraction of the class made candles? Write your answer in simplest form.

CHALLENGE Patterns, Relations, and Functions

What fraction of each figure is shaded?

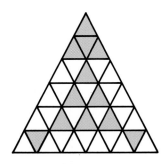 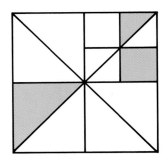 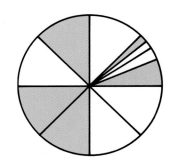

Mixed Numbers

A. A **mixed number** is the sum of a whole number and a fraction.

$5\frac{1}{3}$ means $5 + \frac{1}{3}$.

Every mixed number is equivalent to a fraction.

$$5\frac{1}{3} = 5 + \frac{1}{3} = \frac{15}{3} + \frac{1}{3} = \frac{16}{3}$$

B. You can use a shortcut to write a mixed number as a fraction. Write $5\frac{1}{2}$ as a fraction.

Multiply the whole number by the denominator.	Add the numerator to the product.	Write the sum over the denominator.
$5\frac{1}{2} \longrightarrow 2 \times 5 = 10$	$10 + 1 = 11$	$\frac{11}{2}$

So, $5\frac{1}{2} = \frac{11}{2}$.

C. Fractions greater than 1 can be written as mixed numbers. Write $\frac{34}{6}$ as a mixed number.

$$\frac{34}{6} \longrightarrow \begin{array}{r} 5 \\ 6\overline{)34} \\ \underline{30} \\ 4 \end{array} \begin{array}{l} \leftarrow \text{whole-} \\ \text{number} \\ \text{part} \end{array} \qquad \frac{4}{6} \leftarrow \text{fraction} \qquad 5\frac{4}{6} = 5\frac{2}{3}$$

So, the fraction $\frac{34}{6}$ can be written as the mixed number $5\frac{2}{3}$.

Checkpoint   Write the letter of the correct answer.

Choose the equivalent fraction.

1. $3\frac{2}{3} = $

  a. $\frac{9}{3}$ **b.** $\frac{11}{3}$ **c.** $\frac{12}{3}$ **d.** $\frac{15}{3}$

2. $2\frac{5}{7} = $

  a. $\frac{12}{7}$ **b.** $\frac{19}{7}$ **c.** $\frac{49}{7}$ **d.** $\frac{70}{7}$

Write the mixed number as a fraction.

1. $5\frac{1}{3}$ **2.** $2\frac{1}{2}$ **3.** $6\frac{2}{3}$ **4.** $9\frac{4}{5}$ **5.** $5\frac{3}{4}$ **6.** $7\frac{1}{9}$

7. $2\frac{6}{7}$ **8.** $9\frac{7}{8}$ **9.** $3\frac{4}{5}$ **10.** $1\frac{12}{13}$ **11.** $10\frac{10}{11}$ **12.** $6\frac{1}{9}$

13. $7\frac{1}{3}$ **14.** $1\frac{1}{9}$ **15.** $2\frac{5}{6}$ **16.** $7\frac{8}{9}$ **17.** $5\frac{9}{10}$ **18.** $7\frac{8}{10}$

Write the fraction as a whole number or a mixed number in simplest form.

19. $\frac{22}{5}$ **20.** $\frac{10}{6}$ **21.** $\frac{32}{9}$ **22.** $\frac{45}{7}$ **23.** $\frac{23}{2}$ **24.** $\frac{86}{40}$

25. $\frac{71}{20}$ **26.** $\frac{12}{3}$ **27.** $\frac{15}{9}$ **28.** $\frac{17}{16}$ **29.** $\frac{21}{8}$ **30.** $\frac{23}{5}$

31. $\frac{39}{10}$ **32.** $\frac{5}{4}$ **33.** $\frac{18}{5}$ **34.** $\frac{23}{9}$ **35.** $\frac{17}{10}$ **36.** $\frac{18}{17}$

37. $\frac{36}{7}$ **38.** $\frac{42}{9}$ **39.** $\frac{43}{9}$ **40.** $\frac{25}{7}$ **41.** $\frac{8}{1}$ **42.** $\frac{24}{5}$

Solve. For Problem 44, use the Infobank.

43. Pete is making wooden legs for stools. He needs 4 legs for each stool. If Pete has made 34 legs, how many stools can he make? How many legs will be left?

44. Use the information on page 474 to solve. Find the materials that can be used to make a basket. List the materials which come in $\frac{3}{8}$-in. widths.

CHALLENGE

What fraction of a dollar is each coin?

What fraction are they of $100?

Comparing and Ordering Fractions and Mixed Numbers

A. A number line can be used to compare fractions.

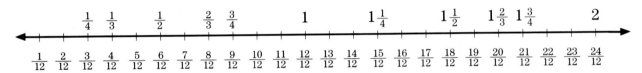

To compare fractions that have like denominators, compare their numerators. From the number line, you can see that $\frac{7}{12} > \frac{5}{12}$, $\frac{15}{12} < \frac{20}{12}$, and $1\frac{1}{4} < 1\frac{2}{3}$.

B. Compare fractions that have unlike denominators by writing equivalent fractions and comparing numerators.

Compare $\frac{3}{5}$ and $\frac{5}{8}$.

Find the **least common multiple (LCM)** of 5 and 8.
The **least common denominator (LCD)** is 40.

$$\frac{3}{5} = \frac{24}{40} \qquad\qquad \frac{5}{8} = \frac{25}{40}$$

Since $24 < 25$, $\frac{24}{40} < \frac{25}{40}$ and $\frac{3}{5} < \frac{5}{8}$.

C. You can also compare mixed numbers. First compare the whole numbers; then compare the fractions.

Compare $3\frac{2}{3}$ and $3\frac{1}{2}$.

$$3 = 3 \qquad \frac{2}{3} = \frac{4}{6} \qquad \frac{1}{2} = \frac{3}{6} \qquad \frac{4}{6} > \frac{3}{6} \qquad \text{So, } 3\frac{2}{3} > 3\frac{1}{2}.$$

D. To order fractions and mixed numbers, compare.

Order $\frac{3}{4}$, $\frac{2}{5}$, and $\frac{5}{6}$.

$$\frac{3}{4} = \frac{45}{60} \qquad \frac{2}{5} = \frac{24}{60} \qquad \frac{5}{6} = \frac{50}{60}$$

So, $\frac{2}{5} < \frac{3}{4} < \frac{5}{6}$.

Order $4\frac{1}{5}$, $4\frac{3}{10}$, and $4\frac{2}{7}$.

$$4 = 4 = 4$$

$$\frac{1}{5} = \frac{14}{70} \qquad \frac{3}{10} = \frac{21}{70} \qquad \frac{2}{7} = \frac{20}{70}$$

So, $4\frac{1}{5} < 4\frac{2}{7} < 4\frac{3}{10}$.

From least to greatest: $\frac{2}{5}$, $\frac{3}{4}$, $\frac{5}{6}$

From greatest to least: $\frac{5}{6}$, $\frac{3}{4}$, $\frac{2}{5}$

From least to greatest: $4\frac{1}{5}$, $4\frac{2}{7}$, $4\frac{3}{10}$

From greatest to least: $4\frac{3}{10}$, $4\frac{2}{7}$, $4\frac{1}{5}$

Compare. Write >, <, or = for ●.

1. $\frac{3}{5}$ ● $\frac{4}{5}$ **2.** $\frac{2}{3}$ ● $\frac{1}{3}$ **3.** $\frac{4}{9}$ ● $\frac{8}{9}$ **4.** $\frac{7}{8}$ ● $\frac{1}{8}$ **5.** $\frac{3}{4}$ ● $\frac{1}{4}$

6. $\frac{6}{7}$ ● $\frac{7}{8}$ **7.** $\frac{5}{9}$ ● $\frac{4}{5}$ **8.** $\frac{2}{3}$ ● $\frac{1}{2}$ **9.** $\frac{3}{8}$ ● $\frac{3}{4}$ **10.** $\frac{9}{10}$ ● $\frac{2}{3}$

11. $\frac{8}{4}$ ● $\frac{7}{8}$ **12.** $\frac{10}{11}$ ● $\frac{5}{6}$ **13.** $\frac{4}{7}$ ● $\frac{8}{9}$ **14.** $\frac{1}{6}$ ● $\frac{9}{10}$ **15.** $\frac{7}{9}$ ● $\frac{3}{5}$

16. $3\frac{1}{6}$ ● $4\frac{5}{6}$ **17.** $2\frac{3}{7}$ ● $2\frac{1}{7}$ **18.** $5\frac{1}{3}$ ● $6\frac{2}{3}$ **19.** $8\frac{1}{4}$ ● $8\frac{3}{4}$

20. $6\frac{1}{5}$ ● $3\frac{1}{8}$ **21.** $4\frac{1}{9}$ ● $4\frac{1}{8}$ **22.** $5\frac{5}{9}$ ● $4\frac{7}{10}$ **23.** $6\frac{2}{3}$ ● $7\frac{8}{9}$

Order from the least to the greatest.

24. $\frac{5}{6}, \frac{2}{9}, \frac{1}{3}$ **25.** $\frac{3}{4}, \frac{1}{4}, \frac{5}{8}$ **26.** $\frac{3}{5}, \frac{3}{10}, \frac{13}{15}, 2\frac{1}{15}$

Order from the greatest to the least.

27. $\frac{1}{6}, \frac{1}{2}, \frac{3}{4}$ **28.** $\frac{2}{3}, \frac{2}{15}, \frac{3}{5}$ **29.** $\frac{4}{7}, \frac{1}{2}, \frac{3}{4}, 1\frac{1}{8}$

Solve.

30. A standard double-bed quilt is 16 patches across and 27 patches long. How many patches are in the quilt?

31. Design your own quilt square. Write problems to compare fractions or whole numbers.

32. A quilt uses 8 triangles and 1 square of red fabric, 12 triangles of black fabric, 4 triangles and 2 squares of checked fabric, and 4 squares of floral fabric. If each triangle is $\frac{1}{4}$ the size of a square, which fabric is used the most?

CALCULATOR

Use a calculator to find each product.

1. 15×15 **2.** 25×25 **3.** 35×35 **4.** 45×45

Find a pattern to help you predict:

5. 65×65 **6.** 75×75 **7.** 85×85 **8.** 95×95

PROBLEM SOLVING
Using a Pictograph

A pictograph is a kind of graph that uses pictures or symbols to represent quantities of items. Use the pictograph below to answer this question. How many shirts were hand-painted?

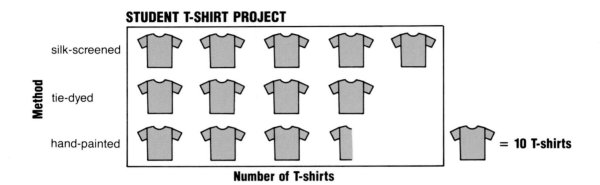

STUDENT T-SHIRT PROJECT

Method / silk-screened / tie-dyed / hand-painted

Number of T-shirts

= 10 T-shirts

- The title tells you that this pictograph shows the number of T-shirts decorated for a student project.

- The key tells you that each symbol stands for 10 T-shirts. This means that half of a T-shirt symbol stands for half of 10, or 5.

- You can find the number of shirts that were hand-painted by counting the symbols in that row. There are $3\frac{1}{2}$ symbols. The 3 symbols stand for 30 shirts; the $\frac{1}{2}$ symbol stands for 5 shirts; so, there is a total of 35 shirts.

Use the T-shirt pictograph to answer each question. Write the letter of the correct answer.

1. How many T-shirts were tie-dyed?

a. 4
b. 40
c. 45

2. Which method of decoration was the most popular?

a. silk-screening
b. tie-dyeing
c. hand-painting

The pictograph below displays the average weekly basket sales in Jane's shop. Use the pictograph to help you solve each question.

JANE'S BASKET SHOP: AVERAGE WEEKLY SALES

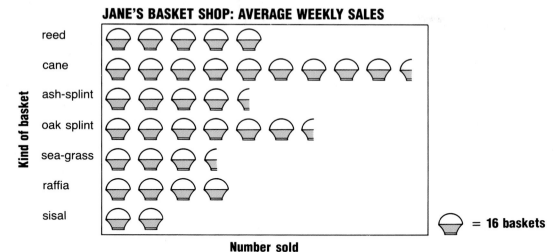

Kind of basket

Number sold

⊖ = 16 baskets

3. How many more reed baskets than raffia baskets were sold weekly?

4. On the average, how many ash-splint baskets are sold in a week?

5. About how many sea-grass baskets are sold in a week?

6. Which kind of basket is the most popular?

7. Which kind of basket is the least popular?

8. Which three kinds of baskets are the best-sellers?

Estimating Sums and Differences

A. Marcy needs at least 9 oz of wool to knit a scarf. Her grandmother gives Marcy $1\frac{3}{4}$ oz of red wool, $2\frac{3}{8}$ oz of green wool, and $3\frac{1}{5}$ oz of yellow wool. Will that be enough?

You do not need to know the exact weight of the wool, only that it weighs at least 9 oz. So, estimate $1\frac{3}{4} + 2\frac{3}{8} + 3\frac{1}{5}$.

Add the whole numbers.

Adjust by approximating the fractions with 0, $\frac{1}{2}$, or 1.
$\frac{3}{4} \approx 1$; $\frac{3}{8} \approx \frac{1}{2}$; $\frac{1}{5} \approx 0$

$1 + 2 + 3 = 6$

Estimate: $6 + 1 + \frac{1}{2} + 0 = 7\frac{1}{2}$.

$\approx$ means "is approximately equal to."

So, $1\frac{3}{4} + 2\frac{3}{8} + 3\frac{1}{5} < 9$.

Marcy doesn't have enough wool to knit a scarf.

Another example:
$4\frac{7}{8} + \frac{1}{9} + \frac{5}{12} + 3\frac{4}{5}$

Think: $4 + 3 = 7$; $\frac{7}{8} \approx 1$; $\frac{1}{9} \approx 0$; $\frac{5}{12} \approx \frac{1}{2}$; $\frac{4}{5} \approx 1$.

Estimate: $7 + 1 + 0 + \frac{1}{2} + 1 = 9\frac{1}{2}$.

B. You can estimate differences in a similar way.

Estimate $6\frac{7}{9} - 2\frac{3}{5}$.

Subtract the whole numbers.

Adjust by comparing the fractional parts.
$\frac{7}{9} > \frac{3}{5}$; so, adjust up.

$6 - 2 = 4$
So, $6\frac{7}{9} - 2\frac{3}{5} > 4$

Estimate 4^+, or slightly more than 4.

Another example:
$12\frac{1}{8} - 9\frac{2}{3}$

Think: $12 - 9 = 3$; $\frac{1}{8} < \frac{2}{3}$; so, adjust down.

Estimate 3^-, or slightly less than 3.

Estimate.

1. $2\frac{6}{7} + 3\frac{7}{9}$ **2.** $4\frac{8}{9} + 2\frac{6}{7}$ **3.** $5\frac{3}{5} + 1\frac{2}{7}$ **4.** $3\frac{1}{9} + 5\frac{9}{10}$

5. $4\frac{7}{8} - 1\frac{3}{7}$ **6.** $3\frac{2}{5} - 1\frac{1}{8}$ **7.** $9\frac{7}{8} - 4\frac{3}{5}$ **8.** $8\frac{3}{7} - 4\frac{4}{5}$

9. $\left(34\frac{1}{8} - 28\frac{3}{7}\right) + \left(11\frac{5}{9} - 4\frac{2}{7}\right)$ **10.** $\left(16\frac{7}{11} + 4\frac{1}{9}\right) - \left(3\frac{4}{9} + 12\frac{3}{10}\right)$

Estimate. Write $>$ or $<$ for ●.

11. $2\frac{6}{7} + 3\frac{8}{9} ● 7$ **12.** $4\frac{3}{4} + 3\frac{9}{10} ● 8$ **13.** $2\frac{1}{8} + 1\frac{5}{9} ● 4$

14. $3\frac{4}{5} + 4\frac{2}{9} ● 9$ **15.** $5\frac{3}{10} + 3\frac{1}{9} ● 8$ **16.** $4\frac{1}{5} + 1\frac{3}{4} ● 6$

17. $3\frac{7}{8} + 2\frac{6}{7} + 4\frac{1}{9} ● 12$ **18.** $\frac{6}{7} + 3\frac{1}{6} + 4\frac{3}{5} ● 8$

19. $5\frac{1}{5} - 2\frac{4}{7} ● 3$ **20.** $6\frac{1}{2} - 2\frac{7}{8} ● 3$ **21.** $7\frac{3}{5} - 2\frac{1}{9} ● 5$

22. $6\frac{1}{7} - 1\frac{4}{5} ● 5$ **23.** $9\frac{3}{4} - 5\frac{2}{5} ● 4$ **24.** $7\frac{1}{5} - 3\frac{2}{9} ● 5$

25. $\left(9\frac{6}{7} - 4\frac{3}{4}\right) + \left(6\frac{1}{8} - 2\frac{2}{3}\right) ● 10$ **26.** $\left(4\frac{7}{8} + 2\frac{6}{7}\right) - \left(1\frac{1}{8} + 2\frac{4}{5}\right) ● 6$

Write the letter of the correct answer. Choose the best estimate.

27. $2\frac{7}{8} + 3\frac{8}{11}$ **a.** about 5 **b.** about 6 **c.** about 7

28. $4\frac{3}{4} + 2\frac{4}{5}$ **a.** about 6 **b.** about 8 **c.** about 9

29. $6\frac{7}{8} - 2\frac{4}{9}$ **a.** about 2 **b.** about 4 **c.** about 8

30. $8\frac{4}{5} - 3\frac{3}{7}$ **a.** about 3 **b.** about 4 **c.** about 5

Solve.

31. During Barclay's yearly leftover-handspun-wool sale, a pound of lamb's wool costs $25.00. Becky buys $3\frac{3}{4}$ oz of grey wool, $4\frac{2}{5}$ oz of white wool, and $2\frac{7}{16}$ oz of brown wool. Does she spend more or less than $25.00?

32. Joan goes on a shopping spree and buys $24\frac{3}{4}$ oz of different-colored wools. She really only needs about 18 oz. Becky offers to buy some of the wool from Joan. She picks three balls weighing $2\frac{4}{5}$ oz, $3\frac{2}{9}$ oz, and $1\frac{7}{8}$ oz. Can Joan let her buy them?

Adding Fractions and Mixed Numbers

A. A toy banjo was constructed in two pieces. The circular body was $\frac{1}{4}$ yd in diameter and the neck was $\frac{3}{4}$ yd long. How long was the banjo?

To add fractions with like denominators, add the numerators. Use the same denominator. Write in simplest form.

$\frac{1}{4} + \frac{3}{4} = \frac{1+3}{4} = \frac{4}{4}$, or **1.**

The banjo was 1 yd long.

B. Add $5\frac{1}{2} + \frac{3}{4} + 1\frac{1}{3}$.

To add fractions and mixed numbers with unlike denominators, find equivalent fractions.

Write each fraction with a common denominator.

Think: The LCD is 12.

$$5\frac{1}{2} = 5\frac{6}{12}$$
$$\frac{3}{4} = \frac{9}{12}$$
$$+ 1\frac{1}{3} = 1\frac{4}{12}$$

Add.

$$5\frac{1}{2} = 5\frac{6}{12}$$
$$\frac{3}{4} = \frac{9}{12}$$
$$+ 1\frac{1}{3} = 1\frac{4}{12}$$
$$6\frac{19}{12}$$

Simplify the sum.

$$6\frac{19}{12} = 6 + 1\frac{7}{12} = 7\frac{7}{12}$$

Checkpoint Write the letter of the correct answer.

Add.

1. $\frac{3}{7} + \frac{5}{14}$ **a.** $\frac{8}{21}$ **b.** $\frac{11}{14}$ **c.** 8   **d.** $\frac{1}{21}$

2. $\frac{3}{5} + \frac{3}{4}$ **a.** $\frac{6}{9}$ **b.** $\frac{6}{5}$ **c.** $\frac{27}{20}$ **d.** $1\frac{7}{20}$

3. $3\frac{5}{6} + 1\frac{2}{3}$ **a.** $1\frac{2}{3}$ **b.** $4\frac{7}{9}$ **c.** $4\frac{2}{3}$ **d.** $5\frac{1}{2}$

4. $2\frac{1}{2} + 4\frac{4}{5} + \frac{3}{4}$ **a.** $8\frac{1}{20}$ **b.** $6\frac{41}{20}$ **c.** 8   **d.** 9

Math Reasoning, page H213

Add. Write the answer in simplest form.

1. $\frac{1}{6} + \frac{5}{6}$ **2.** $\frac{4}{5} + \frac{2}{5}$ **3.** $\frac{7}{12} + \frac{1}{12}$ **4.** $\frac{1}{2} + \frac{1}{2}$ **5.** $\frac{5}{9} + \frac{5}{9}$

6. $\begin{array}{r} \frac{3}{4} \\ + \frac{1}{2} \\ \hline \end{array}$ **7.** $\begin{array}{r} \frac{7}{8} \\ + \frac{3}{4} \\ \hline \end{array}$ **8.** $\begin{array}{r} \frac{11}{12} \\ + \frac{3}{4} \\ \hline \end{array}$ **9.** $\begin{array}{r} \frac{4}{5} \\ + \frac{7}{10} \\ \hline \end{array}$ **10.** $\begin{array}{r} \frac{3}{4} \\ + \frac{2}{7} \\ \hline \end{array}$ **11.** $\begin{array}{r} \frac{2}{15} \\ + \frac{1}{5} \\ \hline \end{array}$

12. $\begin{array}{r} 6\frac{1}{2} \\ + \frac{2}{3} \\ \hline \end{array}$ **13.** $\begin{array}{r} 2\frac{1}{6} \\ + \frac{1}{5} \\ \hline \end{array}$ **14.** $\begin{array}{r} \frac{4}{5} \\ + 1\frac{1}{2} \\ \hline \end{array}$ **15.** $\begin{array}{r} \frac{2}{3} \\ + 7\frac{1}{5} \\ \hline \end{array}$ **16.** $\begin{array}{r} 3\frac{1}{5} \\ + \frac{2}{3} \\ \hline \end{array}$ **17.** $\begin{array}{r} 6\frac{1}{4} \\ + \frac{3}{8} \\ \hline \end{array}$

18. $\begin{array}{r} 7\frac{1}{3} \\ + 3\frac{1}{2} \\ \hline \end{array}$ **19.** $\begin{array}{r} 2\frac{7}{8} \\ + 5\frac{3}{9} \\ \hline \end{array}$ **20.** $\begin{array}{r} 1\frac{4}{5} \\ + 3\frac{1}{3} \\ \hline \end{array}$ **21.** $\begin{array}{r} 2\frac{1}{6} \\ + 3\frac{2}{3} \\ \hline \end{array}$ **22.** $\begin{array}{r} 5\frac{5}{8} \\ + 1\frac{1}{3} \\ \hline \end{array}$ **23.** $\begin{array}{r} 4\frac{5}{9} \\ + 2\frac{2}{3} \\ \hline \end{array}$

24. $6\frac{1}{3} + \frac{1}{2} + \frac{4}{5}$ **25.** $3\frac{1}{2} + \frac{2}{3} + \frac{7}{9}$ **26.** $\frac{1}{6} + 8\frac{1}{3} + 1\frac{1}{4}$

27. $\frac{4}{5} + \frac{1}{8} + 3\frac{2}{5}$ **28.** $1\frac{3}{4} + \frac{1}{2} + \frac{5}{6}$ **29.** $\frac{8}{9} + \frac{5}{6} + 2\frac{1}{3}$

30. $\begin{array}{r} 3\frac{1}{6} \\ 2\frac{1}{5} \\ + \frac{4}{5} \\ \hline \end{array}$ **31.** $\begin{array}{r} 1\frac{1}{8} \\ 3\frac{1}{6} \\ + \frac{1}{2} \\ \hline \end{array}$ **32.** $\begin{array}{r} \frac{2}{3} \\ 1\frac{1}{6} \\ + 4\frac{1}{2} \\ \hline \end{array}$ **33.** $\begin{array}{r} 3\frac{1}{8} \\ \frac{3}{4} \\ + 1\frac{1}{8} \\ \hline \end{array}$ **34.** $\begin{array}{r} 5\frac{1}{6} \\ \frac{2}{5} \\ + 3\frac{3}{10} \\ \hline \end{array}$ **35.** $\begin{array}{r} \frac{4}{5} \\ 1\frac{1}{10} \\ + 4\frac{1}{2} \\ \hline \end{array}$

Solve.

36. A craftsworker worked for $5\frac{1}{2}$ hours Monday, $6\frac{1}{4}$ hours Tuesday, and $7\frac{1}{2}$ hours Wednesday to construct a stringed instrument. How many hours did it take?

37. A wood-carver had two pieces of wood. One piece was $1\frac{3}{8}$ ft long and the other $1\frac{1}{4}$ ft long. Which was the longer piece?

Subtracting Fractions and Mixed Numbers

A. To subtract fractions that have like denominators, subtract the numerators. Use the same denominator.

$$\frac{7}{8} - \frac{3}{8} = \frac{7-3}{8} = \frac{4}{8}, \text{ or } \frac{1}{2}.$$

B. To subtract fractions with unlike denominators, find the LCD.

Subtract $\frac{6}{7} - \frac{2}{3}$.

Write each fraction with a common denominator. Subtract.

$$\begin{array}{r} \frac{6}{7} = \frac{18}{21} \\ - \frac{2}{3} = \frac{14}{21} \\ \hline \frac{4}{21} \end{array}$$

| Think: 21 is the LCD. |

C. To subtract mixed numbers, subtract the fractions. Then subtract the whole numbers.

Subtract $3\frac{3}{4} - 2\frac{1}{2}$.

Find fractions that have a common denominator.	Subtract the fractions.	Subtract the whole numbers.
$3\frac{3}{4} = 3\frac{3}{4}$ $- 2\frac{1}{2} = 2\frac{2}{4}$	$3\frac{3}{4}$ $- 2\frac{2}{4}$ <hr> $\frac{1}{4}$	$3\frac{3}{4}$ $- 2\frac{2}{4}$ <hr> $1\frac{1}{4}$

Checkpoint Write the letter of the correct answer.

Subtract.

1. $\frac{8}{11} - \frac{3}{11}$ **a.** $\frac{5}{11}$ **b.** $\frac{11}{22}$ **c.** $\frac{11}{11}$ **d.** 5

2. $\frac{5}{6} - \frac{1}{3}$ **a.** $\frac{2}{6}$ **b.** $\frac{1}{2}$ **c.** $\frac{4}{6}$ **d.** $\frac{4}{3}$

3. $4\frac{3}{4} - 1\frac{1}{4}$ **a.** 6   **b.** 1   **c.** $\frac{1}{2}$ **d.** $3\frac{1}{2}$

4. $2\frac{19}{24} - 1\frac{3}{8}$ **a.** $1\frac{5}{24}$ **b.** $1\frac{5}{12}$ **c.** $1\frac{10}{12}$ **d.** $4\frac{1}{6}$

Subtract. Write the answer in simplest form.

1. $\frac{6}{7} - \frac{3}{7}$

2. $\frac{9}{11} - \frac{2}{11}$

3. $\frac{3}{4} - \frac{1}{4}$

4. $\frac{4}{5} - \frac{2}{5}$

5. $\frac{7}{9} - \frac{4}{9}$

6. $\frac{12}{21} - \frac{3}{7}$

7. $\frac{13}{24} - \frac{1}{6}$

8. $\frac{1}{2} - \frac{1}{6}$

9. $\frac{2}{3} - \frac{2}{9}$

10. $\frac{3}{4} - \frac{5}{8}$

11. $\begin{array}{r} \frac{19}{21} \\ - \frac{6}{7} \\ \hline \end{array}$

12. $\begin{array}{r} \frac{5}{9} \\ - \frac{1}{3} \\ \hline \end{array}$

13. $\begin{array}{r} \frac{5}{8} \\ - \frac{1}{2} \\ \hline \end{array}$

14. $\begin{array}{r} \frac{3}{7} \\ - \frac{1}{14} \\ \hline \end{array}$

15. $\begin{array}{r} \frac{2}{3} \\ - \frac{1}{6} \\ \hline \end{array}$

16. $\begin{array}{r} \frac{3}{4} \\ - \frac{5}{12} \\ \hline \end{array}$

17. $\begin{array}{r} \frac{7}{8} \\ - \frac{2}{3} \\ \hline \end{array}$

18. $\begin{array}{r} \frac{1}{2} \\ - \frac{5}{11} \\ \hline \end{array}$

19. $\begin{array}{r} \frac{7}{8} \\ - \frac{2}{5} \\ \hline \end{array}$

20. $\begin{array}{r} \frac{5}{6} \\ - \frac{1}{9} \\ \hline \end{array}$

21. $\begin{array}{r} \frac{3}{4} \\ - \frac{2}{5} \\ \hline \end{array}$

22. $\begin{array}{r} \frac{4}{5} \\ - \frac{5}{7} \\ \hline \end{array}$

23. $6\frac{2}{3} - 5\frac{1}{3}$

24. $7\frac{3}{4} - 4\frac{3}{4}$

25. $10\frac{4}{5} - 2\frac{2}{5}$

26. $12\frac{5}{6} - 4\frac{1}{6}$

27. $\begin{array}{r} 4\frac{3}{4} \\ - 1\frac{1}{2} \\ \hline \end{array}$

28. $\begin{array}{r} 5\frac{6}{7} \\ - 3\frac{2}{3} \\ \hline \end{array}$

29. $\begin{array}{r} 2\frac{8}{9} \\ - 1\frac{3}{4} \\ \hline \end{array}$

30. $\begin{array}{r} 3\frac{3}{8} \\ - 2\frac{1}{4} \\ \hline \end{array}$

31. $\begin{array}{r} 4\frac{5}{8} \\ - 2\frac{2}{5} \\ \hline \end{array}$

32. $\frac{7}{8} - \frac{2}{3}$

33. $3\frac{9}{10} - 1\frac{5}{6}$

34. $\frac{33}{41} - \frac{1}{2}$

35. $7\frac{22}{29} - 5\frac{2}{3}$

Solve.

36. Karen bought $\frac{1}{2}$ of a hide. She needed $\frac{3}{8}$ of a hide to make a leather shoulder bag. Did she have enough? How much leather was left?

37. Tanning hides makes them soft. Jerry spends $\frac{1}{2}$ hour on the tanning process. Ron spends $3\frac{1}{4}$ hours tanning. Write a subtraction problem that uses this information.

CHALLENGE   **Patterns, Relations, and Functions**

Study the fractions below.

$\frac{1}{2} - \frac{1}{4} - \frac{1}{8} - \frac{1}{16} - \frac{1}{32} - \frac{1}{64} \cdots$

As you subtract each fraction, what pattern do you notice?

Will you ever reach zero?

Subtracting Mixed Numbers with Renaming

A. Greg has $7\frac{1}{8}$ yd of round reed. He uses $3\frac{3}{8}$ yd for a basket. How much round reed does he have left?

Find $7\frac{1}{8} - 3\frac{3}{8}$.

Write in vertical form.

$$\begin{array}{r} 7\frac{1}{8} \\ -\ 3\frac{3}{8} \\ \hline \end{array}$$

Compare fractions. Rename if necessary.

$$\frac{1}{8} < \frac{3}{8}$$

$$7\frac{1}{8} = 6 + 1\frac{1}{8} = 6\frac{9}{8}$$

Subtract. Simplify if necessary.

$$\begin{array}{r} 7\frac{1}{8} = 6\frac{9}{8} \\ -\ 3\frac{3}{8} = 3\frac{3}{8} \\ \hline 3\frac{6}{8} = 3\frac{3}{4} \end{array}$$

He has $3\frac{3}{4}$ yd of round reed left.

B. Subtract $6\frac{1}{5} - 2\frac{3}{4}$.

Find fractions that have a common denominator.

$$\begin{array}{r} 6\frac{1}{5} = 6\frac{4}{20} \\ -\ 2\frac{3}{4} = 2\frac{15}{20} \\ \hline \end{array}$$

Compare fractions. Rename if necessary.

$$\frac{4}{20} < \frac{15}{20}$$

$$6\frac{4}{20} = 5 + 1\frac{4}{20} = 5\frac{24}{20}$$

Subtract.

$$\begin{array}{r} 6\frac{1}{5} = 5\frac{24}{20} \\ -\ 2\frac{3}{4} = 2\frac{15}{20} \\ \hline 3\frac{9}{20} \end{array}$$

Other examples:

$$\begin{array}{r} 8\phantom{\frac{6}{6}} = 7\frac{6}{6} \\ -\ 2\frac{1}{6} = 2\frac{1}{6} \\ \hline 5\frac{5}{6} \end{array}$$

$$\begin{array}{r} 3\frac{1}{4} = 2\frac{5}{4} \\ -\ 1\frac{3}{4} = 1\frac{3}{4} \\ \hline 1\frac{2}{4} = 1\frac{1}{2} \end{array}$$

Checkpoint Write the letter of the correct answer.

Subtract.

1. $7\frac{7}{9} - 3\frac{4}{9} = \blacksquare$ **a.** $3\frac{3}{9}$ **b.** $4\frac{3}{9}$ **c.** $4\frac{1}{3}$ **d.** $7\frac{1}{3}$

2. $9 - 4\frac{5}{6} = \blacksquare$ **a.** $4\frac{1}{6}$ **b.** 5 **c.** $6\frac{5}{6}$ **d.** $13\frac{5}{6}$

3. $5\frac{1}{4} - 4\frac{1}{3} = \blacksquare$ **a.** $\frac{1}{3}$ **b.** $\frac{11}{12}$ **c.** $1\frac{1}{12}$ **d.** $1\frac{11}{12}$

Subtract. Write the answer in simplest form.

1. $4\frac{1}{4} - 2\frac{3}{4}$ **2.** $5\frac{1}{3} - 3\frac{2}{3}$ **3.** $6\frac{3}{5} - 1\frac{4}{5}$ **4.** $2\frac{3}{8} - 1\frac{7}{8}$

5. $\begin{array}{r} 6\frac{5}{8} \\ -\ 3\frac{3}{4} \\ \hline \end{array}$ **6.** $\begin{array}{r} 3\frac{1}{6} \\ -\ 1\frac{1}{2} \\ \hline \end{array}$ **7.** $\begin{array}{r} 2\frac{2}{5} \\ -\ 1\frac{7}{10} \\ \hline \end{array}$ **8.** $\begin{array}{r} 3\frac{3}{8} \\ -\ 1\frac{1}{2} \\ \hline \end{array}$ **9.** $\begin{array}{r} 9\frac{2}{3} \\ -\ 3\frac{5}{6} \\ \hline \end{array}$ **10.** $\begin{array}{r} 5\frac{3}{5} \\ -\ 2\frac{9}{10} \\ \hline \end{array}$

11. $\begin{array}{r} 5 \\ -\ 3\frac{1}{3} \\ \hline \end{array}$ **12.** $\begin{array}{r} 3 \\ -\ 1\frac{1}{9} \\ \hline \end{array}$ **13.** $\begin{array}{r} 6 \\ -\ 5\frac{7}{9} \\ \hline \end{array}$ **14.** $\begin{array}{r} 12 \\ -\ 6\frac{4}{5} \\ \hline \end{array}$ **15.** $\begin{array}{r} 13 \\ -\ 7\frac{6}{11} \\ \hline \end{array}$ **16.** $\begin{array}{r} 9 \\ -\ 2\frac{2}{3} \\ \hline \end{array}$

17. $8 - 7\frac{1}{4}$ **18.** $19 - 3\frac{2}{3}$ **19.** $7 - 3\frac{5}{6}$ **20.** $5 - 4\frac{4}{7}$

21. $6\frac{2}{3} - 5\frac{6}{7}$ **22.** $3\frac{3}{10} - 1\frac{2}{3}$ **23.** $18\frac{1}{2} - 7\frac{7}{9}$ **24.** $6\frac{1}{4} - 5\frac{3}{5}$

25. $\begin{array}{r} 5\frac{1}{5} \\ -\ 2\frac{2}{3} \\ \hline \end{array}$ **26.** $\begin{array}{r} 2\frac{1}{6} \\ -\ 1\frac{2}{5} \\ \hline \end{array}$ **27.** $\begin{array}{r} 3\frac{1}{8} \\ -\ 1\frac{2}{3} \\ \hline \end{array}$ **28.** $\begin{array}{r} 15\frac{3}{10} \\ -\ 6\frac{2}{3} \\ \hline \end{array}$ **29.** $\begin{array}{r} 17\frac{3}{8} \\ -\ 8\frac{3}{5} \\ \hline \end{array}$ **30.** $\begin{array}{r} 4\frac{1}{12} \\ -\ 3\frac{2}{9} \\ \hline \end{array}$

31. $\begin{array}{r} 9 \\ -\ \frac{13}{15} \\ \hline \end{array}$ **32.** $\begin{array}{r} 6\frac{1}{4} \\ -\ 3\frac{5}{8} \\ \hline \end{array}$ **33.** $\begin{array}{r} 4\frac{1}{4} \\ -\ 1\frac{3}{4} \\ \hline \end{array}$ **34.** $\begin{array}{r} 2 \\ -\ 1\frac{8}{17} \\ \hline \end{array}$ **35.** $\begin{array}{r} 5\frac{1}{6} \\ -\ 2\frac{7}{8} \\ \hline \end{array}$ **36.** $\begin{array}{r} 3 \\ -\ 1\frac{11}{12} \\ \hline \end{array}$

Solve.

37. At the end of the day, Jocelyn had $68\frac{3}{4}$ ft of round reed. If she started the day with $92\frac{1}{2}$ ft, how much round reed did Jocelyn use during the day?

38. Greg started with 50 feet of flat reed. He used $24\frac{1}{2}$ feet on one basket, $12\frac{2}{3}$ feet on another, and $11\frac{1}{4}$ feet on a third. How much did he have left?

MIDCHAPTER REVIEW

Add. Write the answer in simplest form.

1. $\frac{3}{7} + \frac{2}{7}$ **2.** $\frac{5}{8} + \frac{3}{5}$ **3.** $2\frac{4}{9} + \frac{7}{9}$ **4.** $3\frac{3}{4} + 7\frac{11}{16}$ **5.** $2\frac{1}{5} + \frac{9}{11} + 3\frac{7}{10}$

Subtract. Write the answer in simplest form.

6. $\frac{7}{8} - \frac{3}{8}$ **7.** $\frac{5}{9} - \frac{7}{18}$ **8.** $\frac{9}{11} - \frac{3}{4}$ **9.** $4\frac{3}{5} - 2\frac{2}{5}$ **10.** $7\frac{1}{2} - 3\frac{5}{16}$

11. $5\frac{3}{10} - 1\frac{1}{15}$ **12.** $9\frac{5}{8} - 2\frac{7}{8}$ **13.** $12 - 3\frac{5}{6}$ **14.** $2\frac{5}{9} - 1\frac{9}{11}$ **15.** $18\frac{1}{4} - 12\frac{9}{17}$

PROBLEM SOLVING
Estimation

Once you have decided to estimate, you have to decide how accurate your estimate needs to be.

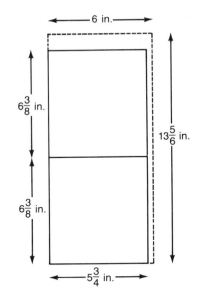

Julia is building a bird feeder. The wooden sides of the feeder are to measure $6\frac{3}{8}$ in. long and $5\frac{3}{4}$ in. wide. Can she cut the 2 sides from a piece of wood $13\frac{5}{16}$ in. long and 6 in. wide?

To solve this problem, you can first draw a sketch. Since $5\frac{3}{4} < 6$, you can see that the piece of wood is wide enough. To discover whether it is long enough, you can round the length of each side to the nearest inch and multiply by 2.

$$6\frac{3}{8} \longrightarrow 6$$
$$2 \times 6 = 12$$

The length of the 2 sides put end to end is about 12 inches.

Of course $13\frac{5}{16}$ is greater than 12, but the lengths are fairly close. You may want to estimate more closely. You can do this by rounding $6\frac{3}{8}$ in. to the nearest $\frac{1}{2}$ in., and then multiplying by 2.

$$6\frac{3}{8} \longrightarrow 6\frac{1}{2}$$
$$2 \times 6\frac{1}{2} = 13$$

Since $13\frac{5}{16} > 13$, the actual length of the piece of wood is greater than the two bird-feeder sides placed end to end. Julia can cut the sides from the piece of wood.

Use estimation to solve each problem. Write an exact answer when needed.

1. George is making a quilt. He wants to use 5 colors. He will need $1\frac{3}{8}$ yards of each color. He finds two matching pieces of red fabric. One is $1\frac{1}{8}$ yards long, the other is $\frac{1}{2}$ yard long. Can he use these pieces as one of his colors?

2. George has five scraps of green fabric. Their lengths are $\frac{5}{8}$ yard, $\frac{1}{5}$ yard, $\frac{1}{4}$ yard, $\frac{3}{8}$ yard, and $\frac{1}{2}$ yard. He needs $1\frac{3}{8}$ yards. Does he have enough green fabric for the quilt?

3. George's quilt will contain 36 squares. For each square, he needs 2 red triangles and 4 blue triangles. How many triangles of each color should he cut for the quilt?

4. George decides to add a white border. The border will measure 10 in. wide and 320 in. long. He has several scraps of white material, that measure 10 in. wide. Their lengths are $8\frac{1}{2}$ in., $19\frac{3}{8}$ in., $33\frac{1}{4}$ in., $41\frac{5}{8}$ in., $48\frac{1}{4}$ in., $61\frac{1}{4}$ in., and $68\frac{1}{4}$ in. Will he have enough fabric to make the border?

5. Elisa is helping George by making the back portion of the quilt. It will measure 80 in. wide and 80 in. long. She is using three pieces of fabric. Each piece measures 80 in. in length. Their widths are $27\frac{1}{2}$ in., $21\frac{3}{4}$ in., and $11\frac{1}{8}$ in. Does she have enough material to make the back?

6. Elisa is also helping to sew the front of the quilt to the back. If George had done this job alone, it would have taken him about $6\frac{3}{4}$ hours to finish it. Elisa works at the same rate as George. How much time should they allow for sewing the back to the front?

Multiplying Fractions

A. When Martha makes patchwork quilts, she sews patches into blocks of 8 first, before sewing the blocks together to form a quilt. Of the part of the quilt shown, $\frac{5}{8}$ is flannel. Of that part, $\frac{4}{5}$ is plaid flannel. What fraction of the block shown is plaid flannel?

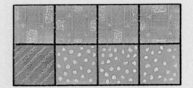

Find $\frac{4}{5}$ of $\frac{5}{8}$. | *Of* means multiply. |

To multiply fractions, multiply the numerators and multiply the denominators. Write the product in simplest form.

$$\frac{4}{5} \times \frac{5}{8} = \frac{4 \times 5}{5 \times 8} = \frac{20}{40} = \frac{1}{2}$$

Of the part of the quilt shown, $\frac{1}{2}$ is plaid flannel.

B. When you multiply fractions, you may want to take a shortcut and simplify first. To simplify, divide the numerators and denominators by a common factor.

Find $\frac{5}{9} \times \frac{21}{25}$.

3 is a common factor of 9 and 21.
Divide each by 3.

$$\overset{}{\underset{3}{\frac{5}{9}}} \times \overset{7}{\frac{21}{25}}$$

5 is a common factor of 5 and 25.
Divide by 5.

$$\overset{1}{\underset{3}{\frac{5}{9}}} \times \overset{7}{\underset{5}{\frac{21}{25}}}$$

Multiply. $\overset{1}{\underset{3}{\frac{5}{9}}} \times \overset{7}{\underset{5}{\frac{21}{25}}} = \frac{1 \times 7}{3 \times 5} = \frac{7}{15}$

Other examples:

$\frac{5}{8} \times \frac{4}{7}$
$\underset{1}{}$

$\underset{2}{\frac{5}{8}} \times \overset{1}{\frac{4}{7}} = \frac{5 \times 1}{2 \times 7} = \frac{5}{14}$

$\frac{3}{7} \times \frac{5}{6} \times \frac{7}{10}$
$\underset{1}{} \quad \underset{1}{} \quad \underset{1}{}$

$\underset{1}{\frac{3}{7}} \times \underset{2}{\frac{5}{6}} \times \underset{2}{\frac{7}{10}} = \frac{1 \times 1 \times 1}{1 \times 2 \times 2} = \frac{1}{4}$

Multiply. Write the answer in simplest form.

1. $\frac{2}{9} \times \frac{1}{3}$
2. $\frac{4}{7} \times \frac{8}{9}$
3. $\frac{3}{4} \times \frac{1}{11}$
4. $\frac{2}{3} \times \frac{4}{5}$
5. $\frac{5}{9} \times \frac{1}{9}$

6. $\frac{1}{3} \times \frac{3}{4}$
7. $\frac{3}{8} \times \frac{4}{9}$
8. $\frac{5}{7} \times \frac{14}{15}$
9. $\frac{12}{17} \times \frac{5}{12}$
10. $\frac{4}{5} \times \frac{1}{8}$

11. $\frac{9}{10} \times \frac{35}{36}$
12. $\frac{7}{8} \times \frac{12}{21}$
13. $\frac{2}{5} \times \frac{8}{9}$
14. $\frac{42}{55} \times \frac{25}{28}$
15. $\frac{8}{9} \times \frac{18}{24}$

16. $\frac{2}{3} \times \frac{1}{4} \times \frac{5}{7}$
17. $\frac{2}{5} \times \frac{1}{4} \times \frac{5}{6}$
18. $\frac{1}{6} \times \frac{1}{2} \times \frac{3}{5}$
19. $\frac{5}{9} \times \frac{2}{3} \times \frac{1}{6}$

20. $\frac{7}{8} \times \frac{8}{9} \times \frac{9}{21}$
21. $\frac{3}{8} \times \frac{2}{7} \times \frac{1}{6}$
22. $\frac{6}{14} \times \frac{1}{3} \times \frac{7}{8}$
23. $\frac{5}{6} \times \frac{12}{25} \times \frac{25}{26}$

24. $\frac{5}{6} \times \frac{1}{2}$
25. $\frac{3}{4} \times \frac{2}{3}$
26. $\frac{1}{2} \times \frac{3}{7}$
27. $\frac{5}{6} \times \frac{1}{10} \times \frac{3}{4}$

28. $\frac{3}{16} \times \frac{5}{9} \times \frac{1}{2}$
29. $\frac{2}{3} \times \frac{9}{10} \times \frac{20}{21}$
30. $\frac{4}{7} \times \frac{3}{5}$
31. $\frac{3}{16} \times \frac{4}{5}$

Solve.

32. Sara had $\frac{3}{4}$ yd of embroidery floss with which to stitch her name. She used $\frac{1}{2}$ of the floss. How much floss did she use?

33. In an embroidery group, $\frac{2}{3}$ of the members use a cross-stitch on their samplers. Of these, $\frac{1}{2}$ also use stem stitch. What part of the embroidery group uses stem stitch?

34. Of Mr. Brooks's class, $\frac{5}{6}$ know how to do the satin stitch. Of these, $\frac{1}{4}$ know how to do the chain stitch. What part of Mr. Brooks's students know how to do the chain stitch?

35. Bob was practicing the French knot on $\frac{3}{4}$ yd of embroidery floss. After 1 hour, he had used up $\frac{3}{4}$ of the embroidery floss he started with. How much embroidery floss did he have left?

ANOTHER LOOK

Write in standard form.

1. $6 \cdot 10^2$
2. $32 \cdot 10^5$
3. $711 \cdot 10^4$
4. $16.8 \cdot 10^3$
5. $72.4 \cdot 10^5$
6. $4.06 \cdot 10^1$
7. $33.92 \cdot 10^6$
8. $12.089 \cdot 10^8$
9. $947.628 \cdot 10^{10}$

Estimating Products and Quotients

A. Handmade quilts are insulated with a material called *batting*. A full-size quilt measures about $8\frac{1}{3}$ feet by $9\frac{1}{2}$ feet. About how many square feet of batting are needed for the quilt?

Estimate $8\frac{1}{3} \times 9\frac{1}{2}$.

Round each factor to the nearest whole number. Then, multiply the rounded factors.

$$8\frac{1}{3} \times 9\frac{1}{2}$$
$$\downarrow \qquad \downarrow$$
$$8 \ \times 10 = 80$$

About 80 square feet of batting are needed for a double quilt.

Other examples:

$\dfrac{3}{8}$ is close to $\dfrac{1}{2}$

$6\frac{1}{4} \times 9\frac{1}{3}$
$\downarrow \qquad \downarrow$
$6 \times 9 = 54^+$

Estimate: 54^+

$9\frac{5}{8} \times 3\frac{3}{4}$
$\downarrow \qquad \downarrow$
$10 \times 4 = 40^-$

Estimate: 40^-

$\frac{3}{8} \times 15\frac{1}{2}$
$\downarrow \qquad \downarrow$
$\frac{1}{2} \times 16 = 8^-$, or $\frac{3}{8} \times 16 = 6^-$

Estimate: 8^- or 6^-

B. $4\frac{7}{8} \div 3\frac{3}{4}$.

Compare the quotient to 1.

$4\frac{7}{8} > 3\frac{3}{4}$. So, the quotient is greater than 1.

Estimate: 1^+

Round the factors to numbers that divide easily.

$$4\frac{7}{8} \div 3\frac{3}{4}$$
$$\downarrow \qquad \downarrow$$
$$4 \div \quad 4$$

Divide the rounded numbers.

$$4 \div 4 = 1$$

Other examples:

$11\frac{2}{3} \div 6\frac{1}{5}$
$\downarrow \qquad \downarrow$
$12 \div \ 6 = 2$

$11\frac{2}{3} > 6\frac{1}{5}$
So, the quotient is greater than 1.

Estimate: 2

$\frac{4}{5} \div 2\frac{1}{3}$
$\downarrow \qquad \downarrow$
$1 \div \quad 2 = \frac{1}{2}$

$\frac{4}{5} < 2\frac{1}{3}$. So, the quotient is less than 1.

Estimate: $\frac{1}{2}$

Estimate.

1. $6\frac{1}{3} \times 4\frac{7}{8}$ 2. $3\frac{3}{4} \times 2\frac{5}{6}$ 3. $1\frac{1}{6} \times 3\frac{1}{4}$ 4. $8\frac{1}{5} \times 3\frac{2}{3}$

5. $5 \times 4\frac{5}{7}$ 6. $3\frac{2}{3} \times 6$ 7. $5\frac{1}{2} \times 2\frac{1}{3}$ 8. $7\frac{2}{5} \times 5$

9. $\frac{7}{16} \times 3\frac{2}{3}$ 10. $\frac{9}{10} \times 7\frac{5}{8}$ 11. $\frac{1}{3} \times 8\frac{5}{8}$ 12. $\frac{3}{4} \times 12\frac{1}{6}$

Estimate. Write > or < for ●.

13. $6\frac{1}{4} \div 3\frac{1}{2}$ ● 1   14. $\frac{3}{8} \div 2\frac{1}{2}$ ● 1   15. $3\frac{1}{5} \div 3\frac{1}{2}$ ● 1

16. $5\frac{1}{8} \div \frac{9}{10}$ ● 1   17. $1\frac{2}{3} \div 5\frac{1}{2}$ ● 1   18. $\frac{15}{16} \div \frac{3}{5}$ ● 1

Estimate.

19. $3\frac{3}{4} \div 2$ 20. $6\frac{1}{3} \div 3\frac{1}{8}$ 21. $3\frac{1}{2} \div 5\frac{7}{8}$ 22. $1\frac{1}{16} \div 4\frac{1}{4}$

23. $5\frac{1}{6} \div 3$ 24. $2\frac{3}{8} \div \frac{7}{8}$ 25. $1\frac{3}{4} \div 5\frac{1}{4}$ 26. $6\frac{1}{4} \div 3\frac{1}{4}$

Estimate. Write > or < for ●.

27. $5\frac{1}{3} \times 6\frac{1}{4}$ ● 30   28. $8\frac{3}{4} \times 2\frac{1}{2}$ ● 27   29. $8\frac{1}{2} \times 1\frac{3}{4}$ ● 10

30. $\frac{7}{9} \times 3\frac{5}{6}$ ● 4   31. $1\frac{1}{3} \times 8\frac{5}{6}$ ● 8   32. $6\frac{3}{4} \times 2\frac{4}{5}$ ● 13

33. $6\frac{1}{2} \div 1\frac{7}{8}$ ● 3   34. $3\frac{4}{5} \div 2$ ● 2   35. $8\frac{1}{3} \div 2\frac{7}{8}$ ● 4

36. $\frac{9}{10} \div 2\frac{7}{8}$ ● $\frac{1}{2}$ 37. $1\frac{1}{3} \div 5\frac{3}{8}$ ● 3   38. $8\frac{5}{8} \div 2\frac{7}{8}$ ● 2

Solve.

39. A baby quilt measures about $2\frac{2}{3}$ feet by $3\frac{1}{2}$ feet. About how many square feet of batting are needed to insulate the quilt?

40. Sue is making a quilt for her mother as a birthday gift. She has about $9\frac{1}{2}$ sections left to quilt. Her mother's birthday is about $4\frac{1}{2}$ weeks away. About how many sections per week must she quilt to finish the gift on time?

Multiplying Mixed Numbers

A. To multiply $1\frac{3}{5} \times 3\frac{1}{8}$, write both mixed numbers as fractions.

Multiply $1\frac{3}{5} \times 3\frac{1}{8}$.

Write fractions for both numbers.

$$1\frac{3}{5} \times 3\frac{1}{8} = \frac{\overset{1}{\cancel{8}}}{\cancel{5}} \times \frac{\overset{5}{\cancel{25}}}{\cancel{8}} = \frac{1 \times 5}{1 \times 1} = 5$$

Multiply $5 \times 2\frac{6}{7}$.

Write whole numbers as fractions.

$$5 \times 2\frac{6}{7} = \frac{5 \times 20}{1 \times 7} = \frac{100}{7} = 14\frac{2}{7}$$

Other examples:

Multiply $3\frac{3}{4} \times \frac{4}{15}$.

$$3\frac{3}{4} \times \frac{4}{15}$$

$$\frac{15}{4} \times \frac{4}{15}$$

$$\frac{\overset{1}{\cancel{15}} \times \overset{1}{\cancel{4}}}{\underset{1}{\cancel{4}} \times \underset{1}{\cancel{15}}} = \frac{1}{1} = 1$$

Multiply $\frac{5}{9} \times 3\frac{6}{7} \times \frac{1}{5}$.

$$\frac{5}{9} \times 3\frac{6}{7} \times \frac{1}{5}$$

$$\frac{5}{9} \times \frac{27}{7} \times \frac{1}{5}$$

$$\frac{\overset{1}{\cancel{5}} \times \overset{3}{\cancel{27}} \times 1}{\underset{1}{\cancel{9}} \times 7 \times \underset{1}{\cancel{5}}} = \frac{3}{7}$$

Checkpoint Write the letter of the correct answer.

Multiply.

1. $3\frac{3}{5} \times 2\frac{2}{9}$ **a.** $6\frac{1}{9}$ **b.** 8   **c.** 10   **d.** 72

2. $8\frac{1}{3} \times 5$ **a.** 15   **b.** 40   **c.** $40\frac{1}{3}$ **d.** $41\frac{2}{3}$

3. $1\frac{2}{7} \times 4\frac{2}{3}$ **a.** 4   **b.** $4\frac{4}{21}$ **c.** 6   **d.** $\frac{126}{7}$

4. $1\frac{3}{4} \times 3\frac{2}{3} \times 3\frac{3}{11}$ **a.** $\frac{21}{4}$ **b.** 9   **c.** $9\frac{3}{22}$ **d.** 21

Multiply. Write the answer in simplest form.

1. $2\frac{4}{5} \times 2\frac{1}{2}$ 2. $5\frac{1}{3} \times 1\frac{3}{4}$ 3. $7\frac{5}{7} \times 4\frac{5}{9}$ 4. $3\frac{7}{11} \times 3\frac{2}{3}$

5. $5\frac{3}{8} \times 3\frac{15}{15}$ 6. $10\frac{2}{3} \times 7\frac{3}{4}$ 7. $5\frac{7}{9} \times 13\frac{1}{2}$ 8. $8\frac{5}{8} \times 2\frac{4}{5}$

9. $13\frac{3}{4} \times 12$ 10. $6\frac{4}{5} \times 20$ 11. $35 \times 3\frac{1}{7}$ 12. $50 \times 7\frac{9}{20}$

13. $3\frac{2}{3} \times \frac{15}{22}$ 14. $\frac{5}{8} \times 4\frac{4}{5}$ 15. $\frac{3}{5} \times 4\frac{1}{2}$ 16. $25\frac{1}{5} \times \frac{4}{5}$

17. $6 \times \frac{7}{12}$ 18. $\frac{8}{15} \times 10$ 19. $24 \times \frac{5}{2}$ 20. $\frac{11}{9} \times 99$

21. $4\frac{1}{4} \times 3\frac{2}{3}$ 22. $6\frac{3}{8} \times 2\frac{4}{9}$ 23. $9 \times 5\frac{2}{3}$ 24. $8\frac{5}{6} \times 12$

25. $5\frac{3}{8} \times 20$ 26. $36 \times 2\frac{1}{3}$ 27. $10 \times \frac{13}{15}$ 28. $\frac{20}{7} \times 84$

29. $4\frac{2}{3} \times 2\frac{1}{2} \times 3\frac{4}{5}$ 30. $3\frac{5}{7} \times \frac{24}{8} \times 3\frac{10}{13}$ 31. $\frac{2}{3} \times 2\frac{1}{8} \times \frac{3}{2}$

Solve.

32. It takes Susan 6 min to complete 1 row of her knitting. About how long will it take her to complete $7\frac{1}{2}$ rows?

33. Bill is making a Mexican hat that will have a $6\frac{1}{2}$-in.-wide brim. The brim is $1\frac{7}{8}$ in. short of that width now. How wide is the brim?

★34. Nancy uses $6\frac{1}{4}$ skeins of wool to make one sweater. How many skeins has Nancy used if she has half-finished her fourth sweater?

★35. Chris needs to knit 120 rows to complete one sweater. It takes him 4 min to knit 1 row. He completed $3\frac{1}{2}$ sweaters this month. How much time did he spend on them?

ANOTHER LOOK

Solve.

1. Cassius makes cameo scenes carved on small pieces of onyx. During the past 18 years, he carved an average of 38 pieces per year. What is the total number of pieces he carved?

2. Eileen constructs lobster traps and sells them for $12.85 each. During her year in Cape Cod, she sold 412 traps. How much money did she earn from these sales?

PROBLEM SOLVING
Writing a Simpler Problem

Some problems look harder than they are. It may help you to solve problems that contain decimals, fractions, or large numbers if you substitute simpler numbers for these numbers. Once you have solved the problem with simpler numbers, solve it with the actual numbers.

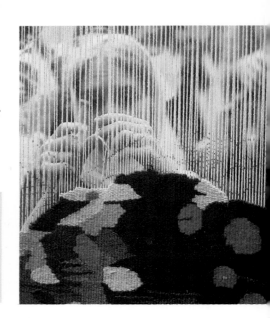

> Last year, a button factory produced 1,283 plastic buttons per week for 46 weeks and 1,720 wood buttons per week for the next 6 weeks. How many buttons did the factory produce during the 52 weeks?

Substitute simpler numbers, and break the problem down into small steps.

1. $1,000 \times 50 = 50,000$ (number of plastic buttons for 46 weeks)

2. $2,000 \times 10 = 20,000$ (number of wood buttons for 6 weeks)

3. $50,000 + 20,000 = 70,000$ (buttons produced in 52 weeks)

Use the actual numbers.

$1,283 \times 46 = 59,018$

$1,720 \times 6 = 10,320$

$59,018 + 10,320 = 69,338$ (buttons produced in 52 weeks)

Write the letter of the better plan for simplifying the problem.

1. Members of the sewing club spend $2.43 for materials to make each pot holder. If the members want to make a $1.69 profit per pot holder, how much should they charge for 15 pot holders?

a. **Step 1:** $2 + $2 = $4
   Step 2: $4 \times 15 = $60

b. **Step 1:** $2 \times 15 = $30
   Step 2: $30 + $2 = $32

Write the letter of the better plan for simplifying the problem.

2. The knitters at the Software Yarn Shop knit 16,800 stitches to make 10 place mats. They produce 386 place mats in 5 days. How many stitches do they knit each day?

a. **Step 1:** $390 \div 10 = 39$
Step 2: $39 \times 5 = 195$
Step 3: $195 \times 17,000 = 3,315,000$

b. **Step 1:** $390 \div 5 = 78$
Step 2: $17,000 \div 10 = 1,700$
Step 3: $1,700 \times 78 = 132,600$

Solve. Simplify the problem if you need to.

3. Mr. Clark's recipe calls for $87\frac{1}{2}$ apples to make 25 bowls of applesauce. If he wants to make 95 bowls of applesauce, how many apples does he need?

4. From 1978 through 1986, the Stoneware Shop dyed 1,570 skeins of wool per year. From 1987 through 1990, the shop dyed 1,610 skeins per year. What is the shop's total production from 1978 to 1990?

5. Sheila makes cotton batik dress fabric. She uses $6\frac{4}{5}$ packages of dye for every 34 dresses. If she wants to make 85 dresses, how many packages of dye does she need?

6. A group of 12 weavers produces $10\frac{1}{2}$ blankets per day. About how many blankets per day should Don expect to weave when he joins the group?

7. The Country Shop produces $20\frac{1}{2}$ dozen candles per day. During the holidays, the shop increases production by $\frac{1}{3}$. How many more candles than normal does the shop produce during a 7-day holiday period?

8. Brad will use 3 bags of tiles for a mosaic floor. The bags contain 4,878 tiles, 6,585 tiles, and 9,681 tiles. Brad uses $\frac{2}{3}$ of the tiles from each bag for the floor. How many tiles does he use?

9. The Antique Artisans make a colonial table set. Each set contains 2 oak chairs and 1 oak table. They use $11\frac{1}{2}$ ft^2 of oak for each chair and $17\frac{3}{4}$ ft^2 of oak for each table. They make 9 sets per week. How much wood do they use per week?

Dividing Fractions

Rhoda has $\frac{3}{4}$ yard of silver beads to be used as spacers in necklaces. If each necklace needs $\frac{3}{8}$ yard of beads, how many necklaces can be made?

Divide $\frac{3}{4} \div \frac{3}{8}$.

Find the **reciprocal** of the divisor.

Two numbers are reciprocals if their product is 1.

$\frac{8}{3} \times \frac{3}{8} = \frac{24}{24} = 1$

So, the reciprocal of $\frac{3}{8}$ is $\frac{8}{3}$.

Multiply by the reciprocal of the divisor.

$\frac{3}{4} \div \frac{3}{8} = \frac{3}{4} \times \frac{8}{3}$

Simplify and multiply.

$\frac{3}{4} \div \frac{3}{8} = \frac{3}{\overset{1}{4}} \times \frac{\overset{2}{8}}{\underset{1}{3}} = \frac{2}{1} = 2$

Two necklaces can be made.

Other examples:

Divide $\frac{3}{5} \div \frac{9}{10}$.

$\frac{3}{5} \div \frac{9}{10} = \frac{3}{5} \times \frac{10}{9} = \frac{\overset{1}{3}}{\underset{1}{5}} \times \frac{\overset{2}{10}}{\underset{3}{9}} = \frac{2}{3}$

Divide $\frac{2}{3} \div \frac{1}{8}$.

$\frac{2}{3} \div \frac{1}{8} = \frac{2}{3} \times \frac{8}{1} = \frac{16}{3} = 5\frac{1}{3}$

Checkpoint   Write the letter of the correct answer.

Divide.

1. $\frac{2}{7} \div \frac{1}{9}$ **a.** $\frac{2}{63}$ **b.** $\frac{7}{18}$ **c.** $1\frac{3}{8}$ **d.** $2\frac{4}{7}$

2. $\frac{1}{4} \div \frac{3}{8}$ **a.** $\frac{3}{32}$ **b.** $\frac{2}{3}$ **c.** $\frac{3}{4}$ **d.** $1\frac{1}{2}$

3. $\frac{3}{4} \div \frac{15}{12}$ **a.** $\frac{45}{48}$ **b.** $1\frac{2}{3}$ **c.** $\frac{3}{5}$ **d.** $\frac{2}{3}$

4. $\frac{7}{8} \div \frac{21}{24}$ **a.** 1   **b.** $\frac{147}{192}$ **c.** $\frac{10}{11}$ **d.** $\frac{7}{8}$

Write the reciprocal.

1. $\frac{3}{4}$
2. $\frac{1}{5}$
3. $\frac{1}{4}$
4. $\frac{4}{5}$
5. $\frac{9}{10}$

6. $\frac{6}{7}$
7. $\frac{7}{9}$
8. $\frac{3}{8}$
9. $\frac{5}{9}$
10. $\frac{7}{8}$

Divide. Write the answer in simplest form.

11. $\frac{1}{3} \div \frac{1}{6}$
12. $\frac{2}{3} \div \frac{2}{9}$
13. $\frac{5}{7} \div \frac{1}{7}$
14. $\frac{3}{4} \div \frac{3}{16}$
15. $\frac{5}{9} \div \frac{5}{18}$

16. $\frac{3}{8} \div \frac{2}{5}$
17. $\frac{1}{3} \div \frac{5}{6}$
18. $\frac{1}{2} \div \frac{6}{7}$
19. $\frac{1}{4} \div \frac{3}{5}$
20. $\frac{1}{6} \div \frac{2}{5}$

21. $\frac{6}{7} \div \frac{4}{5}$
22. $\frac{9}{8} \div \frac{1}{7}$
23. $\frac{4}{5} \div \frac{7}{9}$
24. $\frac{6}{11} \div \frac{5}{33}$
25. $\frac{7}{8} \div \frac{4}{5}$

26. $\frac{4}{9} \div \frac{3}{7}$
27. $\frac{2}{7} \div \frac{4}{11}$
28. $\frac{3}{7} \div \frac{1}{7}$
29. $\frac{1}{5} \div \frac{4}{15}$
30. $\frac{8}{9} \div \frac{18}{25}$

Solve.

31. Beads that are $\frac{1}{16}$ inch in diameter are strung into a necklace. How many beads are needed for $\frac{3}{4}$ inch?

32. Suzanne has $\frac{3}{4}$ yard of cord on which to string beads. How long is $\frac{1}{2}$ this length?

★33. Frank has oblong onyx beads and coral beads. Each onyx bead is $\frac{3}{8}$ in. long, and each coral bead is $\frac{1}{2}$ in. long. How many times a coral bead's length is an onyx bead's length?

CHALLENGE

The large cube on the right is made of twenty-seven smaller cubes. What fraction of the smaller cubes are exposed? What fraction of the smaller cubes have exactly one exposed face? two exposed faces? three? four? five? six? no exposed faces?

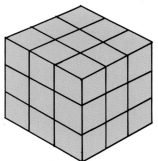

For additional activities, see *Connecting Math Ideas,* page 470.

Dividing Mixed Numbers

A. A dowel is used to make axles for wooden trains. From a dowel $10\frac{2}{3}$ inches long, how many axles can be made if each axle is $2\frac{2}{3}$ inches long?

Divide $10\frac{2}{3} \div 2\frac{2}{3}$.

Since you will divide by $2\frac{2}{3}$, you must find its reciprocal.

$$2\frac{2}{3} = \frac{8}{3} \qquad \frac{8}{3} \times \frac{3}{8} = 1$$

Write fractions for both numbers.

$$10\frac{2}{3} \div 2\frac{2}{3} = \frac{32}{3} \div \frac{8}{3}$$

Four axles can be made.

Multiply by the reciprocal. Simplify.

$$\overset{4}{\underset{1}{\frac{32}{3}}} \times \overset{1}{\underset{1}{\frac{3}{8}}} = \frac{4}{1} = 4$$

B. Divide $3 \div 7\frac{4}{5}$.

Write whole numbers and mixed numbers as fractions.

$$3 \div 7\frac{4}{5} = \frac{3}{1} \div \frac{39}{5}$$

Multiply.

$$\overset{1}{\frac{3}{1}} \times \frac{5}{\underset{13}{39}} = \frac{5}{13}$$

Other examples:

Divide $6\frac{3}{4} \div \frac{5}{8}$.

$$\frac{27}{4} \div \frac{5}{8} = \frac{27}{4} \times \overset{2}{\underset{1}{\frac{8}{5}}} = \frac{54}{5} = 10\frac{4}{5}$$

Divide $8 \div \frac{2}{9}$.

$$8 \div \frac{2}{9} = \frac{8}{1} \times \frac{9}{\underset{1}{\overset{4}{2}}} = \frac{36}{1} = 36$$

Checkpoint Write the letter of the correct answer.

Divide.

1. $3\frac{1}{3} \div 1\frac{1}{5}$ **a.** $\frac{9}{25}$ **b.** $2\frac{7}{9}$ **c.** $2\frac{14}{18}$ **d.** 4

2. $5 \div 1\frac{1}{4}$ **a.** $\frac{1}{4}$ **b.** $\frac{4}{25}$ **c.** 4 **d.** $6\frac{1}{4}$

3. $1\frac{3}{7} \div 1\frac{2}{3}$ **a.** $1\frac{1}{6}$ **b.** $\frac{6}{7}$ **c.** $2\frac{8}{21}$ **d.** $3\frac{3}{7}$

4. $6\frac{3}{5} \div 9$ **a.** $\frac{11}{15}$ **b.** $\frac{3}{5}$ **c.** $1\frac{4}{11}$ **d.** $15\frac{3}{5}$

Math Reasoning, page H214

Divide. Write the answer in simplest form.

1. $3\frac{1}{4} \div 1\frac{3}{4}$ **2.** $4\frac{1}{3} \div 1\frac{2}{3}$ **3.** $4\frac{5}{8} \div 2\frac{1}{8}$ **4.** $2\frac{1}{5} \div 1\frac{3}{5}$

5. $5 \div 2\frac{1}{2}$ **6.** $10 \div 3\frac{1}{3}$ **7.** $16 \div 1\frac{7}{9}$ **8.** $2 \div 1\frac{7}{8}$

9. $2 \div 1\frac{1}{4}$ **10.** $6 \div 3\frac{2}{5}$ **11.** $7 \div 4\frac{1}{9}$ **12.** $12 \div 3\frac{4}{5}$

13. $2 \div \frac{7}{8}$ **14.** $4 \div \frac{3}{4}$ **15.** $12 \div \frac{3}{5}$ **16.** $7 \div \frac{2}{3}$

17. $9\frac{9}{10} \div \frac{4}{5}$ **18.** $6\frac{2}{3} \div \frac{5}{6}$ **19.** $12\frac{1}{3} \div \frac{1}{9}$ **20.** $11\frac{5}{9} \div \frac{1}{4}$

21. $6\frac{6}{7} \div \frac{6}{7}$ **22.** $4\frac{1}{2} \div \frac{1}{3}$ **23.** $9\frac{9}{10} \div \frac{9}{10}$ **24.** $13\frac{1}{10} \div \frac{6}{7}$

25. $9\frac{1}{3} \div 3\frac{2}{3}$ **26.** $14\frac{1}{4} \div \frac{5}{9}$ **27.** $6 \div 3\frac{2}{3}$ **28.** $10\frac{1}{5} \div 5\frac{4}{5}$

29. $7 \div \frac{7}{9}$ **30.** $4 \div 4\frac{5}{9}$ **31.** $5\frac{1}{6} \div 2\frac{1}{4}$ **32.** $6\frac{1}{3} \div \frac{2}{9}$

Solve.

33. Larry bought a piece of wood $34\frac{1}{2}$ inches long to build crossing gates. He cut the wood into 6 pieces of equal length. How long was each piece?

34. George laid down a length of track that was $5\frac{3}{4}$ feet long. He used 5 sections of equal length. How long was each section?

35. Paula wanted to have rugs of equal length for each of her 4 miniature houses. She used up a strip of blue felt $6\frac{3}{4}$ inches long. How long was each rug?

36. In 10 minutes, Lisa's train goes around the track $7\frac{1}{2}$ times. How long does it take the train to go around the track once?

NUMBER SENSE

Two of these answers are unreasonable. Estimate to find them. Tell why they are unreasonable.

1. $2\frac{1}{3} \times \frac{9}{10} = 2\frac{1}{10}$ **2.** $3\frac{3}{8} \times \frac{4}{5} = 5\frac{2}{5}$

3. $5\frac{2}{3} \div 1\frac{1}{6} = 6\frac{5}{6}$ **4.** $3\frac{1}{2} \div \frac{7}{8} = 4$

Decimals and Fractions

Help! The scorekeeper has lost the scorebook and does not know what the batting averages are. The coach has a list of the batting statistics for the starting players through the end of last week, but he does not know which statistic is for which player. The scorekeeper has a piece of scrap paper on which she had computed the current batting averages of 4 starting players, but she does not know which average belongs to which player. She has come to your math class for help.

Here is what she knows:

- Batting statistics up to the end of last week.

| Hits | 24 | 39 | 37 | 23 | 18 | 21 | 21 | 19 | 35 |
| At Bats | 64 | 96 | 80 | 50 | 80 | 70 | 60 | 50 | 63 |

- To find a batting average, divide the number of hits by the number of at bats and show the quotient rounded to the nearest thousandth. Also, drop the zero before the decimal point. Four of the batting averages until today are

    .375   .200   .450   .333

- Statistics from this week for each player:

	At Bats	Hits
Barbara	10	4
Gene	10	0
Fred	11	3
Monica	12	3
Lisa	14	5
Bob	14	5
Daniela	12	4
Juan	10	4
Kelly	10	6

- Other clues:
  Fred insists that his batting average at the end of last week was .375.

  Daniela does not remember her batting average from last week, but she knows she's been at bat a total of 75 times.

150

Juan's batting average at the end of last week included only one nonzero digit.

Kelly's mother knows that Kelly has a total of 43 hits this year.

The girl who has been at bat a total of 72 times knows that all the digits in her current batting average are the same.

The boy whose latest batting average is .200 has a total of 18 hits.

Bob has more hits than anyone else on the team.

Thinking as a Team

1. Use a calculator to convert the batting statistics through the end of last week into decimal form. How can you use this information and the clues to compute the batting statistics for each player?

2. Make a table showing the latest batting statistics in fractional form. Compute the decimal equivalents for each.

3. How would you find the decimal equivalent of $\frac{2}{3}$ on a calculator? Decimals such as 0.666 . . . are called **repeating decimals.** The pattern of the digits is unending. You can write a repeating decimal by putting a bar over the digits that repeat ($0.\overline{6}$). What decimal equivalents in your table are repeating decimals?

4. How would you find the decimal equivalent of $\frac{9}{20}$ on a calculator? Decimals such as 0.45 are called **terminating decimals** because they end instead of repeat. What decimal equivalents in your table are terminating decimals?

5. Find everyone's batting average. Who has the best batting average?

Congratulations! You have analyzed the scorekeeper's data and helped her use logical reasoning to argue to a correct conclusion.

Solving Equations with Fractions

A. A potter needed to make a teapot and teacups. He used $3\frac{3}{4}$ packages of clay for the teapot. If he started with $8\frac{1}{2}$ packages of clay, how much clay did he have left for the teacups?

Clay for the teacups		Clay used for the teapot		Clay started with
x	$+$	$3\frac{3}{4}$	$=$	$8\frac{1}{2}$
x	$+\ 3\frac{3}{4}\ -\ 3\frac{3}{4}$		$=$	$8\frac{1}{2}\ -\ 3\frac{3}{4}$
		x	$=$	$4\frac{3}{4}$

He had $4\frac{3}{4}$ packages of clay left for the teacups.

B. Solve.

$$\frac{3}{4}s = 5$$

$$\frac{3}{4}s = 5$$

$$\frac{4}{3} \cdot \frac{3}{4}s = \frac{4}{3} \cdot \frac{5}{1}$$

Multiply both sides by the reciprocal of $\frac{3}{4}$.

$$s = \frac{20}{3}$$

$$s = 6\frac{2}{3}$$

Check.

$$\frac{3}{4}s = 5$$

$$\frac{3}{4} \cdot 6\frac{2}{3} \stackrel{?}{=} 5$$

$$\overset{1}{\underset{1}{\frac{3}{4}}} \cdot \overset{5}{\underset{1}{\frac{20}{3}}} \stackrel{?}{=} 5$$

$$5 = 5\ \checkmark$$

C. Solve. $\frac{5}{8}d + 4\frac{1}{4} = 16\frac{3}{4}$

$$\frac{5}{8}d + 4\frac{1}{4} = 16\frac{3}{4}$$

$$\frac{5}{8}d + 4\frac{1}{4} - 4\frac{1}{4} = 16\frac{3}{4} - 4\frac{1}{4}$$

$$\frac{8}{5} \cdot \frac{5}{8}d = \frac{8}{5} \cdot 12\frac{1}{2}$$

$$d = \overset{4}{\underset{1}{\frac{8}{5}}} \cdot \overset{5}{\underset{1}{\frac{25}{2}}}$$

$$d = 20$$

152

Solve. Write the answer in simplest form.

1. $x + 1\frac{1}{6} = 5\frac{1}{8}$　　**2.** $z + 2\frac{3}{8} = 8\frac{7}{12}$　**3.** $y - 4\frac{1}{4} = 3\frac{1}{5}$　　**4.** $b - 12\frac{7}{8} = 9\frac{5}{9}$

5. $\frac{1}{6}r = 3$　　　　**6.** $1\frac{3}{4}c = 9\frac{1}{4}$　　**7.** $f \div \frac{2}{5} = 4$　　**8.** $k \div 2\frac{5}{4} = 8\frac{5}{4}$

9. $12\frac{1}{3}h + 3 = 21\frac{1}{3}$ **10.** $3\frac{7}{9}t - 2\frac{8}{9} = 5$ **11.** $5\frac{2}{9}f - 7\frac{2}{3} = 23$ **12.** $3\frac{3}{16}u + \frac{3}{8} = 4\frac{3}{8}$

13. $a + 2\frac{1}{2} = 9$　　**14.** $\frac{1}{8}n = 6\frac{1}{4}$　　**15.** $\frac{1}{2}d + 1\frac{1}{2} = 5$ ★**16.** $12\frac{1}{4} + 3\frac{1}{6} = 21\frac{3}{6}w$

Solve.

17. It takes a potter $\frac{3}{4}$ hour to make 1 bowl. How many bowls will the potter make in 33 hours? (Write an equation, and let b = number of bowls.)

18. A potter used 10 packages of clay to make bowls. If 1 bowl took $1\frac{1}{4}$ packages, how many bowls did he make? (Let b = the number of bowls.)

19. Suppose that you want to buy a set of soup bowls. You consider a set of 8 soup bowls that sells for $20 at a discount store. Then you visit a local potter who sells handcrafted bowls for $5.00 each. The less expensive bowls are mass produced and of lower quality than the pottery bowls. Both types of bowls will serve the same purpose. Would you rather buy more of the less expensive bowls, or fewer bowls of better quality for the same price? Why?

NUMBER SENSE

Mentally match the equations that have the same solution.

1. $a + 2 = 11$

2. $\frac{b}{4} + 6 = 6$

3. $5c + 5 = 30$

4. $12 - 2d = 0$

5. $e + 2 = 10$

a. $4 = \frac{v}{2} + 1$

b. $7 = w - 2$

c. $5 = x + 5$

d. $8 = 4 + \frac{y}{2}$

e. $0 = \frac{z}{5} - 1$

PROBLEM SOLVING
Interpreting the Quotient and the Remainder

Sometimes, when you divide, the answer is not a whole number. If the answer is a quotient with a remainder, be sure your answer really answers the question.

1. Jim gives classes in creating stained-glass windows. He allows a maximum of 8 students per class, and 30 people have applied. How many classes should Jim schedule?

$$\begin{array}{r} 3\text{ R}6 \\ 8\overline{)30} \\ \underline{24} \\ 6 \end{array}$$

Look at the quotient.
Look at the remainder.
Round the quotient up to the next-greater whole number.

Jim should schedule 4 classes.

2. There are $10\frac{2}{3}$ dozen sheets of colored glass given to each class. Each of the 8 students receives an equal amount. How much glass does each student receive?

$10\frac{2}{3} \div 8$ $\frac{32}{3} \div 8$ Look at the quotient.
Look at the remainder.

$\frac{{}^{4}32}{3} \times \frac{1}{8_1}$ $\frac{4}{3} = 1\frac{1}{3}$ Use both the quotient and the remainder.

Each student will receive $1\frac{1}{3}$ dozen, or 16, pieces of glass.

3. Jim is storing glass cutters. He has only 8 boxes. The cutters fit 4 to a box, and there are 34 glass cutters. How many cutters will not be boxed?

$$\begin{array}{r} 8\text{ R}2 \\ 4\overline{)34} \\ \underline{32} \\ 2 \end{array}$$

Look at the quotient.
Look at the remainder.
Use only the remainder.

There will be 2 cutters that will not be boxed.

4. Seven feet of framing are needed to frame each project. If framing is purchased in 8-ft lengths, how many frames can be made from 16 ft of framing?

$$\begin{array}{r} 2\text{ R}2 \\ 7\overline{)16} \\ \underline{14} \\ 2 \end{array}$$

Look at the quotient.
Look at the remainder.
Use only the quotient.

Two frames can be made from 16 ft of framing.

Write the letter of the correct answer.

1. Jackie made a mold for ceramic tiles. The mold produces 8 tiles at a time. If Jackie wants to make 78 tiles, how many times must she fill the mold?

$$78 \div 8 = 9\frac{3}{4}$$

a. 9 times
b. $9\frac{3}{4}$ times
c. 10 times

2. Margo's candle shop produces 700 candles per day. If the shop packs 6 candles to a box, how many boxes are needed per day?

$$700 \div 6 = 116\,\text{R}4$$

a. 116 boxes
b. $116\frac{1}{2}$ boxes
c. 117 boxes

Solve.

3. Samantha buys a piece of canvas that measures 90 square feet. How many paintings that measure 7 square feet can she paint on the canvas?

4. A design for a bowl 10 in. in diameter and 5 in. high calls for $1\frac{3}{4}$ lb of clay. There are 6 lb of clay. How much clay remains if 3 bowls are made?

5. Joanna has 2,000 strands of natural cane. How many baskets can she weave if the pattern for each basket calls for 94 strands of cane?

6. To string a necklace, Jesse needs 236 small beads. The crafts store sells small beads in bags of 75 beads each. How many bags must Jesse buy?

7. Barbara is selling handmade pot holders at 3 for $5.50. What is the lowest price that Barbara should charge for 1 pot holder?

8. Eduardo uses $\frac{3}{4}$ sheet of red glass for each stained-glass window he is working on. If he plans to make 5 windows, how many sheets of red glass does he need to buy?

9. Fiona works in brass. It costs her $12.80 to craft 6 brass nameplates. She sells one to a friend at cost. How much does the friend pay for the nameplate?

★10. Lattia is molding pewter figurines. For every 10.5-ounce figurine, she must pour 12 ounces of molten pewter. What percent of the pewter is waste?

LOGICAL REASONING

At summer camp, each of the 33 campers took exactly one crafts course. A total of 9 campers took the Indian-jewelry course. Of the campers, 8 took the leather class and 14 took a jewelry course. The remaining campers took the stained-glass course. How many campers took the stained-glass course?

VENN DIAGRAM

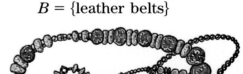

Every Indian-jewelry student is a jewelry student. So, {Indian-jewelry students} is a **subset** of {jewelry students}.
Write: {Indian-jewelry students} ⊂ {jewelry students}.

No students are taking both a jewelry class and the leather class. So, {leather students} and {jewelry students} are **disjoint** sets.

There are $33 - 14 - 8 = 11$ campers taking the stained-glass course.

Write $A \subset B$, $B \subset A$, or A *and* B *are disjoint.*

1. A = {leather belts}
B = {belts}

2. A = {gold jewelry}
B = {silver jewelry}

3. A = {windows}
B = {stained-glass windows}

4. A = {necklaces}
B = {bracelets}

5. A = {metallic jewelry}
B = {silver necklaces}

6. A = {leather crafts}
B = {leather belts}

Use a Venn diagram to solve.

The jewelry class made 24 necklaces from either gemstones or beads. They made 35 bracelets from either silver, beads, or gemstones. They made 23 pieces of jewelry from gems and 19 pieces of jewelry from beads. They made 9 beaded necklaces.

7. How many necklaces were made from gems?

8. How many beaded bracelets did they make?

9. How many bracelets were made from gems?

10. How many bracelets were made from silver?

156

GROUP PROJECT

A Crafty Way to Raise Money

The problem: Your school has been invited to participate in an American Handicrafts Fair to raise money for charity. Your school has been offered a choice of the following three crafts: basket weaving, rug hooking, or beaded jewelry making.

Using the chart and the questions below, decide which handicraft would probably be the wisest choice.

Materials		Cost	Tools	Time to make each	Projected selling price	Estimated number that would be sold
Baskets	wicker	$4.00 per basket	scissors	3 hours	$5.75	200
Rugs	yarn	$44.25 per rug	metal hook	60 hours	$65.00	50
	cotton backing	$7.50 per rug				
Jewelry	beads	$4.50 per necklace	pliers	1 hour	$8.50	125
	string and clasp	$.50 each				

Key Questions
- Which craft item is the least expensive to make?

- Which item is the least time-consuming to make?

- Which item will sell for the highest price?

- Which item will probably sell most successfully?

CHAPTER TEST

Write in simplest form. Then write two fractions that are equivalent to each fraction. (pages 120–121)

1. $\frac{10}{12}$

2. $\frac{35}{56}$

3. $\frac{21}{87}$

Write a fraction for each whole number or mixed number. (pages 122–123)

4. $4\frac{3}{8}$

5. 5

6. $9\frac{2}{5}$

Write a whole number or mixed number for each fraction. (pages 122–123)

7. $\frac{48}{9}$

8. $\frac{85}{5}$

9. $\frac{98}{3}$

Compare. Use >, <, or = for ●. (pages 124–125)

10. $\frac{2}{3}$ ● $\frac{12}{18}$

11. $1\frac{3}{8}$ ● $\frac{15}{8}$

12. $\frac{3}{4}$ ● $\frac{6}{12}$

Order from the greatest to the least. (pages 124–125)

13. $\frac{5}{8}, \frac{2}{3}, \frac{3}{4}, \frac{4}{9}$

14. $2\frac{5}{6}, 2\frac{2}{9}, 2\frac{1}{4}, 2\frac{9}{12}$

15. $1\frac{2}{3}, 1\frac{3}{4}, 2\frac{1}{5}, 1\frac{1}{2}$

Add or subtract. Write the answer in simplest form. (pages 130–135)

16. $\frac{5}{7} + \frac{3}{7} + \frac{4}{7}$

17. $\frac{2}{3} + \frac{7}{9} + \frac{1}{9}$

18. $5\frac{1}{4} + 3\frac{5}{6} + 1\frac{1}{3}$

19. $\frac{5}{8} - \frac{3}{8}$

20. $\frac{1}{2} - \frac{1}{5}$

21. $4\frac{2}{7} - 1\frac{1}{3}$

Estimate. (pages 128–129 and 140–141)

22. $5\frac{3}{4} + 2\frac{4}{5} - 1\frac{3}{5}$

23. $7\frac{1}{6} \times 6\frac{1}{8}$

24. $8\frac{1}{4} \div 2\frac{1}{5}$

Multiply or divide. Write the answer in simplest form. (pages 138–139, 142–143, and 146–149)

25. $\frac{3}{4} \times \frac{4}{5}$

26. $4 \times \frac{8}{9}$

27. $2\frac{1}{2} \times \frac{3}{7}$

28. $\frac{2}{9} \div \frac{4}{5}$

29. $\frac{5}{7} \div 6$

30. $1\frac{3}{4} \div \frac{2}{3}$

Write each decimal as a fraction, and write each fraction as a decimal. (pages 150–151)

31. 0.4 **32.** 0.85 **33.** 0.065 **34.** $\frac{2}{9}$ **35.** $\frac{7}{20}$ **36.** $\frac{4}{15}$

Solve. (pages 152–153)

37. $\frac{3}{5}x = \frac{2}{3}$ **38.** $y \div \frac{3}{5} = 7$ **39.** $\frac{1}{2}d - 1\frac{1}{2} = 7$ **40.** $3\frac{1}{4}x + 2\frac{3}{8} = 5\frac{7}{8}$

Solve. Solve a simpler problem where necessary. (pages 126–127, 136–137, 144–145, and 154–155)

41. The County Fair of Oakley recorded the number of quilts entered in the Best Quilt Contest each year. The results are listed in the pictograph at the right. If the trend of quilt entries continues during the next five years, will the number of entries in 1994 exceed 80 quilts?

QUILTS ENTERED IN CONTEST

Year	
1989	⊠ ⊠ ⊠ ⊠ ⊠ ⊠ ⊠ ⊠
1988	⊠ ⊠ ⊠ ⊠ ⊠ ⊠ ⊠ ◪
1987	⊠ ⊠ ⊠ ⊠ ⊠ ⊠ ◪
1986	⊠ ⊠ ⊠ ⊠ ⊠ ⊠ ◪
1985	⊠ ⊠ ⊠ ⊠ ⊠ ⊠

⊠ **8 quilts**

42. Bert sells necklaces at the fair. If each necklace is made of 3 large ceramic beads and 4 small ceramic beads that have 12 brass spacers on either side of each bead, how many of each item must he buy for 18 necklaces?

43. Use the pictograph to find the average number of quilts entered in the Best Quilt Contest during the last five years. In which year(s) was the number of entries greater than the average? If quilts are shown with no more than 6 per display area, how many display areas were needed in 1989?

BONUS

Use the table to find what fraction of the total cost the small beads are.

Cost of Necklaces	
Large beads	$1.25 each
Small beads	$0.25 each
Spacers	$0.50 bag
Cord and findings	$7.00

RETEACHING

A. Add $1\frac{1}{5} + 4\frac{3}{4} + 1\frac{1}{2}$.

To add mixed numbers that have unlike denominators, find equivalent fractions.

Find the LCM of the denominators 5, 4, and 2. The LCD is 20.

Write each fraction, using like denominators.

$$1\frac{1}{5} = 1\frac{4}{20}$$
$$4\frac{3}{4} = 4\frac{15}{20}$$
$$+ 1\frac{1}{2} = 1\frac{10}{20}$$

Add.

$$1\frac{1}{5} = 1\frac{4}{20}$$
$$4\frac{3}{4} = 4\frac{15}{20}$$
$$+ 1\frac{1}{2} = 1\frac{10}{20}$$
$$6\frac{29}{20}$$

Simplify the sum.

$$6\frac{29}{20} = 6 + 1\frac{9}{20} = 7\frac{9}{20}$$

B. Subtract $4\frac{1}{3} - 1\frac{3}{4}$.

To subtract mixed numbers that have unlike denominators, find fractions that have like denominators.

Rename fractions.

$$4\frac{1}{3} = 4\frac{4}{12}$$
$$- 1\frac{3}{4} = 1\frac{9}{12}$$

Compare fractions.

$$\frac{4}{12} < \frac{9}{12} \quad \textbf{So, rename.}$$
$$4\frac{4}{12} = 3 + 1\frac{4}{12} = 3\frac{16}{12}$$

Subtract.

$$4\frac{1}{3} = 3\frac{16}{12}$$
$$- 1\frac{3}{4} = 1\frac{9}{12}$$
$$2\frac{7}{12}$$

> Subtract the fractions and then the whole numbers.

Add. Write the answer in simplest form.

1. $4\frac{3}{8} + 2\frac{2}{3}$

2. $2\frac{3}{5} + 7\frac{2}{3}$

3. $4\frac{5}{6} + 2\frac{3}{5}$

4. $3\frac{1}{4} + 5\frac{1}{6} + 1\frac{2}{3}$

5. $2\frac{1}{2} + 1\frac{1}{6} + 10\frac{4}{5}$

6. $11\frac{3}{10} + 1\frac{1}{6} + 8\frac{3}{4}$

Subtract. Write the answer in simplest form.

7. $3\frac{2}{5} - 1\frac{9}{10}$

8. $9\frac{1}{8} - 6\frac{1}{2}$

9. $6\frac{1}{3} - 4\frac{5}{6}$

10. $5\frac{1}{4} - 3\frac{5}{6}$

11. $7\frac{1}{7} - 5\frac{1}{3}$

12. $9\frac{2}{3} - 6\frac{7}{8}$

ENRICHMENT

Complex Fractions

A **complex fraction** is a fraction in which the numerator or the denominator or both have a fraction as a term.

You can simplify complex fractions by dividing.

$$\frac{\frac{19}{9}}{\frac{2}{3}} = \frac{19}{9} \div \frac{2}{3}$$

Divide. $\quad \dfrac{19}{9} \div \dfrac{2}{3} = \dfrac{19}{\overset{}{\underset{3}{9}}} \times \dfrac{\overset{1}{3}}{2} = \dfrac{19}{6} = 3\dfrac{1}{6}$

Sometimes you have to simplify the numerator or the denominator or both first.

$$\frac{2\frac{2}{3} + \frac{1}{6}}{\frac{1}{2} + \frac{1}{3}} = \frac{\frac{8}{3} + \frac{1}{6}}{\frac{1}{2} + \frac{1}{3}} = \frac{\frac{16}{6} + \frac{1}{6}}{\frac{3}{6} + \frac{2}{6}} = \frac{\frac{17}{6}}{\frac{5}{6}} =$$

$$\frac{17}{6} \div \frac{5}{6} = \frac{17}{\overset{}{\underset{1}{6}}} \times \frac{\overset{1}{6}}{5} = \frac{17}{5} = 3\frac{2}{5}$$

Simplify.

1. $\dfrac{\frac{1}{4}}{\frac{1}{6}}$ **2.** $\dfrac{\frac{2}{3}}{\frac{1}{3}}$ **3.** $\dfrac{\frac{8}{9}}{\frac{1}{3}}$ **4.** $\dfrac{\frac{4}{5}}{\frac{1}{2}}$

5. $\dfrac{\frac{1}{5}}{\frac{6}{7}}$ **6.** $\dfrac{\frac{4}{7}}{\frac{3}{8}}$ **7.** $\dfrac{\frac{1}{9}}{\frac{7}{8}}$ **8.** $\dfrac{\frac{2}{5}}{\frac{9}{10}}$

9. $\dfrac{\frac{1}{3}}{3}$ **10.** $\dfrac{\frac{1}{3}}{9}$ **11.** $\dfrac{\frac{1}{4}}{2}$ **12.** $\dfrac{\frac{1}{3}}{2}$

13. $\dfrac{\frac{1}{4}}{6}$ **14.** $\dfrac{\frac{6}{7}}{3}$ **15.** $\dfrac{\frac{5}{6}}{2}$ **16.** $\dfrac{\frac{1}{9}}{3}$

17. $\dfrac{\frac{2}{5} + 1\frac{1}{10}}{\frac{1}{2} + \frac{3}{5}}$ **18.** $\dfrac{1\frac{2}{3} - \frac{1}{6}}{\frac{1}{3} + \frac{1}{2}}$ **19.** $\dfrac{\frac{1}{2} + 3\frac{3}{5}}{1\frac{3}{20} + \frac{7}{10}}$ **20.** $\dfrac{1\frac{1}{3} - \frac{3}{5}}{1\frac{1}{2} + \frac{7}{9}}$

21. $\dfrac{\frac{1}{3} + 3\frac{9}{10}}{\frac{1}{6} - \frac{1}{8}}$ **22.** $\dfrac{4\frac{1}{3} + 9\frac{1}{3}}{\frac{1}{2} + 1\frac{1}{4}}$ **23.** $\dfrac{1\frac{6}{7} - \frac{1}{4}}{\frac{1}{9} + \frac{3}{4}}$ **24.** $\dfrac{3\frac{2}{3} + \frac{4}{9}}{1\frac{4}{5} - \frac{2}{3}}$

TECHNOLOGY

This BASIC program renames fractions as decimals.

```
10 PRINT "TYPE THE NUMERATOR": INPUT N
20 PRINT "TYPE THE DENOMINATOR": INPUT D
30 PRINT N "/" D "=" N/D
```

When you RUN this program, your screen might look like this.

```
TYPE THE NUMERATOR
? 2
TYPE THE DENOMINATOR
? 5
2/5 = 0.4
```

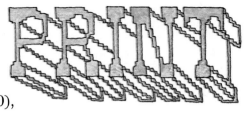

1. Add a line to this program to be sure that the denominator is not zero.

For any two fractions $\frac{a}{b}$ and $\frac{c}{d}$ (where $b \neq 0$ and $d \neq 0$), the product of the fractions is $\frac{a}{b} \cdot \frac{c}{d}$, or $\frac{ac}{bd}$. You can use this program to multiply two fractions.

```
10 PRINT "FIRST NUMERATOR": INPUT A
20 PRINT "FIRST DENOMINATOR": INPUT B
30 PRINT "SECOND NUMERATOR": INPUT C
40 PRINT "SECOND DENOMINATOR": INPUT D
50 LET AC = A * C
60 LET BD = B * D
70 PRINT A "/" B "TIMES" C "/" D "EQUALS" AC "/" BD
```

2. Add two lines to this program to check that the denominators are not zero.

3. Show what your screen will look like when you RUN this program and multiply $\frac{5}{6}$ times $\frac{1}{9}$.

You can use a semicolon to help you print two statements directly following each other. Here is a program that uses semicolons.

```
10 LET A = 7
20 PRINT A; " IS EQUAL";
30 PRINT " TO " ; A
```

When you RUN this program, your screen will look like this.

```
7 IS EQUAL TO 7
```

In line 20, the semicolon after the A made the value of A and the words IS EQUAL print next to each other on the same line. Semicolons do not affect anything that is inside quotation marks. The semicolon at the end of line 20 causes the material from line 30 to print next to the material from line 20.

Here is the fraction-multiplication program rewritten to contain semicolons.

```
10 PRINT "FIRST NUMERATOR"; : INPUT A
20 PRINT "FIRST DENOMINATOR"; : INPUT B
30 PRINT "SECOND NUMERATOR"; : INPUT C
40 PRINT "SECOND DENOMINATOR"; : INPUT D
50 LET AC = A * C
60 LET BD = B * D
70 PRINT A; "/";B; "TIMES"; C; "/";D; "EQUALS"; AC; "/"; BD
```

Notice the semicolon in line 10. It made the question mark from the INPUT statement print right after FIRST NUMERATOR.

4. Write a program to find the sum of two fractions. The expression for the sum of two fractions $\frac{a}{b}$ and $\frac{c}{d}$ is $\frac{ad + bc}{bd}$. Remember to check the denominators to be sure that neither one is zero.

CUMULATIVE REVIEW

Write the letter of the correct answer.

1. Which number is divisible by 9?

a. 291   **b.** 837
c. 982   **d.** not given

2. What is the square root of 81?

a. 9   **b.** 17
c. 27   **d.** not given

3. Evaluate 7^4.

a. 53   **b.** 343
c. 2,401   **d.** not given

4. What is the prime factorization of 54?

a. $3^3 \times 2$ **b.** $3^2 \times 2^3$
c. 34   **d.** not given

5. What is the standard number for 6.75×10^5?

a. 0.00675   **b.** 675,000
c. 6,750,000   **d.** not given

6. What is the LCM of 3, 16, and 24?

a. 24   **b.** 64
c. 48   **d.** not given

7. $106.02 \times 1,000$

a. 0.10602   **b.** 10,602
c. 106,020   **d.** not given

8. Estimate 24.72×0.49.

a. 8   **b.** 10
c. 12^+ **d.** 20^+

9. $712.38 \div 62$

a. 1,149   **b.** 11.49
c. 114.8   **d.** not given

10. 0.703×0.04

a. 0.002802   **b.** 0.02812
c. 0.2812   **d.** not given

11. $0.718116 \div 0.042$

a. 17.098   **b.** 17.98
c. 170.98   **d.** not given

12. Round to the nearest hundredth and subtract: $62.84572 - 3.99398$.

a. 58.8   **b.** 58.84
c. 58.86   **d.** not given

13. By walking 9 km, Max walked 3 km less than four times as far as Joe. Write an equation and solve to find how far Joe walked.

a. $1\frac{1}{2}$ km   **b.** 3 km
c. 24 km   **d.** not given

14. Selina collected 240 cans and bottles to return to the collection center. She had 10 more cans than bottles. Write an equation and solve to find how many cans she had.

a. 110   **b.** 115
c. 230   **d.** not given

Suppose you had a driver's license, and you wanted to buy a car. Which factors would you consider in choosing a car? Which car would you choose, and why would you choose it?

5 MEASUREMENT

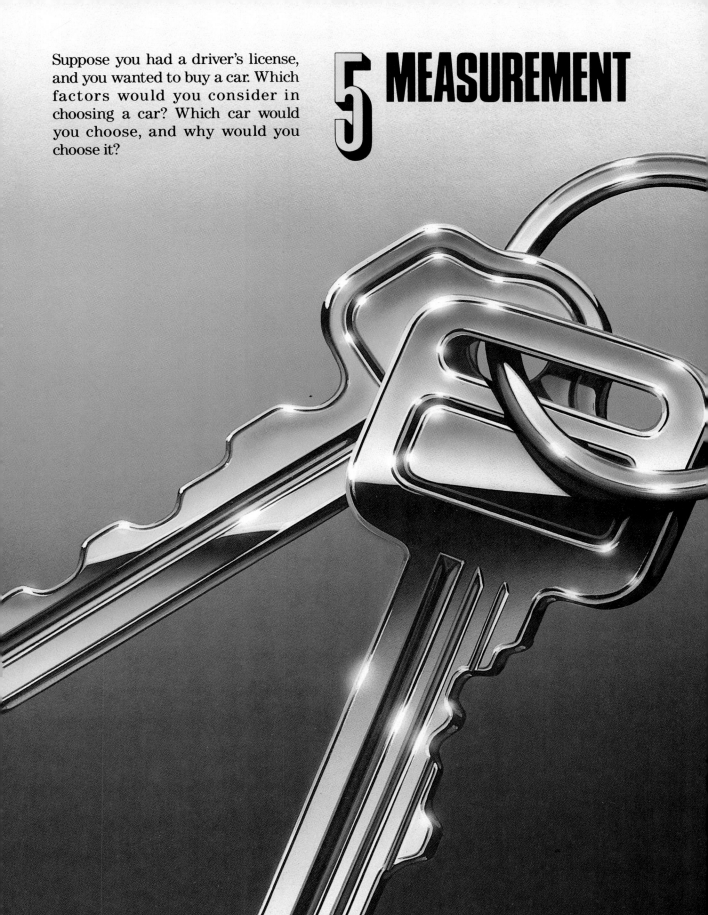

Metric Units of Length

A. The **meter (m)** is the basic metric
unit of length. All other units are related to the meter.

kilometer	hectometer	dekameter	meter	decimeter	centimeter	millimeter
km	hm	dam	m	dm	cm	mm
1,000 m	100 m	10 m	1 m	0.1 m	0.01 m	0.001 m

The width of a car door is about 1 m.

The thickness of a seat belt is about 1 mm.

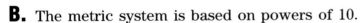

To the nearest centimeter, the car key is 6 cm long.

To the nearest millimeter, the car key is 59 mm long.

B. The metric system is based on powers of 10.

To rename a larger unit with a smaller
unit, multiply.

5 km = ■ m	0.06 m = ■ cm
5 × 1,000 = 5,000	0.06 × 100 = 6
5 km = 5,000 m	0.06 m = 6 cm

To rename a smaller unit with a larger
unit, divide.

300 cm = ■ m	37 m = ■ km
300 ÷ 100 = 3	37 ÷ 1,000 = 0.037
300 cm = 3 m	37 m = 0.037 km

Checkpoint Write the letter of the correct answer.

1. Choose the best measure for the
   length of a gas pedal.

   a. 20 mm   **b.** 20 cm
   c. 200 cm   **d.** 20 m

2. Choose the missing number.
   9 cm = ■ mm

   a. 0.9   **b.** 90
   c. 900   **d.** 9,000

Write the unit used to measure

1. distance on a map

2. the distance between cities.

3. the length of a car.

4. the width of a tire.

Choose the best estimate. Write the letter of the correct answer.

5. the length of a windshield wiper

a. 35 mm   **b.** 35 cm   **c.** 35 m

6. the diameter of a headlight

a. 0.15 km   **b.** 1.5 m   **c.** 15 cm

Complete.

7. 26 km = ▓ m

8. 60 cm = ▓ mm

9. 7 m = ▓ cm

10. 13 m = ▓ cm

11. 2 m = ▓ mm

12. 5 km = ▓ m

13. 8,000 cm = ▓ mm

14. 72 cm = ▓ mm

15. 9 m = ▓ cm

16. 4,000 m = ▓ km

17. 2,000 cm = ▓ m

18. 5,000 mm = ▓ cm

19. 7,600 m = ▓ km

20. 200 m = ▓ km

21. 1,500 mm = ▓ m

22. 1.9 m = ▓ cm

23. 0.6 m = ▓ cm

24. 3.5 km = ▓ m

25. 7 mm = ▓ m

★**26.** 0.2 dm = ▓ m

★**27.** 19 dam = ▓ dm

Solve. For Problem 30, use the Infobank.

28. Car upholstery is sold at the Auto Supply Shop. The clerk has two lengths in blue. One length is 3.04 m long. The other is 189 cm long. Which piece is longer?

29. The distance between two cities is 743.8 km. If Joyce has driven 408.9 km, how much farther does she need to drive to reach the other city?

30. Use the information on page 475 to solve. The Quiet Achiever, a solar-powered car, arrived in Sydney, Australia, on January 7, 1983, after having crossed the entire continent. How many kilometers is it from Port Augusta to Orange?

NUMBER SENSE

Calculate mentally.

1. 100 cm = ▓ m

2. 1 m = ▓ mm

3. 2,000 m = ▓ km

4. 5 m = ▓ cm

5. 40 cm = ▓ mm

6. 10 km = ▓ m

7. 4,000 mm = ▓ m

8. 1 mm = ▓ m

Metric Units of Capacity and Mass

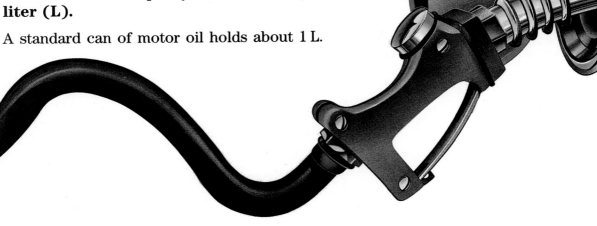

A. The amount of gasoline needed to fill the gas tank of Sharon's car is about 50 L.

The basic unit of capacity in the metric system is the **liter (L).**

A standard can of motor oil holds about 1 L.

1 kL = 1,000 L	1 L = 1,000 mL	1 mL = 0.001 L

B. The **gram (g)** is the basic unit of mass in the metric system.

The mass of a gasoline credit card is about 12 g.

1 kg = 1,000 g	1 g = 1,000 mg	1 mg = 0.001 g

C. To rename one unit of mass or capacity with another unit, multiply or divide by a power of 10.

To rename a larger unit with a smaller unit, multiply.

$$3.8 \text{ kL} = \blacksquare \text{ L}$$
$$3.8 \times 1{,}000 = 3{,}800$$
$$3.8 \text{ kL} = 3{,}800 \text{ L}$$

To rename a smaller unit with a larger unit, divide.

$$500 \text{ g} = \blacksquare \text{ kg}$$
$$500 \div 1{,}000 = 0.5$$
$$500 \text{ g} = 0.5 \text{ kg}$$

Checkpoint Write the letter of the correct answer.

1. Choose the best estimate for the mass of an automobile.

a. 175 g   **b.** 750 kg
c. 1,750 kg   **d.** 1,750 L

2. Choose the missing number. 80 L = ▇ kL

a. 0.08   **b.** 0.8
c. 8   **d.** 80

Write the unit used to measure

1. the mass of a car engine.

2. the capacity of a car's gas tank.

3. the length of the fuel line.

4. a drop of motor oil.

Complete.

5. 1 kg = ▨ g

6. 2 g = ▨ mg

7. 2 L = ▨ mL

8. 90 mg = ▨ g

9. 350 mL = ▨ L

10. 702 L = ▨ kL

11. 7 mL = ▨ L

12. 7,000 L = ▨ kL

13. 1,005 g = ▨ kg

14. 16,000 g = ▨ kg

15. 8,400 mg = ▨ g

16. 5,500 g = ▨ kg

17. 8.2 kg = ▨ g

18. 0.4 L = ▨ mL

19. 6.5 g = ▨ mg

20. 0.025 kL = ▨ mL

21. 0.0525 kg = ▨ g

★22. 4.5 g = ▨ cg

Compare. Write >, <, or = for ●.

23. 1 kg ● 100 g

24. 1 L ● 0.1 kL

25. 1 mg ● 0.001 g

26. 5 kL ● 5,000 L

27. 800 mL ● 8 L

28. 9 g ● 900 mg

29. 3.2 L ● 3,200 mL

30. 0.7 kg ● 70 g

31. 25 mg ● 0.0025 g

32. 19 g ● 0.19 kg

33. 10 L ● 10,000 mL

34. 89 mL ● 0.89 L

35. 0.46 g ● 460 mg

★36. 0.01 kg ● 100,000 mg

★37. 0.56 L ● 5.6 cL

Solve.

38. When the gas tank of Paul's car is empty, it costs $22.80 to fill it. If gasoline costs $0.38 per liter, how many liters does the tank hold?

39. The gas tank of Sarah's car holds 50 liters of gasoline. If gasoline costs $0.30 per liter, how much does it cost Sarah to fill the tank?

40. Select five foreign cars and compare the mass of each. Which car has the largest mass?

★41. Al's car gets 12 km/L of gas. If gas costs $0.35/L, how much will Al spend on gas to drive 60 km?

CHALLENGE

Mr. Stanton is cooking dinner. He must sauté vegetables for exactly 7 min, but he has no clock and his watch is broken. He does, however, have two egg timers—one 3-min timer and one 5-min timer. How can he time 7 min?

Relating Metric Measures

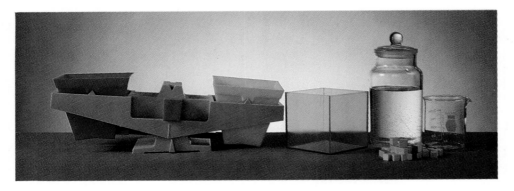

Within the metric system there are simple relationships among the measures of volume, capacity, and mass. This lesson will help you explore these relationships.

The **volume** of an object is the amount of space it occupies. Volume is measured in cubic units. At the right is a picture of a cube with a volume of 1 cubic centimeter ($1\ cm^3$). Each edge of this cube is 1 centimeter (cm) long.

Step 1: Copy the table below. You will complete the table as you work through the rest of this lesson.

CUBES

Edge Length	Volume	Capacity	Mass of Water
1 cm	a. ■	b. ■	c. ■
10 cm	d. ■	e. ■	f. ■
100 cm	g. ■	h. ■	i. ■

Step 2: Take a large hollow cube that has a 10 cm edge.

- Find the volume of the inside of the cube in cubic centimeters. You might use little cubes of volume $1\ cm^3$ to help you.

- Discuss the method you used with your teammates.

- Record your answer next to letter d in the table. Be sure to include the unit of measurement (cm^3).

Step 3: Fill a bottle with water, and then use the water to fill your large cube.

- Use a measuring beaker to measure the amount of water in your cube in millimeters.

- Record the capacity of the cube in milliliters (mL) next to the letter *e* in your table.

Step 4: Find the mass of the water in your large cube. Use a scale or balance.

- How did you adjust for the mass of the cube itself?

- Record your answer in grams (g) next to the letter *f* in your table.

Thinking as a Team _____

Look again at the picture of the cube that has a volume of 1 cm^3.

1. How does the volume of this cube compare to the volume of the large cube?

2. What would be the volume and the mass of the water that would fill the small cube? What is the capacity of the small cube?

3. Record your answers next to the letters *a*, *b*, and *c* in the table. Be sure to include the units of measurement.

4. Imagine a cube that has edges that are 100 cm long. Fill out the last row of the table. A mass of 1,000 kg is 1 metric ton.

5. Discuss the relationships among the volume, the capacity, and the mass of water.

6. Do you think that the same relationships hold for other substances such as sand? Experiment.

For additional activities, see **Connecting Math Ideas**, page 470.

PROBLEM SOLVING
Choosing/Writing a Sensible Question

Asking the right questions can help you organize information and make appropriate decisions.

Jake and Becky decided to publish a newsletter that would feature events and news about cars, trucks, and tractors. Jake named the newsletter *Motor Mouth*. They realized that there would be expenses involved in putting *Motor Mouth* together and in reproducing it. They had enough money for the first issue. After that, they hoped the price of each newsletter would cover its cost of production.

Becky and Jake have to decide on a price per copy for *Motor Mouth.* Answering which of these questions will help them make a decision?

- How much will it cost to reproduce each copy? Computing how much it will cost to reproduce each copy is important. The price per copy will have to be at least as great as that amount.

- How long will it take to write one issue? Because the writers, Becky and Jake, do not plan to receive salaries, this information will not affect the price.

- What supplies, if any, will they have to buy? It is important to determine what supplies they will have to buy. Their cost will be part of the cost of production.

Read each statement. Then formulate questions that Becky and Jake should answer before making a decision.

1. The owner of Taco Stop asked Becky to publish his advertisements in *Motor Mouth.*

2. Ezra offered to write movie reviews for *Motor Mouth* in return for the price of the movie tickets.

3. After the first 2 issues, *Motor Mouth* began to receive from 18 to 30 letters per week. Some offered suggestions. Others contained news and other interesting information. Mary suggested that they publish the letters.

4. People began to ask how much it would cost to subscribe to *Motor Mouth* and have issues mailed to their homes.

5. Sara told them about a county fair that features tractor-pulling and mud-bogging events and suggested that they sell *Motor Mouth* there.

6. Becky took some great photographs of the mud-bogging contest for the newsletter. She shot and developed 2 rolls of film.

7. Both Becky's and Jake's families were planning to go away on vacation for the month of August.

★8. After one year, *Motor Mouth* is selling well and has a large list of subscribers. Several people want to join the staff.

Customary Units of Length

A. The graph at the right shows the total stopping distance (reaction distance + breaking distance) of a car. How many yards will it take for a car to stop if it is going 50 mph?

From the graph, it takes 165 ft to stop. To answer in yards, you need to know the customary units of length.

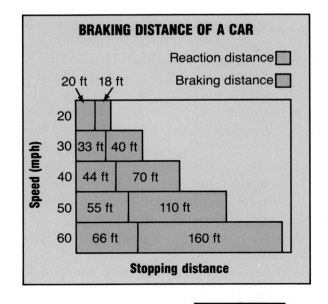

BRAKING DISTANCE OF A CAR

Reaction distance ☐
Braking distance ☐

```
12 inches (in.) = 1 foot (ft)
      36 in. =     3 ft   = 1 yard (yd)
   5,280 ft = 1,760 yd = 1 mile (mi)
```

To rename a smaller unit with a larger unit, divide.

$$165 \text{ ft} = \blacksquare \text{ yd}$$
$$165 \div 3 \quad \longleftarrow \quad \boxed{3 \text{ ft} = 1 \text{ yd}}$$
$$165 \text{ ft} = 55 \text{ yd}$$

The total stopping distance is 55 yd.

To rename a larger unit with a smaller unit, multiply.

$$\tfrac{3}{4} \text{ ft} = \blacksquare \text{ in.}$$
$$\tfrac{3}{4} \times 12 \quad \longleftarrow \quad \boxed{12 \text{ in.} = 1 \text{ ft}}$$
$$\tfrac{3}{4} \text{ ft} = 9 \text{ in.}$$

B. Sometimes when you compute with measures, you have to rename the units.

Add.

```
   5 yd 2 ft
 + 8 yd 2 ft
  13 yd 4 ft,  ←— 1 yd 1 ft
or 14 yd 1 ft
```

Subtract.

```
  4 yd 10 in.  ⟶   3 yd 46 in.
– 2 yd 16 in.  ⟶  – 2 yd 16 in.
                    1 yd 30 in.
```

Choose the best measure. Write the letter of the correct answer.

1. the width of a tire tread

  a. $\frac{1}{2}$ in.   **b.** $\frac{1}{2}$ ft   **c.** $\frac{1}{2}$ yd

2. the height of a car bumper

  a. 10 ft   **b.** 21 in.   **c.** 3 yd

3. the length of a car

  a. 14 in.   **b.** 15 ft   **c.** 12 yd

4. the width of a car headlight

  a. 7 in.   **b.** 12 ft   **c.** 7 yd

Complete.

5. 15 ft = ■ in.

6. 3 mi = ■ yd

7. 16 yd = ■ ft

8. 3 yd = ■ in.

9. 2 mi = ■ yd

10. 11 ft = ■ in.

11. 84 in. = ■ ft

12. 51 ft = ■ yd

13. 10,560 ft = ■ mi

14. 96 in. = ■ ft

15. 144 in. = ■ yd

16. 180 in. = ■ yd

17. $6\frac{1}{2}$ ft = ■ in.

18. $7\frac{1}{3}$ yd = ■ ft

19. $1\frac{1}{5}$ mi = ■ ft

20. $7\frac{1}{4}$ ft = ■ in.

21. $2\frac{1}{2}$ yd = ■ in.

22. $3\frac{1}{2}$ mi = ■ ft

23. 30 in. = ■ ft

24. 60 in. = ■ yd

25. 10 ft = ■ yd

26. 51 in. = ■ ft

27. 2,640 yd = ■ mi

28. 29,040 ft = ■ mi

★**29.** 2 ft 7 in. = ■ in.

★**30.** 4 yd 5 in. = ■ in.

★**31.** 9 yd 2 ft = ■ in.

Add or subtract.

32.   2 ft 4 in.
    + 3 ft 5 in.

33.   8 yd 2 ft
    − 3 yd 1 ft

34.   14 yd 2 ft
    + 6 yd 2 ft

35.   17 ft 4 in.
    − 8 ft 7 in.

Solve.

36. A mechanic installed an exhaust pipe that is $1\frac{2}{3}$ ft long. How many inches long is the pipe?

37. The mechanic joined a pipe that is $1\frac{2}{3}$ ft long to a pipe that is $2\frac{1}{2}$ ft long. Find the total length of the pipe.

NUMBER SENSE

Calculate mentally. Answer in the largest possible unit.

1. 1 ft + 8 in. + 4 in.

2. 9 in. + 7 in. + 8 in.

3. 1 yd + 2 ft + 8 in. + 4 in.

4. 2 ft + 4 ft + 3 ft

5. 2 yd + 30 in. + 6 in.

6. 3 in. + 2 in. + 7 in.

7. 1 ft + 11 in. + 1 in.

8. 2 ft + 8 in. + 4 in.

9. 1 yd + 2 ft + 10 in. + 2 in.

Customary Units of Capacity and Weight

A. In the United States, gasoline and oil are measured in **customary units.** The customary units of capacity are shown below.

> 8 fluid ounces (fl oz) = 1 cup (c)
> 2 c = 1 pint (pt)
> 2 pt = 1 quart (qt)
> 4 qt = 1 gallon (gal)

To rename a larger unit with a smaller unit, multiply.

$$\frac{1}{2} \text{ gal} = \blacksquare \text{ qt}$$

$$\frac{1}{2} \times 4 = 2 \quad \longleftarrow \boxed{4 \text{ qt} = 1 \text{ gal}}$$

$$\frac{1}{2} \text{ gal} = 2 \text{ qt}$$

To rename a smaller unit with a larger unit, divide.

$$144 \text{ fl oz} = \blacksquare \text{ c}$$

$$144 \div 8 = 18$$

$$144 \text{ fl oz} = 18 \text{ c}$$

B. The customary units of weight are shown in this table.

> 16 ounces (oz) = 1 pound (lb)
> 2,000 lb = 1 ton (T)

$$3\frac{1}{4} \text{ T} = \blacksquare \text{ lb}$$

$$3\frac{1}{4} \times 2{,}000 = 6{,}500$$

$$3\frac{1}{4} \text{ T} = 6{,}500 \text{ lb}$$

$$40 \text{ oz} = \blacksquare \text{ lb}$$

$$40 \div 16 = 2\frac{1}{2}$$

$$40 \text{ oz} = 2\frac{1}{2} \text{ lb}$$

Checkpoint   Write the letter of the correct answer.

1. 11 pt = ■

a. $5\frac{1}{2}$ pt   **b.** 5 qt

c. $5\frac{1}{2}$ qt   **d.** 22 qt

2. Choose the best estimate for the weight of an automobile tire.

a. 15 oz   **b.** 15 lb

c. 150 lb   **d.** 1.5 T

Choose the best measure. Write the letter of the correct answer.

1. the capacity of a car's gas tank

   a. 20 c   **b.** 20 pt

   c. 20 qt   **d.** 20 gal

2. the weight of a car

   a. 4,000 oz   **b.** 100 lb

   c. 2 T   **d.** 200 T

Complete.

3. 3 qt = ■ pt

4. 12 gal = ■ qt

5. 5 lb = ■ oz

6. 9 qt = ■ c

7. 3 T = ■ lb

8. 2 c = ■ fl oz

9. 32 fl oz = ■ c

10. 64 oz = ■ lb

11. 12 qt = ■ gal

12. 4,000 lb = ■ T

13. 16 pt = ■ gal

14. 16 c = ■ gal

15. $3\frac{1}{2}$ gal = ■ qt

16. $2\frac{1}{4}$ c = ■ fl oz

17. $5\frac{1}{2}$ lb = ■ oz

18. 24 oz = ■ lb

19. 5,000 lb = ■ T

20. 17 qt = ■ gal

★21. 3 lb 7 oz = ■ oz

★22. 7 gal 3 qt = ■ qt

★23. 47 oz = ■ lb ■ oz

Add or subtract.

24.   3 lb 9 oz
   + 6 lb 7 oz

25.   4 gal 3 qt 1 pt
   + 6 gal 2 qt 1 pt

26.   7 lb 4 oz
   − 2 lb 9 oz

27.   6 gal 1 qt
   − 2 gal 3 qt

Solve.

28. Carol had two 2-gallon containers of gasoline. One container was full and the other half full. How many quarts did she have?

29. Bill pays $11.95 per quart for Shine Perfect car wax. He bought 3 quarts. How much money did he spend?

30. Find out how many gallons of gasoline your local filling station pumps per week. How much is this per month?

31. Auto Tar Remover is sold for $2.79 per quart. If Dennis buys 90 gallons, how much does he pay?

MIDCHAPTER REVIEW

Complete.

1. 17 km = ■ m

2. 4,100 mg = ■ g

3. 22,000 mL = ■ L

4. 288 in. = ■ yd

5. 14 lb = ■ oz

6. 7 gal = ■ qt

PROBLEM SOLVING
Choosing a Strategy or Method

Write the strategy or method you choose. Then solve.

1. A flower shop sells long-stemmed roses for $1.50 each. If the store pays $6.00 per dozen for the roses, how much profit does it make if it sells 5 dozen?

2. A customer in a flower shop bought 3 roses at $1.50 each, 4 gladioli at $0.85 each, and a plant for $12.50. How much did the customer spend?

3. The Grimm Forest has an average of 150 trees per acre. If the forest covers 210 acres, about how many trees are there?

4. On one map, 1 inch equals 24.5 miles. The map shows the distance from Montreal, Quebec, to Burlington, Vermont, to be about 5 inches. What is the approximate distance between those places?

> Estimation
> Using a Graph
> Identifying Extra/Needed Information
> Choosing the Operation
> Solving Multi-step Problems
> Checking for a Reasonable Answer
> Using a Table
> Writing an Equation
> Interpreting the Quotient and the Remainder

5. In a music poll, 55 people said they preferred folk music. This was 12 fewer than those who said they preferred jazz. How many people preferred jazz?

6. Penny caught 10 fish on a camping trip. This number was 2 more than $\frac{2}{3}$ of the number of fish Jan caught. How many fish did Jan catch?

7. The supermarket uses plastic sacks that can hold up to 4 kilograms of groceries. Mr. Jackson's groceries weigh about 22 kilograms. How many sacks should the clerk use?

8. Susan has $30.00 to spend on herself and her brother at the amusement park. Admission tickets cost $9.50 each, and she plans on paying $5.00 each for lunch. Does Susan have enough money?

9. Mrs. McGhee needs 33 feet of wood to complete a fence. The wood is sold in 8-foot sections. How many sections of wood must she buy?

Choose a strategy or method and solve.

10. At a fashion show, each of 50 buyers placed an order for $10,000 worth of fashion items. If $3,000 of each order was spent for jewelry, what was the total spent for other items?

11. A van carries racks of coats from a warehouse to a store. The van carries 320 coats per trip. If the store will sell half the number of coats for $235 and the rest for $350, what is the value of the coats carried in 8 trips?

12. Robbie's mother can spend $9,500 for a new car. She sees a model she likes for $8,754.50, but she wants some options that cost $257.30, $315.75, and $214.47. Does she have enough money to buy the car and the options?

13. Hal wants to buy a car that will cost him a total of $8,568. He can pay for it in 36 monthly payments. His other monthly expenses amount to $76.15, $37.58, $146.25, $322.74, and $176.42. His monthly income is $1,080. Can he afford to buy the car?

Use the double bar graph at the right to solve.

14. On what day did the 1990 attendance first surpass the 1989 attendance?

15. To the nearest thousand, how many more people attended the fair on the Friday of 1989 than on the Friday of 1990?

16. Was the combined attendance on the Fridays of 1989 and 1990 more than or less than the attendance on the Saturday of 1990?

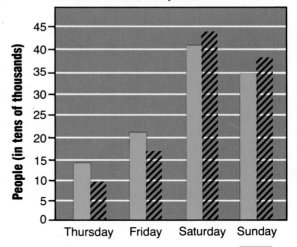

FAIR ATTENDANCE, 1989 AND 1990

People (in tens of thousands)

1989
1990

Precision and Greatest Possible Error

A. Do you think that all items reported as a meter in length are exactly 1 meter long? You can use a centimeter ruler to help you explore how measurements are reported.

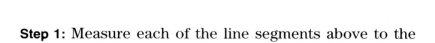

Step 1: Measure each of the line segments above to the nearest centimeter.

- Which line segments have the same measurement to the nearest centimeter?

- Which line segments appear to be exactly equal in length?

Step 2: Measure each of the line segments above to the nearest millimeter.

- Which line segments have the same measurement to the nearest millimeter?

Thinking as a Team

The **precision** of a measurement is related to the unit of measure used. The smaller the unit of measure, the more precise the measurement.

1. Which measurements are more precise, those reported in Step 1 or those reported in Step 2?

2. What is the length of the shortest line segment that could be reported as 7 cm?

3. What is the length of the longest line segment that could be reported as 7 cm?

4. How much more or less than the reported measurement could the actual length of the line segment be?

B. Because the actual measurement could be at most 0.5 units greater or less than the reported measurement, the **greatest possible error** can be written as ±0.5 units. This is read as "plus or minus 0.5 units."

- Do you think any measurement is ever exact? Discuss your reasoning with the group.

- Discuss with your group situations in which different degrees of precision would be necessary. What is the greatest possible error allowable in each situation?

- When the course for a 10-km road race is measured, do you think the greatest possible error is +0.5 km? How precise do you think the measurement should be?

Working as a Team

When serving, a tennis player must hit the ball into the opponent's service court, which is in the shape of a rectangle $13\frac{1}{2}$ feet by 21 feet.

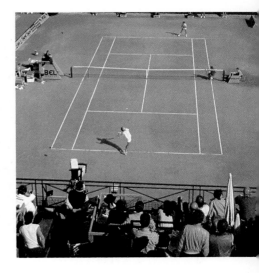

Phyllis and Jorge are painting lines on a tennis court. Phyllis marks off the lines for the service court at 13 feet and 20 feet 6 inches. Jorge insists the measurements should be precise to the nearest inch. Phyllis says that because the measurements are given to the nearest foot, the greatest error allowable is $\frac{1}{2}$ foot either way and the error will make only a very small difference. She tells Jorge that the greatest possible error in area will be only 6 inches × 6 inches, or 36 square inches. Jorge says the error will be much greater. Carefully draw a picture of the court showing how the error in measurement actually affects the area. Then tell who is right.

1. What is the greatest possible error in area?

2. What percent of the total area is this?

3. Do you think that the error in area might be significant in a tennis tournament? Discuss your reasons with the members of your team.

Time and Elapsed Time

Ty left Scranton, Pennsylvania, at 9:30 A.M., and arrived in Wheeling, West Virginia, at 5:15 P.M. How long did the trip take?

The amount of time between events is called the **elapsed time.**

60 seconds (s) = 1 minute (min)	1 week (wk) = 7 d
60 min = 1 hour (h)	1 year (y) = 365 d or 12 months (mo)
24 h = 1 day (d)	100 y = 1 century

$$
\begin{array}{rcl}
5\,\text{h}\,15\,\text{min (P.M.)} \longrightarrow & 17\,\text{h}\,15\,\text{min} = & 16\,\text{h}\,75\,\text{min} \\
-\ 9\,\text{h}\,30\,\text{min (A.M.)} \longrightarrow & -\ 9\,\text{h}\,30\,\text{min} = & -\ 9\,\text{h}\,30\,\text{min} \\
\hline
& & 7\,\text{h}\,45\,\text{min}
\end{array}
$$

Both times now mean "starting from midnight."

The trip took 7 h 45 min.

Checkpoint Write the letter of the correct answer.

1. Choose the correct time for 5 h 45 min after 8:30 A.M.

a. 2:15 A.M. **b.** 2:15 P.M. **c.** 1:75 P.M. **d.** 1:15 P.M.

2. Choose the elapsed time between 10:45 A.M. and 1:15 P.M.

a. 3 h **b.** 3 h 30 min **c.** 2 h 30 min **d.** 2 h 20 min

3. Choose the missing number. 48 min = ■ h

a. $1\frac{1}{4}$ **b.** $\frac{4}{5}$ **c.** 0 **d.** $\frac{24}{30}$

Math Reasoning, page H216

Find the time.

1. 2 h 35 min before 12:15 P.M.

2. 8 h 12 min after 9:00 A.M.

3. 5 h 55 min after 10:30 P.M.

4. 3 h 18 min before 1:10 P.M.

5. 6 h 47 min before 12:50 A.M.

6. 9 h 25 min after 6:00 A.M.

Find the elapsed time between

7. 5:00 A.M. and 3:15 P.M.

8. 8:05 P.M. and 11:00 P.M.

9. 7:21 A.M. and 12 noon.

10. 6:52 A.M. and 2:45 P.M.

11. 4:10 P.M. and 1:20 A.M.

12. 11:20 P.M. and 11:50 A.M.

Write the missing number.

13. 3 min = ■ s

14. $2\frac{1}{2}$ h = ■ min

15. $\frac{3}{4}$ d = ■ h

16. 48 h = ■ d

17. 75 s = ■ min

18. 100 min = ■ h

19. 30 s = ■ min

20. 60 h = ■ d

21. $5\frac{1}{2}$ h = ■ min

Add or subtract.

22.
$$\begin{array}{r} 3\text{ h }20\text{ min} \\ +\ 5\text{ h }30\text{ min} \\ \hline \end{array}$$

23.
$$\begin{array}{r} 5\text{ min }36\text{ s} \\ +\ 10\text{ min }42\text{ s} \\ \hline \end{array}$$

24.
$$\begin{array}{r} 15\text{ h }20\text{ min} \\ -\ 7\text{ h }17\text{ min} \\ \hline \end{array}$$

25.
$$\begin{array}{r} 12\text{ min }15\text{ s} \\ -\ 10\text{ min }45\text{ s} \\ \hline \end{array}$$

Solve.

26. Mr. Thomas drove nonstop from New York City to Washington, D.C. He left New York at 5:00 A.M. If the trip took 5 h 43 min, at what time did he arrive in Washington?

27. Ms. Van Mirt has to be in Denver at 10:30 A.M. She lives 3 h 45 min away. If it takes her 45 min to dress and eat, at what time should she get up in the morning?

28. Plan a four-day car trip to three cities in your area. Outline a time schedule that includes the total driving time.

CHALLENGE

A **hectare** is a measure of land area.

1 hectare (ha) = 10,000 square meters (m^2)

A square field 100 meters on a side would be an example of a hectare. Give the dimensions of another rectangle that would cover 1 hectare. Estimate how many hectares your school yard is.

PROBLEM SOLVING
Using a Formula ($d = rt$)

The distance a vehicle has moved can be calculated when you know the vehicle's average speed and the amount of time for which it has been moving.

To calculate the distance, use the formula $d = rt$, where
d = distance
r = rate of travel (speed)
t = time.

> Rachel is driving from Springfield, Missouri, to Fort Wayne, Indiana. If she drives for 2 hours 15 minutes at 50 miles per hour, how far has she traveled?

To solve a problem by using a formula, follow these general rules.

1. Use the correct formula.

2. Substitute values in the formula.

3. Solve the equation.

4. Write the answer, using the correct unit.

Use the formula $d = rt$, and evaluate.

$t = 2\frac{1}{4}$ hours $\qquad d = rt$

$r = 50$ miles per hour $\quad d = (50)\left(2\frac{1}{4}\right)$

$\qquad\qquad\qquad\qquad\quad d = 112\frac{1}{2}$

She traveled $112\frac{1}{2}$ mi.

You can use other forms of the distance formula to find the time or the rate.

To solve for t: $\quad t = d \div r \quad t = 112\frac{1}{2} \div 50$

To solve for r: $\quad r = d \div t \quad r = 112\frac{1}{2} \div 2\frac{1}{4}$

Write the letter of the formula that will help you solve the problem.

1. A race-car driver drove her car 3.3 kilometers in 1.1 minutes. What was her average speed?

   a. $r = \frac{d}{t}$

   b. $t = \frac{d}{r}$

   c. $d = rt$

2. Mr. Shane drove his car 340 miles. His average speed was 20 mph. How long did his trip take?

   a. $r = \frac{d}{t}$

   b. $t = \frac{d}{r}$

   c. $d = rt$

Solve.

3. Tim drove from Chicago, Illinois, to Evansville, Indiana, in 5 hours 45 minutes. His average speed was 52 mph. About how far is Evansville from Chicago?

4. Durango, Mexico, lies between Mazatlán and Fresnillo. Durango is 325 kilometers from Mazatlán and 291 kilometers from Fresnillo. How far is Mazatlán from Fresnillo by way of Durango?

5. Duncan drove from Davenport, Iowa, to Des Moines, Iowa, a distance of 176 miles. At what rate of speed did he travel if he reached Des Moines in 4 hours?

6. Leaving home, Carol drove at 45 mph for 30 minutes. Then she drove at 30 mph for 15 minutes to reach her office. How far did she drive to reach her office?

7. Jeff and Ann rode on a train from Rome, Italy, to Florence, Italy. The trip took 4.5 hours, and the train's average speed was 96 kilometers per hour. About how far is it from Rome to Florence?

8. Jack drove from his home in Eugene, Oregon, to Portland, Oregon. The distance between the two cities is approximately 173 kilometers. The trip took Jack about $2\frac{1}{2}$ hours. What was his average speed?

9. In 1928, Mr. DeQuincy drove his Model-J Duesenberg 1,845 miles from Los Angeles, California, to St. Louis, Missouri. The trip took 26 hours. To the nearest mile per hour, what was Mr. DeQuincy's average rate of speed?

★10. At 9:00 A.M., Sandi and Kim each begin to drive from Richmond, Virginia, to Harrisburg, Pennsylvania, a distance of 228 miles. Sandi drove at 50 mph, and Kim drove at 55 mph. How much sooner did Kim reach Harrisburg than Sandi?

Time Zones

Mr. McCarthy plans to drive from Washington, D.C., to Seattle, Washington. He will drive 10 h per day. The trip takes 56 h. He leaves on Monday and each day begins driving at 9:00 A.M. by his watch, which remains on D.C. time. When will he arrive in Seattle?

Earth is divided into twenty-four time zones. Universal Coordinated Time is the first time zone. The time changes to one hour earlier for each time zone going west. The time changes to one hour later for each time zone going east. The Continental United States has four time zones.

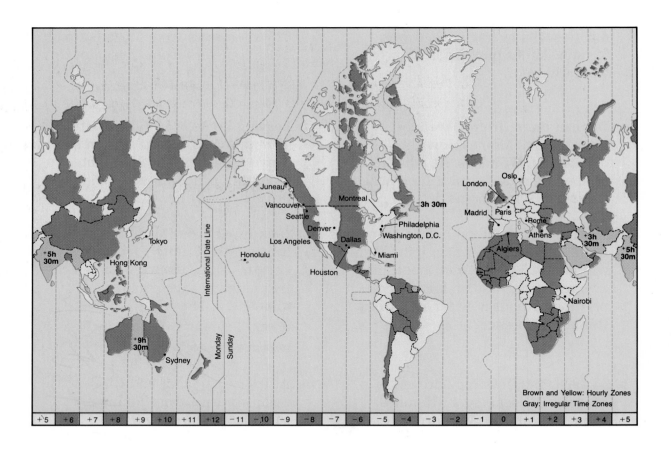

Because Mr McCarthy will pass through four time zones going west, he will arrive in Seattle at 12:00 P.M. Saturday.

It is 9:00 A.M. Friday in Denver. Write the time in each city.

1. Los Angeles   **2.** Houston   **3.** Miami   **4.** Juneau

5. Montreal   **6.** Honolulu   **7.** Seattle   **8.** Philadelphia

It is 4:00 P.M. Tuesday in Paris. Write the time in each city.

9. London   **10.** Oslo   **11.** Athens   **12.** Washington, D.C.

13. Hong Kong   **14.** Nairobi   **15.** Vancouver   **16.** Dallas

It is 5:30 A.M. Thursday in Tokyo. Write the time in each city.

17. Hong Kong   **18.** Sydney   **19.** Paris   **20.** Seattle

21. London   **22.** Athens   **23.** Algiers   **24.** Madrid

Solve. For problem 29, use the Infobank.

25. Ms. Howland drove from Houston to Los Angeles. She left at 8 A.M. and arrived 3 days 2 hours later. What time was it in Los Angeles when she arrived?

26. Mr. Su drove from Seattle to Montreal. When he arrived, it was 7:00 A.M. on Friday. What time and what day was it in Seattle?

27. Plan a two-week trip to the Orient. Determine departure and arrival dates and times for each city on your tour.

28. Ms. Traetta flew from Miami to Sydney, Australia. It was 9:00 P.M. on March 18 when she arrived. What time and date was it in Miami?

29. Use the information on page 475 to solve. The Quiet Achiever is a solar-powered car. Its average velocity is 25 km/h. At this rate, how long would it take the Achiever to travel from Broken Hill to Dubbo?

CHALLENGE

A pilot of a supersonic plane told his young son that when he leaves New York at 10:00 A.M. Eastern time, he arrives in Los Angeles at 9:30 A.M. Pacific time. The young boy looked puzzled and then asked, "If you keep going at the same speed and fly all the way around the world, will you arrive back in New York before you left?" What is wrong with this thinking?

Temperature

The temperature of the burning gases in the cylinder of a car can reach as high as 4,500°F. The cooling system keeps the temperature of the engine between 160°F and 180°F.

Temperature can be measured in degrees Fahrenheit (°F) or degrees Celsius (°C).

Suppose the temperature is ⁻14°C and rises 16°. What is the temperature now?

Look at the Celsius thermometer. Start at ⁻14°C and move 16 units up. The temperature now is 2°C.

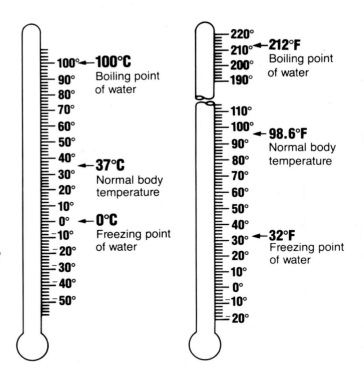

Checkpoint Write the letter of the correct answer.

1. Choose the best estimate for the temperature of a refrigerated apple.

a. 0°C   **b.** 10°C
c. 20°C   **d.** 40°C

2. The temperature is 4°F; it drops 7°. What is the temperature now?

a. ⁻3°F   **b.** 3°F
c. ⁻7°F   **d.** ⁻11°F

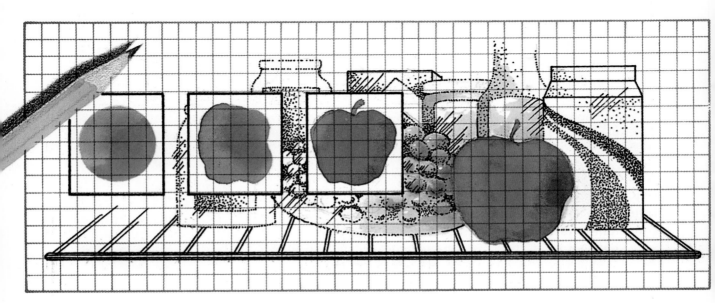

Choose the best estimate. Write the letter of the correct answer.

1. room temperature   **a.** 55°F   **b.** 68°F   **c.** 78°F

2. a medium oven   **a.** 32°F   **b.** 100°F   **c.** 350°F

3. a freezer   **a.** ⁻100°F   **b.** ⁻5°F   **c.** 22°F

Find the temperature.

4. 12°F, rose 15°   **5.** ⁻10°F, dropped 5°   **6.** ⁻7°F, rose 18°

Find the change in temperature.

7. 18°F to 35°F   **8.** ⁻12°F to ⁻17°F   **9.** ⁻18°F to 7°F

Choose the best estimate. Write the letter of the correct answer.

10. a cold day   **a.** 5°C   **b.** 20°C   **c.** 32°C

11. a warm day   **a.** 75°C   **b.** 50°C   **c.** 25°C

Find the temperature.

12. 35.7°C, rose 7°   **13.** ⁻18.2°C, dropped 0.5°   **14.** ⁻12.7°C, rose 18.5°

Find the change in temperature.

15. 38.2°C to 47.9°C   **16.** ⁻12°C to ⁻20.4°C   **17.** ⁻4.6°C to 14.2°C

Solve.

18. An antifreeze composed of ethylene glycol mixed with water has a boiling point of 223°F. How does this compare with the boiling point of water?

19. Research in your school library to find the average temperature inside a carburetor during combustion.

ANOTHER LOOK

Find the product.

1. $4 \cdot 5^2$ **2.** $3^2 \cdot 3^2$ **3.** $2 \cdot 3^2 \cdot 4^2$ **4.** $2^2 \cdot 4^3$ **5.** $2^3 \cdot 7 \cdot 11$

Give the prime factorization of each number.

6. 45   **7.** 36   **8.** 175   **9.** 169   **10.** 572

PROBLEM SOLVING
Using a Road Map

A road map is a good source of information about routes and distances between places.

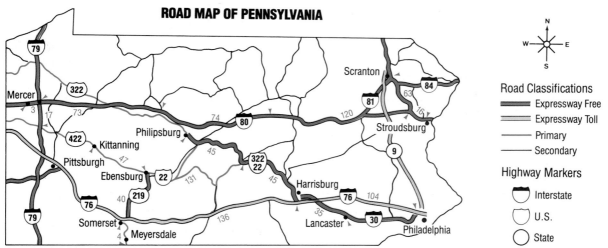

ROAD MAP OF PENNSYLVANIA

This is how data are shown on a road map.

- The map title tells you the area or region that the map shows.

- The map key at the right identifies road classifications and highway markers.

- Mileage is indicated by red numbers between red tick marks.

Karen uses this road map of Pennsylvania to plan her trip from Philipsburg to Harrisburg. She wants to know how many miles she will travel.

- Locate Philipsburg and Harrisburg.

- Find the shortest route that connects them.

- Find the mileage symbols and the numerals along the route between Harrisburg and Philipsburg.

The trip will be 90 miles.

Solve. Use the road map on page 190 to answer each question.

1. Kirby drives from Philadelphia to Lancaster. What road is the most direct route?

2. Monica lives in Meyersdale and is planning to drive to Ebensburg and back. About how many miles will she travel?

3. Millie drove from Kittanning to Ebensburg and from Ebensburg to Somerset. Approximately how many miles did she drive on the expressway, and how many miles did she drive on a primary road?

4. Aaron drove from the junction of routes 79 and 80 to the junction of routes 79 and 422. If he drove at 50 miles per hour, about how long did that trip take him?

5. Mr. Lee is planning to drive from Stroudsburg to Mercer. What is the shortest route? About how long will the trip take him if he drives at 45 mph?

6. Ronnie drove on Route 76 from Philadelphia to Somerset and back. Her company paid her expenses, including gas and a travel allowance of $0.17 per mile. How much was she reimbursed if she spent $17.50 for gas?

7. Mrs. Davis plans to drive from Philadelphia to Harrisburg and then back to Lancaster. Her car gets 21 miles per gallon. About how many gallons of gas will Mrs. Davis use?

8. Anthony wants to drive from Meyersdale to Somerset and then on to Ebensburg. If he averages 49 miles per hour and stops for a half hour to eat lunch, how long will the trip take?

9. Lenny has to drive from Harrisburg to Somerset, but he doesn't want to take a toll road. How much longer will the trip be if he travels on routes 22 and 219?

10. Interstate highways that have even numbers run east and west. Odd numbered interstate highways run north and south. If you left Pittsburgh and traveled an odd-numbered interstate highway, then an even-numbered one, then another odd-numbered one, in what directions would you have gone?

CALCULATOR

Use your calculator and the table to solve.

Distances are given in kilometers.

	Chicago	Denver	Houston	Los Angeles	Miami	New York	St. Louis	Seattle
Denver, CO	1,463							
Houston, TX	1,503	1,408						
Los Angeles, CA	2,806	1,350	2,208					
Miami, FL	1,916	2,762	1,543	3,750				
New York, NY	1,163	2,618	2,279	3,948	1,757			
St. Louis, MO	413	1,257	1,090	2,544	1,719	1,419		
Seattle, WA	2,790	1,642	3,034	1,543	4,385	3,875	2,752	
Washington, DC	953	2,375	1,938	3,682	1,481	346	1,138	3,721

1. Compare the two routes.
   (a) Los Angeles to St. Louis to New York
   (b) Los Angeles to New York
   Which route from Los Angeles to New York is shorter?   how much shorter?

2. Compare these two routes.
   (a) Houston to St. Louis to Washington, D.C.
   (b) Houston to Washington, D.C.
   Which route from Houston to Washington, D.C., is longer? how much longer?

3. Determine the shortest route from Miami to Seattle, stopping at one of the cities on the chart. Which city would you stop at?

4. You are planning a route from Denver to Chicago, that is as close to 2,000 km as possible, making as many stops as you wish. Which route would you use?

5. You have won an airline contest. Your prize is 10,000 km of free flying. You must start from the city nearest you and return to the same city. Which route would you take to use as much of the 10,000 km without going over?

GROUP PROJECT

A Wild and Crazy Car

The problem: Lucky you! In a promotional super-raffle, you alone won the new car, the fabulous Funmobile of the Future! Along with the car, you were given $10,000 to spend on any group of options you want. Choose your options from the list below. Put together a package, and make sure you don't exceed your budget.

Funmobile Options

- Power steering $810.00
- Power brakes $645.00
- Power windows $860.00
- Rear-window wipers $692.00
- Laser defroster $1,350.00
- Deluxe covered roof seats $1,675.00
- OmniScopic see-all windshield $1,815.00
- Telekinetic TV telephone $2,160.00
- Backseat hot tub $2,662.50
- Pseudoconvertible Night Sky Simulator $2,545.00
- Moto-Mini golf course $4,750.00
- Continental climate control $1,235.00
- Solid-gold designer hubcaps (each) $1,672.50
- Accu-Sound SuperStereo system $1,685.00
- Automated ComputoKitchen $4,653.50

CHAPTER TEST

Give the appropriate metric unit to measure each.
(pages 166–169)

1. sack of oranges

2. bottle of vanilla extract

3. a hike

4. slice of melon

Give the appropriate customary unit to measure each.
(pages 174–177)

5. bottle of honey

6. gasoline

7. sack of potatoes

8. length of a shoe

Complete. (pages 166–171 and 174–177)

9. 5,000 cm = ■ m

10. 0.07 L = ■ mL

11. 250 L = ■ kL

12. 8 mL = ■ g of water

13. 0.005 g = ■ mg

14. 6 gal = ■ qt

15. 18 lb = ■ oz

16. 144 oz = ■ lb

17. 5 yd = ■ ft

Add or subtract. (pages 174–177, 182–183)

18. 8 lb 11 oz
     + 2 lb 9 oz

19. 3 yd 2 ft
     + 2 yd 2 ft

20. 5 qt 1 c
     − 3 qt 3 c

21. 6 gal 5 pt
     − 2 gal 5 pt

22. 2 h 45 min
     + 6 h 20 min

23. 5 h 12 min
     − 2 h 35 min

Write the degree change. (pages 188–189)

24. ⁻4°F to ⁻50°F

25. ⁻8°C to 31°C

Find the elapsed time between each. (pages 182–183)

26. 3:00 A.M. and 2:20 P.M.   **27.** 11:15 P.M. and 2:14 A.M.

28. Denver is 7 time zones west of London, England.
If you left London at 1:30 P.M. and flew for 11 hours,
what time would it be in Denver when your plane
arrived? (pages 186–187)

Solve. (pages 168–169, 172–173, 176–177, 184–185, and 190–191)

29. The longest scheduled bus route is Across
Australia Coach Lines, which travels 3,389 mi and
takes about 76 h. To the nearest tenth, what is the
average speed of the bus?

30. Wendell's newspaper route required him to drive
85 mi/d. His map scale was 1.5 cm equals 5 mi.
How many centimeters would represent his route?

31. Wendell earns $1,000 per month delivering
newspapers. He is considering buying a new car
that will cost him $350 per month. Formulate a
question that he should answer before making a
decision.

32. Lynn has used 7,000 mL of car wax this year.
Change this amount to the most appropriate metric
unit.

33. If Dennis wants to fill eight 2-quart containers with
oil, how many gallons of oil must he purchase?

BONUS

Solve.

A bolt has 40 yards of cloth. If a bolt is enough fabric
to upholster $2\frac{1}{2}$ automobiles, how many yards are
necessary for each car? If you can only purchase the
cloth in bolts, how many bolts must you buy for 18
cars?

RETEACHING

The **meter** is the standard metric unit of length. Powers of 10 and metric prefixes are used to name metric units of length.

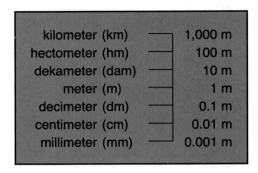

kilometer (km)	—	1,000 m
hectometer (hm)	—	100 m
dekameter (dam)	—	10 m
meter (m)	—	1 m
decimeter (dm)	—	0.1 m
centimeter (cm)	—	0.01 m
millimeter (mm)	—	0.001 m

Use the chart to rename metric units. Count the steps on the chart from the given unit to the desired unit.

To rename 20 km in meters, move the decimal point to the **right** one place for each step you counted **down.** The meter is three steps down. So, move the decimal point three places to the right.

$$20 \text{ km} = 20.000 = 20,000 \text{ m}$$

To rename 500 mm in centimeters, move the decimal point to the **left** one place for each step you counted **up.** The centimeter is one step up. So, move the decimal point one place to the left.

$$500 \text{ mm} = 50.0 = 50 \text{ cm}$$

Complete.

1. 300 cm = ▨ m

2. 250 mm = ▨ m

3. 0.7 m = ▨ mm

4. 0.9 km = ▨ cm

5. 40 cm = ▨ km

6. 0.92 m = ▨ cm

7. 25 cm = ▨ m

8. 0.2 m = ▨ mm

9. 3,500 mm = ▨ m

10. 9 km = ▨ m

11. 1.5 cm = ▨ m

12. 1,400,000 mm = ▨ km

13. 0.32 m = ▨ mm

14. 0.005 m = ▨ cm

15. 520 m = ▨ km

16. 26 mm = ▨ dam

17. 0.027 km = ▨ cm

18. 22,000 m = ▨ km

19. 934,000 cm = ▨ km

20. 340 dm = ▨ hm

21. 0.46 km = ▨ mm

Calculate mentally.

1. 30 cm = ▨ m

2. 500 m = ▨ hm

3. 20 dam = ▨ m

4. 2 hm = ▨ dm

ENRICHMENT

Significant Digits and Accuracy

Significant digits indicate the number of times a unit of measurement is contained in that measurement.

Measurement	120 m	12 m	120.4 m	0.048 cm	3.06 cm
Unit of measure	1 m	1 m	0.1 m	0.001 cm	0.01 cm
Number of units	120	12	1,204	48	306
Significant digits	1, 2, 0	1, 2	1, 2, 0, 4	4, 8	3, 0, 6
Number of significant digits	3	2	4	2	3

When comparing two measurements, the one with the greater number of significant digits is more **accurate.** The one with the smaller unit of measure is more **precise.**

0.048 cm ⟵ more *precise* (unit = 0.001 cm)

3.06 cm ⟵ more *accurate* (three significant digits)

When you compute by using measurement, how you round your answer depends on what operations you are using.

To find the accuracy of a sum or difference, round the answer to the place of the least precise measurement.

$$
\begin{array}{r}
1.6 \ \text{ft} \ \longleftarrow \text{least precise} \\
3.542 \text{ ft} \qquad \text{measurement} \\
+ \ 2.32 \ \text{ft} \\
\hline
7.462 = 7.5 \text{ ft}
\end{array}
$$

(rounded to tenths)

To find the accuracy of a product or quotient, round the answer to the same number of significant digits as the measurement that has the fewest significant digits.

6.09 m × 0.025 m = 0.15225 = 0.15 m

↑ three significant digits ↑ two significant digits ↑ rounded to two significant digits

Compute. Round your answer to the correct number of significant digits.

1. 8.15 m + 7.275 m + 3.7 m

2. 47 in. × 0.902 in.

3. 27.6 ft − 0.048 ft

4. $0.033 \text{ cm}^2 \div 8 \text{ cm}$

CUMULATIVE REVIEW

Write the letter of the correct answer.

1. What is an equivalent fraction for $\frac{12}{14}$?

a. $\frac{6}{7}$ **b.** $1\frac{1}{6}$

c. $\frac{8}{10}$ **d.** not given

2. $8\frac{1}{3} + 4\frac{3}{4}$

a. $3\frac{7}{12}$ **b.** 11

c. $13\frac{1}{12}$ **d.** not given

3. $5\frac{1}{8} - 3\frac{5}{6}$

a. $1\frac{7}{24}$ **b.** $1\frac{1}{2}$

c. $2\frac{1}{14}$ **d.** not given

4. $5\frac{2}{7} \times 3\frac{2}{3}$

a. $15\frac{4}{21}$ **b.** $17\frac{1}{3}$

c. $19\frac{8}{21}$ **d.** not given

5. $4\frac{3}{8} \div 2\frac{3}{4}$

a. $1\frac{12}{19}$ **b.** $2\frac{1}{2}$

c. 4 **d.** not given

6. Choose the GCF of 14, 56, and 91.

a. 3 **b.** 7

c. 14 **d.** not given

7. Simplify
$2.4(16.5 - 5) \div 2(0.951 + 0.549).$

a. 3 **b.** 9.2

c. 15.159 **d.** not given

8. Solve for d: $d - 73 = 126$.

a. 53

b. 126

c. 199

d. not given

9. Solve for x: $\frac{x}{2.4} = 17.03$.

a. 7.1

b. 14.64

c. 40.896

d. not given

10. $402.5\overline{)4{,}037.075}$

a. 1.003

b. 10.03

c. 10.3

d. not given

11. Estimate: $76.59\overline{)759.67}$.

a. 8 **b.** 100

c. 10 **d.** 800

12. Ahmed had $\frac{2}{3}$ of his assets invested. Of his investments, $\frac{3}{4}$ were in mutual funds. What fraction of his money was invested in other ways? Use a simpler problem to write an equation to solve.

a. $\frac{1}{6}$ **b.** $\frac{3}{16}$

c. $\frac{1}{2}$ **d.** not given

13. 5 more than 6 times a number is 23. Write an equation and solve for the number.

a. 3 **b.** 4.67

c. 128 **d.** not given

Suppose you wanted to buy a dog. If you were solely responsible for the purchase and the care of your pet, which kind of dog would you buy? What kind of part-time job would you need in order to purchase and pay for the care of the dog?

6 RATIO, PROPORTION, PERCENT

Ratios and Rates

A. Oceanville has a special lifeguard-training program. The program includes 16 hours of instruction in basic first aid and 8 hours of instruction in cardiopulmonary resuscitation (CPR). What is the ratio of the number of hours of CPR instruction to the number of hours of basic first-aid instruction?

A **ratio** is a comparison of two numbers. The ratio of CPR hours to basic first-aid hours is 8 to 16, or 8:16, or $\frac{8}{16}$. Each ratio is read "8 to 16."

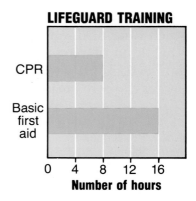

LIFEGUARD TRAINING

CPR

Basic first aid

0   4   8   12   16
Number of hours

The numbers 8 and 16 are called the **terms** of the ratio. The order of terms in a ratio is important. The ratio 16:8 is *not* the same as the ratio 8:16.

$$\frac{8}{16} \quad \longleftarrow \text{ first term}$$
$$\quad \longleftarrow \text{ second term}$$

B. For every 1 hour of CPR instruction, there are 2 hours of basic first-aid instruction. So, you can also use the ratio 1:2 to compare the CPR instruction and the basic first-aid instruction.

These are
equal ratios. $\frac{8}{16} = \frac{1}{2}$ $\longleftarrow$ This ratio is
in **simplest form.**

Equal ratios can be found by multiplying or dividing both terms of a ratio by the same number (not zero).

$$\frac{2}{3} = \frac{2 \times 6}{3 \times 6} = \frac{12}{18} \qquad\qquad \frac{80}{100} = \frac{80 \div 20}{100 \div 20} = \frac{4}{5}$$

C. A **rate** is a ratio that compares two different kinds of units. For example, if John earned $30 in 8 hours, the rate of earnings to hours is

$$\text{dollars} \longrightarrow \frac{30}{8} = \frac{30 \div 8}{8 \div 8} = \frac{3.75}{1}.$$
$$\text{hours} \longrightarrow$$

When the second term is one unit, the rate is called a **unit rate.** The unit rate $\frac{3.75}{1}$ indicates that John earns $3.75 per hour.

Write each ratio in fraction form.

1. 3 to 2   **2.** 6:7   **3.** 9 to 1   **4.** 7 to 10

5. 6 to 17   **6.** 5:4   **7.** 7:5   **8.** 1 to 3

Write each ratio as a fraction in simplest form.

9. $\frac{10}{20}$ **10.** $\frac{9}{6}$ **11.** $\frac{4}{2}$ **12.** 16:6   **13.** $\frac{18}{12}$ **14.** 5 to 45

15. 90:40   **16.** $\frac{15}{10}$ **17.** $\frac{60}{100}$ **18.** 17 to 35   **19.** $\frac{22}{6}$ **20.** 64:24

21. 9:12   **22.** 28 to 7   **23.** 1.2 to 4.8   **24.** 8:80   **25.** 2.6 to 5.2

26. 4 wins to 12 losses   **27.** 8 present to 15 absent

Write three equal ratios.

28. $\frac{1}{3}$ **29.** $\frac{9}{2}$ **30.** $\frac{6}{1}$ **31.** $\frac{7}{5}$

Write the unit rate.

32. 125 yards in 25 seconds   **33.** 180 pages in 3 hours

34. $24 for 3 books   **35.** 28 pounds in 4 weeks

Solve. For Problem 37, use the Infobank.

36. A group of 9 students entered the lifeguard course. All but 2 finished the course. What is the ratio of those finishing the course to those entering?

37. Use the information on page 475 to solve. Wendell's doctor has advised him not to eat any foods that have added salt. Should Wendell have a bowl of Heidi's soup?

ANOTHER LOOK

Find the greatest common factor for each pair of numbers.

1. 4, 12   **2.** 6, 21   **3.** 10, 35   **4.** 14, 63   **5.** 48, 231

Find the least common multiple for each pair of numbers.

6. 3, 7   **7.** 5, 9   **8.** 12, 32   **9.** 16, 44   **10.** 45, 99

Find the least common denominator for each pair of fractions.

11. $\frac{1}{2}, \frac{3}{4}$ **12.** $\frac{2}{3}, \frac{3}{5}$ **13.** $\frac{2}{7}, \frac{3}{4}$ **14.** $\frac{2}{9}, \frac{1}{3}$ **15.** $\frac{3}{4}, \frac{7}{12}$

Proportions

A. Lori is comparing catalogs of two computer schools. One catalog states that 27 out of 30 of our graduates find jobs. The other catalog states that 90 out of 100 of our graduates find jobs. So, Lori compares the ratios 27:30 and 90:100.

An equation that shows that two ratios are equal is called a **proportion.** You can use **cross products** to determine whether two ratios are equal.

$$\frac{27}{30} \overset{?}{=} \frac{90}{100}$$

extremes → 27 ⟋ 90 ← means
means → 30 ⟍ 100 ← extremes

$$27 \cdot 100 \overset{?}{=} 30 \cdot 90$$
$$2{,}700 = 2{,}700$$

The cross products are equal. So, the ratios are equal.
$\frac{27}{30} = \frac{90}{100}$ is a proportion.

Two ratios such as $\frac{27}{30}$ and $\frac{64}{70}$ are not equal, because their cross products are not equal.

$$\frac{27}{30} \quad \overset{⟋}{⟍} \quad \frac{64}{70}$$
$$27 \cdot 70 \overset{?}{=} 30 \cdot 64$$
$$1{,}890 \neq 1{,}920$$

B. Sometimes you are given a proportion that has a variable in one of its ratios. You *solve* the proportion when you find the correct value for x. You can use cross products.

Cross multiply.	Solve.	Check: $\frac{24}{40} \overset{?}{=} \frac{15}{25}$.

$$\frac{24}{40} = \frac{15}{x}$$

$$24 \cdot x = 40 \cdot 15$$

$$\frac{24x}{24} = \frac{600}{24}$$

$$24x = 600 \qquad x = 25$$

$$\frac{3}{5} = \frac{3}{5} \; ✔$$

Other examples:

$$\frac{14}{10} = \frac{x}{15}$$
$$14 \cdot 15 = 10 \cdot x$$
$$210 = 10x$$
$$\frac{210}{10} = \frac{10x}{10}$$
$$21 = x$$

Check: $\frac{14}{10} \overset{?}{=} \frac{21}{15}$.

$$\frac{7}{5} = \frac{7}{5} \; ✔$$

$$\frac{1.25}{x} = \frac{5}{9}$$
$$1.25 \cdot 9 = x \cdot 5$$
$$11.25 = 5x$$
$$\frac{11.25}{5} = \frac{5x}{5}$$
$$2.25 = x$$

Check: $\frac{1.25}{2.25} \overset{?}{=} \frac{5}{9}$.

$$\frac{1.25 \times 4}{2.25 \times 4} = \frac{5}{9}$$

$$\frac{5}{9} = \frac{5}{9} \; ✔$$

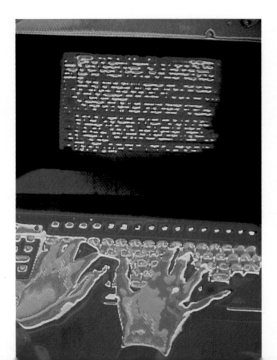

Are the ratios equal? Write *yes* or *no*.

1. $\dfrac{3}{6}, \dfrac{5}{4}$

2. $\dfrac{18}{6}, \dfrac{6}{2}$

3. $\dfrac{6}{9}, \dfrac{10}{15}$

4. $\dfrac{20}{4}, \dfrac{106}{21}$

5. $\dfrac{4}{16}, \dfrac{12}{48}$

6. $\dfrac{30}{40}, \dfrac{80}{100}$

7. $\dfrac{4}{8}, \dfrac{105}{210}$

8. $\dfrac{50}{60}, \dfrac{60}{50}$

Solve each proportion.

9. $\dfrac{6}{9} = \dfrac{8}{x}$

10. $\dfrac{6}{5} = \dfrac{30}{x}$

11. $\dfrac{21}{28} = \dfrac{6}{x}$

12. $\dfrac{12}{4} = \dfrac{15}{x}$

13. $\dfrac{4}{12} = \dfrac{x}{15}$

14. $\dfrac{8}{20} = \dfrac{x}{25}$

15. $\dfrac{15}{21} = \dfrac{x}{35}$

16. $\dfrac{20}{12} = \dfrac{x}{33}$

17. $\dfrac{12}{x} = \dfrac{8}{10}$

18. $\dfrac{16}{x} = \dfrac{8}{4}$

19. $\dfrac{9}{x} = \dfrac{60}{80}$

20. $\dfrac{36}{x} = \dfrac{45}{50}$

21. $\dfrac{x}{10} = \dfrac{36}{20}$

22. $\dfrac{x}{18} = \dfrac{6}{9}$

23. $\dfrac{x}{4} = \dfrac{180}{30}$

24. $\dfrac{x}{50} = \dfrac{21}{75}$

25. $\dfrac{1.2}{x} = \dfrac{6}{9}$

26. $\dfrac{10}{14} = \dfrac{x}{10.5}$

27. $\dfrac{9}{3.5} = \dfrac{18}{x}$

28. $\dfrac{x}{3.6} = \dfrac{60}{80}$

Write a proportion and solve for x.

29. The ratio of 18 to 15 is equal to the ratio of x to 40.

★30. The ratio of $13\frac{1}{2}$ to $3\frac{3}{8}$ is equal to the ratio of 48 to x.

Solve.

31. One school states that 3 of every 5 students have part-time jobs. Another school says that 60 of every 100 students have part-time jobs. Are these equal ratios?

32. A school admits 3 of every 4 people who apply. If 120 people apply, how many will probably be admitted?

33. A school states that 80 of its 96 graduates in computer science found jobs in their field. What is this ratio in simplest form?

CHALLENGE

Use the digits 1, 2, 3, 6, 7, 9, and 0 to find the value each letter represents in the problem below.

```
   SUN
 + FUN
 -----
  SWIM
```

PROBLEM SOLVING
Writing a Proportion

Sometimes you can use a proportion to solve a problem.

> Patrick is studying to become a chef. For one of his assignments, he has to convert a recipe that yields 16 servings to one that will yield 6 servings. The recipe, for an eggplant casserole, calls for $\frac{2}{3}$ cup of grated cheese. How much will he need for the recipe that will yield only 6 servings?

To find out how much cheese he needs, write a proportion.

Let n = the amount of cheese required in the 6-serving recipe.

$$\underset{\substack{\text{servings in the} \\ \text{original recipe}}}{\overset{\substack{\text{cheese in the} \\ \text{original recipe}}}{}} \quad \frac{\frac{2}{3}}{16} = \frac{n}{6} \quad \underset{\substack{\text{servings in the} \\ \text{new recipe}}}{\overset{\substack{\text{cheese in the} \\ \text{new recipe}}}{}}$$

You cannot rename either fraction, and so, the next step is to cross multiply.

$$16 \cdot n = \frac{2}{3} \cdot 6$$

Solve for n.
$$16n = 4$$
$$n = \frac{4}{16} \text{ or } \frac{1}{4}$$

Patrick will need $\frac{1}{4}$ cup of cheese.

- Why is it usually important to keep a specific ratio between ingredients when changing the amount of servings for a recipe?

Write the letter of the correct proportion.

1. Anthony's assignment is to make chili for 80 people. He has a recipe that serves 35 people. It calls for 8 pounds of ground beef. How many pounds of ground beef will he need in order to serve 80 people?

   a. $\frac{80}{8} = \frac{8}{n}$ b. $\frac{1}{10} = \frac{35}{n}$ c. $\frac{8}{35} = \frac{n}{80}$

2. Jack needs 2 quarts of salad dressing for 80 people. The recipe for 3 cups of salad dressing calls for $\frac{1}{4}$ cup of vinegar. How much vinegar will Jack need for 2 quarts of dressing?

   a. $\frac{\frac{1}{4}}{8} = \frac{8}{n}$ b. $\frac{2}{3} = \frac{n}{\frac{1}{4}}$ c. $\frac{\frac{1}{4}}{3} = \frac{n}{8}$

Solve. Use a proportion when appropriate.

3. For the final exam, the students at the Culinary Institute are making dinner for all the teachers. Mark is supposed to make 17 loaves of bread. If he uses $5\frac{3}{4}$ cups of whole-wheat flour for 2 loaves, how many cups will he need to use for 17 loaves?

4. Angela has been assigned to make her famous sauce. Her recipe calls for boiling the sauce until it is reduced by $\frac{1}{3}$. If she wants $3\frac{1}{3}$ cups of reduced sauce, how many cups will she need to begin with?

5. Carol conducted a survey to find out how many people preferred fried chicken to roasted chicken. She found that the ratio of fried-chicken lovers to roasted-chicken lovers was 7 to 4. If 224 people preferred fried chicken, how many people were polled in the survey?

6. Raul made a fruit drink by using 1 part orange concentrate to 1 part lemon concentrate to 6 parts water. If he used 24 ounces of orange concentrate, how much water did he use? If there were 130 calories in each 8-ounce cup, how many calories were there in 24 ounces of fruit drink?

7. Sue usually buys avocados for guacamole at $0.89 each. Avocados are on sale at $0.79 each or 2 for $1.50. If she decides to spend $7.00 on avocados, how many can she buy, and how much money will she have left?

8. The Griffin Restaurant offers a dinner for $27.50. The owner's cost for each dinner is $25.00, giving him a 10% profit. To increase the profit to 13%, how much more will he need to charge for this dinner?

Scale Drawings

A. Enrique is studying to be a landscape architect. He prepares a scale drawing that has a scale of 2 cm = 1 m. In his drawing, a spruce tree is located 11 cm from the building. What is the actual distance from the tree to the building?

Let x = the actual distance from the tree to the building. Use the scale to write a proportion.

$$\text{distance in drawing (cm)} \longrightarrow \frac{2}{1} = \frac{11}{x} \longleftarrow \text{distance in drawing (cm)}$$
$$\text{actual distance (m)} \longrightarrow \phantom{\frac{2}{1}} \phantom{\frac{11}{x}} \longleftarrow \text{actual distance (m)}$$

$$2x = 11$$
$$\frac{2x}{2} = \frac{11}{2}$$
$$x = 5.5$$

Cross multiply and find x.

The actual distance is 5.5 m.

B. Suppose you plan to use the scale 1 cm = 4 m to prepare a scale drawing. If the actual length of an object is 10 m, what will be its length in the scale drawing?

Let x = the length in the drawing. Write a proportion.

$$\text{length in drawing (cm)} \longrightarrow \frac{1}{4} = \frac{x}{10} \longleftarrow \text{length in drawing (cm)}$$
$$\text{actual length (m)} \longrightarrow \phantom{\frac{1}{4}} \phantom{\frac{x}{10}} \longleftarrow \text{actual length (m)}$$

$$10 = 4x$$
$$\frac{10}{4} = \frac{4x}{4}$$
$$2.5 = x$$

Cross multiply and find x.

The length in the drawing will be 2.5 cm.

Checkpoint Write the letter of the correct answer.

Find the missing measurement.

1. Scale: 1 cm = 2 m
Drawing measurement: 6 cm
Actual measurement: ▦

   a. 3 cm   **b.** 12 cm

   c. 3 m   **d.** 12 m

2. Scale: 3 in. = 5 ft
Actual measurement: 10 ft
Drawing measurement: ▦

   a. $1\frac{1}{2}$ in.   **b.** 6 in.

   c. 6 ft   **d.** 150 ft

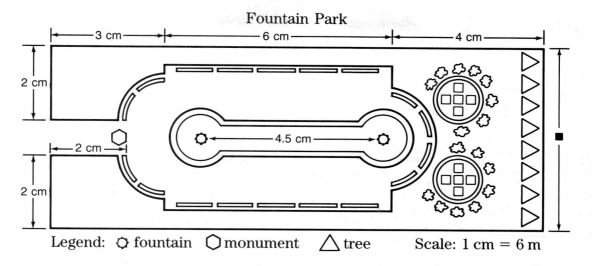

Fountain Park

Legend: ○ fountain ◯ monument △ tree   Scale: 1 cm = 6 m

1. Use a centimeter ruler to find the width of the park in the drawing.

Use the scale drawing to find the actual

2. length of the park.

3. width of the park.

4. width of the park entrance.

5. distance between the fountains.

Solve.

6. The lawn area in front of a post office is 3 meters wide. How wide should it be in a scale drawing if a scale of 1 cm = 0.5 m is used?

7. A landscape architect is preparing a scale drawing of a shrub border that has a scale of $\frac{1}{2}$ in. = 1 ft. If the border is $35\frac{1}{2}$ ft long, how long should it be in the drawing?

8. A scale drawing of the town park is prepared that has a scale of 1 cm = 8 m. If the distance from the drinking fountain to the bandstand is 8.5 cm, what is the actual distance?

9. Choose a rectangular area, such as a classroom or school yard, and find its length and width. Select an appropriate scale, and prepare a scale drawing based on your measurements.

CHALLENGE

You have 6 toothpicks. How can you arrange them so you have four equilateral triangles, all having sides 1 toothpick long?

The Meaning of Percent

A. This year's graduating class at Lakeland High School has 100 students, and 17 of them plan to attend the community college. You can express this information

as a ratio.	as a fraction.	as a decimal.
17 to 100, or 17:100	$\frac{17}{100}$	0.17

You can also use a percent. **Percent (%)** means "per hundred."

So, 17% of Lakeland's graduates plan to attend the community college.

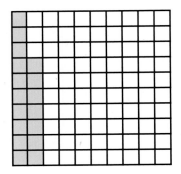

The 10-by-10 figure represents the 100 graduates. Of the squares, 17 are shaded.

B. To write a percent for a fraction, you can find an equivalent fraction that has 100 as the denominator.

Write $\frac{1}{2}$ as a percent.

$$\frac{1}{2} = \frac{x}{100}$$
$$\frac{1}{2} = \frac{1 \cdot 50}{2 \cdot 50} = \frac{50}{100}$$

The fraction $\frac{1}{2} = \frac{50}{100}$, or 50%.

Write $\frac{7}{5}$ as a percent.

$$\frac{7}{5} = \frac{x}{100}$$
$$\frac{7}{5} = \frac{7 \cdot 20}{5 \cdot 20} = \frac{140}{100}$$

The fraction $\frac{7}{5} = \frac{140}{100}$, or 140%.

C. To write a percent for the ratio of a part to the whole, find an equal ratio that has 100 as the second term.

Express the ratio 9:20 as a percent.

$9{:}20$ is $\dfrac{9}{20}$ ← part ← whole

$$\frac{9}{20} = \frac{x}{100}$$
$$900 = 20x$$
$$\frac{900}{20} = \frac{20x}{20}$$
$$45 = x$$

The ratio 9:20 is equal to 45:100, or 45%.

Express the ratio 3 to 800 as a percent.

3 to 800 is $\dfrac{3}{800}$ ← part ← whole

$$\frac{3}{800} = \frac{x}{100}$$
$$300 = 800x$$
$$\frac{300}{800} = \frac{800x}{800}$$
$$0.375 = x$$

The ratio 3 to 800 is equal to 0.375:100, or 0.375%.

Write as a percent.

1. $\frac{12}{100}$ **2.** $\frac{3}{100}$ **3.** 99 of 100 **4.** 7:100

5. $\frac{77}{100}$ **6.** 13 per hundred **7.** 11:100 **8.** 1 of 100

9. $\frac{3}{10}$ **10.** $\frac{10}{10,000}$ **11.** $\frac{7}{10}$ **12.** $\frac{426}{200}$

13. $\frac{3}{2}$ **14.** $\frac{3}{5}$ **15.** $\frac{9}{1,200}$ **16.** $\frac{12}{25}$

Write each ratio as a percent.

17. 7:50 **18.** 13:20 **19.** 5:8 **★20.** 1 to 3

21. 5 students of 100 students **22.** 2 scholarships per 25 students

Solve. For Problem 24, use the Infobank.

23. Of the 100 graduates at Lakeland High School, 31 plan to attend an out-of-state college. What percent plan to attend an out-of-state college?

24. Use the information on page 475 to solve. In grams, what is the United States Recommended Daily Allowance of protein?

25. This year, Fairview High School has a graduating class of 80 students. Of the 80 students, 6 plan to enter the military. What percent plan to enter the military?

26. Of this year's 80 graduates at Fairview High School, 57 have found summer jobs. What percent have found summer jobs?

27. Survey 10 of your classmates to determine the career that each is preparing for. Write each result as a fraction and then as a percent.

NUMBER SENSE

Change each fraction to a percent.

1. $\frac{3}{4}$ **2.** $\frac{2}{5}$ **3.** $\frac{9}{10}$ **4.** $\frac{4}{5}$ **5.** $\frac{6}{5}$

6. $\frac{1}{4}$ **7.** $\frac{5}{4}$ **8.** $\frac{3}{20}$ **9.** $\frac{3}{25}$ **10.** $\frac{41}{50}$

Percents and Decimals

A. Ben plans to become a reporter. This summer he is working part-time in a newsroom and spends 35% of his salary for school expenses.

You can write a decimal to describe the part of Ben's salary spent for school expenses.

35% means 35 per 100, or $\frac{35}{100}$.
35% = 0.35

B. You can use a shortcut to write a percent as a decimal. Move the decimal point two places to the left and omit the percent sign.

18% = 0.1 8 = 0.18
225% = 2.2 5 = 2.25

3.5% = 0.0 3 5 = 0.035
0.6% = 0.0 0 6 = 0.006

> Add zeros as necessary.

C. You can also write a decimal as a percent. Move the decimal point two places to the right and write the percent sign.

0.32 = 0 3 2.% = 32%
0.07 = 0 0 7.% = 7%

4 = 4 0 0.% = 400%
0.015 = 0 0 1.5 % = 1.5%

> Add zeros as necessary.

Checkpoint Write the letter of the correct answer.

Write as a decimal.

1. 12.5%

a. 0.125
b. 1.25
c. 12.5
d. 1,250.0

2. 220%

a. 0.22
b. 2.20
c. 22
d. 2,200.0

Write as a percent.

3. 0.71

a. 0.0071%
b. 0.71%
c. 7.1%
d. 71%

4. 0.0075

a. 0.000075%
b. 0.75%
c. 7.5%
d. 75%

Math Reasoning, page H217

Write as a decimal.

1. 13%   2. 99%   3. 8%   4. 62%

5. 150%   6. 500%   7. 354%   8. 247%

9. 1.8%   10. 0.9%   11. 12.5%   12. 6.25%

Write as a percent.

13. 0.83   14. 0.32   15. 0.60   16. 0.07

17. 3.68   18. 5.00   19. 1.04   20. 7.50

21. 0.4   22. 6   23. 1.2   24. 9

25. 0.005   26. 1.005   27. 0.0057   28. 0.0125

Copy and complete the table.

Percent	8.25%	925%	31. ■	32. ■
Decimal	29. ■	30. ■	0.0038	0.0125

Solve.

33. The staff issued a special edition of the paper for the opening of the baseball season. The number of copies printed of the special edition was 2.1 times the usual number. What percent was this?

34. Gwen questioned the reporters about their education. Of 10 reporters, 4 had gone to journalism school. What percent went to journalism school? Write this percent as a decimal.

35. When Gwen works overtime, she earns 1.5 times her regular wage. What is this number written as a percent?

36. In a newspaper or a magazine, find a graph that has percents. Redraw the graph. Use decimals for the percents.

FOCUS: REASONING

"My name is William McShane. I have as many brothers as sisters, but each of my sisters has twice as many brothers as sisters."

QUESTION: How many boys and how many girls are there in the McShane family?

Percents and Fractions

A. Before entering the state veterinary school, 75% of the students completed four years of college. What fraction of the students is this?

To write a percent as a fraction, use 100 as the denominator and write the answer in simplest form.

$$75\% = \frac{75}{100} = \frac{75 \div 25}{100 \div 25} = \frac{3}{4}$$

$\frac{3}{4}$ of the students completed four years of college.

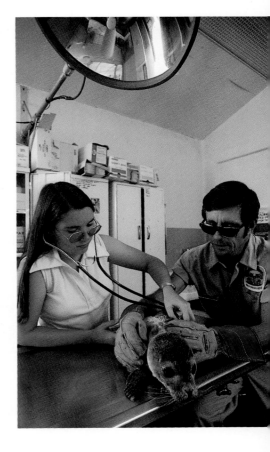

B. There are two ways to write a fraction as a percent. One way is to find an equivalent fraction that has a denominator of 100.

$$\frac{1}{4} = \frac{25}{100} = 25\%$$

The other way is to use division to find a decimal.

Division is convenient for a fraction such as $\frac{7}{8}$ because the denominator 8 is not a factor of 100.

$$\frac{1}{4} \longrightarrow \begin{array}{r} 0.25 = 25\% \\ 4\overline{)1.00} \end{array}$$

Sometimes you must divide beyond the hundredths place.

$$\frac{7}{8} \longrightarrow \begin{array}{r} 0.875 = 87.5\%, \text{ or } 87\frac{1}{2}\% \\ 8\overline{)7.000} \end{array}$$

Other examples:

percents to fractions

$$28\% = \frac{28}{100} = \frac{7}{25}$$

$$83\frac{1}{3}\% = \frac{83\frac{1}{3}}{100} = 83\frac{1}{3} \div 100$$
$$= \frac{\overset{5}{\cancel{250}}}{3} \times \frac{1}{\cancel{100}} = \frac{5}{6}$$
$$_{2}$$

$$165\% = \frac{165}{100} = \frac{33}{20} = 1\frac{13}{20}$$

fractions to percents

$$\frac{2}{5} = \frac{40}{100} = 40\%$$

$$\frac{2}{3} = \begin{array}{r} 0.66\frac{2}{3} \\ 3\overline{)2.00} \end{array} = 66\frac{2}{3}\%$$

$$1\frac{3}{5} = \underbrace{1}_{100\%} + \underbrace{\frac{3}{5}}_{60\%} = 160\%$$

212

Write as a fraction, a whole number, or a mixed number. Express all fractions in simplest form.

1. 10%

2. 25%

3. 95%

4. 56%

5. $12\frac{1}{2}\%$

6. $14\frac{2}{7}\%$

7. $2\frac{1}{2}\%$

8. $66\frac{2}{3}\%$

9. 175%

10. 280%

11. 200%

12. 550%

Write as a percent.

13. $\frac{1}{2}$

14. $\frac{7}{10}$

15. $\frac{22}{25}$

16. $\frac{49}{50}$

17. $\frac{1}{11}$

18. $\frac{5}{12}$

19. $\frac{11}{40}$

20. $\frac{4}{7}$

21. $1\frac{4}{5}$

22. $3\frac{1}{2}$

23. $2\frac{2}{3}$

★24. $5\frac{1}{9}$

Copy and write the missing fraction, mixed number, or percent.

25. $91\frac{2}{3}\% = $ ■

26. ■$\% = \frac{1}{6}$

27. $62\frac{1}{2}\% = $ ■

28. ■$\% = 32.5$

29. $112\frac{1}{2}\% = $ ■

★30. ■$\% = \frac{80}{30}$

Solve.

31. Of all veterinarians, $\frac{1}{3}$ are specialists in treating small animals. What percent of veterinarians specialize in this area?

32. Of the 36,000 veterinarians in the United States, 7.5% work for the federal government. What is this percent written as a fraction?

33. A student in veterinary school estimates that she spends $\frac{1}{8}$ of her time working with animals. What is this fraction written as a percent?

34. A young veterinarian who borrowed money to attend school spends $16\frac{2}{3}\%$ of his income to repay the loan. What fraction of his income is this?

ANOTHER LOOK

Divide. Write the quotient in simplest form.

1. $\frac{3}{4} \div \frac{3}{8}$

2. $\frac{6}{9} \div \frac{1}{3}$

3. $\frac{4}{5} \div \frac{6}{10}$

4. $\frac{9}{15} \div \frac{2}{6}$

5. $\frac{8}{3} \div \frac{3}{4}$

6. $\frac{7}{6} \div \frac{3}{5}$

7. $\frac{4}{9} \div \frac{11}{6}$

8. $\frac{18}{13} \div \frac{6}{5}$

PROBLEM SOLVING
Making an Organized List/Acting it Out

Making an organized list can help you solve certain word problems. Here is an example.

Bernard is teaching a course in job hunting to eight college students. He wants to set up interviews in which every student will meet with every other student. How many meetings will take place?

Students
Phil
Annette
Rodrigo
Twyla
Griffin
Miko
Sal
Lee

Use slips of paper with the names of the students to *act out* the different combinations of students.

Make an organized list of each pair. Use each student's first initial.

P–A, P–R, P–T, P–G, P–M, P–S, P–L
A–R, A–T, A–G, A–M, A–S, A–L
R–T, R–G, R–M, R–S, R–L
T–G, T–M, T–S, T–L
G–M, G–S, G–L
M–S, M–L
S–L   A total of 28 meetings will take place.

Remember that each pair of students needs to meet only once. For example, A–P is the same pair as P–A.

Solve.

1. Bill is registering for night classes at a local college. He can take two classes on Wednesday night, but there are four offered that interest him: English literature, BASIC, sociology, and journalism. Complete the list of the course combinations Bill could take. Use the first initial of each course.

   E–B, ■–■, ■–■
   B–S, ■–■,
   ■–■

2. The writing-workshop instructor puts students together in groups of three to criticize one another's work. The students in the workshop are Verna, Maurice, Ophelia, Seth, Carla, and Andrea. Complete the list of combinations of six students in groups of three.

   V–M–O, V–M–S, ■–■–■, ■–■–■,
   V–O–S, V–O–C, ■–■–■,
   ■–■–■, V–S–A, V–C–A
   M–O–S, ■–■–■, ■–■–■,
   ■–■–■, M–S–A, M–C–A
   ■–■–■, O–S–A, O–C–A
   ■–■–■

Solve.

3. Deborah is a textbook designer. For a two-color geometric figure, she must choose from four color overlays: black, red, blue, and yellow. List all the possible color combinations for the geometric figure.

4. Liza's chamber-music class is giving a benefit concert of works by Haydn, Mozart, Dvořák, and Brahms. Liza will play two pieces with the class. Make a list of all the combinations of works she could play.

5. Lori is a floral designer. She wants to use five colors in a particular arrangement of flowers. She has white carnations, yellow daisies, blue iris, orange lilies, red chrysanthemums, lavender chrysanthemums, pink tulips, and green ferns. Make a list of all the color combinations Lori could use in her arrangement.

6. Frederico is an apprentice tiler. He is installing a floor based on a design that uses tiles of four colors. Frederico can use eight colors: earth, copper, gray, turquoise, white, olive, lemon, and black. Make a list that shows each combination of colors Frederico could use.

7. Kevrok has a reading list of twelve novels for his American literature course—one each by Twain, James, Irving, Dreiser, Crane, Fitzgerald, Hemingway, Faulkner, Warren, Mailer, Roth, and Barth. His professor told him to read any ten from the list. How many combinations of novels could Kevrok read?

8. Drew is a carpentry teacher. His students work with pine, oak, cherry, walnut and maple wood finishes. Drew can only supervise two types of wood finishes each class. Make a list of all the wood finish combinations that Drew could supervise.

Finding the Percent of a Number

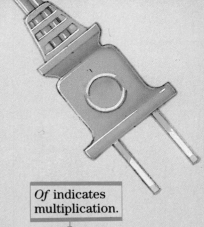

A. Janine is an apprentice electrician. Her four-year apprenticeship combines classroom instruction with practical experience. In her first year, she is paid 40% of the hourly wage for union electricians. If that wage is $15 per hour, what is her hourly wage in the first year?

Of indicates multiplication.

Let x = the number.

Write an equation and solve.

Janine earns $6 per hour in the first year.

Think: What number is 40% of 15?

$$x = 0.40 \cdot 15$$
$$x = 6$$

You can also use a fraction to solve the problem.

$$40\% = \frac{40}{100} = \frac{2}{5}$$

Write an equation and solve. The answer is the same.

$$x = \frac{2}{5} \cdot 15$$
$$x = 6$$

B. To find a percent of a number, sometimes it is easier to use a fraction. At other times, it is easier to use a decimal.

Find $66\frac{2}{3}\%$ of 510.

Use a fraction. $66\frac{2}{3}\% = \frac{2}{3}$

Write an equation and solve.

Think: What number is $66\frac{2}{3}\%$ of 510?

$$x = \frac{2}{3} \cdot 510$$
$$x = 340$$

What is 7.5% of 68?
Use a decimal. $7.5\% = 0.075$
Write an equation and solve.

$$x = 0.075 \cdot 68$$
$$x = 5.1$$

Other examples:

Find 0.2% of 800.
$$x = 0.002 \cdot 800$$
$$x = 1.6$$

Find 175% of 60.
$$x = 1.75 \cdot 60$$
$$x = 105$$

Reasoning, page H218

Find the percent of the number.

1. 10% of 20
2. 70% of 200
3. 50% of 80
4. 75% of $40

5. 8% of 48
6. 30% of 50
7. 15% of $30
8. 2% of 250

9. $66\frac{2}{3}$% of 33
10. $12\frac{1}{2}$% of 72
11. $16\frac{2}{3}$% of $96
12. $6\frac{1}{4}$% of 64

13. 1.5% of 400
14. 0.5% of 444
15. 7.5% of $160
16. 2.75% of 200

17. 260% of 20
18. $37\frac{1}{2}$% of 80
19. 0.9% of $300
20. $14\frac{2}{7}$% of 84

Solve.

21. Find 63% of 500.

22. 110% of 96 is what number?

23. What is $84\frac{2}{3}$% of $150?

24. Find 7.5% of $2,100.

25. 0.5% of 65 is what number?

26. Find 0.08% of 500.

27. What number is 85.5% of 70?

28. What number is 99.5% of 200?

29. During one 40-hour week, Janine spent 25% of her time in class. How many hours did she spend in class?

30. On Jason's current electrical job, there are 3 experienced electricians for every apprentice. What is the ratio of experienced electricians to apprentices?

31. A second-year apprentice earns 55% of the union wage, and a third-year apprentice earns 75% of it. If the union wage is $15 per hour, what is the difference in hourly earnings between a second- and a third-year apprentice?

32. There are 560,000 licensed electricians in the United States. Of these, 52% are construction electricians. How many construction electricians are there?

MIDCHAPTER REVIEW

Write as a percent.

1. $\frac{4}{5}$
2. $\frac{7}{7}$
3. $3\frac{7}{10}$
4. 0.54
5. 3.08

Write as a decimal and as a fraction or mixed number.

6. 20%
7. 42%
8. 360%
9. 37.5%
10. $62\frac{1}{2}$%

Finding What Percent

A. Gifford Hospital has a 35-hour training course for volunteer workers. Students in the course spend 21 hours on patient care. What percent of the course is spent on patient care?

Let n = the percent.

Write an equation.

Solve.

Think: What percent of 35 is 21?

$$n \cdot 35 = 21$$
$$35n = 21$$
$$\frac{35n}{35} = \frac{21}{35}$$
$$n = \frac{3}{5} = 0.60, \text{ or } 60\%$$

So, 60% of the course is spent on patient care.

B. What percent of 6 is 15?

$$n \cdot 6 = 15$$
$$6n = 15$$
$$\frac{6n}{6} = \frac{15}{6}$$
$$n = 2.5, \text{ or } 250\%$$

3 is what percent of 750?

$$3 = n \cdot 750$$
$$3 = 750n$$
$$\frac{3}{750} = \frac{750n}{750}$$
$$0.004 = n \qquad 0.004 \longrightarrow 0.4\%$$
$$0.4\% = n$$

Another example:

What percent of $19.50 is $6.50?

$$n \cdot 19.5 = 6.5$$
$$19.5n = 6.5$$
$$\frac{19.5n}{19.5} = \frac{6.5}{19.5}$$
$$n = \frac{1}{3}, \text{ or } 33\frac{1}{3}\%$$

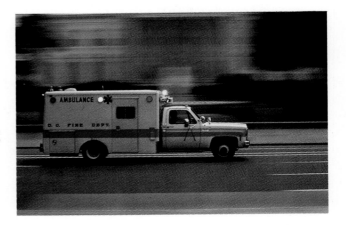

Checkpoint   Write the letter of the correct answer.

1. What percent of 20 is 5?

a. 100%   **b.** 25%   **c.** 40%   **d.** 400%

2. What percent of 72 is 90?

a. 1.25%   **b.** 80%   **c.** 125%   **d.** 2.8%

3. What percent of 16 is 6?

a. 96%   **b.** $266\frac{2}{3}\%$ **c.** $37\frac{1}{2}\%$ **d.** 10%

4. What percent of 50 is 0.5?

a. 1%   **b.** 25%   **c.** 100%   **d.** 49.5%

Find the percent.

1. What percent of 50 is 10?

2. 1.6 is what percent of 6.4?

3. 4.5 is what percent of 90?

4. What percent of 485 is 97?

5. What percent of 110 is 60.5?

6. 1,250 is what percent of 5,000?

7. 9 is what percent of 6?

8. 34 is what percent of 17?

9. 81.25 is what percent of 65?

10. What percent of 10 is 12?

11. 1.5 is what percent of 300?

12. What percent of 400 is 2?

13. 0.15 is what percent of 300?

14. What percent of 200 is 0.125?

15. 30 is what percent of 36?

16. What percent of 24 is 4?

17. 98 is what percent of 1,000?

18. 12.5 is what percent of 40?

19. 6 is what percent of 600?

20. What percent of 180 is 4.5?

★21. Suppose x and y are whole numbers, and x is 15% of y. List three pairs of possible values for x and y.

Solve.

22. A volunteer course was started that had 25 people. Of those enrolled, 4 volunteers transferred to another course. What percent completed the original course?

23. The hospital has 180 volunteers. Teenagers comprise $\frac{1}{3}$ of the volunteers. What percent of the volunteers are teenagers?

24. In one group, all 18 volunteers plan careers in medicine. Of this number, 3 plan to become surgeons. What percent of the volunteer group plans to become surgeons?

25. Hospital officials would like volunteers to contribute a total of 900 hours per week. Last week, volunteers contributed a total of 840 hours. What percent of the desired total is this?

NUMBER SENSE

Compute mentally by changing percents to fractions.

1. 60% of 15

2. 75% of 240

3. $33\frac{1}{3}$% of 420

4. 40% of 35

5. 45% of 80

6. $12\frac{1}{2}$% of 80

7. 140% of 250

8. $87\frac{1}{2}$% of 160

Finding the Total Number

A. Andrew earns $480 per week as a computer programmer trainee. This amount is 75% of the salary for an experienced programmer. What is the salary of an experienced programmer?

Let x = the number.

Write an equation.

Think: 75% of what number is 480?

$$0.75 \cdot x = 480$$

Solve.

$$0.75x = 480$$
$$\frac{0.75x}{0.75} = \frac{480}{0.75}$$
$$x = 640$$

An experienced programmer earns $640 per week.

B. In some problems, it is easier to use a fraction for the percent.

54 is $66\frac{2}{3}\%$ of what number?

$$54 = \frac{2}{3} \cdot x \qquad \boxed{66\frac{2}{3}\% = \frac{2}{3}}$$

$$54 = \frac{2}{3}x$$

$$\frac{3}{2} \cdot 54 = \frac{3}{2} \cdot \frac{2}{3}x$$

$$81 = x$$

So, 54 is $66\frac{2}{3}\%$ of 81.

Other examples:

0.3% of what number is 12?

$$0.003 \cdot x = 12$$
$$0.003x = 12$$
$$\frac{0.003x}{0.003} = \frac{12}{0.003}$$
$$x = 4{,}000$$

91 is 130% of what number?

$$91 = 1.3 \cdot x$$
$$91 = 1.3x$$
$$\frac{91}{1.3} = \frac{1.3x}{1.3}$$
$$70 = x$$

Checkpoint Write the letter of the correct answer.

1. 10 is 50% of what number?

a. 0.2   **b.** 5   **c.** 20   **d.** 25

2. $12\frac{1}{2}\%$ of what number is 8?

a. 1   **b.** 16   **c.** 0.64   **d.** 64

Find the number.

1. 10% of what number is 30?

2. 40 is 80% of what number?

3. 16 is 25% of what number?

4. 81 is 90% of what number?

5. 65% of what number is 260?

6. 92% of what number is 50.6?

7. $12\frac{1}{2}$% of what number is 4?

8. $87\frac{1}{2}$% of what number is 70?

9. $6\frac{1}{4}$% of what number is 2?

10. $23\frac{1}{3}$ is $16\frac{2}{3}$% of what number?

11. 0.5% of what number is 2.5?

12. 0.04% of what number is 1?

13. 147 is 350% of what number?

14. 42 is 100% of what number?

15. 12.75 is 15% of what number?

16. 68.75 is 55% of what number?

17. 0.325 is 20% of what number?

18. 75% of what number is 14.25?

★19. If x is 125% of y, then y is what percent of x?

★20. If x is 45% of y, then y is what percent of x?

Solve.

21. A company employs 180 computer programmers. This is 45% of the employees in the company. How many employees are there in the company?

22. Susan earns 60% of the salary of a systems analyst. If a systems analyst earns $900 per week, how much does Susan earn?

23. Computer Graphics Inc. spent $1,400 advertising for new programmers. If this amount was 125% of the budgeted amount, how much had been budgeted?

NUMBER SENSE

Choose the correct answer.

1.	10% of 130	a. 1.3	b. 13	c. 130	d. 1,300
2.	1% of 200	a. 0.2	b. 2	c. 20	d. 200
3.	100% of 40	a. 0.4	b. 4	c. 40	d. 4,000
4.	10% of 70	a. 0.7	b. 7	c. 70	d. 700
5.	100% of 350	a. 3.5	b. 35	c. 350	d. 35,000
6.	1% of 500	a. 0.5	b. 5	c. 50	d. 500

PROBLEM SOLVING
Using a Formula ($I = prt$)

Interest is a fee someone pays for borrowing money from a bank or a lending agency. Interest is also the set fee that a bank pays to customers for the use of their money. The amount of money borrowed or saved is called the *principal,* and the interest rate is a percent of the principal. Time is expressed in years.

Maureen is planning a career as a forest ranger. The books for the second semester of her sophomore year in college will cost $350. She can pay only $50 of her book bill and will have to borrow the rest. If the bank agrees to lend her the money for 6 months at an interest rate of 8%, how much interest will she pay?

To solve a problem by using a formula, follow these general rules.

1. Use the correct formula.
2. Substitute values in the formula.
3. Solve the equation.
4. Write the answer.

To calculate the interest, use the formula $I = prt$, where

I = interest

p = principal ($350 − $50 = $300)

r = rate (8%)

t = time $\left(6 \text{ months or } \frac{1}{2} \text{ year} = 0.5\right)$.

Therefore, $I = \$300 \times 0.08 \times 0.5 = \$12$.

Maureen will pay $12 in interest.

You can use other forms of the interest formula to find the principal, the rate, or the time.

To calculate the principal, use $p = I \div rt$.
To calculate the rate, use $r = I \div pt$.
To calculate the time in years, use $t = I \div pr$.

Write the letter of the correct form of the interest formula.

1. Mark paid $1,500 in interest on money he borrowed for 3 years in order to attend a computer-training program. If the interest rate was 10%, how much did he borrow?

    a. $t = I \div pr$
    b. $r = I \div pt$
    c. $I = prt$
    d. $p = I \div rt$

2. Christine wants to borrow $2,000 in order to take a foreign-language course. If she borrows the money for 2 years at an interest rate of 12%, how much will she pay in interest?

    a. $t = I \div pr$
    b. $r = I \div pt$
    c. $I = prt$
    d. $p = I \div rt$

Solve. Use the correct form of the interest formula.

3. Joan borrowed $3,000 from her father to use as a down payment on a new car. She agreed to pay him back at a yearly rate of $12\frac{1}{2}\%$ over a period of 3 years. How much interest will she pay him?

4. Ralph's college tuition for one year is $5,500. He pays 20% down and takes out a loan for the balance at a rate of 6% a year for 6 years. What is the total amount he will repay?

5. On a loan of $804, Arthur paid interest that amounted to $192.96 over 2 years. He made monthly payments of $41.54. What was the rate of interest at which he borrowed the money?

6. Mr. and Mrs. Whitkin drove 478 miles from Houston, Texas, to Tulsa, Oklahoma, to take their son back to college. If their average driving speed was 52 miles per hour, how long—to the nearest hour—did it take them to reach Tulsa?

7. At the end of 45 months, Cindy paid $1,881 in interest on money she borrowed to go to a business school. If she paid interest at an annual rate of $15\frac{1}{5}\%$ on the loan, how much did she borrow?

★8. The Carsons bought their son a personal computer that cost $1,850. They paid 10% down and agreed to

pay the balance plus interest in equal monthly payments for 24 months. If the annual interest rate is 16%, how much are their monthly payments, rounded to the nearest dollar?

Percent Using Proportions

A. Of the 120 students in one barber school, 85% are less than 25 years old. How many students are less than 25 years old?

You can use a proportion to find a percent of a number. In this problem, you want to find 85% of 120.

REMEMBER: 85% means $\frac{85}{100}$. Set up another ratio that equals $\frac{85}{100}$. Let x = the number of students less than age 25.

Write a proportion.

part $\longrightarrow$ $\frac{85}{100} = \frac{x}{120}$ $\longleftarrow$ part
whole $\longrightarrow$ $\phantom{\frac{85}{100} = \frac{x}{120}}$ $\longleftarrow$ whole

Cross multiply and solve.

$$85 \cdot 120 = 100 \cdot x$$
$$10{,}200 = 100x$$
$$102 = x$$

So, 102 students are less than 25 years old.

B. You can use a proportion to find what percent one number is of another.

What percent of 24 is 3?

Write a proportion.

part $\longrightarrow$ $\frac{x}{100} = \frac{3}{24}$
whole $\longrightarrow$

Cross multiply and solve.

$$x \cdot 24 = 100 \cdot 3$$
$$24x = 300$$
$$x = 12\frac{1}{2}$$

So, 3 is $12\frac{1}{2}$% of 24.

C. You can use a proportion to find a number when you know a percent of the number.

20% of what number is 1.7?

Write a proportion.

part $\longrightarrow$ $\frac{20}{100} = \frac{1.7}{x}$
whole $\longrightarrow$

Cross multiply and solve.

$$20 \cdot x = 100 \cdot 1.7$$
$$20x = 170$$
$$x = 8.5$$

So, 20% of 8.5 is 1.7.

Use a proportion to solve each problem.

1. What is 40% of 160?
2. Find 25% of 48.
3. What number is 15% of 400?
4. What is 150% of 30?
5. What percent of 50 is 35?
6. 16 is what percent of 48?
7. 2.2 is what percent of 8.8?
8. What percent of 600 is 3?
9. 60% of what number is 63?
10. 1.9 is 10% of what number?
11. 18 is 200% of what number?
12. 175 is 25% of what number?
13. What number is 7% of 300?
14. 22 is 55% of what number?
15. What percent of 140 is 7?
16. Find 75% of 150.
17. 65 is what percent of 120?
18. What is $33\frac{1}{3}$% of 99?
19. 1.1 is what percent of 55?
20. What is 87.5% of 56?

Solve.

21. An apprentice barber earns about $260 a week. This is about 65% of what an experienced barber earns. How much does an experienced barber earn?

22. Of the 112,000 barbers in this country, 5% are women. Use a proportion to find the number of women barbers.

23. The training program at one barber school lasts 10 months. Tuition costs $1,900. In addition, the student must buy a personal set of tools for $600. Tools make up what percent of the combined cost of tuition and tools?

CHALLENGE

Rita owns a boutique. When an item arrives, Rita marks it up 60% from the buying price. If it does not sell after 9 weeks, she takes 25% off its price. Four weeks later, if it is still in the shop, she takes 30% off that price. If it sells at this price, does she earn or lose money on it? What percent of the original buying price is her earnings or her loss?

Percent of Increase and Decrease

A. A technical college is expanding its program in civil engineering. There are now 60 students in the program. If there will be 15 more students next year, what is the percent of increase?

Let n = the percent.

Think: What percent of 60 is 15?

$$n \cdot 60 = 15$$

Write an equation.

$$60n = 15$$

Solve.

$$n = \frac{15}{60} \quad \longleftarrow \text{ amount of change}$$
$$\phantom{n = \frac{15}{60}} \quad \longleftarrow \text{ original amount}$$

The percent of increase is 25%.

$$n = \frac{1}{4}, \text{ or } 25\%$$

Suppose that the enrollment was originally 80 students, and it decreased by 16. What is the percent of decrease?

Let n = the percent.

Think: What percent of 80 is 16?

$$n \cdot 80 = 16$$

Write an equation.

$$80n = 16$$

Solve.

$$n = \frac{16}{80}$$

$$n = \frac{1}{5}, \text{ or } 20\%$$

The percent of decrease is 20%.

B. Sometimes you need to compute the amount of change before you can find the percent of increase or decrease.

At the start of a term, there were 20 students in one surveying class. At the end, there were only 18. What is the percent of decrease?

Compute the amount of change.

$$20 - 18 = 2$$

Write an equation and solve it.

$$n \cdot 20 = 2$$
$$20n = 2$$
$$n = \frac{2}{20} = \frac{1}{10}, \text{ or } 10\%$$

The percent of decrease is 10%.

Find the percent of increase or decrease.

1. Original value: 50
   Increase: 18

2. Original price: $21
   Decrease: $7

3. Original value: 90
   Increase: 15

4. Original price: $100
   New price: $140

5. Original value: 500
   New value: 625

6. Original value: 22
   New value: 33

7. Original value: 50
   New value: 35

8. Original value: 240
   New value: 96

9. Original price: $72
   New price: $60

10. Original Price: $12
    New price: $15

11. Original price: $15
    New price: $12

12. Change: 10
    Original value: 200

Find the missing number.

★13. Original value: ■
     New value: $18.90
     Percent of
     increase: 12.5%

★14. Original value: ■
     New value: $44.50
     Percent of
     decrease: $28\frac{4}{7}$%

★15. Original value: ■
     Increase: 72,000
     Percent of
     increase: 56.25%

Solve.

16. Last year, Les earned $8.50 per hour working on a surveying job. This year he has been offered $9.35 per hour for the same job. What is the percent of increase?

17. Carolyn needs a total of 72 credits for an associate degree in civil-engineering technology. If 6 of those are credits in surveying, what percent are credits in surveying?

18. Paul spent $28.80 on a school jacket. If the same jacket sold for $21.60 last semester, what is the percent of increase?

19. Compare the number of students in your class now with the number at the beginning of the school year. Find the percent of increase or decrease.

FOCUS: REASONING

Write the conclusion.

If this item did not cost less, you did not buy it on sale.

If you bought this item at Relangers, it did not cost less.

You bought this item on sale.

PROBLEM SOLVING
Using a Circle Graph

A circle graph shows how a total amount is divided into parts. For example, the circle graph below was divided into parts based on the percent each part is of the whole. The larger the percent, the larger the part.

Use the circle graph to answer this question. How many students plan to enter the field of medicine?

CAREER CHOICES OF 160 STUDENTS AT WILSON HIGH SCHOOL

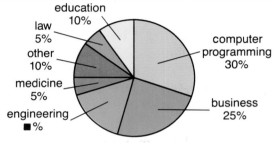

education 10%
law 5%
other 10%
medicine 5%
engineering ■%
computer programming 30%
business 25%

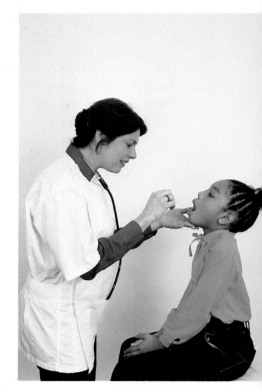

- The title tells you that this graph shows the career choices made by 160 students at one school.

- Each part of the graph shows what percent of the students have chosen a particular career. These percents must add up to 100%.

- The size of each part shows the size of its percent. Find the part labeled *medicine*. What percent is this part?

The graph tells you that 5% of the students have chosen medicine.

Find 5% of 160.

Use a fraction. $5\% = \frac{5}{100} = \frac{1}{20}$

Write an equation, and solve. $x = \frac{1}{20} \cdot 160$

$x = 8$

A total of 8 students plan to enter the field of medicine.

Can you use the circle graph on page 228 to answer
each question? Write *yes* or *no*.

1. Did more students choose computer programming as a career than any other category?

2. How many career choices are there in the category labeled *other*?

3. Is the number of students who chose computer programming as a career double the number of students who chose engineering as a career?

Use the circle graph on page 228 to solve each
problem. If you cannot use the circle graph to answer
a question, write *not enough information.*

4. What percent of the students plan to have careers in engineering?

5. How many students plan to have careers in engineering?

6. How many students plan to follow a career in business?

7. How many students plan to have a career in law?

8. Which other field was chosen by the same number of students as law?

9. How many more students plan to enter computer programming than the field of education?

10. Which two fields combined represent the career choices of more than half the students?

11. How many students plan to have careers in farming and agriculture?

12. If half the students who chose business as a career intend to become accountants, how many students plan to become accountants?

13. One fourth of the students who chose engineering as a career intend to become electrical engineers. How many students are planning to become electrical engineers?

14. Notice that 10% of the students chose a career in the category labeled *other*. If three fourths of the students in this category chose a military career, how many students plan to enter the military?

MATH COMMUNICATION

Read this want ad.

FOR RENT: Sunny apt on Green St Seattle Wash. Liv rm, lg bdrm, kit & laun rm w/ w/d. Tel eves (206) 687–2478, ask for Mr Toms.

The ad contains some familiar abbreviations. An abbreviation is a quick way of writing a word that is used frequently.

When you read mathematics, you will find many abbreviations for commonly used terms.

Match the abbreviation with its meaning.

1. A.M.   **a.** ante morem   **b.** second

2. s   **c.** commutative   **d.** minute

3. cm   **e.** mile   **f.** subtract

4. mi   **g.** ante meridiem   **h.** centimeter

Write an appropriate abbreviation for each missing word in each sentence below.

5. A pint of liquid will fill two 1-■ measures.

6. One ■ equals a thousandth of a meter.

7. Eighteen inches is $1\frac{1}{2}$ ■.

8. Nine feet equals 108 ■.

9. A fence that measures 3,520 yd is about 2 ■ long.

10. A hundredth of a meter is 1 ■.

11. Ten o'clock, between midnight and noon, is 10:00 ■.

12. Twelve ■ is about 3 months.

13. Four quarts equals one ■.

14. A cup of liquid is 8 ■.

15. Ten hours past 10:30 in the morning is 8:30 ■.

16. Jack drove his car 4,312 meters, or 4.312 ■.

17. Lenna's lasagna called for $\frac{1}{2}$ cup tomato sauce or 4 ■.

18. When he applied for a library card, Carl had to fill in the ■, ■, and ■ he was born.

19. In 1984, Gabriella Dorio ran the 1,500-m run in 4 ■ 03.26 ■.

20. In July, the average temperature in Egypt is about 34°■.

GROUP PROJECT

Teachers for a Day

The problem: You and your classmates are going to become teachers for one week. You will have 6 hours per day to teach the subjects you are learning about now. You must decide who will teach each subject, how it will be taught, and how teaching time will be budgeted for each day of the week. Consider the questions below. Discuss them with your classmates, and make a schedule for the week.

Key Questions

- How will you decide who will teach which subject? Will you have a different teacher for each subject?

- Which of the listed subjects will you teach?
    Science   Art
    Social Studies   Music
    Math   Home economics
    English   Industrial arts
    Foreign Language   Physical education

- What other subjects should be included?

- Do some subjects require more time than others to teach?

- What activities should you include (for example: lunch, assembly, study hall)?

TEACHING SCHEDULE

	Monday	Tuesday	Wednesday	Thursday	Friday
9:00					
9:45					
10:30					
11:15					
12:00					
12:45					
1:30					
2:15					
3:00					

CHAPTER TEST

Solve the proportions. (pages 202–203)

1. $\frac{7}{a} = \frac{28}{44}$
2. $\frac{3}{5} = \frac{y}{30}$
3. $\frac{b}{9} = \frac{2}{3}$

The scale of a drawing is 1.5 cm = 10 m. (pages 206–207)

4. What length does 6 cm represent?

5. How many centimeters represent 25 m?

On a drawing, $7\frac{1}{2}$ cm represents 135 m. (pages 206–207)

6. The scale is 1 cm = ■ m?

7. What distance does 3 cm represent?

Write each fraction or decimal as a percent. (pages 208–213)

8. $\frac{4}{5}$
9. $2\frac{19}{50}$
10. 0.83
11. 3.097

Write each percent as a fraction and as a decimal. (pages 208–213)

12. 32%
13. 21.6%
14. 620%
15. 0.3%

Solve. (pages 216–221)

16. 26% of 480

17. 2.8% of 325

18. 130% of 67

19. 338 is what percent of 845?

20. 987 is what percent of 282?

21. 0.5 is what percent of 200?

22. 160 is 25% of what number?

23. 1,050 is 140% of what number?

24. 75.85 is $9\frac{1}{4}$% of what number?

25. 180.9 is 22.5% of what number?

Give the percent of the increase or the decrease. (pages 226–227)

26. $260 is marked up to $338.

27. $400 is marked down to $340.

28. 180 is changed to 259.2.

29. 46 is changed to 43.47.

Solve. (pages 204–205, 214–215, 222–223, and 228–229)

30. A magazine conducted a survey to find how many high school graduates preferred the sales profession to one in advertising. The published report stated that the ratio of potential salespersons to advertisers was 3 to 2. If 621 graduates preferred sales, how many graduates were polled in this survey?

31. Sue tutors new secretaries in dictation. She tutors only two students at a time. There are four secretaries who have applied: Dorinda, Lois, Ella, and Christopher. Use the initial of each name to find the possible combinations she could teach.

32. John earned $350 at his job. If he invests this money at 8.75% simple interest yearly, how much will he earn in 1 year?

Use the circle graph at the right for Exercises 33–34.

33. Angadish College offers 4 different programs. If the total student body is 13,145 students, how many students are there in the business program?

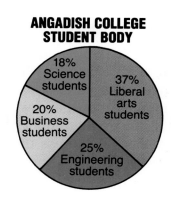

ANGADISH COLLEGE
STUDENT BODY

18% Science students

37% Liberal arts students

20% Business students

25% Engineering students

34. Suppose the total of business and engineering students is 6,525. Find the number of students in the student body.

BONUS

Solve.

After last year's graduation, 95 students of a class of 475 went into business. This year, 130 students of a class of 520 went into business after graduation. In terms of percent, how many more students went into business this year?

RETEACHING

$\frac{1}{2}$, 0.5, and 50% all have the same value.

A. To change a fraction to a decimal, divide its numerator by its denominator.

Express $\frac{5}{8}$ as a decimal and as a percent.

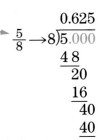

$$\frac{5}{8} = 0.625$$

To change a decimal to a percent, multiply the decimal by 100 and write the percent sign.

$$0.625 \cdot 100 = 62.5\%$$

So, $\frac{5}{8} = 0.625 = 62.5\%$

B. To write a percent as a decimal, move the decimal point two places to the left and remove the percent sign.

Express 45% as a decimal and as a fraction.

$$45\% = 0.45$$

To rewrite the decimal as a fraction, write the decimal (without the decimal point) in the numerator. The denominator is the power of 10 indicated by the number of places in the decimal. Express the fraction in simplest form.

$$0.45 = \frac{45}{100} = \frac{9}{20}$$

So, $45\% = 0.45 = \frac{9}{20}$

Copy and complete the chart at right.

Fraction	Decimal	Percent
$\frac{3}{4}$	**1.** ■	**2.** ■
3. ■	0.52	**4.** ■
$\frac{7}{8}$	**5.** ■	**6.** ■
7. ■	**8.** ■	60%
9. ■	**10.** ■	25%
11. ■	0.375	**12.** ■
$\frac{17}{20}$	**13.** ■	**14.** ■
15. ■	0.4	**16.** ■

ENRICHMENT

Inverse Proportions

The formula used to compute distance is

$$\text{rate} \times \text{time} = \text{distance}.$$

With this formula, different pairs of rate and time factors can produce a distance of 200 mi.

r	×	t	=	d
100	×	2	=	200
50	×	4	=	200
40	×	5	=	200
20	×	10	=	200

Notice that if distance, d, remains constant, the time, t, increases as the rate, r, decreases. Rate is said to be **inversely proportional** to time. Since the rate multiplied by the time is constant, we can express this relation as $rt = k$, where k is the constant.

Write the following relation as a formula. Use k as the constant.

If a fixed sum of money is to be spent, the number of articles, n, that can be bought is inversely proportional to the cost, c, of an article.

Since the product of n and c must be constant, the formula is

$$nc = k.$$

Write each relation as a formula. Use k as the constant.

1. If the area of a rectangle is constant, the length varies inversely with the width.

2. If annual income is fixed, the principal that must be invested varies inversely with the rate of interest.

3. If a weekly salary is fixed, the amount of money earned per hour varies inversely with the number of hours worked.

★4. If a force remains constant, the amount of mass used varies inversely with its acceleration.

235

TECHNOLOGY

You can use the INTEGER FUNCTION with BASIC to round a number down to the nearest integer. If you enter PRINT INT(2.7), your computer will print this. 2

For negative numbers, INT also rounds numbers downward. INT does not simply cut off the decimal part of a number. If you enter PRINT INT($-12 - 0.5$), the computer will print this. -13.

Write what the instruction will print.

1. PRINT INT (9.6)   **2.** PRINT INT (-1.5)

3. PRINT INT (3.55)   **4.** PRINT INT ($-5*0.5$)

5. PRINT INT (13/3)   **6.** PRINT INT ($-9/4$)

Here is a program that tells whether a number is even or odd. If you divide an even number by 2, the result will always be an integer. If you divide an odd number by 2, the result is never an integer.

```
10 PRINT "TYPE A NUMBER"; : INPUT N
20 IF N/2 = INT (N/2) THEN PRINT N; "IS EVEN"
30 IF N/2 < > INT (N/2) THEN PRINT N; "IS ODD"
```

7. Write two runs of this program, one showing an odd number and the other showing an even number.

8. Write a program to test whether a number is evenly divisible by 3.

Sometimes you want to round a number to the nearest integer, instead of rounding down. This means that any number that has a decimal of 0.5 or greater, will be rounded up, and any number that has a decimal of less than 0.5 will be rounded down.

Here's how to use the INT function to round a number.

```
10 PRINT "TYPE A DECIMAL"; : INPUT D
20 LET N = INT (D + .5)
30 PRINT D; "ROUNDS TO"; N
```

If you type the number 4.7 into this program, the computer will add .5 to it and produce 5.2. The integer value of 5.2 is 5. The rounded value of 4.7 is 5.

If you type the number 4.3 into this program, the computer will add .5 to it and produce 4.8. The integer value of 4.8 is 4, so the rounded value of 4.3 is 4.

9. Edit (replace lines or write new lines) the program to tell you whether the number is rounded up or down. Here are some sample RUNs of your program.

   ```
   TYPE A DECIMAL ? 8.5
   8.5 ROUNDS UP TO 9
   ```

   ```
   TYPE A DECIMAL ? 5.2
   5.2 ROUNDS DOWN TO 5
   ```

10. Write a program that will round numbers to the nearest ten.

CUMULATIVE REVIEW

Write the letter of the correct answer.

1. Complete: $284.7 \text{ m} = \blacksquare \text{ km}$.

   a. 0.2847   b. 2.847
   c. 28.47   d. not given

2. Choose the appropriate unit to measure cranberry juice.

   a. meters   b. liters
   c. grams   d. not given

3. $7 \times 42.95 \text{ L}$

   a. 30.035 L   b. 300.65 L
   c. 3006.5 L   d. not given

4. Complete: $0.038 \text{ g} = \blacksquare \text{ mg}$.

   a. 0.0038   b. 0.38
   c. 3.8   d. not given

5. Complete: $7 \text{ gal } 8 \text{ pt} = \blacksquare \text{ qt}$.

   a. 29   b. 30
   c. 32   d. not given

6. $18 \text{ ft } 9 \text{ in.} - 11 \text{ ft } 11 \text{ in.}$

   a. 6 ft 10 in.   b. 7 ft 2 in.
   c. 7 ft 11 in.   d. not given

7. Write 0.64 as a fraction.

   a. $\frac{2}{3}$ b. $\frac{3}{5}$
   c. $\frac{16}{25}$ d. not given

8. Order $\frac{2}{3}, \frac{3}{7}, \frac{7}{19}$ from the least to the greatest.

   a. $\frac{7}{19}, \frac{3}{7}, \frac{2}{3}$ b. $\frac{3}{7}, \frac{2}{3}, \frac{7}{19}$
   c. $\frac{3}{7}, \frac{7}{19}, \frac{2}{3}$ d. not given

9. Solve for r: $\frac{2}{3}r = \frac{4}{5}$.

   a. $\frac{5}{6}$ b. 1
   c. $1\frac{1}{5}$ d. not given

10. Solve for c: $24c = 168$.

    a. 7   b. 144
    c. 3,032   d. not given

11. Solve for m: $\frac{m}{8} - 41 = 23$.

    a. 8   b. 64
    c. 512   d. not given

12. $28.34 \div 1{,}000$

    a. 0.02834
    b. 2.834
    c. 2,834
    d. not given

13. Andrea drove 297 mi in 5 h 24 min. At what rate did she drive?

    a. 50 mph
    b. 55 mph
    c. 60 mph
    d. not given

14. At Lily's yarn sale, Lilycot costs $1.75 per 35-g ball. Lilycot used to cost $3.25 per ball. How much would it cost to knit a sweater requiring 900 g of Lilycot?

    a. $43.75
    b. $45.50
    c. $81.25
    d. not given

You are only 50 feet below a cave entrance. The temperature is 10°C. The tunnel to your right is 6 feet wide. All the other tunnels are 2 feet wide. What is your next move? Finish writing the text for the new computer game, Spelunking Adventure. The player's goal is to find the cave exit without becoming stuck or frozen. Remember too, that cave temperatures often fall well below zero and that players may move in any direction.

7 INTEGERS, RATIONALS, REALS

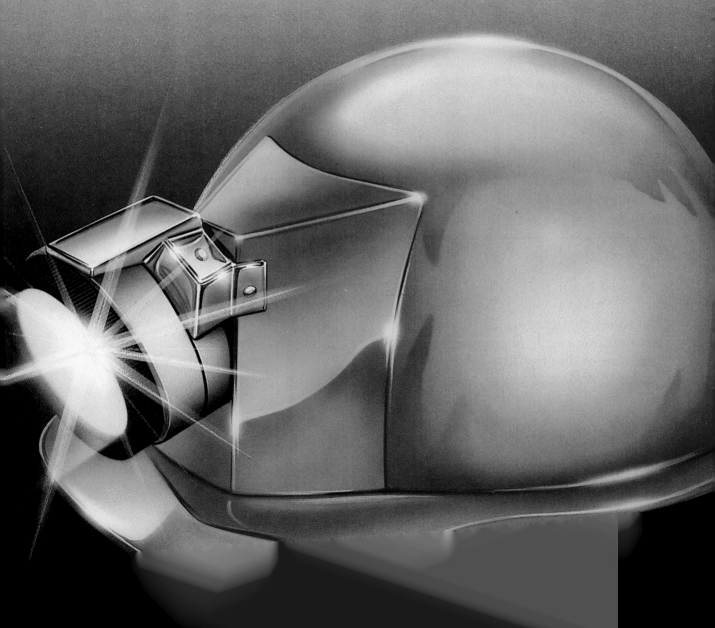

The Meaning of Integers

A. **Integers** are located at whole-number distances from zero (0) on a number line. Integers to the left of zero are **negative,** and integers to the right of zero are **positive.** Although zero is an integer, it is neither positive nor negative.

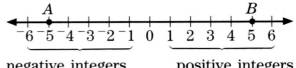

negative integers   positive integers

Point A is at negative 5 ($^-5$).
Point B is at positive 5 ($^+5$), or (5).
Positive integers are customarily written without the positive sign.

B. Each integer has an opposite that is an equal distance from zero in the opposite direction.

$^-6$ is the opposite of 6.
4 is the opposite of $^-4$.
0 is the opposite of 0.

C. An integer's **absolute value** is its distance from zero. The distance is never negative.

The absolute value of $^-5$ is 5.
Write $|^-5| = 5$.

The absolute value of 5 is 5.
Write: $|5| = 5$.

D. Integers increase in value from left to right on the number line, and decrease in value from right to left.

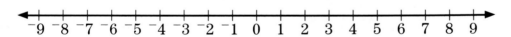

$^-8$ is to the left of $^-5$.   So, $^-8 < {}^-5$.   2 is to the right of $^-4$.   So, $2 > {}^-4$.

To order the integers 7, $^-6$, 4, 0, and $^-3$ from the least to the greatest, think of them on a number line. Write them in order from left to right.

$^-6, {}^-3, 0, 4, 7$

To order the same integers from the greatest to the least, think of the numbers from right to left.

$7, 4, 0, {}^-3, {}^-6$

Checkpoint   Write the letter of the correct answer.

1. Which of the following is *not* true?

a. $|^-3| = 3$ **b.** $|6| = {}^-6$
c. $|0| = 0$ **d.** $^-3 < 7$

2. Order $^-3$, 0, 4, and $^-7$ from the least to the greatest.

a. 0, $^-3$, 4, $^-7$ **b.** 0, 4, $^-3$, $^-7$
c. $^-3$, $^-7$, 0, 4   **d.** $^-7$, $^-3$, 0, 4

Write an integer for each point on the number line.

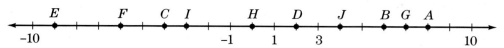

1. Point *A*   **2.** Point *B*   **3.** Point *C*   **4.** Point *D*   **5.** Point *E*

6. Point *F*   **7.** Point *G*   **8.** Point *H*   **9.** Point *I*   **10.** Point *J*

Write each phrase as an integer.

11. 80°F below zero   **12.** a gain of 23 yards

13. 7 ft below flood stage   **14.** 200 miles above sea level

Write the opposite of each integer.

15. 13   **16.** ⁻8   **17.** 25   **18.** ⁻110   **19.** ⁻76

Find the absolute value.

20. |24| **21.** |⁻7| **22.** |⁻91| **23.** |28| **24.** |⁻96|

Compare. Write >, <, or = for ●.

25. ⁻9 ● 4   **26.** ⁻7 ● ⁻5   **27.** 0 ● ⁻3   **28.** ⁻1 ● ⁻1

29. 6 ● ⁻5   **30.** 8 ● ⁻8   **31.** ⁻62 ● ⁻47   **32.** 26 ● ⁻27

Order each set of integers from the least to the greatest.

33. 4, ⁻4, ⁻7, ⁻9   **34.** 42, 0, ⁻41, ⁻1   **35.** 6, 7, 9, ⁻7, ⁻6

36. 1, ⁻2, ⁻4, ⁻6, 0   **37.** 20, ⁻21, 10, ⁻19   **38.** 0, ⁻5, 6, 9, ⁻10

Order each set of integers from the greatest to the least.

39. 21, 3, ⁻8, 0, 8   **40.** 1, 0, ⁻1, 3, 4   **41.** ⁻14, ⁻17, ⁻8, ⁻10, ⁻6

42. 11, ⁻10, 14, 7, ⁻6   **43.** 8, 14, ⁻15, 17, ⁻3   **44.** ⁻21, 16, 7, ⁻5, ⁻4

CHALLENGE

To compare the absolute value of two integers,
compare their distances from zero.

|⁻8| > |⁻5| |⁻4| < |⁻5| |⁻3| > |2|

Compare. Write >, <, or = for ●.

1. |⁻35| ● |⁻9| **2.** |42| ● |⁻42| **3.** |⁻61| ● |28| **4.** |72| ● |⁻3|

Properties of Integers

The properties for the addition and multiplication of whole numbers also apply to integers. The letters a, b, and c represent integers.

Addition Properties	Examples	For any a, b, c
Commutative Property	$3 + {}^-8 = {}^-8 + 3$	$a + b = b + a$
Associative Property	$({}^-7 + 2) + {}^-4 = {}^-7 + (2 + {}^-4)$	$(a + b) + c = a + (b + c)$
Identity Property	${}^-3 + 0 = {}^-3 \qquad 0 + {}^-8 = {}^-8$	$a + 0 = a \qquad 0 + a = a$
Opposites Property	$9 + {}^-9 = 0 \qquad {}^-6 + 6 = 0$	$a + {}^-a = 0 \qquad {}^-a + a = 0$

Multiplication Properties	Examples	For any a, b, c
Commutative Property	${}^-5 \cdot 6 = 6 \cdot {}^-5$	$a \cdot b = b \cdot a$
Associative Property	$({}^-2 \cdot 9) \cdot {}^-1 = {}^-2 \cdot (9 \cdot {}^-1)$	$(a \cdot b) \cdot c = a \cdot (b \cdot c)$
Distributive Property	${}^-6 \cdot (3 + 10) = ({}^-6 \cdot 3) + ({}^-6 \cdot 10)$	$a \cdot (b + c) = (a \cdot b) + (a \cdot c)$
Property of Zero	${}^-12 \cdot 0 = 0 \qquad 0 \cdot {}^-7 = 0$	$a \cdot 0 = 0 \qquad 0 \cdot a = 0$
Identity Property	${}^-8 \cdot 1 = {}^-8 \qquad 1 \cdot {}^-5 = {}^-5$	$a \cdot 1 = a \qquad 1 \cdot a = a$

Use the properties to find the missing integer.

1. $7 + {}^-11 = \blacksquare + 7$

2. ${}^-12 + 0 = \blacksquare$

3. ${}^-5 + (3 + {}^-10) = ({}^-5 + \blacksquare) + {}^-10$

4. ${}^-8 \cdot 0 = \blacksquare$

5. ${}^-9 \cdot (6 \cdot 5) = ({}^-9 \cdot 6) \cdot \blacksquare$

6. $13 \cdot {}^-18 = {}^-18 \cdot \blacksquare$

7. $5 + {}^-5 = \blacksquare$

8. $7 \cdot ({}^-10 + 6) = (7 \cdot \blacksquare) + (7 \cdot 6)$

9. ${}^-4 \cdot \blacksquare = {}^-20 \cdot {}^-4$

10. $(17 + \blacksquare) + {}^-1 = 17 + (8 + {}^-1)$

11. $16 \cdot ({}^-8 \cdot \blacksquare) = (16 \cdot {}^-8) \cdot 14$

12. ${}^-22 \cdot (6 + \blacksquare) = ({}^-22 \cdot 6) + ({}^-22 \cdot 5)$

13. ${}^-3 \cdot 0 = n$

14. $n \cdot 1 = {}^-12$

15. $n + 0 = {}^-32$

16. ${}^-19 + n = 10 + {}^-19$

17. $(n + 0) + 6 = {}^-4 + (0 + 6)$

18. ${}^-4 + n = 0$

Use the Commutative Property to write an equivalent expression.

19. ${}^-8 + 7$

20. $13 \cdot {}^-9$

21. ${}^-22 \cdot {}^-20$

22. $43 + {}^-81$

23. $n + 2$

24. $3 \cdot r$

25. $x + {}^-9$

26. $y \cdot {}^-8$

Use the Associative Property to write an equivalent expression.

27. $10 + ({}^-9 + {}^-15)$

28. $(38 \cdot {}^-2) \cdot {}^-3$

29. $7 \cdot (56 \cdot {}^-31)$

30. ${}^-9 + ({}^-6 + x)$

31. ${}^-8 \cdot (y \cdot {}^-4)$

32. $(16 \cdot {}^-16) \cdot {}^-r$

Use the Distributive Property to write an equivalent expression.

33. $5 \cdot ({}^-8 + 10)$

34. $(6 \cdot y) + (6 \cdot x)$

35. $({}^-8 \cdot 21) + ({}^-8 \cdot 5)$

36. $x \cdot (6 + 4)$

★37. $({}^-37 + 3) \cdot {}^-16$

★38. $({}^-8 + 8) \cdot y$

CALCULATOR

To find the prime factorization of a number on a calculator, divide by the lowest prime number (2, 3, 5, 7, 11, ...) until you get a whole number. Continue to divide each resulting quotient by the least prime number that gives a whole number as an answer. $40 \div 2 \rightarrow 20 \div 2 \rightarrow 10 \div 2 \rightarrow 5$ So $40 = 2^3 \cdot 5$. Use a calculator to find the prime factorization.

1. 24

2. 100

3. 525

4. 1,617

Adding Integers

A. The entrance to a cave is 20 m below the surface. The main chamber's floor is 30 m below the entrance. Write an integer for the location of the main chamber's floor. To find the location of the main chamber's floor, use a number line and start at 0. Add $^-20 + {}^-30$.

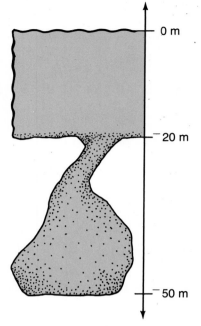

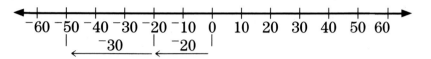

Begin at 0, and move left to 20. From there, move left 30 more.

The main chamber's floor is 50 m below the surface. This is written as $^-50$.

B. **If two integers have the same sign, add their absolute values, and use the sign of the addends.**

$$20 + 30 \rightarrow |20| + |30| \rightarrow 50 \qquad {}^-20 + {}^-30 \rightarrow |20| + |30| \rightarrow {}^-50$$

C. You can also add integers with unlike signs.

Add $6 + {}^-5$.

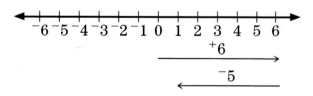

Begin at 0, and move right to 6. From there, move 5 to the left.

$$6 + {}^-5 = 1$$

Add $^-6 + 5$.

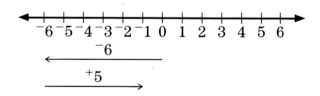

Begin at 0, and move left to $^-6$. From there, move 5 to the right.

$$^-6 + 5 = {}^-1$$

To find the sum of two integers that have different signs, subtract their absolute values. Then use the sign of the addend that has the greater absolute value.

$$6 + {}^-5 \rightarrow |6| - |{}^-5| \rightarrow 1$$
$$^-6 + 5 \rightarrow |{}^-6| - |5| \rightarrow {}^-1$$

Add. Use the number line.

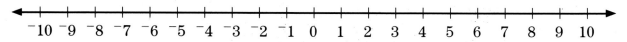

1. 3 + 2
2. ⁻4 + ⁻3
3. ⁻5 + 2
4. 3 + ⁻1
5. (⁻4 + 2) + ⁻1
6. (⁻2 + ⁻3) + ⁻4
7. (6 + ⁻1) + ⁻2
8. (⁻3 + ⁻2) + 0

Add.

9. 7 + 4
10. ⁻3 + ⁻6
11. ⁻10 + ⁻21
12. 18 + 32
13. 12 + ⁻8
14. 6 + ⁻2
15. ⁻7 + 18
16. 18 + ⁻7
17. ⁻10 + 8
18. 25 + ⁻30
19. 81 + ⁻72
20. ⁻72 + 81
21. ⁻7 + 9
22. ⁻46 + ⁻1
23. 12 + ⁻12
24. 62 + ⁻80
25. 3 + ⁻114
26. ⁻7 + 8
27. ⁻356 + ⁻85
28. ⁻211 + 437
29. ⁻2 + (⁻6 + ⁻8)
30. (⁻2 + ⁻6) + ⁻8
31. (⁻9 + ⁻22) + 0
32. 14 + (⁻3 + 6)
33. (28 + 30) + ⁻18
34. 28 + (30 + ⁻18)
35. (⁻10 + ⁻10) + 25
36. 47 + (⁻130 + ⁻2)
37. (⁻45 + 8) + ⁻23
38. ⁻611 + (89 + 12)
39. (⁻611 + 89) + 12
40. (338 + 109) + ⁻447

Solve. For Problem 42, use the Infobank.

41. The depth of the deepest point in the Atlantic Ocean is 30,246 ft below sea level. The deepest point in the Pacific Ocean is 5,052 ft lower. What is the depth of the deepest point in the Pacific Ocean?

42. Use the information on page 476 to solve. Find the span of years between the founding of Geneva and the founding of Madrid.

NUMBER SENSE

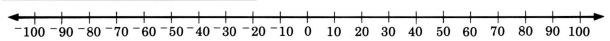

Solve.

1. Start at 0. Add 30. Subtract 40. Add 10. Subtract 50.

2. Start at 0. Subtract 50. Add 20. Subtract 40. Add 70. Add 20.

3. Start at ⁻20. Subtract 30. Add 60. Add 20. Subtract 80. Add 100.

Subtracting Integers

A scientist stationed at the McMurdo research station in Antarctica recorded a temperature drop of 4°F between morning and evening. The temperature in the morning was ⁻28°F. What was the temperature after the drop?

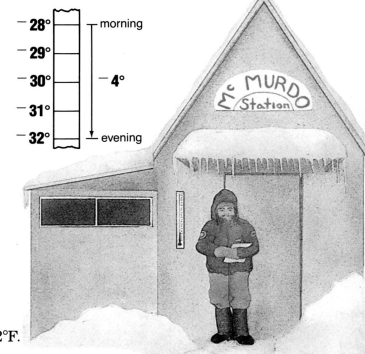

To find the temperature at McMurdo, subtract.

Refer to the picture of the thermometer. ⁻28 − 4 = ⁻32

Another way to subtract an integer is to add its opposite.

⁻28 − 4
⁻28 + ⁻4 = ⁻32

The temperature after the drop was ⁻32°F.

Other examples:

Subtract.

⁻7 − ⁻6	10 − 12	25 − ⁻14
↓ ↓	↓ ↓	↓ ↓
⁻7 + 6 = ⁻1	10 + ⁻12 = ⁻2	25 + 14 = 39
⁻7 − ⁻6 = ⁻1	10 − 12 = ⁻2	25 − ⁻14 = 39

Checkpoint Write the letter of the correct answer.

Subtract.

1. ⁻5 − 2   **a.** ⁻10   **b.** ⁻7   **c.** ⁻3   **d.** 3

2. 9 − ⁻4   **a.** ⁻13   **b.** ⁻5   **c.** 5   **d.** 13

3. ⁻11 − ⁻2   **a.** ⁻14   **b.** ⁻9   **c.** 9   **d.** 13

4. 4 − 14   **a.** ⁻18   **b.** ⁻10   **c.** ⁻4   **d.** 18

Rewrite each using addition.

1. $^-5 - 6$ **2.** $9 - {^-4}$ **3.** $7 - 9$ **4.** $^-4 - {^-6}$

5. $14 - 20$ **6.** $^-10 - 30$ **7.** $^-11 - {^-2}$ **8.** $8 - {^-9}$

Subtract.

9. $^-9 - 7$ **10.** $^-6 - 2$ **11.** $^-12 - 18$ **12.** $18 - {^-12}$

13. $14 - {^-3}$ **14.** $7 - {^-8}$ **15.** $21 - {^-1}$ **16.** $4 - {^-10}$

17. $^-5 - {^-4}$ **18.** $^-11 - {^-6}$ **19.** $^-8 - {^-5}$ **20.** $8 - 5$

21. $^-17 - {^-19}$ **22.** $^-6 - {^-3}$ **23.** $^-56 - {^-61}$ **24.** $^-18 - {^-18}$

25. $7 - 41$ **26.** $15 - 20$ **27.** $38 - 167$ **28.** $49 - 50$

29. $12 - {^-8}$ **30.** $^-37 - 40$ **31.** $37 - {^-40}$ **32.** $8 - {^-111}$

33. $63 - 78$ **34.** $^-301 - {^-28}$ **35.** $538 - 746$ **36.** $^-80 - {^-80}$

Compute. Perform operations within parentheses first.

37. $^-7 + (6 + 8)$ **38.** $3 - ({^-4} + 2)$ **39.** $^-12 - ({^-6} + {^-9})$

40. $({^-18} - 4) + {^-7}$ **41.** $^-36 - (4 + {^-8})$ **42.** $101 + ({^-7} - {^-7})$

43. $({^-36} - 31) + 18$ **44.** $({^-146} - 52) + {^-27}$ **45.** $^-87 + ({^-87} - 0)$

Solve.

46. The average temperature in Antarctica is $^-60°F$. In the winter, the temperature can drop another 60°. What would this temperature be?

47. If the temperature is $^-46°C$ in the morning at an Antarctic research center, how many degrees must the temperature rise to reach 0°C?

48. In Chicago the high for a day was 7°F and the low was $^-4°F$. What was the difference between the two temperatures?

49. In Fargo, North Dakota, the high for a day was $^-5°F$ and the low was $^-17°F$. What was the difference between the two temperatures?

PROBLEM SOLVING
Using Graphs

The broken-line graph below shows variations in the average monthly temperature in Fairbanks, Alaska.

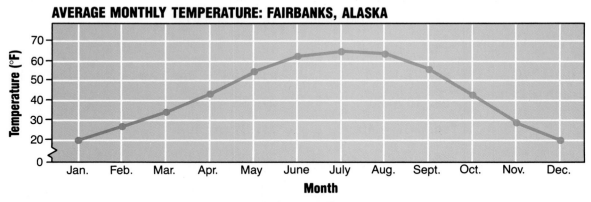

AVERAGE MONTHLY TEMPERATURE: FAIRBANKS, ALASKA

- The title describes the purpose of the graph.

- The scale along the vertical axis shows the temperature in degrees Fahrenheit. The temperature did not go below 20°F, and so, the graph shows a break in the scale between 20°F and 0°F.

- The labels along the horizontal axis show the months.

- Each point on the graph shows the average temperature for the month. Lines between the points make the graph easy to read.

The bar graph below shows the average monthly temperature in Juneau, Alaska.

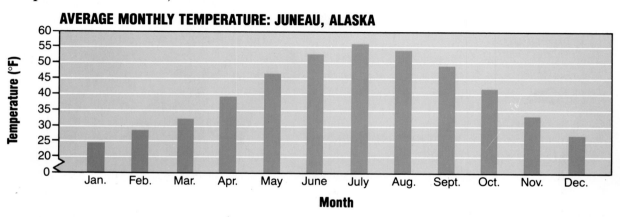

AVERAGE MONTHLY TEMPERATURE: JUNEAU, ALASKA

Can you use the broken-line graph or the bar graph to
answer each question? Write either *yes* or *no*.

1. What is the lowest average
temperature in Fairbanks?

2. What was the temperature in
Fairbanks on August 5?

3. What is the hottest month in
Juneau?

4. What was the temperature on the
coldest day on record in
Barrow?

Use the broken-line graph to answer each question.

5. Between which months does the
average temperature in Fairbanks
increase?

6. Between which months does the
average temperature in Fairbanks
decrease?

7. Between which months does the
average temperature not vary by
more than 5 degrees?

8. Which average temperature change
was greater, September to October
or October to November?

Use the bar graph to answer each question.

9. Between which months does the
average temperature in Juneau
increase?

10. Between which months does the
average temperature in Juneau
decrease?

11. What is the difference in degrees
between the highest and the lowest
average temperatures in
Juneau?

12. Which is the hottest month in
Juneau?

Use the broken-line graph and the bar graph to answer
each question.

13. Which city has the highest average
temperature? During which month?

14. Which city has the lowest average
temperature? During which months?

15. Which city has the greatest
temperature increase between two
months; between which months
and how many degrees of
difference?

16. Which city has the least
temperature difference between
two months; which months and
how many degrees of difference?

Classwork/Homework, page H100

Multiplying Integers

Dominick uses his video camera to record the actions of his remarkable pet turtle.

When the turtle moves forward and Dominick plays the video tape in reverse, what action appears on the screen? When the turtle moves backward, how does it appear on the screen if the tape is played normally? What would happen if the turtle were backing up and Dominick played the tape in reverse?

How does the remarkable turtle provide a model for finding the sign when you multiply integers?

The following patterns suggest the rules that you might have discovered above.

Do you see a pattern developing in the right-hand column? Copy and complete the table.

$$3 \times 3 = 9$$
$$3 \times 2 = 6$$
$$3 \times 1 = 3$$
$$3 \times 0 = 0$$

How does the pattern suggest a general rule for multiplying a positive number by a negative number?

$$3 \times {}^-1 = \blacksquare$$
$$3 \times {}^-2 = \blacksquare$$
$$3 \times {}^-3 = \blacksquare$$

Do you recall why it is true that $3 \times {}^-3$ equals ${}^-3 \times 3$?

Copy and complete this table. Do you see a pattern in the right-hand column?

$${}^-3 \times 3 = {}^-9$$
$${}^-3 \times 2 = {}^-6$$
$${}^-3 \times 1 = {}^-3$$
$${}^-3 \times 0 = 0$$

How does this pattern suggest a general rule for finding the product of two negative numbers?

$${}^-3 \times {}^-1 = \blacksquare$$
$${}^-3 \times {}^-2 = \blacksquare$$
$${}^-3 \times {}^-3 = \blacksquare$$

Thinking as a Team

Copy and complete the table shown below, using what you have learned about determining the sign of the product of two integers.

Discuss with your group how you determine the sign. Discuss ways to remember the rules for the sign of a product.

Sign of first number	Sign of second number	Sign of product
positive	positive	■
positive	negative	■
negative	positive	■
negative	negative	■

1. What happens when more than two integers are multiplied?

   Is $^-2 \times {}^-3 \times 4$ positive or negative?

   What about $^-2 \times {}^-3 \times {}^-4$?

   What about $^-2 \times {}^-3 \times {}^-4 \times {}^-5$?

   Discuss with your group the methods you used to find these products?

2. Describe the patterns for the products when more than two negative integers are multiplied.

3. On a local quiz show a player gets 10 points (+10) for each correct answer and loses 5 points ($^-5$) for each incorrect answer. After eight answers, the player has earned the following number of points:

   $$10 + 10 + {}^-5 + 10 + {}^-5 + {}^-5 + {}^-5 + 10$$

   Describe several different ways to find the player's score.

4. Mr. Cyan told his children, "Be careful, that chemical is not nonpoisonous!" How could Mr. Cyan have warned his children by using a simpler phrase?

Dividing Integers

Just as multiplication and division of whole numbers are related, so are multiplication and division of integers. With that in mind, try these multiplication and division exercises mentally. Use multiplication to check the division results.

$$7 \times 5 = \blacksquare \qquad 35 \div 7 = \blacksquare$$
$$^-7 \times 5 = \blacksquare \qquad ^-35 \div ^-7 = \blacksquare$$
$$7 \times ^-5 = \blacksquare \qquad ^-35 \div 7 = \blacksquare$$
$$^-7 \times ^-5 = \blacksquare \qquad 35 \div ^-7 = \blacksquare$$

Did you get the correct sign in each case? Which answers are negative? Which are positive?

1. What is the relationship between multiplication of integers and division of integers? Use what you have learned about multiplication of integers to write a set of rules for the division of integers. When is the quotient positive? When is the quotient negative?

2. Can you use a calculator to divide integers? Not all calculators accept data in the same way. To divide 35 by ⁻7 on many calculators, you could do this:

   $$\boxed{3} \; \boxed{5} \; \boxed{\div} \; \boxed{7} \; \boxed{^+\!/\!_-} \; \boxed{=}$$

   Does your calculator work this way? What display results? Do any calculators in your group work differently?

3. You use the same order of operations to simplify expressions that contain integers as you use to simplify expressions that contain whole numbers. Simplify the following expressions.

   $$^-75 \div (^-5 - 10)$$
   $$200 \div (^-25 \div 10)$$
   $$[18 \div (^-2)] \div [3 \times (^-3)]$$

You are writing a social studies report on the companies that have opened in your city during the last year. In the newspaper you read the total sales and the total costs of each company for different periods of time. To find the company's profit or loss, you can subtract total costs from total sales. If the number is positive, then it is a profit. If the number is negative, then it is a loss.

Copy the table. Use positive and negative integers to represent the missing figures.

Company	Time Period	Total Sales	Total Costs	Profit or Loss	Yearly Profit or Loss	Monthly Profit or Loss
Perelli Plastics	3 mos.	80,000	89,000	⁻9,000	▪	▪
Smith Foundry	6 mos.	158,000	140,000	▪	▪	▪
Dirks Tires	4 mos.	56,000	64,000	▪	▪	▪
Kraus Metal Co.	2 mos.	24,000	20,000	▪	▪	▪
A-1 Advertising	3 mos.	19,000	17,600	▪	▪	▪
Diamax Inc.	8 mos.	132,000	136,000	▪	▪	▪

Thinking as a Team

Review how you found the yearly and monthly figures for each company.

- Are the yearly and monthly figures exact? What does the yearly figure for each company mean? Do you think that the yearly and monthly figures are more accurate for some companies than for others? Discuss your answers and reasoning with the other teams in your class.

Integers as Exponents

A. You can use integers as exponents. Study the pattern.

$$10^1 = 10$$
$$10^0 = 1$$
$$10^{-1} = \frac{1}{10}$$
$$10^{-2} = \frac{1}{10^2} = \frac{1}{10 \cdot 10} = \frac{1}{100}$$

Other examples:

$$5^{-1} = \frac{1}{5}$$
$$3^{-2} = \frac{1}{3^2} = \frac{1}{3 \cdot 3} = \frac{1}{9}$$
$$10^{-3} = \frac{1}{10^3} = \frac{1}{10 \cdot 10 \cdot 10} = \frac{1}{1,000}$$

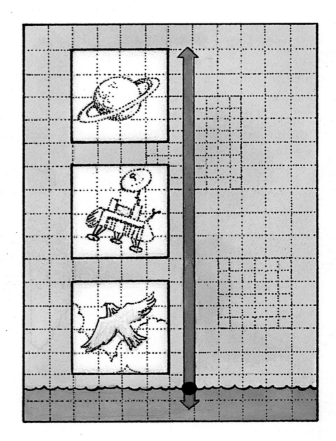

B. A very large number can be written in **scientific notation** by writing the number as a product of two factors. One factor is between 1 and 10. The other factor is a power of 10.

$$42,500 = 4.25 \cdot 10,000$$

So, $42,500 = 4.25 \cdot 10^4$.

C. Numbers less than 1 can be written in scientific notation by using a negative power of 10. To write $3.76 \cdot 10^{-4}$ in standard form, move the decimal point four places to the left.

$$3.76 \cdot 10^{-4} = 0\ 0\ 0\ 0\ 3.7\ 6$$

So, $3.76 \cdot 10^{-4} = 0.000376$.

D. Simplify $4^2 \cdot 4^3$.

$$4^2 \cdot 4^3 = (4 \cdot 4) \cdot (4 \cdot 4 \cdot 4) = 4^5 = 1,024$$

You can also multiply powers with the same base by addng the exponents.

$$4^2 \cdot 4^3 = 4^{(2 + 3)} = 4^5$$

Another example:

$$3^4 \cdot 3^{-5} = 3^{(4 + {}^-5)} = 3^{-1}$$

E. Simplify $6^4 \div 6^2$.

$$6^4 \div 6^2 = \frac{6 \cdot 6 \cdot 6 \cdot 6}{6 \cdot 6} = 6 \cdot 6 = 6^2 = 36$$

You can also divide powers with the same base by subtracting the exponents.

$$6^4 \div 6^2 = 6^{(4 - 2)} = 6^2$$

Another example:

$$8^{-2} \div 8^{-5} = 8^{({}^-2 - {}^-5)} = 8^3$$

Write as fractions with positive exponents.

1. 2^{-2} **2.** 4^{-3} **3.** 8^{-6} **4.** 14^{-5}

5. 21^{-8} **6.** 30^{-10} **7.** 142^{-14} **8.** 1^{-20}

Write in scientific notation.

9. 0.143 **10.** 0.089 **11.** 0.0406 **12.** 0.000461

13. 0.000092 **14.** 0.000723 **15.** 0.00846 **16.** 0.000452

Write in standard form.

17. $2.5 \cdot 10^{-2}$ **18.** $3.78 \cdot 10^{-4}$ **19.** $1.6 \cdot 10^{-6}$ **20.** $7.219 \cdot 10^{-5}$

21. $3.84 \cdot 10^{-8}$ **22.** $9.92 \cdot 10^{-9}$ **23.** $4.32 \cdot 10^{-3}$ **24.** $5.702 \cdot 10^{-7}$

Simplify.

25. $2^{-2} \cdot 2^{-4}$ **26.** $5^{-1} \cdot 5^{-5}$

27. $8^{-9} \cdot 8^{-2}$ **28.** $12^2 \cdot 12^{-2}$

29. $7^{-6} \cdot 7^4$ **30.** $16^{-8} \cdot 16^{-8}$

31. $10^{-6} \cdot 10^5$ **32.** $22^{-10} \cdot 22^{-3}$

33. $6^{-4} \div 6^{-2}$ **34.** $9^{-6} \div 9^{-5}$

35. $7^{-1} \div 7^{-1}$ **36.** $5^{-4} \div 5^0$

37. $\dfrac{8^{-2}}{8^{-5}}$ **38.** $\dfrac{13^{-6}}{13^{-10}}$

39. $\dfrac{21^{-6}}{21^4}$ **40.** $\dfrac{36^8}{36^{-7}}$

For additional activities, see
Connecting Math Ideas on page 471.

MIDCHAPTER REVIEW

Compute.

1. $^-6 + 3 + {}^-9$ **2.** $^-63 + 19 + {}^-7$ **3.** $^-6 + {}^-3 + {}^-4$ **4.** $6 + {}^-13 + {}^-7$

5. $49 - 63$ **6.** $^-4 - {}^-4$ **7.** $8 - {}^-11$ **8.** $^-7 - 8$

9. $2 \cdot {}^-3$ **10.** $^-12 \cdot {}^-2$ **11.** $1 \cdot {}^-1$ **12.** $^-13 \cdot 7$

13. $\dfrac{32}{-8}$ **14.** $^-40 \div {}^-2$ **15.** $\dfrac{^-25}{-5}$ **16.** $^-144 \div 12$

Simplify.

17. $6^{-2} \cdot 6^{-3}$ **18.** $10^{-3} \cdot 10^{13}$ **19.** $23^{-4} \div 23^0$ **20.** $7^{-4} \div 7^{-2}$

PROBLEM SOLVING
Choosing a Strategy or Method

Write the strategy or method you choose. Then solve.

Estimation
Using a Graph
Choosing the Operation
Solving Multi-step Problems
Checking for a Reasonable Answer
Writing an Equation
Interpreting the Quotient and the Remainder
Using a Formula
Using a Road Map
Making an Organized List

1. For 9 years, an automobile maker produced an average of 3,425,600 cars per year. In the tenth year, the company made 2,747,500 cars. What was the average production rate for 10 years?

2. From 1984 through 1989, Artie grew an average of $173\frac{1}{2}$ bushels of tomatoes per year. In 1990, he grew $185\frac{3}{4}$ bushels. What was the average number of bushels grown through 1990?

3. A hardware store sells solder in 25-foot rolls. Jerry needs 137 feet of solder. How many rolls does he need to buy?

4. A magazine distributor packs magazines in bundles of 50. How many bundles can be made from 35,700 magazines?

5. In 1987, the most money spent by a single advertiser was $1,557,800,000. Of this, 21% was spent on network TV. How much money did this advertiser spend on network TV?

6. How much of the total amount spent on advertising in Exercise 5 was not spent on network TV?

7. Last month, Robbie used the rowing machine $7\frac{1}{2}$ hours more than his father did. Robbie used the rowing machine for $35\frac{3}{4}$ hours. For how many hours did his father use the machine?

8. Carl made 6 equal payments on a new pair of ice skates. Each payment was $18.42. What was the total cost of the skates?

9. Susan has saved $150.00 to have 2 new tires put on her car. The tires cost $52.50 each, and the labor costs $18.50. Balancing costs $11.75. Does Susan have enough money to pay for everything?

10. On Wednesday, 22 students visited a museum and paid a total of $116.60 for admission. They all paid the same amount. About how much was the admission per student?

Solve if possible. Identify any needed information.

11. On their vacation, Marie and her family went from Portland, Maine, to Cleveland, Ohio. They spent $535.00. What were their average daily expenses?

12. Chris and Anita began to hike at 7:35 one morning. They hiked for $2\frac{1}{2}$ hours, stopped for 20 minutes, and hiked again for $1\frac{3}{4}$ hours. What time was it then?

Choose a strategy or method and solve.

13. A man on a unicycle set a record by traveling 100 miles in about $7\frac{3}{4}$ hours. What was his average rate of speed for the distance, rounded to the nearest mile per hour?

14. A team of cyclists rode at an average speed of 21 miles per hour for 2 hours 36 minutes. How far did they ride?

15. Dave's father bought a stereo for $857.50. He paid $90 down and arranged to finance the rest for one year at 19%. How much did he pay for the stereo?

16. Antonia paid $420.75 in interest on a loan of $1,700 for a period of 18 months. What was the rate of interest on the loan?

17. Use the map at the right. What major route would you take from Macon to Atlanta, and how far would you travel?

18. Use the map at the right. Driving at an average speed of 48 miles per hour, how long would it take to go from Chattanooga, Tennessee, to Atlanta, Georgia?

19. Look back at the problems you have solved. Which of these problems seemed difficult? What strategy or method did you use? Is there more than one way to solve these problems? Share ideas with your classmates.

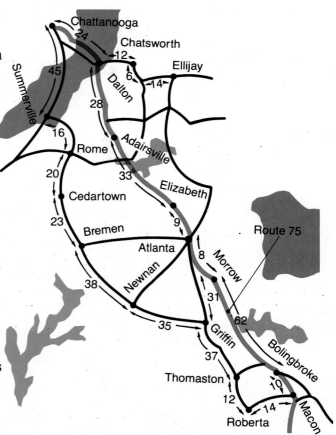

Rational Numbers

A. A **rational number** is a number that can be written as a ratio of two integers, where the denominator is not zero. Integers, fractions, and mixed numbers are rational numbers.

$^-3 = \frac{^-3}{1}$ So, $^-3$ is rational.

$^-1\frac{3}{5} = \frac{^-8}{5}$ So, $^-1\frac{3}{5}$ is rational.

$0.75 = \frac{3}{4}$ So, 0.75 is rational.

$0.\overline{3} = \frac{1}{3}$ So, $0.\overline{3}$ is rational.

Every rational number can be named by a terminating or a repeating decimal. A number such as 0.010010001 . . . is nonterminating and nonrepeating. 0.010010001 . . . represents a number that is not rational.

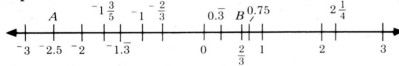

Point A is the rational number $^-2\frac{1}{2}$, or $^-2.5$.
Point B is the rational number $\frac{2}{3}$.
$^-\frac{2}{3}$ and $\frac{2}{3}$ are opposites. $^-2.5$ and 2.5 are opposites.

B. To compare two rational numbers, compare as you would compare integers. The number to the right on a number line is greater. The number to the left on the number line is less.

$$^-3 < {}^-1.\overline{3} \qquad 2\frac{1}{4} > {}^-\frac{2}{3}$$

To order the rational numbers 0.75, 0, $^-1\frac{3}{5}$, $^-\frac{2}{3}$, and $\frac{2}{3}$ from the least to the greatest, think of the number line from the left to the right.

$$^-1\frac{3}{5},\ {}^-\frac{2}{3},\ 0,\ \frac{2}{3},\ 0.75$$

To order the same rational numbers from the greatest to the least, think of the number line from the right to the left.

$$0.75,\ \frac{2}{3},\ 0,\ {}^-\frac{2}{3},\ {}^-1\frac{3}{5}$$

Write the rational number for each point.

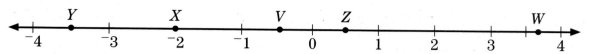

1. Point V **2.** Point W **3.** Point X **4.** Point Y **5.** Point Z

Write the opposite of the rational number.

6. $^-4\frac{1}{2}$ **7.** 28 **8.** $^-0.95$ **9.** $\frac{8}{15}$ **10.** $2\frac{4}{5}$

Compare. Use $>$, $<$, or $=$ for ●.

11. $\frac{1}{2}$ ● $\frac{1}{4}$ **12.** $^-6$ ● $^-\frac{2}{3}$ **13.** $\frac{4}{5}$ ● $^-\frac{3}{8}$ **14.** 2 ● $\frac{2}{1}$

15. $^-1.4$ ● $^-\frac{3}{5}$ **16.** $1\frac{1}{2}$ ● $\frac{4}{9}$ **17.** $6\frac{1}{4}$ ● 6.25 **18.** $^-\frac{3}{2}$ ● $^-\frac{15}{10}$

19. $\frac{4}{7}$ ● $0.\overline{5}$ **20.** 9.6 ● $8\frac{3}{8}$ **21.** $^-5$ ● $^-\frac{1}{5}$ **22.** $1\frac{1}{8}$ ● $1.\overline{1}$

23. 4 ● $\frac{24}{6}$ **24.** 37.5 ● $37\frac{1}{2}$ **25.** $8\frac{1}{8}$ ● $^-8$ **26.** $^-6.\overline{3}$ ● $^-6\frac{1}{3}$

Order from the greatest to the least.

27. $^-\frac{3}{2}$, 2, 0.2

28. $1\frac{1}{8}$, $1.\overline{3}$, $^-0.6$

29. $^-4$, $^-\frac{4}{2}$, $^-1\frac{3}{8}$, 4.7

30. $\frac{3}{7}$, $2\frac{1}{7}$, $^-6.\overline{3}$, $^-2\frac{1}{7}$

Order from the least to the greatest.

31. $^-2.4$, $^-\frac{9}{2}$, $^-3$

32. $1\frac{5}{7}$, $\frac{13}{7}$, $1.\overline{5}$

33. $^-3\frac{1}{2}$, $^-3.\overline{5}$, $\frac{7}{8}$, 4

34. $^-1\frac{1}{5}$, $\frac{7}{9}$, $1.\overline{4}$, 2.0

CHALLENGE

Between any two different rational numbers there is an infinite number of rational numbers. For example, between 2.7 and 2.8 there are 2.75, 2.76, 2.763, 2.764, and so on.

Name four rational numbers between each pair of rational numbers.

1. $^-1.35$, $^-1.34$ **2.** $\frac{2}{3}$, $\frac{3}{4}$ **3.** $1\frac{1}{3}$, 1.4

Adding and Subtracting Rational Numbers

A. The deepest part of the Pacific Ocean was measured to be 6.77 mi below sea level in 1951. Eight years later, the deepest part was measured to be 0.08 mi lower. What was the new lowest depth?

To add and subtract rational numbers, combine the rules for adding and subtracting integers and fractions.

To add two rational numbers that have the same signs, add their absolute values and use the sign of the addends.

Add $^-6.77 + {^-0.08}$.

$^-6.77 + {^-0.08} = |^-6.77| + |^-0.08| = {^-6.85}$

The new lowest depth is 6.85 mi.

Other examples:

Add $\frac{3}{4} + \frac{1}{2}$.

$$\frac{3}{4} + \frac{1}{2} = \left|\frac{3}{4}\right| + \left|\frac{2}{4}\right| = \frac{3+2}{4} = 1\frac{1}{4}$$

Add $^-\frac{3}{4} + {^-\frac{1}{2}}$.

$$^-\frac{3}{4} + {^-\frac{1}{2}} = {^-\left(\frac{3}{4} + \frac{2}{4}\right)} = {^-\left(\frac{3+2}{4}\right)} = {^-1\frac{1}{4}}$$

To add two rational numbers that have different signs, find the difference between their absolute values, and use the sign of the addend that has the greater absolute value.

Add $^-\frac{3}{7} + \frac{1}{3}$.

$$^-\frac{3}{7} + \frac{1}{3} = {^-\left(\frac{9}{21} - \frac{7}{21}\right)} = {^-\left(\frac{9-7}{21}\right)} = {^-\frac{2}{21}}$$

Add $0.32 + {^-0.4}$.

$$0.32 + {^-0.4} = {^-(0.40 - 0.32)}$$
$$= {^-0.08}$$

B. To subtract a rational number, add its opposite.

Subtract $^-\frac{4}{5} - \frac{2}{5}$.

$$^-\frac{4}{5} - \frac{2}{5} = {^-\frac{4}{5}} + {^-\frac{2}{5}} = \frac{^-4 + {^-2}}{5}$$
$$= {^-\frac{6}{5}} = {^-1\frac{1}{5}}$$

Subtract $\frac{7}{8} - {^-\frac{5}{8}}$.

$$\frac{7}{8} - {^-\frac{5}{8}} = \frac{7}{8} + \frac{5}{8} = \frac{12}{8} = 1\frac{4}{8} = 1\frac{1}{2}$$

Subtract $^-12.5 - 10.4$.

$$^-12.5 - 10.4 = {^-12.5} + {^-10.4}$$
$$= {^-22.9}$$

Subtract $^-2.26 - {^-4.31}$.

$$^-2.26 - {^-4.31} = {^-2.26} + 4.31 = 2.05$$

Add. Simplify when necessary.

1. $\frac{2}{3} + {}^-\frac{1}{3}$
2. ${}^-\frac{3}{4} + \frac{3}{4}$
3. ${}^-\frac{1}{6} + {}^-\frac{5}{6}$
4. ${}^-\frac{4}{5} + {}^-\frac{3}{5}$

5. $\frac{7}{8} + {}^-\frac{5}{8}$
6. $\frac{3}{4} + {}^-\frac{7}{8}$
7. ${}^-\frac{2}{5} + {}^-\frac{3}{10}$
8. ${}^-\frac{5}{7} + {}^-\frac{3}{14}$

9. $\frac{4}{27} + {}^-\frac{1}{9}$
10. ${}^-\frac{1}{5} + \frac{2}{7}$
11. ${}^-\frac{3}{8} + 2$
12. ${}^-4 + {}^-\frac{4}{15}$

13. $0.4 + {}^-0.7$
14. ${}^-2.1 + {}^-3.5$
15. ${}^-6.21 + {}^-4.13$

16. ${}^-7.24 + 2.18$
17. ${}^-2.4 + 3.12$
18. $0.3 + {}^-3.12$

19. ${}^-2.86 + {}^-2$
20. $1.76 + {}^-0.06$
21. ${}^-4 + {}^-0.04$

Subtract. Simplify when necessary.

22. ${}^-\frac{3}{8} - \frac{1}{8}$
23. ${}^-\frac{7}{16} - {}^-\frac{5}{16}$
24. $\frac{2}{5} - \frac{3}{5}$
25. $\frac{4}{7} - {}^-\frac{6}{7}$

26. ${}^-\frac{9}{10} - {}^-\frac{3}{10}$
27. ${}^-\frac{4}{7} - \frac{3}{14}$
28. ${}^-\frac{8}{15} - \frac{3}{5}$
29. ${}^-\frac{3}{4} - {}^-\frac{7}{8}$

30. ${}^-\frac{5}{9} - \frac{5}{18}$
31. $\frac{2}{3} - {}^-\frac{1}{2}$
32. $3 - {}^-\frac{4}{5}$
33. ${}^-\frac{1}{9} - {}^-2$

34. $1.2 - {}^-0.7$
35. ${}^-3.6 - {}^-2.1$
36. ${}^-4.52 - 0.76$

37. ${}^-5.35 - {}^-5.35$
38. $0.67 - {}^-1.2$
39. $3.82 - {}^-2.34$

40. ${}^-7.6 - 0.05$
41. ${}^-12.4 - {}^-14.57$
42. ${}^-0.22 - 1.02$

Solve.

43. The brightness of stars is called their *visual magnitude*. Sirius has a magnitude of ${}^-1.58$. Alpha Centauri has a magnitude 1.64 greater than Sirius. What is the magnitude of Alpha Centauri?

44. The brightest star in the Leo constellation has a visual magnitude of 1.36. The star Canopus has a visual magnitude of ${}^-0.86$. What is the difference between their visual magnitudes?

NUMBER SENSE

Write the reciprocal.

1. ${}^-\frac{1}{2}$
2. $\frac{4}{5}$
3. ${}^-\frac{7}{8}$
4. ${}^-2$
5. $1\frac{3}{4}$

6. ${}^-2\frac{5}{7}$
7. $4\frac{3}{4}$
8. ${}^-2\frac{1}{3}$
9. ${}^-1\frac{5}{6}$
10. $1\frac{7}{8}$

PROBLEM SOLVING
Checking That the Solution Answers the Question

Some problems call for answers that are not just numbers with labels. Pay special attention to the question that is asked in a problem. Be sure that your answer actually answers the question.

> Deepstar-4000, a minisub used for undersea exploration, can reach a maximum depth of 4,000 ft. During one trip, it descended to a depth of 2,200 ft; then it descended another 650 ft. Did it descend to within 100 ft of its maximum depth?

Which is the correct answer?

a. 2,850 ft
b. 1,150 ft
c. No, it did not descend to within 100 ft of its maximum depth.

$$
\begin{array}{r}
2,200 \\
+ \quad 650 \\
\hline
2,850
\end{array}
\qquad
\begin{array}{r}
4,000 \\
- \quad 100 \\
\hline
3,900
\end{array}
$$

$2,850 < 3,900$

> The number of feet to which the minisub must descend if it is to be within 100 feet of its maximum depth

The correct answer is c. The problem does not ask for a numerical solution; it asks a question that can only be answered with a yes or no.

On another trip, Deepstar-4000 descended to a depth of 3,200 ft; then it descended another 250 ft. How far did it descend in all?

Which is the correct answer?
a. 3,450 ft
b. No, it did not descend to within 100 ft of its maximum depth.
c. 2,950 ft

The correct answer is a. This time, the problem requires a numerical solution. It is a matter of simple addition.

Which statement answers the question? Write the letter of the correct answer.

1. A chart used by a scientist has a scale from 0 to $^-325$ ft. Every $^-25$ ft, there is a special mark on the scale. Are there more than 15 special marks on the scale?

a. Yes, there are more than 15 special marks.

b. No, there are fewer than 15 special marks.

c. 13 special marks

2. The maximum depth of a minisub is 3,945 ft. A trip calls for the minisub to descend first to a depth of 1,945 ft and then to descend another 1,890 ft. Will the sub descend to within 200 ft of its maximum depth?

a. 3,835 ft   **b.** 110 ft

c. Yes, it will descend to within 200 ft of its maximum depth.

Solve.

3. The minisub's marine biologist arranged 3 microscopic sea creatures by size, from the largest to the smallest. The creatures were labeled as follows:
 a. 1.75×10^{-5} meters
 b. 0.95×10^{-6}
 c. 1.21×10^{-4}.
Was the order **c, b, a**?

4. A minisub touched the ocean bottom in one spot at 3,450 ft. Its mechanical arm reached out and dug $\frac{1}{8}$ ft into the ocean floor. Then the arm probed 4 times deeper. Was the depth of the last probe greater or less than 3,460 ft from sea level?

5. An explorer minisub descends in stages of 400 ft at a time. The descent takes 8 min per stage. After 32 min, is the sub above or below 1,800 ft?

6. A minisub was transported on a truck that drove 8.4 kilometers in 24 minutes. What was the rate of speed of the truck in kilometers per hour?

7. The ocean depth at one place is $\frac{3}{5}$ mi. A minisub descended to $\frac{2}{3}$ of the depth. Did the sub descend more than 2,000 ft?

8. A sea creature measures 4.75×10^{-2} meters long. It has tiny stripes every 0.25×10^{-3} meters. Does the creature have more than 180 stripes?

9. A robot minisub descends at a rate of 5 meters per minute. It reaches the end of its cable in 15 minutes. Can the robot minisub descend below 100 meters?

10. A minisub descended to a depth of $2\frac{1}{8}$ mi. It then ascended $\frac{3}{8}$ mi before descending $2\frac{3}{8}$ mi. What depth is the minisub at now?

Multiplying and Dividing Rational Numbers

A. To multiply rational numbers, use the rules for multiplying integers, decimals, and fractions.

If two rational numbers have like signs, their product is positive.

Multiply $^-\frac{1}{3} \cdot {}^-\frac{1}{2}$.

$^-\frac{1}{3} \cdot {}^-\frac{1}{2} = \frac{^-1 \cdot {}^-1}{3 \cdot 2} = \frac{1}{6}$

Multiply $^-0.4 \cdot {}^-1.2$.

$^-0.4 \cdot {}^-1.2 = 0.48$

If two rational numbers have unlike signs, their product is negative.

Multiply $^-\frac{1}{2} \cdot \frac{3}{4}$.

$^-\frac{1}{2} \cdot \frac{3}{4} = \frac{^-1 \cdot 3}{2 \cdot 4} = {}^-\frac{3}{8}$

Multiply $4.2 \cdot {}^-3.1$.

$4.2 \cdot {}^-3.1 = {}^-13.02$

B. Divide rational numbers by combining the rules for dividing integers, decimals, and fractions.

If two rational numbers have like signs, their quotient is positive.

Divide $^-1\frac{1}{2} \div {}^-\frac{3}{8}$.

$^-1\frac{1}{2} \div {}^-\frac{3}{8} = {}^-\frac{3}{2} \div {}^-\frac{3}{8}$
$= {}^-\frac{3}{2} \cdot {}^-\frac{8}{3}$
$= \frac{^-3 \cdot {}^-8}{2 \cdot 3} = \frac{24}{6} = 4$

Divide $^-4.5 \div {}^-18.0$.

$^-4.5 \div {}^-18.0 = 0.25$

If two rational numbers have unlike signs, their quotient is negative.

Divide $\frac{3}{4} \div {}^-\frac{3}{8}$.

$\frac{3}{4} \div {}^-\frac{3}{8} = \frac{3}{4} \cdot {}^-\frac{8}{3} =$
$\frac{3 \cdot {}^-8}{4 \cdot 3} =$
$^-\frac{24}{12} = {}^-2$

Divide $1.2 \div {}^-0.4$.

$1.2 \div {}^-0.4 = {}^-3$

Checkpoint Write the letter of the correct answer.

Multiply or divide.

1. $^-\frac{2}{3} \cdot {}^-\frac{4}{5}$ **a.** $^-\frac{8}{15}$ **b.** $^-\frac{10}{12}$ **c.** $\frac{8}{15}$ **d.** $\frac{6}{15}$

2. $\frac{1}{8} \cdot {}^-\frac{4}{5}$ **a.** $\frac{5}{20}$ **b.** $^-\frac{1}{10}$ **c.** $^-\frac{5}{32}$ **d.** $\frac{4}{10}$

3. $^-1\frac{1}{4} \div {}^-\frac{5}{8}$ **a.** $\frac{25}{32}$ **b.** $^-\frac{2}{1}$ **c.** $\frac{1}{2}$ **d.** 2

Multiply. Simplify when necessary.

1. $^-\dfrac{3}{8} \cdot \dfrac{1}{4}$ **2.** $\dfrac{1}{2} \cdot ^-\dfrac{5}{16}$ **3.** $^-\dfrac{7}{9} \cdot \dfrac{3}{4}$ **4.** $^-\dfrac{2}{5} \cdot ^-\dfrac{5}{8}$

5. $\dfrac{4}{7} \cdot ^-\dfrac{7}{8}$ **6.** $^-\dfrac{5}{9} \cdot ^-\dfrac{2}{3}$ **7.** $\dfrac{7}{12} \cdot \dfrac{3}{4}$ **8.** $^-\dfrac{2}{15} \cdot \dfrac{7}{11}$

9. $1\dfrac{1}{4} \cdot ^-\dfrac{3}{8}$ **10.** $^-\dfrac{5}{6} \cdot ^-2\dfrac{5}{8}$ **11.** $^-2\dfrac{3}{5} \cdot 4$ **12.** $^-1\dfrac{1}{9} \cdot ^-2\dfrac{3}{7}$

13. $\dfrac{1}{4} \cdot ^-\dfrac{2}{5}$ **14.** $\dfrac{2}{3} \cdot ^-1\dfrac{1}{4}$ **15.** $^-1\dfrac{2}{5} \cdot ^-4$ **16.** $^-\dfrac{1}{4} \cdot ^-3$

17. $0.7 \cdot ^-3.5$ **18.** $^-1.2 \cdot ^-4.4$ **19.** $^-3.7 \cdot 3.71$

20. $^-2.63 \cdot ^-1.45$ **21.** $^-4.3 \cdot 0.08$ **22.** $^-14.67 \cdot ^-6.2$

23. $^-9.5 \cdot 3.703$ **24.** $^-1.14 \cdot ^-0.07$ **25.** $^-6.2 \cdot ^-1.45$

Divide. Simplify when necessary.

26. $^-\dfrac{3}{4} \div \dfrac{1}{8}$ **27.** $^-\dfrac{5}{8} \div ^-\dfrac{2}{3}$ **28.** $\dfrac{1}{2} \div ^-\dfrac{3}{5}$ **29.** $^-\dfrac{7}{8} \div ^-\dfrac{3}{8}$

30. $^-\dfrac{1}{4} \div \dfrac{1}{4}$ **31.** $\dfrac{3}{8} \div ^-\dfrac{5}{16}$ **32.** $\dfrac{5}{9} \div ^-\dfrac{3}{8}$ **33.** $^-\dfrac{1}{2} \div ^-\dfrac{14}{15}$

34. $\dfrac{3}{8} \div ^-2$ **35.** $^-1\dfrac{5}{3} \div ^-\dfrac{7}{16}$ **36.** $^-\dfrac{3}{4} \div 4$ **37.** $^-5 \div \dfrac{7}{7}$

38. $^-4.8 \div ^-0.6$ **39.** $^-2.5 \div 1.5$ **40.** $7.28 \div ^-0.08$

41. $^-6.66 \div ^-1.11$ **42.** $^-9.39 \div 0.3$ **43.** $^-1.2 \div ^-1.44$

44. $^-18.3 \div 0.183$ **45.** $^-3.185 \div ^-2.45$ **46.** $^-0.8 \div ^-3.2$

NUMBER SENSE

Copy and complete the table.

	1%	10%	100%
98			
540			
1,900			
3,000			

Real Numbers

Every point on the number line corresponds to a real number. For example, point A corresponds to the real number 2. The point midway between A and B must correspond to 2.5. What number corresponds to the point one unit to the left of 2.5?

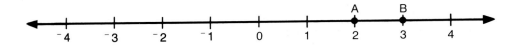

A real number in decimal form may repeat or terminate, or it may neither repeat nor terminate. Real numbers that repeat or terminate are called **rational** numbers.

2.5 terminates. The decimal equivalent of $2\frac{1}{3}$ is 2.333.... This decimal repeats and can be written $2.\overline{3}$.

Thinking as a Team

1. Copy the number line shown above. Then show the approximate location of each of the following real numbers. Which numbers, as decimals, are repeating? Which terminate? You may use your calculator.

    1.5 $^-1$ $\frac{1}{3}$ $^-1.\overline{6}$ $\frac{3}{4}$ 0 2.7 $1\frac{5}{8}$

2. Do you or any of your friends have a calculator that has a $\boxed{\sqrt{}}$ key? If so, press $\boxed{2}$ $\boxed{\sqrt{}}$ on this calculator. Does the decimal form of $\sqrt{2}$ appear to repeat? How about $\sqrt{3}$? $\sqrt{4}$? $\sqrt{5}$?

Real numbers that cannot be written as terminating or repeating decimals are called **irrational** numbers. The square root of a whole number is either another whole number or an irrational number. Thus $\sqrt{4}$ is rational, but $\sqrt{6}$ is irrational. Numbers such as 0.10110111011110... are also irrational because, although their digits follow a pattern, they do not repeat.

Thinking as a Team ⎯⎯⎯⎯⎯

You can estimate the square root of a number by using perfect squares that are near the number.

1. $\sqrt{5}$ is between $\sqrt{4}$ and $\sqrt{9}$, and so $\sqrt{5}$ is between what two numbers?

2. How can you estimate $\sqrt{5}$ to the nearest tenth?

3. What is $\sqrt{20}$ to the nearest tenth?

4. Enter any number on your calculator. Is the number shown on your display rational or irrational? Can your calculator actually display an irrational number?

5. Are the numbers $\frac{1}{11}$, $\frac{1}{7}$, and $\frac{1}{13}$ rational or irrational? How do you know?
   Using your calculator, look at the decimal form of $\frac{1}{11}$, $\frac{1}{7}$, and $\frac{1}{13}$. Can you tell whether each of these decimals is rational from looking at your calculator? Why or why not?

Classify the following real numbers as rational or irrational. Your calculator will help.

$$\sqrt{9} \qquad \frac{1}{-6} \qquad \sqrt{8} \qquad 1.2 \qquad {}^-4 \qquad 0.\overline{7} \qquad \sqrt{7} \qquad \frac{3}{5} \qquad \frac{1}{11} \qquad 0$$

Which of these numbers are integers? Which are whole numbers? Can a number be both rational and irrational?

Thinking as a Team ⎯⎯⎯⎯⎯

1. In this Venn Diagram, each circle represents one of the following number sets: real numbers, rational numbers, irrational numbers, integers, and whole numbers. Identify each of these sets with the letters A, B, C, D, and E.

2. Decide which of the following statements are true:

   All rational numbers are real numbers.
   If a number is an integer, then it is rational.
   If a number is negative, then it is not a whole number.
   Some rational numbers are irrational.
   Every rational number is an integer.

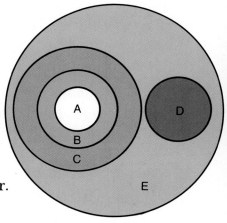

Graphing Real Numbers

You have used real numbers to locate points on a number line. You can also use real numbers to locate points in a plane, called a **coordinate plane,** or a **real-number plane.**

The x-axis and y-axis are real-number lines. Their intersection is the **origin,** and is described by the **ordered pair** (0,0).

Every point in the real-number plane can be described by an ordered pair of real numbers.
The x-axis and the y-axis divide the real-number plane into four **quadrants.**

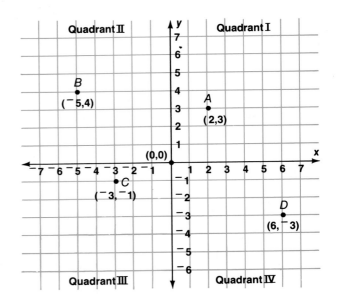

Ordered pairs in Quadrant I have the form $(+,+)$. $(2,3)$ are the coordinates of point A in Quadrant I.

Ordered pairs in Quadrant II have the form $(-,+)$. $(^-5,4)$ are the coordinates of point B in Quadrant II.

Ordered pairs in Quadrant III have the form $(-,-)$. $(^-3,^-1)$ are the coordinates of point C in Quadrant III.

Ordered pairs in Quadrant IV have the form $(+,-)$. $(6,^-3)$ are the coordinates of point D in Quadrant IV.

Graph the ordered pair $(^-4,2)$.

To graph $(^-4,2)$, move 4 to the left of the origin (0,0) along the x-axis. Then move 2 up from the x-axis.

Graph the ordered pair $\left(1\frac{1}{2}, ^-2\right)$.

To graph $1\frac{1}{2}$, move right $1\frac{1}{2}$, or $\frac{1}{2}$ of the way between 1 and 2 along the x-axis. Then move 2 down from the x-axis.

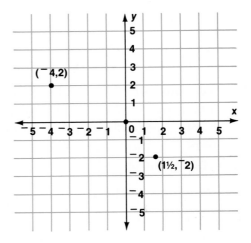

Write the quadrant in which each point is located.

1. (4,3)

2. (2,⁻1)

3. $\left(\frac{^-3}{4},6\right)$

4. (⁻7,⁻2.$\bar{3}$)

5. (3,⁻1)

6. (3.1,2)

7. $\left(\frac{7}{8},\frac{^-5}{9}\right)$

8. (⁻2,4)

Match each ordered pair with a point in the real-number plane at the right.

9. (⁻2,1)

10. (4,6)

11. $\left(\frac{3}{4},^-3\right)$

12. (5,1.3)

13. (⁻1.$\bar{6}$,⁻3)

14. (2,3)

15. $\left(\frac{^-7}{9},2\frac{2}{3}\right)$

16. (⁻2,5)

17. (⁻4,⁻0.5)

18. (3,⁻3.3)

19. $\left(5\frac{1}{8},^-3\frac{7}{11}\right)$

20. (5.5,3.5)

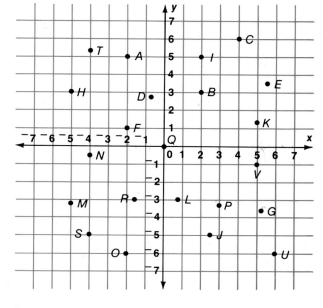

Write an ordered pair for each point in the real-number plane at the right.

21. *H*   **22.** *I*   **23.** *J*

24. *M*   **25.** *O*   **26.** *Q*

27. *S*   **28.** *T*   **29.** *U*   **30.** *V*

On graph paper, draw a real-number plane like the one above. Graph each point and connect the points in order. Connect the last point to the first and name the figure.

31. (⁻2,2), (4,2), (2,⁻2), (⁻4,⁻2)

32. (⁻6,3), (⁻6,⁻3), (6,⁻3), (6,3)

33. (1,⁻3), (1,3), (⁻5,⁻3)

34. (⁻4,4), (⁻4,⁻4), (4,⁻4), (4,4)

35. (⁻2,2), (⁻1,2), (2,⁻2), (2,2), (3,2), (3,⁻3), (1,⁻3), (⁻1,⁻1), (⁻1,⁻3), (⁻2,⁻3)

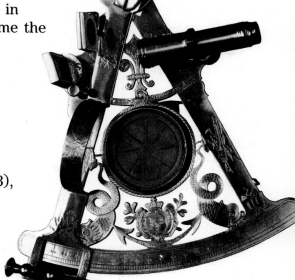

PROBLEM SOLVING
Solving Multistep Problems/Making a Plan

You may need to make more than one calculation to solve some problems. Before you can answer the question that is asked, you may have to find some data that are not stated. You can often compute with the numbers that are stated to find the numbers you need. Making a plan can help you solve such problems.

> Ms. Cronin, a geologist, discovered some plant fossils in a cave 30 meters below sea level. The next day, she dug 25 centimeters deeper and found more plant fossils. On the third day, she dug twice as far as on the second day and found several insect fossils. How many meters below sea level were the insect fossils Ms. Cronin discovered on the third day?

Unstated data: number of meters dug the second day
number of meters dug the third day

Plan

___ **1.** Rename 25 centimeters with meters.

___ **2.** Multiply Step 1's answer by 2.

___ **3.** Add the total number of meters found in steps 1 and 2 to the depth of the cave.

Rename 25 centimeters with meters; divide 25 by 100.

$25 \div 100 = 0.25$ $25\,cm = 0.25\,m$

Multiply 0.25 m by 2 to find the number of meters dug the third day.

$0.25 \times 2 = 0.50$ She dug 0.50 m.

Add the answers found in steps 1 and 2 to the depth of the cave.

$30 + 0.25 + 0.50 = 30.75$

The insect fossils Ms. Cronin discovered on the third day were 30.75 meters below sea level.

Complete the plan for solving each problem by writing
the missing steps.

1. After digging for 3 days, a geologist discovered plant fossils at a distance of 24.5 m below sea level. On Thursday, he dug 185 cm deeper and found more plant fossils. On Friday, he dug three times as far as on Thursday and found several animal fossils. How many meters below sea level were the animal fossils?

___ **1.**

___ **2.**

___ **3.**

2. Ms. Cronin recorded the depths at which fossils were found on a recent search. She recorded findings at depths of 0.66 meters, 0.62 meters, 64.5 centimeters, and 65.4 centimeters. At what depth was the deepest fossil found?

___ **1.**

___ **2.**

___ **3.**

Make a plan for each problem. Solve.

3. From a floating platform, a drill is lowered to a depth of 6.2 kilometers. The drill goes 9.5 meters into the sea floor and then is withdrawn 750 centimeters. How many meters below sea level did the tip of the drill reach?

4. A section of a petrified tree measures 1,296 cm long. A geologist cuts it into 4 sections, and each section is cut in half to form a research sample. How many meters are in a research sample?

5. From a cavern 1.75 kilometers below sea level, a diver releases a flare that travels to the surface of the sea at the rate of 15 meters per second. How many meters from the surface was the flare 12 seconds after firing?

6. Ms. Cronin took out a loan to build a laboratory for examining and displaying fossils. She repaid a total of $18,562.50 on a loan of $16,500. What was the rate of interest on the 1-year loan?

7. The maximum depth of the Atlantic Ocean is 8.65 kilometers. A geologist took a water sample from a level that was $\frac{2}{5}$ this depth. At how many meters from the surface was the sample taken?

8. Ms. Cronin supervised 2 research sites. At the first site her assistants dug 1.6 m the first day and 2.4 m the next day. At the second site they dug 1.7 m the first day and 2.2 m the second day. At which site was the deeper hole dug?

CALCULATOR

Most savings accounts pay compound interest. This means that the bank pays interest on both the money in the account and the interest earned. The formula for computing compound interest is:

$$a = p \cdot \left(1 + \frac{r}{n}\right)^{(n \cdot y)}$$

a = amount of money after all of the interest is paid
p = the principal, or the money deposited
r = the annual rate of interest written as a decimal
n = the number of times a year interest is compounded
y = the number of years the principal is left in the account

Harry deposits $1,000 into his savings account. This account earns 10% interest, compounded quarterly (4 times a year). How much money will be in the account if he leaves it in for a year?

Press: 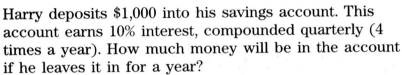 ← The display should show 4. This tells you what the exponent will be.

Press:  ← The display should show 1.025. Raise this number to the exponent found in the first step.

Press:  ← The display should show 1.1038128. Multiply this by the principal.

Press:  ← The display should show 1103.8128. Round this amount to the nearest hundredth.

There will be $1,103.81 in the account at the end of a year.

Use a calculator to solve.

1. Ronnie deposits $2,000 into an account that earns 8% interest, compounded twice a year. How much money will be in the account if she leaves it in for 2 years?

2. Pablo deposits $4,000 into an account that earns 12% interest, compounded yearly. How much money will be in the account if he leaves it in for 3 years?

3. In the example, suppose that Harry had rounded 1.025 to 1.03 before calculating the interest. Would the error have been very great? Explain.

272

GROUP PROJECT

Circling the World

The problem: The first circumnavigation of the world occurred in the 1500's. The sea voyage, undertaken by Ferdinand Magellan, took three years. Today, you can travel around the world in a fraction of that time. You can travel by ship, by jet, and, to a great extent, by car, train, or bus. Using the questions below, plan a trip around the world. Draw your route on a map.

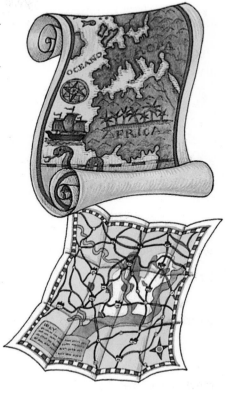

Key Questions

• How many weeks, months, or years will you allow for your trip?

• How many stops will you make?

• At which places will you stop?

• How long will you stay in each place?

• How will you travel from each place to the next? What forms of transportation will you use?

• What preparations will you make before leaving on your trip?

• Can you estimate how much your trip will cost?

• Suppose you want to spend the least time traveling and the most time visiting places. What would be the minimum amount of time you'd have to allow for traveling?

• How many miles do you plan to travel each day?

CHAPTER TEST

Compare. Write >, <, or = for ●. (pages 240–241)

1. ⁻3 ● ⁻3

2. ⁻6 ● ⁻2

3. 4 ● ⁻5

Order from the greatest to the least. (pages 240–241 and 258–259)

4. 16, ⁻3, 37, ⁻49, 2, ⁻24

5. ⁻1$\frac{1}{2}$, ⁻2, 0.5, $\frac{4}{7}$

Add, subtract, multiply, or divide. (pages 244–247 and 250–253)

6. ⁻10 + ⁻4 + 3

7. ⁻21 − 4 − ⁻3

8. ⁻2 · 21

9. ⁻4 · ⁻5

10. 32 ÷ ⁻8

11. ⁻81 ÷ ⁻9

Write in scientific notation. (pages 254–255)

12. 0.187

13. 0.00586

14. 0.00604

Compare. Write >, <, or = for ●. (pages 258–259)

15. ⁻1.2 ● ⁻$\frac{4}{9}$

16. $\frac{6}{11}$ ● ⁻1$\frac{1}{3}$

17. 9.6 ● 9$\frac{3}{5}$

Add, subtract, multiply, or divide. (pages 260–261 and 264–265)

18. ⁻$\frac{1}{5}$ + $\frac{2}{5}$ − $\frac{4}{5}$

19. ⁻$\frac{3}{5}$ · ⁻$\frac{4}{11}$

20. ⁻$\frac{2}{3}$ · $\frac{3}{8}$

21. ⁻3.7 + ⁻2.8 − ⁻3.5

22. ⁻$\frac{4}{5}$ ÷ $\frac{1}{6}$

23. ⁻7.68 ÷ ⁻3.2

Write as a terminating or a repeating decimal. (pages 266–267)

24. ⁻$\frac{5}{11}$

25. $\frac{5}{8}$

26. $\frac{7}{18}$

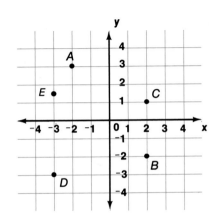

Use the graph for Exercises 27–31. (pages 268–269)
Write the ordered pair for each point.

27. A

28. C

Write the point for the ordered pair.

29. (2,⁻2)

30. $\left(⁻3, 1\frac{1}{2}\right)$

31. (⁻3,⁻3)

Solve. Use the graph to answer Exercises 32–35. Make sure that your solution answers the question. (pages 248–249, 256–257, 262–263, and 270–271)

32. During Expedition TLO, Marcel recorded the temperature at 12 noon and at 12 midnight for a week. Find the average temperature at midnight for the week.

33. Was the difference in temperature for Day 4 greater than or less than the difference in temperature for Day 7?

34. What was the difference in temperature between noon on Day 2 and noon on Day 6?

35. What was the average temperature at 12 noon for the week? Round your answer to the nearest tenth of a degree.

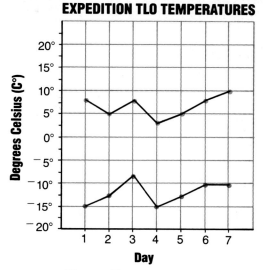

EXPEDITION TLO TEMPERATURES

Degrees Celsius (C°)

Day

Blue = 12 noon
Red = 12 midnight

BONUS

Solve.

If one day the temperature was ⁻15°C at midnight, ⁻10°C at 3 A.M., ⁻3°C at 6 A.M., 0°C at 9 A.M., and 5°C at noon, which interval showed the greatest degree of change in temperature? What was the change in degrees?

RETEACHING

A. Recall that a number in scientific notation is the product of a number between 1 and 10 and a power of 10. When a number smaller than 1 is expressed in scientific notation, the power of 10 has a negative exponent.

Express 659,000 in scientific notation.

$$659,000 = 6.59 \cdot 10,000$$
$$= 6.59 \cdot 10^5 \longleftarrow \text{scientific notation}$$

Express 0.00286 in scientific notation.

$$0.00286 = 2.86 \cdot 0.001$$
$$= 2.86 \cdot 10^{-3} \longleftarrow \text{scientific notation}$$

The exponent shows how many places the decimal point must be moved to write the number in standard form. Move the decimal point to the right with a positive exponent. Move the decimal point to the left with a negative exponent.

B. To multiply (or divide) numbers that are powers of the same base, use the following rules.

1. To multiply powers of the same base, add exponents.
2. To divide powers of the same base, subtract exponents.

Multiply $5^4 \cdot 5^3$.
$$5^4 \cdot 5^3 = 5^{4+3} = 5^7 \quad \text{Add exponents.}$$
$$\text{Base remains the same.}$$

Divide $7^5 \div 7^2$.
$$7^5 \div 7^2 = 7^{5-2} = 7^3 \quad \text{Subtract exponents.}$$
$$\text{Base remains the same.}$$

Express each number in scientific notation.

1. 2,300

2. 60,350

3. 84,000

4. 750,000

5. 0.000426

6. 0.0583

7. 0.000063

8. 0.00000312

Multiply or divide.

9. $8^2 \cdot 8^3$

10. $6^{-2} \cdot 6^3$

11. $5 \cdot 5^4$

12. $2^{-4} \cdot 2^{-2}$

13. $5^4 \div 5$

14. $3^6 \div 3^{-2}$

15. $4^7 \div 4^5$

16. $9^{-2} \div 9^3$

ENRICHMENT

Adding and Subtracting with Radicals

In a **radical expression** such as $3\sqrt{2}$, the number under the radical sign is called the **radicand.** The number in front of the radical sign is called the **coefficient.** If two radical expressions have the same radicand, they are called **like radicals.**

$5\sqrt{2}$ and $7\sqrt{2}$ are like radicals because they both contain the same radicand (2).

Like radical expressions can be combined by adding (or subtracting) their coefficients.

Add. $5\sqrt{2} + 7\sqrt{2} = (5 + 7)\sqrt{2}$
$= 12\sqrt{2}$

Subtract. $3\sqrt{6} - 5\sqrt{6} = (3 - 5)\sqrt{6}$
$= {}^-2\sqrt{6}$

Only expressions containing like radicals can be combined. However, some expressions that appear to have no like radicals can be combined after each radical is simplified.

Simplify and combine $\sqrt{75} - \sqrt{27} + \sqrt{12}$.

$\sqrt{75} = \sqrt{25 \cdot 3} = \sqrt{25} \cdot \sqrt{3} = 5\sqrt{3}$
$\sqrt{27} = \sqrt{9 \cdot 3} = \sqrt{9} \cdot \sqrt{3} = 3\sqrt{3}$
$\sqrt{12} = \sqrt{4 \cdot 3} = \sqrt{4} \cdot \sqrt{3} = 2\sqrt{3}$

Think:
$\sqrt{a \cdot b} = \sqrt{a} \cdot \sqrt{b}$

$5\sqrt{3} - 3\sqrt{3} + 2\sqrt{3} = (5 - 3 + 2)\sqrt{3}$
$= 4\sqrt{3}$

Check with a calculator:

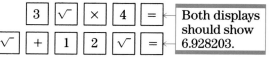

| 3 | √ | × | 4 | = | ← | Both displays should show 6.928203. |

| 7 | 5 | √ | − | 2 | 7 | √ | + | 1 | 2 | √ | = | ← |

Simplify and combine where possible.

1. $4\sqrt{10} + 2\sqrt{10} - 5\sqrt{10}$

2. $7\sqrt{7} - 2\sqrt{7} + 3\sqrt{7} + 3\sqrt{7}$

3. $\sqrt{5} + 7\sqrt{2} - 4\sqrt{2} + 7\sqrt{5}$

4. $4\sqrt{3} + 6\sqrt{2} + 4\sqrt{11} - \sqrt{3}$

5. $3\sqrt{44} + \sqrt{99} - 7\sqrt{11}$

6. $12\sqrt{7} - \sqrt{63} + 5\sqrt{112}$

7. $2\sqrt{13} - 4\sqrt{13} + \sqrt{13}$

8. ${}^-6\sqrt{3} + {}^-2\sqrt{3} + 14\sqrt{3}$

9. ${}^-3\sqrt{2} + 4\sqrt{17} + {}^-2\sqrt{2} - {}^-\sqrt{17}$

10. $\sqrt{5} - \sqrt{5} + \sqrt{23} + {}^-6\sqrt{3}$

CUMULATIVE REVIEW

Write the letter of the correct answer.

1. What is $3:7$ written as a fraction?

   a. $\frac{7}{21}$ b. $\frac{3}{7}$

   c. $2\frac{1}{3}$ d. not given

2. Solve for c: $\frac{3}{5} = \frac{c}{15}$.

   a. 3   b. 9

   c. 25   d. not given

3. What is 723% written as a fraction?

   a. $\frac{723}{1,000}$ b. $\frac{723}{100}$

   c. 723   d. not given

4. What is 4.03 written as a percent?

   a. $4\frac{3}{100}$ b. 40.3%

   c. $40\frac{3}{10}$ d. not given

5. What is 24.6% of 242?

   a. 59.532   b. 584.32

   c. 4,953.2   d. not given

6. What is $4\frac{3}{5}$ written as a percent?

   a. 4.6%   b. 60%

   c. 460%   d. not given

7. What is the temperature change from 33°C to ⁻5°C?

   a. 28°C   b. 38°C

   c. 39°C   d. not given

8. $3.25 \text{ m} + 7.10 \text{ cm} = \blacksquare \text{ cm}$

   a. 10.35   b. 332.10

   c. 396   d. not given

9. Choose the appropriate unit to measure flour.

   a. inches   b. quarts

   c. pounds   d. not given

10. $4\frac{2}{5} \times 7\frac{1}{8}$

    a. $\frac{176}{285}$ b. $28\frac{1}{20}$

    c. $32\frac{7}{20}$ d. not given

11. What is $\frac{3}{7}$ written as a decimal rounded to the nearest hundredth?

    a. 0.42   b. 0.429

    c. 0.43   d. not given

12. Of 11, 43, and 57, which is not prime?

    a. 11   b. 43

    c. 57   d. not given

13. Janice wanted to bake a dozen muffins, but the recipe she had would yield 36. How much milk should she use if the recipe called for $2\frac{1}{4}$ c?

    a. $\frac{1}{3}$ c   b. $\frac{3}{4}$ c

    c. $\frac{5}{5}$ c   d. not given

14. Ed's map has a scale of 1 in. = 20 mi. The distance between two cities on this map is 8.45 in. How far apart are the cities?

    a. 4.9 mi   b. 52.25 mi

    c. 169 mi   d. not given

Which factors do you think affect the cost of advertising on national television programs? Think of a product you would like to sell. Plan when and how you would advertise it. Can you come up with equations that you could use to show the costs of making the commercial and of showing it once, twice, or ten times?

8 EQUATIONS AND INEQUALITIES
One Variable

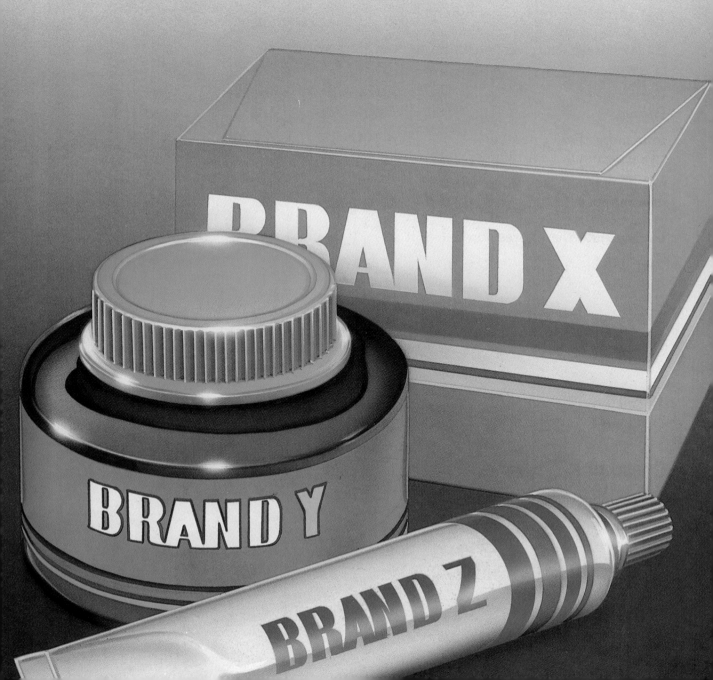

Algebraic Expressions

A. TV station WYZX programs 2 more hours of news during the afternoon than it programs during the morning. An **algebraic expression** can represent this relationship.

Let m equal the amount of news programming during the morning. Then $m + 2$ will equal the amount of news programming during the afternoon.

The variable m represents a number.

B. Algebraic expressions can be written from word phrases.

Word Phrase	Algebraic Expression
four more than a number	$n + 4$
twice as much as a number	$2n$
negative seven plus three fourths of a number	$^-7 + \frac{3}{4}n$

C. Evaluate the expression $2 + y$, if $y = {}^-1$, 0, and 3.

$$
\begin{array}{ccc}
2 & + & y \\
\downarrow & & \downarrow \\
2 & + & {}^-1 \\
& 1 &
\end{array}
\qquad
\begin{array}{ccc}
2 & + & y \\
\downarrow & & \downarrow \\
2 & + & 0 \\
& 2 &
\end{array}
$$

$$
\begin{array}{ccc}
2 & + & y \\
\downarrow & & \downarrow \\
2 & + & 3 \\
& 5 &
\end{array}
$$

Checkpoint   Write the letter of the correct answer.

1. An algebraic expression for seven less than m would be 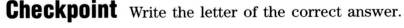.

   a. $7 < m$ **b.** $m - 7$ **c.** $m + 7$ **d.** $7 - m$

2. Evaluate ^-4c, when $c = 5$.

   a. $^-20$ **b.** $^-1\frac{1}{4}$ **c.** $^-\frac{4}{5}$ **d.** 20

Write each as an algebraic expression.

1. eight less than y

2. four multiplied by x

3. the total of a and 6

4. five more than d

5. c decreased by 6

6. r times 3

7. 7 divided by a

8. c divided by 4

9. twice the sum of t and 5

10. a increased by 11

Evaluate each expression, if the variable equals 0, 1, 2, 3, and 4.

11. $3 + t$

12. $t - 4$

13. $4t$

14. $\frac{m}{3}$

15. $b + 11$

16. $20 - y$

17. $3(x + 2)$

18. $2x - 3$

19. $16 + 3w$

Evaluate each expression, if the variable equals $^-3$, $^-2$, $^-1$, 0, and 1.

20. $m + 1$

21. $m - 5$

22. $5x$

23. $4(x - 3)$

24. $\frac{(y + 2)}{3}$

25. $\frac{4}{(6 + y)}$

26. $3m + 5$

27. $10 - 2y$

28. $(m + 2) \cdot 2$

Solve.

29. WYZX broadcasts a dance program each day of the week. Write an expression that represents the number of times the program is broadcast in a given number (w) of weeks.

30. The total number of soap operas that were aired last year was p. If the same number of soap operas were aired daily, write an expression to show how many shows were aired each day.

31. In 1984, people in 63.8 million households in the United States watched public television at least once per month. If the number is projected to be 95.7 million households in 1994, how many more households can be expected to watch public television in 1994?

Solving One-Step Equations

To solve equations that have real numbers, remember the rules for operations that involve real numbers.

A. Solve and check.

$$x + 3 = {}^-12$$
$$x + 3 - 3 = {}^-12 - 3$$
$$x = {}^-15$$

Check.
$${}^-15 + 3 \overset{?}{=} {}^-12$$
$${}^-12 = {}^-12 \ \checkmark$$

$$x + {}^-3 = {}^-12$$
$$x + {}^-3 - ({}^-3) = {}^-12 - ({}^-3)$$
$$x = {}^-9$$

Check.
$${}^-9 + {}^-3 \overset{?}{=} {}^-12$$
$${}^-12 = {}^-12 \ \checkmark$$

B. Solve and check one-step equations that involve real numbers. Remember that operations must be performed on both sides of an equation.

$$d - \frac{1}{8} = \frac{{}^-3}{4}$$
$$d - \frac{1}{8} + \frac{1}{8} = \frac{{}^-3}{4} + \frac{1}{8}$$
$$d = \frac{{}^-6}{8} + \frac{1}{8}$$
$$d = \frac{{}^-5}{8}$$

$$d - \frac{{}^-1}{8} = \frac{{}^-3}{4}$$
$$d - \frac{{}^-1}{8} + \frac{{}^-1}{8} = \frac{{}^-3}{4} + \frac{{}^-1}{8}$$
$$d = \frac{{}^-6}{8} - \frac{1}{8}$$
$$d = \frac{{}^-7}{8}$$

Other examples:

$${}^-4c = 12$$
$$\frac{{}^-4c}{{}^-4} = \frac{12}{{}^-4}$$
$$c = {}^-3$$

Check.
$${}^-4 \cdot {}^-3 \overset{?}{=} 12$$
$$12 = 12 \ \checkmark$$

$$\frac{{}^-y}{2.5} = {}^-5$$
$$\frac{{}^-y}{2.5} \cdot {}^-2.5 = {}^-5 \cdot {}^-2.5$$
$$y = 12.5$$

Check.
$$\frac{{}^-12.5}{2.5} \overset{?}{=} {}^-5$$
$${}^-5 = {}^-5 \ \checkmark$$

Checkpoint Write the letter of the correct answer.

Solve.

1. $y - 3 = {}^-15$; $y = \blacksquare$

a. ${}^-12$ **b.** ${}^-5$ **c.** 12 **d.** 18

2. $0.2c = {}^-20$; $c = \blacksquare$

a. ${}^-100$ **b.** ${}^-10$ **c.** 10 **d.** 100

3. $y - {}^-12 = 15$; $y = \blacksquare$

a. ${}^-3$ **b.** $-\frac{4}{5}$ **c.** 3 **d.** 27

4. $\frac{1}{2}x = {}^-4$; $x = \blacksquare$

a. ${}^-8$ **b.** ${}^-2$ **c.** 2 **d.** 8

Solve and check.

1. $a + 3 = {}^-19$

2. $c + \frac{3}{4} = \frac{5}{8}$

3. ${}^-2.8 + x = 3.2$

4. $e - 6 = {}^-12$

5. $g - 16 = {}^-4$

6. $y - 4.3 = {}^-2.1$

7. $7x = {}^-21$

8. $9y = {}^-36$

9. $5.3x = {}^-21.2$

10. ${}^-\frac{x}{4} = {}^-13$

11. $\frac{y}{2} = {}^-26$

12. $\frac{m}{2.5} = {}^-10$

13. ${}^-5 + t = 17$

14. $a + {}^-2 = {}^-9$

15. $r - {}^-3 = 6$

16. ${}^-7 - p = {}^-9$

17. ${}^-6d = 42$

18. $8c = {}^-64$

19. ${}^-\frac{m}{3} = {}^-8$

20. $\frac{r}{5} = {}^-3$

21. $a + \frac{1}{2} = {}^-1\frac{1}{2}$

22. $c - \left({}^-\frac{2}{3}\right) = \frac{1}{9}$

23. $4x = {}^-\frac{3}{5}$

24. $\frac{\frac{y}{2}}{3} = {}^-6$

25. $c + {}^-0.5 = {}^-2.8$

26. ${}^-1.7 + y = 3.2$

27. $d + 0.8 = {}^-3.2$

28. $y - 0.7 = 0.4$

29. ${}^-0.6\,m = 0.72$

30. $2.3y = {}^-9.2$

31. ${}^-\frac{r}{0.7} = {}^-0.6$

32. ${}^-\frac{t}{0.3} = 5$

33. $\frac{0.4}{x} = {}^-0.2$

Solve. For Problem 35, use the Infobank.

34. The audience for a new movie's first night was 320. This was twice the number of people who attended the movie the second night. If x represents the second night's audience, how many people attended the movie the second night? (HINT: Use an equation to solve.)

35. Use the information on page 476 to solve. A TV set projects 60 frames per second. In which region or country would you find this TV set? Write an equation and solve. (HINT: Let x = the number of pictures per second.)

NUMBER SENSE

Compute mentally.

1. $7z = 14$

2. $y + 8 = 20$

3. $\frac{a}{6} = 4$

4. $f - 15 = 15$

5. $\frac{h}{4} = 5$

6. $m + 9 = {}^-1$

7. $3r = {}^-18$

8. $18 + k = 12$

9. $t + {}^-6 = 4$

10. ${}^-12v = 0$

11. ${}^-\frac{u}{2} = 4$

12. $b - {}^-5 = 10$

Solving Two-Step Equations

TICKETS

A. At the Bijou, movie tickets for adults cost $5 each, and tickets for children under 12 years of age cost $2 each. One evening, the total ticket sales were $374. If 12 child tickets were sold, how many adult tickets were sold?

A two-step equation can be used to answer the question.

If you let x represent the number of adults, then $5x$ represents the cost of the adult tickets. The cost of the child tickets was $12 \cdot \$2$, or $24.

$$5x + 24 = 374$$
$$5x + 24 - 24 = 374 - 24$$
$$5x = 350$$
$$\frac{5x}{5} = \frac{350}{5}$$
$$x = 70$$

To check, let $x = 70$.
$$5 \cdot 70 + 24 \overset{?}{=} 374$$
$$350 + 24 \overset{?}{=} 374$$
$$374 = 374 \ ✔$$

That evening, 70 adult tickets were sold.

B. To solve a two-step equation, you must "undo" both operations.

Solve $\frac{x}{0.03} - 0.5 = 3.5$.

$$\frac{x}{0.03} - 0.5 = 3.5$$
$$\frac{x}{0.03} - 0.5 + 0.5 = 3.5 + 0.5$$
$$\frac{x}{0.03} = 4$$
$$\frac{x}{0.03} \cdot 0.03 = 4 \cdot 0.03$$
$$x = 0.12$$

Check.
$$\frac{0.12}{0.03} - 0.5 \overset{?}{=} 3.5$$
$$4 - 0.5 \overset{?}{=} 3.5$$
$$3.5 = 3.5 \ ✔$$

Another example: Solve $\frac{2}{3}x - {}^-4 = 26$.

$$\frac{2}{3}x - {}^-4 - {}^+4 = 26 - {}^+4$$
$$\frac{2x}{3} \cdot \frac{3}{2} = 22 \cdot \frac{3}{2}$$
$$x = 33$$

Check.
$$\frac{2}{3} \cdot 33 - {}^-4 \overset{?}{=} 26$$
$$22 - {}^-4 \overset{?}{=} 26$$
$$26 = 26 \ ✔$$

Solve and check.

1. $5x + 7 = 32$ **2.** $8y + 9 = 49$ **3.** $2g - 18 = 42$ **4.** $9m - 9 = 72$

5. $\frac{b}{2} + 7 = 10$ **6.** $\frac{p}{9} + 1 = 8$ **7.** $\frac{x}{5} - 3 = 2$ **8.** $\frac{c}{5} - 1 = 9$

9. $0.5r - 7 = 13$ **10.** $8d - 0.9 = 4.7$ **11.** $3.6y + 3.2 = 15.8$

12. $0.06x + 3.6 = 3.6042$ **13.** $0.08t - 4 = 16$ **14.** $\frac{s}{0.5} + 4 = 8$

15. $\frac{e}{6} + 2.7 = 6$ **16.** $\frac{w}{3.2} - 14 = 27$ **17.** $\frac{t}{3} - 4.25 = 7.25$

18. $\frac{2}{5}t + 7 = 21$ **19.** $3g + \frac{4}{5} = 9\frac{4}{5}$ **20.** $\frac{3}{4}z - 2 = 4$ **21.** $7n - \frac{3}{7} = 20\frac{4}{7}$

22. $\frac{5}{6}r + 20 = 40$ **23.** $\frac{2}{3}p - 6 = 2$ **24.** $6c - \frac{1}{3} = 11\frac{2}{3}$ **25.** $9a + \frac{7}{10} = 3\frac{2}{5}$

26. $^-7x + 8 = {}^-20$ **27.** $^-5c + 5 = {}^-15$ **28.** $4y - {}^-3 = {}^-25$ **29.** $^-7f + {}^-3 = {}^-45$

30. $\frac{^-s}{3} - 4 = {}^-10$ **31.** $\frac{^-b}{5} + 8 = 14$ **32.** $\frac{^-x}{1} - 9 = {}^-15$ **33.** $\frac{^-z}{7} + 4 = 8$

Write an equation for each and solve.

34. Six more than eight times a number is thirty. What is the number? (HINT: Let n = the number.)

35. Five less than a number divided by four is two. What is the number? (HINT: Let n = the number.)

36. In one year, the Orpheum presents 21 movies, which is 5 more than the number of movies presented by the Bijou. How many movies does the Bijou present? (HINT: Let m = the number of movies at the Bijou.)

37. If film is projected at the rate of 24 frames per second, how many frames will be projected in 3 minutes? (HINT: Let f = the number of frames.)

NUMBER SENSE

Compute mentally.

1. $21 \div 3 = \blacksquare$ **2.** $75 \div 25 = \blacksquare$ **3.** $220 \div 11 = \blacksquare$ **4.** $240 \div 3 = \blacksquare$

5. $150 \div 5 = \blacksquare$ **6.** $144 \div 6 = \blacksquare$ **7.** $81 \div 3 = \blacksquare$ **8.** $120 \div 40 = \blacksquare$

9. $720 \div 8 = \blacksquare$ **10.** $360 \div 12 = \blacksquare$ **11.** $164 \div 4 = \blacksquare$ **12.** $275 \div 11 = \blacksquare$

Word Problems from Equations

A. You can write word problems from equations.

What word problem could be represented by $3m + 9 = 15$?

Let \$9 be the cost of a blank cassette tape.
Let \$3 be the cost of a movie rental at Video Corner.
Let \$15 be the total that Neville Adams spent at Video Corner for tapes and movies.

Here is a possible word problem: Neville Adams rented movies at \$3 each at Video Corner and bought one blank cassette tape for \$9. His total bill was \$15. How many movies did he rent?

Solve.
$$3m + 9 = 15.$$
$$3m = 6$$
$$m = 2$$

Check.
$$3(2) + 9 \stackrel{?}{=} 15$$
$$6 + 9 \stackrel{?}{=} 15$$
$$15 = 15 \checkmark$$

He rented 2 movies.

B. What word problem could be represented by $4c + 6 = {}^-2$?

Let 4 be the number of free prizes.
Let \$6 be the profit from the sale of sandwiches.
Let $^-$\$2 be the net loss from the day's receipts at the street fair.

Here is a possible word problem: The owners of one booth at the street fair gave away 4 free prizes and earned \$6 profit on the sandwiches they sold. If $^-$\$2 is the net loss from the day's receipts, how much did it cost the owners for each prize they gave away?

Solve.
$$4c + 6 = {}^-2$$
$$4c = {}^-8$$
$$c = {}^-2$$

Check.
$$4({}^-2) + 6 \stackrel{?}{=} {}^-2$$
$${}^-8 + 6 \stackrel{?}{=} {}^-2$$
$${}^-2 = {}^-2 \checkmark$$

It cost the owners \$2 for each prize they gave away, or $^-$\$2.

Match the equation to the word problem.

1. $2v = 8$ **2.** $2k + 8 = 40$ **3.** $8r + 40 = 640$ **4.** $\frac{g}{2} = 8$

a. Edna watched television twice as much as she watched her VCR. If she watched television for 8 hours, how much time did she spend watching her VCR?

b. Tommy paid $40 as a down payment on a new television/VCR package. He paid the balance in 8 equal installments. If the total cost was $640, how much was each payment?

c. Marvin's television set was half as old as his radio. If his television set was 8 years old, how old was his radio?

d. Because Rudy had cable TV, he could watch 8 more stations than Pam. Counting twice the stations that they both could watch, they could watch 40 stations in all. How many stations could Pam watch?

Write a word problem for each equation.

5. $v - 3 = 27$

Let 3 be the number of videotapes returned to the manufacturer.

6. $\frac{u}{21} = 5$

Let $21 be the cost of one radio.

Write a word problem for each equation. Then solve and check.

7. $x - 10 = 31$ **8.** $a + 7 = 9$ **9.** $6p = 204$

10. $\frac{b}{3} = 1$ **11.** $z - 4 = 3$ **12.** $\frac{m}{10} = 9$

MIDCHAPTER REVIEW

Evaluate each algebraic expression if the variable equals $^-2$, $^-1$, 0, 3, and 4.

1. $x + 7$ **2.** $4a - 12$ **3.** $\frac{6}{(f + 8)}$

Solve and check.

4. $y + 19 = 8$ **5.** $v - 36 = 40$ **6.** $\frac{1}{4}p = {}^-8$

7. $9z - 2 = {}^-20$ **8.** $\frac{^-r}{1.6} + 4 = 12$ **9.** $^-7m - \frac{7}{8} = 48\frac{1}{8}$

PROBLEM SOLVING
Writing an Equation

Writing a problem in equation form will often help you find the solution to a word problem.

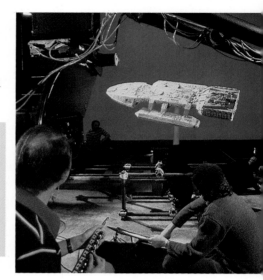

> Jerry Davis recently directed a cast of 38 people in the movie *Thunderbolt*. The cast consisted of 20 more than $\frac{3}{5}$ of the number of people in the cast of another movie called *Skytrail*. How many people were there in the cast of *Skytrail*?

— 1. List what you know and what you need to find.

Know

- There were 38 people in the cast of *Thunderbolt*.

- *Thunderbolt's* cast contained 20 more than $\frac{3}{5}$ of the number of people in the cast of *Skytrail*.

Find

- the number of people in the cast of the movie *Skytrail*

— 2. Think about how you can use the given information to form an equation. Use a variable to represent the number you need to find. Let $n =$ number of people in the cast of *Skytrail*.

<u>number of people in the cast of *Thunderbolt*</u>   was   20   more than $\frac{3}{5}$ of the number of people <u>in the cast of *Skytrail*</u>

$$38 \quad = \quad 20 \quad + \quad \frac{3}{5}n$$

Think: You can rewrite this equation as $\frac{3}{5}n + 20 = 38$.

— 3. Solve the equation and write the answer.

$$\frac{3}{5}n + 20 = 38 \qquad \frac{3}{5}n + 20 - 20 = 38 - 20$$

$$\frac{3}{5}n = 18 \qquad \frac{5}{3} \cdot \frac{3}{5}n = 18 \cdot \frac{5}{3}$$

$n = 30$; There were 30 people in the cast of *Skytrail*.

Write the letter of the correct equation.

1. The Majestic Theater will show 17 cartoons during a festival. This is $\frac{1}{3}$ the number of cartoons it plans to show during the year. How many cartoons will the theater show during the year?

   a. $n + \frac{1}{3} = 17$

   b. $\frac{1}{3}n = 17$

   c. $n - 17 = \frac{1}{3}$

2. Last week 274 people attended the premiere of a movie. This number was 14 fewer than twice the number of people who attended the last premiere at this theater. How many people attended the last premiere?

   a. $274 = 2n - 14$

   b. $\frac{274}{2} = n - 14$

   c. $274 + 14 = \frac{n}{2}$

Solve. Use an equation where appropriate.

3. One Hollywood studio owns enough science fiction movies to show 2 movies a day for 52 days. This number is 20 more than a rival studio owns. How many science fiction movies does the rival studio own?

4. Mr. Von Meck directed a cast of 19 people in a new movie. This cast had 3 fewer people than $\frac{2}{3}$ of the cast in his previous movie. How many actors and actresses were cast in his previous movie?

5. In April 5,530 people saw films at the Fox Theater. This number was 122 fewer than $\frac{4}{5}$ of the attendance at that theater in March. How many people saw films at the Fox Theater in March?

6. The special effects for *Skytrail*, a new adventure movie, cost $2,370,000. This was $\frac{1}{5}$ of the total cost of making the movie. How much did it cost to make *Skytrail*?

7. Anna manages a movie theater that features classic movies. Anna has scheduled 23 musical comedies for an upcoming movie festival. The number of musical comedies scheduled is 5 more than 3 times the number of mysteries scheduled for the festival. How many mysteries has Anna scheduled for the festival?

8. Tom's costume for his new role cost $2,560. In his previous role his costume cost $30 more than $\frac{1}{8}$ of the cost of the costume for his new role. How much did his costume for his previous role cost?

PROBLEM SOLVING
Guessing and Checking

Sometimes you can solve a problem by using the conditions given, first to guess at and then to check the answer.

Number Explorers is a TV math show that presents everything from games to plays. Sally, a game contestant, has to guess two 2-digit numbers that meet the following requirements.

1. Each of the two numbers has two different digits.
2. Both numbers must have the same digits, but the digits are reversed.
3. The sum of the 2 digits must be 12.
4. The product of the 2 digits must be a number cubed.

For the first guess, Sally picks two numbers that meet requirements 1 and 3—they are 2-digits, and the sum of the 2 digits is 12. The first guess is 57 and 84.

Then, she checks them against the other requirements and finds that the numbers 57 and 84 do not meet requirement 2—they must have the same digits but those digits must be reversed. Her second guess is 48 and 84.

When she checks this guess against requirement 4, she finds that the product of the two digits—32—is not a number cubed.

Sally continues to guess and check until she finds the pair of numbers that meets all four requirements.

Of all the possible pairs of numbers, only 39 and 93 meet the fourth requirement. The product of their digits—27—equals a number cubed—3. The 2-digit numbers are therefore 39 and 93.

Solve. If you use the guess-and-check strategy, show your guesses and how you checked them.

1. For a party, the people who work on *Number Explorers* baked giant loaves of bread in geometric shapes. They bought 28 bags of flour, rye flour in 2-pound bags and wheat flour in 5-pound bags. They bought the same number of pounds of each kind of flour. How many bags of each kind of flour did they buy?

2. One contestant must find a 2-digit number that is less than 20. When each of its digits is squared and the two squared numbers are added together, their sum is 3 less than the original number. What is the number?

3. To find the number of production workers on the show, find this number. It is a 2-digit number between 75 and 90. When its digits are added together and the sum is squared, the answer is the original number. What is the number of workers?

4. One contestant wins a prize by correctly guessing a 3-digit number between 140 and 160. When each digit is cubed and the three cubed numbers are added together, the sum equals the number. What is the number?

5. One week, the show features automorphic numbers. An *automorphic number* is one whose square ends with the number. An example is 25, whose square is 625. There are 2 automorphic numbers between 2 and 10. What are they?

6. Contestants on the show are given prizes based on the number of points they score. For every 3 points, a contestant is given $25 worth of prizes. Linda Randizi scored 969 points. How much money were her prizes worth?

Inequalities

A. An inequality is a number sentence that has any of the following symbols: $>$, $<$, $\geq$, $\leq$, or $\neq$.

$\geq$ means "is greater than or equal to."
$\leq$ means "is less than or equal to."

Word Sentence	*Inequality*
The temperature is less than $^-10°F$.	$t < {}^-10$
The cost is greater than or equal to $5.	$c \geq 5$
The weight of the fish plus 5 oz is less than or equal to 32 oz.	$f + 5 \leq 32$

A drop of $3°C$ in the temperature results in a temperature greater than $^-12°C$. $\quad t - 3 > {}^-12$

B. You can solve an inequality by finding all the values in the **replacement set** that make the inequality a true statement.

Solve $x < {}^-3$. Use the replacement set $\{^-5, {}^-4, {}^-3\}$.

Try $^-5$.	Try $^-4$.	Try $^-3$.
$x < {}^-3$	$x < {}^-3$	$x < {}^-3$
$^-5 \bullet {}^-3$	$^-4 \bullet {}^-3$	$^-3 \bullet {}^-3$
$^-5 < {}^-3$ ✔	$^-4 < {}^-3$ ✔	$^-3 = {}^-3$
$^-5$ is a solution.	$^-4$ is a solution.	$^-3$ is not a solution.

So, the values $^-5$ and $^-4$ in the replacement set are solutions to the inequality.

Other examples:

Solve. Use all real numbers as the replacement set.

$$p + 7 \geq 0 \qquad\qquad \frac{x}{2} < {}^-2$$

Try 7.	$7 + 7 \bullet 0$	$14 \geq 0$ ✔	Try 0.	$\frac{0}{2} \bullet {}^-2$	$0 > {}^-2$
Try 0.	$0 + 7 \bullet 0$	$7 \geq 0$ ✔	Try $^-4$.	$\frac{^-4}{2} \bullet {}^-2$	$^-2 = {}^-2$
Try $^-7$.	$^-7 + 7 \bullet 0$	$0 \geq 0$ ✔	Try $^-5$.	$\frac{^-5}{2} \bullet {}^-2$	$^-2\frac{1}{2} < {}^-2$ ✔
Try $^-8$.	$^-8 + 7 \bullet 0$	$^-1 < 0$			

So, all real numbers $\geq {}^-7$ are solutions of the inequality.

So, all real numbers $< {}^-4$ are solutions of the inequality.

Math Reasoning, page H222

Match each statement with an inequality.

1. The weight is greater than 6 pounds.

2. The watermelons weigh less than 6 kg.

3. The length of the rope is greater than 20 feet.

4. The cost of 6 peaches is greater than or equal to $1.

5. One quarter of the number of lemons in the basket is less than 20.

a. $6p \geq 1$

b. $w > 6$

c. $w < 6$

d. $l > 20$

e. $\frac{1}{4}f < 20$

Use the replacement set {0,1,2,3,4,5,6,7}.
Solve.

6. $x < 4$ **7.** $a \geq 3$ **8.** $y < 2$ **9.** $b \geq 5$

10. $r \leq 7$ **11.** $c \leq 4$ **12.** $b \leq 1$ **13.** $g < 3$

14. $m \geq 3 + 4$ **15.** $r > 7 - 3$ **16.** $d < 1 \cdot 4$ **17.** $h > \frac{10}{2}$

Use the replacement set {⁻5,⁻4,⁻3,⁻2,⁻1,0,1,2,3,4,5}.
Solve.

18. $x + 2 > 5$ **19.** $y + {}^-1 \leq {}^-3$ **20.** $t - 5 < 0$

21. $3r \geq {}^-3$ **22.** $\frac{s}{4} \leq {}^-1$ **★23.** ${}^-2n > 6$

Use the replacement set of all real numbers.
Solve.

24. $q + 10 > 2$ **25.** $x - 21 > {}^-5$ **26.** $\frac{y}{3} \leq {}^-19$

27. $12m < 252$ **28.** $\frac{p}{7} \leq {}^-52$ **★29.** $33x \neq 2{,}508$

CALCULATOR

Compare. Use >, <, or = for ●.

1. $\sqrt{3} + \sqrt{7} \; ● \; \sqrt{10}$ **2.** $\sqrt{13} \; ● \; \sqrt{2} + \sqrt{11}$ **3.** $\sqrt{3} + \sqrt{5} \; ● \; \sqrt{7} + \sqrt{1}$

4. $\sqrt{13} - \sqrt{5} \; ● \; \sqrt{8}$ **5.** $\sqrt{15} - \sqrt{12} \; ● \; \sqrt{3}$ **6.** $\sqrt{11} - \sqrt{3} \; ● \; \sqrt{13} - \sqrt{5}$

7. $\sqrt{3} \cdot \sqrt{4} \; ● \; \sqrt{12}$ **8.** $\sqrt{2} \cdot \sqrt{8} \; ● \; \sqrt{16}$ **9.** $\sqrt{2} \cdot \sqrt{3} \cdot \sqrt{5} \; ● \; \sqrt{30}$

10. $\frac{\sqrt{20}}{\sqrt{5}} \; ● \; \sqrt{4}$ **11.** $\frac{\sqrt{9}}{\sqrt{3}} \cdot \sqrt{2} \; ● \; \sqrt{6}$ **12.** $\frac{\sqrt{8}}{\sqrt{4}} \cdot \sqrt{2} \; ● \; \sqrt{4}$

Solving One-Step Inequalities

A movie needs extras for a crowd scene. Each extra is paid $50. If the budget allows no more than $4,500 for extras, how many can be hired?

Let x represent the number of extras. Then, $50x \leq 4{,}500$.

To solve an inequality, solve the related equation. Then write the correct inequality for the solution.

$50x \leq 4{,}500$
$50x = 4{,}500$ Use the related equation.
$\frac{50x}{50} = \frac{4{,}500}{50}$ Divide by 50.
$x = 90$ Think: Is $x \leq 90$ the solution?

Test any value less than 90 to find out.
If you try 0 for x, $50 \cdot 0 \leq 4{,}500$. So, $x \leq 90$.

No more than 90 extras can be hired.

Other examples:

Solve $a + 7.5 \geq 9.4$.
Use the related equation.

$$a + 7.5 = 9.4$$

$a + 7.5 - 7.5 = 9.4 - 7.5$
$a = 1.9$ Is $a \leq 1.9$ the solution?
Try 10 for a. $\frac{10}{2.5} > 2$. So, $a \leq 1.9$.

Solve $\frac{4}{5}s \geq 20$.
Use the related equation.

$$\frac{4}{5}s = 20$$

$\frac{4}{5}s \cdot \frac{5}{4} = \overset{5}{\cancel{20}} \cdot \frac{5}{\underset{1}{\cancel{4}}}$

$s = 25$ Is $s \geq 25$ the solution?
Try 30 for s. $\frac{4}{5} \cdot 30 \geq 20$.
So, $s \geq 25$.

Solve $\frac{p}{7} \neq 49$.
Use the related equation.

$$\frac{p}{7} = 49$$

$\frac{p}{7} \cdot 7 = 49 \cdot 7$
$p = 343$
So, $p \neq 343$.

Solve $t - 4 \leq 6$.
Use the related equation.

$$t - 4 = 6$$

$t - 4 + 4 = 6 + 4$

$t = 10$ Is $t \leq 10$ the solution?
Try 8 for t. $8 - 4 \leq 6$.
So, $t \leq 10$.

Solve.

1. $x + 2 < 8$

2. $a + 4 \geq 9$

3. $r - 1 > 7$

4. $x - 5 \leq 3$

5. $3g > 24$

6. $7b < 21$

7. $\frac{d}{6} \leq 10$

8. $\frac{m}{4} > 6$

9. $x - 0.3 \neq 0.7$

10. $y + 1.3 \geq 2.4$

11. $c + 2.4 > 4.2$

12. $k - 4.8 \leq 6.3$

13. $0.6m \leq 3.6$

14. $1.2t > 4.8$

15. $\frac{q}{2.7} \geq 0.3$

16. $\frac{m}{1.6} < 0.6$

17. $a - \frac{1}{4} \geq \frac{3}{4}$

18. $c - \frac{3}{8} > \frac{4}{8}$

19. $s + \frac{1}{3} \geq \frac{2}{5}$

20. $y + \frac{1}{8} \leq \frac{4}{5}$

21. $\frac{1}{2}c \geq \frac{3}{5}$

22. $\frac{2}{3}t \leq \frac{4}{5}$

23. $\frac{r}{\frac{1}{3}} \neq \frac{2}{3}$

24. $\frac{y}{\frac{1}{5}} \leq \frac{2}{5}$

25. $e - 7 \neq {}^{-}3$

26. $x - 3 > {}^{-}8$

27. $x + 5 > {}^{-}3$

28. $g + 9 \leq {}^{-}18$

29. $\frac{y}{3} \leq 2$

30. $\frac{d}{5} > 5$

31. $6m < {}^{-}3.6$

32. $3r < 12$

Solve.

33. Last week, 7 people were selected for a scene in the school play. The director wants no more than 29 people in the scene. Write an inequality, and solve to find how many more people can be selected for the scene.

34. The leading player, Angela Greene, receives a salary of $175 per day. How many days will it take her to earn $2,275?

CHALLENGE

To simplify expressions such as $2x + 4 + 3x + 7$, first, group the like terms, variables with identical variables, and whole numbers with whole numbers.

Add the like terms.

$$2x + 3x + 4 + 7$$
$$5x \quad + \quad 11$$

Simplify each expression.

1. $4x + 3x + 7 + 10$

2. $6y + 8 + 3y + 4$

3. $7 + 12 + 19z + 1 + 2z$

4. $5a + 3 + 176 + 18a + a$

PROBLEM SOLVING
Making a Table To Find a Pattern

You can use a table to help you find a pattern that will enable you to solve a problem.

> To help promote its new movie, *Galaxy Dragonfighter*, Fallotte Enterprises created a video game about the movie's hero. For the next week, Fallotte is offering cash prizes to players who score high in the game. A score of 75,000 points in a single game wins a $2 prize. Scoring 77,250 points wins $2.50, scoring 79,500 wins $3.00, and so on. Shawn won $5.00. How many points did he score?

Make a table.

Points Scored	Prize
75,000	$2.00
77,250	$2.50
79,500	$3.00

The table makes it easier to see the pattern. For every 2,250 points scored, the player wins another $0.50. To find out how many points Shawn scored, continue the table until you reach the prize that he won—$5.00.

Points Scored	Prize
75,000	$2.00
77,250	$2.50
79,500	$3.00
81,750	$3.50
84,000	$4.00
86,250	$4.50
88,500	$5.00

Shawn scored at least 88,500 points.

Solve. Make a table if needed.

1. Julie scored 95,250 points playing the *Galaxy Dragonfighter* game. What was the cash prize that she won?

2. How many points would a player have to score to win the top prize—$8.00?

3. *The Danville Times* charges $31.75 for a 3-line classified advertisement. A 4-line ad costs $41.10, a 5-line ad costs $50.45, a 6-line ad costs $59.80, and so on. How much will Mr. Simmons pay if he wants to take out a help-wanted ad that runs 9 lines?

4. How much would it cost to place a 7-line ad in *The Danville Times*?

5. To rent 4 video tapes at the Tape City Video Shop, you need $63.80. To rent 5 tapes, you need $67.60; to rent 6 tapes, you need $71.40; and so on. If you need a membership in order to rent even 1 tape and if you get 3 tapes rent free when you buy a membership, how much does a membership cost? How much does it cost to rent 9 tapes?

6. A throng of Hollywood stars arrived at the gala opening of a new movie. The first person through the door of the theater was the star of the movie. Each time the theater doors opened thereafter, 4 more stars entered than had entered previously. If the theater doors opened and closed 15 times, how many stars attended the opening of the movie? Copy and complete the table.

Door openings	1	2	3	4	5	6	7	8	9	10	11	12	13	14	15
Stars entered	1	5	9												
Total stars	1	6	15												

7. After the doors had opened 9 times, how many stars were there in the theater?

Solving Two-Step Inequalities

Shigeko has 7 scenes left to tape for her television drama. She has already spent 56 days on the project, which must be finished in a total of 84 days or less. How many days can she spend on the average on each remaining scene?

The problem can be represented as a two-step inequality. Let x represent the number of days she can spend on each scene; then $7x$ represents the total time that remains.

$$7x + 56 \leq 84$$

$$7x + 56 - 56 = 84 - 56 \qquad \text{Use the related equation.}$$

$$7x = 28$$

$$\frac{7x}{7} = \frac{28}{7}$$

$$x = 4 \qquad \text{Is } x \leq 4 \text{ the solution?}$$

Try 0 for x. $7 \cdot 0 + 56 \leq 84$ So, $x \leq 4$.

She can spend on the average 4 days or less on each remaining scene.

Another example:

Solve. Use the replacement set of real numbers.

$$\frac{x}{2} + 4 < 7$$

$$\frac{x}{2} + 4 - 4 = 7 - 4 \qquad \text{Use the related equation.}$$

$$\frac{x}{2} = 3$$

$$\frac{x}{2} \cdot 2 = 3 \cdot 2$$

$$x = 6 \qquad \text{Is } x < 6 \text{ the solution?}$$

Try 2 for x. $\frac{2}{2} + 4 < 7$. So, $x < 6$.

Any number less than 6 will be in the solution set.

Checkpoint Write the letter of the correct answer.

Solve.

1. $2x + 3 < 9$ **a.** $x < 3$ **b.** $x = 3$ **c.** $x < 6$ **d.** $x < 12$

2. $4x + 4 \leq 16$ **a.** $x \geq 3$ **b.** $x \leq 3$ **c.** $x \leq 5$ **d.** $x > 3$

Solve.

1. $2x + 3 < 5$

2. $4a - 2 > 6$

3. $3y - 1 < 5$

4. $6z + 3 > 15$

5. $\frac{b}{2} + 4 > 2$

6. $\frac{k}{3} - 1 > 1$

7. $\frac{d}{12} + 4 \geq 7$

8. $\frac{t}{8} - 7 \geq 7$

9. $7c - 5.7 > 51$

10. $8.2g + 8 < 24.4$

11. $1.2t + 4 > 100$

12. $1.2m - 4 \leq 2$

13. $\frac{t}{3} - 0.2 \geq 0.6$

14. $\frac{c}{12} + 1.6 > 1.7$

15. $\frac{m}{0.5} - 3.1 \leq 59$

16. $\frac{y}{0.6} + 4 > 8$

17. $7y - \frac{2}{5} < 48\frac{3}{5}$

18. $6c - 2\frac{1}{4} < 39\frac{3}{4}$

19. $\frac{2}{3}y + 9 \geq 21$

20. $\frac{3}{5}n + 8 > 17$

21. $\frac{m}{3} + \frac{1}{8} \neq \frac{4}{8}$

22. $\frac{x}{2} - \frac{3}{4} \leq \frac{3}{4}$

23. $\frac{l}{2} - \frac{1}{5} > \frac{3}{5}$

24. $\frac{d}{4} + \frac{1}{12} < \frac{4}{12}$

25. $8e + 4 < 36$

26. $9s - {}^-7 \geq 25$

27. $4b + {}^-2 \neq {}^-6$

28. $2m - 9 > 19$

29. $\frac{a}{2} + {}^-9 \geq 6$

30. $\frac{z}{6} - 14 \leq 2$

31. $\frac{r}{7} - {}^-3 > 4$

32. $\frac{n}{4} + 2 < 7$

Solve. For Problem 34, use the Infobank.

33. Write an inequality; then solve. Toby and Sam are saving to buy a TV that costs $147. If Toby has saved $25 more than Sam, but they do not have enough as yet, how much have they each saved?

34. Use the information on page 476 to solve. What is the number of frames projected by a TV set in Europe if it has projected 2,500 lines. Write an equation; then solve. (HINT: Let x = the number of frames projected.)

NUMBER SENSE

How can we estimate $\frac{348 \times 17}{9}$?

Think about numbers that are easier to compute mentally.

$350 \times \frac{18}{9}$		$\frac{360}{9} \times 20$	$\frac{350 \times 20}{10}$
350×2	or	40×20	or 350×2
700		800	700

Both 700 and 800 are good estimates.

Think of easier numbers, and estimate. Other estimates are possible.

1. $\frac{478 \times 36}{7}$

2. $\frac{713 \times 65}{8}$

3. $\frac{94 \times 198 \times 14}{7 \times 46}$

Graphing Equations and Inequalities

The solution to an equation or an inequality can be shown as a point or a set of points on a number line.

$x = 3$

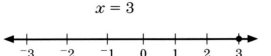

$x > 3$

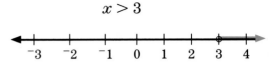

The open circle indicates the solution does not include 3.

Graph $\frac{y}{2.5} > 2$.

Use the related equation to solve.

$$\frac{y}{2.5} = 2$$
$$\frac{y}{2.5} \cdot 2.5 = 2 \cdot 2.5$$
$$y = 5 \quad \text{Is } y > 5 \text{ the solution?}$$

Try 10. $\frac{10}{2.5} > 2$. So, $y > 5$.

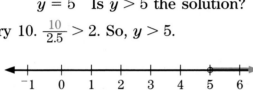

The ray indicates that all real numbers greater than 5 are solutions; 5 is not a solution.

Graph $45x \le 270$.

Use the related equation to solve.

$$45x = 270$$
$$\frac{45x}{45} = \frac{270}{45}$$
$$x = 6 \quad \text{Is } x \le 6 \text{ the solution?}$$

Try 0. $45 \cdot 0 \le 270$. So, $x \le 6$.

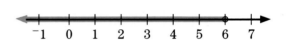

The ray indicates that all real numbers less than or equal to 6 are solutions.

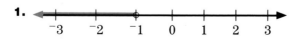

Checkpoint Write the letter of the correct answer.

Choose the equation or inequality that matches each graph.

1.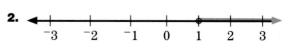

a. $x = {}^-1$ b. $x > {}^-1$

c. $x < {}^-1$ d. $x \ge {}^-1$

2.

a. $a \le 1$ b. $a \ge 1$

c. $a > 1$ d. $a < 1$

Solve and graph the inequality.

1. $x - 8 > 7$

2. $z + 5.5 > 8$

3. $\frac{y}{2} \leq 3$

4. $4c > 12$

5. $\frac{1}{4}a \geq 4$

6. $w - {}^-7 \leq 15$

7. $\frac{3}{4}r < 3$

8. $7c \neq 2.8$

9. $2x - 5 < 1$

10. $\frac{y}{2} + 5 > 6$

11. $0.3p + 0.3 \leq 1.2$

12. $\frac{m}{2} + {}^-2 < 10$

13. $3b + \frac{2}{3} \geq 3\frac{10}{15}$

14. $\frac{c}{2.5} - 7 \leq 3.4$

15. $\frac{3}{5}n + 2 > 5$

★16. $\frac{5}{9}g + 2.7 \neq 4.75$

Solve and graph the equation.

17. $c - 9 = 3$

18. $b - 1.28 = 8.72$

19. $9t = 7$

20. $a - 8 = {}^-4$

21. $\frac{{}^-x}{4} = \frac{3}{4}$

22. $p + 0.78 = 18$

23. ${}^-4c = {}^-16$

24. $\frac{e}{6} = \frac{2}{3}$

25. $2x + 10 = 18$

26. ${}^-12 + p = 4$

27. $x + 5.7 = 18.3$

28. ${}^-2b - 5 = {}^-7$

29. $\frac{r}{2} - 2 = 2$

★30. $\frac{s}{2} + 2 = 2$

★31. ${}^-4c - 8 = {}^-8$

★32. ${}^-k + 3 = {}^-4$

Solve.

33. Time the lengths of commercials in minutes during an hour of TV programming. Write equations to represent the relation between the total commercial time and the remaining time. Solve to find the program time. Graph the solution.

★34. Maria sells station time for commercials. Yesterday she sold 2 minutes more than she sold the day before. These two days are still less than her record total sale of 8 minutes in two days. Write and graph an inequality to represent the number of minutes sold yesterday and the day before.

CHALLENGE   Patterns, Relations, and Functions

To solve these inequalities, test values for the variable, and graph the solution set.

1. ${}^-x > 2$

2. ${}^-y < {}^-6$

3. $\frac{x}{2} + 4 \geq 7$

4. ${}^-5a + 4 \leq 24$

PROBLEM SOLVING
Using a Schedule

A plane schedule shows you where and when each plane stops along its route. You can use a time-zone map to find the difference in time between two places that are in different time zones.

> The International Film and Video Convention is being held in New York City. Travis will travel from Chicago, Illinois, to New York, New York. Here is the plane schedule he will use.

Here is the information you should study on this kind of schedule:

- The main heading tells you where the plane leaves from.

- The subheading tells you where the plane is flying to.

- The columns show you the plane's departure time, its arrival time, and the flight number.

- The *a* or the *p* after the times shows you whether the time is A.M. or P.M.

- The capital letters *(CST)* show the time zone of the city of departure *(Central Standard Time)*.

Use the schedule and the time-zone map on page 186 to answer this question.

Travis decides to take the 2:00 P.M. flight to New York. At what time will he arrive, and how long will the flight take?

Look at the schedule. Locate the entry under New York that shows the 2:00 P.M. departure time. Now look at the time-zone map on page 186. Chicago is in the Central time zone, and New York is in the Eastern time zone. When it is 4:54 P.M. in New York, it is 3:54 P.M. in Chicago. The flight will take 1 hour 54 minutes.

Chicago, Illinois (CST)		
To New York, New York		
Leave	Arrive	Flight
6:15a	9:09a	928
6:44a	9:42a	256
7:00a	9:55a	900
8:00a	10:53a	902
8:35a	11:27a	258
9:00a	11:55a	904
10:00a	12:52p	906
11:00a	1:49p	908
11:15a	2:20p	304
11:30a	2:22p	518
11:46a	3:22p	390
11:48a	2:47p	760
12:00p	2:50p	910
1:00p	3:50p	912
2:00p	4:54p	914
2:15p	5:11p	122
2:15p	5:30p	790
3:00p	5:53p	916
4:00p	7:00p	918
4:43p	7:59p	152
4:43p	7:43p	584
4:44p	8:39p	782
5:00p	7:59p	920
5:10p	8:18p	104
6:00p	8:57p	922
7:00p	10:00p	924
8:00p	10:50p	926
8:15p	11:14p	220
8:15p	11:14p	308

Use the plane schedule on page 302 to solve each problem. Write either *true* or *false*.

1. Flight 518 leaves Chicago at 11:30 A.M. and arrives in New York at 2:22 P.M.

2. If Travis takes Flight 920, he will arrive in New York at 8:39 P.M.

3. Flight 760 takes 5 minutes longer than Flight 914.

4. If Travis takes Flight 928, the trip will take him 1 hour and 54 minutes.

Use the plane schedules on pages 302 and 303 to answer each question.

5. Elaine, an independent filmmaker from Seattle, Washington, has to change planes in Denver, Colorado, before flying to New York. Which flights could she take from Seattle if she wants to arrive in New York by 6:00 P.M.?

6. Elaine, flying from Seattle, takes the earliest possible connecting flight in Denver and arrives in New York on time. How much time did she spend on the entire trip?

★7. Donald, a film critic, wants to leave Denver, Colorado, before 8:00 in the morning. He can fly directly to New York or fly to Chicago, change planes, and save some money on plane fare. Which flight takes more time? How much more time does it take?

★8. Donald decides to save money and change planes in Chicago, but his plane is late and he doesn't arrive in Chicago until 11:35 A.M. Which flights could he take from Chicago and still arrive in New York before 5:00 P.M.? How long would each flight take?

Seattle, Washington (PST)		
To Denver, Colorado		
Leave	Arrive	Flight
6:35a	10:04a	210
8:00a	11:27a	288
12:05p	3:27p	18
2:15p	6:37p	748
2:55p	6:17p	434
3:30p	10:15p	1257

Denver, Colorado (MST)		
To Chicago, Illinois		
Leave	Arrive	Flight
7:35a	10:40a	518
10:12a	1:28p	26
10:54a	3:08p	576
11:01a	2:15p	916
11:03a	3:50p	482
11:04a	3:55p	670
12:55p	4:05p	376
4:00p	7:18p	296
4:09p	8:52p	328
5:35p	8:47p	276
6:57p	11:01p	636
7:15p	10:19p	254
8:35p	11:39p	278
3:00a	6:01a	888
To New York, New York		
Leave	Arrive	Flight
7:35a	3:22p	518
8:15a	1:40p	164
10:12a	4:54p	26
10:51a	5:50p	642
11:00a	4:35p	210
11:01a	5:53p	916
11:09a	4:51p	160
12:25p	6:00p	162
12:55p	8:39p	376
4:20p	9:55p	174
4:21p	10:00p	178
3:00a	9:42a	888

LOGICAL REASONING

A. Logical statements are always either true or false. Two statements are equivalent if each is true when the other is true. The table below shows that statements p and q are equivalent.

p: x is greater than or equal to 8.
q: x is not less than 8.

	p	q
if $x < 8$	false	false
if $x = 8$	true	true
if $x > 8$	true	true

B. A statement such as "*If* tomorrow is Thursday, *then* the weather will be clear" is a **conditional statement.** The statement only promises clear weather if tomorrow is a Thursday. So, it is only false on a Thursday that is not clear. This relationship is shown in the **truth table.**

p: Tomorrow is Thursday.
q: The weather will be clear.

Notice that the conditional statement **if p, then q** is true unless p is true and q is false.

p	q	if p, then q
true	true	true
true	false	false
false	true	true
false	false	true

C. The statement **if q, then p** is the **converse** of the statement **if p, then q.** If a conditional statement is true, its converse may or may not be true.

Statement: If $x > 5$, then $x > 2$. ⟵ true for any x
Converse: If $x > 2$, then $x > 5$. ⟵ false for $x = 3$ or $x = 4$

Solve by using p: Mr. Watson's car is green.
q: Mr. Watson's car is a two-door.

1. Is the statement **if p, then q** *true* or *false* if Mr. Watson's car is

a. a brown two-door?
b. a green two-door?

c. a green four-door?
d. a blue four-door?

2. Write the converse of **if p, then q.** Is the converse true or false if Mr. Watson's car is

a. a red five-door?
b. a green two-door?

c. a blue two-door?
d. a green four-door?

GROUP PROJECT

Choose Your Channel

The problem: Your class is in charge of the prime-time schedule for a new TV network. Divide the class into 7 teams. Each team will be responsible for the schedule for one night. Look in TV guides to find out what the competition is doing. Then decide what kinds of shows to do, and make out a schedule like the one below to create balanced programming for the week.

Key Facts

- You must compete with the other networks to attract a share of the viewing audience.

- You need sponsors and advertisers, and so, your shows cannot be too controversial; but you also cannot let your advertisers determine the content of your programming.

- Each team must convince the rest of the class to approve its schedule.

Key Questions

- How do you decide whether a show should be 1 hour or $\frac{1}{2}$ hour long?

- What kinds of shows will you schedule?

- At what time would you schedule news? movies? variety shows? family shows? series?

- What kinds of specials would you schedule?

	Mon.	Tue.	Wed.	Thurs.	Fri.	Sat.	Sun.
P.M. VIEWING							
8:00	?	?	?	?	?	?	?
8:30	?	?	?	?	?	?	?
9:00	?	?	?	?	?	?	?
9:30	?	?	?	?	?	?	?
10:00	?	?	?	?	?	?	?
10:30	?	?	?	?	?	?	?

CHAPTER TEST

Evaluate each expression if the variable equals 0, $^-3$, and 2. (pages 280–281)

1. $a + 4$

2. $3b$

3. $\frac{x}{5}$

Solve. (pages 282–285)

4. $^-3x = {}^-24$

5. $\frac{a}{^-2.7} = 4.1$

6. $b - {}^-\frac{1}{4} = \frac{3}{8}$

7. $^-4d + 2 = 18$

8. $\frac{s}{3.2} - {}^-6 = 2$

9. $^-\frac{5}{6}m - 3 = 7$

10. $\frac{g}{^-3} + 17 = 32$

11. $0.6k - {}^-8 = 11.6$

12. $\frac{z}{^-\frac{1}{5}} + {}^-2 = 13$

Write a word problem for each equation then solve and check. (pages 286–287)

13. $n - 18 = 40$

14. $\frac{p}{7} = 5$

15. $2x = 174$

16. $r + 25 = 180$

17. $6t = 48$

18. $\frac{15}{z} = 5$

Solve. (pages 294–295 and 298–299)

19. $x + 5 > {}^-3$

20. $a - {}^-\frac{4}{7} < 1\frac{1}{2}$

21. $\frac{y}{6.2} \geq 3.4$

22. $\frac{t}{0.4} + 2 > 3$

23. $\frac{d}{4} + \frac{2}{9} < 1\frac{1}{18}$

24. $2x - {}^-3 \neq 6$

Solve and graph each equation. (pages 300–301)

25. $3e - 4 = 11$

26. $\frac{f}{^-5} - 5 = {}^-7$

27. $\frac{t}{^-2} - 4 = 9$

Solve and graph each inequality. (pages 300–301)

28. $3a - 7 > 8$

29. $\frac{c}{2.5} - 4 \leq 6$

30. $5c + {}^-3 > 12$

Solve. (pages 288–289, 290–291, 296–297, and 302–303)

31. José read the schedule to plan his TV viewing. Would it be possible for him to watch the entire drama on Channel 16 at 9 P.M. and also to watch the comedy on Channel 15 at 9:30 P.M.?

TV Programs This Evening		
9:00	(15)	Sports
	(16)	Drama
9:30	(15)	Comedy
10:00	(14)	Film
	(16)	Sports

32. The cost of special effects for a new movie was $3,472,800. This amount was $\frac{1}{5}$ of the total cost of making the movie. Write an equation and solve to find the cost of making the movie.

33. A game show contestant must find a 3-digit number that is divisible by 3 and by 5. The first two digits (but not the third) are the same and the sum of the 3 digits is less than 20. What is the number?

34. In May 2,345 people attended a comedy film at the Century Theater. This was 106 fewer than $\frac{3}{4}$ of the attendance at that theater in December. Write an equation and solve to find how many people attended the Century Theater in December.

35. *The Village Gazette* charges $29.75 for a 4-line advertisement. A 5-line ad costs $38.20, a 6-line ad costs $46.65, a 7-line ad costs $55.10, and so on. How much will Mrs. Webb pay for a 10-line ad?

BONUS

Solve.

For $126.94, Lynne purchased 3 movies and rented 4 films. If the rental fee was $2.86 per film, write an equation and solve to find the cost of purchasing a movie.

RETEACHING

To solve an algebraic equation means to find the values of the variable that make the equation true. If there is one operation in the variable expression, use the inverse operation on both sides of the equation. If there are two operations in the variable expression, add or subtract first, and then solve for the variable.

Solve.
$$1.8x + 1.6 = 7.9$$
$$1.8x + 1.6 - 1.6 = 7.9 - 1.6$$
$$1.8x = 6.3$$
$$\frac{1.8x}{1.8} = \frac{6.3}{1.8}$$
$$x = 3.5$$

To check, let $x = 3.5$.
$$1.8 \cdot 3.5 + 1.6 \overset{?}{=} 7.9$$
$$6.3 + 1.6 \overset{?}{=} 7.9$$
$$7.9 = 7.9 \; \text{✔}$$

Solve.
$$\frac{3}{4}x - 3 = {}^-9$$
$$\frac{3}{4}x - 3 + 3 = {}^-9 + 3$$
$$\frac{3}{4}x = {}^-6$$
$$\frac{4}{3} \cdot \frac{3}{4}x = \frac{4}{3} \cdot {}^-6$$
$$x = {}^-8$$

To check, let $x = {}^-8$.
$$\frac{3}{4} \cdot {}^-8 - 3 \overset{?}{=} {}^-9$$
$${}^-6 - 3 \overset{?}{=} {}^-9$$
$${}^-9 \overset{?}{=} {}^-9 \; \text{✔}$$

Solve and check.

1. $9x - 18 = 72$

2. $\frac{1}{2}x + 3 = 12$

3. $\frac{x}{5} - 3 = 6.5$

4. $8x - 0.9 = 4.7$

5. $\frac{3}{4}x + 6 = 21$

6. $\frac{2}{3}x - 6 = 2$

7. $6x - \frac{1}{3} = 12\frac{2}{3}$

8. $^-5x + 10 = 25$

9. $^-7x + 3 = {}^-39$

10. $\frac{x}{^-2} + 4 = 8$

11. $\frac{3}{4}x - 4 = 2$

12. $\frac{x}{1.6} - 3.2 = 3.2$

13. $\frac{x}{0.5} + 4 = 8$

14. $0.2x + 3.2 = 6$

15. $\frac{x}{3} - 4.25 = 7.25$

16. $\frac{x}{7} + 4 = 8$

17. $4x + 1.2 = {}^-5.6$

18. $^-6x - {}^-3 = {}^-7.8$

19. $\frac{x}{9} + 17 = 46$

20. $^-3x + 21 = 63$

21. $\frac{^-x}{8} - 10\frac{1}{2} = {}^-30$

22. $\frac{x}{13} + {}^-4 = {}^-4$

23. $16x - {}^-7.5 = 76.3$

24. $^-9x + {}^-1\frac{3}{8} = 64\frac{5}{8}$

25. $\frac{5}{x} - 1.7 = 0.3$

26. $\frac{^-3}{5}x + 6 = 5\frac{1}{4}$

27. $\frac{14}{x} - {}^-7.2 = 17.2$

ENRICHMENT

Solving Algebraic Equations in One Variable With Exponents

An algebraic equation is called a **quadratic or second-degree equation** when 2 is the largest exponent used. Every quadratic equation has two roots or solutions.

When the quadratic equation has only one variable term, its two roots are found by

1. isolating the variable term.
2. taking the square root of each side.
3. checking the resulting roots.

Solve. $x^2 = 64$

$$x = \pm \sqrt{64}$$

> $\pm$ means one root is positive and the other is negative.

$$x = {}^{\pm}8$$

Check. $8^2 \overset{?}{=} 64 \qquad (^-8)^2 \overset{?}{=} 64$

$\qquad 64 = 64 \; \boldsymbol{\swarrow} \qquad 64 = 64 \; \boldsymbol{\swarrow}$

So, the two roots of $x^2 = 64$ are 8 and $^-8$.

Solve. $\qquad 4x^2 = x^2 + 48$

$$4x^2 - x^2 = 48$$
$$3x^2 = 48$$
$$x^2 = 16$$
$$x = \pm \sqrt{16}$$
$$x = {}^{\pm}4$$

Check. $4(4)^2 \overset{?}{=} 4^2 + 48 \qquad 4(^-4)^2 \overset{?}{=} (^-4)^2 + 48$

$\qquad 4 \cdot 16 \overset{?}{=} 16 + 48 \qquad 4 \cdot 16 \overset{?}{=} 16 + 48$

$\qquad\quad 64 = 64 \; \boldsymbol{\swarrow} \qquad\qquad 64 = 64 \; \boldsymbol{\swarrow}$

The roots are 4 and $^-4$.

Solve and check.

1. $x^2 = 49$ **2.** $x^2 = 121$ **3.** $x^2 = 625$ **4.** $x^2 = 20$

5. $x^2 = 72$ **6.** $x^2 = 125$ **7.** $3x^2 = 12$ **8.** $4x^2 = 36$

9. $6x^2 = 96$ **10.** $5x^2 = 90$ **11.** $7x^2 = 686$ **12.** $10x^2 = 360$

309

TECHNOLOGY

You can use BASIC to solve computational problems that contain exponents. For example, to find the value of 2^3, you can type this. PRINT 2^3
The computer will print this. 8

On some computers, you use the ↑ symbol instead of the ^ symbol. Other computers may use other symbols.

Write what the instruction will print.

1. PRINT 8^2   **2.** PRINT 5^3   **3.** PRINT 2^4   **4.** PRINT 10^5

If you give the computer an instruction with several operations, it will use the same rules for computing that you have learned. The computer does operations in the following order:

1. Operations within parentheses
2. Exponents
3. Multiplication and division (left to right)
4. Addition and subtraction (left to right)

If a multiplication operation and a division operation occur in the same exercise, the computer will first do the computation that is on the left.

Write what the computer will print when you give this instruction:

5. PRINT 5 * 2^2   **6.** PRINT (5 * 2)^2
7. PRINT 16 − 4^2   **8.** PRINT (2 * 5)^3/(2^2)

Scientific Notation is a shorthand way to write very large or very small numbers. Your computer uses scientific notation to represent any number that has more than 9 digits. For instance, 670,000,000,000 is represented as 6.7 E 11.

This means 6.7 times 10^{11}. Another way to think of this is to move the decimal point 11 places to the right.

The number 0.000000000067 is represented as 6.7 E −11.

This means 6.7 times 10^{-11}, or move the decimal point 11 places to the left.

The computer always moves the decimal point far enough so that the number to the left of the E is a number between 1 and 10, followed by a decimal point and the number of decimal places needed up to 8.

Write what the instruction will print.

9. PRINT .00000000000038

10. PRINT 7300000000000000

11. PRINT 11^9

12. PRINT 10^10

13. PRINT 10^−17

CUMULATIVE REVIEW

Write the letter of the correct answer.

1. $7 + {}^-14$

   a. $^-21$ b. $^-7$
   c. 7 d. not given

2. $^-72 - {}^-31$

   a. $^-103$ b. $^-41$
   c. 41 d. not given

3. $^-23 \times {}^-14$

   a. $^-9$ b. 37
   c. $^-122$ d. not given

4. Order from the greatest to the least: $^-7, 4, {}^-82, {}^-14$.

   a. $4, {}^-7, {}^-14, {}^-82$
   b. $^-82, {}^-14, {}^-7, 4$
   c. $^-82, 4, {}^-7, {}^-14$
   d. not given

5. What is 0.07824 written in scientific notation?

   a. 7.824×10^{-3} b. 7.824×10^{-2}
   c. $7,824 \times 10^{-2}$ d. not given

6. Order $^-5\frac{4}{5}, 7.25, {}^-43.3, 2\frac{1}{8}$ from the least to the greatest.

   a. $^-43.3, {}^-5\frac{4}{5}, 2\frac{1}{8}, 7.25$
   b. $2\frac{1}{8}, {}^-5\frac{4}{5}, 7.25, {}^-43.3$
   c. $7.25, 2\frac{1}{8}, {}^-5\frac{4}{5}, {}^-43.3$
   d. not given

7. 3.54 is what percent of 472?

   a. 13%   b. 25%
   c. 76%   d. not given

8. 299.04 is 84% of what number?

   a. 234   b. 356
   c. 451   d. not given

9. Complete: 272 oz = ▇ lb.

   a. 17   b. 23
   c. 27.2   d. not given

10. 7 h 42 min + 16 h 39 min

    a. 9 h 3 min
    b. 23 h 3 min
    c. 24 h 21 min
    d. not given

11. What is $\frac{52}{9}$ as a mixed number?

    a. $5\frac{2}{9}$ b. $5\frac{7}{9}$
    c. $7\frac{2}{9}$ d. not given

12. Frieda left New York when the temperature was 42°F. When she arrived in Nome, Alaska, the temperature was 9°F below zero. What was the change in the number of degrees?

    a. 33°F   b. 51°F
    c. 52°F   d. not given

13. Floyd's savings account pays an annual yield of 6.03% interest. To the nearest dollar, how much interest did he gain on $2,000 over a 3-year period if the interest was reinvested each year?

    a. $361   b. $371
    c. $384   d. not given

What is the most popular spectator sport in your school? Do boys and girls have the same favorites or different ones? Does the answer differ according to the age of the people you question? How would you take a sample that would give you reliable information about the preferences of the students in your school?

9 STATISTICS AND PROBABILITY

Arranging Data

A. Between 1954 and 1976, Hank Aaron hit 755 home runs. The number of home runs he hit each year is listed below.

13, 39, 24, 44, 20, 27, 40, 32, 38, 12, 26, 31, 44, 47, 10, 44, 45, 39, 34, 30, 44, 29, 40

In how many of the years did Hank Aaron hit 40 or more home runs?

It is easier to find the answer if the numerical information, or **data,** is organized into intervals. In the **frequency table** at the right, the data (number of home runs per year) is organized into **intervals.** The size of each interval, called its **width,** is 10 home runs ($20 - 10 = 10$, $30 - 20 = 10$, and so on). For each year's number, a **tally mark** is made next to the appropriate interval. The **relative frequency** is the ratio of the frequency for the interval to the total frequency.

Hank Aaron hit 40 or more home runs in 8 of the 23 years, or about 35% of the time.

$\frac{8}{23} \approx 0.35$, or 35%

NUMBER OF HOME RUNS

Intervals	Tally	Frequency	Relative frequency
10–19	III	3	13%
20–29	IHI1	5	22%
30–39	IHI1 II	7	30%
40–49	IHI1 III	8	35%
Total		23	100%

B. Find the range for the set of data given above.

The **range** is the difference between the greatest and the least number in a set of data. You can tell from the frequency table that the greatest number is between 40 and 49, and that the least number is between 10 and 19.

> Greatest number = 47
> Least number = 10
> Range = 47 − 10 = 37

So, the range for the given set of data is 37.

Use the data to solve Exercises 1–6.

The most home runs hit per year in each of the major leagues for 1980–1989 was 48, 41, 31, 22, 37, 39, 40, 39, 36, 43, 37, 40, 37, 40, 49, 49, 39, 42, 47, and 36.

1. Make a frequency table. Start with 20 and use intervals that have a width of 5. (The first interval is 20–24.)

2. For how many years did the major leaguers hit 45 or more home runs?

3. For what percent of the years were 30–34 home runs hit?

4. For what percent of the years were 35–39 home runs hit?

5. Which interval of home runs has the greatest frequency?

6. What is the range of the home runs hit?

Use the data to solve Exercises 7–11.

The average number of points per game of the NBA scoring leaders for 1965–1989 was 34.7, 33.5, 35.6, 27.1, 28.4, 31.2, 31.7, 34.8, 34.0, 30.8, 34.5, 31.1, 31.1, 27.2, 29.6, 33.1, 30.7, 32.3, 28.4, 30.6, 32.9, 30.3, 37.1, 35.0, and 32.5.

7. Make a frequency table. Start with 25 and use intervals that have a width of 5. (The first interval is 25–29.9.)

8. What is the range for this set of data?

9. Which interval has the greatest frequency?

10. In how many years was the average 35 or above?

11. What percent of the scoring leaders had an average between 25 and 29.9?

Solve. For Problem 13, use the Infobank.

12. Make a frequency table to organize this data of the years of football played by the all-time leading scorers.

13. Use the information on page 477 to solve. Which scoring champion had the highest scoring average for one season? During which year did he accomplish this?

ALL-TIME LEADING SCORERS

Player	Years played	Player	Years played
Bahr	13	Bakken	17
Blanda	26	Cappelletti	11
Cox	15	Groza	17
Leahy	15	Moseley	16
Stenerud	19	Turner	16

Median, Mode, and Mean

A. The first women's Olympic long-jump competition occurred in 1948, and the record jump was $18 \text{ ft } 8\frac{1}{4}$ in. The distances for a high school women's long-jump competition are listed in the table.

Find the median and mode for this set of data.

High School Women's Long Jump	
12 ft 6 in.	11 ft 4 in.
15 ft 8 in.	9 ft 9 in.
12 ft 2 in.	10 ft 1 in.
14 ft 7 in.	16 ft 2 in.
14 ft 6 in.	16 ft 9 in.

The **median** is the middle number in a set of data when the numbers are listed in order. When there are two middle numbers, add the two middle numbers and divide by 2 to find the median.

$$\frac{12 \text{ ft } 6 \text{ in.} + 14 \text{ ft } 6 \text{ in.}}{2} = 13 \text{ ft } 6 \text{ in.}$$

The median is 13 ft 6 in.

The **mode** is the number that appears most often in the set. In the given set of data, there is no mode because all of the long jumps are of different distances. A set of data can have more than one mode. For example, the following set of data has two modes.

38, 21, 29, 38, 5, 21

Both 38 and 21 are modes.

B. The Olympic Pentathlon is a contest of five events. What is the mean score for the five scores shown at the right?

The **mean,** or **average,** is the sum of the numbers divided by the number of addends. To find the mean score, add the scores and divide by the number of events.

PENTATHLON

Event	Score
Riding	1,100
Fencing	956
Swimming	1,300
Shooting	978
Running	1,135

$$\frac{1,100 + 956 + 1,300 + 978 + 1,135}{5} = \frac{5,469}{5} = 1,093.8$$

The mean score for the Pentathlon is 1,093.8 points.

The mean, median, and mode are called **measures of central tendency.**

316

For each set of data find the median, mode, and mean.
Round to the nearest thousandth.

Set of data	Median	Mode	Mean
78, 96, 83, 78, 94	1. ■	2. ■	3. ■
132, 249, 365, 418, 253, 372	4. ■	5. ■	6. ■
5,697; 5,432; 5,574; 5,459; 5,357; 5,495; 5,697; 5,459	7. ■	8. ■	9. ■
0.5, 0.8, 0.6, 1.1, 0.9, 0.1, 0.5	10. ■	11. ■	12. ■
1.12, 2.37, 3.46, 1.29, 2.87, 3.46	13. ■	14. ■	15. ■
4.002, 4.215, 3.84, 4.215, 3.906, 3.84, 3.002, 4.215	16. ■	17. ■	18. ■
$6, 3\frac{1}{2}, 4\frac{3}{4}, 5\frac{1}{4}, 5, 4\frac{1}{2}, 4\frac{3}{4}, 4\frac{3}{4}$	19. ■	20. ■	21. ■
$7\frac{2}{3}, 6\frac{1}{2}, 4, 5\frac{1}{3}, 8, 7\frac{1}{2}$	22. ■	23. ■	24. ■
7 ft 5 in., 12 ft 3 in., 7 ft 9 in., 6 ft 5 in., 10 ft 6 in., 7 ft 9 in.	25. ■	26. ■	★27. ■
3 lb 8 oz, 2 lb 15 oz, 4 lb 3 oz, 3 lb, 4 lb 5 oz, 2 lb 8 oz, 3 lb 10 oz	28. ■	29. ■	★30. ■

Solve. For Problem 33, use the Infobank.

The table lists the salary distribution for twelve professional basketball players.

31. Find the median, mode, and mean.

★**32.** Imagine that the highest-paid player retires and is replaced by another player. If the mean of the team members' salaries is now $325,000, what is the salary of the new player?

33. Use the information on page 477 to solve. To the nearest whole number, find the mean number of points that Bob McAdoo scored over the years that he was NBA scoring leader.

Salary	Frequency
$70,000	1
$100,000	1
$130,000	1
$250,000	3
$400,000	2
$600,000	2
$750,000	1
$1,000,000	1

Bar Graphs and Histograms

A. The average age of athletes in different sports varies. This chart lists the mean (average) age of Olympic athletes in four sports.

Graphs are used to make it easy to see relationships among data. To make several comparisons between two sets of data, draw a **double-bar graph.**

MEAN AGE

Sport	Men	Women
Canoeing	24.2	22.0
Diving	21.3	21.1
Gymnastics	23.6	17.8
Swimming	19.2	16.3

1. Choose a scale. Be sure that the largest number on the scale is greater than the largest number that will be plotted. The break in the vertical scale shows that the portion of the graph between 0 and 15 is not being shown.

2. Label the axes of the graph.

3. Draw a bar for each item. You can use vertical bars or horizontal bars.

4. Make a key and choose a title for your graph.

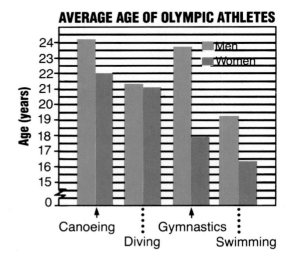

AVERAGE AGE OF OLYMPIC ATHLETES

B. The Wheatly Municipal Swim Club conducted a survey of the ages of its members. Draw a histogram to show the distribution of the data.

A **histogram** is a bar graph that shows the frequencies of intervals of data. The histogram below is made from the table at the right.

To make a histogram, follow these steps.

1. Make a frequency table.

2. Choose a scale.

3. Label the axes of the histogram.

4. Draw a bar to show the frequency of each interval of data.

5. Choose a title for your histogram.

Age	Frequency	Age	Frequency
0–9	58	40–49	56
10–19	66	50–59	43
20–29	42	60–69	21
30–39	74	70–79	15

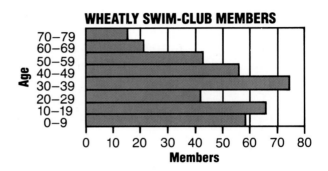

WHEATLY SWIM-CLUB MEMBERS

318

Use the tables in Exercises 1 and 2 to make bar graphs.

1. COLLEGE FOOTBALL STADIUMS

School	Capacity
Alabama	59,000
Florida	72,000
Iowa State	50,000
Michigan U.	102,000
Utah U.	35,000
Virginia U.	42,000

2. LEADING LIFETIME PASSERS

Player	Yards
Joe Montana	27,533
Otto Graham	23,584
Danny White	21,959
Roger Staubach	22,700
Sonny Jurgensen	32,224
Boomer Esiason	14,825

Use the tables in Exercises 3 and 4 to make double-bar graphs.

3. NATIONAL HOCKEY LEAGUE

Team	87–88 Wins	88–89 Wins
N.Y. Islanders	39	28
Washington	38	41
Philadelphia	38	36
N.Y. Rangers	36	37
New Jersey	38	27
Pittsburgh	36	40

4. RECORD AUTO SPEEDS

Year	Indianapolis	Daytona
1983	162.117	155.979
1984	163.621	150.994
1985	152.982	172.265
1986	170.722	148.124
1987	162.175	176.263
1988	149.809	137.531
1989	167.581	148.466

For Exercises 5–7, refer to the table on the years of football played by the leading rushers. Choose intervals that have widths of 2 years, beginning with 6–7.

5. How many intervals are needed?

6. Make a frequency table.

7. Graph the information in a histogram.

ALL-TIME LEADING RUSHERS

Player	Years played	Player	Years played
Payton	13	Simpson	11
Dorsett	12	Dickerson	6
Brown	9	Perry	16
Harris	13	Campbell	8
Riggins	14	Taylor	10

PROBLEM SOLVING
Using a Scattergram

A **scattergram** is a useful tool for showing whether a correlation exists between two sets of data.

The graph below is a scattergram. It shows the batting average and the age of each member of the Hodge's Hardware Little League team. A dashed line drawn through the points, as shown, makes it easy to see a correlation between the two sets of data.

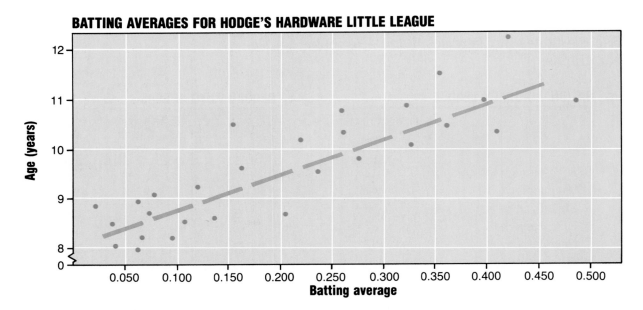

BATTING AVERAGES FOR HODGE'S HARDWARE LITTLE LEAGUE

From the scattergram, you can see that as a player's age increases, that player's batting average also increases. This is known as a **positive correlation** because both sets of data increase or decrease together, and the dashed line slants upward to show a positive correlation.

In a **negative correlation,** one set of data increases as the other decreases. The dashed line slants downward to show a negative correlation.

If no dashed line can be drawn close to the points, there is said to be **no correlation** between the two sets of data.

Use the scattergram below to solve.

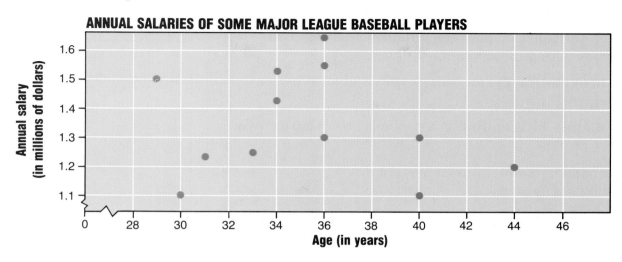

ANNUAL SALARIES OF SOME MAJOR LEAGUE BASEBALL PLAYERS

1. What correlation, if any, do you see between the two sets of data?

2. What does the answer to Question 1 tell you about the relationship between the two sets of data.

3. What correlation would you expect to see if you graphed a similar scattergram for accountants?

For each scattergram below, write *positive correlation,* *negative correlation* or *no correlation.*

4.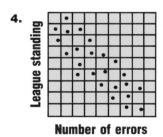

Number of errors

5.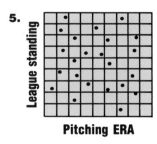

Pitching ERA

6.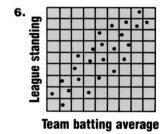

Team batting average

Tell which kind of correlation you would probably see in each scattergram.

7. A scattergram that shows the distance from an archery target and shooting accuracy.

8. A scattergram that shows the speed at which a discus is tossed and the time it stays aloft.

9. A scattergram that shows the weight of goalies and the number of saves they made.

10. A scattergram that shows the speed of ski jumpers and the length of their jumps.

Broken-Line Graphs

The table at the right lists baseball attendance from 1982 to 1989. Compare the attendance at baseball games during these years.

A **broken-line graph** usually shows change over a period of time.

A **double broken-line** graph is used to compare two sets of data.

To make a double broken-line graph, follow these steps.

1. Round the data to an appropriate scale unit. In this case, the numbers are already rounded to the nearest million.

2. Draw a graph, and use the chosen scale unit to label the vertical axis. Then label the horizontal axis. Note that the periods of time are generally represented on the horizontal axis.

3. To plot on the graph the data points from one league, start at 1982 on the horizontal axis. For the American League, place the dot halfway between 22 million and 24 million, directly above 1982. Continue in this manner to plot the remaining points for the American League.

BASEBALL ATTENDANCE (IN MILLIONS)

| Year | League | |
	American	National
1982	23	22
1983	24	22
1984	24	22
1985	24	22
1986	25	22
1987	27	25
1988	28	24
1989	30	25

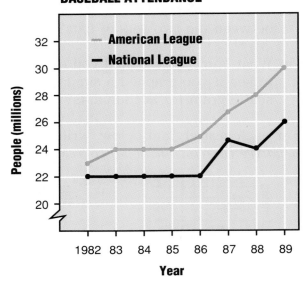

BASEBALL ATTENDANCE

4. Use line segments to connect all the points for the American League in order. Then plot the points for for the National League, and connect them in the same way. Make a key and choose a title for your graph.

Between which years was there the greatest increase in the National League?

The greatest increase occurred between 1986 and 1987.

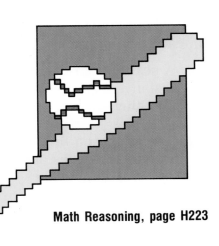

1. Use the data to make a broken-line graph.

LEAGUE BOWLING AVERAGES

Year	Averages
1985	219.834
1986	221.662
1987	218.535
1988	223.699
1989	212.844
1990	216.645

2. Use the data to make a double broken-line graph.

BOATS (MILLIONS)

Year	Inboard	Sail
1985	1.1	0.9
1986	1.3	0.9
1987	1.2	1.0
1988	1.2	1.0
1989	1.3	1.1
1990	1.4	1.1

Solve.

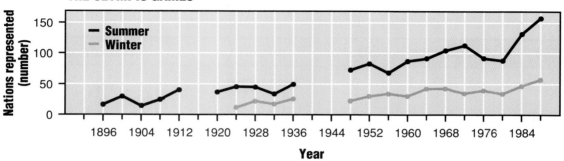

THE OLYMPIC GAMES

3. Are more nations represented in the summer or in the winter games?

4. Why are there two breaks in the graph?

MIDCHAPTER REVIEW

Use the data to solve Exercises 1–4.

The best player on the local women's basketball team scored 318 points during the season. The number of points she scored in each game are 16, 18, 10, 20, 21, 6, 17, 15, 20, 12, 15, 18, 10, 18, 20, 21, 9, 14, 18, and 20.

1. What is the range of points she scored during the season?

2. Find the mean, median, and mode or modes for this set of data.

3. Make a frequency table for her scores. Use an interval width of 5, starting with 5–9.

4. Draw a broken-line graph with the data.

Circle Graphs

A. The chart at the right lists the favorite sports of 872 students.

A **circle graph** is often used to show how a whole quantity is divided into parts. Circle graphs are used to display data in fraction, decimal, or percent form.

To make a circle graph, follow these steps.

1. Find the percent of the total for each item.

2. Calculate the measure of each central angle.

3. Use a protractor to draw each central angle.

4. Label the graph and choose a title.

FAVORITE SPORTS

Sport	Number of students
Soccer	123
Softball	67
Tennis	297
Volleyball	318
Other	67

Sport	Number of students	Percent of total	Central angles of graph
Soccer	123	$\frac{123}{872} \approx 14\%$	14% of 360° ≈ 50°
Softball	67	$\frac{67}{872} \approx 8\%$	8% of 360° ≈ 29°
Tennis	297	$\frac{297}{872} \approx 34\%$	34% of 360° ≈ 122°
Volleyball	318	$\frac{318}{872} \approx 36\%$	36% of 360° ≈ 130°
Other	67	$\frac{67}{872} \approx 8\%$	8% of 360° ≈ 29°
Total	872	100%	360°

B. Which two sports together were preferred by about $\frac{2}{3}$ of the students?

Look at the graph.

You can see that together volleyball and tennis were preferred by about $\frac{2}{3}$ of the students.

FAVORITE SPORTS

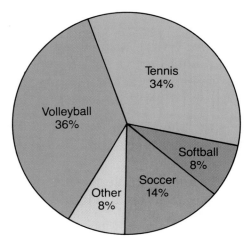

Use each set of data to make a circle graph.

1. groups of people watching the Super Bowl on television

Men	Women	Teens	Children
48%	35%	7%	10%

2. groups of people watching the World Series on television

Men	Women	Teens	Children
52%	38%	5%	5%

3. COLLEGE FOOTBALL GAMES ALABAMA

Won	Lost	Tied
641	226	43

4. COLLEGE FOOTBALL GAMES TULSA

Won	Lost	Tied
421	261	26

5. AFTER-SCHOOL FALL SPORTS CLUBS

Sport	Number of participants
Football	73
Gymnastics	42
Ice hockey	24
Soccer	85
Volleyball	164

6. AFTER-SCHOOL SPRING SPORTS CLUBS

Sport	Number of participants
Basketball	98
Soccer	128
Softball	66
Tennis	90
Track	28

Selecting an Appropriate Format • Tell which type of graph would best display the data.

7. the percent of earnings spent for food, rent, clothing, utilities, and entertainment

8. the monthly profit earned by a company for a year

9. the frequency of scores between 50 and 60, 60 and 70, 70 and 80, and 80 and 90 on a math test

10. the heights of the six tallest buildings in the United States

11. the daily high and low temperatures for a city for a month

12. the weights of 26 members of a football team

PROBLEM SOLVING
Using a Sample

Sampling is a method of obtaining information. It can be used to draw conclusions about the opinions of a particular population by questioning a representative group.

Castle Rock is going to have a referendum on the ballot in the upcoming election. It asks if the town should raise money for the library by increasing taxes. *The Castle Rock Newsletter* conducted a poll before the election to find out if the referendum would pass. They used a sample of 125 people of a population of 7,250.

ARE YOU IN FAVOR OF THE REFERENDUM?	
Yes	60
No	50
Undecided	15

What percent of the sample favored the referendum?

60 of 125
$60 \div 125 = 0.48$
$0.48 = 48\%$
48% of the sample favored the referendum.

You can use this poll to make predictions about the whole population if you assume that the views of the people in the sample are representative of those of the whole population.

According to the poll, how many in the total population favor the referendum?

$48\% = 0.48$
$0.48 \times 7,250 = 3,480$

About 3,500 people in Castle Rock favor the referendum.

Use the table below to answer the exercises.

The Metropolis, a daily newspaper, conducted a poll on the performance of the mayor after two years in office. They questioned three groups of 400 people each, of the city's 30,000 population. They carefully chose the people they questioned so that the views of the people in the sample would be representative of the whole population. (The numbers in parentheses show the percent of the total population that each age group represents.)

AGE GROUP	18–30 (36%)	31–60 (30%)	OVER AGE 60 (12%)
Approve	192	168	144
Disapprove	164	156	176
Undecided	44	76	80
Total	400	400	400

1. Which age group(s) approved of the mayor's performance by more than 40%?

2. According to the poll, how many people in the total population aged 18–30 (to the nearest 100) disapproved of the mayor's performance?

3. In which age group were 20% of the people undecided?

4. From the results of the survey, *The Metropolis* predicts that the mayor will be reelected during the next election. Do you agree or disagree with the prediction? Explain.

5. What is meant by the statement "they carefully chose the people they questioned"?

6. Suppose the mayor is in the 18–30 age group. Do you think this fact would bias the results of those people in the 18–30 age group? Explain.

Possible Outcomes

A. For gym class, Bob may be assigned to football or soccer in the fall. He may be assigned to baseball, jogging, or tennis in the spring. What are the **possible outcomes?**

You can use a **tree diagram** to find the number of possible outcomes.

Each branch of the tree lists a possible outcome.

Count the possible outcomes.

The tree diagram lists 6 possible outcomes.

TREE DIAGRAM

Fall assignment	Spring assignment	Possible outcomes
football	baseball	football–baseball
	jogging	football–jogging
	tennis	football–tennis
soccer	baseball	soccer–baseball
	jogging	soccer–jogging
	tennis	soccer–tennis

The **sample space** consists of the 6 possible outcomes. You can use these letters to list the outcomes: *FB, FJ, FT, SB, SJ,* and *ST.*

F stands for football, *B* stands for baseball, and so on.

B. Both the fall sports can be paired with all the spring sports. You can multiply to find the total number of possible outcomes.

number of possible outcomes for first assignment	times	number of possible outcomes for second assignment	=	number of possible outcomes for both assignments
↓	↓	↓	↓	↓
2	·	3	=	6

If you are making two or more choices, the total number of possible outcomes is the product of the number of possible outcomes for each choice.

Math Reasoning, page H223

You are going to spin these two spinners.

First spinner

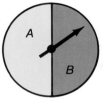
Second spinner

1. Copy and complete the tree diagram to show the possible outcomes.

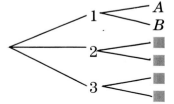

2. Copy and complete the sample space.
1A, 1B, 2A, ■, ■, ■

3. How many possible outcomes are there?

4. Is the number of possible outcomes equal to 3 · 2?

You are going to choose one card from each row.

5. Draw a tree diagram to show the possible outcomes.

6. List the outcomes in space.
★+, ★√, ★✳,

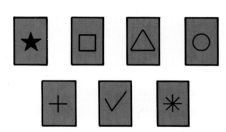

7. How many possible outcomes are there?

8. Is the number of possible outcomes equal to 4 · 3?

Solve.

9. Bob has 5 shirts in his closet and 3 pairs of pants. He is going to choose one shirt and one pair of pants. How many different outfits can he choose?

10. Maria has 4 skirts and 6 blouses in her closet. She is going to choose one skirt and one blouse. How many different outfits can she choose?

11. There are 3 routes from Ashton to Centerville and 3 routes from Centerville to Sterling. How many routes are there from Ashton to Sterling through Centerville?

12. There are 2 routes from Plainedge to Bellmore and 4 routes from Bellmore to Talmont. How many routes are there from Plainedge to Talmont through Bellmore?

Permutations and Combinations

Ms. Baker rushed into her eighth grade class one day and exclaimed, "The mayor has decided that our class will send a team to represent the city in the state Mathematics Challenge! We have to pick three representatives from the ten students in the class, and I think they should go to the competition as equal partners."

"I disagree," said John, the resident mathematics whiz. "Let's send a captain, assistant captain, and a secretary. I think that the team will be better organized that way."

Ms. Baker thought for a moment and responded, "Very well, John, if you can tell me in three tries how many teams are possible if we go along with my idea or with your idea, then I'll agree to your proposal."

"That's easy, ten times three equals thirty teams," John said quickly.

"Haste makes waste," Ms. Baker replied. "Try again."

John started to hedge. "Well, both proposals involve the same number of possible teams, right?"

"Wrong!" said Ms. Baker. The class got more excited as John grew nervous.

Thinking as a Team

What is John to do? How is it possible that one proposal would result in more teams than the other proposal? Discuss with your teammates. Try to determine which proposal would result in more teams and, if possible, the number of teams involved in each proposal.

John did not understand the difference between ordered arrangements, or permutations, and unordered arrangements, or combinations. Ms. Baker's proposal involved combinations. John's proposal involved permutations.

John decided to try a simple experiment to help him see the difference between permutations and combinations. He would make organized lists to see how many permutations and combinations could be made if 2 team members were being chosen from a group of 4 students: Allen, Biff, Carla, and Dione. Complete each of the lists on your own.

Combinations

Allen–Biff
Allen–Carla
Allen–Dione. . . .

Permutations

Allen–Biff, Biff–Allen
Allen–Carla, Carla–Allen
Allen–Dione. . . .

Thinking as a Team

1. How many combinations are there?

2. How many ways can each combination be ordered?

3. How many permutations are there?

4. Can you generalize about whether there will be more combinations or more permutations for any arrangement of things?

5. How can you relate the number of combinations, the number of ways in which each combination can be ordered, and the number of permutations?

When is order important? When is order unimportant? Determine whether order is important in finding the number of arrangements in each problem.

- You are inviting four of your friends for a dinner.

- You are mixing five different components for fertilizer for your garden.

- You are placing three of your records on a turntable to be played.

- You are planning a party, and you plan to ask six guests to park their six cars in your driveway.

Thinking as a Team

1. Different members of your team may interpret each of the four problems differently. Discuss your answers and the various interpretations involved.

2. Explain how Ms. Baker's proposal involved combinations, whereas John's proposal involved permutations.

Numbers of Permutations and Combinations

A. To satisfy Ms. Baker's request from the last lesson, John had to find the number of possible combinations and the number of possible permutations when 3 students are selected from a class of 10 students.

Thinking as a Team

John chose one combination of 3 students to examine. He started to make a list to determine all of the permutations that can be formed using those 3 students. Copy and complete the list.

Combination	Permutations		
	Captain	*Asst. Capt.*	*Secretary*
John, Kim, Alice	John	Alice	Kim
	John	Kim	Alice

How many permutations are there?

Choose another combination of 3 students and find how many permutations there are. What numerical relationship is there between the combinations and the permutations for each combination?

To solve John's problem you need to find the number of combinations of 3 students there are in a group of 10 students. Would you make a list? Why not?

It is easier to find the number of permutations; then you divide to find the number of combinations. You can find the total number of permutations or teams by multiplying.

- In a class of 10 students, how many possible choices are there for captain?
- After a captain is selected, how many students are left to choose an assistant from?
- How many choices are there left for secretary?

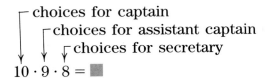

$$10 \cdot 9 \cdot 8 = \blacksquare$$

- What is the total number of permutations?
- How many combinations are there?
- How many teams are possible using John's idea?
- How many teams are possible using Ms. Baker's idea?

B. Some special notation is used in discussing permutations and combinations.

In the case you just solved, you found the numbers of permutations possible when 3 objects are chosen from a group of 10 objects. This is written as $_{10}P_3$.

$$_{10}P_3 = 10 \cdot 9 \cdot 8 = 720$$

number of choices   number of positions

The notation 3! is used to show the product of 3 and all counting numbers less than 3, and is read "three factorial."

$$3! = 3 \cdot 2 \cdot 1 = 6$$

In the case you just solved you found that the number of ways in which 3 objects can be ordered is 3! or 6. You then found the number of combinations possible for 3 objects chosen from a group of 10 objects by dividing $_{10}P_3$ by 6. This can be written:

$$_{10}C_3 = \frac{_{10}P_3}{3!} = \frac{10 \cdot 9 \cdot 8}{3 \cdot 2 \cdot 1} = 120$$

Thinking as a Team

Discuss the solutions to each of the following with other teams.

1. In how many ways can a president and vice president be chosen in a class of 15 students?
2. How many basketball teams of 5 members each can be made from a group of 12 students?
3. How many committees of 3 can be formed from a class of 18 students?

Probability

A. Mr. Thomas has a bag of tennis balls. Of them, 3 are green, 2 are white, and 1 is yellow. He is going to pick a tennis ball without looking. This is called picking a tennis ball **at random.** He is **equally likely** to pick any one of the tennis balls.

What is the **probability** of picking a green tennis ball?

The probability of picking a green tennis ball can be written as P(G).

$$P(G) = \frac{\text{number of favorable outcomes}}{\text{number of possible outcomes}}$$

There are 6 possible outcomes; 3 of the outcomes are favorable because there are 3 green tennis balls.

So, P(G) = $\frac{3}{6}$ = $\frac{1}{2}$.

The probability of picking a green tennis ball is $\frac{1}{2}$, or 50%.

B. An event consists of 0, 1, or more possible outcomes.

What is the probability of picking a red tennis ball?

Since there is no red tennis ball in the bag, the event is **impossible.** If an event will never occur, the probability is 0.

P(red) = 0

What is the probability of picking a white, yellow, or green tennis ball?

Since any one of the tennis balls will be either white, yellow, or green, the event is **certain.** If an event will always occur, the probability is 1.

P(white, yellow, or green) = 1

C. What is the probability of not picking a white tennis ball?

Since 4 tennis balls are not white, there are 4 possible favorable outcomes.

P(not white) = $\frac{4}{6}$ = $\frac{2}{3}$

D. There are 5 cards in a hat. They are 1, 2, 3, 4, and 5. If a card is picked at random, what is the probability that it is greater than 3? Since there are 2 cards greater than 3, P(greater than 3) = $\frac{2}{5}$.

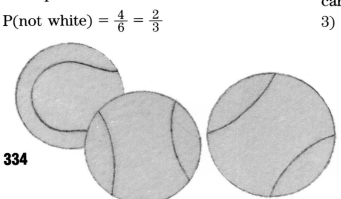

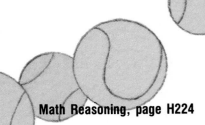

Find each probability in Exercises 1–32.

Toss a number cube once. The numbers on the 6 faces
are 1, 2, 3, 4, 5, and 6.

1. P(5)

2. P(odd)

3. P(3 or 6)

4. P(less than 5)

5. P(not 1)

6. P(9)

7. P(greater than 3)

8. P(even or odd)

9. P(2, 3, or 4)

Choose 1 marble without looking.

10. P(blue)

11. P(yellow)

12. P(not green)

13. P(green or yellow)

14. P(white)

15. P(not yellow)

16. P(not red and not blue)

Pick 1 card at random.

17. P(blue)

18. P(A)

19. P(green or red)

20. P(F)

21. P(vowel)

22. P(A or B)

23. P(not D)

24. P(blue or C)

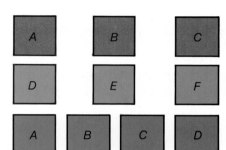

Pick 1 card at random.

25. P(even)

26. P(less than 4)

27. P(a multiple of 4)

28. P(a multiple of 2)

29. P(a prime)

30. P(a factor of 25)

31. P(greater than 4)

32. P(a factor of 24)

Solve.

33. In a raffle for a 10-speed bike, 250
tickets are sold. What is the
probability of winning if you buy 10
tickets?

34. Sue collects old dimes. She has 6
dimes from 1941, 5 dimes from
1932, and 1 dime from 1930 in her
pocket. If she picks 1 dime, what is
the probability she will pick a dime
older than 1932?

Independent Events

A. Mr. Ramos has 2 caps that have a fish on them, 3 caps that have a boat on them, and 1 cap that has waves on it. Without looking, he picks a cap from the box. He puts it back. He picks another cap. What is the probability that he picks a cap that has a fish followed by a cap that has a boat?

Find the probability of each event. Since Mr. Ramos replaces the first hat, the outcome of the second event does not depend on the outcome of the first event. These are **independent events.**

$P(\text{fish}) = \frac{2}{6} \text{ or } \frac{1}{3}$

$P(\text{boat}) = \frac{3}{6} \text{ or } \frac{1}{2}$

If A and B are independent events, you can multiply to find the probability of event A and event B both occurring.

$P(A,B) = P(A) \cdot P(B)$

$P(\text{fish, boat}) = P(\text{fish}) \cdot P(\text{boat}) = \frac{1}{3} \cdot \frac{1}{2} = \frac{1}{6}$

So, the probability of picking a hat that has a fish followed by a hat that has a boat is $\frac{1}{6}$.

B. Toss a coin and then spin the spinner. What is the probability of tossing heads and spinning red?

$P(\text{heads}) = \frac{1}{2} \qquad P(\text{red}) = \frac{2}{5}$

$P(\text{heads, red}) = P(\text{heads}) \cdot P(\text{red}) = \frac{1}{\underset{1}{2}} \cdot \frac{\overset{1}{2}}{5} = \frac{1}{5}$

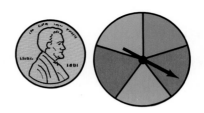

The probability of tossing heads and spinning red is $\frac{1}{5}$.

Checkpoint Write the letter of the correct answer.

Use the coin and spinner above to find the probability.

1. P(heads, green) = ■

a. $\frac{1}{10}$ **b.** $\frac{7}{10}$ **c.** $\frac{1}{5}$ **d.** $\frac{1}{2}$

2. P(red or blue, tails) = ■

a. $\frac{5}{8}$ **b.** $\frac{2}{5}$ **c.** $\frac{1}{2}$ **d.** $\frac{4}{5}$

Math Reasoning, page H224

Find each probability in Exercises 1–27.

Toss a number cube 2 times. The numbers on the 6 faces are 1, 2, 3, 4, 5, and 6.

1. P(1,6) **2.** P(2,7) **3.** P(even, odd)

4. P(1 or 2, 3) **5.** P(not 6, 3) **6.** P(greater than 3, 1)

Spin both spinners.

7. P(red, 2) **8.** P(green, 6)

9. P(yellow, 2 or 4) **10.** P(red, 4 or 8)

11. P(not red, even) **12.** P(not green, not 8)

13. P(red, odd) **14.** P(green or blue, 4 or 8)

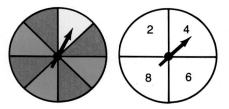

Pick 1 marble at random, replace it, and pick another marble at random.

15. P(blue, red) **16.** P(red, yellow)

17. P(green, green) **18.** P(blue, not blue)

19. P(red or green, blue)

Pick 1 marble at random from each bag.

★**20.** P(red, blue, yellow)

★**21.** P(blue, red, yellow)

★**22.** P(three reds)

Solve.

23. Alim and Lina each choose at random a number from 1 to 4. What is the probability that they choose the same number?

24. Kara tosses a coin 2 times. The first time she tosses heads. What is the probability that she tosses tails the second time?

CHOOSING THE METHOD

Decide which method you would use to compute each exercise: mental math, calculator, or paper and pencil. Explain your answer.

1. 500 × 30 **2.** 49 × 51 **3.** 0.23 × 41.2 **4.** 6.10 × 20.5

PROBLEM SOLVING
Selecting Notation

In the past, you have used symbols for variables to help solve a word problem. In mathematics, it is possible to use different kinds of notation or symbols to represent the facts of a problem and to assist you in finding the solution.

> The water boy for the football team needed exactly 5 liters of water to fill the water dispenser. If he had only a 7-liter container and a 3-liter container, how could he fill and empty these two containers so that he could return from the locker room with exactly 5 liters of water?

- You can order pairs to represent the water in each container at any given time.

For example, the ordered pair (5,2) means

$$\left(\begin{array}{c} 5 \text{ liters of water} \\ \text{in 7-liter container} \end{array} \right) \text{ and } \left(\begin{array}{c} 2 \text{ liters of water} \\ \text{in 3-liter container} \end{array} \right)$$

The sequence $(0,0) \rightarrow (0,3) \rightarrow (3,0)$ means that 3 liters of water were first poured into the 3-liter container. These 3 liters were then poured into the 7-liter container.

- Use the ordered pairs to represent the sequence of pourings needed to obtain exactly 5 liters.

$(0,3) \rightarrow (3,0) \rightarrow (3,3) \rightarrow (6,0)$
$(6,3) \rightarrow (7,2) \rightarrow (0,2) \rightarrow (2,0)$
$(2,3) \rightarrow (5,0)$

An ordered pair is one of many different kinds of notation that is helpful in solving problems.

Another type of notation which you have used earlier in this chapter is *P(G)*. On page 334, the notation *P(G)* represents the probability of picking a green tennis ball.

Select the appropriate notation, and solve. Write the letter of the correct answer.

1. There are 5 members of a handball club. They decided that every member of the club should play every other member once. Use geometric notation to find out how many games had to be played. (HINT: use a dot to represent a member of the club and a line segment to represent a game played.)

a. 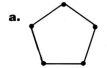   b.    c.   d.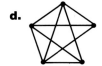

2. How many combinations of 10¢ stamps and 2¢ stamps equal 46¢ worth of postage? Choose the notation that represents the correct combinations. The first number of each ordered pair represents 10¢ stamps, and the second number represents 2¢ stamps.

a. (5,1), (1,7), (3,4), (4,10), (2,13)
b. (4,3), (2,13), (2,8), (2,18)
c. (1,20), (2,10), (1,18)
d. (4,3), (3,8), (2,13), (1,18)

Solve. Use notation where appropriate.

3. While hiking, 2 friends decide to separate. They have a water jug that contains 6 pints of water. They also have a 4-pint canteen and a 1-pint canteen. How can 2 friends divide the water evenly between themselves? Use ordered pairs.

4. Janine sells perfume at a department store. She earns $3 per hour plus $0.50 commission on every bottle she sells. One day, she works from 10:00 A.M. to 3:00 P.M. and sells 14 bottles of perfume. How much did she earn that day?

5. Jack Griffin pays for $3.75 worth of bandages with a $5 bill. How many combinations of dimes and nickels might Jack receive in change?

Dependent Events

A. Mrs. Waltham went to watch sailboat races with friends. She brought 2 tuna sandwiches and 5 cheese sandwiches in a picnic basket. Mrs. Waltham picked a sandwich at random and took it from the basket. Her friend Kim picked a sandwich at random from the basket. What is the probability they both picked tuna sandwiches?

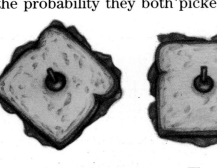

These two events are **dependent events.** The outcome of the first choice affects the probabilities of the outcomes of the second choice because the first sandwich was not replaced.

Find the probability of each event.

$$P(\text{tuna}) = \frac{2}{7}$$

$$P(\text{tuna after tuna}) = \frac{1}{6}$$ ← There is 1 tuna sandwich left.
← There are 6 sandwiches left.

$$P(\text{tuna, then tuna}) = P(\text{tuna}) \cdot P(\text{tuna after tuna}) = \frac{\overset{1}{\cancel{2}}}{7} \cdot \frac{1}{\underset{3}{\cancel{6}}} = \frac{1}{21}$$

The probability that they both picked tuna sandwiches is $\frac{1}{21}$.

B. Pick a marble from the bag without looking. Do not replace it. Pick another marble. What is the probability of picking a red and then a green marble?

$$P(\text{red}) = \frac{3}{10} \qquad P(\text{green after red}) = \frac{4}{9}$$

$$P(\text{red, then green}) = P(\text{red}) \cdot P(\text{green after red}) = \frac{\overset{1}{\cancel{3}}}{\underset{5}{\cancel{10}}} \cdot \frac{\overset{2}{\cancel{4}}}{\underset{3}{\cancel{9}}} = \frac{2}{15}$$

Checkpoint Write the letter of the correct answer.

Refer to the bag of marbles above.

1. P(red, then blue) = ▧

a. $\frac{3}{10}$ **b.** $\frac{1}{15}$ **c.** $\frac{2}{9}$ **d.** $\frac{2}{45}$

2. P(blue, then blue) = ▧

a. $\frac{1}{9}$ **b.** $\frac{1}{15}$ **c.** $\frac{1}{5}$ **d.** $\frac{1}{45}$

Find each probability in Exercises 1–22. Assume that the marbles and cards are picked at random.

Pick a marble. Do not replace it. Pick a second marble.

1. P(green, then red)   **2.** P(red, then blue)

3. P(green, then blue)   **4.** P(blue, then green)

5. P(not green, then green) **6.** P(yellow, then red)

7. P(red, then red)   **8.** P(not blue, then blue)

Pick a marble. Do not replace it. Pick a second marble.

9. P(blue, then red)   **10.** P(red, then green)

11. P(blue, then green)   **12.** P(not blue, then blue)

13. P(red, then red)   **14.** P(blue, then blue)

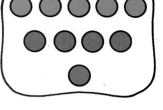

Pick a card. Do not replace it. Pick a second card.

15. P(red 1, then blue 1)   **16.** P(2, then 4)

17. P(red, then blue)   **18.** P(3, then red 4)

19. P(red or blue, then 3)   **20.** P(not 2, then not 3)

★**21.** P(1 or 3, then 2 or 4) ★**22.** P(not odd, then 3)

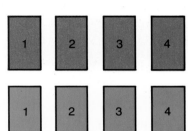

CHALLENGE

There were 9 boxes in a grab bag, 5 red and 4 green. All the boxes felt the same. There were calculators in 4 of the red boxes and in 2 of the green boxes. Sarah reached in and chose a box without looking.

What is each probability?

1. Sarah chose a red box.

2. Sarah chose a green box.

3. Sarah chose a box containing a calculator.

4. Sarah chose a box containing a calculator if she chose a green box.

5. Sarah chose a box containing a calculator if she chose a red box.

6. Sarah chose a red box if the box she chose contained a calculator.

Prediction

A. In this lesson your team will conduct an experiment by gathering sample data and making a prediction.

Working as a Team _____

1. Gather a sample of between 50 and 100 pennies.

2. Describe your sample to the class. How can pennies be categorized?

3. Use a bar graph or a histogram to display the minting dates of the coins in your sample.

4. Before you choose a penny at random, about how old would you expect it to be? Would you use the mean, the median, or the mode of your sample to help you make this prediction?

Thinking as a Team _____

Use your sample of pennies to make the predictions:

1. What percent of pennies now in circulation were minted before 1975?

2. What is the probability that a penny now in circulation was minted more than 20 years ago?

3. Of those pennies now in circulation, in what year were more minted than in any other?

4. About 50% of the pennies now in circulation were minted prior to what year?

Now share your team's sample data with the class. Using the class data, find or predict:

5. The total number of pennies sampled

6. The class distribution of minting dates

7. The probability that a penny now in circulation was minted more than 20 years ago.

8. The percent of pennies in circulation that were minted before 1975. Is this different from your team's prediction? Why?

9. Do you think that your team's predictions are likely to be more or less accurate than the class-based predictions? Why?

10. Place the class data on minting dates on a double-bar graph to compare it to your team's sample data. How can you use a graph to show clearly the similarities of or the differences between these two groups of data?

11. How can you find out how many coins are actually minted each year?

B. The license plate on Ceanne's new car reads 586 BUG. If every license plate contains 3 letters and 3 digits, what do you think is the probability that any license plate chosen at random will spell a 3-letter word in the English language?

Thinking as a Team

1. Could you list all possible 3-letter sequences that could appear on license plates? How would you do it?

2. Should your list include sequences in which the same letter appears twice?

3. How could you gather data from an experiment to make a prediction?

4. What are the advantages of making a list? What are the advantages of doing an experiment?

5. How would you decide what method to use?

6. Can you think of another way to solve the problem?

Classwork/Homework, page H142

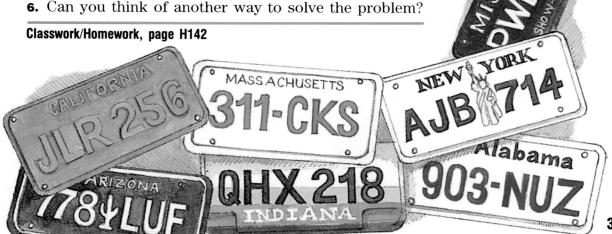

PROBLEM SOLVING
Interpreting a Graph

Graphs are helpful tools for showing and comparing information. Sometimes, however, the comparison can be misleading; so, you must be careful to correctly interpret the given information.

These graphs show the total yardage gained by the football teams of 2 colleges in each of the first 6 games of the season.

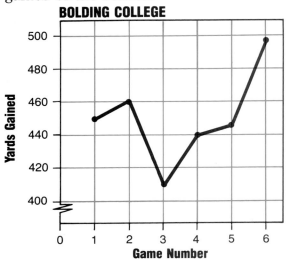

BOLDING COLLEGE

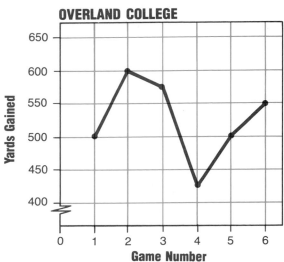

OVERLAND COLLEGE

Use the information shown on the graphs to answer the question.

Which school gained the greater number of yards in one game?

At first glance, it may seem that Bolding gained more, during the sixth game. But the vertical axis of the left graph is shown in steps of 20 yards, whereas that of the right graph is shown in steps of 50 yards. The greatest number of yards gained by Bolding, in the sixth game, is 490 yards. In the second game, Overland gained 600 yards.

The greater number of yards gained in one game was achieved by Overland College, in the second game.

Use the graphs on page 344 to answer these questions.

1. How many yards did Bolding College gain in the second game?

2. How many yards did Overland College gain in the first game?

3. Which college gained the least number of yards in a single game, how many yards were gained, and in which game?

The graphs below represent the number of runs scored in each game of a six-game series by two high schools.

CENTRAL HIGH SCHOOL

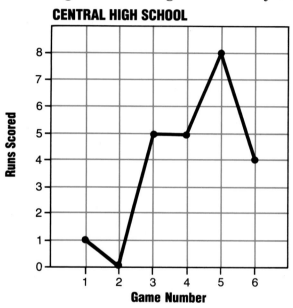

NEWTON HIGH SCHOOL

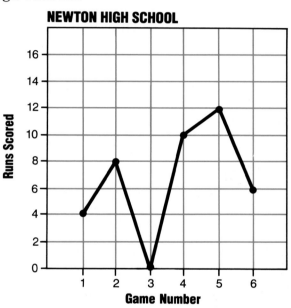

4. Which school had the greater number of runs in one game, and how many runs was it?

5. Which school scored the fewer number of runs in the 6-game series, and how many runs did it score?

6. How many runs did each school score in the fourth game?

7. Which school scored the same number of runs in two consecutive games, how many runs were scored, and in which games?

CALCULATOR

To find the mean of these test scores, you could add them on a calculator and divide by the total number of scores.

Scores: 20, 25, 26, 29, 26, 24

Press: $\boxed{2}\,\boxed{0}\,\boxed{+}\,\boxed{2}\,\boxed{5}\,\boxed{+}\,\boxed{2}\,\boxed{6}\,\boxed{+}\,\boxed{2}\,\boxed{9}\,\boxed{+}\,\boxed{2}\,\boxed{6}\,\boxed{+}\,\boxed{2}\,\boxed{4}\,\boxed{\div}\,\boxed{6}\,\boxed{=}$

The mean is 25. Another way to find the mean is to pick a number less than or equal to the least number as a "benchmark." Suppose 20 is chosen as the benchmark. Add the differences between each number and the benchmark. Then find the mean of the differences.

Scores: 20, 25, 26, 29, 26, 24

difference from 20: 0, 5, 6, 9, 6, 4

Press: $\boxed{0}\,\boxed{+}\,\boxed{5}\,\boxed{+}\,\boxed{6}\,\boxed{+}\,\boxed{9}\,\boxed{+}\,\boxed{6}\,\boxed{+}\,\boxed{4}\,\boxed{\div}\,\boxed{6}\,\boxed{=}$

The mean of the differences is 5. Add it to the benchmark, 20. You get 25. The advantage of this method is that you have smaller numbers to enter and can check the total on the screen more easily as you go.

Find the mean of these numbers, using benchmarks. Find the differences mentally.

1. Test scores of 52, 54, 56, 50, 58; use 50 as the benchmark.

2. Prices of $100, $120, $110, $115, $130; use $100 as the benchmark.

3. Scores of 38, 35, 32, 33, 31, 39, 40, 41

4. Heights of 55 in., 56 in., 57 in., 58 in.

5. Weights of 150 lb, 160 lb, 152 lb, 161 lb, 155 lb, 158 lb

GROUP PROJECT

Rules of the Game

The problem: Your class is in charge of setting up a sports competition. All of you are tired of the same old sports. You decide to come up with a new kind of competition. How will you agree on which events to include and what the rules will be? Referring to the facts and the questions below, plan the competition, and write a book of rules.

Key Facts

- Many sports consist of a combination of events. The decathlon, for instance, features ten events, including races, jumping, and javelin throwing. The modern pentathlon consists of horseback riding, swimming, running, fencing, and marksmanship.

- Recently developed sports include the triathlon, which consists of swimming, cycling, and running.

- Games in which goals are scored include field hockey, ice hockey, soccer, and polo, which is played on horseback.

- Scoring differs from sport to sport, and winners may be decided on the basis of points, fastest times, highest and farthest marks, or a combination of these methods.

Key Questions

- Will players compete individually or in teams?

- How many events will there be?

- Will you need a field or other special area? If so, what will be its dimensions? How will you indicate boundary lines or goal lines?

- How will the events be scored?

CHAPTER TEST

TY COBB'S SEASON
BATTING AVERAGES

1921	0.389
1922	0.401
1923	0.340
1924	0.338
1925	0.378

FREQUENCY TABLE

Interval	Frequency	Relative Frequency
0.330–0.349		

Use Ty Cobb's season batting averages to solve
Exercises 1–5. (pages 314–317)

1. Make a frequency table. Start with 0.330 and use
   intervals of 0.020.

2. What is the range of these batting averages?

3. What is the median?

4. What is the mean?

5. Is there a mode?

6. A baseball player is practicing hitting. Each time at
   bat there are two possible outcomes: to get a hit
   (H), or to miss the ball (M). Draw a tree diagram
   to show the possible outcomes for four times at
   bat. How many possible outcomes are there?
   (pages 328–329)

7. A team is holding elections. There are 5 members
   running for three positions: manager, captain, and
   treasurer. In how many ways can the three
   positions be filled? (pages 330–333)

8. There are 9 members on the school basketball
   team. How many different combinations of 5 can
   be formed from the 9 members? (pages 330–333)

If a number cube is tossed, what is the probability that
the number on the cube will be (pages 334–335)

9. even?   10. odd?   11. less than 3?   12. 5?

348

A number cube is tossed twice. Find the probability.
(pages 336–337)

13. P(two 3's) **14.** P(even, odd) **15.** P(less than 3, 6)

Pick a card. Do not replace it. Pick a second card.
Find each probability. (pages 340–341)

16. P(blue, then green)

17. P(2, then 4)

18. P(1 or 4, then 2 or 3)

19. P(4, then blue)

You are going to toss a number cube 300 times.
Predict the number of times the outcome will be
(pages 342–343)

20. 6. **21.** even. **22.** less than 3.

23. There are 4 members on the chess team. They
decide that every member should play every other
member once. Use geometric notation to find out
how many games have to be played. (pages 338–
339)

Woodville has a referendum on the ballot for the
upcoming election. A newspaper conducted a poll on
the referendum. The poll used a sample of 450 voters
of a voting population of 2,500 people. The results of
the poll are listed below. (pages 326–327)

Yes	279
No	117
Undecided	54

24. What percent of Woodville's voting population was
included in the newspaper poll?

25. What percent of voters in the sample favored the
referendum?

RETEACHING

Statisticians frequently use data in order to make comparisons. To help make meaningful comparisons, they use the range, mode, median, and mean.

Paul received the following scores on his mathematics tests during the second marking period: 99, 75, 86, 66, 80, 100, 75, and 76.

Arrange the scores from the greatest to the least.

$$100, 99, 86, 80, 76, 75, 75, 66$$

The **range** is the difference between the highest and the lowest scores.

$$100 - 66 = 34$$

range = 34

The **mode** is the score that occurs most frequently.

mode = 75

The **median** is the middle number of the scores. If there are an even number of scores, add the two middle numbers and divide by 2.

median = 78

The **mean** is the sum of the scores divided by the number of scores.

$$\frac{657}{8} = 82.125$$

mean = 82.125

Find the range, mode, median, and mean for each set of numbers. Round to the nearest hundredth.

1. 23, 21, 31, 29, 31
2. 10, 4, 12, 8, 14, 4, 4
3. 62, 68, 64, 60, 65, 68
4. 95, 79, 86, 80, 95, 75
5. 86, 92, 92, 85, 75
6. 170, 100, 200, 150, 170, 85
7. 8, 3, 6, 5, 9, 5
8. 6, 10, 12, 17, 24, 35, 1
9. 50, 75, 75, 40, 90, 65, 35
10. 75, 70, 80, 95, 135, 135, 135
11. 35, 40, 50, 60, 70
12. 85, 75, 90, 70, 70, 100, 80
13. 110, 130, 122, 138, 114, 125, 136
14. 15, 17, 20, 20, 20, 22, 23, 24, 26
15. 24, 36, 48, 24, 30, 49, 40, 25, 26, 30
16. 24, 30, 22, 17, 36, 51, 81, 24, 31, 49, 13, 18, 25
17. 134, 137, 134, 136, 133, 135, 135, 134, 130, 135, 134

ENRICHMENT

The Normal Curve

Try this experiment. Toss 10 pennies all at once, and count the number of pennies that turn up heads. Record the number. Repeat this procedure 99 more times. Use the data to make a frequency-distribution table. The table probably will look something like the one at the right.

Notice that the values closest to the center have the highest frequency, and the values closest to the ends have the lowest frequency. This pattern of scores is called a **normal distribution.** When a normal distribution is graphed, a bell-shaped curve results that is called a **normal curve.**

Number of heads per toss	Tally	Frequency
0	I	1
1	II	2
2	III	3
3	HHI HHI I	11
4	HHI HHI HHI IIII	19
5	HHI HHI HHI HHI HHI	25
6	HHI HHI HHI HHI	20
7	HHI HHI II	12
8	HHI	5
9	I	1
10	I	1

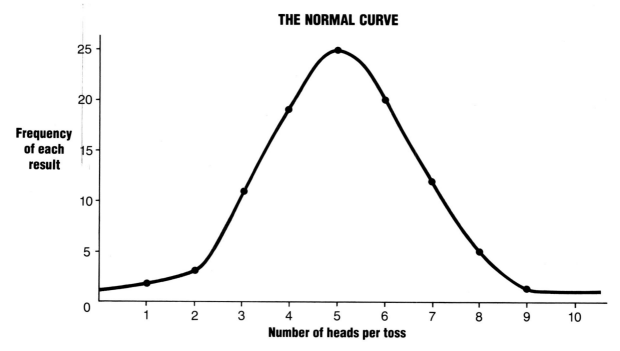

THE NORMAL CURVE

Frequency of each result (vertical axis)

Number of heads per toss (horizontal axis)

Draw a frequency-distribution table of the heights of all the boys in the eighth grade. Graph the distribution. Is the graph a normal curve?

CUMULATIVE REVIEW

Write the letter of the correct answer.

1. Evaluate ^-7g when $g = 6$.

   a. $^-42$
   b. $\frac{-6}{7}$
   c. $1\frac{1}{4}$
   d. not given

2. Solve for t: $^-6t = 84$.

   a. $^-24$
   b. $^-14$
   c. 90
   d. not given

3. Solve for y: $\frac{y}{-4} - 16 = 4$.

   a. $^-80$
   b. $^-16$
   c. $^-5$
   d. not given

4. 70 is 7 more than 3 times a number. Use an equation to solve.

   a. 21
   b. $25\frac{2}{3}$
   c. 189
   d. not given

5. Solve for n: $\frac{n}{7} < 21$.

   a. $n < 3$
   b. $n < 28$
   c. $n < 147$
   d. not given

6. $\frac{4}{7} + \frac{-2}{7}$

   a. $\frac{-2}{7}$
   b. $\frac{2}{7}$
   c. $\frac{6}{7}$
   d. not given

7. $\frac{-3}{4} \times \frac{-2}{11}$

   a. $\frac{-3}{22}$
   b. $\frac{8}{23}$
   c. $\frac{1}{3}$
   d. not given

8. A $68.00 item now sells for $80.24. Calculate the percent of increase.

   a. 15%
   b. 17%
   c. 18%
   d. not given

9. Jack's flight left New York at 7:35 A.M. Eastern time and landed in San Diego at 11:10 A.M. Pacific time. For how long did he fly?

   a. 3 h 35 min
   b. 4 h 25 min
   c. 6 h 35 min
   d. not given

10. Jenny bought 17 pages of sheet music and 3 guitar picks. She paid a total of $42.15. The picks were 3 for $0.50. Use an equation to find the cost of a page of sheet music.

    a. $2.13
    b. $2.45
    c. $3.45
    d. not given

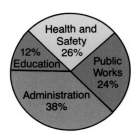

11. The circle graph shows how the budget for the town of Millindale is spent. What is the ratio of the amount spent on education to the amount spent on public works?

    a. 1:2
    b. 2:1
    c. 2.1:1
    d. not given

The design of every house includes geometric shapes. Which geometric shapes can you find in the design of the house in which you live? Use at least five different geometric shapes to make a design for a new house.

10 GEOMETRY

Basic Ideas

Terms and ideas in geometry	Picture
point *A*: is an exact location in space.	• *A*
line *CD*, or *DC*: $\overleftrightarrow{CD}$ or $\overleftrightarrow{DC}$ names a straight path of points that continues infinitely in two directions. Another name for $\overleftrightarrow{CD}$ is line *l*.	*C* ... *D* *ℓ*
ray *EC*, or *EF*: $\overrightarrow{EC}$ or $\overrightarrow{EF}$ names part of a line that has one endpoint and continues infinitely in one direction.	*E* *C* *F*
angle *XYZ*, or *ZYX*: $\angle XYZ$ or $\angle ZYX$ names two rays with a common endpoint. Another name for $\angle XYZ$ is $\angle Y$, or $\angle 1$.	*X* *Y* 1 *Z*
line segment *GH*, or *HG*: $\overline{GH}$ or $\overline{HG}$ names part of a line with two endpoints.	*G* *H*
plane *T*: is a flat surface that continues infinitely in all directions.	*T*
intersecting lines: $\overleftrightarrow{AB}$ and $\overleftrightarrow{CD}$ are lines that meet at a point *P*.	*A* *D* *P* *C* *B*
parallel lines: $\overleftrightarrow{RS}$ and $\overleftrightarrow{TU}$ are lines in a plane that do not intersect.	*R* *S* *T* *U*
skew lines: $\overleftrightarrow{AB}$ and $\overleftrightarrow{CD}$ are lines that do not intersect and are not parallel. Skew lines lie in different planes.	*A* *B* *C* *D*
congruent segments: $\overline{LM}$ and $\overline{QR}$ are two line segments that have the same length. $\overline{LM} \cong \overline{QR}$. The symbol $\cong$ means "is congruent to."	*L* •———————• *M* *Q* •———————• *R*
midpoint: *M* marks a point that separates a line segment into two congruent segments.	2 cm 2 cm *X* *M* *Y*

354

Name the figure.

1. •————————▶

2. (two intersecting rays forming an X)

3. •

4. (two parallel lines/arrows)

5. (parallelogram/plane with arrows)

6. •————————•

7. ◀————————▶

Write the symbol for each figure.

8. *N* •

9. ◀——•——•——▶
R   S

10. •————————▶
P   M

11. •————————•
K   L

Draw and label each figure.

12. point *F*

13. $\overline{BC}$

14. plane *J*

15. $\overleftrightarrow{EF}$

16. $\overrightarrow{GH}$

17. $\overleftrightarrow{EF}$ is parallel to $\overleftrightarrow{GH}$.

18. $\overleftrightarrow{KL}$ intersects $\overleftrightarrow{MN}$.

Points *A*, *B*, *C*, and *D* lie on the same line.

◀——•————————•————•————————•——▶
   A   **B**   **C**   **D**

19. Name all the line segments that have these points as endpoints.

20. Name all the rays that have these points as endpoints.

Write *true* if the statement is true. Write *false* if it is false.

21.
$AB \cong CD$

22. (E–F and G–H segments)
$EF \cong GH$

23.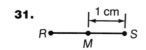
$JK \cong LM$

24.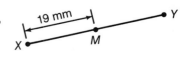
$NP \cong RS$

Use the number line to complete each statement.

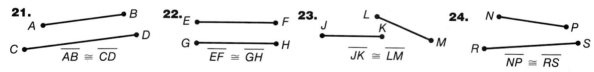

A F B   C G D   E
‾6 ‾5 ‾4 ‾3 ‾2 ‾1 0 1 2 3 4 5 6 7

25. $\overline{AB} \cong$ ▨

26. $\overline{CB} \cong$ ▨

27. $\overline{AC} \cong$ ▨

28. The midpoint of $\overline{AB}$ is ▨.

29. The midpoint of $\overline{CD}$ is ▨.

Find the length of each segment whose midpoint is *M*.

30. (segment A–M–C with 1.5 cm marked from A to M)

31. (segment R–M–S with 1 cm marked from M to S)

32. (segment X–M–Y with 19 mm marked from X to M)

Angles and Angle Measure

A. For any **angle,** the common endpoint is called the **vertex,** and the rays are called the **sides** of the angle.

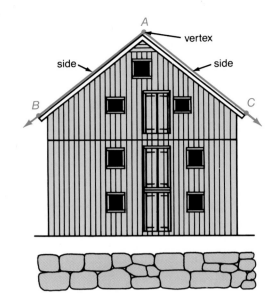

Find the measure of the angle formed at the peak of the roof shown in the drawing.

To find the measure of an angle, use an instrument called a **protractor.** Place the center of the protractor at A (the peak of the roof). Place the 0° mark of one scale on one side of the angle. Read that same scale where the other side of the angle intersects it. The angle formed at the peak of the roof is 101°. You can write m$\angle BAC = 101°$. m means "measure of."

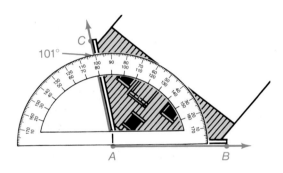

B. An angle can be classified according to its measure (m).

acute
(less than 90°)

indicates a right angle

right
(90°)

obtuse
(greater than 90°
but less than 180°)

straight
(180°)

C. Two angles whose measures have a sum of 90° are **complementary** angles.

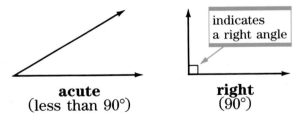

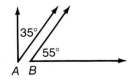

$\angle A$ and $\angle B$ are *complements* of each other.

D. Two angles whose measures have a sum of 180° are **supplementary** angles.

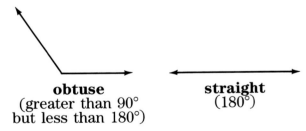

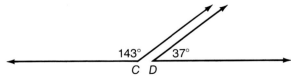

$\angle C$ and $\angle D$ are *supplements* of each other.

Use a protractor to measure each angle.

1.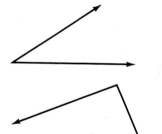

2.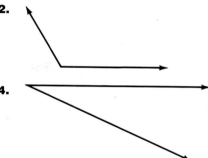

3.

4.

Draw an angle that has the given measure.

5. 27°   **6.** 124°   **7.** 90°   **8.** 61°   **9.** 180°

Use the angle shown to complete.

10. Its vertex is ▪.

11. Its sides are ▪.

12. Three ways to identify the angle are ▪.

Classify each angle as *acute*, *right*, *obtuse*, or *straight*.

13. 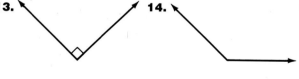   **14.**   **15.**   **16.**

17. 148°   **18.** 180°   **19.** 17°   **20.** 83°   **21.** 90°

Classify each pair of angles as *complementary*, *supplementary*, or *neither*.

22. 67°, 13°   **23.** 141°, 39°   **24.** 2°, 88°   **25.** 45°, 45°

Find the complement of an angle that has the given measure.

26. 31°   **27.** 74°   **28.** 11°   **29.** 48°   **30.** 86°

Find the supplement of an angle that has the given measure.

31. 64°   **32.** 112°   **33.** 13°   **34.** 128°   **35.** 160°

Solve.

36. Draw and label the complementary angles that have equal degree measures.

★37. What is the degree measure of an angle that is 4 times the measure of its supplement?

Constructing Congruent Line Segments and Angles

In geometry, a **construction** is a drawing for which only a compass and a straightedge are used.

A. Construct a line segment congruent to $\overline{AB}$.

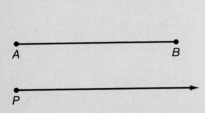

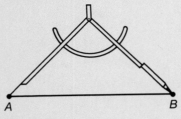

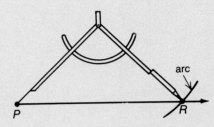

Draw a ray, and label its endpoint P.

Open the compass to the length of $\overline{AB}$.

Using the same compass opening, place the compass point on P, and draw an arc. $\overline{PR} \cong \overline{AB}$

B. Construct an angle congruent to $\angle S$.

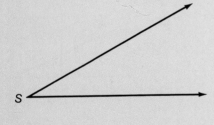

Draw a ray $\overrightarrow{LM}$.

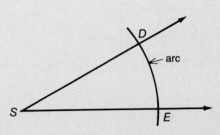

Place the compass point at S, and draw an arc that intersects both sides of $\angle S$. Label the points D and E.

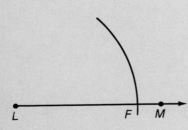

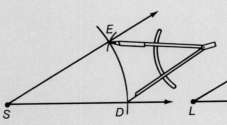

Using the same compass opening, place the compass point at L, and draw an arc. Label the point F on $\overrightarrow{LM}$.

Place the compass points on D and E.

Use the same compass opening to draw an arc from F that intersects the first arc at G. Draw $\overrightarrow{LG}$. $\angle L \cong \angle S$

358

Copy the figures, and use them to construct the following.

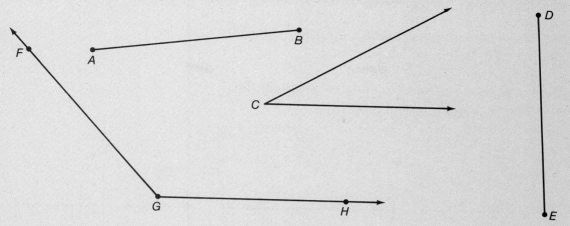

1. Construct a line segment congruent to $\overline{AB}$.

2. Construct an angle congruent to $\angle C$.

3. Construct a line segment congruent to $\overline{DE}$.

4. Construct an angle congruent to $\angle FGH$.

★ 5. Construct a line segment whose length is equal to the length of $\overline{AB}$ + the length of $\overline{DE}$.

★ 6. Construct an angle whose measure is equal to $m\angle FGH - m\angle C$.

Draw the figure, and construct a figure congruent to it.

7. Draw a line segment. Construct a line segment congruent to it.

8. Draw a right angle. Construct an angle congruent to it.

9. Draw complementary angles. Construct angles congruent to them.

10. Draw supplementary angles. Construct angles congruent to them.

CHALLENGE

Find the diameter of this circle.

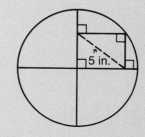

5 in.

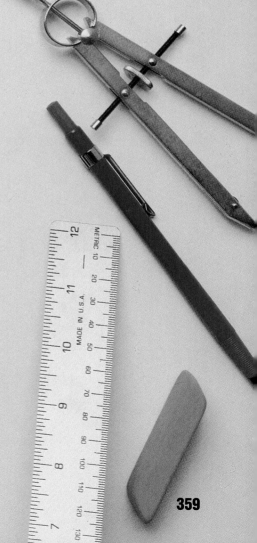

Bisecting Line Segments and Angles

Architects use a straightedge and a compass to bisect line segments and angles on blueprints.

A. To **bisect a line segment** means to divide it into two congruent segments. Bisect $\overline{AB}$.

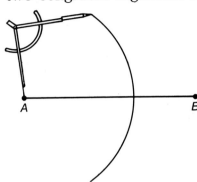
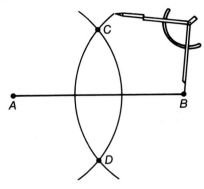
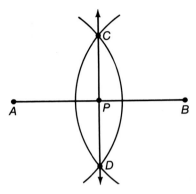

Open the compass to more than $\frac{1}{2}$ the length of $\overline{AB}$. Place the compass point at A, and draw an arc.

Without changing the compass opening, place the compass point at B, and draw another arc. Label the intersections C and D.

Use a straightedge to connect points C and D. $\overleftrightarrow{CD}$ bisects $\overline{AB}$ at P. $\overline{AP} \cong \overline{PB}$. $\overleftrightarrow{CD}$ is the bisector of AB.

B. To **bisect an angle** means to divide it into two congruent angles. Bisect $\angle Y$.

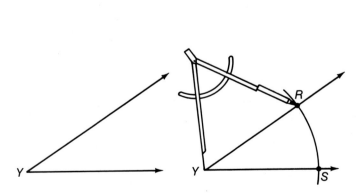
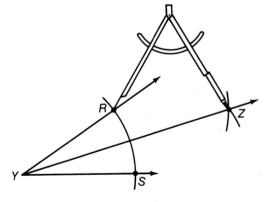

Place the compass point at Y, and draw an arc that intersects both sides of $\angle Y$. Label the points R and S.

Use the same compass opening to draw intersecting arcs from R and S. Label the point Z. Draw $\overrightarrow{YZ}$. $\overrightarrow{YZ}$ bisects $\angle Y$. $\angle RYZ \cong \angle ZYS$. $\overrightarrow{YZ}$ is the bisector of $\angle RYS$.

Math Reasoning, page H225

Use the figures to complete.

1.

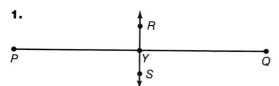

$\overleftrightarrow{RS}$ bisects $\overline{PQ}$.

$\overline{PY} \cong$ ■

2.

$\overrightarrow{VX}$ bisects $\angle TVW$.

$\angle WVX \cong$ ■

Complete.

3. $\overleftrightarrow{EF}$ bisects $\overline{GH}$ at N.

$\overline{GN} \cong$ ■

4. $\overrightarrow{MK}$ bisects $\angle LMN$.

$\angle LMK \cong$ ■

Copy each figure. Use each to construct the following:

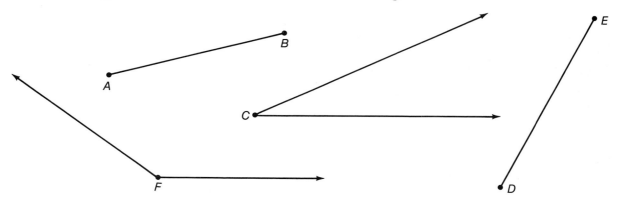

5. the bisector of $\overline{AB}$

7. the bisector of $\overline{DE}$

6. the bisector of $\angle C$

8. the bisector of $\angle F$

Draw any triangle.

9. Construct the bisector of each side of the triangle. Do these bisectors intersect at one point?

10. Construct the bisector of each angle in the triangle. Do the angle bisectors intersect at one point?

ANOTHER LOOK

Evaluate. Use the replacement set $\{^-2, ^-1, 0, 1, 2\}$.

1. $7 + n$

2. $n - 11$

3. $21n$

4. $\frac{n}{4}$

5. $\frac{2}{3} + n$

6. $n - 17.8$

7. $0.052n$

8. $\frac{n}{\frac{9}{11}}$

PROBLEM SOLVING
Working Backward

Some problems give the final result of a series of operations and ask for the original number. You work backward to solve such problems.

> James led a tour through the historic nineteenth-century storefronts in Kansas City. Then, $\frac{2}{5}$ of the group left for lunch. The tour went on to the nation's first major shopping center, which was built in 1922. Half of the remaining group stayed there. James took the last 6 people on a special bus tour. How many people were there on the tour originally?

1. Arrange the information given in the problem into ordered steps.

2. Write an equation for each step.

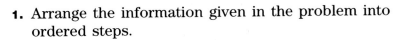

the number of people in the tour	the number after $\frac{2}{5}$ left	half in the center	other half with James
x	$x - \frac{2}{5}x = \frac{3}{5}x$	$\frac{1}{2}y = z$	$z = 6$
	$\frac{3}{5}x = y$		

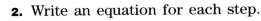

3. Work backward, and solve each equation.

How many people were with the tour in the shopping center?

Since $z = 6$ and $\frac{1}{2}y = z$, then $\frac{1}{2}y = 6$.

$$2 \cdot \frac{1}{2}y = 2 \cdot 6$$

$$y = 12$$

How many people were with the tour originally?

Since $y = 12$ and $\frac{3}{5}x = y$, then $\frac{3}{5}x = 12$.

$$\frac{5}{3} \cdot \frac{3}{5}x = \frac{5}{3} \cdot 12$$

$$x = 20$$

There were originally 20 people on the tour.

Check your answer.

	number in tour	that number minus $\frac{2}{5}$ of it	$\frac{1}{2}$ the difference
	20	$20 - \left(\frac{2}{5} \cdot 20\right)$	$\frac{1}{2} \cdot 12 = 6$
		$20 - 8 = 12$	The answer is correct.

Work backward. Then write the letter of the correct answer.

1. Of her weekly allowance, Sara spent $\frac{1}{6}$ to buy 12 postcards of historic houses and $\frac{1}{3}$ to buy a book about architecture. Sara had $7.50 of her weekly allowance left after these purchases. What is Sara's weekly allowance?
   a. $12.50   b. $15.00   c. $22.50

2. Thelma had some baseball cards. She gave 11 to her brother and divided the remainder equally among herself and 3 friends. Her share consisted of 19 cards. How many cards did she have originally?
   a. 90   b. 48   c. 87

Solve.

3. Mrs. Cole's class visited the Mount Pleasant Estate. Half the class toured the grounds. Of those who did not tour the grounds, $\frac{1}{3}$ began the tour in the drawing room and 5 began in the kitchen. This left 3, who began the tour in the basement. How many students were there in the class?

4. A team of three painters painted one tower of a suspension bridge. The first painter painted $\frac{1}{4}$ of the tower. The second painter painted $\frac{1}{2}$ the remaining part. The third painter painted a 24-foot section. That left a 16-foot section to be painted by all three painters. How tall is the bridge tower?

5. The idea for a national monument in St. Louis was conceived 14 years before construction began. It took 20 years to build the Great Archway, but 2 of those years were spent finishing the interior. St. Louis planned a twenty-fifth birthday party to commemorate the building of the exterior of the arch. The party was held in 1990. In which year was the idea for the monument conceived?

6. It took 4 months to pour all the concrete required to build the Hoover Dam. In March, 0.62 million cubic meters of concrete were poured. In April, 0.21 million cubic meters less than the March amount were poured. In May, twice the April amount was poured. That left 0.63 million cubic meters to be poured in June. How many cubic meters of concrete are there in the dam?

Perpendicular and Parallel Lines

A. In the drawing shown on the right, line *l* is parallel to line *m*, or *l*‖*m*. Line *n* is perpendicular to line *p*, or *n*⊥*p*. **Perpendicular** lines intersect to form right angles.

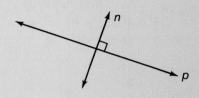

Line *t* is a **transversal** that intersects lines *l* and *m* forming eight angles. Since *l*‖*m*, the following angle relationships are true. For example, ∠1 and ∠3, and ∠6 and ∠8 are **vertical angles** and are congruent. ∠1 and ∠2, and ∠6 and ∠7 are **adjacent angles** and are supplementary. ∠4 and ∠6, and ∠3 and ∠5 are **alternate interior angles** and are congruent. Finally, ∠2 and ∠6, and ∠4 and ∠8 are **corresponding angles** and are congruent.

B. Construct a line parallel to line *l*.

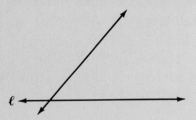

Draw a line that intersects line *l* at any point.

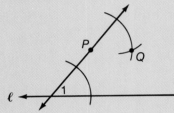

At any point *P* on this line, construct an angle congruent to ∠1. Label the point *Q*.

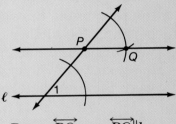

Draw $\overleftrightarrow{PQ}$. $\overleftrightarrow{PQ}$‖*l*

C. Construct a line perpendicular to line *l*.

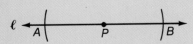

With the compass opening the same, draw two arcs from *P* that intersect *l*. Label the points *A* and *B*.

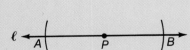

Open the compass farther and place its point at *A* and then at *B*, draw intersecting arcs. Label the point *Q*.

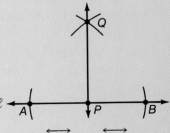

Draw $\overleftrightarrow{PQ}$. $\overleftrightarrow{PQ}$⊥*l*

Identify each pair of lines as *parallel* or as *perpendicular*.

1. a pair of lines that intersect to form right angles

2.

3.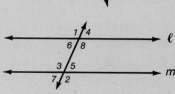

In the given figure, $l \parallel m$. Identify each pair of angles as *vertical*, *adjacent*, *alternate interior*, or *corresponding* angles.

4. ∠1 and ∠8

5. ∠3 and ∠8

6. ∠6 and ∠7

7. ∠3 and ∠5

8. ∠4 and ∠5

9. ∠5 and ∠7

10. ∠1 and ∠6

11. ∠5 and ∠6

12. ∠2 and ∠5

13. ∠4 and ∠6

14. ∠2 and ∠3

In the same figure, name each pair of angles as *congruent* or *supplementary*.

15. ∠7 and ∠8

16. ∠4 and ∠2

17. ∠7 and ∠1

18. ∠6 and ∠4

19. ∠5 and ∠6

20. ∠2 and ∠3

21. ∠4 and ∠1

22. ∠1 and ∠3

23. ∠7 and ∠2

Complete. Use the same figure as above.

24. If m∠6 = 57°, m∠4 = ▨

25. If m∠6 = 57°, m∠1 = ▨

In the given figure, $\overleftrightarrow{AB} \parallel \overleftrightarrow{CD}$. Write *true* if the angles are congruent. Write *false* if the angles are not congruent.

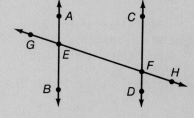

26. ∠AEG ≅ ∠BEF

27. ∠DFH ≅ ∠DFG

28. ∠AEH ≅ ∠CFH

29. ∠BEH ≅ ∠GFC

30. ∠DFH ≅ ∠HFC

31. ∠EFD ≅ ∠CFH

Use this figure to find the measure of each angle. $l \parallel m$ and m∠6 = 145°.

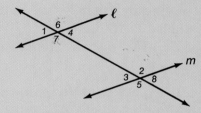

32. m∠7

33. m∠5

34. m∠2

35. m∠8

Solve.

36. Draw a line. Construct a line parallel to it.

37. Draw a line. Construct a line perpendicular to it.

Classifying Triangles

The Southport Savings Bank in Southport, Connecticut, was built in 1854. Notice the triangle-shaped roof. What kind of a triangle is it?

A **triangle** is a closed figure that has three line segments that form its **sides.** You can use the **vertices** of a triangle to name it. Triangle *ABC* is written △*ABC*.

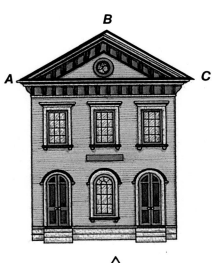

A. A triangle can be named according to the lengths of its sides.

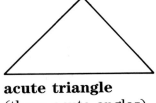

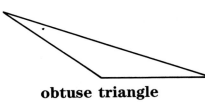

shows congruent sides

shows congruent angles

scalene triangle
(no congruent sides)

isosceles triangle
(two congruent sides)

equilateral triangle
(three congruent sides)

The roof of the bank forms an isosceles triangle.

B. A triangle also can be named according to the measures of its angles.

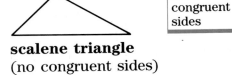

acute triangle
(three acute angles)

obtuse triangle
(one obtuse angle)

right triangle
(one right angle)

The roof of the bank also forms an obtuse triangle.

C. In any triangle, the sum of the measures of the angles is 180°.
$33° + 132° + 15° = 180°$

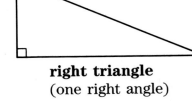

An **exterior angle** of a triangle is formed by extending a side of the triangle. The measure of an exterior angle of a triangle is equal to the sum of the measures of the two opposite interior angles of the triangle. In the figure, $m\angle 4 = m\angle 1 + m\angle 2$.

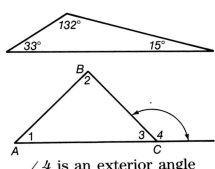

∠4 is an exterior angle of △*ABC*.

Math Reasoning, page H225

Complete.

1. A triangle that has at least two congruent sides is called ■.

2. A triangle that has a 97° angle is called ■.

3. If the sum of the measures of two angles of a triangle is 124°, the measure of the third angle is ■.

4. In the accompanying figure, the measure of the exterior angle is ■.

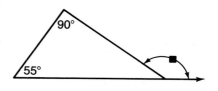

Name each triangle according to the lengths of its sides.

5.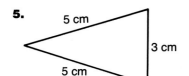
5 cm
3 cm
5 cm

6.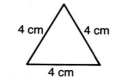
4 cm   4 cm
4 cm

7.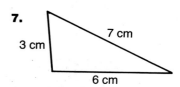
3 cm   7 cm
6 cm

Name each triangle according to the measures of its angles.

8.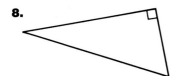

9.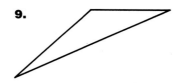

10.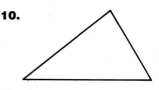

Given the measure of two angles of a triangle, find the measure of the third angle.

11. 48° and 71°   **12.** 90° and 15°   **13.** 117° and 27°   **14.** 13° and 141°

15. 90° and 45°   **16.** 30° and 60°   **17.** 60° and 60°   **18.** 30° and 90°

Draw each figure.

19. an acute scalene triangle   **20.** an equilateral triangle

21. an isosceles right triangle   **22.** an obtuse scalene triangle

23. an equiangular triangle   **24.** a right scalene triangle

25. an obtuse isosceles triangle   **26.** an acute isosceles triangle

Determine the measure of each angle in the figure.

27. m∠1   **28.** m∠2

29. m∠3   **30.** m∠4

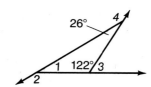

Polygons

A. The figures shown below are examples of **polygons**. A polygon is named according to the number of its sides.

A **regular polygon** has congruent sides and congruent angles.

Sides	Polygon
three	triangle
four	quadrilateral
five	pentagon
six	hexagon
seven	heptagon
eight	octagon
nine	nonagon
ten	decagon

pentagon

regular pentagon

quadrilateral

hexagon

B. Here are some kinds of **quadrilaterals**.

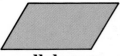

parallelogram
opposite sides parallel and congruent

rectangle
parallelogram has four right angles

square
rectangle has four congruent sides

rhombus
parallelogram has four congruent sides

trapezoid
quadrilateral has only two parallel sides

C. A **diagonal** is a line segment other than a side that joins two vertices of a polygon.

The diagonals in this 5-sided polygon (pentagon) divide it into $5 - 2$, or 3 triangles. So, the sum of the measures of the pentagon's interior angles is $3 \cdot 180$. For a polygon of n sides, the interior angle sum is $(n - 2) \cdot 180$.

For a pentagon $ABCDE$,
sum for $ABCDE = (n - 2) \cdot 180$
$(5 - 2) \cdot 180$
$3 \quad \cdot 180 = 540$

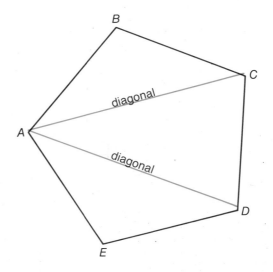

Name each polygon. Indicate if it is regular.

1.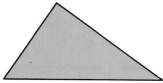

2.

3.

4.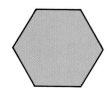

5.

6.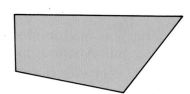

7. Trace the hexagon. How many diagonals can be drawn from any one vertex?

8. Trace the octagon. How many diagonals can be drawn from any one vertex?

Name each quadrilateral.

9.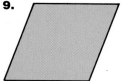

10.

11.

12.

For each polygon, find the sum of the measures of the interior angles.

13. triangle

14. octagon

15. pentagon

16. nonagon

17. hexagon

18. quadrilateral

19. decagon

20. heptagon

MIDCHAPTER REVIEW

In the figure at right, $\overline{AB} \| \overline{CD}$. Identify each of the following.

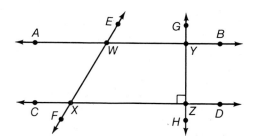

1. a point

2. four lines

3. two rays

4. two line segments

5. two acute angles

6. two obtuse angles

7. two straight angles

8. two right angles

9. two congruent angles

10. two supplementary angles

11. two vertical angles

12. two adjacent angles

13. two corresponding angles

PROBLEM SOLVING
Choosing a Strategy or Method

Write the strategy or method you choose. Then solve.

| Estimation |
| Using a Graph |
| Choosing the Operation |
| Solving Multi-step Problems |
| Guessing and Checking |
| Making a Table to Find a Pattern |
| Writing an Equation |
| Interpreting the Quotient and the Remainder |
| Using a Formula |
| Making an Organized List |
| Using a Sample |

1. The Washington Monument is 555 feet tall. A statue in Ana's town is 27 feet less than $\frac{1}{3}$ of the Washington Monument's height. How tall is the statue?

2. Boston's Freedom Trail is a $1\frac{1}{2}$ mile path of landmarks. On one map $\frac{1}{4}$ inch represents the length of the trail. What does 1 inch represent on the map?

3. Ted had a total of 24 dimes and quarters with a value of $3.75. He had 6 more dimes than quarters. How many dimes did he have?

4. A football team scored 37 points by making some 7-point touchdowns and fewer than five 3-point field goals. How many touchdowns did the team make?

5. Cathy works at the mall 4 days each week. The distance from her house to work is 15.2 miles. How many miles does she travel each week going to and from work?

Use the survey of 200 votes for Exercises 6–9.
STUDENTS' VOTES ON THE TEN MOST USEFUL INVENTIONS

Rank	Invention	Votes	Rank	Invention	Votes
1	Electric light	38	6	Airplane	15
2	Computer	35	7	TV	12
3	Car	30	8	Radio	10
4	Telephone	24	9	Zipper	8
5	Plastic	16	10	Typewriter	6

6. What percent of the students voted for the radio?

7. How many more people voted for the electric light than for TV?

8. What percent of the students voted for inventions that did not make the top-ten list?

★9. The town has 1,250 students. What percent of the town's students participated in the survey?

10. The Cathedral of Saint John the Divine in New York City will be the world's largest cathedral when completed. The ratio of the length to the width is 15:8. The width is 320 feet. What is the length?

11. Each tower of the World Trade Center stands 411.6 meters tall. An architectural model of the towers uses a scale of 4 mm equals 1 m. How tall is the model?

Use the broken-line graph below for Exercises 12–13.

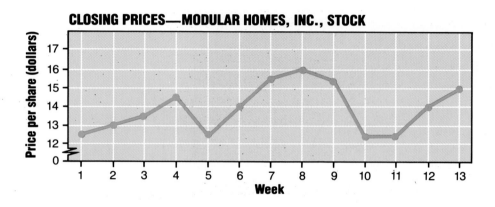

CLOSING PRICES—MODULAR HOMES, INC., STOCK

12. During which week did the Modular Homes stock close at its highest price?

13. Between which weeks did Modular Homes stock experience the greatest drop in price?

Use the circle graph at the right for Exercises 14–16.

14. If a total of 240 people were interviewed, how many prefer biking?

15. How many more people prefer jogging than biking and jumping rope?

16. Which two exercises have a combined percent that equals jogging's percent?

FAVORITE EXERCISES

Jumping Rope 5%
22% Swimming
40% Jogging
15% Biking
18% Walking

Circles

The Hirshhorn Museum in Washington, D.C., shown below, is noted for its distinctive circular design.

A **circle** is a set of all points in a plane that are the same distance from one point called the **center.**

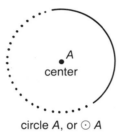

circle *A*, or ⊙ *A*

A compass is used to construct a circle or part of a circle. The distance from the compass point to a point on the circle is the **radius** of the circle.

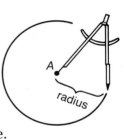

PARTS OF A CIRCLE

Radius: $\overline{AB}$ is a line segment from the center of the circle to any point on the circle.

Chord: $\overline{CD}$ is a line segment whose endpoints are on the circle.

Diameter: $\overline{EF}$ is a chord that passes through the center of the circle and has the length of two radii. $d = 2r$

Arc: $\overparen{BE}$ is part of the circle.

Central angle: $\angle BAE$ is an angle whose vertex is the center of the circle.

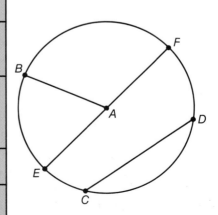

Name each part of the circle.

1. the center

2. the diameter

3. three chords

4. the longest chord

5. the radii

6. five arcs

7. the central angles   8. obtuse central angle   9. acute central angle

10. intersecting chords   11. shortest chord

Classify each segment as a *chord*, a *radius*, or a *diameter*. *H* is the center.

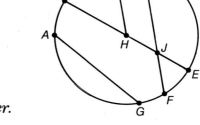

12. $\overline{BE}$ 13. $\overline{AG}$ 14. $\overline{HC}$

15. $\overline{DF}$ 16. $\overline{BH}$ 17. $\overline{HE}$

18. Name two central angles of circle *H*.

For each statement, write *always*, *sometimes*, or *never*.

19. All radii of a circle are the same length.

20. A central angle has its vertex on the circle.

★21. Small circles have measures less than 360° and large circles have measures more than 360°.

22. All points of a circle are the same distance from the center of the circle.

23. Chords are diameters.

24. Some arcs are line segments.

25. Circles are congruent.

26. All circles are regular polygons.

27. The longest chord of any circle is its diameter.

28. A radius of a circle is half the length of the circle's diameter.

Solve. Use the Infobank.

29. Use the information on page 477 to solve. Look at the design of the house pictured. Find the geometric shapes that have been used in this design. Draw a house of your own, using as many geometric shapes as you can.

Congruent Polygons

Congruent polygons are polygons that have the same size and shape. For example, the dome of the Roundhouse in Baton Rouge, Louisiana, consists of hundreds of congruent hexagons.

The corresponding parts of congruent polygons also are congruent. The slash marks on the sides and the angles of each polygon indicate the corresponding parts that are congruent.

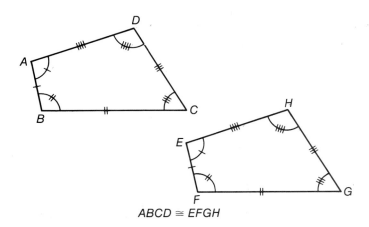

ABCD ≅ EFGH

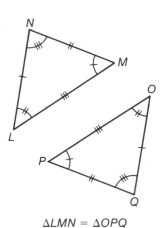

△LMN = △OPQ

For quadrilaterals *ABCD* and *EFGH*:

Corresponding sides	Corresponding angles
$\overline{AB} \cong \overline{EF}$	$\angle A \cong \angle E$
$\overline{BC} \cong \overline{FG}$	$\angle B \cong \angle F$
$\overline{CD} \cong \overline{GH}$	$\angle C \cong \angle G$
$\overline{DA} \cong \overline{HE}$	$\angle D \cong \angle H$

For congruent triangles *LMN* and *OPQ*:

Corresponding sides	Corresponding angles
$\overline{LM} \cong \overline{OP}$	$\angle L \cong \angle O$
$\overline{MN} \cong \overline{PQ}$	$\angle M \cong \angle P$
$\overline{NL} \cong \overline{QO}$	$\angle N \cong \angle Q$

When naming congruent polygons, be sure to list congruent vertices in the same order. For example,

$\triangle LMN \cong \triangle OPQ$ means that $\angle L \cong \angle O$, $\angle M \cong \angle P$, and $\angle N \cong \angle Q$.

Find the pair of polygons that appears to be congruent.

1.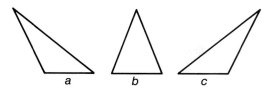

2.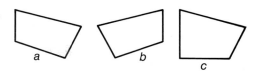

3.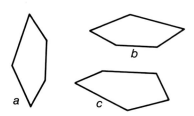

4.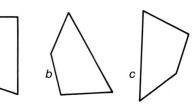

Use the congruent triangles to answer the following.

5. Name three pairs of congruent angles.

6. Name three pairs of congruent sides.

7. Complete: $\triangle RCX \cong \triangle$ ▨

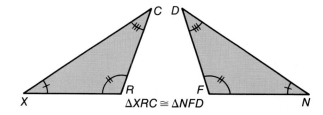

$\triangle XRC \cong \triangle NFD$

Use the congruent quadrilaterals to answer the following.

8. Name the congruent quadrilaterals.

9. Name four pairs of congruent sides.

10. Name four pairs of congruent angles.

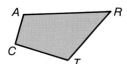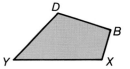

Use quadrilaterals $CDNR$ and $LTYZ$ to find the measure of each segment or angle. $CDNR \cong LTYZ$

11. $\overline{LT}$
12. $\angle Y$
13. $\overline{ZL}$

14. $\angle N$
15. $\overline{DN}$
16. $\angle L$

17. $\angle R$
18. $\angle D$
19. $\angle R + \angle C + \angle D + \angle N$

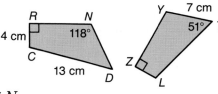

Solve.

★20. Quadrilateral $ZABC$ has two right angles. Must it be a parallelogram? If possible, draw one figure that is a parallelogram, and one that is not.

★21. Each diagonal drawn through quadrilateral $PQRS$ divides it into two congruent triangles. Is $PQRS$ a parallelogram?

Constructing Congruent Triangles

Two triangles are congruent if

a. three pairs of sides are congruent. This is called **side-side-side congruence,** or **SSS.**
$\overline{AB} \cong \overline{DE}$, $\overline{BC} \cong \overline{EF}$, $\overline{CA} \cong \overline{FD}$

b. two pairs of sides and the included pair of angles are congruent. This is called **side-angle-side congruence,** or **SAS.**
$\overline{AB} \cong \overline{DE}$, $\overline{BC} \cong \overline{EF}$, $\angle B \cong \angle E$

c. two pairs of angles and the included pair of sides are congruent. This is called **angle-side-angle congruence,** or **ASA.**
$\angle C \cong \angle F$, $\angle B = \angle E$, $\overline{CB} \cong \overline{FE}$

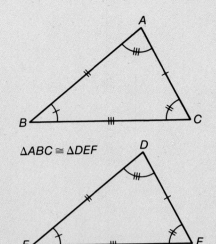

$\triangle ABC \cong \triangle DEF$

Use the SSS congruence to construct a triangle congruent to $\triangle GHJ$.

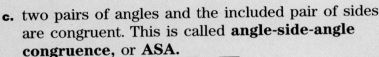

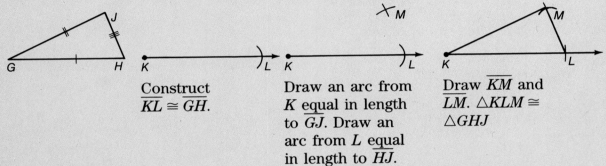

Construct $\overline{KL} \cong \overline{GH}$.

Draw an arc from K equal in length to $\overline{GJ}$. Draw an arc from L equal in length to $\overline{HJ}$.

Draw $\overline{KM}$ and $\overline{LM}$. $\triangle KLM \cong \triangle GHJ$

Use the SAS congruence to construct a triangle congruent to $\triangle DEF$.

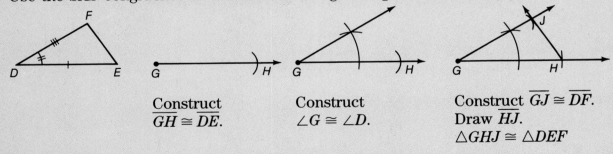

Construct $\overline{GH} \cong \overline{DE}$.

Construct $\angle G \cong \angle D$.

Construct $\overline{GJ} \cong \overline{DF}$. Draw $\overline{HJ}$. $\triangle GHJ \cong \triangle DEF$

Use the ASA congruence to construct a triangle congruent to $\triangle RST$.

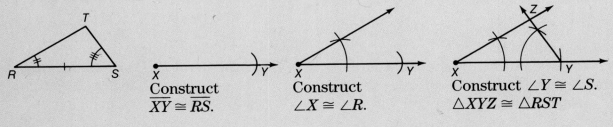

Construct $\overline{XY} \cong \overline{RS}$.

Construct $\angle X \cong \angle R$.

Construct $\angle Y \cong \angle S$. $\triangle XYZ \cong \triangle RST$

Write *SSS*, *SAS*, or *ASA* to show the congruence indicated by the markings.

1.
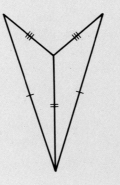

2.
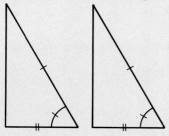

3.
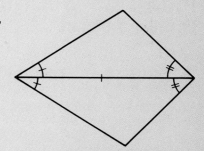

4.
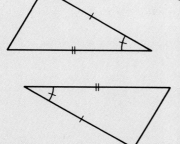

5.
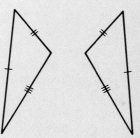

6.
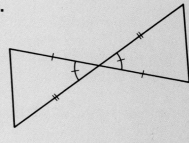

Draw an acute triangle and label it *ABC*.
Draw an obtuse triangle and label it *DEF*.
Use the triangles to complete exercises 7 through 12.

7. Use SSS congruence to construct a triangle congruent to △*ABC*.

8. Use SAS congruence to construct a triangle congruent to △*DEF*. (Copy sides $\overline{DE}$, $\overline{DF}$, and ∠*D*.)

9. Use ASA congruence to construct a triangle congruent to △*ABC*. (Copy ∠*A*, ∠*B*, and side $\overline{AB}$.)

10. Use ASA congruence to construct a triangle congruent to △*DEF*. (Copy ∠*F*, ∠*E*, and side $\overline{EF}$.)

11. Use SAS congruence to construct a triangle congruent to △*ABC*. (Copy sides $\overline{AC}$, $\overline{CB}$, and ∠*C*.)

12. Use SSS congruence to construct a triangle congruent to △*DEF*.

★**13.** Use the two line segments to construct an isosceles triangle.

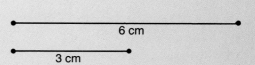

6 cm

3 cm

PROBLEM SOLVING
Drawing a Picture

Sometimes it is easier to solve a problem by drawing a picture before you try to do any computation. Then you can see what you are being asked to compute.

Bookworms are the larvae of a beetle, and they destroy books. Suppose a bookworm begins its trip on the first page of the first volume of a 3-volume work on architecture. The bookworm burrows in a straight line from volume 1 into volume 2 and volume 3. It stops at the last page of the third volume. If each volume is 75 millimeters thick and each cover of each volume is 3 millimeters thick, how far does the bookworm travel?

Make a picture to help you solve the problem.

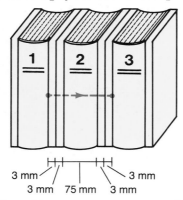

By looking at the picture you can see that the first page of volume 1 is actually on the *right* side of the book (imagine taking the book off the shelf and opening it to the first page). You can also see that the last page of volume 3 is on the *left* side of the book. So, the bookworm burrows through the cover of volume 1, through all of volume 2, and through the cover of volume 3.

$3 \text{ mm} + 3 \text{ mm} + 75 \text{ mm} + 3 \text{ mm} + 3 \text{ mm} = 87 \text{ mm}$

The bookworm travels 87 millimeters.

Write the letter of the drawing you would use to solve each problem.

1. On one wall of an architect's office there are 6 shelves spaced the same distance apart. The bottom of the first is 15 in. from the floor. The bottom of the fourth is 48 in. from the floor. The top of the top shelf is 24 in. below the ceiling. Each shelf is 2 in. thick. How high is the room?

2. The architect's office is on the fourth floor of a building. The fourth floor is 48 ft above the street. The distance between each floor above the fourth is 11 ft. The top floor is 24 ft below the roof. There are 6 floors above street level. How tall is the building?

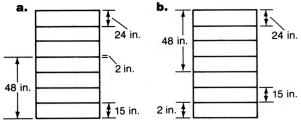

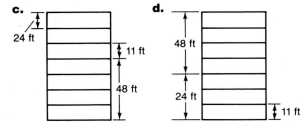

Draw a picture, and solve each problem.

3. The Diagnostic Clinic is an 8-story medical building. Standing outside the building, you see that each story consists of windows 2 meters high. Each window is surrounded on all sides by 1 meter of concrete. What is the height of the building?

4. Fran always sits in a certain seat in the theater. Her favorite seat is located in the fourth row from the front and the twelfth row from the back of the hall. Her seat is 2 seats from the right aisle and 7 seats from the left aisle. How many seats are there in the auditorium?

★5. A 2-volume set of books sits on a library bookshelf. Volume 1 sits to the left of volume 2. The cover of each book is 1.4 mm thick. Each group of 10 pages of these volumes measures 1 mm. Find the distance from the last page of volume 2 to page 60 of volume 1.

6. Jo-Jo is delivering three packages to offices in the Empire State Building. He takes the elevator 28 floors to deliver the first package. He takes the elevator another 19 floors to deliver the second package. He then rides the elevator down 13 floors to deliver the last package. He finds that he is now $\frac{1}{3}$ of the way up the building. How many floors does the Empire State Building have?

Similar Polygons

A. **Similar polygons** are two polygons that have the same shape.

is similar to

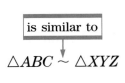

$\triangle ABC \sim \triangle XYZ$

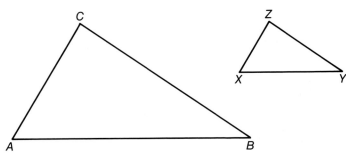

The corresponding angles of similar polygons are congruent.

$$\angle A \cong \angle X$$
$$\angle B \cong \angle Y$$
$$\angle C \cong \angle Z$$

The lengths of the corresponding sides of similar polygons are proportional.

$$\frac{\text{length of } \overline{AB}}{\text{length of } \overline{XY}} = \frac{\text{length of } \overline{BC}}{\text{length of } \overline{YZ}} = \frac{\text{length of } \overline{CA}}{\text{length of } \overline{ZX}}$$

B. In the drawing at the right, $ABCD \sim LMNO$. To find the length of $\overline{LM}$, use a proportion.

$$\frac{5}{600} = \frac{2}{n}$$
$$5n = 1{,}200$$
$$n = 240 \text{ cm}$$

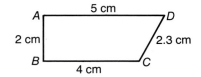

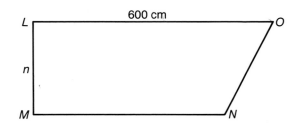

The length of $\overline{LM}$ is 240 cm (2.4 m).

Checkpoint

Write the letter of the correct answer.

Polygon $ANXDT \sim$ polygon $YGCRB$.

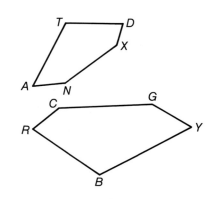

1. The angle that is congruent to $\angle D$ is ▒.

a. $\angle A$ **b.** $\angle Y$ **c.** $\angle R$ **d.** $\angle B$

2. Complete the proportion. $\frac{\overline{AT}}{\overline{YB}} = \frac{\overline{NX}}{▒}$

a. $\overline{BR}$ **b.** $\overline{YG}$ **c.** $\overline{BY}$ **d.** $\overline{GC}$

Math Reasoning, page H226

Do the polygons appear similar? Write *yes* or *no*.

1.

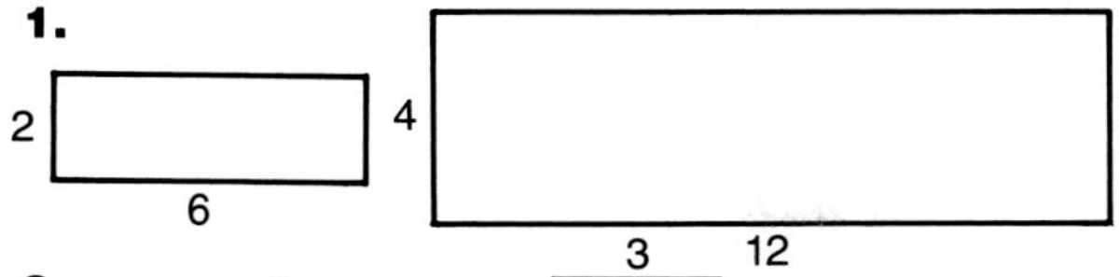

2.

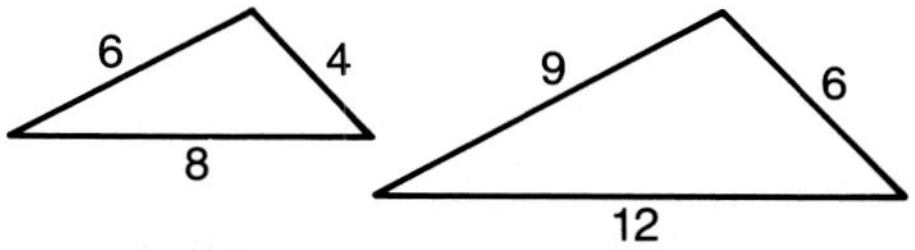

3.

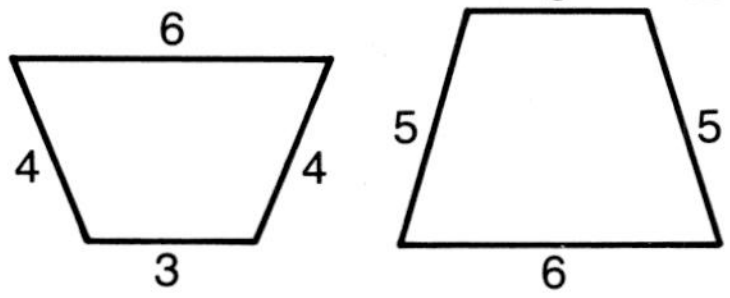

4.

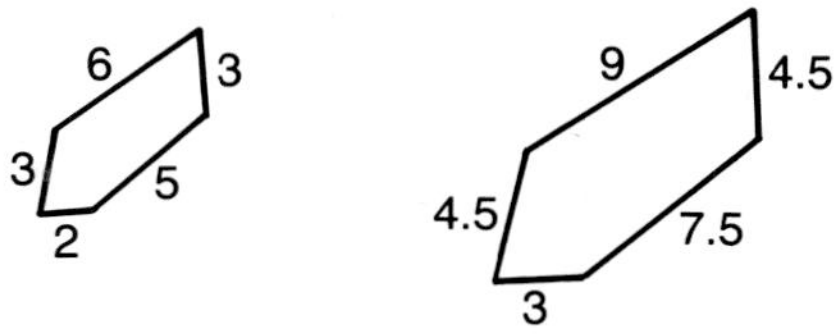

Complete.

Quadrilateral *ABCD* ~ quadrilateral *FEHG*.

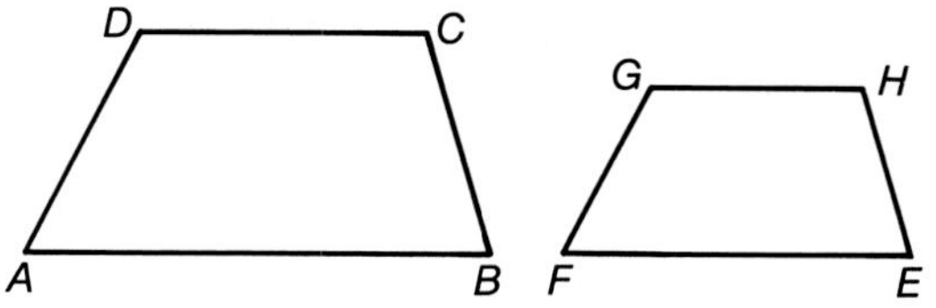

5. $\angle A \cong$ ■

6. $\angle C \cong$ ■

7. $\angle D \cong$ ■

8. $\angle B \cong$ ■

$\triangle DXN \sim \triangle YRC$

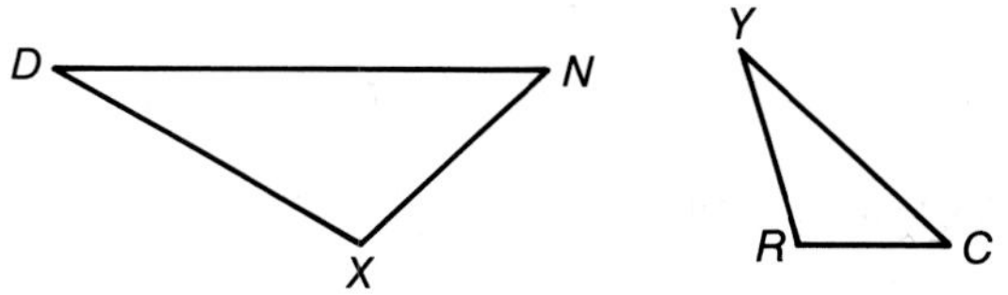

9. $\dfrac{\text{length of } \overline{DX}}{\text{length of } \overline{YR}} = \dfrac{\text{length of ■}}{\text{length of ■}}$

Polygon *VARYCX* ~ polygon *PLTBYN*. Find the length of each segment.

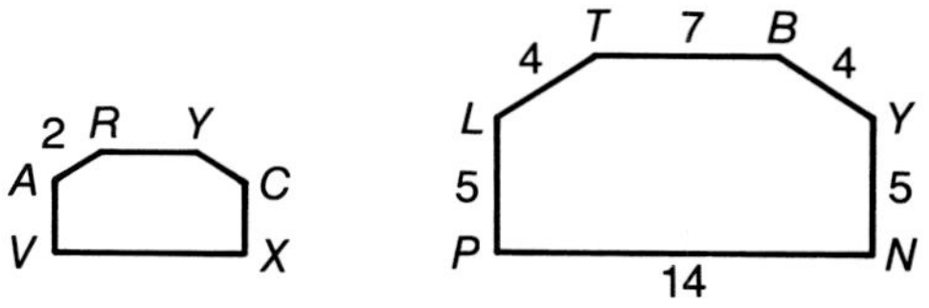

10. $\overline{AV}$

11. $\overline{YC}$

12. $\overline{VX}$

13. $\overline{RY}$

The polygons in each pair are similar. Find the measure of each side or each angle.

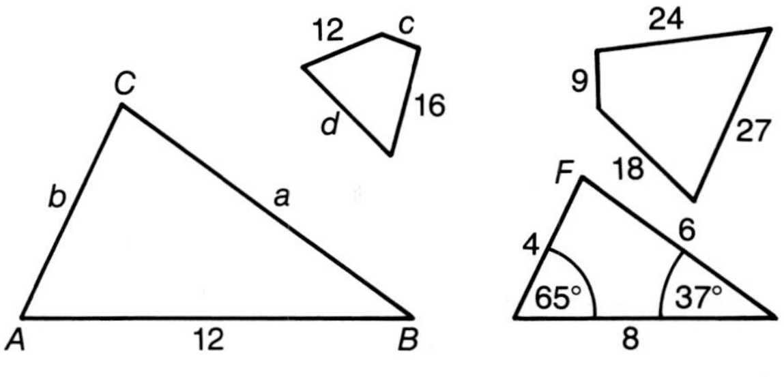

14. $a =$ ■

15. $b =$ ■

16. $c =$ ■

17. $d =$ ■

18. $\angle A =$ ■

19. $\angle B =$ ■

20. $\angle C =$ ■

21. $\angle F =$ ■

Solve.

22. To find the height of the Statue of Liberty, Debi put a 2-m stick in the ground. The stick cast a 1.5-m shadow. If the Statue of Liberty casts a 35-m shadow, how high is the statue?

23. Use the sketch to find the width of the Grand Canyon.

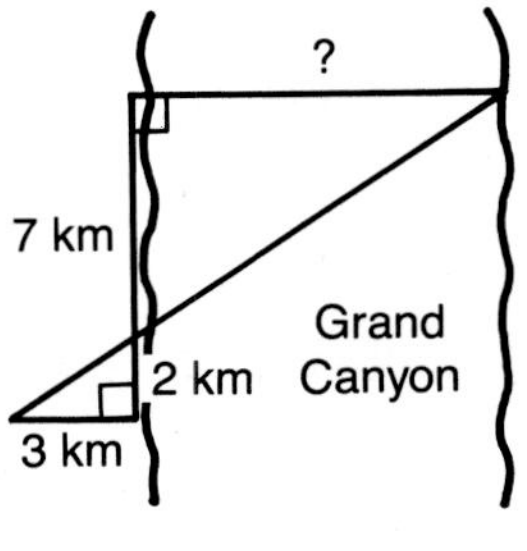

Symmetry and Reflections

The surfaces of many buildings are symmetrical. That is, a line placed in the proper position divides a face of the building into two identical parts. The faces of the Chrysler Building in New York are symmetrical.

A. Some figures have many **lines of symmetry,** while others have none.

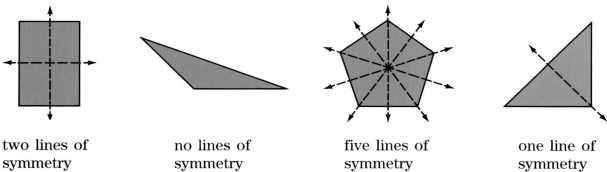

| two lines of symmetry | no lines of symmetry | five lines of symmetry | one line of symmetry |

B. It is also possible to draw the mirror image, or the **reflection,** of a given figure about a line of symmetry. A figure and its reflection are congruent.

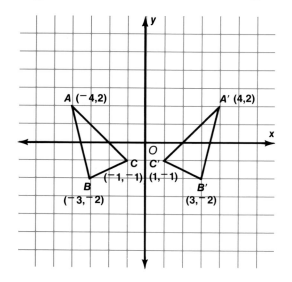

$\triangle A'B'C'$ is the reflection $\triangle ABC$ about the y-axis. The y-axis is the line of symmetry. (Read A' as "A prime.")

Note that the reflection of point $A(^-4,2)$ about the y-axis is $A'(4,2)$. Similarly, the reflection of $B(^-3,^-2)$ about the y-axis is $B'(3,^-2)$, and the reflection of $C(^-1,^-1)$ is $C'(1,^-1)$. The reflection of each point has the same y-coordinate, and the x-coordinate of each point differs in sign only.

Math Reasoning, page H226

Trace the following figures. Draw all the lines of symmetry. Write the number of lines of symmetry that each figure has.

1.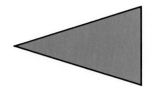

2.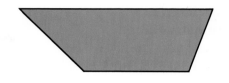

3.

4.

5.

6.

Find the coordinates of the reflection point about the *x*-axis.

7. (6,1)   **8.** (⁻2,3)   **9.** (0,4)

Find the coordinates of the reflection point about the *y*-axis.

10. (4,2)   **11.** (2,⁻7)   **12.** (⁻1,⁻5)

Plot the reflection in a coordinate plane.

13. Plot the points (4,1), (3,5), and (⁻3,2). Connect the points to form a triangle. Plot its reflection about the *x*-axis.

14. Plot the points (⁻6,5), (⁻2,4), (⁻1,⁻3), and (⁻5,6). Connect the points to form a polygon. Plot its reflection about the *y*-axis.

Solve.

15. If a figure is cut along its line of symmetry, will each piece also have a line of symmetry? Why?

CHALLENGE

In geometry, it is proved that if two angles of one triangle are congruent to two angles of another triangle, then the two triangles are similar.

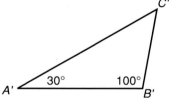

△ABC ~ △A'B'C'

Find the missing lengths in each pair of similar triangles.

1.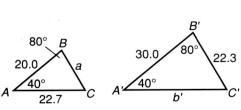

2.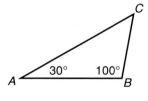

3.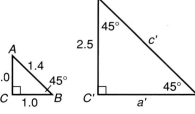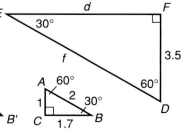

Translations and Rotations

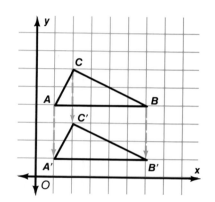

A. A 200-year-old house was located at the corner of New Street and Main Street. A high-rise apartment building was planned for that block, and the house was moved to the corner of New Street and Forest Street.

When an entire geometric figure is moved without changing its shape, the movement is called a **transformation.** When a figure is moved, or **translated,** along a line, like the house described above, all parts remain parallel to their former position, and the figure's size and shape do not change.

The diagram shows each point of $\triangle ABC$ moved 3 units down. $\triangle A'B'C'$ is a **translation** of $\triangle ABC$.

The vertices of $\triangle ABC$ are (1,4), (2,6), and (6,4). The vertices of $\triangle A'B'C'$ are (1,1), (2,3), and (6,1).

B. A **rotation** is another type of transformation or movement. In a rotation, a figure is moved about a point. All the figure's parts keep their original distance from the point and do not change their size or shape.

To rotate $\triangle RST$ around point O along the rotation arrow,

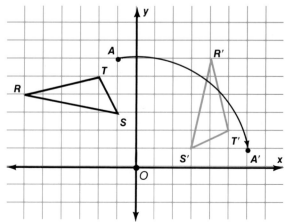

1. use tracing paper to trace $\triangle RST$, and then draw a dot on the copy at A (the end of the rotation arrow).

2. place the pencil point on O, and turn the paper until the dot is on the tip of the arrowhead.

3. press down on the pencil to outline $\triangle RST$. This figure, $\triangle R'S'T'$, is the rotation of $\triangle RST$.

384

For each of the following, draw a graph and find the coordinates of the translation.

1. $A(6,5)$; $B(2,3)$
   Translate 4 units left.

2. $C(2,^-3)$; $D(4,1)$; $E(6,^-1)$
   Translate 5 units up.

3. $F(1,^-4)$; $G(^-5,2)$; $H(^-7,^-2)$;
   $J(^-3,^-5)$
   Translate 6 units right.

4. $K(^-2,^-1)$; $L(^-5,4)$; $M(^-6,1)$
   Translate 5 units right and
   4 units down.

Trace each figure, point O, and the rotation arrow.
Then draw the rotation of the given figure about point
O, along the rotation arrow.

5.
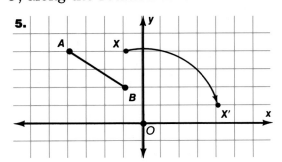

6.
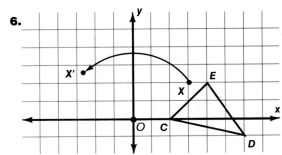

7.
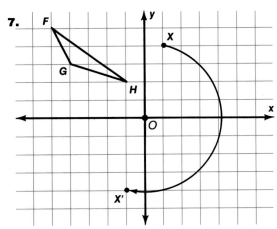

8.
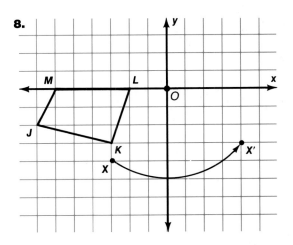

CHALLENGE

You are visiting Washington, D.C. You want to know the height of the Washington Monument. The easiest way to find out would be to ask someone, but you want to figure it out yourself. Devise several ways of measuring it.

PROBLEM SOLVING
Using Outside Sources Including the Infobank

Some problems do not contain all the information necessary to find the answer. To solve these problems, you will need to use an outside source to find the missing information. Sometimes, the information is found in an Infobank, such as the one on pages 473–478. Otherwise, you can look in an encyclopedia, an almanac, or other outside sources.

> How many more privately owned houses were started in 1983 than in 1981 in the midwestern United States?

To answer this question, you need to know how many houses were started in 1981 and how many were started in 1983 in the midwestern United States. If this information were not given in the table below, you would have to consult an outside source that has the particular information.

**NEW, PRIVATELY OWNED HOUSING UNITS
STARTED BY REGION: 1981 TO 1983
(negative sign (⁻) indicates decrease)**

| Region | Number (in thousands) | | | Percent change | |
	1981	1982	1983	1981–1982	1982–1983
Northeast	117.0	117.0	176.5	0.0	50.9
Midwest	166.0	148.0	214.1	⁻10.8	44.7
South	562.0	591.2	926.8	5.2	56.8
West	240.0	205.8	370.9	⁻14.3	80.2

To answer the question above, you need to compare.

$$\begin{array}{r} 214.1 \text{ thousands of houses started in 1983} \\ -\ 166.0 \text{ thousands of houses started in 1981} \\ \hline 48.1 \text{ thousands more houses started in 1983} \end{array}$$

Notice that to answer the question, you do not need the information about other regions of the country, about 1982, or about the percent change.

Would you need to use an outside source to answer each question? Write *yes* or *no*.

1. If 40% of the houses started in the Midwest in 1981 were ranch-style houses, how many midwestern ranch houses were started that year?

2. Stella builds log cabins. She uses 245 logs per cabin. She uses 75% of the logs for the walls. How many logs make up the roof?

Solve each problem. Use the Infobank on page 473 and the chart on page 386 to obtain additional information.

3. The Niger River is 2,597 miles long. If Jason traveled 42% of the river's length, how far would he travel?

4. Laura has traveled 3,000 miles along the Amazon River. What percent of the river has she traveled?

5. In 1989, Michael Jordan scored 2,633 points in the National Basketball Association (NBA). How many more points did he score in 1987?

6. What was the average increase in housing starts from 1982 to 1983 for all regions of the United States?

7. How old was the city of Geneva when Budapest was founded in A.D. 100?

8. In 1974, Bob McAdoo scored 2,261 points in the NBA. In 1975, he scored 570 more. How many points did he score in 1975?

9. How many more privately owned houses were started in the Midwest than in the Northeast from 1981 to 1983?

10. Ralph is using 2 decks of 52 cards each to build card houses. His biggest house contains 73 cards. How many more cards would he have used if he wanted this house to contain 75% of the cards?

MATH COMMUNICATION

When you read English sentences, you begin at the left and read to the right.

Mathematics sentences are equations or inequalities. Equations and inequalities have a left side and a right side.

$$\underbrace{7 \cdot 8}_{\text{left}} = \underbrace{56}_{\text{right}} \qquad \underbrace{5 - 2}_{\text{left}} \neq \underbrace{8}_{\text{right}}$$

You can start reading on the left side or the right side. No matter in which direction the sentence is read, the mathematical statement is equivalent.

Look at this mathematical sentence. It is an equation.

$$7 \cdot 8 = 56$$

Read the left side first: Seven times eight *is equal to* fifty-six.

Read the right side first: Fifty-six *is equal to* seven times eight.

You can start on either side. The equals sign indicates that the two expressions are equivalent.

Look at this mathematical sentence. It is an inequality.

$$5 - 2 \neq 8$$

Read the left side first: Five minus two *is not equal to* eight.

Read the right side first: Eight *is not equal to* five minus two.

You can start on either side. Read either way both statements are true.

Write each in words from left to right and then from right to left.

1. $13 + 5 = 2 \cdot 9$ **2.** $6 \cdot 9 > 45 - 2$ **3.** $38 \div 2 < 15 + 6$ **4.** $x - 6 = 14$

5. $24 \div 3 \geq x - 2$ **6.** $40 - x \leq \frac{x}{2}$ **7.** $x + y > 17$ **8.** $x^2 + y < 5$

GROUP PROJECT

The Ideal Recreation Center

The problem: Your community is going to build a
recreation center for teenagers. Meet with your
classmates, and design the center. Look at the facts
and questions below. Then make a scale drawing of
the ideal center.

Key Facts
- The community has a limited amount of money to
  spend on the project. Construction is costly.

- The ground floor of the building must not exceed
  1,500 square feet.

- There should be a separate room provided for each
  activity.

Key Questions
- What kinds of activities will the center
  accommodate?

- How large should the rooms be?

- Should sports activities take place in the center? If
  so, which ones and how much space will they
  require?

- What source of energy should be used to heat the
  building?

- Should any of the rooms be used for more than one
  activity?

- Will there be a room reserved for refreshments?

- Should there be a second floor?

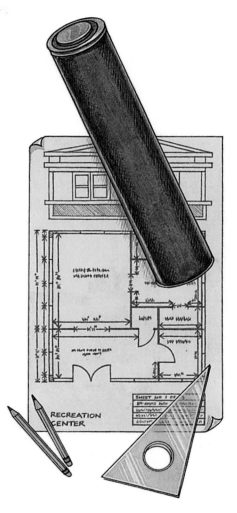

RECREATION
CENTER

Use the figure to answer Exercises 1–10. (pages 354–357 and 364–365)

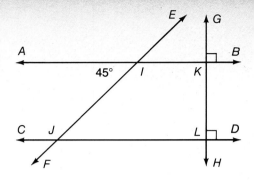

1. Name the lines that intersect at *J*.

2. Name a point on line *AB*.

3. Which line is parallel to $\overleftrightarrow{AB}$?

4. Which line is perpendicular to $\overleftrightarrow{AB}$?

5. Is ∠*AIJ* an acute angle, an obtuse angle, or a right angle?

6. Name the supplement of ∠*AIJ*.

7. What is the measure of the complement of ∠*AIJ*?

Find the measure of each angle. (pages 364–365)

8. ∠*EIK*   9. ∠*KIJ*   10. ∠*IJL*

11. Copy $\overline{WX}$ and construct the perpendicular bisector. (pages 364–365)

12. Construct a line parallel to $\overleftrightarrow{WX}$. (pages 364–365)

Use the figure *ABCD* to answer Exercises 13–17. The opposite sides are parallel and congruent. (pages 366–369)

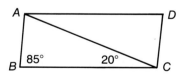

13. Is the triangle *ABC* scalene, right, or equilateral?

14. What is the measure of ∠*CAB*?

15. Copy ∠*ABC* and construct the bisector.

16. Name the quadrilateral, *ADCB*.

17. What is the measure of ∠*BAD*?

Use the circle with center *I* to answer Exercises 18–20. (pages 372–373)

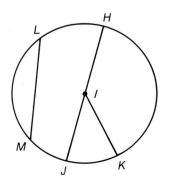

18. Name a chord.

19. Name a radius.

20. Name a diameter.

21. Does the diagram show *SSS*, *SAS*, or *ASA* congruence? (pages 374–377)

22. Find the length of x for the pair of similar triangles. (pages 380–381)

Use the figures for Exercises 23–25. (pages 382–385)

23. Name a translation of Figure *A*.

24. Name a reflection of Figure *A*.

25. Name a rotation of Figure *A*.

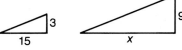

Solve. (pages 356–357, 362–363, 368–369, 372–373, and 378–379)

26. A triangle has an exterior angle of 140° and an opposite interior angle of 80°. What are the measures of the other two interior angles? Draw a picture to help you find the answer.

27. What is the sum of the measures of the interior angles of a quadrilateral whose opposite sides are parallel and congruent? What is the name of the figure?

28. If an angle is $\frac{1}{2}$ the measure of its complement, what is the measure of the angle?

29. If the central angle of a circle is 40°, what is its supplement?

30. The blueprints for a new arts institute call for $\frac{5}{8}$ of the tower's floors to be galleries and $\frac{1}{4}$ to be administration. Of the remaining floors, $\frac{1}{3}$ will be studios, 3 will be devoted to a performance hall, and 1 will be for maintenance. How many floors will the tower have?

BONUS

Solve.

How many lines of symmetry are there in an isosceles triangle? a square? a regular octagon? a regular pentagon?

RETEACHING

Perpendicular and parallel lines can be constructed
with a compass and a straightedge.

A. When two lines in a plane meet to
form a right angle, they are
perpendicular.

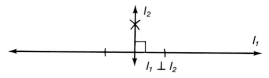

B. When two lines in a plane do not
intersect, they are parallel.

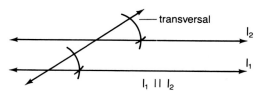

C. When parallel lines are intersected by a transversal,
special pairs of angles are formed. If $l_1 \| l_2$, the
following angle relationships are true:
Vertical angles are congruent.

$\angle 1 \cong \angle 4$, $\angle 2 \cong \angle 3$, $\angle 5 \cong \angle 8$, $\angle 6 \cong \angle 7$

Corresponding angles are congruent.

$\angle 2 \cong \angle 6$, $\angle 1 \cong \angle 5$, $\angle 4 \cong \angle 8$, $\angle 3 \cong \angle 7$

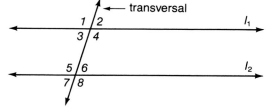

Alternate interior angles are congruent. $\angle 3 \cong \angle 6$,
$\angle 4 \cong \angle 5$

Adjacent angles, such as $\angle 1$ and $\angle 2$, and $\angle 6$ and $\angle 8$,
are supplementary. Recall that supplementary angles
are two angles whose measures have a sum of 180°.

In the given figure, $r \| s$.
If $m\angle 1 = 135°$, find

1. $m\angle 2$ **2.** $m\angle 5$ **3.** $m\angle 3$ **4.** $m\angle 6$

5. $m\angle 4$ **6.** $m\angle 8$ **7.** $m\angle 7$

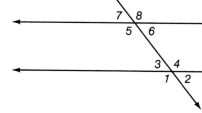

8. Name a pair of corresponding angles.

9. Name a pair of vertical angles.

10. Name a pair of alternate interior angles.

Write *true* or *false*.

11. $\angle 1 \cong \angle 7$ **12.** $\angle 5 \cong \angle 8$ **13.** $\angle 2 \cong \angle 6$ **14.** $\angle 1 \cong \angle 8$

ENRICHMENT

Constructing Regular Polygons

A regular polygon is a polygon whose sides all have the same length and whose angles all have the same measure. An equilateral triangle is a regular triangle.

To construct a regular triangle, use a compass and a straightedge.

1. Use a straightedge to draw $\overline{AB}$.

2. Open the compass to the length of $\overline{AB}$.

3. With the compass on point A, draw an arc above $\overline{AB}$.

4. With the compass on point B, draw another arc that intersects the first arc. Label the point C.

5. Draw $\overline{AC}$ and $\overline{BC}$.

$\triangle ABC$ is an equilateral or regular triangle.

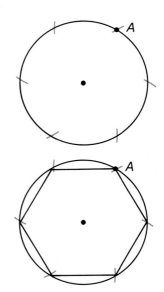

You can also use a compass and a straightedge to construct a regular hexagon.

1. Draw a circle.

2. Open the compass to the length of a radius. With the compass on any point on the circle, draw an arc that intersects the circle. Place the compass on the point where the arc intersects the circle, and draw another arc. Continue around the circle until you have six arcs.

3. Draw chords between the arcs as shown.

Use only a compass and a straightedge to construct

1. a regular hexagon without drawing a circle.
   (HINT: Use regular triangles.)

2. a regular dodecagon (twelve-sided figure).
   (HINT: First construct a regular hexagon.)

A LOGO program is called a **procedure.** Here are some LOGO commands.

FD   This makes the turtle move forward the number of steps shown.

BK   This moves the turtle backward.

RT   This makes the turtle turn to the right the number of degrees shown.

LT   This makes the turtle turn to the left.

PU   This moves the turtle without drawing a line.

PE   This makes the turtle erase as it moves.

PD   This makes the turtle draw again after PU or PE.

REPEAT   This command makes the turtle repeat commands given in the following brackets the number of times shown. For instance, this procedure draws a square.
TO SQUARE
REPEAT 4 [RT 90 FD 50]
END

You can use more than one REPEAT statement in a LOGO procedure. This procedure draws a row of squares.

TO SQUARE ROW
REPEAT 3 [REPEAT 4 [RT 90 FD 50] PU RT 90 FD 50 LT 90 PD]
END

You can also use a variable in a LOGO procedure. This procedure draws squares that have any length sides.

TO SQUARE :SIDE
REPEAT 4 [FD :SIDE RT 90]
END

The variable :SIDE allows you to plug in any length of side. Command the turtle SQUARE 50, and it will draw a square that has sides 50 steps long. Always use a colon (:) when placing a variable.

1. The commands below should draw the following figure. They are out of order. Rewrite the procedure in the correct order.

TO CROSS
FD 40 RT 90 FD 20 FD 40 RT 90
LT 90 RT 90 FD 20 FD 40 FD 40
LT 90 FD 40 FD 20 RT 90 RT 90
LT 90 FD 40 FD 40 FD 20 RT 90
RT 90 FD 40
END

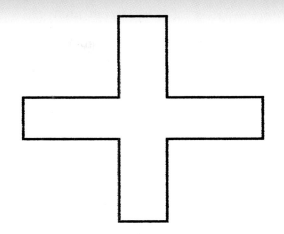

2. Write a procedure to draw this figure. Write it so that the sides can be any length. Use the REPEAT command.

3. Write a procedure that will take the turtle out of the maze without hitting any of the walls.

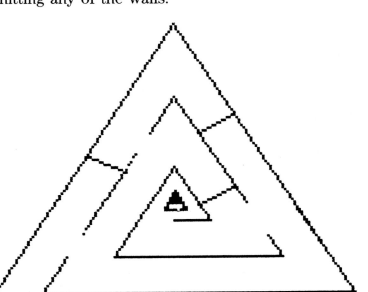

CUMULATIVE REVIEW

Write the letter of the correct answer.

1. What is the mean of 7, 8, 6, 4, 6, 7, 7, 3?

a. 3   **b.** 6
c. 7   **d.** not given

2. What is the median of 234, 6, 3, 12, 96, 7, 9?

a. 9   **b.** 52
c. 96   **d.** not given

3. What is the mode of 1, 7, 3, 6, 7, 5, 9?

a. 5   **b.** 6
c. 7   **d.** not given

4. What is the range of 9, 12, 18, 15, 16, 5, 8?

a. 10   **b.** 13
c. 15   **d.** not given

5. There are 7 marbles. If only 2 are striped, what is your probability of picking striped marbles without looking on your first two tries, if you do not return the first marble to the group?

a. $\frac{1}{49}$ **b.** $\frac{1}{21}$
c. $\frac{2}{7}$ **d.** not given

6. What is the probability of tossing an odd number with a 6-sided number cube?

a. $\frac{1}{6}$ **b.** $\frac{1}{3}$
c. $\frac{1}{2}$ **d.** not given

7. Solve for z: $\frac{2}{3}z + 4 \geq 12$.

a. $z \geq 12$ **b.** $z \geq 24$
c. $z \geq 32$ **d.** not given

8. Which sentence is shown by the graph?

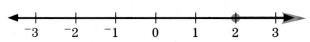

a. $y < 2$ **b.** $y > 2$
c. $y \geq 2$ **d.** not given

9. Given a map that has a scale where 1.5 cm equals 50 km, what distance does 4.5 cm represent?

a. 22.5 km   **b.** 100 km
c. 300 km   **d.** not given

10. There are 1,200 students at Montville Junior High School. In a sampling of 100 students, 8 are found to be studying music. How many students can you expect to be studying music in the entire school?

a. 8   **b.** 96
c. 800   **d.** not given

11. XQR's stock opened on Monday at $38\frac{1}{4}$ and closed for the day down $\frac{1}{4}$. On each day during the rest of the week it closed down twice as much as the day before. What was the closing price of XQR on Friday?

a. $30\frac{1}{2}$ **b.** $30\frac{3}{4}$
c. 37   **d.** not given

The Pentagon, a five-sided building in Washington, D.C., is the largest office building in the world. It covers 29 acres of land and has 3,705,397 square feet of space. Why is it important to know the area or the volume of a building? List all the reasons you can think of.

11 PERIMETER, AREA, VOLUME

Perimeter

A. A restaurant has only small square tables. To seat large groups together the restaurant follows these two rules:

1. Only one person can sit on one side of the table.

2. At least one side of a table must be placed next to the side of another table.

Here are some different ways that six tables can be arranged.

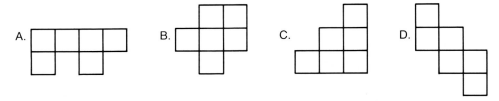

Does each arrangement seat the same size party?

How many people can be seated at each arrangement?

Which arrangement seats the largest party? the smallest party?

The restaurant wants to put crepe paper on the edge of each table where someone will be sitting. If each table is 3 feet on a side, how much crepe paper do they need for the largest party? for the smallest party?

Make a different arrangement of six tables. Compare this arrangement with the ones above. Can you seat more people, less people, or the same number as the largest party above? How much crepe paper will be needed for this arrangement?

Thinking as a Team

Twelve tables are to be arranged to seat one party. Use tiles or square pieces of paper to show the different arrangements, then compare your arrangements with the other members of the team. Record your results.

1. Show how the tables can be arranged to seat four different-sized parties.

Math Reasoning, page H227

2. What is the largest party that can be seated? Show how you would arrange the twelve tables. How much crepe paper will be needed?

3. What is the smallest party that can be seated using all twelve tables? How much crepe paper will be needed?

4. Try several other numbers of tables and have each member of the team show how the tables can be arranged.

5. Which arrangement allows for seating of the largest party? the smallest party? Do you see a pattern? Describe it.

B. The diagrams below show the floor plan of two diffferent restaurants. Each restaurant wants to put molding around the entire perimeter of the floor. How much molding will be needed?

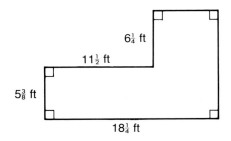

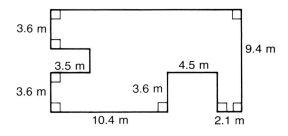

Working as a Team

You are working for the summer at a kennel. Your boss wants you to fence in a rectangular track in a pasture as a dog run. He has marked out the four corners of the interior rectangle and you install a total of 1,260 ft of fencing along the perimeter of this rectangle. The width of the run will be 22 ft. What is the outer perimeter of the run?

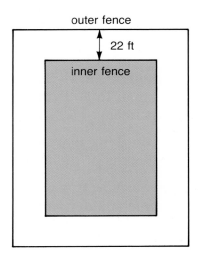

The Pythagorean Rule

A. In a right triangle the side opposite the right angle is called the **hypotenuse.** The two other sides are called the **legs.** This lesson will explore the relationship among these three sides.

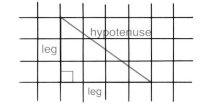

- Using a sheet of graph paper, draw a right triangle with legs of length 3 cm and 4 cm. Measure the length of the hypotenuse. Copy the table and record your measurement.

- Draw another right triangle with legs of length 5 cm and 12 cm and then another right triangle with legs of length 6 cm and 8 cm. Measure the length of each hypotenuse and record your measurements on the table.

- Using another sheet of graph paper, draw another right triangle with legs of any length, and measure the length of the hypotenuse. Record your measurements on the table.

- Can you find a relationship among the entries in each row of this table?

leg	leg	hypotenuse
3	4	■
5	12	■
6	8	■

Thinking as a Team

1. Copy and complete the table at the right by squaring each entry in the table above. Can you find a relationship among the entries in each row of this table? Write a rule to show this relationship?

$(\text{leg})^2$	$(\text{leg})^2$	$(\text{hypotenuse})^2$
9 ■ ■	16 ■ ■	■ ■ ■

The rule that shows this relationship is called the Pythagorean Rule. Pythagoras was an ancient Greek mathematician.

2. Do you think that this rule works no matter what the lengths of the legs are?

Draw a right triangle with legs of any length. Use a centimeter ruler and a calculator to predict the length of the hypotenuse to the nearest millimeter. Was your prediction correct?

B. Suppose that you know the length of the hypotenuse and the length of one leg of a right triangle. How do you find the length of the other leg? Look at the diagram at right and complete the table below it. You may want to use a calculator.

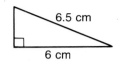

(leg)^2	(leg)^2	(hypotenuse)^2
■	36	42.25

C. In this activity you will use the rule you have discovered to help you compare the sizes of square roots.

Step 1: Draw a right triangle with legs each 1 centimeter long.

- According to the rule that you have written, how many centimeters long is the hypotenuse of this triangle?

- Use a ruler to find the length of the hypotenuse to the nearest tenth of a centimeter.

Step 2: Draw a 1-cm line perpendicular to the first hypotenuse. Now draw a hypotenuse to make a new right triangle.

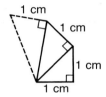

- What are the lengths of the legs of this triangle?

- What length can you predict for its hypotenuse?

- Use a ruler to find the hypotenuse to the nearest tenth of a centimeter.

Step 3: Continue to draw perpendicular lines 1 cm long and hypotenuses to create new right triangles. Measure each hypotenuse and draw new right triangles until you can make a table listing the square roots of the numbers from 1 to 10 to the nearest tenth.

Thinking as a Team ————————————

- Use your calculator to compute to the nearest tenth the square roots of the numbers from 1 to 10. How close to correct were your answers to the above problems? How do you explain the discrepancies?

Trigonometric Ratios

The word **trigonometry** means "triangle measure." You can use the relationship between the sides and the angles of a right triangle to find missing parts of the triangle.

In right triangle ABC, the ratios of sides are given the following special names:

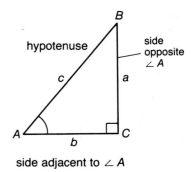

The **sine** of $\angle A = \dfrac{\text{length of side opposite } \angle A}{\text{length of hypotenuse}}$, or $\sin A = \dfrac{a}{c}$.

The **cosine** of $\angle A = \dfrac{\text{length of side adjacent to } \angle A}{\text{length of hypotenuse}}$, or $\cos A = \dfrac{b}{c}$.

The **tangent** of $\angle A = \dfrac{\text{length of side opposite } \angle A}{\text{length of side adjacent to } \angle A}$, or $\tan A = \dfrac{a}{b}$.

In a right triangle, the trigonometric ratios are the same for a certain angle, no matter what the size of the triangle. The trigonometric ratios for some angles measuring 46° through 64° are listed in the table at the right.

You can use one of the three trigonometric ratios to find an unknown side of a right triangle.

Angle Measure	Sin	Cos	Tan
46°	0.719	0.695	1.04
47°	0.731	0.682	1.07
48°	0.743	0.669	1.11
49°	0.755	0.656	1.15
50°	0.766	0.643	1.19
51°	0.777	0.629	1.23
52°	0.788	0.616	1.28
53°	0.799	0.602	1.33
...	...	...	...
60°	0.866	0.500	1.73
61°	0.875	0.485	1.80
62°	0.883	0.469	1.88
63°	0.891	0.454	1.96
64°	0.899	0.438	2.05

Find the length of $\overline{BC}$ (or side a).

To find a to the nearest tenth, use the sine ratio.

$\sin \angle A = \dfrac{a}{c}$

$\sin 48° = \dfrac{a}{8}$

$0.743 \approx \dfrac{a}{8}$

$5.944 \approx a$

So, $a \approx 5.9$.

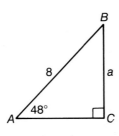

Another example:

Find $\tan B$. Then find the measure of $\angle B$ to the nearest degree.

$\tan B = \dfrac{21}{20} = 1.05$

$\tan 46° \approx 1.04$

$\tan 47° \approx 1.07$

Since 1.05 is closer to 1.04, $\angle B$ is closer to 46°.

402

Use the table to find the value.

1. tan 45°   **2.** tan 30°

3. sin 45°   **4.** sin 20°

5. tan 40°   **6.** cos 30°

Angle Measure	Sin	Cos	Tan
19°	0.326	0.946	0.344
20°	0.342	0.940	0.364
21°	0.358	0.934	0.384
22°	0.375	0.927	0.404
23°	0.391	0.921	0.424
24°	0.407	0.914	0.445
25°	0.423	0.906	0.466
26°	0.438	0.899	0.488
27°	0.454	0.891	0.510
28°	0.469	0.883	0.532
29°	0.485	0.875	0.554
30°	0.500	0.866	0.577
31°	0.515	0.857	0.601
32°	0.530	0.848	0.625
33°	0.545	0.839	0.649
34°	0.559	0.829	0.675
35°	0.574	0.819	0.700
36°	0.588	0.809	0.727
37°	0.602	0.799	0.754
38°	0.616	0.788	0.781
39°	0.629	0.777	0.810
40°	0.643	0.766	0.839
41°	0.656	0.755	0.869
42°	0.669	0.743	0.900
43°	0.682	0.731	0.933
44°	0.695	0.719	0.966
45°	0.707	0.707	1.00

Use the table to find the measure of ∠A.

7. tan ∠A = 0.404   **8.** tan ∠A = 1.000

9. sin ∠A = 0.358   **10.** sin ∠A = 0.602

11. cos ∠A = 0.891   **12.** cos ∠A = 0.719

13. tan ∠A = 0.649   **14.** sin ∠A = 0.515

Use the triangles shown and the tables on this page and on page 402 to find each trigonometric ratio to the nearest hundredth. Then find each angle to the nearest degree.

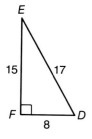

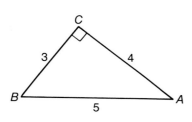

15. sin ∠A   **16.** cos ∠A   **17.** tan ∠A   **18.** sin ∠D

19. cos ∠D   **20.** tan ∠D   **21.** sin ∠B   **22.** cos ∠B

23. tan ∠B   **24.** sin ∠E   **25.** cos ∠E   **26.** tan ∠E

Use the trigonometric ratios listed in the table to find the side indicated. Round to the nearest tenth.

27.

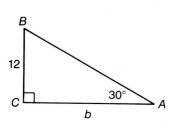

28.

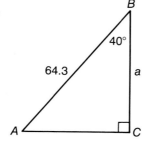

29.

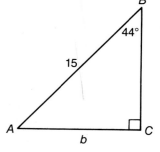

Circumference of a Circle

What is the circumference of The Rainbow, a Ferris wheel in Japan, if its diameter is 70.1 m?

The perimeter of a circle is called its **circumference.** The ratio of a circle's circumference (C) to its diameter (d) is the same in every circle. The Greek letter π **(pi)** represents the ratio. $\frac{C}{d} = \pi$

π is a nonterminating, nonrepeating decimal.

$\pi = 3.141592653589793\ldots$

Two common approximations for π are shown below.

$\pi \approx 3.14$ or $\pi \approx \frac{22}{7}$

The ratio can also be written as

$C = \pi d,$ or $C = 2\pi r.$ ← $\boxed{d = 2r}$

A. To find the circumference of the Ferris wheel, use the formula $C = \pi d$, and use 3.14 for π.

$C = \pi d$
$C \approx 3.14 \cdot 70.1$
$C \approx 220.114$

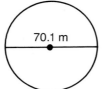

70.1 m

The circumference of the Ferris wheel, to the nearest hundredth, is 220.11 m.

B. Find the circumference of the circle. Use the formula $C = 2\pi r$, and use $\frac{22}{7}$ for π.

$C = 2\pi r$
$C \approx 2 \cdot \frac{22}{7} \cdot 126$
$C \approx 792$

126 ft

The circumference is approximately 792 ft.

Checkpoint Write the letter of the correct answer.

1. If $d = 49$ in., compute the circumference. Use $\frac{22}{7}$ for π.

a. 77 in. **b.** 154 in.

c. 308 in. **d.** 1,078 in.

2. If $r = 11.5$ ft, compute the circumference. Use 3.14 for π.

a. 36.115 ft **b.** 72.22 ft

c. 415.265 ft **d.** 7,222 ft

Math Reasoning, page H227

Find the circumference. Use 3.14 for π, and round to the nearest hundredth.

1.
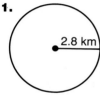
2.8 km

2.
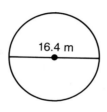
16.4 m

3.
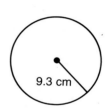
9.3 cm

Find the circumference. Use $\frac{22}{7}$ for π.

4.
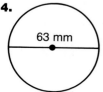
63 mm

5.

35.7 cm

6.

28.14 cm

Find the circumference. Use 3.14 for π, and round to the nearest hundredth.

7. $r = 11.3$ m   **8.** $d = 10$ m   **9.** $d = 84.14$ m   **10.** $r = 2.6$ cm

11. $d = 7.3$ m   **12.** $d = 11.6$ cm   **13.** $d = 15.2$ dm   **14.** $d = 100$ km

Find the circumference. Use $\frac{22}{7}$ for π.

15. $r = 49$ ft   **16.** $r = 105$ in.   **17.** $r = 7\frac{1}{2}$ in.   **18.** $d = 20\frac{1}{2}$ ft

19. $d = 45$ yd   **20.** $r = 12\frac{1}{2}$ mi   **21.** $r = 28$ yd   **22.** $d = 70$ ft

Find the radius or the diameter. Use 3.14 for π, and round to the nearest tenth.

★23. $C = 37.68$ cm
$r = $ ▓

★24. $C = 14.13$ cm
$r = $ ▓

★25. $C = 28.26$ m
$d = $ ▓

★26. $C = 92.4$ cm
$r = $ ▓

★27. $C = 39.25$ m
$d = $ ▓

★28. $C = 20.41$ cm
$r = $ ▓

★29. $C = 150.72$ mm
$r = $ ▓

★30. $C = 37.68$ m
$r = $ ▓

Solve. Round to the nearest hundredth when necessary.

31. The Louisiana Superdome has a diameter of 680 ft. Find the circumference of the Superdome. Use 3.14 for π.

32. The circular entrance to the longest tunnel in the world is 15.5 ft in diameter. Find the circumference of the entrance. Use 3.14 for π.

PROBLEM SOLVING
Solving Multistep Problems/Making a Plan

A problem may need more than one step in order to be solved. Making a plan can help you solve such problems.

> Beginning on May 4, 1957, David Kwan walked from Singapore to London, a distance of 18,500 miles, in 82 weeks. He walked for 8 hours each day. How fast did he walk?

Needed data: miles walked in 1 week
             miles walked in 1 day

Plan

Step 1: Find the number of miles walked in 1 week.

Step 2: Find the number of miles walked in 1 day.

Step 3: Find the number of miles walked in 1 hour.

Step 1:

miles walked in 1 week $=$ total miles $\div$ total weeks

$n \quad = \quad 18,500 \quad \div \quad 82$

$n \quad = \quad 226$

He walked 226 miles per week.

Step 2:

miles walked in a day $=$ miles a week $\div$ days in a week

$x \quad = \quad 226 \quad \div \quad 7$

$x \quad = \quad 32$

He walked 32 miles per day.

Step 3:

miles walked in 1 hour $=$ miles a day $\div$ hours a day

$y \quad = \quad 32 \quad \div \quad 8$

$y \quad = \quad 4$

He walked 4 miles per hour.

Write the steps you would take to complete each plan.

1. The largest sculpture in the world, carved into Mount Rushmore, shows the faces of four Presidents: Washington, Lincoln, Jefferson, and Theodore Roosevelt. The head of Washington is about 20 yards in height. If the ratio of a man's head to his total height is about 1 to 8, how many feet tall would the complete statue of Washington be?

Step 1:

Step 2: Find the number of feet in the statue's height.

2. The first nonstop transpacific airplane flight occurred in 1931. Hugh Herndon and Clyde Pangborn took off from Sabishiro Beach, Japan, dropped their landing gear, and flew to a spot near Wenatchee, Washington. Their average air speed was about 2 miles per minute. The trip was about 4,860 miles long. For how many days were they in the air?

Step 1:

Step 2:

Step 3: Find the number of days it took them to fly.

Make a plan for each problem. Solve.

3. In 1981, President and Mrs. Reagan bought some dishes for the White House. The dishes cost $106,172 for 508 place settings. How much more would the same dishes have cost if they had bought 600 place settings?

4. The peregrine falcon is the fastest-moving animal in the world. It has been electronically timed at 217 mph. How far could it go if it were able to fly at this rate for 2 minutes? (Round your answer to the nearest mile.)

5. The two highest mountains in the world are Mount Everest and Mount Godwin Austen, both in the Himalayas. Their heights are 29,028 feet and 28,741 feet, respectively. If you could put one on top of the other and then place them into the deepest trench in the Pacific Ocean (the Mindanao Deep, which is 37,782 feet in depth), how far would they rise above the ocean's surface?

6. The fastest-growing tree ever recorded was an *Albizzia falcata*, which was planted on June 17, 1974, in Sabah, Malaysia. In 13 months, it grew from a seed to a height of 35 feet 3 inches. Assuming that it grew at a steady rate, how tall would it have been in 2 years if it had continued to grow at the same rate? (Round your answer to the nearest foot.)

Area of Squares, Rectangles, and Parallelograms

The area of a polygon (**A**) is the number of unit squares enclosed by the polygon. A unit square that has a side of 1 cm has an area of 1 square centimeter (1 cm²).

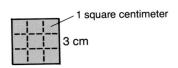

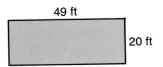

A. To find the area of a square whose side is 3 cm, multiply.

$A = \text{side} \cdot \text{side, or } \boldsymbol{A = s^2}.$
$A = 3^2 = 3 \cdot 3 = 9$

The area of the square is 9 cm².

B. To find the area of a rectangle whose length is 49 ft and whose width is 20 ft, multiply.

$A = \text{length} \cdot \text{width, or } \boldsymbol{A = lw}.$
$A = 49 \cdot 20 = 980$

The area of the rectangle is 980 ft².

C. If a parallelogram and a rectangle have equal bases and equal heights, then they are equal in area.

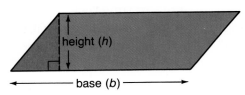

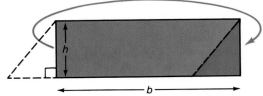

To find the area of a parallelogram whose base is 4.5 cm and whose height is 2.5 cm, multiply.

$A = \text{base} \cdot \text{height, or } \boldsymbol{A = bh}.$
$A = 4.5 \cdot 2.5 = 11.25$

The area of the parallelogram is 11.25 cm².

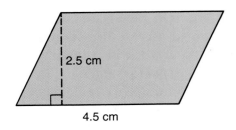

Checkpoint Write the letter of the correct answer.

1. The area of a rectangle whose length is 4.6 m and whose width is 3.9 m is ■.

   a. 8.5 m²   **b.** 17 m

   c. 17.94 m   **d.** 17.94 m²

2. The area of a parallelogram whose base is 85 mm and whose height is 60 mm is ■.

   a. 145 mm²   **b.** 290 mm

   c. 5,100 mm   **d.** 5,100 mm²

Find the area of the polygon.

1.
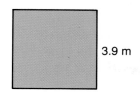
3.7 cm

7.6 cm

2.
3.9 m

3.9 m

3.
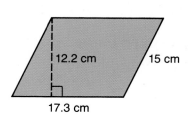
12.2 cm   15 cm

17.3 cm

Find the area of each square.

4. $s = 14.2$ m   **5.** $s = 1.5$ m   **6.** $s = 2.5$ cm   **7.** $s = 10$ m

Find the area of each rectangle.

8. $l = 18.3$ yd
$w = 8.9$ yd

9. $l = 4\frac{1}{2}$ in.
$w = 7$ in.

10. $l = 13.1$ in.
$w = 9.3$ in.

11. $l = 16$ ft
$w = 5\frac{1}{4}$ ft

12. $l = 4\frac{1}{2}$ mi
$w = 2$ mi

13. $l = 7$ in.
$w = 5\frac{1}{2}$ in.

14. $l = 2.5$ ft
$w = 1.5$ ft

★15. $l = 20$ ft
$w = 18$ in.

Find the area of each parallelogram.

16. $b = 5.1$ cm
$h = 11.8$ cm

17. $b = 9.3$ m
$h = 6$ m

18. $b = 14.3$ cm
$h = 8$ cm

19. $b = 5.75$ m
$h = 18$ m

20. $b = 52$ cm
$h = 44.6$ cm

21. $b = 15$ m
$h = 12.4$ m

22. $b = 11.8$ m
$h = 9.6$ m

★23. $b = 8.6$ m
$h = 64$ cm

Solve.

24. Find the area.

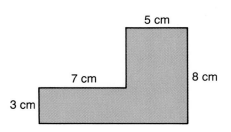
5 cm

7 cm   8 cm

3 cm

25. Find the area of the deck.

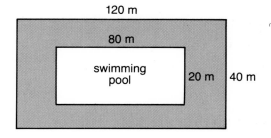
120 m

80 m

swimming
pool   20 m   40 m

26. Bev is installing carpet. If her living room is 7 yd long by 4 yd wide, and her hall is 8 yd long by 2 yd wide, how many square yards of carpet will she need?

27. Bill is painting a wall that measures 30 ft long by 12 ft high. If a can of paint covers 400 ft² and Bill has one can, will he have enough paint?

Area of Triangles and Trapezoids

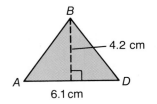

A. Find the area of $\triangle ABD$ to the nearest tenth, if the base AD is 6.1 cm and the height is 4.2 cm.

The area of a triangle is $\frac{1}{2}$ the area of a parallelogram that has the same height and base.

Note that parallelogram $ABCD$ at the right has a height of 4.2 cm and a base of 6.1 cm.

Since the formula for the area of a parallelogram is $A = bh$, the formula for the area of a triangle is $A = \frac{1}{2}bh$.

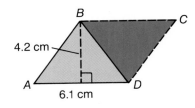

To find the area of $\triangle ABD$, multiply.

$A = \frac{1}{2}\text{base} \cdot \text{height}$, or $\boldsymbol{A = \frac{1}{2}bh}$.

$A = \frac{1}{2} \cdot 6.1 \cdot 4.2$

$A = 12.81$

The area of $\triangle ABD$, to the nearest tenth, is 12.8 cm^2.

B. The area of a trapezoid is $\frac{1}{2}$ the area of a certain parallelogram.

Parallelogram $ABEF$ is formed by two trapezoids equal in area. The area, A, of parallelogram $ABEF = bh$. Since $b = b_1 + b_2$, $A = (b_1 + b_2)h$. The area of trapezoid $ABCD$ is $\frac{1}{2}$ the area of parallelogram $ABEF$.

$A = \frac{1}{2} \cdot (\text{base}_1 + \text{base}_2) \cdot \text{height}$, or $\boldsymbol{A = \frac{1}{2}(b_1 + b_2)h}$.

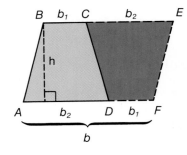

Use the formula to find the area of trapezoid $ABCD$.

$A = \frac{1}{2}(15 + 9) \cdot 12$

$A = \frac{1}{2} \cdot 24 \cdot 12$

$A = 144$

The area of trapezoid $ABCD$ is 144 ft^2.

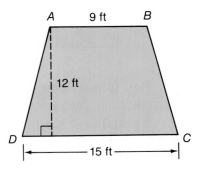

410

Find the area of the triangle or the trapezoid. Round
to the nearest tenth.

1.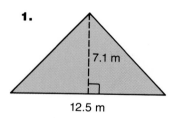
7.1 m
12.5 m

2.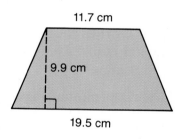
8.2 cm
8.7 cm
13.8 cm

3.
11.7 cm
9.9 cm
19.5 cm

Find the area of each triangle. Round to the
nearest tenth.

4. base = 18.5 m, height = 5.2 m

5. base = 13.5 m, height = 11 m

6. base = 4.3 m, height = 9 m

7. base = 15.5 cm, height = 3.4 cm

8. base = 1.9 km, height = 2.6 km

9. base = 0.4 km, height = 2.6 km

Find the area of each trapezoid. Round to the
nearest tenth.

10. bases = 6.2 cm, 12.8 cm
height = 5.7 cm

11. bases = 6.3 m, 8.5 m
height = 5 m

12. bases = 19 m, 6 m
height = 9 m

13. bases = 63 mm, 82 mm
height = 45 mm

14. bases = 11 mm, 15 mm
height = 12 mm

15. bases = 4.5 m, 6.25 m
height = 12 m

Given the area, find the height of the polygon.

★16. triangle, $A = 100 \text{ ft}^2$
base = 20 ft

★17. trapezoid, $A = 32 \text{ in.}^2$
bases = 7 in., 9 in.

★18. triangle, $A = 20 \text{ yd}^2$
base = 4 yd

★19. trapezoid, $A = 100 \text{ mi}^2$
bases = 15 mi, 5 mi

Find the area of each composite polygon by adding or
subtracting the areas of the parts.

20.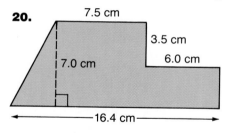
7.5 cm
3.5 cm
7.0 cm
6.0 cm
16.4 cm

21.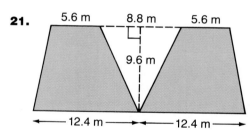
5.6 m   8.8 m   5.6 m
9.6 m
12.4 m   12.4 m

Area of a Circle

The world's largest working clock has a radius of 29.5 ft. Find the area of the clock face.

The approximate area of a circle can be found by cutting the circle into wedge-shaped sections and then rearranging the pieces to form a figure that has the approximate shape of a parallelogram.

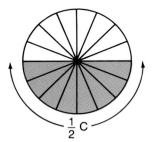

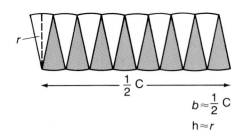

The area of the parallelogram = bh, or

$A = \frac{1}{2}C \cdot r$.

To find the formula for the area of a circle, substitute $2\pi r$ for C.

$A = \frac{1}{2} \cdot 2\pi r \cdot r$, or $\boldsymbol{A = \pi r^2}$

Use the formula to find the area of the clock face to the nearest tenth. Use 3.14 for π.

$A = \pi r^2$
$A \approx 3.14 \cdot 29.5 \cdot 29.5$
$A \approx 2{,}732.59$

The area of the clock face, to the nearest tenth, is $2{,}732.6 \text{ ft}^2$.

Another example:

Find the area of the circle.

$A = \pi r^2$
$A \approx 3.14 \cdot 6 \cdot 6$
$A \approx 113.04$

Think:
If $d = 2r$,
then $r = \frac{1}{2}d$.

12 cm

The area is about 113.04 cm^2.

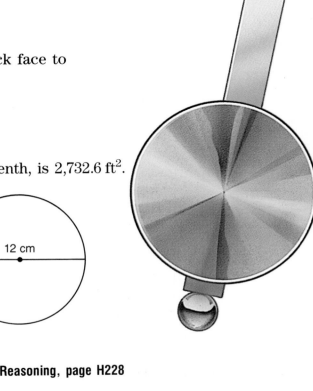

412

Find the area of each circle. Use 3.14 for π, and round to the nearest tenth.

1.

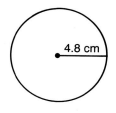

4.8 cm

2.

19.6 cm

3.

2.9 cm

Find the area of each circle. Use $\frac{22}{7}$ for π.

4. $r = 14$ ft   **5.** $r = 280$ in.   **6.** $d = 14$ yd   **7.** $d = 84$ in.

8. $d = 196$ in.   **9.** $d = 91$ in.   **10.** $r = 147$ in.   **11.** $r = 119$ in.

Find the area of each circle. Use 3.14 for π, and round to the nearest tenth.

12. $r = 6.6$ cm   **13.** $d = 8.2$ km   **14.** $d = 1$ m   **15.** $r = 2.5$ m

16. $r = 15.1$ dm   **17.** $r = 17.7$ cm   **18.** $d = 9$ m   **19.** $r = 0.5$ m

Use the given area to find the radius of the circle. Use 3.14 for π.

20. $A = 50.24$ cm^2 **21.** $A = 78.5$ mm^2 **22.** $A = 153.86$ m^2 **23.** $A = 113.04$ m^2

24. $A = 254.34$ km^2 **25.** $A = 200.96$ m^2 **26.** $A = 452.16$ km^2 **27.** $A = 907.46$ dm^2

Find the area of each shaded region. Use 3.14 for π, and round to the nearest tenth.

28.

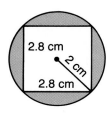

2.8 cm
2 cm
2.8 cm

29.

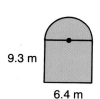

9.3 m

6.4 m

30.

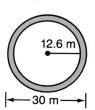

12.6 m

30 m

MIDCHAPTER REVIEW

Find the missing side of each right triangle. $m\angle C = 90°$.

1. $a = 5$ cm, $b = 12$ cm   **2.** $a = 48$ m, $c = 102$ m   **3.** $b = 32$ km, $c = 40$ km

Use the table on page 403 to find the measure of $\angle A$.

4. $\tan \angle A = 0.445$ **5.** $\sin \angle A = 0.616$ **6.** $\cos \angle A = 0.707$ **7.** $\tan \angle A = 1.000$

PROBLEM SOLVING
Using a Picture

To solve certain problems, you may need to find information in a picture.

> Matt built a scale model of a Saber Royale. Each 1 inch of the model represents 2 inches of an actual Saber. What is the height of Matt's model?

To answer this problem, you need to know the actual height of a Saber Royale. You can find this information in the picture below.

The height of a Saber Royale is 5 ft 10 in., or 70 in.

To find the height of Matt's model, you multiply the actual height by the scale of Matt's model.

$$1 \text{ inch} = 2 \text{ inches}$$
$$\text{So, } 70 \times \frac{1}{2} = 35.$$

The height of Matt's model is 35 inches.

Use the picture below to solve.

1. How long is the windshield of Matt's model?

2. How tall is the windshield of an actual Saber Royale?

3. What is the diameter of each tire of Matt's model?

4. Is the Saber longer from the seat to the front of the car than from the seat to the back of the car?

SABER ROYALE

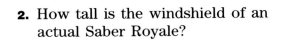

A family tree is a model of a family's history. You can use a family tree to find information about a family.

Brenda Thornton is researching her family history. The chart she made is shown below. How much younger is Brenda's mother than Brenda's Aunt Lily?

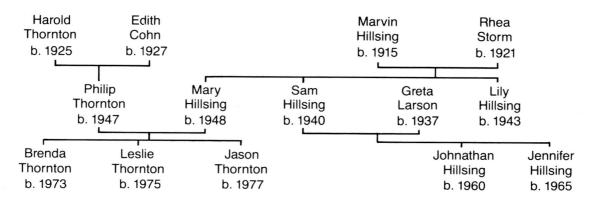

To solve this problem, you first have to find on the chart the people mentioned in the problem.

Brenda's mother is listed as Mary Hillsing. Brenda's aunt—her mother's sister—is listed as Lily Hillsing.

Once you have located the people, you can subtract their years of birth to find the difference in their ages.

$$\begin{array}{r} 1948 \text{ Mary Hillsing (Brenda's Mother)} \\ - 1943 \text{ Lily Hillsing (Brenda's Aunt)} \\ \hline 5 \end{array}$$

Brenda's mother is 5 years younger than Brenda's aunt.

Use the family tree to solve.

5. What is the difference in age between Brenda's two grandfathers?

6. Greta Larson married Sam Hillsing in 1959. How old was she when she married him?

7. Brenda's birthday is July 27. Leslie's is March 27. How many months older is Brenda?

8. Mary Hillsing was married when she was 23 years old. What year was that?

Solid Figures

All of the figures pictured so far in this chapter are 2-dimensional figures. **Solid figures** are 3-dimensional. In this lesson you will explore solid figures.

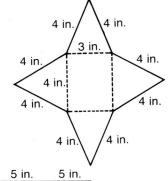

Draw the figures shown below and at the right on posterboard or some other kind of thin cardboard. Use the measurements indicated. You may find it helpful to use a compass to make the triangles.

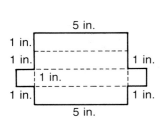

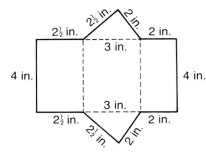

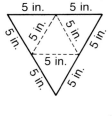

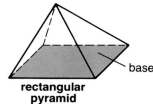

rectangular
pyramid

base

Cut out the figures along the outside lines. Fold them along the broken lines to make the solid figures shown. You can use cellophane tape to fasten the sides together.

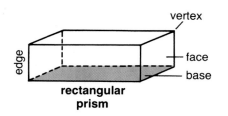

vertex

edge

face

base

**rectangular
prism**

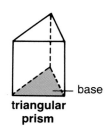

base

**triangular
prism**

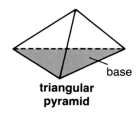

base

**triangular
pyramid**

Working as a Team

1. Describe the two different kinds of prisms that you have made. Use terms such as *faces, edges, vertices,* and *congruent.*

2. In which ways are rectangular prisms and triangular prisms alike? How are they different?

3. A cube is a rectangular prism in which all of the faces are in the shape of congruent squares. On posterboard draw a figure that can be cut out and folded into a cube.

416

4. What do you think a hexagonal prism would look like? Make one using straws for edges and clay for vertices.

5. Describe the two different kinds of pyramids you have made.

6. In which ways are rectangular pyramids and triangular pyramids alike? How are they different?

7. What do you think a pentagonal pyramid would look like? Make one using straws for edges and clay for vertices.

All of the solid figures that you have made so far are called **polyhedrons.** All of the faces of a polyhedron have the shape of polygons. A prism is a polyhedron that has at least two congruent faces that are parallel. A pyramid is a polyhedron whose one base is a polygon and whose other faces are triangles that share one vertex.

Working as a Team

1. Can you make a solid figure that is not a polyhedron?

2. Using poster board, make a cylinder and a cone.

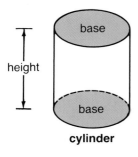

cylinder

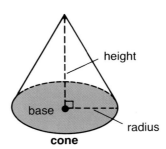

cone

3. Describe the two kinds of solid figures that you have just made. Are they polyhedrons?

4. Another kind of solid figure is a sphere. How many examples of spheres can you think of? Share them with the class.

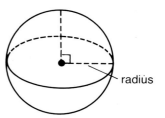

5. What can you say about the distance from the center of all points on the surface of a sphere?

Surface Area of Prisms and Pyramids

You can discover how to find the **surface area** of a polyhedron.

A. Trace the pattern shown below on posterboard, label it, and cut it out.

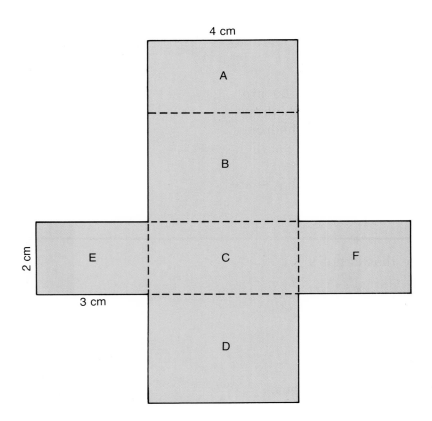

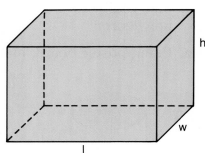

Now fold the pattern along the broken lines and assemble the figure. It should look like the solid figure shown to the right. Use l, w, or h to label the edges of each face.

What is the name of this solid figure?

How many faces does this solid figure have? Copy the table. Measure the dimensions of each face, find the area, and write it in the table.

What formula did you use to find the area of a face?

Which pairs of faces are congruent?

Surface Area	
Face	**Area in Square Units**

418

How can you find the combined area of a pair of congruent faces?

How can you find the surface area of the entire polyhedron?

Thinking as a Team

Replace the dimensions you used to find the prism's surface area with the variables *l*, *w*, and *h*. Try to write a formula for the surface area of a rectangular prism. Use *l*, *w*, and *h*.

1. What formula did you discover?

2. How would you change the formula to find the surface area of a triangular prism? What formula would you use to find the area of the triangular bases?

B. Trace the pattern at the right on posterboard, and cut it out.

Now fold the pattern along the broken lines, and assemble the figure.

- What is the name of this solid figure?

- Examine each face and label its dimensions.

- Which pairs of faces are congruent?

- How can you find the surface area of the entire polyhedron?

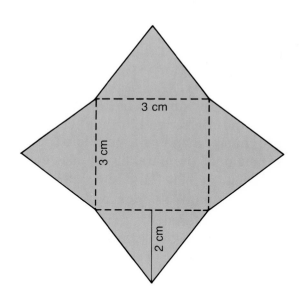

Thinking as a Team

1. Can you use this procedure to find the surface area of other polyhedrons?

2. Try to write a formula for the surface area of a rectangular pyramid.

Surface Area of Cylinders and Cones

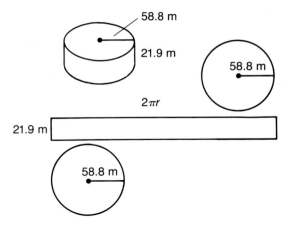

58.8 m

21.9 m

58.8 m

$2\pi r$

21.9 m

58.8 m

A. One of the largest cylindrical oil tanks in the world is located in Saudi Arabia. The tank is 21.9 m high, and the radius of its circular base is 58.8 m.

Find the surface area of the oil tank.

A cylinder can be cut apart and flattened to form a rectangle and two circles as shown. The area of the rectangle that is formed is called the **lateral area.**

To find the surface area (S) of a cylinder, use the formula

S = lateral area + 2 · area of circular base.

$S = 2\pi rh + 2\pi r^2$
$S \approx 2 \cdot 3.14 \cdot 58.8 \cdot 21.9 + 2 \cdot 3.14 \cdot 58.8 \cdot 58.8$
$S \approx 8,086.8816 + 21,712.723$
$S \approx 29,799.604$

The surface area of the oil tank is about 29,799.6 m^2.

B. The lateral surface of a cone can be cut and rearranged in the approximate shape of a parallelogram. The height of the parallelogram is equal to the slant height (l) of the cone. The base of the parallelogram is $\frac{1}{2}$ the cone's circumference, or πr. To find the surface area of a cone, use the formula

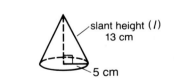

slant height (l)
13 cm

5 cm

l

$2\pi r$

πr

$S = \pi r^2 + \pi rl$
$S \approx 3.14 \cdot 5 \cdot 5 + 3.14 \cdot 5 \cdot 13$
$S \approx 78.5 + 204.1$
$S \approx 282.6$

The surface area of the cone is about 282.6 cm^2.

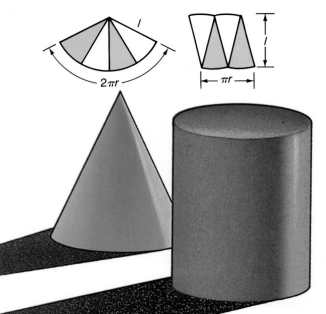

Math Reasoning, page H228

Find the surface area. Use 3.14 for π, and round to the nearest tenth.

1. 7.1 cm
15.5 cm

2. 8.6 m
3.3 m

3. 11.3 cm
10.8 cm
4.9 cm

4. 4.7 dm
9.5 dm
10.6 dm

5. 12.8 m
14.7 m

★6.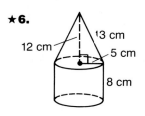
12 cm
13 cm
5 cm
8 cm

Find the surface area of each cylinder. Use 3.14 for π, and round to the nearest tenth.

7. radius = 12 cm
height = 15 cm

8. diameter = 14 dm
height = 8 dm

9. radius = 60 mm
height = 75 mm

10. diameter = 25 cm
height = 5 cm

11. diameter = 4.8 m
height = 12.3 m

12. radius = 7.6 dm
height = 11.9 dm

13. diameter = 4 dm
height = 2.1 dm

14. height = 1 m
radius = 1 m

15. height = 0.9 m
radius = 0.1 m

Find the surface area of each cone. Use 3.14 for π, and round to the nearest tenth.

16. radius = 5 cm
slant height = 13 cm

17. radius = 6.7 cm
slant height = 9.1 cm

18. radius = 11.9 cm
slant height = 18.1 cm

19. radius = 1.1 m
slant height = 5 m

20. radius = 21 m
slant height = 8 m

★21. slant height = 400 mm
radius = 300 mm

Solve.

22. The cone-shaped front of a space satellite has a diameter of 4.5 m and a slant height of 12.1 m. Find the surface area.

23. A cylindrical oil tank has a diameter of 34.4 m and a height of 15.7 m. Find the surface area of the oil tank.

★24. A conical mound of sand has a lateral surface area of 2,355 m². If the radius of the base is 10 m, what is the slant height of the mound?

★25. What is the surface area of the largest cylinder that would fit in your classroom?

PROBLEM SOLVING
Checking for Hidden Assumptions

Sometimes when solving a problem, you assume conditions that do not apply to that problem. If you are stuck on a problem, it is a good idea to check for assumptions you are making that are confusing the problem.

Draw a picture of an equilateral pentagon (one with congruent sides).

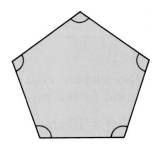

The sketch at the right shows what you usually think of as an equilateral pentagon. But this pentagon has congruent sides *and* congruent angles. Can you draw an equilateral pentagon without five congruent angles?

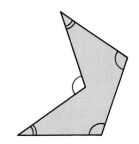

If you are having trouble making the drawing, you should think about the assumptions you are making. A pentagon is a five-sided figure. Any fact other than that may be an assumption. You might be assuming that the pentagon has to be convex. The drawing at the right is a solution to the problem. It is a pentagon with five congruent sides that is not convex.

True or false: x^2 is always greater than x.

Your initial response might be that this is true. For the numbers you try, it is always true.

But the question asks whether this is *always* true. Is the statement true for all numbers? Check for hidden assumptions.

You might be assuming that x is always a whole number. But the symbol x can stand for *any* number. If x is a fraction that is less than 1, x^2 will be *less* than x. The statement which at first seemed obviously true is actually false.

Write the letter of each assumption that is correct to make. Then answer the question.

1. True or false: $x + y$ is always greater than $x - y$.

a. x is greater than y.
b. x and y are real numbers.
c. x and y are whole numbers.

2. Line A and line B are both perpendicular to the same line C. Must line A and line B be parallel?

a. Line A intersects line B.
b. Lines A, B, and C are in one plane.
c. Line A intersects line C.

Solve. Be careful to check for assumptions you might be making in each problem.

True or false: $\frac{n}{n}$ always equals 1.

4. True or false: $0 \cdot n$ always equals 0.

5. Line A is perpendicular to line B. Is it possible for line C to be perpendicular to both A and B? If so, how?

6. Is it possible to start on spot A, walk 10 miles south, then walk 10 miles east, and then walk 10 miles north, and return to spot A?

7. A monkey is climbing a 10-foot tree. It climbs 3 feet each hour, and then falls back 2 feet. At this rate, how many hours does it take the monkey to reach the top of the tree?

8. Shown below are the floor plans of two houses. Copy each floor plan and try to draw one line, without lifting your pencil, that crosses each wall of each room once and only once.

★9. You have a chessboard and 32 dominoes. The chessboard has 64 squares. Each domino can cover 2 squares. You remove 2 opposite corners of the chessboard and take away 1 domino. Is it possible to cover the 62 squares with 31 dominoes? Explain. (HINT: Solve a simpler problem. Try 16 squares and 8 dominoes.)

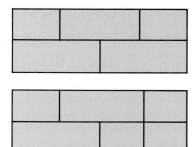

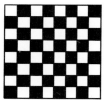

Volume of Prisms and Pyramids

A. What is the volume of a typical cassette case that is 1.5 cm high, 11 cm long, and 7 cm wide?

The **volume (*V*)** of a solid figure is the number of unit cubes that can fit inside the figure. A unit cube that measures 1 cm along each edge is called a **cubic centimeter (cm³)**.

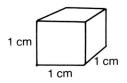

Use this formula to find the volume of a rectangular prism.

V of a prism = area of base · height

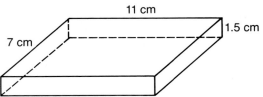

$V = Bh$, or $V = lwh$
$V = (11 \cdot 7) \cdot 1.5$
$V = 77 \cdot 1.5$
$V = 115.5$

The volume of the cassette case is 115.5 cm³.

B. Use this formula to find the volume of a cube.

V of a cube = area of base · height

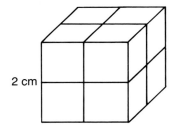

$V = e^3$
$V = 2^3$
$V = 8$

The volume of the cube is 8 cm³.

C. The volume of a pyramid is equal to $\frac{1}{3}$ the volume of a prism that has the same base and height.

V of a pyramid = $\frac{1}{3}$ area of base · height

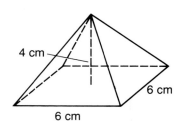

$V = \frac{1}{3}Bh$
$V = \frac{1}{3}(6 \cdot 6) \cdot 4$
$V = \frac{1}{3} \cdot 36 \cdot 4$
$V = 48$

The volume of the pyramid is 48 cm³.

For additional activities, see **Connecting Math Ideas,** page 472.

Find the volume of each polyhedron. Round to the nearest tenth.

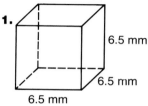

1. 6.5 mm, 6.5 mm, 6.5 mm

2. 6.3 m, 0.5 m, 8 m

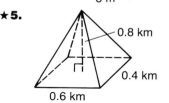

3. 9.9 cm, 8 cm, 15 cm

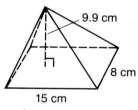

4. 8.8 cm, 15 cm, 15 cm

★5. 0.8 km, 0.4 km, 0.6 km

★6. 14.6 cm, 24 cm, 10.4 cm

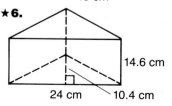

Find the volume of each polyhedron. Round to the nearest tenth.

7. rectangular prism
length = 5.2 cm, width = 4.4 cm,
height = 4 cm

8. rectangular pyramid
length = 75 m, width = 72 m,
height = 60 m

9. cube
edge = 3.5 dm

10. hexagonal prism
Base = 240 m^2, height = 11 m

11. rectangular prism
length = 8.1 cm, width = 4.7 cm,
height = 9.2 cm

12. rectangular pyramid
length = 3 m, width = 2.1 m,
height = 3.5 m

★13. rectangular pyramid
length = 0.15 km, width = 25 m
height = 10 m

★14. triangular prism
height = 15 ft, Base = 8 in.^{2}

Solve.

15. The Vehicle Assembly Building where the Apollo rocket was put together is a rectangular prism 716 ft long, 518 ft wide, and 525 ft high. Write the volume in scientific notation.

16. The pyramid at Cholula, Mexico, has the greatest volume of any structure built. Its base area is 1,400 ft^2 and its height is 177 ft. Find its volume.

NUMBER SENSE

Estimate which costs more.

1. 52% of $55 *or* 23% of $85

2. 48% of $950 *or* 127% of $425

Volume of Cylinders and Cones

A. A university art class painted the campus water tank to look like a giant soup can. The tank is 120 ft high and has a diameter of 30 ft. Find the volume of the tank.

To find the volume (V) of a cylinder that is 120 ft high and has a diameter of 30 ft, multiply the area of its base by the height of the cylinder.

V of a cylinder = area of base · height; or $V = Bh$

$V = \pi r^2 \cdot h$
$V \approx 3.14 \cdot 15 \cdot 15 \cdot 120$
$V \approx 84{,}780$

The volume of the water tank is 84,780 ft^3.

B. The volume of any cone is equal to $\frac{1}{3}$ the volume of a cylinder that has the same base and height. To find the volume of a cone that is 120 ft high and has a radius of 15 ft, use the formula

Volume of a cone = $\frac{1}{3}$ Base · height, or $V = \frac{1}{3}Bh$.

$V = \frac{1}{3}\pi r^2 \cdot h$

$V \approx \frac{1}{3} \cdot 3.14 \cdot 15 \cdot 15 \cdot 120$

$V \approx 28{,}260$

The volume of the cone is 28,260 ft^3.

Checkpoint Write the letter of the correct answer.

Use 3.14 for π, and round to the nearest tenth.

1.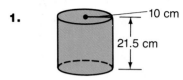

The volume of the cylinder is

  a. 1,350.2 cm^3.
  b. 6,751 cm^2.
  c. 6,751 cm^3.
  d. 675.1 cm^3.

2.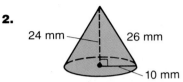

The volume of the cone is

  a. 7,536 mm^3.
  b. 2,512 mm^3.
  c. 502.4 mm^3.
  d. 2,721.3 mm^3.

3.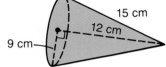

The volume of the cone is

  a. 226.1 cm^3
  b. 3,052.1 cm^3
  c. 1,017.4 cm^3.
  d. 1,271.7 cm^3.

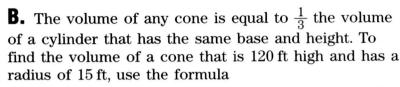
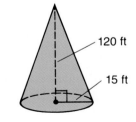

Find the volume. Use 3.14 for π, and round to the nearest tenth.

1.
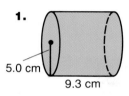
5.0 cm
9.3 cm

2.
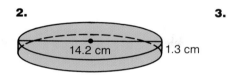
14.2 cm
1.3 cm

3.
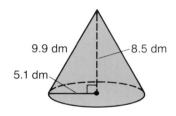
9.9 dm
8.5 dm
5.1 dm

4.
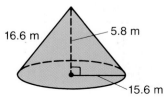
16.6 m
5.8 m
15.6 m

5.
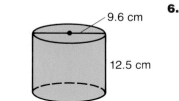
9.6 cm
12.5 cm

6.
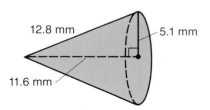
12.8 mm
5.1 mm
11.6 mm

Find the volume. Use 3.14 for π, and round to the nearest tenth.

7. cylinder
radius = 7.6 cm
height = 14 cm

8. cone
radius = 3.3 m
height = 8.7 m

9. cylinder
radius = 16.5 cm
height = 25 cm

10. cone
Base = 116.8 cm^2
height = 15 cm

11. cylinder
diameter = 1 m
height = 25 cm

12. cone
diameter = 7.2 cm
height = 7.2 cm

★13. cylinder
circumference = 12.56 cm
height = 9.1 cm

★14. cone
circumference = 6.28 dm
height = 18 dm

Find the volume of the shaded portion. Use 3.14 for π, and round to the nearest tenth.

15.
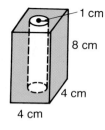
1 cm
8 cm
4 cm
4 cm

16.
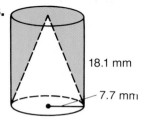
18.1 mm
7.7 mm

★17.
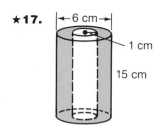
6 cm
1 cm
15 cm

Solve. Use 3.14 for π.

18. A large, conical mound of sand has a diameter of 45 ft and a height of 20 ft. Find the volume.

19. A cylindrical column is 90 ft high and has a diameter of $6\frac{1}{2}$ ft. Find its volume.

PROBLEM SOLVING
Choosing a Formula

A formula can help you solve certain kinds of problems.

Stacy's class is making scale models of famous buildings. The students will place their models on a carpeted rectangular platform 5 feet long and 4 feet wide. How large a carpet is needed for the platform?

To solve the problem, you must choose the correct formula. To choose the correct formula, think about these questions.

- Which geometric figure is described in the problem?

- Which measurements are given in the problem?

- What do you need to solve for?

- In which unit of measurement should the answer be expressed?

The problem describes a rectangle 5 feet long and 4 feet wide. You need to find the area of the rectangle. The area will be expressed in square feet.

Which formula will help you solve this problem?

    a. $A = s^2$ **b.** $C = \pi d$ **c.** $A = lw$

Since you are finding the area of a rectangle, $A = lw$ is the formula you would use. After you choose the correct formula, substitute the measurements in the formula. Check to make sure you are using units that are alike, and solve the problem.

$$A = lw$$
$$A = 5 \cdot 4$$
$$A = 20$$

The carpeting must be 20 ft^2.

Write the letter of the correct formula.

1. Ralph is making a model of a Greek amphitheater. The radius of the circular stage is $2\frac{1}{4}$ inches. How much flooring is needed for the stage in the model?

a. $S = r^2 + rl$
b. $A = \pi r^2$
c. $A = \frac{1}{2}bh$

2. Lisa is making a model of the Great Pyramid. The base of the pyramid is a square, 6 inches by 6 inches. Each side is a triangle 7 inches high. What is the surface area of the wood Lisa needs to make the model?

a. $S = \pi r^2 + \pi rl$
b. $S = s^2 + 4\left(\frac{1}{2}sl\right)$
c. $A = \frac{1}{2}(b_1 + b_2)h$

Several students are working on a scale model of the Pantheon in Rome. For each section of the model, write the correct formula, and solve.

3. Find the length of side c that forms part of the triangular roof. Side a is 5 inches long, side b is 3 inches long. Angle ACB is a right angle.

4. Find the volume of the rectangular porch that measures 10 inches long by 4 inches wide by 6 inches high.

5. Find the surface area of the circular column that measures $\frac{1}{2}$ inch in diameter and 6 inches in height.

6. Find the circumference of the base of the dome, the diameter of which is 14 inches.

7. How large is the light opening in the dome? The opening is a circle that has a 1-inch radius.

8. Find the volume of the rotunda, a cylindrical space that has a radius of 7 inches and a height of 12 inches.

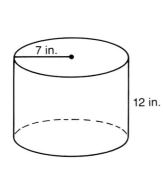

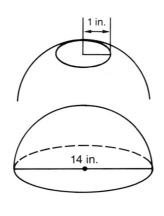

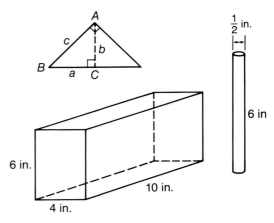

CALCULATOR

A calculator can be very useful when you are working with geometric formulas. Sometimes it is better to rewrite the formula so computation is easier.

Example: Find the perimeter of a rectangle that has a length of 8.2 cm and a width of 4.9 cm.

$P = 2l + 2w = 2 \cdot (l + w)$

Press: $\boxed{2}\ \boxed{\times}\ \boxed{8}\ \boxed{.}\ \boxed{2}\ \boxed{=}\ \boxed{M+}\ \boxed{2}\ \boxed{\times}\ \boxed{4}\ \boxed{.}\ \boxed{9}\ \boxed{=}\ \boxed{M+}\ \boxed{RM}$

  or

Press: $\boxed{8}\ \boxed{.}\ \boxed{2}\ \boxed{+}\ \boxed{4}\ \boxed{.}\ \boxed{9}\ \boxed{\times}\ \boxed{2}\ \boxed{=}$ The display should show 26.2.

$P = 26.2$ cm

As you can see, the second formula used fewer keys and would work on calculators that do not have a memory. However, on some calculators, you must press " = " after "4.9."

Example: Find the surface area of a sphere with a radius of 5 cm. (Use 3.14 for π.)

$SA = 4\pi r^2$

Press: $\boxed{4}\ \boxed{\times}\ \boxed{3}\ \boxed{.}\ \boxed{1}\ \boxed{4}\ \boxed{\times}\ \boxed{5}\ \boxed{\times}\ \boxed{5}\ \boxed{=}$ The display should show 314.

$SA = 314$ cm^2

Use a calculator to solve each exercise. Round the answer to the same number of digits as the measurement that is either the *least precise* (Exercises 1–2) or the *least accurate* (Exercises 3–6). See page 197 for the rules on rounding answers.

Find the perimeter.
  1. rectangle: $l = 5.3$ in., $w = 2.9$ in.   **2.** square: $s = 4.5$ cm

Find the surface area of each sphere.
  3. $r = 6.5$ cm   **4.** $r = 12.5$ in.

The volume of a sphere equals $\frac{4}{3}\pi r^3$.
Find the volume.
  5. $r = 7.5$ cm   **6.** $r = 5.9$ in.

GROUP PROJECT

A Graph of the Future

The problem: How much have you thought about your future? Do you have career plans? Do your classmates have career plans? You can find out by taking a survey. Write a questionnaire that asks about career plans. Then make a circle graph to show your findings.

Key Questions

- Do you think that the careers the class members hope to pursue will vary a great deal?

- How will you categorize the career choices for your circle graph?

- Do some of the careers require college training? specialized training?

- Do you think that your class's career choices are similar to those of the other students in your school? your town? the country?

- What conclusions can you draw from looking at the results of your graph?

CHAPTER TEST

Find the perimeter or circumference of each figure.
(pages 398–399 and 404–405)

1.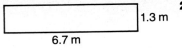
6.7 m, 1.3 m

2.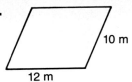
10 m, 12 m

3.
15 m

Find the area of the figure. Use $\pi = 3.14$. (pages 408–413)

4.
15 cm, 7 cm

5.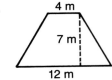
4 m, 7 m, 12 m

6.
4 in.

7.
12 m

8.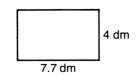
4 dm, 7.7 dm

9.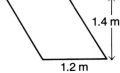
1.4 m, 1.2 m

Use the right triangle ABC to answer Exercises 10–12.
(pages 400–401)

10. $b = 4$ cm, $a = 3$ cm, $c = \blacksquare$ cm

11. $b = 15$ m, $a = 36$ m, $c = \blacksquare$ cm

12. $b = 16$ cm, $a = 12$ cm, $c = \blacksquare$ cm

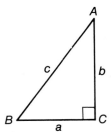

Find the surface area and volume of each figure. Use
$3.14 = \pi$. (pages 418–421 and 424–427)

13.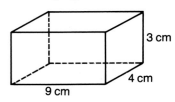
3 cm, 4 cm, 9 cm

14.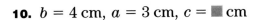
8 m, 3 m, 10 m, 5 m, 5 m

15.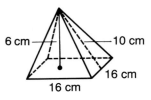
6 cm, 10 cm, 16 cm, 16 cm

16.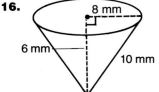
8 mm, 6 mm, 10 mm

17.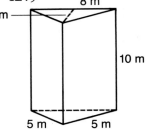
4 cm, 6 cm

18.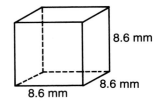
8.6 mm, 8.6 mm, 8.6 mm

Use the right triangle and the table at the right to solve to the nearest inch. (pages 402–403)

19. $m\angle B = 49°$, $a = 17$ in., $b = $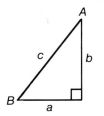

20. $m\angle A = 56°$, $a = 14$ in., $c = $ ▨

21. $m\angle B = 51°$, $c = 4.4$ in., $a = $ ▨

Angle	Sin	Cos	Tan
49°	0.755	0.656	1.15
50°	0.766	0.643	1.19
51°	0.777	0.629	1.23
52°	0.788	0.616	1.28
53°	0.799	0.602	1.33
54°	0.809	0.588	1.38
55°	0.819	0.574	1.43
56°	0.829	0.559	1.48

Solve. (pages 422–423, and 428–429)

22. The largest poster made was 311 ft 4 in. long and 141 ft 10 in. wide. What was its area in square inches?

23. The largest rope ever made had a radius of 7.48 inches, to the nearest inch. What was its circumference?

24. The tallest load-bearing stone columns measure 69 feet tall. If the base of one column was 5 feet in diameter, what would the surface area of a column be?

25. The largest cartoon ever exhibited covered five stories of a university building in 1954. If it was 50 feet by 150 feet, what was its area?

Use the picture to solve. (pages 414–415)

26. Each floor of the building at right is identical. Each side of the building is identical. Find the area of the glass in the building.

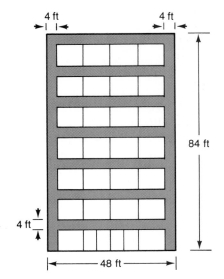

BONUS

Solve.

The largest cherry pie was baked in Charlevoix, Michigan, in 1976. If the pie had a diameter of 14 feet 4 inches and a depth of 24 inches, what was its volume in cubic inches?

RETEACHING

The Pythagorean rule states the relationship among the sides of a right triangle. In a right triangle, if a and b are the legs, and c is the hypotenuse, then $a^2 + b^2 = c^2$.

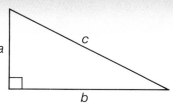

A. To find the length of the hypotenuse, use the formula.

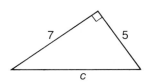

$$a^2 + b^2 = c^2$$
$$5^2 + 7^2 = c^2$$
$$25 + 49 = c^2$$
$$74 = c^2$$
$$8.602 \approx c$$

The hypotenuse is 8.602.

B. To find the length of the missing side, use the formula.

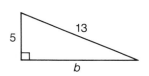

$$a^2 + b^2 = c^2$$
$$5^2 + b^2 = 13^2$$
$$25 + b^2 = 169$$
$$b^2 = 144$$
$$b = 12$$

The missing side is 12.

Find the length of each missing side. Use the tables on pages 82 and 83.

1.

2.
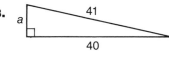

3.
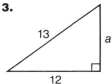

4.

5.
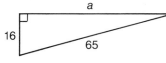

6.
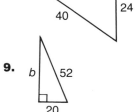

7.
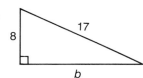

8.
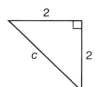

9.

10.
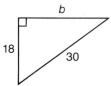

11.

12.

13.

14.

15.

ENRICHMENT

Volume of a Sphere

To compute the volume of a basketball or any other sphere, use the formula

$$V = \frac{4}{3}\pi r^3.$$

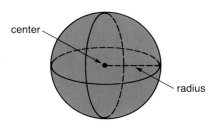

Find the volume of a soccer ball that has a 6-inch radius. (Use 3.14 for π.)

$$V = \frac{4}{3}\pi r^3$$

$$V = \frac{4}{3} \cdot 3.14 \cdot 6^3$$

$$V = \frac{4}{3} \cdot 3.14 \cdot 216$$

$$V = 4 \cdot 3.14 \cdot 72$$

$$V = 904.32$$

The volume is 904.32 in.³

Find the volume of each sphere. Use 3.14 for π.
Round to the nearest tenth.

1. $r = 9$ in. **2.** $d = 10$ ft **3.** $d = 24$ m **4.** $r = 2$ cm

Solve. Use 3.14 for π. Round your answer to the nearest tenth.

5. What is the volume of a beach ball that has a diameter of 2 feet?

6. A spherical natural gas tank has a diameter of 32 yards. Find the volume of gas it can contain.

7. A marble has a diameter of 1.6 cm. Find its volume.

8. A hollow rubber ball has an outer diameter of 7 cm. If it has an inner diameter of 6.5 cm, what is the volume of rubber contained in the shell?

435

CUMULATIVE REVIEW

Write the letter of the correct answer.

1. What kind of line segment is $\overline{CD}$?

a. diameter
b. radius
c. chord
d. not given

2. What is the size of the supplement of a 40° angle?

a. 25°
b. 50°
c. 140°
d. not given

3. What kind of polygon is *ABCD*?

a. square
b. rhombus
c. parallelogram
d. not given

4. Classify triangle *ABC*.

a. equilateral
b. scalene
c. right
d. not given

5. Select the congruent triangle.

a.
b.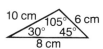

c.
d. not given

6. Which line segments are perpendicular?

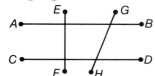

a. $\overline{AB}$ and $\overline{CD}$
b. $\overline{AB}$ and $\overline{EF}$
c. $\overline{AB}$ and $\overline{GH}$
d. not given

7. In how many ways could you arrange 5 records on a shelf?

a. 25
b. 60
c. 120
d. not given

8. How many combinations could you make from 6 different fruits added to 3 kinds of muffins?

a. 9
b. 20
c. 120
d. not given

9. An equilateral triangle has an area of 12 in.^{2}. If you bisect each side of the triangle and connect the points, you have another, smaller equilateral triangle. What is the area of this new triangle? Draw a picture to help you solve the problem.

a. 3 in.^{2}
b. 6 in.^{2}
c. 8 in.^{2}
d. not given

10. Dorothy lives in Brooklyn. She has to be in Islip by 1:00 P.M. What is the latest train she can take?

a. 10:23 A.M.
b. 11:30 A.M.
c. 12:19 P.M.
d. not given

Leave			Arrive		
New York	Brook-lyn	Ja-maica	Bay Shore	Islip	Great River
10:32	10:23	10:51	11:33	11:37	11:41
11:32	11:30	11:51	12:33	12:37	—
12:32	12:19	12:51	1:33	1:37	—
1:32	1:31	1:51	2:33	2:37	2:41
2:40	2:39	3:00	3:47	3:51	3:55
3:23	3:23	3:44	4:33	4:37	

436

Suppose you wanted to send someone a three-dimensional picture of
your geographic area. How would
you show distance? How would you
show elevation?

12 EQUATIONS AND INEQUALITIES
Two Variables

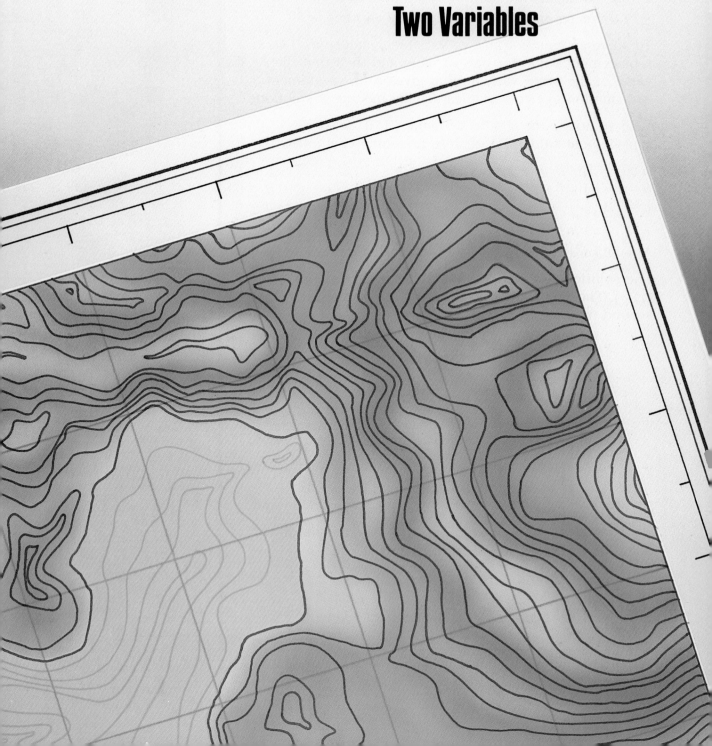

Equations in Two Variables

A. Equations such as $3x = y$, $x + y = 8$, and $\frac{y}{x} = 3$ are examples of equations in two variables.

$3x = y$ means one number is 3 times another number.
$x + y = 8$ means the sum of two numbers is 8.
$\frac{y}{x} = 3$ means one number divided by another is 3.

To solve an equation in two variables, choose a replacement value for one variable and then find the value of the other variable that gives a true statement. An equation in two variables usually has many solutions.

Find solutions for $y = 3x$ by using $^-1$, 0, and 2 as replacement values for x. Here are some examples.

If $x = ^-1$,   If $x = 0$,   If $x = 2$,
$y = 3 \cdot {}^-1$ $y = 3 \cdot 0$ $y = 3 \cdot 2$
$y = {}^-3$ $y = 0$ $y = 6$

A solution is $(^-1,^-3)$.   A solution is $(0,0)$.   A solution is $(2,6)$.

The solutions are usually written as ordered pairs, (x, y). The first number represents the x-value; the second number represents the y-value.

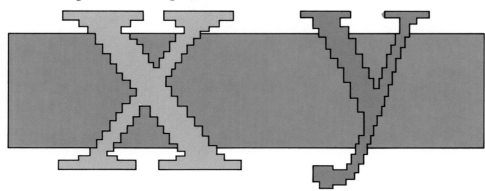

B. You can test an ordered pair in a given equation to determine whether it is a solution to the equation.

Is $(2,6)$ a solution for $\frac{y}{x} = 3$?

Replace y with 6. $\longrightarrow \frac{6}{2} \overset{?}{=} 3$
Replace x with 2. $\nearrow \quad 3 = 3$
So, $(2,6)$ is a solution for $\frac{y}{x} = 3$.

Is $(^-2,3)$ a solution for $x - 2y = 6$?

Replace x with $^-2$. $\longrightarrow {}^-2 - 2(3) \overset{?}{=} 6$
Replace y with 3. $\xrightarrow{\hspace{3cm}} {}^-8 \neq 6$
So, $(^-2,3)$ is *not* a solution for $x - 2y = 6$.

To solve each equation, use 3 as the replacement value for x. Write each solution as an ordered pair.

1. $x + y = 7$

2. $x - y = 3$

3. $2x + y = 7$

4. $x + y = 12$

5. $x - 2y = 11$

6. $5x - y = 4$

7. $3x + 2y = 13$

8. $x + y = 0$

9. $x - y = 0$

10. $2x - y = 7$

11. $5x + y = 17$

12. $x + 4y = 14$

Use $^-1$, 0, and 2 as replacements for x. Write the solutions for each equation as ordered pairs.

13. $x + y = 4$

14. $2x + y = 13$

15. $y - x = 8$

16. $2y - x = 0$

17. $3x + 2y = 6$

18. $3x - 2y = 6$

19. $4x + 2y = 8$

20. $4x - 2y = 8$

21. $5x - y = 4$

22. $7x - 3y = 6$

23. $x + 3y = 9$

24. $2x + 2y = 5$

Decide whether the ordered pair is a solution of $5x + y = 12$. Write *yes* or *no*.

25. $(2,2)$

26. $(7,1)$

27. $(12,0)$

28. $(1,7)$

29. $(0,12)$

30. $(3,^-3)$

31. $(^-3,3)$

32. $(4,^-8)$

Write the letter of the equation next to its meaning.

33. The sum of two numbers is 10.

a. $6x = 3y$

34. The difference between two numbers is 6.

b. $\frac{1}{4}x + 4y = 12$

35. 6 times a number is 3 times another number.

c. $x - y = 6$

36. 2 times a number divided by another number is 12.

d. $x + y = 10$

37. $\frac{1}{4}$ of a number plus 4 times another number is 12.

e. $\frac{2x}{y} = 12$

CHALLENGE Patterns, Relations, and Functions

If x = the length of one side of a regular polygon, and y = the perimeter of that polygon, which polygon is represented by each of the following equations?

1. $y = 3x$

2. $y = 4x$

3. $y = 5x$

4. $y = 6x$

Solving Equations in Two Variables

A. Equations in two variables can be solved if you make a table of values. Choose values for x, and solve the equation for the values of y.

Solve $y = 7 - x$.

x	$y = 7 - x$	y
$^-1$	$y = 7 - (^-1)$	8
0	$y = 7 - 0$	7
1	$y = 7 - 1$	6
2	$y = 7 - 2$	5

The ordered pairs $(^-1,8)$, $(0,7)$, $(1,6)$, and $(2,5)$ are solutions to the equation. More solutions are possible.

B. Solve $2x + y = 5$.

x	$2x + y = 5$	y
$^-2$	$2(^-2) + y = 5$	9
0	$2(0) + y = 5$	5
2	$2(2) + y = 5$	1
4	$2(4) + y = 5$	$^-3$

The ordered pairs $(^-2,9)$, $(0,5)$, and $(2,1)$, and $(4,^-3)$ are four solutions to the equation.

Checkpoint   Write the letter of the correct answer.

1. A solution for $y = 4x - 3$ is $x = 1$, $y = \blacksquare$.

a. 2   **b.** 7

c. 1   **d.** 12

2. A solution for $2x + y = 4$ is the ordered pair $\blacksquare$.

a. $(4,0)$ **b.** $(1,2)$

c. $(2,1)$ **d.** $(^-2,6)$

440

Solve for y using $^-1$ and 2 as replacements for x.

1. $y = x - 4$ **2.** $y = 3 - x$ **3.** $y = 2x + 5$

4. $3x - y = 5$ **5.** $5x + y = 4$ **6.** $^-2x + y = 9$

7. $3x - 2y = 10$ **8.** $5x - y = 20$ **9.** $2x + 5y = 10$

Make a table of values for each equation. Use $^-1, 0, 1,$ and 2 as the replacement values for x.

10. $y = 3x$ **11.** $y = 3x + 2$ **12.** $y = 3x - 2$

13. $y = {}^-x$ **14.** $y = 2x - 3$ **15.** $y = 2 - 3x$

16. $y = 2x + 1$ **17.** $^-2x + y = {}^-1$ **18.** $3x - 2y = 7$

Find three solutions for each equation. Write as ordered pairs.

19. $y - x = 10$ **20.** $x + y = 8$ **21.** $2x + 3y = 6$

22. $3x + y = 9$ **23.** $3x - y = 6$ **24.** $2x + y = 12$

25. $x - 3y = 6$ **26.** $3y = x + 1$ **27.** $y + 3 = 4x$

For each equation, write the ordered pair that is *not* a solution.

28. $x = 8y$ $(0,0), (1,1), (8,1), \left(4, \frac{1}{2}\right)$

29. $3y + x = 15$ $(0,5), (15,0), (0,15), (9,2)$

30. $x + 2y = 7$ $(0,7), (7,0), \left(\frac{1}{2}, 3\frac{1}{4}\right), \left(0, 3\frac{1}{2}\right)$

31. $4x - 3y = {}^-12$ $(0,4), \left(^-4, ^-1\frac{1}{3}\right), (^-3,0), \left(^-4\frac{1}{2}, 2\right)$

ANOTHER LOOK

Write and solve an equation for each.

1. The Beatles have sold 1,004 million records and tapes, which is 46 million less than 5 times the number ABBA has sold. How many records and tapes has ABBA sold?

2. In 1976, 80-year-old George Burns became the oldest Academy Award winner. The youngest winner, Shirley Temple, won her Academy Award in 1934 when she was 2 years less than $\frac{1}{10}$ of George's age. How old was Shirley when she won her Academy Award?

PROBLEM SOLVING
Making a Diagram

When solving a problem that involves directions, you may want to draw a diagram.

Carl entered a circular park that measures 6 km in diameter. He entered from the northernmost point of the park. He walked due south for 1 km and stopped at a monument. Then he walked about 2.25 km due east to a food vendor at the edge of the park. From there, he walked due south 2 km to another monument and finally, 2.25 km due west to a fountain. How far is the fountain from the food vendor?

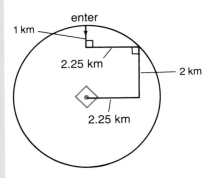

- Draw a picture.

- Use your picture to solve the problem.

  The fountain is located in the center of the circle. The distance from the fountain to the food vendor is the radius of the circle. The radius of the circle is 3 km.

The distance between the fountain and the vendor is 3 km.

Write the letter of the correct answer.

1. Becky left a restaurant that was located on Third Street and drove north along Third Street for 2 km. She drove west on Sixth Avenue for 5 km and then south on 11 Street for 2 km. At that point, how far was Becky from the restaurant?

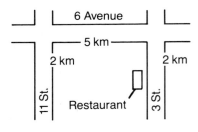

a. 9 km   **b.** 5 km   **c.** 14 km

2. Smithtown, Branchville, and Garfield form a right triangle. Branchville is located 12 km due east of Smithtown. Garfield is located 5 km due south of Branchville. Find the distance from Smithtown to Garfield.

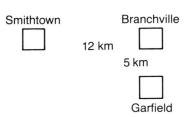

a. 17 km   **b.** 12.5 km   **c.** 13 km

Draw a picture. Then solve each problem.

3. The shape of a summer camp is like that of a square. It measures 10 km on each side. Warren entered the camp from the center of the south side and walked 2 km due north. He then walked 3 km due east and then 7 km due north. At that point, how far was he from the western border of the camp?

4. Albert stood in the center of a circular pool. He took 2 steps toward the edge of the pool and was then 9 m from the edge. If each of Albert's steps measured 1 m, what is the diameter of the pool?

5. Mr. Paxton wants to carpet an L-shape room. The main part of the room measures 5 m by 3 m. The rest of the room measures 4 m by 2 m. The carpet costs $17.95 per square meter. How much will it cost Mr. Paxton to carpet the room?

6. Ralph followed a map made by his friend Sheila. He began his walk at a large rock and walked 11 paces west, 5 paces north, 2 paces east, 13 paces south, 9 paces west, and 8 paces north. If each pace is equal to 1 meter, how far from the rock did Ralph end his walk?

7. The state of Colorado has a rectangular shape that measures 578 km by 458 km. The longer sides are the northern and southern borders of the state. A helicopter begins a trip in the northwest corner and flies south until it reaches the southwest corner. It then flies east until it reaches the southeast corner. How far is the helicopter from the northwest corner at this point? Round your answer to the nearest kilometer. You may use a calculator to solve this problem.

Relations and Functions

A. A relation (R) is a set of ordered pairs (x,y). An example is $R = \{(1,7), (2,4), (3,3), (2,6), (5,1)\}$. A function (F) is a relation where each x value has only one y value, for example $F = \{(2,3), (3,5), (4,7), (5,9), (6,11)\}$. If a relation is a function, then for every value of x, there is one and only one value of y.

Function		
x	y	
2	3	(2,3)
3	5	(3,5)
4	7	(4,7)
8	4	(8,4)
9	2	(9,2)

Not a function		
x	y	
1	4	(1,4)
2	4	(2,4)
3	6	(3,6)
2	6	(2,6)
5	1	(5,1)

For $x = 2$, there are two values of y.

B. Sometimes you can use a rule to describe a function. For example, $y = {}^{-}3x + 2$ is a rule for a function that multiplies every real number by $^{-}3$ and adds 2. The table of values shows some of the solutions to this equation.

x	$y = {}^{-}3x + 2$	y
0	$y = {}^{-}3(0) + 2$	2
1	$y = {}^{-}3(1) + 2$	$^{-}1$
2	$y = {}^{-}3(2) + 2$	$^{-}4$

Some solutions are $(0,2)$, $(1,{}^{-}1)$, and $(2,{}^{-}4)$.
The set $\{(0,2), (1,{}^{-}1), (2,{}^{-}4)\}$ is a function because for each x-value, there is one and only one value of y.

Checkpoint Write the letter of the correct answer.

1. If $(1,3)$, $(2,4)$, $(3,6)$, $(4,5)$, and (x,y) are ordered pairs of a function, then (x,y) could be ■.

a. $(1,5)$ **b.** $(6,3)$ **c.** $(4,2)$ **d.** $(3,1)$

2. If the relation $\{(x,3), (2,5), (3,7), (4,9)\}$ is a function, then x could be ■.

a. 1   **b.** 2   **c.** 3   **d.** 4

444

Write *yes* if the relation is a function. Write *no* if it is not.

1. {(0,2), (1,2), (1,4)}
2. {(0,1), (0,2), (0,3)}

3. {(1,4), (2,4), (3,4)}
4. {(0,0), (1,4), (1,⁻4)}

5. {(2,4), (3,4), (3,5), (4,6)}
6. {(1,1), (2,2), (3,3), (4,4)}

7. {(5,6), (⁻2,4), (⁻1,6), (4,3)}
8. {(⁻1,3), (⁻2,3), (⁻3,3), (⁻4,3)}

9. {(1,2), (1,3), (1,4)}
10. {(0,⁻2), (1,⁻3), (2,⁻4)}

11. {(5,3), (3,5), (4,⁻2)}
12. {(⁻1,3), (⁻2,4), (⁻3,5), (⁻2,6)}

13. {(1,2), (1,3), (2,1), (2,3)}
14. {(2,6), (3,6), (5,7), (6,2)}

Make a table of values for each equation using 2,1,0⁻1,⁻2, as replacements for x. Is the set of solutions a function?

15. $y = x + 6$
16. $x + y = 11$
17. $y = 3x + 4$

Write the rule if the given relation is a function. Write *no* if it is not a function.

★**18.** {(0,0), (1,1), (3,3), (4,4)}
★**19.** {(1,4), (2,5), (0,3), (3,6)}

★**20.** {(0,0), (1,2), (2,4), (3,6)}
★**21.** {(0,2), (1,1), (0,1), (5,⁻3)}

Solve. For Problem 22, use the Infobank.

22. Use the information on page 478 to solve. How many points would you have to eliminate to turn the graphed relation (Graph A) into a graph of a function?

89707

40769

CHALLENGE **Patterns, Relations, and Functions**

Archeologists often use a system of tags to identify the various artifacts discovered during a dig. If you think about the tags as ordered pairs (x = the tag number; y = the actual artifact), why is it crucial that the ordered pairs be a function? If you let x = the artifact and y = the tag number, what effect would that have on the tag system?

The Real-Number Plane

A. You have used whole numbers, integers, rational numbers, and irrational numbers as coordinates of points on the real-number line. You can use ordered pairs of real numbers to represent points on a **real-number plane.** The horizontal **x-axis** and the vertical **y-axis** are perpendicular number lines. They intersect at a point (0,0) called the **origin.** The coordinate axes divide the plane into four quadrants.

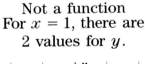

In Quadrant I, all ordered pairs are in the form $(^+,^+)$.

In Quadrant II, all ordered pairs are in the form $(^-,^+)$.

In Quadrant III, all ordered pairs are in the form $(^-,^-)$.

In Quadrant IV, all ordered pairs are in the form $(^+,^-)$.

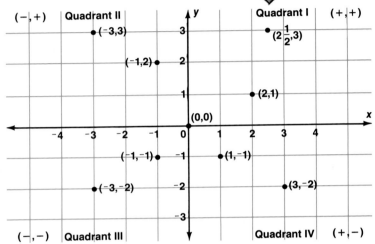

B. Since a function has only one y value for each x value, you can examine the graph to see if it is a graph of a function.

Function	Function	Not a function For $x = 1$, there are 2 values for y.

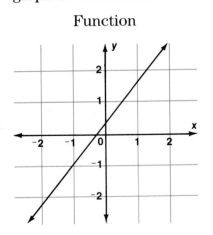
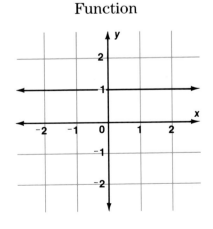
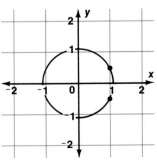

If a vertical line passes through more than one point, the graph is *not* a graph of a function.

Math Reasoning, page H229

Write Quadrant *I, II, III,* or *IV* for each ordered pair.

1. $(4,7)$ **2.** $(2,^-1)$ **3.** $(^-2,4)$ **4.** $(^-1,6)$ **5.** $(^-1,^-3)$

6. $(^-2,^-5)$ **7.** $(1,4)$ **8.** $(3,^-4)$ **9.** $(^-3,1)$ **10.** $(5,8)$

Use the same pair of coordinate axes to graph and label each point. Connect the points in alphabetical order. Write *yes* if the figure is a graph of a function. Write *no* if it is not.

11. $B\ (^-4,^-7)$ **12.** $F\ (0,1)$ **13.** $D\ (^-2,^-3)$ **14.** $A\ (^-5,^-9)$

15. $E\ (^-1,^-1)$ **16.** $G\ (1,3)$ **17.** $C\ (^-3,^-5)$ **18.** $H\ (2,5)$

Draw another pair of axes. Graph and label each point. Connect the points in alphabetical order. Write *yes* if the figure is a graph of a function. Write *no* if it is not.

19. $P\ (0,^-4)$ **20.** $M\ (2,3)$ **21.** $R\ (4,0)$ **22.** $L\ (0,4)$

23. $N\ (4,0)$ **24.** $Q\ (^-2,^-3)$ **25.** $S\ (^-2,3)$ **26.** $O\ (2,^-3)$

Write *yes* if the graph is a graph of a function. Write *no* if it is not.

27.
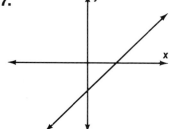

28.
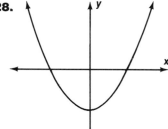

29.
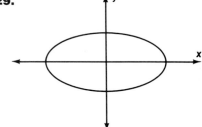

Solve. For Problem 30, use the Infobank.

30. Use the information on page 478 to solve. Is the graph of $xy = 1$ a function? In which quadrants would $xy = {}^-1$ be graphed?

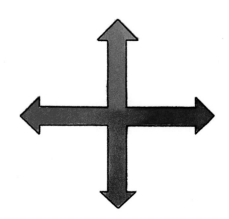

MIDCHAPTER REVIEW

Find three solutions for each equation. Write as ordered pairs.

1. $2x - y = 3$ **2.** $3y = x + 2$ **3.** $y + 4 = 2x$ **4.** $2x - y = 6$

PROBLEM SOLVING
Choosing a Strategy or Method

Write the strategy or method you choose. Then solve.

> Estimation
> Using a Table
> Choosing the Operation
> Solving Multi-step Problems
> Guessing and Checking
> Making a Table to Find a Pattern
> Writing an Equation
> Interpreting the Quotient
>   and the Remainder
> Using a Formula
> Making an Organized List
> Working Backward

1. The attendance at a soccer game was 71,500, which is 5,200 more than $\frac{4}{5}$ of the attendance at a football game. How many people attended the football game?

2. One container holds a maximum of 500 gallons. This is 150 gallons more than $\frac{2}{3}$ of the capacity of another container. How many gallons does the second container hold?

3. One city's new art museum will be rectangular, 160 feet long, and 102 feet wide. What will the area of the building be?

4. Brad swam for 45 minutes on Monday. On Tuesday, he swam $1\frac{1}{3}$ times as long. Wednesday, he swam $\frac{2}{3}$ as long as he swam on Monday. How many hours did he swim in all?

5. Ann has a piece of fabric 5 yards wide and 3 yards long. She needs to cut a piece of $2\frac{1}{2}$ feet by $2\frac{2}{3}$ feet from the fabric. How many square feet of fabric will be left?

6. A circular pool in a museum's courtyard has a diameter of 8 feet. What is the circumference of the pool?

7. Joshua buys a piece of wood that is 75 inches long. How many pieces, each 8 inches long, can he cut from this piece?

8. Michelle spent $0.89 for a soda and $2.75 for a sandwich. She gave the cashier $10.00. How much change did she receive?

9. Lucy's car averages 25.8 miles per gallon of gasoline. At this rate, how far can she drive on 8.5 gallons?

Choose a strategy or method and solve.

10. The Martins are planning a trip to Europe. Mrs. Martin wants to buy a road map of France for $7.85, one of Spain for $6.59, one of Italy for $9.35, and one of Greece for $8.25. She has $31.00. Can she buy all the maps?

11. In a bookstore, Howard sees a world globe for $31.75, a large map of the United States for $15.30, a map of Asia for $12.75, and a road atlas for $9.35. Can he buy all the items with $70.00?

12. Tanya is drawing a map of her town. She is using a scale of $\frac{3}{4}$ inch = 6 miles. How many inches would represent a distance of 9 miles?

13. One fruit-punch recipe calls for $1\frac{1}{2}$ quarts apple juice to make 15 servings. How much juice is needed to make 35 servings?

Use the table for Exercises 14–15.

Some American Colleges and Universities				
Name	State	Year founded	Students	Teachers
Beloit	Wisconsin	1846	1,079	97
Bowdoin	Maine	1794	1,371	116
Harvard	Massachusetts	1636	6,537	689
Oberlin	Ohio	1833	2,898	226
Stanford	California	1891	12,341	1,219
Yale	Connecticut	1701	10,448	1,741

14. Which school on the list has the most students? Does that school have the most teachers?

15. What is average age (number of years since these schools were founded) of these schools?

16. From the lesson, choose one problem that you have already solved. Show how the problem can be solved by a different method.

Graphing Equations in Two Variables

In an earlier lesson, you found ordered-pair solutions to an equation in two variables by using a table of values. The solutions from the table of values can be graphed on the coordinate axes. The graphs in this lesson are straight lines.

To graph $y = 4 - 2x$, list some solutions in a table of values.

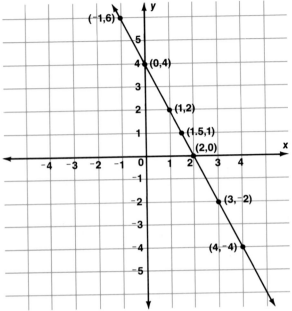

x	$y = 4 - 2x$	y	Solutions
0	$y = 4 - 2(0)$	4	$(0,4)$
1	$y = 4 - 2(1)$	2	$(1,2)$
2	$y = 4 - 2(2)$	0	$(2,0)$
3	$y = 4 - 2(3)$	$^-2$	$(3,^-2)$

Graph the solutions. Draw a line through the solutions you have graphed. All the points on the line, such as $(^-1,6)$, $(1.5,1)$, and $(4,^-4)$ are solutions.

Another example: Graph the equation $2x - y = 4$.

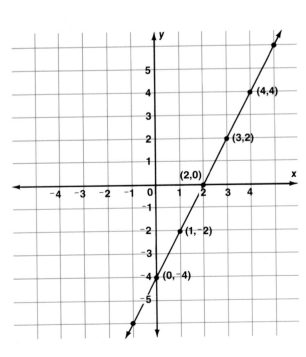

x	y	Solutions
$^-1$	$^-6$	$(^-1,^-6)$
0	$^-4$	$(0,^-4)$
2	0	$(2,0)$
5	6	$(5,6)$

Other points on the line include $(1,^-2)$, $(3,2)$, and $(4,4)$.

450

Copy and complete each table of values. Then graph
each set of solutions.

1.

x	y = x − 5	y
0	y = 0 − 5	
1	y = 1 − 5	
2	y = 2 − 5	

2.

x	y = 2x + 1	y
0	y = 2(0) + 1	
1	y = 2(1) + 1	
2	y = 2(2) + 1	

3.

x	y = 2x	y
0	y = 2(0)	
1	y = 2(1)	
2	y = 2(2)	

Make a table of values for each equation. Then graph
each set of solutions.

4. $2x + y = 14$

5. $3x - y = 8$

6. $2x + 5y = 10$

7. $3x + 4y = 12$

8. $4x - 2y = 8$

9. $2x + 3y - 12 = 0$

10. $y = 4x$

11. $3y = 4x$

12. $y = {}^-3x$

13. $3x = {}^-5y$

14. $x + y = 4$

15. $y - x = 5$

16. $2x + y = 10$

17. $x + 3y = 5$

18. $3x - y = 8$

19. $x + y = 7$

20. $2x - y = 11$

21. $x - y = {}^-4$

22. $2x + 3y + 12 = 0$

★23. $y = \frac{1}{2}x$

★24. $y = \frac{2}{3}x$

For each equation make a table of values that has
three values for x. Graph the points and use the graph
to find two other points on the line.

25. $x + y = {}^-1$

26. $2x - y = 3$

27. $x = 3y$

28. $3y - 4 = x$

29. $y = x$

30. $y - x = 1$

Match each graph with its equation.

a.
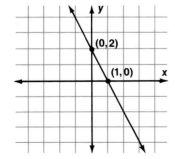

b.
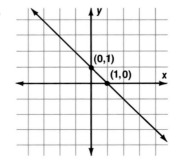

c.
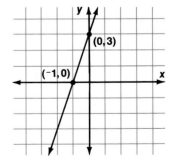

31. $y = 1 - x$

32. $y = 2 - 2x$

33. $y = 3x + 3$

Graphing Pairs of Equations

Look at the pair of equations shown below.

$$2x + y = 4$$
$$3x - y = 11$$

Such a pair of equations is called a **system of equations.** A solution to a system of equations is an ordered pair that is a solution to both equations. You can graph a system of equations to find its solution. Begin by graphing each equation on the same set of axes.

x	y = 4 − 2x	y	Solutions
0	y = 4 − 2(0)	4	(0,4)
1	y = 4 − 2(1)	2	(1,2)
2	y = 4 − 2(2)	0	(2,0)

x	y = 3x − 11	y	Solutions
0	y = 3(0) − 11	⁻11	(0,⁻11)
1	y = 3(1) − 11	⁻8	(1,⁻8)
2	y = 3(2) − 11	⁻5	(2,⁻5)

The coordinates of the point of intersection (3,⁻2) are the solution to the system.
Check the solution (3,⁻2) in each equation.

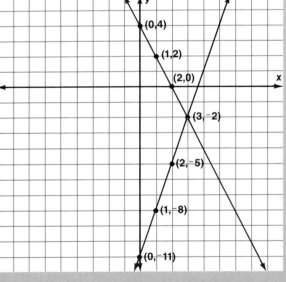

$$2x + y = 4$$
$$2(3) + (^-2) \overset{?}{=} 4$$
$$6 - 2 \overset{?}{=} 4$$
$$4 = 4$$

$$3x - y = 11$$
$$3(3) - (^-2) \overset{?}{=} 11$$
$$9 + 2 \overset{?}{=} 11$$
$$11 = 11$$

Graph each system of equations on the same set of
axes to find the solution. Check each solution.

1. $x + y = 6$
   $x - y = 2$

2. $x + y = 8$
   $x - y = 4$

3. $x + 2y = 15$
   $y = 2x$

4. $x + 3y = 19$
   $x - 3y = 1$

5. $3x = 4y + 17$
   $2x = {}^-3y$

6. $x + y = 3$
   $x - y = 1$

7. $2x + y = 6$
   $y - x = 3$

8. $x + y = 9$
   $x - y = 3$

9. $x + 2y = 8$
   $x - 2y = 4$

10. $y + 3x = 8$
    $y - 3x = 8$

11. $x + 2y = 14$
    $3y + x = 18$

12. $y = 3x$
    $x + y = 8$

13. $y = 3x$
    $x - y = 2$

14. $x + y = 12$
    $x - y = 2$

15. $3x + 2y = 9$
    $x + y = 3$

16. $5x + 2y = 11$
    $4x - 3y = 18$

17. $x + y = 12$
    $x - y = 4$

18. $x + 2y = 8$
    $x - 2y = 4$

19. $5x + 4y = 27$
    $x - 11 = 2y$

20. $2x + y = 12$
    $x = 9 - 2y$

21. $3x - y = 13$
    $2x - 16 = {}^-3y$

22. $2x + y = 17$
    $5x = 25 + y$

23. $x - 2y = 8$
    $2y = 3x - 16$

24. $6y = x$
    $5y = 2x - 14$

Use the system of equations $x + 9y = 12$ and
$x - 3y = 6$ to solve.

25. Graph the system of equations to find the solution.
    In which quadrant is the solution?

26. At which point does $x + 9y = 12$ intersect the
    y-axis? the x-axis?

27. At which point does $x - 3y = 6$ intersect the
    y-axis? the x-axis?

28. Is each equation an equation of a function?

ANOTHER LOOK

Compare. Write $>$, $<$, or $=$ for ●.

1. 14.82 ● 14.83

2. 31.09 ● 31.092

3. 17.7 ● 17.69

4. 126.91 ● 128.9

5. 7.621 ● 7.66

6. 553.9 ● 553.90

Inequalities in Two Variables

Mathematical statements such as $y > x$ and $y \leq x$ are inequalities in two variables. These inequalities may be graphed by first graphing the related equation.

To graph $y > x$, first graph $y = x$.

x	$^-1$	0	1
y	$^-1$	0	1

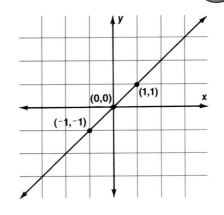

The straight line $y = x$ divides the plane into two half planes. Only the ordered pairs in one half plane make the inequality $y > x$ true.

Choose the test point $(2,1)$ to see whether it makes the inequality true.

$y > x$; $1 > 2$ is false. So, $(2,1)$ is not a solution of $y > x$. The half plane that does not include $(2,1)$ should be shaded. The broken line shows that points on the line $y = x$ are not solutions.

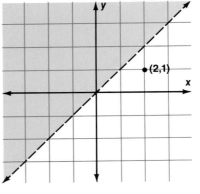

To graph $y \leq x$, graph $y = x$ again. You can use the same test point.

$y \leq x$; $1 \leq 2$ is true. So, the half plane that includes $(2,1)$ should be shaded. The solid line shows that points on the line are solutions.

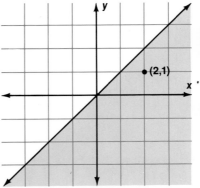

If the inequality does not go through the origin, you can use $(0,0)$ as the test point.

Math Reasoning, page H230

454

Write *yes* if the ordered pair is a solution of the inequality. Write *no* if it is not.

1. $y > 2x$; $(2,1)$

2. $y < x + 2$; $(3,^-1)$

3. $y \geq 2x - 1$; $(3,2)$

4. $y \geq x + 2$; $(4,3)$

5. $2x - y \leq 0$; $(5,4)$

6. $y < x - 1$; $(10,3)$

7. $x - y > 4$; $(3,2)$

8. $x + y < 6$; $(1,2)$

9. $3x - y \leq 6$; $(4,11)$

10. $x - 2y < 3$; $(4,1)$

Match the graph with the inequality.

11. $y \geq ^-x$

a.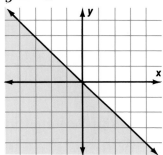

12. $y \leq ^-x$

b.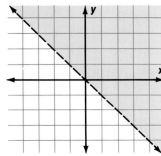

13. $y > ^-x$

c.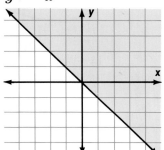

Match the graph with the inequality. Use $(0,0)$ as the test point.

14. $y > x + 1$

a.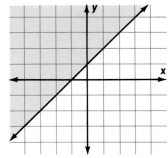

15. $y \geq x + 1$

b.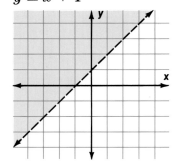

16. $y < x + 1$

c.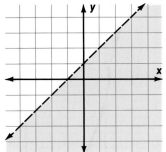

NUMBER SENSE

Compute mentally.

1. $15 + ^-6 - 7$

2. $12 - 8 - ^-6$

3. $28 - ^-16 + 8$

4. $^-66 - ^-21 + 7$

5. $18 + 62 - ^-10$

6. $^-7 + ^-8 - ^-26$

7. $^-36 - 18 + ^-80$

8. $9 - 7 + ^-6 - ^-4$

9. $^-5 - ^-5 + 10 + ^-12$

Graphing Inequalities in Two Variables

You can graph the solutions of an inequality in two variables
by first graphing the solutions of its related equation.

Solve. $\qquad y > 5 - 2x$

Write a related
equation. $\qquad y = 5 - 2x$

Make a table of values.

x	y = 5 − 2x	y	Solutions
1	$y = 5 - 2(1)$	3	(1,3)
0	$y = 5 - 2(0)$	5	(0,5)
⁻1	$y = 5 - 2(^-1)$	7	(⁻1,7)
⁻2	$y = 5 - 2(^-2)$	9	(⁻2,9)

Graph the solutions on coordinate axes.

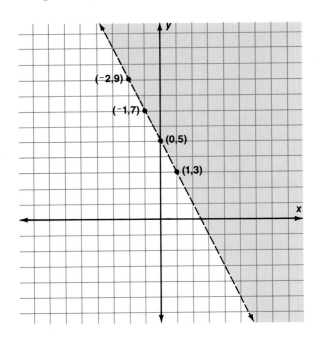

Use a broken line for $>$ or $<$. Choose
(0,0) as a test point to see if it makes
the inequality true. $y > 5 - 2x$; $0 > 5$ is
not true. The half plane that includes
(0,0) is not shaded.

Solve. $\qquad y \le 2x + 4$

Write a related
equation. $\qquad y = 2x + 4$

Make a table of values.

x	y = 2x + 4	y	Solutions
1	$y = 2(1) + 4$	6	(1,6)
0	$y = 2(0) + 4$	4	(0,4)
⁻1	$y = 2(^-1) + 4$	2	(⁻1,2)
⁻2	$y = 2(^-2) + 4$	0	(⁻2,0)

Graph the solutions on coordinate axes.

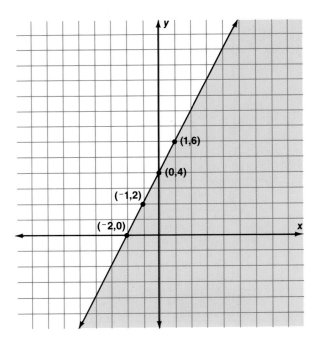

Use a solid line for $\ge$ or $\le$. Choose
(0,0) as a test point to see if it makes
the inequality true. $y \le 2x + 4$; $0 \le 4$ is
true. The half plane that includes (0,0) is
shaded.

456

Make a table of values for each inequality. Then graph the solutions.

1. $x + y < 6$

2. $x + 2y > 15$

3. $x + 4y \le 7$

4. $x \le 2y + 1$

5. $y \le 2x$

6. $x - y \ge 2$

7. $y - x < {}^-2$

8. $3x - 4y > 6$

9. $x - 2y \ge 4$

10. $y - x < 1$

11. $y \ge 2x + 1$

12. $2x - y \le 8$

13. $2x + y \le 5$

14. $3x - y \le 9$

15. $3x + y < 7$

16. $2x + y \ge 8$

17. $2x - y < 4$

18. $y > 3x$

19. $x + y \le 12$

20. $x - y > 2$

21. $x \le {}^-2y$

22. $y \le 4x$

23. $2x + 3y \le 9$

24. $x + 2y \le 6$

Write an inequality for each. Then graph it.

25. Twice a number x is less than three added to a number y.

26. A number y is more than two added to three times a second number x.

27. One number minus a second number is more than six.

★28. The sum of two numbers minus two is less than zero.

★29. The difference of two numbers divided by seven is less than four.

★30. The sum of two numbers divided by three is less than two times their difference.

CHALLENGE

Find the volume of each solid. Round to the nearest tenth.

1.

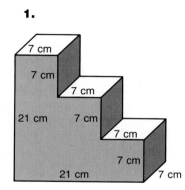

2.

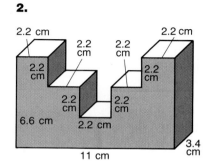

3.

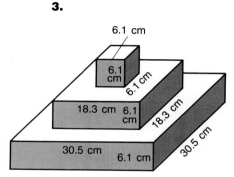

PROBLEM SOLVING
Choosing a Strategy or Method

Write the strategy or method you choose. Then solve.

Estimation
Drawing a Picture
Choosing the Operation
Solving Multi-step Problems
Guessing and Checking
Making a Table to Find a Pattern
Writing an Equation
Selecting Notation
Making an Organized List
Working Backward

1. Mark is making a map of his neighborhood. Starting in front of his house, he walks 3 blocks east to the post office. He then turns right and walks 4 blocks to the library. Turning right again, he walks 2 blocks, makes another right, and walks 2 blocks to the school. At the school, he turns west, walks 1 block, turns right, and walks 2 blocks. Does he end up at home? How many blocks does he have to walk to the library?

2. David is making a physical map of the area in which he lives. Forests make up $\frac{1}{3}$ of the map. Mountains make up $\frac{1}{2}$ the remaining land. Of the remaining area, residential areas make up 40 mi^2, leaving 27 mi^2 for Lake Gemini. How many square miles does David's map cover?

3. TV station WBBQ broadcasts national football games. It charges advertisers $15,750 for 15 seconds of prime time, $23,625 for 30 seconds, and $55,125 for 90 seconds. How much would 75 seconds of prime time cost?

4. A group of 6 people go to a restaurant. They can only get 2 tables that have 3 chairs each. How many different seating combinations could there be?

5. At a concert, 8 singers will sing solos and then duets. If each singer sings a duet with every other singer, how many duets will be performed?

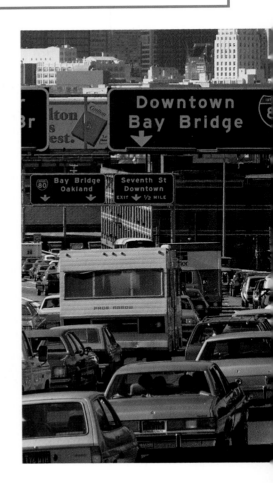

Choose a strategy or method and solve.

6. There is a 3-digit number. The sum of all three digits is 16. The first digit equals the sum of the remaining digits. The difference between the second and the third digits is 2. What is the number?

7. Murray has a green tie and an orange tie; a silver shirt and a striped shirt; a pink jacket and a purple jacket. List the different combinations of ties, shirts, and jackets he can wear.

8. Johnny, Ray, and Gene are camping. They have a jar that contains 12 quarts of juice, an empty 8-quart container, and an empty 4-quart container. Describe how they can divide the juice equally among themselves.

9. Acme Car Rental charges $26.50 to rent a car for one day. To rent a car for 2 days costs $40.00. For 3 days, the charge is $53.50, and so on. How much would it cost to rent a car for 6 days?

10. Sybil's family drove from Seattle, Washington, to Dallas, Texas. After driving 849 mi, they arrived in Salt Lake City, Utah. Driving 1,175 miles farther, they arrived in Oklahoma City, Oklahoma. From there, they drove back 263 mi to get something they left behind. Then, they drove 628 mi to Dallas. How many miles long is the route they took to Dallas?

11. Sonja took a walk around a right triangular block near her home in San Francisco, California. The perimeter of the block was 540 feet, and the area of the block was 12,150 square feet. If one of the sides of the block adjacent to the right angle was 135 feet long, how long was the longest side of the block?

12. There is a 4-digit number. The first digit is 2 greater than the second digit. The fourth digit is 3 greater than the third digit. The second and fourth digits are the same. The sum of the last two digits is 9. What is the number?

13. Choose one problem that you've already solved in this lesson. Show how you could use another method to solve this problem.

LOGICAL REASONING

You can use several statements to reach a new conclusion. The conclusion is said to be **valid** if it is impossible for the statements to be true and the conclusions to be false. Otherwise the conclusion is said to be **invalid.** Be sure to consider how *all, some,* and *none* are used before you reach a conclusion or before you determine whether a given conclusion is valid or invalid. Is the conclusion below valid or invalid?

Statements: Some of the spotted pets are dogs.
None of the spotted pets are black.
Conclusion: None of the dogs are black.

Think: You know that none of the spotted pets are black. If a dog is spotted, it is not black. But a dog does not have to be spotted. So, the conclusion is *invalid.*

Determine whether the conclusions are *valid* or *invalid.*

Statements

1. ● None of the members of the swim team play polo.
   ● All the divers are members of the swim team.

2. ● Some lizards hide under bushes.
   ● All snakes hide under bushes.

3. ● All elephants are hungry.
   ● None of the zoo animals are hungry.
   ● Some of the zoo animals have two legs.

4. ● Some of Angela's pets are rabbits.
   ● Some of the rabbits have black feet.

Conclusions

a. None of the divers play polo.
b. Some of the polo players are divers.

a. Some lizards are snakes.
b. All lizards are snakes.

a. There are no elephants in the zoo.
b. No animals with two legs are hungry.

a. All of Angela's pets have black feet.
b. None of Angela's pets have black feet.

GROUP PROJECT

Marathon Map

The problem: The members of the town's Athletic Club are planning a marathon, and your school has been asked to assist them. Your class is going to plan the course. Use the following information to work with your classmates in creating a map of the course. Your marathon map should be drawn to scale.

Key Facts

- A marathon is 26 miles and 385 yards long.

- No part of the course can be covered more than once. The course should pass through as many neighborhoods as possible.

- The course must vary in difficulty.

Key Questions

- Is there a natural route for such a race in your town?

- Can certain roads be closed during the race?

- Do you want to include places along the route where spectators can watch?

- What requirements must be followed in determining where to locate the starting line? the finish line?

- Can the course accommodate a large number of runners?

- Will your map include the locations of
  water stations?
  security personnel?
  timers?
  medical facilities?

CHAPTER TEST

Solve. Use 5 as the replacement value for x. Write each solution as an ordered pair. (pages 438–439)

1. $x + y = 7$

2. $2x + y = 13$

3. $x - 2y = 3$

4. $2x + 3y = 1$

5. $5x - y = 0$

6. $3x - 2y = 25$

Prepare a table of values for each equation and graph. (pages 440–441, 450–451)

7. $y = 2x + 1$

8. $x + y = 7$

9. $^-2x + y = {}^-1$

10. $2x + y = 16$

Prepare a table of values, and graph each system of equations on the same set of axes. (pages 452–453)

11. $x + y = 6$
$x - y = 2$

12. $x + 2y = 14$
$3y + x = 19$

13. $x + y = 6$
$x = 9 - 2y$

14. $2x + y = 10$
$x - y = 5$

Prepare a table of values for each inequality and graph the solutions. (pages 454–457)

15. $x \leq 3$

16. $2x - y > 3$

17. $3x + 2y \leq 8$

Solve. Draw a picture if necessary.
(pages 442–443 and 452–457)

18. Bob's house is 4 km due south of Town Hall. His house is 6 km due west of the post office. The train station is 9 km due east of Town Hall. How far is the post office from the train station?

19. Write a system of equations. Then solve by graphing.

3 times one number minus a second number is 14; twice one number plus a second number is 16.

20. Write and graph this inequality: One number is greater than three added to twice a second number.

21. Write and graph this inequality: Four times one number is less than 5 more than $\frac{1}{2}$ a second number.

BONUS

Solve.

Graph the equations $x + y = 4$, $x + 2 = y$, and $y = 2x + 4$. Write the points of intersection as ordered pairs.

RETEACHING

The equation $y = 5 - x$ is an equation in two variables that means that one number is equal to 5 minus another number. The solutions to this equation can be graphed as a line.

First, solve the equation by choosing a replacement value for one variable and then finding the value of the other variable that makes the statement true. Make a table of values.

x	y = 5 − x	y
2	3 = 5 − 2	3
1	4 = 5 − 1	4
7	⁻2 = 5 − 7	⁻2
⁻1	6 = 5 − ⁻1	6
4	1 = 5 − 4	1

(2,3)
(1,4)
(7,⁻2)
(⁻1,6)
(4,1)

The ordered pairs (2,3), (1,4), (7,⁻2), (⁻1,6), and (4,1) are solutions to the equation $y = 5 - x$. Many other solutions are possible.

Next, draw a pair of coordinate axes and graph the solutions from the table of values. Then, draw a line through the solutions that you have graphed.

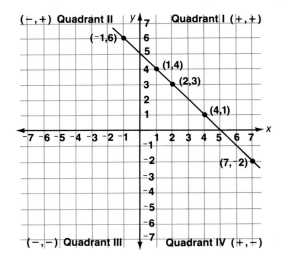

Make a table of values for each equation. Then graph each set of solutions.

1. $y = 9 - x$

2. $y = 2 - x$

3. $y = 6 - x$

4. $y = 14 + 2x$

5. $y = 6 - 4x$

6. $y = 3x$

7. $x - y = {}^-2$

8. $2x = {}^-4y$

9. $2x - y = 7$

ENRICHMENT

Graphing Parallel Lines

Graph the system of equations on the
same pair of axes.

$y = 2x$
$y = 2x + 4$

x	y = 2x	y
2	y = 2(2)	4
0	y = 2(0)	0
⁻2	y = 2(⁻2)	⁻4

Solutions
(2,4)
(0,0)
(⁻2,⁻4)

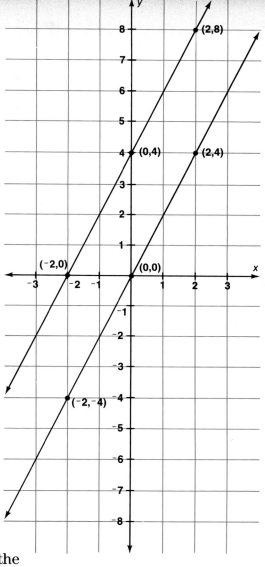

x	y = 2x + 4	y
2	y = 2(2) + 4	8
0	y = 2(0) + 4	4
⁻2	y = 2(⁻2) + 4	0

Solutions
(2,8)
(0,4)
(⁻2,0)

As you can see from the graph at right,
the line $y = 2x$ is parallel to the line
$y = 2x + 4$.

Graph each system of equations. State whether the
lines are *parallel* or *not parallel*.

1. $y = 3x$
$\quad y = 3x - 6$

2. $y = 4x + 2$
$\quad y = 4x + 4$

3. $y = 5x + 10$
$\quad y = 5x + 5$

4. $x + y = 7$
$\quad 2x + 2y = 4$

5. $y = 2 - 4x$
$\quad y + 4x = 4$

6. $3x - 3y = 6$
$\quad y = x$

7. $y = 4x + 4$
$\quad y = 3x + 3$

8. $5y - 5x = 5$
$\quad x = y + 2$

9. $7x + 7y = 14$
$\quad 3x + 3y = 6$

465

TECHNOLOGY

This procedure uses the REPEAT command, two variables, and division to draw a polygon that has any length side and any size angle.

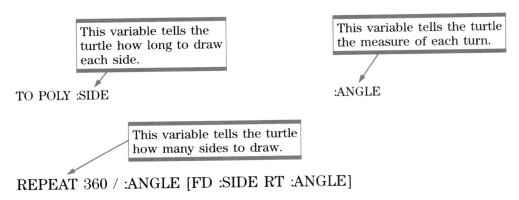

This variable tells the turtle how long to draw each side.

This variable tells the turtle the measure of each turn.

TO POLY :SIDE

:ANGLE

This variable tells the turtle how many sides to draw.

REPEAT 360 / :ANGLE [FD :SIDE RT :ANGLE]

END

HINT: In drawing any polygon, the turtle makes one complete turn of 360°. Therefore, the measure of any single turn the turtle makes divided by 360° will tell the turtle how many sides to draw.

Write the number of sides each of these figures would have if they were drawn by using the POLY procedure.

1. POLY 60 120
2. POLY 100 90
3. POLY 30 45
4. POLY 60 72

Use this table for Exercises 5–8.

Measure of each turn	120°	90°	72°	60°	45°	40°
Number of sides	3	4	5	6	8	9

Write POLY procedures to draw each of the following figures.

5.

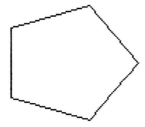

6.

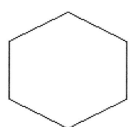

7.

8.

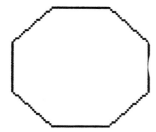

CUMULATIVE REVIEW

Write the letter of the correct answer.

1. What is the length of the hypotenuse in a right triangle that has legs of 5 meters and 12 meters?

a. $\sqrt{119}$ m   b. 13 m
c. 60 m   d. not given

2. What is the circumference? Use 3.14 for π.

a. 7.85 cm   b. 15.7 cm
c. 19.63 cm   d. not given

3. Choose the correct ratio for the cosine of $\angle A$.

a. $\frac{a}{c}$ b. $\frac{a}{b}$
c. $\frac{b}{c}$ d. not given

4. Find the area. Use 3.14 for π.

a. 9.42 m^2
b. 18.84 m^2
c. 28.26 m^2
d. not given

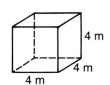

5. Find the surface area.

a. 60 m^2
b. 96 m^2
c. 160 m^2
d. not given

6. Find the volume.

a. 15 cm^3
b. 50 cm^3
c. 60 cm^3
d. not given

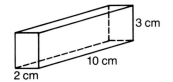

7. Which quadrant is $(^-8,2)$ in?

a. Quadrant I   b. Quadrant II
c. Quadrant III   d. not given

8. Which is the alternate interior angle for $\angle 3$?

a. $\angle 1$
b. $\angle 5$
c. $\angle 2$
d. not given

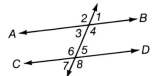

9. The two polygons are similar. What is the measure of side $\overline{AB}$?

a. 10
b. 16
c. 20
d. not given

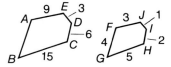

10. A triangular prism has a height of 12 cm and a base of 24 cm^2. What is its volume?

a. 144 cm^3 b. 288 cm^3
c. 576 cm^3 d. not given

11. George timed his weekly workout on the school track. According to his scattergram, what would you expect his average running time to be for Week 5?

a. 90   b. 100
c. 110   d. not given

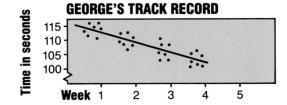

GEORGE'S TRACK RECORD

Connecting Math Ideas

Page 13   Identifying Relationships

Some problems can be solved by using a logic table.

James, Martin, and Tasha play in the school band. One plays the drum, one plays the trumpet, and one plays the flute. Copy the table and use the clues to find who plays each instrument. Use an X to show that a possibility cannot be true. Use a $\sqrt{}$ when you are certain that a possibility is true.

Clue 1: James is a senior.
Clue 2: James and the trumpet player practice together after school.
Clue 3: Martin and the flute player are sophomores.

	Drum	Trumpet	Flute
James			
Martin			
Tasha			

Page 39   Exploring Other Number Systems

The example at the right shows an ancient Hindu method of adding the whole numbers 2, 32, 143, and 335.

Sum of ones: $2 + 2 + 3 + 5 = $ 12
Sum of tens: $3 + 4 + 3 = $ 10
Sum of hundreds: $1 + 3 = $ 4
Sum of the sums: 512

Use the ancient Hindu method to find the following sums.

1. $8 + 16 + 22 + 145$

2. $5 + 22 + 45 + 202$

3. $36 + 123 + 465 + 62$

4. $56 + 732 + 128 + 3 + 19$

Page 75   Extending the Investigation of Number Patterns

This is a famous number sequence called the **Fibonacci sequence.**

$$1, 1, 2, 3, 5, 8, 13, 21, \ldots$$

The **Golden Number,** or Golden Ratio, is 1.618 . . . If you divide any number in the Fibonacci sequence by the previous number, the quotient is an approximation of the Golden Number. For example, $13 \div 8 = 1.625$.

Use a calculator and the Fibonacci sequence to find 5 approximations for the Golden Number.

Page 85 Extending Scientific Notation

You can add two numbers written in scientific notation if the numbers have the same power of 10.

Example: $4.5 \times 10^3 + 3.2 \times 10^3 = (4.5 + 3.2) \times 10^3$
$$= 7.7 \times 10^3$$

Add. Write the sum in scientific notation.

1. $4.66 \times 10^5 + 1.2 \times 10^5$ **2.** $2.78 \times 10^2 + 5.01 \times 10^2$ **3.** $9.23 \times 10^7 + 2 \times 10^7$

Page 109 Solving Application Problems by Solving Linear Equations

A formula can be solved as an equation if you know the values of all but one of the variables.

Example: Use the formula $U = P \div n$ where $U =$ the unit price, $P =$ the total price, and $n =$ the number of units to find the total price of a 305-gram can of soup that has a unit price of $0.002.

$U = P \div n$ ◄——— Replace U with 0.002 and n with 305.
$0.002 = P \div 305$
$0.002 \times 305 = P \div 305 \times 305$
$0.61 = P$ ◄——— The total price is $0.61.

Use the formula $U = P \div n$ to find the missing value of the variable.

1. $U = \$0.03$ per gram
$P = \square$
$n = 68$ grams

2. $U = \$0.12$ per foot
$P = \square$
$n = 25$ feet

3. $U = \square$
$P = \$5.62$
$n = 8$ pounds

Page 147 Drawing Three-Dimensional Figures from Different Perspectives

Look at the cube at the bottom of page 147.

1. What do you know about the shape of each side of the large cube?

2. Draw what you would see if you looked at the large cube from the top.

3. Suppose you removed one small cube from the large cube. Draw how the small cube would look if it were in the same position as the large cube.

Page 171 Relating Metric Measures

You can find the volume, capacity, and mass of rectangular containers that are not cubes.

Example: length = 4 cm, height = 5 cm, width = 6 cm
Volume = length × width × height
$$= 4 \times 5 \times 6$$
$$= 120 \text{ cm}^3, \text{ capacity} = 120 \text{ mL, mass} = 120 \text{ g}$$

Copy and complete the chart for each container of water.

Length	Width	Height	Volume	Capacity	Mass
1. 8 cm	7 cm	2 cm	112 cm³	▩ mL	▩ g
2. 8 m	5 m	3 m	▩ m³	▩ kL	▩ t
3. 7 m	5 m	400 cm	▩ m³	▩ kL	▩ t

Page 255 Extending Scientific Notation

You can multiply numbers that are written in scientific notation.

Example: $(2.3 \cdot 10^3) \cdot (8.5 \cdot 10^2) = (2.3 \cdot 8.5) \cdot (10^3 \cdot 10^2)$
$$= 19.55 \cdot 10^5$$
$$= 1.955 \cdot 10^6$$

Multiply. Write the product in scientific notation.

1. $(4.2 \cdot 10^3) \cdot (7.1 \cdot 10^4)$ **2.** $(8.2 \cdot 10^3) \cdot (4.5 \cdot 10^5)$

3. $(6 \cdot 10^5) \cdot (4.8 \cdot 10^{-2})$ **4.** $(3.1 \cdot 10^8) \cdot (8.7 \cdot 10^{-3})$

Page 319 Investigating Formats for Presenting Data

The stem-and-leaf plot at the right is a useful way to display data. The numbers on the left are called the stems, and the numbers on the right are called the leaves. The stem and leaf 5 | 2 represents a test score of 52.

Test Scores

```
5 | 2358
6 | 0034688
7 | 0112455788
8 | 00123358899
9 | 13478
```

1. Tell how many test scores are shown in the stem-and-leaf plot.

2. What is the median of the test scores?

3. Make a stem-and-leaf plot of the data shown for Exercises 1–6 on page 315.

Page 325 Investigating Formats for Presenting Data

A box-and-whisker graph is another way to display data. The box-and-whisker graph below displays the data for math class quiz scores.

Example:

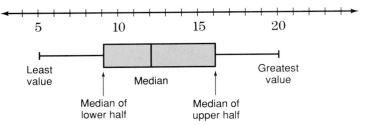

Use the data below for Exercises 1–4.
Weights (in kilograms): 32, 33, 34, 34, 36, 40, 41, 43, 45, 47, 48, 49, 50, 52, 54, 58, 62, 63, 65, 68, 71

1. Find the median of the data.

2. Find the median of the lower half of the data (from 32 to 47).

3. Find the median of the upper half of the data (from 49 to 71).

4. What is the least value? the greatest value?

5. Using the box-and-whisker graph shown above as an example and your answers to Exercises 1–4, make a box-and-whisker graph for the data.

Page 425 Exploring the Volume of Pyramids and Prisms

Draw these figures using the dimensions given. Then assemble the pyramid and prism.

1. Fill the pyramid with sand. Then pour this sand into the prism. Repeat this process until the prism is full.

2. How many times did you pour sand from the pyramid into the prism?

3. Write a sentence to tell how the volume of the pyramid compares to the volume of the prism.

4. Based on your experiment, write the formulas for the volume of the pyramid and the volume of the prism.

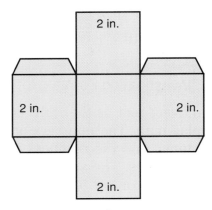

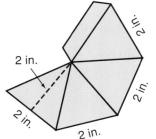

Infobank

APPROXIMATE LENGTH OF PRINCIPAL RIVERS OF THE WORLD

River	Miles	Kilometers
Amazon	3,912	6,296
Mississippi/Missouri	3,880	6,240
Niger	2,600	4,184
Nile	4,180	6,690
Yangtze	3,602	5,797

SPECIFIC GRAVITY OF MINERALS

Mineral	Specific gravity
Barite	4.50
Graphite	2.09–2.23
Magnesite	2.98–3.44
Olivine	3.22–4.39

NUTRITIONAL VALUE OF VEGETABLES, FRESH COOKED, PER CUP

	Carbohydrates (grams)	Protein (grams)
Broccoli	7.0	4.8
Cauliflower	5.1	2.9
Celery	4.7	1.2
Corn	31.0	5.3
Green beans	6.8	2.0
Okra	9.6	3.2
Peas	19.4	8.6
Spinach	6.5	5.4

ADVENTURES IN TRAVELING

Announces New Low
Bus & Van Rentals

Weekly rates:
43-passenger bus $3,278.75
47-passenger bus $3,583.75
12 passenger van $1,134.00

CUBES AND CUBE ROOTS

N	N^3	$\sqrt[3]{N}$	N	N^3	$\sqrt[3]{N}$
1	1	1.000	26	17,576	2.962
2	8	1.260	27	19,683	3.000
3	27	1.442	28	21,952	3.037
4	64	1.587	29	24,389	3.072
5	125	1.710	30	27,000	3.107
6	216	1.817	31	29,791	3.141
7	343	1.913	32	32,768	3.175
8	512	2.000	33	35,937	3.208
9	729	2.080	34	39,304	3.240
10	1000	2.154	35	42,875	3.271
11	1331	2.224	36	46,656	3.302
12	1728	2.289	37	50,653	3.332
13	2197	2.351	38	54,872	3.362
14	2744	2.410	39	59,319	3.391
15	3375	2.466	40	64,000	3.420
16	4096	2.520	41	68,921	3.448
17	4913	2.571	42	74,088	3.476
18	5832	2.621	43	79,507	3.503
19	6859	2.668	44	85,184	3.530
20	8000	2.714	45	91,125	3.557
21	9261	2.759	46	97,336	3.583
22	10,648	2.802	47	103,823	3.609
23	12,167	2.844	48	110,592	3.634
24	13,824	2.884	49	117,649	3.659
25	15,625	2.924	50	125,000	3.684

BASKET-WEAVING SUPPLIES

Material	Available sizes	Amount sold
Sea grass	$\frac{3}{16}$ in.	3-lb coil (600 ft)
Flat reed	$\frac{1}{4}$ in., $\frac{3}{8}$ in., $\frac{1}{2}$ in., $\frac{5}{8}$ in.	by the lb
Flat oval reed	$\frac{1}{4}$ in., $\frac{3}{8}$ in.	by the lb
Round reed	$\frac{3}{8}$ in., $\frac{1}{2}$ in., $\frac{5}{8}$ in.	by the lb
Fiber rush	$\frac{3}{32}$ in., $\frac{4}{32}$ in., $\frac{5}{32}$ in., $\frac{6}{32}$ in.	by the lb (250 ft)
White ash or oak	$\frac{5}{8}$ in.	15-strand bundle (6–8 ft)

DISTANCES FROM PERTH TO SYDNEY

Perth–Coolgardie. 537
Perth–Nullarbor. 1,418
Perth–Port Augusta 2,051
Perth–Broken Hill 2,404
Perth–Dubbo. 3,067
Perth–Orange 3,100
Perth–Sydney 3,278

HEIDI'S HEARTY CHICKEN NOODLE SOUP
19 ounces

INGREDIENTS: chicken stock, chicken, enriched egg noodles, mushrooms, carrots, celery, sauterne wine, corn starch, water, salt, sweet peppers, potato starch, yeast extract, hydrolyzed plant protein, monosodium glutamate, natural flavoring, and dehydrated parsley

**Nutrition information
per serving**

Serving size	$9\frac{1}{2}$ oz (269 g)
Servings per container	2
Calories	140
Protein (g)	12
Total carbohydrates (g)	12
simple sugars (g)	1
complex carbohydrates (g)	11
Fat (g)	7
Sodium	1,070 mg/serving

Percentage of U.S. Recommended Daily Allowance (U.S. RDA)

Protein	25%	Riboflavin	10%
Vitamin A	20%	Niacin	20%
Vitamin C	2%	Calcium	2%
Thiamine	6%	Iron	10%

FOUNDING (ESTABLISHMENT) OF FOUR EUROPEAN CITIES

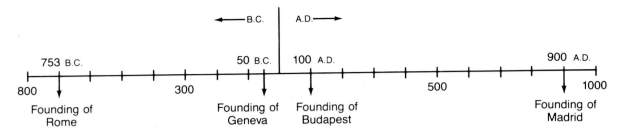

753 B.C. — Founding of Rome
50 B.C. — Founding of Geneva
100 A.D. — Founding of Budapest
900 A.D. — Founding of Madrid

TELEVISION SYSTEMS OF THE WORLD

Region or country	Number of lines per frame	Number of pictures per second
United Kingdom	405–625	25
North America, South America, Japan	525	30
Europe, Australia, Africa, Eurasia	625	25
France and French dependents	625–819	25

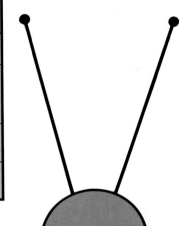

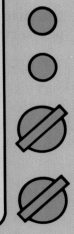

In movies, the illusion of movement is created by projecting a series of still pictures, one after another.

In television, each frame is "drawn" by an electronic scanning spot that races across the screen in straight horizontal lines from top to bottom. When it has finished, it has completed one frame, and returns to the top to begin another. It takes two frames to make one picture. The process is so fast that what we see is moving pictures.

NBA SCORING LEADERS

Year	Scoring champion	Pts	Avg	Year	Scoring champion	Pts	Avg
1950	George Mikan, Minneapolis	1,865	27.4	1970	Jerry West, Los Angeles	2,309	31.2
1951	George Mikan, Minneapolis	1,932	28.4	1971	Lew Alcindor, Milwaukee	2,596	31.7
1952	Paul Arizin, Philadelphia	1,674	25.4	1972	Kareem Abdul-Jabar, Milwaukee	2,822	34.8
1953	Neil Johnston, Philadelphia	1,564	22.3	1973	Nate Archibald, Kansas City-Omaha	2,719	34.0
1954	Neil Johnston, Philadelphia	1,759	24.4	1974	Bob McAdoo, Buffalo	2,261	30.8
1955	Neil Johnston, Philadelphia	1,631	22.7	1975	Bob McAdoo, Buffalo	2,831	34.5
1956	Bob Pettit, St. Louis	1,849	25.7	1976	Bob McAdoo, Buffalo	2,427	31.1
1957	Paul Arizin, Philadelphia	1,817	25.6	1977	Pete Maravich, New Orleans	2,273	31.1
1958	George Yardley, Detroit	2,001	27.8	1978	George Gervin, San Antonio	2,232	27.2
1959	Bob Pettit, St. Louis	2,105	29.2	1979	George Gervin, San Antonio	2,365	29.6
1960	Wilt Chamberlain, Philadelphia	2,707	37.6	1980	George Gervin, San Antonio	2,585	33.1
1961	Wilt Chamberlain, Philadelphia	3,033	38.4	1981	Adrian Dantley, Utah	2,452	30.7
1962	Wilt Chamberlain, Philadelphia	4,029	50.4	1982	George Gervin, San Antonio	2,551	32.3
1963	Wilt Chamberlain, San Francisco	3,586	44.8	1983	Alex English, Denver	2,326	28.4
1964	Wilt Chamberlain, San Francisco	2,948	36.9	1984	Adrian Dantley, Utah	2,418	30.6
1965	Wilt Chamberlain, San Fran., Phila.	2,534	34.7	1985	Bernard King, New York	1,809	32.9
1966	Wilt Chamberlain, Philadelphia	2,649	33.5	1986	Dominique Wilkins, Atlanta	2,366	30.3
1967	Rick Barry, San Francisco	2,775	35.6	1987	Michael Jordan, Chicago	3,041	37.1
1968	Dave Bing, Detroit	2,142	27.1	1988	Michael Jordan, Chicago	2,868	35.0
1969	Elvin Hayes, San Diego	2,327	28.4	1989	Michael Jordan, Chicago	2,633	32.5

ABSTRACT REPRESENTATION OF A HOUSE: GREENVILLE, DELAWARE

AMERICA'S TALLEST BUILDINGS AND MONUMENTS

Structure	Height (ft)
A. Lake Point Towers, Chicago, tallest apartment building	640
B. Peachtree Center Plaza, Atlanta, tallest hotel	754
C. Chrysler Building, New York	1,046
D. Empire State Building, New York	1,250 without mast 1,472 with mast
E. World Trade Center, New York	1,377
F. Sears Tower, Chicago, tallest office building	1,454 without mast 1,559 with mast
G. Statue of Liberty, New York	301 including pedestal
H. Washington Monument, Washington, D.C.	555
I. San Jacinto Column, Texas, tallest monument column	570
J. Gateway Arch, St. Louis, Missouri	630

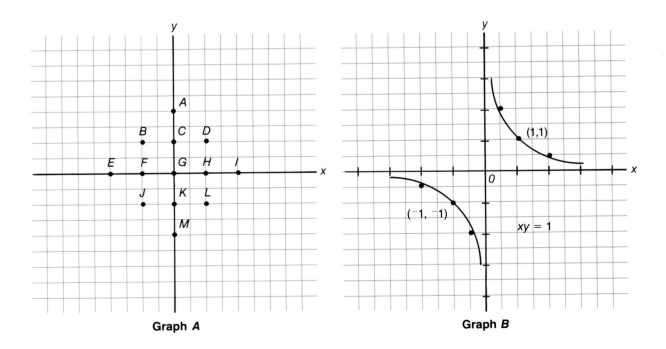

Graph *A*

Graph *B*

STUDENT HANDBOOK

Write the number in standard form.

1. 964 trillion, 200 billion, 701 million, 16 thousand

2. 18 trillion, 322 million, 941 thousand, 1

3. one million, thirty thousand, six hundred seventy-eight

Write the short word name for each number.

4. 73,079,937

5. 9,251,865,804

6. 100,200,600,900,700

Write the value of each underlined digit.

7. 43,<u>5</u>06,971,384

8. 6<u>2</u>1,335,954,628,168

Solve.

9. Hector went to visit his sister Luisa at Yale University. He was impressed with the libraries there. Luisa told him that Yale has more than 8,391,707 books. How would Hector write this number in expanded form?

Write >, <, or =.

1. 674,476 ◯ 476,674

2. 98,697,996 ◯ 100,402,140

3. 24,671 ◯ 24,617

4. 200,020,020 ◯ 200,020,200

5. 678,675 ◯ 678,675

6. 111,111,111 ◯ 11,111,111

7. forty-nine million ◯ forty-nine billion

8. two hundred twenty trillion ◯ two hundred two trillion

Write each group of numbers from the greatest to the least.

9. 27,490,179; 22,790,197; 24,790,719; 6,947,791; 24,400,420

Write each group of numbers from the least to the greatest.

10. 999,999; 55,555; 9,999; 555,555; 55,555,555

11. 8,808; 80,880; 88,008; 8,080; 80,808

Solve.

12. In 1980, the estimated population of Australia was 13,548,448. In 1980, the estimated population of the Netherlands was 13,060,115. Which country had a larger estimated population?

13. In 1980, the estimated population of the Fiji Islands was 588,068. In 1980, the estimated population of Mongolia was 1,594,800. Which country had a larger estimated population?

Write the missing number.

1. $757 + 468 = 468 + \underline{\quad ? \quad}$

2. $9{,}003 - 0 = \underline{\quad ? \quad}$

3. $759 + 0 = \underline{\quad ? \quad}$

4. $(15 + 47) + 26 = 15 + (\underline{\quad ? \quad} + 26)$

5. $287 - 287 = \underline{\quad ? \quad}$

6. $217 + 308 = \underline{\quad ? \quad} + 217$

7. $94 + (62 + 22) = (94 + 62) + \underline{\quad ? \quad}$

8. $6{,}280 + 0 = \underline{\quad ? \quad}$

9. $104 - 0 = \underline{\quad ? \quad}$

10. $5{,}091 - 5{,}091 = \underline{\quad ? \quad}$

11. $7{,}462 + 6{,}186 = \underline{\quad ? \quad} + 7{,}462$

12. $80 + 246 = 246 + \underline{\quad ? \quad}$

13. $41{,}001 + 0 = \underline{\quad ? \quad}$

14. $175 - 0 = \underline{\quad ? \quad}$

15. $(31 + 91) + 58 = 31 + (\underline{\quad ? \quad} + 58)$

16. $9 + 0 = \underline{\quad ? \quad}$

17. $19{,}539 - 19{,}539 = \underline{\quad ? \quad}$

18. $1{,}763 - 1{,}763 = \underline{\quad ? \quad}$

19. $4{,}891 + 9{,}746 = 9{,}746 + \underline{\quad ? \quad}$

20. $39 + (25 + 10) = (39 + 25) + \underline{\quad ? \quad}$

21. $615 - 0 = \underline{\quad ? \quad}$

22. $47 + 86 = \underline{\quad ? \quad} + 47$

23. $16 + (37 + 91) = (16 + 37) + \underline{\quad ? \quad}$

24. $503 - 0 = \underline{\quad ? \quad}$

25. $601 - 601 = \underline{\quad ? \quad}$

26. $999 + 0 = \underline{\quad ? \quad}$

27. $275 + 353 = \underline{\quad ? \quad} + 275$

28. $(41 + 19) + 15 = \underline{\quad ? \quad} + (19 + 15)$

29. $61{,}580 - 0 = \underline{\quad ? \quad}$

30. $697 - 697 = \underline{\quad ? \quad}$

31. $(15 + 50) + 54 = 15 + (\underline{\quad ? \quad} + 54)$

32. $45 - 0 = \underline{\quad ? \quad}$

33. $6{,}743 + 0 = \underline{\quad ? \quad}$

34. $(27 + 18) + 98 = 27 + (\underline{\quad ? \quad} + 98)$

35. $9{,}132 - 9{,}132 = \underline{\quad ? \quad}$

36. $413 + 62 = 62 + \underline{\quad ? \quad}$

37. $397 - 0 = \underline{\quad ? \quad}$

38. $9{,}007 + 0 = \underline{\quad ? \quad}$

39. $452 + 810 = 810 + \underline{\quad ? \quad}$

40. $550 - 550 = \underline{\quad ? \quad}$

The Ecology Club is collecting aluminum cans, glass bottles, and newspapers for recycling. The club will use money from the sale of these items to buy posters, T-shirts, paint, and membership cards. The club has to place an order before it knows exactly how much it will take in from the items.

Here is some information:

- Renting a truck costs about $55 a day.
- Supplies, such as twine, bags, scissors, and gloves, cost $25 per week.
- Within 3 weeks, the club will collect $210–$362.50 worth of cans and bottles.
- Within 3 weeks, the club will collect $372–$672 worth of newspapers.

300 Posters $225
100 T-shirts $175
8 Gallons of paint $80
500 Membership cards $100

Answer each question to help the club make choices about which combination of items to order. You may have to go back and revise figures as you work.

1. How much money will the club collect from the sale of cans, bottles, and newspapers after 3 weeks? Should the club underestimate or overestimate the amount? Why?

2. How much money should the club plan to spend for renting a truck if the truck is needed for only 2 days to make deliveries to the recycling plant? Should they underestimate or overestimate the amount? Why?

3. How much should the club plan to spend for supplies? Should they underestimate or overestimate the amount? Why?

4. How much money should the club expect to take in from the sale of bottles, cans, and newspapers after paying for the truck and for supplies?

5. What is the greatest amount of money the club can expect to earn after expenses?

6. Which two items should the club order? Explain why.

Write > or <.

1. 4,235 + 7,186 $\bigcirc$ 11,000

2. 5,134 + 4,389 $\bigcirc$ 10,000

3. $79.65 + $28.57 $\bigcirc$ $100

4. $564.39 + $228.88 $\bigcirc$ $800

5. 51,764 + 9,275 + 23,459 $\bigcirc$ 80,000

6. 36,297 + 58,498 $\bigcirc$ 100,000

7. 492,716 + 236,459 $\bigcirc$ 750,000

8. 789,265 + 976,296 $\bigcirc$ 1,600,000

Estimate each sum.

9.
```
   5,237
   1,789
   3,465
 + 7,559
```

10.
```
   4,369
      87
   9,063
 + 4,527
```

11.
```
  $ 9.53
    0.07
    0.39
 +  15.18
```

12.
```
  3,276,546
     11,327
  2,176,549
+ 1,527,461
```

13.
```
   4,937
   2,175
   5,186
 + 7,559
```

14.
```
   2,759
     175
 + 6,108
```

15.
```
  $39.88
    0.79
 +  1.08
```

16.
```
  4,175,268
    895,317
+ 2,105,639
```

Solve. Use the information in the table to answer these questions.

17. On which two days was the total attendance about 25,000?

18. On which two days was the total attendance about 50,000?

19. On which two days did the total attendance exceed 100,000?

State Fair	
Day	**Attendance**
Monday	12,654
Tuesday	17,859
Wednesday	7,236
Thursday	9,389
Friday	29,358
Saturday	85,465

Write > or <.

1. 8,165 − 2,089 ◯ 6,000

2. 5,896 − 1,547 ◯ 4,000

3. 6,129 − 387 ◯ 6,000

4. 19,537 − 5,387 ◯ 14,000

5. $48.65 − $19.85 ◯ $20.00

6. $96.37 − $9.55 ◯ $85.00

7. 26,576 − 19,865 ◯ 10,000

8. 82,179 − 19,583 ◯ 60,000

9. 486,925 − 95,467 ◯ 400,000

10. 689,278 − 417,885 ◯ 200,000

11. 5,176,429 − 875,265 ◯ 4,000,000

12. 18,752,469 − 7,895,265 ◯ 10,000,000

Estimate.

13.
```
  4,836
−   978
```

14.
```
  7,234
− 4,187
```

15.
```
  $79.56
−  15.89
```

16.
```
  $118.87
−   79.59
```

17.
```
  53,476
−  8,958
```

18.
```
  81,647
− 25,879
```

19.
```
  74,529
− 25,287
```

20.
```
  435,276
−  89,197
```

Solve.

21. About how many more people attended Thursday than Wednesday?

22. Did over 25,000 more people attend Friday than attended Thursday?

23. About how many more people attended Saturday than Monday?

24. Did 5,000 more people attend Tuesday than Monday?

Date	Attendance
Monday	14,567
Tuesday	18,081
Wednesday	5,869
Thursday	30,287
Friday	54,895
Saturday	61,457

Add or subtract. Check your answers by estimating.

1. 4,887,472
\+ 1,633,993

2. 411,392
860,128
341,274
\+ 602,835

3. $90,751.04
\- 61,562.46

4. 435 billion
\+ 125 billion

5. $3,839.58
58.20
514.36
\+   967.26

6. 9,704,152
\-   48,345

7. 635 trillion
\- 558 trillion

8. 1,546,360
\+   42,350

9. 7,933,066
\- 4,278,109

10. 94 million
\+ 8 million

11. 394,012
679,293
5,653
\+ 424,844

12. $9,034,842
\-   595,961

13. 237 billion
\- 54 billion

14. $21,126.75
\+   47.05

15. 1,470,422
\-   315,683

16. 385,807
583,415
923,847
\+ 782,044

17. 625,363
9,402
339,930
\+ 415,806

18. 3,459,408
\- 2,234,005

19. 857 million
\+ 115 million

20. $84,237.11
\+ 35,681.25

21. 210 trillion
\- 13 trillion

22. $173,820
976,472
7,341
\+   14,399

23. 6,247,768
\+   126,544

24. 5,783,504
\-   24,064

25. 7,014,499 − 227,192 = _____?_____

26. 9,467,977 + 6,285,461 = _____?_____

27. 22,036 + 3,191 + 91,838 = _____?_____

28. 7,462,023 − 6,386,803 = _____?_____

29. _____?_____ − 817,456 = 123,739

30. 9,624,004 − _____?_____ = 9,326,417

Use the information in the table. Solve each problem using the four-step plan.

- State the problem in your own words.
- Tell which tools you will use.
- Solve the problem.
- Check your solution.

OLDEST NATIONAL PARKS		
Park	Year	Area (Acres)
Yellowstone	1872	2,219,785
Kings Canyon	1890	461,901
Sequoia	1890	402,482
Yosemite	1890	761,170

1. How old is Yellowstone National Park?

2. Suppose you could transplant parks. How many Yosemite National Parks

3. How many acres of land were set aside as national parks in 1890?

4. List the four oldest parks in order from smallest to largest.

5. An average acre in Sequoia National Park contains about 50 trees. About how many trees are there in Sequoia National Park?

6. An average camper uses 1.5 acres of land during a visit. How many campers can Yosemite accommodate at one time?

7. The National Park Service manages 68,234,091 acres of federal land. How many Yellowstone National Parks could fit in this area?

8. The summit of Yosemite's highest mountain is 3,960 meters above sea level. The lowest point in Death Valley is 86 meters below sea level. How high above the lowest point is the summit of Yosemite's highest mountain?

Use with pages 16–17.

Write the decimal.

1. five hundred ninety-eight thousandths

2. thirteen thousand, five hundred twenty-two hundred-thousandths

3. one millionth

4. one thousand one millionths

5. one and ninety-eight hundredths

Write the word name for each number.

6. 0.4786

7. 13.925684

8. 143.75669

9. 0.46539

10. 5.01

Write the value of each underlined digit.

11. 0.92<u>5</u>84

12. 23,809.2<u>3</u>809

13. 57,174.4<u>7</u>601

14. 0.602<u>4</u>58

15. 2373.28789<u>9</u>

Write >, <, or =.

1. 229.783938 ◯ 229.7839348

2. 0.999999 ◯ 1

3. 5,674.0123 ◯ 5,674.123

4. 6.00002 ◯ 6.000002

5. 323,956.987453 ◯ 323,956.985753

6. 8.034 ◯ 80.34

7. 1.019872 ◯ 1.919872

8. 1.00000 ◯ 1.00

9. 0.333 ◯ 0.3333

10. 10.0 ◯ 100.00000

11. 57.345 ◯ 57.345

12. 0.99999 ◯ 0.1

Write each group of decimals from the least to the greatest.

13. 0.656, 0.565, 0.6565, 0.56565, 0.65

14. 0.456789, 0.6789, 0.56789, 0.789, 0.89

15. 0.000666, 0.066006, 0.00666, 0.006066, 0.006606

16. 0.53298, 0.52398, 0.54398, 0.54298, 0.534

Write each group of decimals from the greatest to the least.

17. 0.747447, 0.744774, 0.477447, 0.747474, 0.774774

18. 0.9286, 0.9386, 0.8386, 0.9376, 0.928

19. 0.564897, 0.563997, 0.563897, 0.564997, 0.564887

20. 0.000003, 0.003, 0.0003, 0.00003, 0.03

Use with pages 20–21.

Round to the nearest whole number.

1. 0.9111 **2.** 0.1605 **3.** 23.47108 **4.** 55.555

5. 7.553 **6.** 0.894 **7.** 15.823 **8.** 83.001

Round to the nearest tenth or to the nearest ten cents.

9. 93.451 **10.** $0.88 **11.** 0.94738 **12.** $1.6302

13. 0.387 **14.** 14.567 **15.** 8.3219 **16.** $75.099

Round to the nearest hundredth or to the nearest cent.

17. 0.96679 **18.** $40.6731 **19.** $0.8263 **20.** 9.14131

21. $7.5681 **22.** 0.01895 **23.** 5.36521 **24.** $27.8095

Round to the nearest thousandth.

25. 0.87835508 **26.** 19.99999

27. 521.802267 **28.** 0.044133

29. 46.905371 **30.** 5.000932

Round to the nearest ten-thousandth.

31. 402.98434892 **32.** 7,017.53268

33. 0.5678687 **34.** 70.3295681

35. 0.22225 **36.** 5.605987

The chart below shows some famous ocean voyages, the ships that made them, and the distance and duration of the voyages.

Year	From	To	Ship	Distance (Nautical miles)	Duration
1840	Halifax	Liverpool	*Brittania*	2,610	9 days 21 hours
1854	Liverpool	New York	*Baltic*	3,037	9 days 17 hours
1928	San Pedro	Honolulu	*USS Lexington*	2,226	3 days 1 hour
1944	Halifax	Vancouver	*St. Roch*	7,295	86 days
1950	Japan	San Francisco	*USS Boxer*	5,000	7 days 19 hours
1962	New York	Capetown	*African Comet*	6,786	12 days 16 hours

Do you need the Infobank above to solve the problems?
Write *yes* or *no*.

1. The *Brittania* was the first Cunard liner. Cunard was named after Sir Samuel Cunard, who was born in 1787 and died in 1865. How many years did he live?

2. The *St. Roch* was the first vessel to complete the Northwest Passage in one season. How many more miles was its voyage than the voyage of the *Brittania* from Halifax to Liverpool?

Solve. Use the Infobank above for any additional information you need.

3. In 1846, the *Yorkshire* traveled from Liverpool to New York in 16 days. How much less time did the *Baltic* take for the same voyage?

4. The *Yorkshire* covered 3,150 miles on its voyage. How many more miles was this than the *Baltic's* voyage between the same places?

5. In 1970 a ship sailed from Capetown to Liverpool via New York, and followed the courses taken by the *African Comet* and the *Baltic*. How many miles was the voyage?

6. Write the ships in order from the voyage that took the longest amount of time to the voyage that took the shortest amount of time.

7. Is the order for question 6 the same as the order of the ships according to the distance of the voyages?

8. In 1959, Max Conrad flew 5,000 miles solo from Chicago to Rome. It took him 1 day 10 hours. How much longer did it take the *USS Boxer* to cover the same distance?

The figure shows the progress of a white-water kayak race.

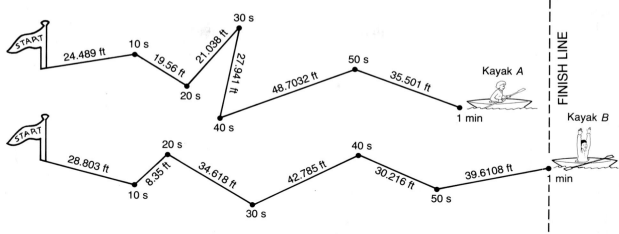

Estimate and write each answer to the nearest whole number.

1. How many feet did kayak *A* travel in 40 s?

2. How many feet did kayak *B* travel in 40 s?

3. Which kayak traveled farther in 40 s?

4. How much farther did kayak *A* travel between the 40-s mark and the 50-s mark than between the 50-s mark and the 1-min mark?

5. How many feet did kayak *B* travel between the 40-s mark and the 1-min mark?

6. How far did kayak *B* travel in the race?

7. How many feet did kayak *A* travel between the 40-s mark and the 1-min mark?

8. How much farther did kayak *B* travel between the 30-s mark and the 40-s mark than between the 10-s mark and the 20-s mark?

9. How far did kayak *A* travel in the race?

10. The direct distance from the start to the finish line is 158.307 ft. How far out of the way did kayak *B* travel?

Add. Check your answer by estimating.

1. 0.6927
\+ 0.836

2. 0.1159
0.5367
\+ 0.2863

3. 5.651
89.261
87.2426
\+ 23.1546

4. $70.11
\+ 25.62

5. 0.6966
0.5125
\+ 0.3957

6. 45.4789
\+ 46.2787

7. $29.03
76.27
61.58
\+ 10.42

8. 0.3978
0.302
0.9564
\+ 0.48

9. $26.87
\+ 59.47

10. 73.468
84.1951
6.1828
\+ 0.254

11. 71.8132
20.746
\+ 61.9367

12. 0.605
\+ 0.8183

13. 0.143
0.9764
0.7341
\+ 0.17

14. $6,222.03
931.91
\+   5.15

15. 0.3156
\+ 0.7223

16. $50.65
5.49
\+   0.75

17. 63.2108
\+ 1.367

18. 8.269
4.8265
87.923
\+ 3.7442

19. 0.4727
8.285
\+ 0.9864

20. $531.93
360.28
35.68
\+   4.86

21. 3.7575
4.7014
\+ 2.8869

22. 75.6743
0.8
\+ 4.62

23. $5,794.84
\+   885.72

24. 86.3726
69.4605
64.1016
\+ 94.2732

25. 0.9835 + 0.4978

26. 0.7452 + 0.6173

27. 6.492 + 9.977

28. 4.394 + 6.5653

29. 4.385 + 58.923

30. 7.4921 + 1.7796

Subtract. Check your answer by estimating.

1. 17.5082
    − 12.6201

2. 28.7988
    − 14.1648

3. 9.5102
    − 9.3928

4. $39.28
    − 5.58

5. 74.5897
    − 30.5261

6. 87
    − 7.613

7. $3.98
    − 2.10

8. 67.9105
    − 17.0366

9. 51.5364
    − 5.7

10. 89.4739
    − 51.3134

11. 65.666
    − 8.3425

12. 99.7057
    − 70.7603

13. 3.8203
    − 1.676

14. 6.4977
    − 1.8483

15. 44.8889
    − 10.0428

16. 7.059
    − 2.6153

17. 89.4739 − 51.3134

18. 57.5240 − 7

What is purple and 5,000 miles long? Subtract. Then copy the puzzle.
Write the letter of each problem on the line that has the first two
digits of the answer.

A   84.232
  − 51.877

E   5
  − 2.3614

G   9.28713
  − 7.56349

P   62.618
  − 34.259

T   12.489
  − 5.322

O   9.1
  − 6.887

F   4.28951
  − 3.64728

N   114.32
  − 73.88

R   3.99442
  − 1.84357

H   7.22
  − 6.1834

I   6.43892
  − 2.56183

W   55.410
  − 14.882

L   14.927
  − 10.333

C   7.52578
  − 5.21953

$$\frac{?}{71}\ \frac{?}{10}\ \frac{?}{26}\ \frac{?}{17}\ \frac{?}{21}\ \frac{?}{32}\ \frac{?}{28}\ \frac{?}{26}$$

$$\frac{?}{40}\ \frac{?}{32}\ \frac{?}{45}\ \frac{?}{45}\ \frac{?}{22}\ \frac{?}{06}\ \frac{?}{23}\ \frac{?}{10}\ \frac{?}{38}\ \frac{?}{40}\ \frac{?}{32}$$

NUMBER OF DEMOCRATIC AND REPUBLICAN SENATORS

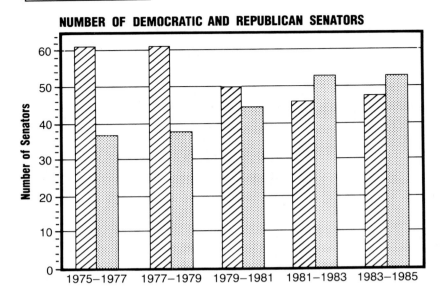

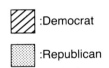

:Democrat

:Republican

Use the double-bar graph above to answer each question.

1. Which party controlled the Senate during six of the ten years shown in the graph?

2. In which years did the Democratic party have the greater number of members in the Senate?

3. In which years did the Republican party have the fewest members in the Senate?

4. In which years did the majority hold the greatest number of seats? How many more seats did the majority party hold during those years?

5. In which years was the majority the smallest? How many more seats did the majority party hold during those years?

Complete.

1. $640 \times 36 = 36 \times$ ___?___

2. $4 \times (3 + 6) = (4 \times 3) + (4 \times$ ___?___ $)$

3. $72 \div 1 =$ ___?___

4. $5 \times (7 \times 8) = (5 \times 7) \times$ ___?___

5. $84 \times 0 =$ ___?___

6. $9{,}029 \times 1 =$ ___?___

7. $144 \div 6 = 24$
$6 \times 24 =$ ___?___

8. $17 \times 4 = 68$
$68 \div 17 =$ ___?___

9. $95 \times 3 = 3 \times$ ___?___

10. $23 \times (6 \times 7) = (23 \times 6) \times$ ___?___

11. $16 \times (17 + 8) = (16 \times 17) +$
$(16 \times$ ___?___ $)$

12. $49 \times 0 =$ ___?___

13. $54 \div 1 =$ ___?___

14. $835 \times 1 =$ ___?___

15. $720 \div 8 = 90$
$8 \times 90 =$ ___?___

16. $36 \times 4 = 144$
$144 \div 4 =$ ___?___

17. $390 \times 0 =$ ___?___

18. $30 \times (2 + 6) = (30 \times 2) +$
$(30 \times$ ___?___ $)$

19. $1{,}864 \div 1 =$ ___?___

20. $9 \times (42 \times 71) = (9 \times 42) \times$ ___?___

21. $55 \times 7 = 7 \times$ ___?___

22. $4 \times 1 =$ ___?___

23. $546 \div 2 = 273$
$273 \times 2 =$ ___?___

24. $707 \times 3 = 2{,}121$
$2{,}121 \div 707 =$ ___?___

25. $85 \times 1 =$ ___?___

26. $696 \div 1 =$ ___?___

27. $16 \times 94 = 94 \times$ ___?___

28. $84 \times (3 \times 2) = (84 \times 3) \times$ ___?___

29. $45 \times (46 + 19) = (45 \times 46) +$
$(45 \times$ ___?___ $)$

30. $1{,}561 \times 0 =$ ___?___

31. $22 \times 23 = 506$
$506 \div 23 =$ ___?___

32. $7{,}007 \div 1{,}001 = 7$
$1{,}001 \times 7 =$ ___?___

Find the product or quotient.

1. $\dfrac{4,900}{700}$

2. 10×500

3. $1,200 \times 30$

4. $290,000 \div 1,000$

5. $\dfrac{\$9,000}{600}$

6. $15,000 \div 300$

7. $\dfrac{5,600}{800}$

8. $4,000 \times 70$

9. 600×60

10. $\dfrac{782,000}{100}$

11. $320 \div 80$

12. $\dfrac{\$47,500}{100}$

13. 70×60

14. 500×30

15. $210,700 \div 700$

16. 404×100

17. $\dfrac{6,400}{400}$

18. $1,500 \times 50$

19. $\dfrac{84,000}{70}$

20. $9,200 \div 100$

21. $\dfrac{9,400,000}{10,000}$

22. 731×10

23. $100,000 \div 100$

24. $\dfrac{\$6,300}{70}$

25. 450×300

26. $210 \times 7,000$

27. 506×30

Solve.

28. The Whatzit Tooyou Opinion Company is asking people if they would like the White House to be painted blue. The company mailed 4,250 questionnaires. Each one contained 100 questions. If every person returns the questionnaire, how many answers will the company receive?

Write the most reasonable estimate.

1. 34 × 73   a. over 2,100   b. under 2,100

2. 8 × 469   a. over 3,200   b. under 3,200

3. 18 × 368   a. over 8,000   b. under 8,000

4. 29 × 468   a. over 15,000   b. under 15,000

5. 7)3,468   a. 50   b. 500   c. 5,000

6. 9)35,689   a. 40   b. 400   c. 4,000

7. 5)423,826   a. 800   b. 8,000   c. 80,000

Decide how many digits there are in each quotient. Then estimate.

8. 4)7,354

9. 6)2,543

10. 9)45,372

11. 53)4,934

12. 28)13,762

Use the data in the chart to estimate.

13. About how many daily papers does Bob deliver

   a. in a week?

   b. in a month?

   c. in a year?

Bob's Newspaper Deliveries	
Daily (Mon.–Sat.)	48
Sunday	93

14. About how many Sunday papers does Bob deliver

   a. in a month?   b. in a year?

Write the letter of the information that is not needed.

1. A radio show host gets paid $2,680 per month. He hosts 2 shows each week, and the average length of each show is $4\frac{1}{2}$ hours. How much does he receive per show?

   a. He gets paid $2,680 per month.

   b. He hosts 2 shows each week.

   c. Each show averages $4\frac{1}{2}$ hours.

2. A radio station charges $3.76 per second of weekday advertising, and $5.26 per second on weekends. Hopscotch, Inc., runs a 30-second ad each weekday. How much does it pay the station each week?

   a. The charge is $3.76 per second.

   b. The weekend charge is $5.26.

   c. Hopscotch runs a 30-second ad each weekday.

Solve.

3. WXYZ Radio has a competition that attracts 630 entries for a $250 prize. Molly gets paid $7.50 per hour for checking the entries, which takes her 2 minutes each. How much does WXYZ pay Molly to check the entries?

4. In one nonleap year, a radio announcer called every 50th number in the local telephone directory. There are 18,150 people listed in the telephone directory. If he dialed one person per day, how many days were there that he did not make a call?

5. One radio station has an average of 12 minutes of advertising per hour. The station broadcasts 14 hours per day. How much advertising time can it sell each week?

6. A radio station invites 42 listeners to visit the station. Each listener is given a certificate that costs the station $1.75 and a radio that costs the station $14.63. How much did the station pay for the radios?

7. WXYZ's Twilight Hour show reaches 45,500 listeners, and its Midnight Mood show reaches 8,955 listeners. There are 3,420 people who listen to both shows. How many listeners does WXYZ reach with the two shows?

8. A radio station installs an emergency generator that uses 12 gallons of gasoline per hour. The station decides to store enough gasoline to run for 6 days. Gasoline costs $1.23 per gallon. How much gasoline does the station need?

Multiply.

1. 99,319
   × 47

2. 85,064
   × 226

3. 8,613
   × 92

4. 58,214
   × 7

5. 53,556
   × 783

6. 42,312
   × 21

7. $89,456
   × 63

8. 287,431
   × 120

9. 8,016
   × 75

10. 42,914
   × 716

11. 83,382
   × 52

12. $99.37
   × 61

13. 5,312
   × 3

14. $370.04
   × 71

15. 7,891
   × 729

16. 29,907
   × 757

17. 186,439
   × 27

18. 5,221
   × 974

19. 9,491
   × 66

20. 3,050
   × 6

21. 3 × 407 billion

22. 7 × 106 million

23. 8 × 69 million

24. 8 × 14 trillion

Solve.

25. In 1976, the solar probe *Helios B* reached a speed of 149,125 mph. At this speed, how far would it travel in 12 hours?

26. Earth orbits the sun at about 66,641 mph. About how far does Earth travel in 48 hours?

Divide.

1. 310 ÷ 6

2. $3,045 ÷ 33

3. 25,965 ÷ 45

4. 6,201 ÷ 7

5. 391 ÷ 72

6. $1,175 ÷ 47

7. 221,044 ÷ 428

8. 328 ÷ 5

9. 624 ÷ 8

10. $42 ÷ 3

11. 3,544 ÷ 4

12. 2,111 ÷ 18

13. $\frac{1,856}{7}$

14. $\frac{7,875}{9}$

15. $\frac{217}{3}$

16. $\frac{391}{72}$

17. $\frac{\$998}{74}$

18. $\frac{6,177}{71}$

19. $\frac{535}{15}$

20. $\frac{21,859}{54}$

21. $\frac{295}{4}$

22. 72)28,990

23. 469)418,718

24. 8)416

25. 783)749,331

26. 35)14,168

27. 16)4,736

Solve.

28. The Crunchy Breakfast Cereal Company decided to introduce its new cereal by sending an equal number of sample boxes to homes in 72 neighborhoods throughout the state. The company sent out 13,536 sample boxes. How many homes in each neighborhood received a sample?

Write the letter of the answer that describes the correct way to estimate to solve the problem.

1. Charlotte is sending a boat anchor by freight. The anchor weighs 96 pounds, and Charlotte believes that the freight charges are $1.42 per pound. How much money should she take to the freight office to be sure that she has enough?

   a. Overestimate the weight, and underestimate the charges.

   b. Overestimate both the weight and the charges.

   c. Underestimate both the weight and the charges.

2. Ralph wants to photograph the end of a boat race. The race is 138 miles long, and the fastest boat is expected to average 87 miles per hour. How long after the start of the race should Ralph arrive at the finish line?

   a. Overestimate the miles, and underestimate the speed.

   b. Overestimate both the miles and the speed.

   c. Underestimate the miles, and overestimate the speed.

Solve by estimation.

3. A race starts at 12:15 P.M. Judith's boat is docked 27 miles from the starting line, and can travel at an average speed of 11 miles per hour. If Judith leaves at 10:00 A.M., will she arrive at the race before it begins?

4. A ferry charges $5.85 for each car it carries, and $1.55 for each person in the car. Marco and 3 friends are riding in a car and want to take the ferry. They have $12.50 among them. Is it enough for the ferry ride?

5. Overnight docking at a marina costs $23.20. The price is reduced by $1.95 for each member of the boat's crew who eats at the Marina café. To the nearest dollar, about how much does it cost Jacob to dock if 3 members of his crew eat at the café?

6. The captain of a fishing boat needs to buy 42 feet of wood to make repairs to the deck. The wood costs $4.83 per foot. To the nearest $10, how much will the captain pay for the wood to repair the deck?

7. Thelma is organizing a fishing contest at the lake near her house. The prize for catching the largest fish is $50. The entry fee for the first 12 people to enter is $3.80, and all other contestants pay $4.15. If 20 people enter the contest, how much (to the nearest $10) will Thelma have left after paying the prize money?

Compute.

1. 0.006×100

2. $32.58 \div 10$

3. $22.88 \times 1,000$

4. 30.8×10

5. 0.007×100

6. $1.6 \div 10$

7. $0.5 \div 1,000$

8. $476.7 \div 10$

9. $0.004 \times 1,000$

10. 0.077×10

11. 10.2761×10

12. $98.95 \div 100$

13. $52.04 \div 1,000$

14. 0.25×100

15. 2.316×10

16. $0.74 \div 10$

17. $189.7 \div 1,000$

18. 5.778×100

19. 5.316×100

20. 16.64×10

21. $0.06 \div 1,000$

22. $68.96 \div 10$

23. $0.85 \div 1,000$

24. 32.14×100

25. 38.652×10

26. $21.5 \div 10$

27. $0.38 \div 100$

28. $619.5 \div 1,000$

29. 0.01116×100

30. 0.59×10

31. $78.64 \div 10$

32. $2,041 \div 1,000$

33. 71.3×100

34. $0.2413 \times 1,000$

35. $799.8 \div 10$

36. $645.8 \div 100$

37. 7.8×10

38. 4.004×100

Use with pages 56–57.

Use the numbers in the box to answer the questions.

1. Which decimals are close to but greater than 1?

2. Which decimals are close to but less than 1?

3. Which decimals are close to but greater than one half?

4. Which decimals are close to but less than one half?

0.499	1.038–1.109
0.0099	0.98, 0.900, 0.897
0.48236	0.51
1.109	0.9001
0.49	0.499, 0.48236

Estimate to find the most sensible answer.

5. 3.17×17.15 a. 5.44   b. 54.37   c. 543.66

6. 0.624×0.482 a. 0.30   b. 3.01   c. 30.08

7. 3.009×2.156 a. 6.49   b. 64.87   c. 648.74

8. 0.98×4.86 a. 0.47628   b. 4.76   c. 47.62

9. 3.68×0.512 a. 0.1884   b. 1.884   c. 18.84

10. 7.38×4.15 a. 3.063   b. 30.62   c. 306.3

Estimate. Adjust by writing + or − where possible.

11. 4.28×5.76

12. 1.34×7.8

13. 0.98×12.5

14. 0.489×2.4

15. 3.56×1.12

16. 0.503×4.31

17. 3.45×1.1123

18. 12.4×5.78

19. 0.894×3.44

Solve.

20. The typical American eats 96.3 pounds of beef each year. If the average price of beef is $2.42 per pound, about how much is spent on beef by each American?

21. The typical American eats about 73.5 pounds of hamburger each year. If the average price of hamburger is $1.19, about how much is spent on hamburger?

Multiply. Round the product to the nearest cent where necessary.

1. $3.71
   × 0.06

2. 0.739
   × 0.008

3. 26.342
   × 0.697

4. 0.781
   × 29.6

5. 6.186
   × 3.05

6. $33.56
   × 68.5

7. 4.059
   × 4.13

8. 0.0213
   × 0.71

9. 55.36875
   × 1.03

10. 4.302
    × 0.009

11. 20.9413
    × 0.03

12. $2.97
    × 3.3

13. 0.010
    × 0.02

14. 226.479
    × 2.31

15. $7.98
    × 2.6

16. 6.91532
    × 1.78

17. 3.9 × 6.1

18. 0.698 × 3.07

19. 0.02 × 0.048

20. 0.0213 × 0.71

21. 1.8 × 5.8 × 7.4

22. 3.743 × 15

Solve. Round to the nearest cent if necessary.

23. Tracy wants to sell a gold bracelet she never wears. She wants to buy a video cassette recorder that costs $270. Her bracelet contains 0.78 ounces. If the jeweler will pay $380.35 per ounce for her bracelet, how much money will Tracy have left after she buys the video cassette recorder?

Write the letter of the operation you would use to solve each problem.

1. The distance from San Antonio, Texas to Dallas, Texas is 250 miles. The distance from San Antonio to Corpus Christi , Texas is 153 miles. What is the distance from Dallas to Corpus Christi via San Antonio?

   a. addition

   b. subtraction

   c. multiplication

2. The Mississippi–Missouri River System is 3,740 miles long. The Missouri river is 2,683 miles long. How long is the Mississippi after the Missouri meets it?

   a. addition

   b. subtraction

   c. multiplication

Solve.

3. Mount Washington in New Hampshire is 2,096 yards high. How many feet is the mountain? (There are 3 feet to a yard.)

4. Big Elk Peak in Idaho is 9,478 feet tall. How many feet have you traveled if you went to the top and came down?

5. The distance from Milwaukee, Wisconsin to Chicago, Illinois is 87 miles. Julia drives from one city to the other 8 times per week. How much is her total mileage?

6. The Republic of Andorra lies between France and Spain. The border it shares with France is 37.3 miles, and the border it shares with Spain is 40.4 miles. How long is Andorra's border?

7. The border of China is 17,445 miles long. Its border with Mongolia is 2,904 miles long. Its border with the Soviet Union is 4,673 miles long, and its border with all other countries is 5,822 miles long. How long is China's coastline?

8. The highest point in Alabama is 2,400 feet high. The lowest point is 500 feet high. How much higher is the highest point than the lowest point?

9. The Gobi desert is 500,000 square miles, and the Kalahari desert is 225,000 square miles. The Sahara desert is 2,775,000 square miles larger than the two other deserts combined. How many square miles is the Sahara?

10. The world's largest island, Greenland, is 2.75 times larger than the world's second largest island, New Guinea. New Guinea covers 306,000 square miles. How many square miles does Greenland cover?

Divide. Round the quotient to the nearest thousandth or to the nearest cent where necessary.

1. $620.1 \div 8$

2. $1{,}863.36 \div 288$

3. $8.33 \div 2$

4. $\dfrac{749.331}{783}$

5. $\dfrac{14.4}{36}$

6. $\dfrac{1.819}{4}$

7. $\$196.32 \div 64$

8. $0.1293 \div 5$

9. $38.35 \div 65$

10. $5.351 \div 7$

11. $14.88 \div 62$

12. $2.984 \div 2$

13. $58.6219 \div 328$

14. $6.177 \div 71$

15. $206.6 \div 4$

16. $\dfrac{31.80}{32}$

17. $\dfrac{3.835}{65}$

18. $\dfrac{841.2}{6}$

19. $215\overline{)\$241.7893}$

20. $47\overline{)117.5}$

21. $673\overline{)58.2614}$

22. $22\overline{)1.122}$

23. $318\overline{)\$418.71}$

24. $7\overline{)535.1}$

25. $4\overline{)84.12}$

26. $55\overline{)2.530}$

27. $151\overline{)23.426}$

Use with pages 64–65.

Divide. Round your answer to the nearest thousandth or to the nearest cent where necessary.

1. $\dfrac{1.352}{0.8}$

2. $0.016 \div 0.04$

3. $\dfrac{0.624}{0.078}$

4. $\dfrac{\$6.45}{8.6}$

5. $\dfrac{428}{6.4}$

6. $7.5 \div 0.15$

7. $5.632 \div 3.2607$

8. $\$1.40 \div 2.818$

9. $\dfrac{4.346}{0.2173}$

10. $\dfrac{0.87571}{9.218}$

11. $8,564 \div 32.54$

12. $\dfrac{6.7}{2.264}$

13. $7.4\overline{)3,500.8}$

14. $0.87\overline{)0.00435}$

15. $0.004\overline{)0.00372}$

16. $2.818\overline{)1,409}$

17. $5.8\overline{)\$15.95}$

18. $8.04\overline{)0.602}$

Solve.

19. Mandy is trying to create a liquid that will not evaporate. Her beaker contains 47.5 mL of solution. She wants to put an equal amount of the solution into test tubes by using an eyedropper that holds 0.98 mL. How many times can she fill the eyedropper completely?

Holt, Rinehart and Winston, Publishers • 8

Complete the plan for each problem by writing the missing steps.

1. The purchasing committee for the Student Council Bookstore is ordering supplies. Notebook paper is shipped in boxes of 24 packages each. The committee orders 30 boxes of paper. If the cost of the paper is $0.22 per package, find the total cost of the order.

   Step 1: Find the cost of a box of paper.

   Step 2: ___?___

2. The bookstore sold 321 packages of notebook paper during the first month of the school year. The store paid $0.22 for each package of paper. It sells each package of paper for $0.30. How much profit did the bookstore make on the paper?

   Step 1: Find the amount received for the paper.

   Step 2: ___?___

   Step 3: ___?___

Make a plan for each problem. Solve.

3. A package holds 24 pencils. Pencils are shipped in boxes of 10 packages each. If each pencil costs $0.12 and the bookstore purchasing committee orders 15 boxes of pencils, what is the cost of the order?

4. The bookstore sold 4 boxes of pencils last month. Each box has 10 packages of pencils, and each package contains 24 pencils. If the pencils sell for $0.15 each and cost $0.12 each, how much profit did the bookstore make on the pencils?

5. The bookstore also sells graph paper at $0.03 per sheet. The store buys the graph paper in packs of 200 sheets each. If each pack costs $4.58, how much profit was made from selling 2 packs of graph paper?

6. The bookstore started the year with a cash balance of $37.62. If the receipts for September were $321.72 and the expenditures were $325.18, what was the balance at the end of September?

Write *yes* or *no*.

Is the number divisible by 2?

1. 8,356
2. 53,775
3. 437
4. 29
5. 1,274
6. 322
7. 2,180
8. 33,455

Is the number divisible by 3?

9. 243
10. 1,200
11. 6,801
12. 11
13. 15
14. 25,006
15. 421
16. 100,005

Is the number divisible by 4?

17. 76,521
18. 390,062
19. 973
20. 48
21. 886
22. 567
23. 2,004
24. 6,935

Is the number divisible by 5?

25. 13
26. 95,215
27. 3,750
28. 102,211
29. 26
30. 500,909
31. 638
32. 773

Is the number divisible by 6?

33. 672
34. 34
35. 611
36. 48,928
37. 199
38. 47,068
39. 21
40. 5,940

Is the number divisible by 9?

41. 155
42. 81
43. 77
44. 5,001
45. 563
46. 4,292
47. 6,885
48. 19

Is the number divisible by 10?

49. 300
50. 400,000
51. 6,020
52. 909
53. 25,005
54. 170
55. 898
56. 50,000

Write as a product of factors and evaluate.

1. 4^3 **2.** 3^4 **3.** 2^5

4. 10^3 **5.** 8^2 **6.** 5^5

Rewrite and evaluate each. Use exponents.

7. $8 \times 8 \times 8$ **8.** $2 \times 2 \times 2$ **9.** 11×11

10. $4 \times 4 \times 4 \times 4 \times 4$ **11.** $5 \times 5 \times 10 \times 10$ **12.** $7 \times 7 \times 7 \times 7$

Find the square root. Use this table.

13. $\sqrt{16}$ **14.** $\sqrt{49}$

15. $\sqrt{144}$ **16.** $\sqrt{361}$

17. $\sqrt{21}$ **18.** $\sqrt{14}$

19. $\sqrt{256}$ **20.** $\sqrt{484}$

21. $\sqrt{39}$ **22.** $\sqrt{576}$

23. $\sqrt{22}$ **24.** $\sqrt{43}$

25. $\sqrt{625}$ **26.** $\sqrt{1,024}$

27. $\sqrt{47}$ **28.** $\sqrt{33}$

29. $\sqrt{2,116}$ **30.** $\sqrt{50}$

31. $\sqrt{28}$ **32.** $\sqrt{34}$

n	n^2	$\sqrt{n}$	n	n^2	$\sqrt{n}$
1	1	1.000	26	676	5.099
2	4	1.414	27	729	5.196
3	9	1.732	28	784	5.292
4	16	2.000	29	841	5.385
5	25	2.236	30	900	5.477
6	36	2.449	31	961	5.568
7	49	2.646	32	1,024	5.657
8	64	2.828	33	1,089	5.745
9	81	3.000	34	1,156	5.831
10	100	3.162	35	1,225	5.916
11	121	3.317	36	1,296	6.000
12	144	3.464	37	1,369	6.083
13	169	3.606	38	1,444	6.164
14	196	3.742	39	1,521	6.245
15	225	3.873	40	1,600	6.325
16	256	4.000	41	1,681	6.403
17	289	4.123	42	1,764	6.481
18	324	4.243	43	1,849	6.557
19	361	4.359	44	1,936	6.633
20	400	4.472	45	2,025	6.708
21	441	4.583	46	2,116	6.782
22	484	4.690	47	2,209	6.856
23	529	4.796	48	2,304	6.928
24	576	4.899	49	2,401	7.000
25	625	5.000	50	2,500	7.071

Solve. Use the table of square roots. Round to the nearest tenth.

33. The area of a square carpet is 42 m². What is the length of each side?

34. The area of a square garden is 27 m². What is the length of each side?

Write in scientific notation.

1. 400

2. 800

3. 1,100

4. 2,000

5. 6,500

6. 8,300

7. 9,800

8. 33,000

9. 41,000

10. 76,000

11. 59,350

12. 304,685

13. 680,000

14. 93,215,000

15. 8,499,315

16. 54,975,000

17. 1,110,000

18. 476,000,000

19. 888,888

20. 6,981

21. 33,450

Express in standard form.

22. 6×10^2

23. 5×10^4

24. 3.7×10^3

25. 8.9×10^4

26. 4.4×10^5

27. 1.1×10^2

28. 3.56×10^5

29. 7.38×10^7

30. 4.07×10^6

31. 5.289×10^8

32. 6.12345×10^{10}

33. 9.751×10^9

Solve.

34. The longest biography in publishing history is that of Sir Winston Churchill. The book contains about 7,620,000 words. Express this number in scientific notation.

35. The Library of Congress in Washington, D.C., is one of the world's largest libraries. It contains over 80,798,000 items, including books, maps, and other documents. Express this number in scientific notation.

Read each problem. Without computing the exact answer, write the letter of the most reasonable answer.

1. Alan ordered 45 windows for a house he was building. The bill came to $1,647. What was the price of each window?

   a. $3.60

   b. $36

   c. $72

2. A brick weighs 2.3 kilograms. Sheila is calculating the weight of a stack of 37 bricks. What is the closest answer?

   a. 85 kilograms

   b. 95 kilograms

   c. 120 kilograms

3. There are 144 nails in a box. If Rosa has 3,000 nails, about how many boxes does she have?

   a. about 12

   b. about 15

   c. about 20

4. Katsiko is estimating quantities of supplies he needs from a building plan. He has to find the cube root of 64,000. What is the answer?

   a. 400

   b. 40

   c. 4,000

5. A hardware company designed a new lock for private garages. In the first month of sale, 3,258 locks were sold for $17.25 each. What was the total amount paid?

   a. $5,500

   b. $55,000

   c. $550,000

6. Antonio is deciding how many lamps he will need for an apartment complex. Each apartment has 13 lamps, and there are 87 apartments in the complex. How many lamps does he need?

   a. 1,100

   b. 1,500

   c. 950

7. The Verrazano Narrows bridge in New York is 1,300,000 millimeters long. The Delaware River bridge is 500,000 millimeters long. What is the sum of the lengths in meters?

   a. 18×10^3 meters

   b. 1.8×10^2 meters

   c. 1.8×10^3 meters

8. A building supply catalog has 9,346 items listed in it. The catalog is 124 pages long. About how many items are there per page?

   a. about 95

   b. about 125

   c. about 75

Use after pages 86–87.

Write all the factors of the number.

1. 63

2. 33

3. 91

4. 12

5. 16

6. 119

7. 9

8. 17

9. 57

10. 20

11. 125

12. 35

13. 39

14. 74

15. 7

16. 26

17. 52

18. 66

Write *prime* or *composite*.

19. 109

20. 17

21. 18

22. 29

23. 79

24. 52

25. 72

26. 19

27. 39

28. 96

29. 91

30. 59

31. 47

32. 144

33. 2

34. 71

35. 57

36. 36

37. 13

38. 189

39. 300

40. 3

Write the prime factorization of each number using exponents.

1. 950

2. 104

3. 192

4. 84

5. 81

6. 448

7. 196

8. 414

9. 222

10. 670

Draw a factor tree for each number. Then write the prime factorization with and without exponents.

11. 720

12. 279

13. 2310

Write the number for each prime factorization.

14. $2^2 \times 3^2 \times 11$

15. $2 \times 3 \times 7^2$

16. $2^4 \times 3 \times 5^2$

17. $2^2 \times 3 \times 13$

18. $3^2 \times 5^2$

19. $2^3 \times 3^2$

20. $2^2 \times 5^2$

21. $2^3 \times 3^2 \times 11$

22. $2 \times 3 \times 5^2$

23. $11 \times 13 \times 5^2$

24. $5 \times 7 \times 11$

25. $2 \times 3 \times 11^2$

Write the GCF. Find it by listing the factors.

1. 16, 24   2. 15, 35   3. 24, 72

4. 42, 105   5. 63, 81   6. 24, 49

7. 18, 27, 45   8. 35, 84   9. 12, 20, 28

10. 24, 36, 60   11. 26, 208   12. 88, 121

Write the GCF. Find it by using prime factorization.

13. 60, 140   14. 96, 128   15. 40, 64

16. 64, 96, 112   17. 81, 108   18. 34, 51

19. 72, 180   20. 15, 80   21. 21, 56

22. 25, 225   23. 60, 84, 114   24. 552, 648

25. 39, 65, 91   26. 115, 138, 184   27. 133, 152

List the first five nonzero multiples of each number.

1. 4

2. 30

3. 13

4. 8

5. 50

6. 17

7. 70

8. 19

9. 15

10. 60

Write the LCM. Find it by listing multiples.

11. 8, 6

12. 12, 48, 72

13. 5, 37

14. 14, 35

15. 12, 18

16. 8, 24

17. 23, 5

18. 3, 7

19. 10, 40, 50

Write the LCM. Find it by using prime factorization.

20. 12, 28, 45

21. 14, 52

22. 32, 48

23. 60, 90

24. 21, 70

25. 22, 35

26. 12, 36, 48

27. 36, 72

28. 8, 24

UTILITY RATES

Electric	
service charge . . . . $7.65 per month	
first 300 Kwh . . . . 7.918¢ per Kwh	
next 700 Kwh . . . . 4.87¢ per Kwh	
over 1,000 Kwh . . . . 4.168¢ per Kwh	

Gas	
service charge . . . . $7.80 per month	
first 6,000 cu ft . . . . $7.06 per 1,000 cu ft	
over 6,000 cu ft . . . . $6.39 per 1,000 cu ft	

Water	
service charge . . . . $18.27 per quarter	
first 6,000 cu ft . . . . $1.266 per 100 cu ft	
over 6,000 cu ft . . . . $1.005 per 100 cu ft	

Kwh = Kilowatt hours
Cu ft = cubic feet

Use the rate tables above to solve. Note that the service charge must be paid even if no gas, electricity, or water is used.

1. The Alvarez family will be out of town for 3 months (1 quarter). How much will it cost to maintain service for all three utilities for this period?

2. The Williams' largest gas bill was last January when they used 19,200 cubic feet of gas. How much was the bill?

3. The Williams family used 6,700 cubic feet of gas this month. How much will they have to pay for the gas?

4. A family used 1,270 Kwh of electricity last month. How much did they pay for the electricity?

5. In December of last year, the DeAngelis family used 2,450 Kw hours of electricity. Calculate the electric bill.

6. The Washington's water bill this quarter is based on their using 2,000 cubic feet of water. Calculate the water bill.

7. If one cubic foot of water is about 7.5 gallons, how many gallons of water did the Washington family use during the quarter?

8. The Washington family has a swimming pool that holds 1,800 cubic feet of water. If the family had filled the pool during the quarter, how much more would their bill have been?

The table below shows the long-distance rates charged by a phone company for direct-dial calls.

Distance to Called Place (Airline Miles)	Weekday Full Rate 8 AM–9 PM		Evening 35% Discount 9 PM–11 PM		Night 11 PM–8 AM & Weekend 60% Discount	
	initial 1 min	each addl min	initial 1 min	each addl min	initial 1 min	each addl min
1–16 miles	$0.23	$0.15	$0.14	$0.10	$0.09	$0.06
17–30 miles	.33	.21	.21	.14	.13	.09
31–55 miles	.43	.28	.27	.19	.17	.12
56–100 miles	.53	.34	.34	.23	.21	.14
101–172 miles	.62	.40	.40	.26	.24	.16
173–244 miles	.69	.45	.44	.30	.27	.18
245–316 miles	.75	.49	.48	.32	.30	.20

Use the rate table to solve.

1. Linda called Inez at 12 noon on Wednesday. Inez lives 90 miles away. How much did the call cost if Linda and Inez talked for 12 minutes?

2. How much would Linda have saved if she had made a call of the same length to Inez at 9:30 P.M. on Wednesday?

3. How much would Linda have saved if she had made a call of the same length to Inez at 11:30 P.M.?

4. Ben lives in Indianapolis, 294 miles from his aunt. At 8:00 P.M. on Saturday, Ben called his aunt and talked for 17 minutes. How much did the call cost?

5. The EZ Company does business with a bank 40 miles away. The president of EZ makes a 5-minute call to the bank at 10:00 A.M. on Friday. How much does the call cost?

6. The EZ Company makes 25 weekly calls to an insurance company, 185 miles away. The calls last an average of 15 minutes each and occur between 9:30 A.M. and 4:30 A.M. on weekdays. How much does the company pay per week for the 25 calls?

7. If the EZ Company could call the insurance company at 7:30 A.M., how much would it save each week on the 25 phone calls?

Simplify.

1. $6 + 9 \cdot 3$

2. $12 - 8 + 7$

3. $16 + 32 \div 4$

4. $24 - (17 - 5)$

5. $6 + 10^2$

6. $31 - 7 \cdot (14 - 10)$

7. $(15 - 6)^2$

8. $70 - 3 \cdot (15 - 2)$

9. $(8^2 + (13 - 4)^2) \div 5$

10. $7 + 9^2$

11. $18 \div 6 + 11$

12. $300 - 36 \cdot 8$

13. $17 + (3 + 2)^3$

14. $4 \cdot 16 + 8 - 9 \div 3$

15. $64 \div 4 + 4$

Rewrite using parentheses to make each answer true.

16. $21 \div 3 + 4 = 3$

17. $9 + 3 \div 2 + 10 = 1$

18. $9 - 2 \cdot 3 = 21$

19. $3.8 + 4.4 \div 2 = 6$

20. $30 \div 5 + 10 = 2$

21. $2.4 - 0.4 \cdot 6 = 12$

22. $30 \div 5 + 1 = 5$

23. $4 + 2 \cdot 6 = 36$

24. $40 \div 4 - 2 + 8 = 0$

Simplify each expression. Then write the letter of the expression on the line or lines above its simplified form.

H. $(264 \div 3) + 2 \cdot 17 + (196 - 70)$

I. $(840 \div 5) \div (104 \div 26)$

T. $333 \div 9 + 74 \cdot (9 - 5) \div 8 + 17$

N. $145 - 28 \cdot 2 - (12 \cdot 5) \div 3 - 21$

L. $(44 + 31) \div (2 \cdot 17 - 9) + 6 - 2$

O. $68 - (32 + 17) + (90 \cdot 6)$

C. $56 - (21 \cdot 4 - 38) + 5^2$

K. $(4 + 5)^2 \cdot 4 + 130 - 7$

G. $500 \div 5^2 \cdot 10 \div (77 - 75)^2 + 9$

S. $16 + 8^2 \div 32 \cdot (3 + 7)^2 - 216$

Where did Sir Galahad study?

$$\frac{?}{447} \quad \frac{?}{48} \quad \frac{?}{42} \quad \frac{?}{59} \quad \frac{?}{248} \quad \frac{?}{91} \qquad \frac{?}{0} \quad \frac{?}{35} \quad \frac{?}{248} \quad \frac{?}{559} \quad \frac{?}{559} \quad \frac{?}{7}$$

Write T for true if the replacement value is a solution. Write F for false if it is not.

1. $a + 8 = 9$, if $a = 2$

2. $3 \times b = 18$, if $b = 6$

3. $\frac{15}{b} = 3.25$, if $b = 4$

4. $c - 8 = 3$, if $c = 12$

5. $5.6 + c = 7$, if $c = 1.4$

6. $\frac{a}{6} = 1$, if $a = 6$

7. $3d = 24$, if $d = 9$

8. $9 + d = 12$, if $d = 4$

9. $7.2 - a = 5.2$, if $a = 2$

10. $a - 7 = 3$, if $a = 10$

11. $\frac{c}{4} = 2$, if $c = 12$

12. $3c = 15$, if $c = 5$

Find the solution. Use the replacement set $\{0, 1, 2, \ldots\}$

13. $x + 3.6 = 7.6$

14. $36 = m - 27$

15. $g + 49 = 51$

16. $105 = z + 47$

17. $7 + e = 18$

18. $\frac{99}{a} = 3$

19. $96 - x = 18$

20. $19d = 171$

21. $14 - v = 14$

22. $\frac{f}{6} = 6$

23. $39 = 13a$

24. $10.6f = 53$

25. $103 = 71 + b$

26. $s - 106 = 34$

27. $446 = 307 + n$

28. $4.4 = \frac{17.6}{x}$

29. $\frac{308}{b} = 77$

30. $95 + z = 107$

31. $27a = 324$

32. $136 = r + 27$

33. $11 = \frac{121}{r}$

34. $c + 26 = 95$

35. $147 = 49w$

36. $c - 3 = 115$

Write the operation you would use to solve each problem.

1. The tallest tree in the world is the Howard Libby redwood tree, 366 feet tall. The tallest spruce tree is a 126-foot blue spruce in Colorado. How many times taller is the redwood than the spruce?

   a. add   **b.** subtract   **c.** multiply   **d.** divide

2. White pine trees average 100 feet in height. Scotch pine trees average 30 feet less in height. About how tall are most scotch pines?

   a. add   **b.** subtract   **c.** multiply   **d.** divide

Solve.

3. The diameter of a mature chestnut oak is about 2.5 feet. The diameter of a mature sequoia is about 20 feet. About how many times greater is the diameter of the sequoia than the oak?

4. The General Sherman sequoia tree is 272 feet high. Its lowest branch is 130 feet high. How many feet of the tree contain branches?

5. The fastest-growing tree is a type of silk tree which has grown as fast as 2.7 feet in one month. How tall might a tree like this grow in $\frac{1}{2}$ a year?

6. The wood of a black ironwood tree weighs up to 93 pounds per cubic foot. The wood of the lightest balsa wood tree is 37.2 times lighter. What is the balsa wood's weight per cubic foot?

7. The northernmost tree, a Sitka spruce, took 98 years to grow 28 cm. About how many years did it take to grow one cm?

8. The tallest recorded apple tree was 70 feet high. The tallest known shellbark hickory tree was 1.5 times taller. How tall was the hickory?

Solve.

1. $x - 14 = 99$

2. $186 + c = 747$

3. $z + 14 = 63$

4. $83 - n = 65$

5. $2.7 + c = 9.4$

6. $m - 3 = 12.9$

7. $a + 108 = 306$

8. $25.6 + r = 74.4$

9. $s - 214 = 36$

10. $99 - n = 46$

11. $11.7 + t = 109.8$

12. $v + 175 = 203.2$

13. $36 - s = 14$

14. $b - 83 = 207.2$

15. $f - 13 = 221$

16. $154 - g = 78$

17. $b + 7.2 + 2.1 = 11.4$

18. $19 + z = 101$

19. $14.5 + r = 22.7$

20. $w + 22 = 104.8$

21. $a - 18.3 = 24.1$

22. $11.7 - b = 4.2$

23. $z - 27.2 = 36.1$

24. $204 + c = 807$

25. $59.6 + m = 83.2$

26. $n + 3.5 = 10.2$

27. $201 - s = 174$

28. $t - 114.3 = 236.1$

29. $b + 19 = 30$

30. $25.3 + v = 108$

31. $19.2 + a = 19.2$

32. $c - 7 - 2 = 9$

33. $22 + t = 121$

34. $336 + b = 407$

Write the equation.

35. The sum of 18 and a number, x, is 36.

36. A number, r, decreased by 6 is 136.2.

37. 49 decreased by a number, z, is 11.

38. The sum of a number, b, and 207 is 404.

Solve.

1. $7z = 84$

2. $\frac{r}{3} = 38$

3. $\frac{c}{30} = 0.5$

4. $\frac{m}{15} = 6$

5. $202n = 404$

6. $6n = 96$

7. $\frac{r}{0.4} = 50$

8. $\frac{t}{5} = 3.5$

9. $19m = 228$

10. $\frac{a}{80} = 7$

11. $36b = 540$

12. $\frac{m}{0.1} = 6$

13. $45n = 315$

14. $\frac{x}{15} = 2.5$

15. $\frac{r}{9} = 0.3$

16. $7s = 182$

17. $23a = 184$

18. $5.5c = 335.5$

19. $\frac{w}{3.2} = 8.5$

20. $\frac{m}{21} = 5.8$

21. $\frac{y}{5} = 0.016$

22. $1.05n = 60.27$

23. $6.2m = 80.6$

24. $\frac{e}{5} = 1.4$

25. $\frac{s}{12} = 0.8$

26. $78k = 81.12$

Write the equation and solve.

27. If 72 is 8 times a number, a, what is the number?

28. A number, c, divided by 0.4 is 10. What is c?

29. A number, j, times 4.8 is 33.6. What is j?

30. A number, t, divided by 4.2 is 1.9. What is t?

Solve.

1. $5z + 7 = 32$

2. $\frac{s}{3} + 3 = 5$

3. $\frac{a}{8} - 3 = 9$

4. $4w - 6 = 14$

5. $\frac{b}{4} + 13 = 17$

6. $9c + 12 = 21$

7. $10h - 34 = 66$

8. $\frac{x}{10} + 8 = 13$

9. $\frac{m}{6} - 6 = 0$

10. $16n - 28 = 4$

11. $5k - 2 = 43$

12. $\frac{z}{3} + 4 = 13$

13. $4v - 22 = 22$

14. $4y - 8 = 20$

15. $\frac{c}{5} + 7 = 12$

16. $\frac{d}{4} + 3 = 33$

17. $3r + 15 = 75$

18. $\frac{b}{3} + 17 = 48$

19. $8t - 14 = 82$

20. $5x + 6 = 41$

21. $\frac{v}{2} - 4 = 26$

22. $\frac{p}{2} - 5 = 9$

23. $0.5j + 2 = 6$

24. $4y + 15 = 67$

Write a two-step equation and solve.

25. The sum of 9 and $\frac{1}{3}$ of a number, x, is 13. What is the number?

26. The sum of 7 and three times a number, a, is 16. What is the number?

27. The sum of 8 and $\frac{1}{4}$ of a number, b, is 10. What is the number?

28. The sum of 11 and four times a number, c, is 55. What is the number?

Write the letter of the correct equation.

1. The Mark 2 model of the Trans computer costs $785. This is $45 less than 1.5 times the cost of the Mark 1 model. How much does the Mark 1 model cost?

   a. $1.5n - 45 = 785$

   b. $1.5n = 785 - 45$

   c. $n + 45 = 785 - 1.5$

2. The Mark 1 model has a memory storage of 32K. The memory of the Mark 2 model is 10K more than 5 times the memory of the Mark 1. How many K's is the Mark 2's memory?

   a. $n + 10 = 32 \times 5$

   b. $\frac{n}{5} = 32 + 10$

   c. $n - 10 = 32 \times 5$

Write an equation, and solve.

3. The Gant printer can print 600 characters per minute. The Nole printer can print 20 characters per minute more than 1.8 times the characters per minute of the Gant printer. How many characters per minute can the Nole printer print?

4. The weight of a hard disk unit of a computer is 0.5 times the total weight of the printer and the terminal. The hard disk unit weighs 14.85 kilograms, and the terminal weighs 10.6 kilograms. How many kilograms does the printer weigh?

5. A pack of 10 soft disks costs $6 less than 4 printer ribbons. Each printer ribbon costs $7.80. What is the cost of each soft disk?

6. Max has $65.00. He buys 5 copies of a computer manual, and his change is $2.75. How much does each copy of the manual cost?

7. The total memory of two computers is 192K. The second computer has double the memory of the first computer. How much memory does the second computer have?

8. Katrine has programmed a computer so that any number she enters will be squared and then the square will be doubled. If she enters the number 1.2 what will the computer show?

Write two equivalent fractions for each.

1. $\frac{7}{11}$

2. $\frac{2}{3}$

3. $\frac{2}{5}$

4. $\frac{1}{3}$

Write the fraction in simplest form.

5. $\frac{56}{72}$

6. $\frac{26}{28}$

7. $\frac{40}{110}$

8. $\frac{9}{54}$

9. $\frac{48}{64}$

10. $\frac{28}{35}$

11. $\frac{18}{24}$

12. $\frac{24}{48}$

13. $\frac{51}{68}$

14. $\frac{24}{84}$

15. $\frac{45}{99}$

16. $\frac{12}{48}$

Find the missing term.

17. $\frac{40}{52} = \frac{d}{13}$

18. $\frac{60}{75} = \frac{u}{15}$

19. $\frac{2}{3} = \frac{34}{t}$

20. $\frac{63}{75} = \frac{21}{w}$

21. $\frac{16}{18} = \frac{48}{p}$

22. $\frac{24}{64} = \frac{s}{16}$

23. $\frac{18}{99} = \frac{6}{r}$

24. $\frac{75}{125} = \frac{3}{k}$

25. $\frac{21}{28} = \frac{a}{4}$

26. $\frac{44}{121} = \frac{j}{11}$

27. $\frac{6}{7} = \frac{54}{h}$

28. $\frac{24}{42} = \frac{f}{7}$

Solve.

29. The Benny Button Company supplies 105 clothing manufacturers with an equal number of buttons each month. The Benny Brass Button is their best-selling button, and 45 companies order only Benny Brass Buttons. If the Benny Button Company ships 315 cases of buttons per month, how many cases are there of Benny Brass Buttons?

30. The Benny Button Company ships 63 cases of buttons by truck each month, 140 cases of buttons by train, and 112 cases by air. What is the fraction of buttons shipped by truck, train, and air in simplest form?

Use with pages 120–121.

Write each mixed number as a fraction.

1. $5\frac{5}{12}$

2. $7\frac{9}{16}$

3. $6\frac{2}{9}$

4. $14\frac{2}{3}$

5. $146\frac{3}{8}$

Write each fraction as a whole number or a mixed number in simplest form.

6. $\frac{374}{22}$

7. $\frac{30}{14}$

8. $\frac{222}{35}$

9. $\frac{100}{7}$

10. $\frac{216}{44}$

For each number on the left, find its equivalent on the right. Use a straightedge to sight along an imaginary line connecting the dots next to the two numbers. The line will pass through a number and a letter. Use the number and corresponding letter to answer the riddle. Do not write in this book.

11. $1\frac{2}{3}$ •   • 4

12. $\frac{12}{5}$ •   **3**   **T** • $\frac{41}{4}$
                        I

13. $2\frac{3}{4}$ •   **S** • $\frac{45}{7}$

14. $8\frac{1}{2}$ •   **O**   **6** • $2\frac{2}{5}$

15. $\frac{28}{11}$ • **T**   **10**   **U** • $\frac{5}{3}$

16. $6\frac{3}{7}$ •   **13**   **11**   **7** • $2\frac{6}{11}$
                     5

17. $10\frac{1}{4}$ •   **2**   • $\frac{94}{7}$
                              4

18. $6\frac{1}{2}$ •   **N**   **N** • $\frac{11}{4}$

19. $13\frac{3}{7}$ •   **1**   • $\frac{17}{2}$

20. $\frac{76}{5}$ • **I**   • $\frac{66}{7}$
            G   **S**

21. $\frac{24}{6}$ •   **C**   • $\frac{30}{3}$
            8   **9**

22. $9\frac{3}{7}$ •   • $\frac{13}{2}$
                              12

23. 10 • **R**   • $15\frac{1}{5}$

How can you tell the age of a telephone?

$\frac{?}{1}$ $\frac{?}{2}$ $\frac{?}{3}$ $\frac{?}{11}$ $\frac{?}{7}$ $\frac{?}{6}$ $\frac{?}{5}$ $\frac{?}{13}$ $\frac{?}{9}$ $\frac{?}{10}$ $\frac{?}{4}$ $\frac{?}{12}$ $\frac{?}{8}$

Use with pages 122–123.

Compare. Write $>$, $<$, or $=$. Use the LCD.

1. $\frac{12}{19}$ ◯ $\frac{23}{40}$

2. $\frac{1}{6}$ ◯ $\frac{2}{8}$

3. $6\frac{3}{7}$ ◯ $6\frac{4}{7}$

4. $\frac{18}{4}$ ◯ $\frac{30}{7}$

5. $\frac{4}{7}$ ◯ $\frac{3}{7}$

6. $\frac{22}{7}$ ◯ $\frac{68}{28}$

7. $\frac{19}{54}$ ◯ $\frac{7}{21}$

8. $2\frac{3}{8}$ ◯ $2\frac{4}{11}$

9. $1\frac{22}{35}$ ◯ $1\frac{4}{7}$

10. $\frac{6}{11}$ ◯ $\frac{66}{121}$

11. $\frac{41}{23}$ ◯ $\frac{29}{16}$

12. $2\frac{2}{3}$ ◯ $2\frac{5}{9}$

13. $\frac{5}{9}$ ◯ $\frac{14}{25}$

14. $\frac{12}{17}$ ◯ $\frac{25}{33}$

15. $7\frac{8}{19}$ ◯ $7\frac{24}{57}$

16. $\frac{18}{21}$ ◯ $\frac{5}{6}$

17. $\frac{6}{7}$ ◯ $\frac{4}{9}$

18. $\frac{13}{8}$ ◯ $\frac{7}{4}$

19. $6\frac{5}{9}$ ◯ $6\frac{3}{5}$

20. $4\frac{42}{55}$ ◯ $4\frac{5}{7}$

21. $\frac{16}{91}$ ◯ $\frac{9}{50}$

22. $3\frac{6}{15}$ ◯ $3\frac{2}{3}$

23. $\frac{42}{8}$ ◯ $\frac{85}{17}$

24. $\frac{6}{11}$ ◯ $\frac{12}{23}$

Write the numbers in order from the least to the greatest.

25. $\frac{3}{8}$, $\frac{6}{8}$, $\frac{1}{4}$, $\frac{5}{4}$

26. $\frac{3}{10}$, $\frac{2}{3}$, $\frac{3}{8}$, $\frac{1}{2}$

27. $5\frac{3}{5}$, $5\frac{3}{8}$, $5\frac{2}{10}$, $4\frac{1}{4}$

28. $\frac{15}{6}$, $2\frac{1}{7}$, $3\frac{1}{4}$, $\frac{50}{14}$

Solve.

29. Marie drank $1\frac{2}{3}$ cups of juice. Roger drank $1\frac{3}{5}$ cups of juice. Who drank more juice?

30. Lila has two different recipes for banana bread. Recipe A uses $3\frac{3}{4}$ cups of bananas. Recipe B uses $3\frac{7}{8}$ cups of bananas. Which recipe uses less?

PIZZA PALACE SALES

Monday	☺ ☺ ☺ ☺ ☺ ☺
Tuesday	☺ ☺ ☺ ☺ ☺ ☺ ◖
Wednesday	☺ ☺ ☺ ☺ ☺ ☺
Thursday	☺ ☺ ☺ ☺ ☺ ☺ ☺ ☺
Friday	☺ ☺ ☺ ☺ ☺ ☺ ☺ ☺ ◖
Saturday	☺ ☺ ☺ ☺ ☺ ☺ ☺ ◖
Sunday	☺ ☺ ☺ ☺ ☺ ☺ ◖

☺ = 50 pizzas

The pictograph above shows the average sales of pizzas for various days of the week. Use the pictograph to solve.

1. On which day are the most pizzas sold?

2. On which days are the least pizzas sold?

3. How many more pizzas are normally sold on Thursday than on Sunday?

4. What is the average number of pizzas sold per week?

5. How many more pizzas does the Palace normally sell during the week (Monday through Friday) than on weekends?

6. When there is a Friday night football game, the Pizza Palace sales are usually 1.6 times the normal Friday sales. About how many are sold on a football Friday?

7. During a holiday weekend the sales on Friday, Saturday, and Sunday are usually 1.5 times the usual sales. Calculate the sales for each of these three days during the holiday weekend. (Round to the nearest whole number.)

8. If the average profit on a pizza is $2.63, how much profit does the Pizza Palace earn on the sales of pizzas during an average week?

Write > or <.

1. $1\frac{1}{9} + 2\frac{3}{8}$ ◯ 3

2. $2\frac{4}{5} + 1\frac{7}{8}$ ◯ 5

3. $4\frac{8}{9} + 3\frac{6}{7}$ ◯ 9

4. $7\frac{8}{11} + 6\frac{7}{9}$ ◯ 13

5. $6\frac{1}{7} + 5\frac{3}{19}$ ◯ 11

6. $8\frac{1}{7} + 13\frac{2}{21}$ ◯ 22

7. $4\frac{7}{9} + 2\frac{6}{11}$ ◯ 7

8. $4\frac{5}{6} + 1\frac{9}{11}$ ◯ 7

9. $14\frac{5}{6} + 9\frac{8}{9}$ ◯ 23

10. $\frac{4}{7} + \frac{5}{9}$ ◯ 1

11. $2\frac{6}{11} + 3\frac{5}{8}$ ◯ 6

12. $6\frac{3}{17} + 2\frac{2}{19}$ ◯ 9

13. $14\frac{8}{11} + 1\frac{3}{4}$ ◯ 16

14. $3\frac{9}{10} + 1\frac{5}{7}$ ◯ 5

15. $7\frac{2}{3} + 6\frac{5}{7}$ ◯ 14

16. $4 - 2\frac{1}{8}$ ◯ 2

17. $3\frac{1}{5} - 1\frac{7}{8}$ ◯ 1

18. $8\frac{7}{8} - 5\frac{1}{5}$ ◯ 3

19. $9\frac{7}{8} - 2\frac{1}{15}$ ◯ 7

20. $5\frac{4}{7} - 1\frac{3}{11}$ ◯ 4

21. $12\frac{3}{5} - 5\frac{9}{10}$ ◯ 6

22. $6\frac{2}{11} - 1\frac{5}{7}$ ◯ 3

23. $15\frac{7}{8} - 3\frac{2}{19}$ ◯ 12

24. $20\frac{7}{8} - 10\frac{3}{7}$ ◯ 10

Solve.

25. Do the apples and oranges weigh more than 8 pounds altogether?

26. Do the bananas and berries weigh more than 4 pounds altogether?

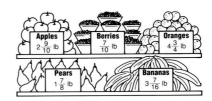

Apples $2\frac{9}{10}$ lb Berries $\frac{7}{10}$ lb Oranges $4\frac{3}{4}$ lb Pears $1\frac{7}{8}$ lb Bananas $3\frac{7}{16}$ lb

27. Which two bags of fruit weigh about 5 pounds?

28. Is the total weight of all five bags of fruit more than 12 pounds?

Add. Write the answer in simplest form.

1. $\dfrac{3}{8}$
$\dfrac{1}{8}$
$+\dfrac{3}{8}$

2. $5\dfrac{2}{5}$
$+\,4\dfrac{1}{5}$

3. $\dfrac{3}{5}$
$+\dfrac{1}{5}$

4. $3\dfrac{1}{4}$
$+\,4\dfrac{1}{2}$

5. $\dfrac{1}{6}$
$+\dfrac{1}{4}$

6. $\dfrac{1}{6}$
$+\dfrac{1}{2}$

7. $\dfrac{8}{9}$
$+\dfrac{5}{9}$

8. $3\dfrac{2}{3}$
$+\,7\dfrac{2}{3}$

9. $\dfrac{4}{10}$
$\dfrac{3}{10}$
$+\dfrac{1}{10}$

10. $2\dfrac{3}{6}$
$+\,1\dfrac{1}{6}$

11. $7\dfrac{2}{5}$
$+\,8\dfrac{1}{5}$

12. $\dfrac{1}{8}$
$\dfrac{3}{16}$
$+\dfrac{1}{2}$

13. $\dfrac{1}{3}$
$+\dfrac{2}{5}$

14. $2\dfrac{3}{12}$
$+\,7\dfrac{3}{4}$

15. $9\dfrac{1}{10}$
$+\,10\dfrac{1}{6}$

16. $4\dfrac{2}{3}$
$+\,3\dfrac{8}{9}$

17. $\dfrac{2}{3}$
$\dfrac{5}{8}$
$+\dfrac{5}{6}$

18. $3\dfrac{1}{2}$
$+\,5\dfrac{1}{6}$

19. $\dfrac{5}{9}$
$+\dfrac{2}{3}$

20. $\dfrac{5}{12}$
$\dfrac{1}{4}$
$+\dfrac{2}{3}$

21. $\dfrac{1}{6}+\dfrac{2}{3}+\dfrac{5}{12}$

22. $5\dfrac{1}{4}+3\dfrac{3}{8}+4\dfrac{5}{8}$

23. $\dfrac{1}{7}+\dfrac{3}{7}+\dfrac{2}{7}$

24. $5\dfrac{1}{9}+7\dfrac{4}{9}+3\dfrac{8}{9}$

Solve.

25. Viola made a fruit mix with $1\dfrac{1}{2}$ cup raisins, $1\dfrac{1}{3}$ cup dried apples, and $1\dfrac{1}{4}$ cup dried apricots. How much fruit did she use in all?

26. Marc used two pieces of wood that were $15\dfrac{5}{8}$ in. long and $17\dfrac{3}{4}$ in. long. What was the total length of the wood used?

Subtract. Write the answer in simplest form.

1. $\dfrac{5}{6}$
$-\dfrac{1}{3}$

2. $17\dfrac{4}{5}$
$-10\dfrac{7}{10}$

3. $12\dfrac{5}{8}$
$-9\dfrac{1}{4}$

4. $\dfrac{3}{5}$
$-\dfrac{2}{5}$

5. $9\dfrac{1}{2}$
$-3\dfrac{1}{8}$

6. $11\dfrac{1}{2}$
$-1\dfrac{3}{7}$

7. $\dfrac{9}{10}$
$-\dfrac{3}{10}$

8. $18\dfrac{1}{3}$
$-10\dfrac{2}{9}$

9. $\dfrac{2}{9}$
$-\dfrac{1}{6}$

10. $15\dfrac{1}{3}$
$-14\dfrac{1}{6}$

11. $\dfrac{4}{5}$
$-\dfrac{7}{10}$

12. $10\dfrac{1}{3}$
$-10\dfrac{1}{9}$

13. $9\dfrac{1}{2}$
$-5\dfrac{1}{3}$

14. $\dfrac{3}{4}$
$-\dfrac{1}{3}$

15. $10\dfrac{1}{2}$
$-4\dfrac{3}{9}$

16. $20\dfrac{5}{6}$
$-16\dfrac{1}{2}$

17. $3\dfrac{1}{2}$
$-2\dfrac{1}{4}$

18. $\dfrac{3}{5}$
$-\dfrac{3}{10}$

19. $18\dfrac{1}{4}$
$-13\dfrac{1}{6}$

20. $18\dfrac{4}{7}$
$-5\dfrac{1}{2}$

21. $19\dfrac{1}{2}$
$-14\dfrac{1}{3}$

22. $\dfrac{5}{6}$
$-\dfrac{4}{9}$

23. $8\dfrac{9}{10}$
$-5\dfrac{5}{6}$

24. $4\dfrac{8}{9}$
$-1\dfrac{1}{2}$

25. $19\dfrac{7}{8}$
$-11\dfrac{1}{2}$

26. $\dfrac{4}{5} - \dfrac{1}{2}$

27. $8\dfrac{4}{5} - 2\dfrac{1}{4}$

28. $12\dfrac{8}{9} - 7\dfrac{5}{9}$

29. $22\dfrac{5}{7} - 6\dfrac{2}{3}$

Solve.

30. Peter picked $4\dfrac{1}{2}$ pounds of strawberries and ate $\dfrac{1}{3}$ pound. Ellen picked $4\dfrac{1}{4}$ pounds of strawberries and ate $\dfrac{1}{6}$ pound. Who has more left and how much?

Subtract. Write the answer in simplest form.

1. $16\frac{1}{5}$
   $- 15\frac{1}{2}$

2. $19\frac{1}{2}$
   $- 14\frac{1}{3}$

3. $17\frac{4}{5}$
   $- 10\frac{7}{10}$

4. 16
   $- 7\frac{3}{5}$

5. $8\frac{4}{5}$
   $- 2\frac{1}{4}$

6. $16\frac{2}{5}$
   $- 5\frac{4}{5}$

7. 9
   $- 2\frac{1}{5}$

8. $16\frac{3}{4}$
   $- 5\frac{4}{5}$

9. $12\frac{5}{8}$
   $- 9\frac{1}{4}$

10. $9\frac{1}{2}$
    $- 3\frac{3}{8}$

11. $12\frac{1}{6}$
    $- 10\frac{5}{9}$

12. 19
    $- 2\frac{1}{2}$

13. $15\frac{1}{3}$
    $- 14\frac{1}{6}$

14. 5
    $- 2\frac{7}{9}$

15. $18\frac{1}{3}$
    $- 10\frac{2}{3}$

16. $13\frac{1}{2}$
    $- 3\frac{3}{5}$

17. $4\frac{8}{9}$
    $- 1\frac{1}{9}$

18. $10\frac{1}{4}$
    $- 3\frac{2}{3}$

19. $18\frac{4}{7}$
    $- 5\frac{1}{2}$

20. $10\frac{1}{3}$
    $- 10\frac{1}{9}$

21. 5
    $- 3\frac{2}{3}$

22. $3\frac{1}{2}$
    $- 2\frac{1}{2}$

23. 14
    $- 1\frac{5}{6}$

24. $9\frac{3}{4}$
    $- 5\frac{1}{3}$

25. $19\frac{7}{8}$
    $- 11\frac{1}{2}$

26. $12\frac{1}{9} - 11\frac{1}{2}$

27. $10\frac{1}{2} - 4\frac{3}{7}$

28. $11\frac{3}{4} - 2\frac{9}{10}$

29. $20 - 2\frac{3}{10}$

30. $11\frac{4}{7} - 1\frac{3}{7}$

31. $10\frac{2}{3} - 9\frac{1}{6}$

32. $18\frac{1}{4} - 13\frac{1}{6}$

33. $13 - 6\frac{8}{9}$

34. $10\frac{2}{6} - 7\frac{3}{6}$

35. $10\frac{3}{4} - 2\frac{1}{3}$

Use estimation to solve.

1. Cindy is building a workbench. She has to hammer a nail through two pieces of wood, each $\frac{9}{16}$ inches thick, into the top of a support. If she wants the nail to go at least $\frac{3}{4}$ inch into the support, can she use a $1\frac{3}{4}$-inch nail?

2. One part of the workbench is made from 3 pieces of wood each measuring $7\frac{3}{8}$ inches by 7 inches. Can Cindy cut the pieces from a board measuring $7\frac{1}{4}$ inches by 24 inches?

3. It took Cindy $1\frac{1}{4}$ hours to buy the wood, $2\frac{3}{4}$ hours to build the bench, $1\frac{1}{2}$ hours to paint it, and $\frac{1}{4}$ hour to set it up in the garage. Did she spend more than 5 hours on the project?

4. Otto needs five strips of wood, measuring $4\frac{3}{8}$ inches, $7\frac{1}{2}$ inches, $9\frac{3}{4}$ inches, $6\frac{1}{8}$ inches, and $8\frac{5}{8}$ inches long. Can he cut the strips from a one-yard length of wood strip?

5. George has a board of wood 6 feet long. From it, he cuts 2 pieces that are each $18\frac{1}{8}$ inches long, a piece $15\frac{1}{4}$ inches long, and a piece $7\frac{5}{8}$ inches long. About how long, to the nearest inch, is the piece of wood that he has left over?

6. Gayle, Mario, and Geoff are building a cabinet. Gayle cuts a piece of wood $25\frac{3}{4}$ inches long, Mario cuts a piece $25\frac{7}{16}$ inches long, and Geoff cuts 2 pieces that are each $12\frac{15}{16}$ inches long. Who cut the most wood?

Multiply. Write the answer in simplest form.

1. $\frac{2}{3} \times \frac{9}{10}$

2. $\frac{1}{6} \times \frac{1}{9} \times \frac{3}{4}$

3. $\frac{2}{3} \times \frac{5}{6} \times \frac{3}{8}$

4. $\frac{1}{6} \times \frac{1}{9}$

5. $\frac{1}{9} \times \frac{9}{10}$

6. $\frac{1}{4} \times \frac{2}{3}$

7. $\frac{1}{2} \times \frac{5}{8} \times \frac{4}{5}$

8. $\frac{1}{7} \times \frac{1}{5}$

9. $\frac{4}{5} \times \frac{5}{7}$

10. $\frac{2}{5} \times \frac{1}{2}$

11. $\frac{2}{3} \times \frac{1}{2}$

12. $\frac{2}{9} \times \frac{3}{4} \times \frac{7}{8}$

13. $\frac{6}{7} \times \frac{1}{6}$

14. $\frac{3}{8} \times \frac{2}{8}$

15. $\frac{3}{4} \times \frac{4}{9} \times \frac{1}{2}$

16. $\frac{7}{8} \times \frac{3}{8} \times \frac{3}{10}$

17. $\frac{1}{8} \times \frac{2}{3}$

18. $\frac{3}{4} \times \frac{7}{9}$

19. $\frac{1}{6} \times \frac{1}{3}$

20. $\frac{2}{7} \times \frac{6}{7}$

21. $\frac{2}{5} \times \frac{1}{2} \times \frac{1}{7}$

22. $\frac{3}{10} \times \frac{5}{9}$

23. $\frac{5}{6} \times \frac{3}{8}$

24. $\frac{1}{8} \times \frac{1}{4}$

25. $\frac{12}{17} \times \frac{1}{2}$

26. $\frac{6}{7} \times \frac{1}{5}$

27. $\frac{9}{10} \times \frac{2}{3}$

28. $\frac{5}{6} \times \frac{2}{15}$

29. $\frac{3}{7} \times \frac{14}{15}$

30. $\frac{2}{9} \times \frac{3}{5}$

Solve.

31. Larry had $\frac{3}{4}$ can of shellac. He used $\frac{2}{3}$ of it. What part of the can of shellac did Larry use?

32. Helen had $\frac{2}{3}$ of a box of pipe cleaners. She used $\frac{5}{6}$ of them to make a mobile. What part of the box of pipe cleaners did she use?

Write > or <.

1. $2\frac{1}{8} \times 1\frac{1}{9}$ ◯ 2

2. $3\frac{2}{7} \times 2\frac{1}{6}$ ◯ 12

3. $4\frac{1}{7} \times 2$ ◯ 8

4. $5\frac{2}{3} \times 4\frac{3}{4}$ ◯ 30

5. $3\frac{4}{9} \times 5$ ◯ 20

6. $2\frac{3}{4} \times 2\frac{7}{8}$ ◯ 9

7. $6 \times 5\frac{7}{11}$ ◯ 30

8. $\frac{7}{8} \times 5$ ◯ 5

9. $8\frac{1}{9} \times 2\frac{1}{5}$ ◯ 16

10. $3\frac{1}{7} \times 12\frac{7}{8}$ ◯ 36

11. $4\frac{4}{5} \times 2$ ◯ 8

12. $14\frac{7}{8} \times 2\frac{9}{11}$ ◯ 45

13. $\frac{4}{5} \div \frac{1}{9}$ ◯ 1

14. $\frac{1}{9} \div \frac{4}{5}$ ◯ 1

15. $1\frac{1}{2} \div 2$ ◯ 1

16. $2\frac{1}{4} \div 1\frac{7}{8}$ ◯ 1

17. $7\frac{3}{4} \div 8\frac{1}{9}$ ◯ 1

18. $5\frac{1}{3} \div 2\frac{7}{8}$ ◯ 1

Estimate.

19. $15\frac{1}{7} \div 4\frac{11}{12}$

20. $6\frac{1}{7} \div 1\frac{8}{9}$

21. $5\frac{1}{8} \div \frac{9}{10}$

22. $28\frac{7}{8} \div 8\frac{1}{4}$

23. $10\frac{2}{3} \div 4\frac{1}{7}$

24. $6\frac{1}{7} \div 1\frac{3}{4}$

25. $5\frac{7}{8} \div 2\frac{9}{11}$

26. $8\frac{1}{11} \times 7\frac{2}{19}$

27. $3\frac{8}{9} \times 7\frac{10}{13}$

28. $14\frac{1}{6} \times 2\frac{1}{15}$

29. $1\frac{1}{9} \times 5\frac{1}{8}$

30. $\frac{9}{10} \times 5\frac{4}{5}$

Multiply. Write the answer in simplest form.

1. $4\frac{1}{5} \times 1\frac{3}{7}$

2. $\frac{3}{4} \times 2\frac{8}{9} \times \frac{9}{10}$

3. $\frac{2}{5} \times 85$

4. $6\frac{9}{10} \times 1\frac{1}{3} \times 2\frac{1}{3}$

5. $8\frac{1}{5} \times 5\frac{5}{6}$

6. $2\frac{1}{2} \times 8\frac{7}{10} \times 2\frac{3}{8}$

7. $10\frac{1}{2} \times 8\frac{5}{7} \times 5\frac{1}{6}$

8. $10 \times \frac{2}{5} \times \frac{1}{3}$

9. $4\frac{1}{6} \times 2\frac{1}{5}$

10. $2\frac{2}{7} \times 8\frac{3}{4} \times 32\frac{5}{8}$

11. $6\frac{5}{8} \times 1\frac{3}{5}$

12. $48 \times \frac{2}{3}$

13. $10\frac{5}{6} \times 6\frac{2}{5}$

14. $36 \times \frac{2}{9}$

15. $70 \times \frac{4}{5} \times 2\frac{2}{3}$

16. $\frac{4}{9} \times 27$

Complete each problem. Then find the fraction below that is the same as the fraction in your answer. Write the matching code letters to solve the riddle.(You won't use all letters.)

17. $8\frac{3}{7} \times 5\frac{5}{6}$ $\boxed{A}$

18. $10\frac{3}{10} \times 2\frac{1}{2}$ $\boxed{S}$

19. $1\frac{1}{8} \times 2\frac{7}{9}$ $\boxed{T}$

20. $4\frac{2}{3} \times 3\frac{5}{6}$ $\boxed{E}$

21. $1\frac{1}{3} \times 3\frac{3}{10}$ $\boxed{P}$

22. $9\frac{1}{10} \times 3\frac{3}{7}$ $\boxed{G}$

23. $7\frac{4}{5} \times 2\frac{1}{6}$ $\boxed{A}$

24. $2\frac{3}{10} \times 5\frac{5}{6}$ $\boxed{R}$

25. $6\frac{1}{4} \times 4\frac{4}{7}$ $\boxed{R}$

26. $7\frac{1}{3} \times 8\frac{1}{2}$ $\boxed{F}$

27. $6\frac{1}{3} \times 6\frac{3}{8}$ $\boxed{H}$

28. $5\frac{7}{9} \times 3\frac{1}{2}$ $\boxed{Y}$

$\underline{}$ $\underline{}$ $\underline{}$ $\underline{}$ $\underline{}$ $\underline{}$ $\underline{}$ $\underline{}$ $\underline{}$
?   ?   ?   ?   ?   ?   ?   ?   ?

Write the letter of the better plan for simplifying each problem.

1. It took 11 carpenters $4\frac{1}{2}$ hours to cut 1,260 dowels. How long would it take one carpenter working at the same speed to cut 196 dowels?

   a. step 1: 200 × 10 = 2,000

   step 2: 2,000 ÷ 5 = 400

   step 3: 1,200 ÷ 400 = 3

   b. step 1: 1,250 ÷ 5 = 250

   step 2: 250 ÷ 10 = 25

   step 3: 200 ÷ 25 = 8

2. A fence painter uses $8\frac{3}{4}$ gallons of paint for every 210 feet of fence. How much paint would he use to paint 752 feet of fence?

   a. step 1: 200 ÷ 10 = 20

   step 2: 800 ÷ 20 = 40

   b. step 1: 750 + 200 = 950

   step 2: 950 ÷ 10 = 95

Solve. Simplify the problem if you need to.

3. A bricklayer uses 1,785 bricks to build 15 fireplaces. If he builds 6 fireplaces in 2 days, how many bricks does he use per day?

4. Phillip has three boxes of nails. The boxes contain 126 nails, 240 nails, and 342 nails. If he uses $\frac{5}{6}$ of the nails, how many nails will he have left?

5. Louise needs 164 feet of board for a client's wooden floor. The wood costs $3.40 per foot, and Louise wants to make $1.25 for every foot of board that she installs. How much does she charge the client for installing the floor?

6. Roger uses $7\frac{1}{4}$ cans of putty to set 29 windows. He expects to set 210 windows this week. How much putty will he use?

7. Dawson Construction built 53 houses each year from 1971 to 1980. From 1981 to 1985, it built 76 houses each year. How many houses did Dawson Construction build from 1971 to 1985?

8. Jance Buildings constructed 140 houses from 1978 to 1982. If construction was increased by $\frac{1}{5}$, how many houses would Jance build from 1983 to 1987?

Divide. Write the answer in simplest form.

1. $\frac{3}{5} \div \frac{9}{10}$

2. $\frac{1}{10} \div \frac{9}{10}$

3. $\frac{19}{81} \div \frac{1}{3}$

4. $\frac{7}{27} \div \frac{4}{9}$

5. $\frac{1}{6} \div \frac{1}{4}$

6. $\frac{1}{10} \div \frac{1}{3}$

7. $\frac{4}{7} \div \frac{4}{5}$

8. $\frac{3}{8} \div \frac{3}{5}$

9. $\frac{1}{3} \div \frac{1}{2}$

10. $\frac{3}{22} \div \frac{2}{11}$

11. $\frac{1}{7} \div \frac{1}{6}$

12. $\frac{1}{2} \div \frac{3}{4}$

13. $\frac{1}{12} \div \frac{2}{3}$

14. $\frac{2}{15} \div \frac{4}{5}$

15. $\frac{7}{12} \div \frac{7}{9}$

16. $\frac{4}{9} \div \frac{1}{2}$

17. $\frac{1}{5} \div \frac{3}{5}$

18. $\frac{1}{8} \div \frac{1}{3}$

19. $\frac{1}{15} \div \frac{3}{5}$

20. $\frac{2}{3} \div \frac{4}{5}$

21. $\frac{5}{28} \div \frac{1}{4}$

22. $\frac{2}{27} \div \frac{1}{3}$

23. $\frac{3}{50} \div \frac{1}{10}$

24. $\frac{8}{27} \div \frac{1}{3}$

25. $\frac{3}{8} \div \frac{3}{4}$

26. $\frac{70}{99} \div \frac{7}{9}$

27. $\frac{3}{10} \div \frac{9}{10}$

28. $\frac{3}{10} \div \frac{2}{5}$

29. $\frac{7}{72} \div \frac{1}{6}$

30. $\frac{10}{21} \div \frac{6}{7}$

Divide. Write the answer in simplest form.

1. $3\frac{1}{2} \div 1\frac{7}{8}$

2. $1\frac{3}{4} \div 4\frac{1}{2}$

3. $1\frac{1}{5} \div 1\frac{1}{2}$

4. $4\frac{1}{3} \div 2\frac{1}{2}$

5. $3\frac{1}{6} \div 2$

6. $7\frac{1}{3} \div \frac{1}{3}$

7. $7\frac{1}{2} \div 2\frac{7}{9}$

8. $3\frac{1}{2} \div 3$

9. $9\frac{1}{5} \div 2$

10. $3\frac{1}{3} \div 1\frac{5}{9}$

11. $\frac{9}{10} \div 9\frac{3}{4}$

12. $4\frac{2}{3} \div 2\frac{2}{3}$

13. $4\frac{5}{8} \div \frac{7}{8}$

14. $8\frac{1}{3} \div 4$

15. $8\frac{1}{4} \div \frac{3}{4}$

16. $1\frac{1}{2} \div 1\frac{1}{2}$

17. $1\frac{2}{7} \div 1\frac{1}{5}$

18. $3\frac{1}{5} \div 4\frac{4}{7}$

19. $4\frac{1}{4} \div 3$

20. $\frac{1}{6} \div 10\frac{3}{4}$

21. $9\frac{2}{7} \div 1\frac{5}{7}$

22. $6\frac{2}{5} \div \frac{7}{10}$

23. $6\frac{1}{6} \div \frac{2}{3}$

24. $9\frac{1}{3} \div 1\frac{1}{3}$

25. $4\frac{2}{7} \div 1\frac{1}{2}$

26. $10\frac{3}{4} \div 2$

27. $6\frac{1}{2} \div 1\frac{1}{6}$

28. $4\frac{1}{3} \div 1\frac{5}{8}$

29. $2\frac{1}{4} \div 6\frac{3}{4}$

30. $7\frac{1}{10} \div \frac{3}{8}$

Write a decimal for each fraction or mixed number. Use a bar to show repeating decimals.

1. $\frac{18}{25}$

2. $\frac{7}{20}$

3. $2\frac{7}{22}$

4. $4\frac{6}{25}$

5. $\frac{29}{50}$

6. $12\frac{80}{91}$

7. $\frac{5}{24}$

8. $7\frac{86}{90}$

9. $\frac{27}{40}$

Write a fraction or mixed number, in simplest form, for each decimal.

10. $0.\overline{2}$

11. 4.8125

12. 9.3

13. 0.765

14. $3.\overline{3}$

15. $9.\overline{5}$

16. 13.96

17. 0.125

18. $4.\overline{8}$

Compare. Write $<$, $>$, or $=$.

19. 0.34 $\bigcirc$ $\frac{1}{3}$

20. 0.125 $\bigcirc$ $\frac{1}{8}$

21. 0.55 $\bigcirc$ $\frac{12}{20}$

22. $\frac{5}{7}$ $\bigcirc$ 0.714281

23. $\frac{8}{9}$ $\bigcirc$ 0.89

24. 0.756 $\bigcirc$ $\frac{19}{25}$

Solve.

25. There are 100 beads on Julie's necklace. Of these, 0.45 are blue. What fraction of the beads are blue?

26. Out of 1,000 tickets for the crafts fair, all but 150 were sold. What part of the tickets were sold? Write the answer as a decimal and as a fraction in simplest form.

Solve. Write the answer in simplest form.

1. $x + 2\frac{1}{3} = 7$

2. $n - 4\frac{3}{5} = 12\frac{1}{3}$

3. $\frac{1}{9}a + 3\frac{2}{3} = 4\frac{1}{2}$

4. $1\frac{3}{4}b - 13 = 2\frac{1}{4}$

5. $3\frac{1}{3}w + \frac{2}{3} = 20\frac{1}{2}$

6. $3\frac{3}{10}r \div 2\frac{1}{3} = 1\frac{5}{6}$

7. $\frac{1}{2}g + \frac{4}{3} = 7$

8. $\frac{4}{9}s - 2 = 14$

Copy and solve each equation. To unscramble the limerick, write the words from each box in the order given.

$3X \div 5 = 9$ $X = \underline{\quad?\quad}$ WHEN HE ROSE	$\frac{5}{3}X = 15$ $X = \underline{\quad?\quad}$ EXCEEDINGLY NEAT	$2X \div 3 = 14$ $X = \underline{\quad?\quad}$ WHO WAS SO
$5\frac{1}{4}X = 42$ $X = \underline{\quad?\quad}$ ON HIS HEAD	$3\frac{2}{3}X = 44$ $X = \underline{\quad?\quad}$ THERE WAS A	$1\frac{3}{5}X = 32$ $X = \underline{\quad?\quad}$ HIS FEET
$\frac{5}{12}X + 1 = 21$ $X = \underline{\quad?\quad}$ OUT OF BED	$7X - 3 = 39$ $X = \underline{\quad?\quad}$ DID DIRTY	$\frac{8}{9}X = 2\frac{2}{3}$ $X = \underline{\quad?\quad}$ HE STOOD
$3\frac{3}{7}X - 5 = 19$ $X = \underline{\quad?\quad}$ FROM CRETE	$\frac{X}{23} + 13 = 14$ $X = \underline{\quad?\quad}$ YOUNG FELLOW	$5X - 2\frac{3}{7} = 7\frac{4}{7}$ $X = \underline{\quad?\quad}$ AND NEVER

12, 23, 7
21, 9
15, 48
3, 8
2, 6, 20

Write the letter of the correct answer.

1. Albert wants to put 250 eggs in cartons that hold a dozen eggs each. How many cartons will he need?

   a. 20 cartons

   b. $20\frac{5}{6}$ cartons

   c. 21 cartons

2. Hassan is reading a 4-volume set of cookbooks. Each book has 250 pages. He is now on page 437. How many pages of the second book has he finished?

   a. 187 pages

   b. 63 pages

   c. $\frac{187}{250}$ book

Solve.

3. Chef Salim prepares 35 tea sandwiches in 2 minutes. After 7 minutes and 45 seconds, how many whole sandwiches has she prepared if she makes them at her regular speed?

4. It takes Ruth 2 minutes to chop 3 pounds of celery into small pieces. How long will it take her to chop $5\frac{1}{2}$ pounds?

5. Talal's kitchen floor measures 110 feet square. He wants to cover the floor with tiles that measure $7\frac{1}{2}$ feet square each. How many tiles will he need?

6. Sadako's new restaurant has 8 rooms. To paint the rooms, he needs 10 gallons of paint. He has already used $3\frac{1}{4}$ gallons of paint. How many rooms has he completed painting if he is painting 1 at a time?

7. Betty is selling her old paperback cookbooks at 3 for $3.50. A customer wants only one book. What is the price she should charge if she does not want to lose money?

8. A grocery chain sells melons at 3 for $4.00. The computer that it uses to calculate prices drops all fractions of a cent. How much does one melon cost?

9. In making loaves of whole wheat bread, a baker uses $2\frac{1}{2}$ pounds of flour to make 5 loaves. The baker purchases flour in 50-pound bags. How many loaves have been made if $22\frac{1}{4}$ pounds of flour have been used so far?

10. The bakery ships loaves of bread in boxes that hold 2 dozen loaves each. If the bakery ships 372 loaves to a restaurant, how many boxes of bread are delivered to the restaurant?

kilometer (km)	hectometer (hm)	dekameter (dm)	meter (m)	decimeter (dm)	centimeter (cm)	millimeter (mm)
1,000 m	100 m	10 m	1 m	0.1 m	0.01 m	0.001 m

Write the unit used to measure

1. the thickness of a phone book.

2. the width of an ocean.

3. the thickness of a quarter.

4. the length of a swimming pool.

Complete. Use the chart to help you.

5. 9,100 cm = ___?___ m

6. 49 cm = ___?___ m

7. 25,000 mm ___?___ m

8. 27 m = ___?___ mm

9. 16 km = ___?___ m

10. 4.33 m = ___?___ cm

11. 855 cm = ___?___ m

12. 58,000 m = ___?___ km

13. 3.779 km = ___?___ m

14. 71 m = ___?___ cm

15. 0.53 m = ___?___ cm

16. 5.28 m = ___?___ cm

17. 10,000 cm = ___?___ m

18. 570 m = ___?___ km

19. 5 m = ___?___ cm

20. 6,528 m = ___?___ km

21. 3.848 m = ___?___ mm

22. 16 km = ___?___ m

23. 923 mm = ___?___ m

24. 100 m = ___?___ cm

25. 4,300 m = ___?___ km

26. 5,062 m = ___?___ km

27. 10 km = ___?___ m

28. 741 cm = ___?___ m

29. 8.4 m = ___?___ m

30. 9.790 m = ___?___ mm

31. 9,000 cm = ___?___ m

32. 1,800 cm = ___?___ m

kilogram (kg)	gram (g)	milligram (mg)
1,000 g	1,000 mg	0.001 g

kiloliter (kL)	liter (L)	milliliter (mL)
1,000 L	1,000 mL	0.001 L

Write the unit used to measure

1. a raindrop.

2. the mass of a person.

3. the capacity of a milk pitcher.

4. the mass of an orange.

Complete. Use the charts to help you.

5. 15,000 mL = _____?_____ L

6. 62 kL = _____?_____ L

7. 0.378 L = _____?_____ mL

8. 6,622 mL = _____?_____ L

9. 39,000 g = _____?_____ kg

10. 513 g = _____?_____ mg

11. 918 g = _____?_____ kg

12. 1,785 mg = _____?_____ g

13. 3,186 mL = _____?_____ L

14. 642 L = _____?_____ kL

15. 47 kg = _____?_____ g

16. 65 g = _____?_____ kg

17. 49.992 kg = _____?_____ g

18. 5.828 L = _____?_____ mL

19. 50 kL = _____?_____ L

20. 313.103 kg = _____?_____ g

21. 500 mg = _____?_____ g

22. 8,906 g = _____?_____ kg

23. 23 L = _____?_____ mL

24. 80.044 g = _____?_____ mg

Solve.

25. Phyllis has a piece of cheese with a mass of 258 g. Irene has a piece of cheese with a mass of 0.3 kg. Whose piece of cheese has the greater mass?

26. Brian drank 575 mL of juice. Robert drank 0.55 L of juice. Who drank more juice?

Copy and complete the chart.

Length	Width	Height	Volume	Capacity	Mass
1. 12 cm	8 cm	10 cm	—————— cm³	—————— mL	—————— g
2. 40 mm	20 mm	111 mm	—————— cm³	—————— mL	—————— g
3. 6 m	2 m	90 cm	—————— m³	—————— kL	—————— t
4. 30 m	14 m	8 m	—————— m³	—————— L	—————— t
5. 50 cm	25 cm	60 cm	—————— cm³	—————— L	—————— kg
6. 650 mm	10 cm	2 m	—————— cm³	—————— mL	—————— g
7. 50 m	35 m	75 mm	—————— m³	—————— kL	—————— t
8. 65 cm	40 cm	3 m	—————— cm³	—————— mL	—————— g
9. 15 m	6 m	9 m	—————— m³	—————— kL	—————— t
10. 8 cm	7 cm	12 cm	—————— cm³	—————— mL	—————— g

Solve.

11. An empty container has a mass of 240 grams. When filled with water, the container and the water have a total mass of 875 grams. How many milliliters of water are there in the container?

12. The inside dimensions of a fish tank are 50 cm by 25 cm by 30 cm. Find the mass of water in the tank when it is full. Express your answer in kilograms.

13. The volume of a juice carton is 960 cm³. How many liters of juice does it hold?

14. A gas station pumps 2,000 L of gas each day. How long does it take the station to use up a 14-kL delivery?

Steve and Leiko opened a frozen yogurt parlor across the street from the Mason Junior High and High School. The shop sells 15 flavors of homemade, wholesome, all-natural frozen yogurt with no preservatives. After the first few weeks of business, Steve and Leiko have some decisions to make.

Read each statement, and write a question that Steve and Leiko should answer before making a decision.

1. Business has been very good in the first few weeks. Some friends say that the prices are too low and should be raised.

2. Some kids suggested that the store add at least 3 or 4 tables and have even more flavors.

3. As business increases, Steve and Leiko find it hard to make enough frozen yogurt. They want to hire someone to help them.

4. The cost of the ingredients for making frozen yogurt is increasing. The landlord wants to raise the rent.

5. The yearbook staff of the school asks them to buy an ad. Other salespersons from the town newspapers and several magazines also solicit their business.

6. One of their customers told her mother how good their frozen yogurt was. Her mother wants Steve to cater a party for her friends.

7. Leiko wants to print a newsletter on a regular basis to inform customers about health and nutrition.

8. The kids want the owners to install a public telephone, a juke box, and video game machines.

12 inches (in.) = 1 foot (ft)
36 in. = 3 ft = 1 yard (yd)
5,280 ft = 1,760 yd = 1 mile (mi)

Write the unit used to measure

1. the height of a refrigerator.

2. a tennis court.

3. the distance to the moon.

4. the width of a shelf.

What is the middle of India? Find the equivalent on the right for each measurement on the left. Write the letters of your answers horizontally on a separate sheet of paper. Then read across to answer the riddle.

5. $\frac{1}{4}$ ft

6. 1,104 in.

7. 84 ft

8. 32 in.

9. 92 yd

10. $\frac{3}{4}$ mi

11. $20\frac{1}{3}$ yd

12. 63 ft

13. 129 in.

14. 440 yd

H. 92 ft

L. $2\frac{2}{3}$ ft

T. 61 ft

D. $\frac{1}{4}$ mi

T. 3 in.

E. 276 ft

E. 28 yd

T. 3,960 ft

R. $10\frac{3}{4}$ ft

E. 21 yd

8 fluid ounces (fl oz) = 1 cup (c)
2 c = 1 pint (pt)
2 pt = 1 quart (qt)
4 qt = 1 gallon (gal)

16 ounces (oz) = 1 pound (lb)
2,000 lb = 1 ton (T)

Write the unit used to measure

1. the weight of an airplane.

2. the amount of juice in a glass.

3. the capacity of a swimming pool.

4. the weight of a marble.

Complete. Use the charts to help you.

5. 22 c = _____?_____ pt

6. $4\frac{3}{4}$ lb = _____?_____ oz

7. 159 lb = _____?_____ oz

8. 55,000 lb = _____?_____ T

9. 148 qt = _____?_____ gal

10. 43 pt = _____?_____ qt _____?_____ pt

11. 192 oz = _____?_____ lb

12. 300 oz = _____?_____ lb

13. 32,000 lb = _____?_____ T

14. 14 c = _____?_____ fl oz

15. $40\frac{1}{10}$ T = _____?_____ lb

16. 7 qt 3 pt = _____?_____ pt

17. $23\frac{1}{4}$ gal = _____?_____ qt

18. 21 c = _____?_____ pt

19. 7 T = _____?_____ lb

20. 240 fl oz = _____?_____ c

21. 12 qt 3 pt = _____?_____ pt

22. 29 pt = _____?_____ qt

Solve.

23. A large apple weighs 7 ounces. If Peter and John each eat an apple a day, how many pounds of apples do they eat in 2 weeks?

24. A recipe for soup uses 1 quart beef broth, 1 pint tomato juice, and 1 cup of milk. How many 1-cup servings will it make?

Estimation	Choosing the Operation	Using a Table
Using a Graph	Solving Multi-step Problems	Writing an Equation
Identifying Extra/Needed Information	Checking for a Reasonable Answer	Interpreting the Quotient and the Remainder

Write the strategy or method you choose. Then solve.

1. To start her company, Maria needs $160,000. Each of 5 investors is paying $15,000, and 4 others are paying $17,000 each. Maria has to invest the rest herself. How much money will she need?

2. A manufacturer in Boston pays Carlos $0.37 per mile one way to deliver its product in Atlanta, 1037 miles away. On the return trip, Carlos is paid $0.24 per mile to deliver another product in Boston. How much money does Carlos make after 7 round-trips?

3. The Johnsons are getting ready to move to New York. They can pack 12 books in each box. If they have 546 books, how many boxes will they need for books?

4. Mrs. Lee wants to buy a new car. She sees one for $10,750. The car has 4 options, costing $389, $429, $318, and $211. With all the options, about how much will the car cost?

Use the graph at the right for Exercises 5–8.

5. By which year has California's population surpassed New York's?

6. About how many people lived in California in 1980?

7. Which state had the biggest increase in population? When and how much was it?

8. About how many more people lived in California than in New York in 1970?

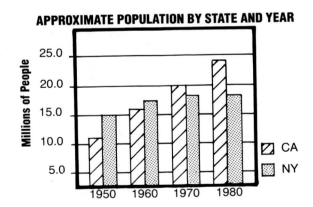

APPROXIMATE POPULATION BY STATE AND YEAR

Millions of People — 25.0, 20.0, 15.0, 10.0, 5.0
Years: 1950, 1960, 1970, 1980
☒ CA ☒ NY

Estimation	Choosing the Operation	Writing an Equation
Using a Graph	Solving Multi-step Problems	Interpreting the Quotient
Identifying Extra/Needed	Checking for a Reasonable Answer	and the Remainder
Information	Using a Table	

Write the strategy or method you choose. Then solve.

1. Roberto wants to buy a $43 gift for his father. He finished one odd job in 4 hours at $3.75 an hour. He is now working at a job which pays $4.00 an hour. How many hours does he have to work to earn the money he needs?

2. Andrea had $20.00. She bought 4 paper pads at $1.19 each, 3 notebooks at $1.89 each, and a book at $4.95. Now she wants to use the remaining money to buy as many pens at $0.79 each as possible. How many pens can she buy?

3. In 1950, there were about 48.4 million $50-bills in the United States. About how much money did these bills amount to?

4. An armored truck traveled at 42 miles per hour for a quarter of a mile. If the truck traveled at the same speed for 5.8 hours, about how far did it go?

5. It takes Una 15 minutes to walk to school. This is 10 minutes more than $\frac{1}{2}$ the time it takes Lin to walk to school. How long does it take Lin?

6. Oscar drove 4 hours at 55 mph, and then drove 45 miles at 50 mph. Then he drove for $2\frac{1}{2}$ hours at 52 mph. How far did he go?

7. Last year, 78 students had perfect attendance records. That was $\frac{2}{3}$ the number of students that had perfect records this year. How many had perfect records this year?

8. In the last 4 months, Jeremy has rented 18 videos. This is 4 more than twice the number of videos he rented during the previous 4 months. How many videos has Jeremy rented in the last 8 months?

9. The gas tank in Art's truck holds 12 gallons. The truck gets 18 miles per gallon. If Art fills the tank just before leaving on a 678-mile trip, how many more times will he have to fill the tank during the trip?

10. Rachel bought 16 rose bushes for $5.95 each. She also bought 8 gardenias for $3.98 each and 7 jasmine plants for $2.65 each. She gave the clerk eight $20-bills. How much change did she receive?

Two measures for a length are given. Write the more precise measure.

1. 42 cm; 422 mm

2. $3\frac{1}{2}$ in.; $3\frac{3}{4}$ in.

3. 37 in.; 3 ft.

4. 2,120 m; 2 km

5. 2 mi; 3,522 yd

6. 8 cm; 83 mm

7. 4.2 m; 423 cm

8. 12 m; 1,206 mm

9. 7 ft; 82 in.

10. 7 km or 700 m

11. 15 km or 15,000 m

12. 6 g or 6,012 mg

13. 6 ft or 73 in.

14. 1 ft or 14 in.

15. 500 mm or 50 cm

16. 3,300 m or 3 km

17. 2 yd or 71 in.

18. 10 m or 100 cm

Find the greatest possible error of measurement.

19. 435 mm

20. 3,840 cm

21. 367 cm

22. 76 mm

23. 8,845 m

24. 7,355 km

25. 295 km

26. 26 cm

27. 22 mm

28. 617 km

29. 3 m

30. 549 mm

31. 600 cm

32. 5 cm

33. 4 km

34. 78,125 km

35. 4.17 dm

36. 9.85 m

Use with pages 180–181.

60 seconds (s) = 1 minute (min)
60 min = 1 hour (h)
24 h = 1 day (d)

Find the time.

1. 3 h 13 min before 6:45 A.M.

2. 6 h 27 min after 3:10 P.M.

Find the elapsed time between

3. 1 P.M. and 11 A.M.

4. 12:37 A.M. and 3 P.M.

5. 3:15 A.M. and 3:02 P.M.

Write the missing number.

6. $3\frac{1}{2}$ h = ____?____ min

7. 18 h = ___?___ d

8. $2\frac{1}{2}$ min = ____?____ s

9. 360 s = ___?___ min

This is a typical weekday for Rocky Rhodes.

Wake up	7:05	Work	9:10–12:30	Bus home	5:40–6:10	Television	7:30–8:30
Breakfast	30 min	Lunch	40 min	Nap	20 min	Extra office work	8:30–9:30
Bus to office	8:20–9:00	Work	1:30–5:30	Supper	50 min	Go to bed	11:15

10. How much time does Rocky spend sleeping? ___?___ minutes.

11. How much time does he spend eating? ___?___ hours ___?___ minutes

12. How much time at home does he spend that is unaccounted for on this table? ___?___ hours ___?___ minutes

13. How much time does he spend doing office work? ___?___ minutes

Write the letter of the correct answer to each problem.

1. In 1.3 hours, a pilot flew a twin-engine propeller plane 403 miles. What was the average speed of the aircraft?

   a. 310 mph b. 313 mph c. 303 mph

2. Captain Roberts piloted a 727 jet 3,200 miles across the United States at an average speed of 510 miles per hour. How long did the flight take?

   a. 6.25 hours b. 6.27 hours c. 6.30 hours

Solve.

3. Lin flew from San Francisco, California, to Phoenix, Arizona, in 1 hour 30 minutes. The plane flew at an average speed of 406 miles per hour. About how far is Phoenix from San Francisco?

4. New York City is located between Washington, D.C., and Boston, Massachusetts. New York is 227 miles from Washington and 185 miles from Boston. How far is Boston from Washington by way of New York?

5. Leslie takes a train from Pittsburgh, Pennsylvania, to Philadelphia, a distance of 260 miles. What is the train's average speed if Leslie reaches Philadelphia in 4 hours 20 minutes?

6. A test pilot flew a jet at the rate of 1,855 miles per hour for 0.6 of an hour. Then the pilot flew the plane for 0.8 of an hour at 1,900 miles per hour. How far did the plane travel during its test flight?

7. Juaquin flew from San Diego, California, to Denver, Colorado. The trip took $2\frac{3}{4}$ hours, and the plane traveled at an average speed of 466 miles per hour. About how far is it from San Diego to Denver?

8. At 9:00 A.M., Seigi and Roberta took separate flights from Boston to Miami, Florida, a distance of 1,236 miles. Seigi's plane flew at 620 mph for 550 miles and then flew the rest of the way at 505 mph. Roberta's plane averaged 570 mph but stopped for 1 hour in Charleston, South Carolina. About how much earlier than Roberta did Seigi arrive in Miami?

9. In 1927, Charles Lindbergh flew 3,600 miles from New York City to Paris, France. The trip took $33\frac{1}{2}$ hours. What was Lindbergh's average rate of speed?

10. In 1903, the Wright Brothers flew 120 feet in 12 seconds in one of the first plane flights. What was their plane's average rate of speed?

Use the time-zone map on page 186 of your textbook to answer the following questions.

It is 6:00 P.M. Wednesday in Washington, D.C. Write the time in each city.

1. Houston

2. Vancouver

3. Hong Kong

4. Algiers

5. Philadelphia

6. Oslo

7. Honolulu

8. Athens

It is 7:45 A.M. Monday in Paris. Write the time in each city.

9. Seattle

10. Nairobi

11. Sydney

12. Denver

13. Miami

14. Madrid

15. Tokyo

16. Oslo

It is 3:20 P.M. Friday in Tokyo. Write the time in each city.

17. Athens

18. Vancouver

19. Honolulu

20. Paris

21. Montreal

22. Los Angeles

23. Houston

24. Miami

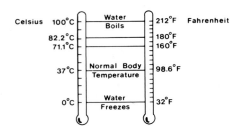

Write the letter of the best estimate.

1. the freezing point of water   **a.** 32°C   **b.** 0°C   **c.** 100°C

2. a warm day   **a.** 45°F   **b.** 80°F   **c.** 197°F

3. inside a refrigerator   **a.** 2°C   **b.** 45°C   **c.** 66°C

4. inside a freezer   **a.** 50°F   **b.** 69°F   **c.** 20°F

Find the temperature.

5. 36°F, rose 14°

6. 17°C, dropped 13°

7. ⁻5.5°C, rose 26°

8. ⁻12°F, dropped 6°

9. 78°F, rose 6°

10. 9.5°C, dropped 1.7°

11. 112.4°C, rose 42.3°

12. 100°F, dropped 64°

13. ⁻16°F, rose 124°

14. 2.7°C, dropped 18°

Find the change in temperature.

15. ⁻12°F to ⁻27°F

16. ⁻30.7°C to ⁻45.3°C

17. 100°F to 167°F

18. 70°C to 98°C

19. 32°F to 6°F

20. ⁻14.6°C to ⁻22.8°C

21. ⁻5°F to 6°F

22. 75°C to 98°C

23. 68°F to 202°F

24. 27.3°C to 98.4°C

25. 14°F to ⁻16°F

26. 6°C to ⁻1°C

Solve. Use the road map to answer each question.

CALIFORNIA

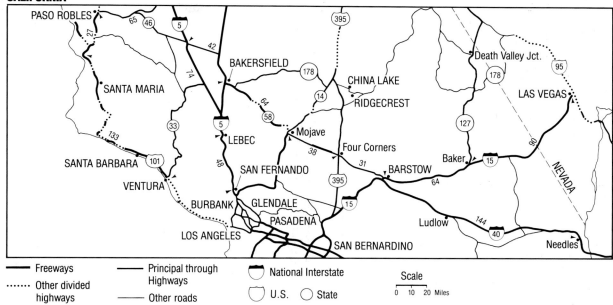

— Freeways —— Principal through Highways National Interstate Scale

····· Other divided highways —— Other roads U.S. State 0 10 20 Miles

1. Martin drives from Las Vegas, Nevada, to Ludlow, California, via Barstow, California. What are the numbers of the highways he will drive on?

2. About how far along the freeways is it from Las Vegas, Nevada, to Needles, California (on Route 40 near Arizona)?

3. Samuel drives on Route 58 from Bakersfield to Barstow. His car travels 20 miles per gallon. If he has 6 gallons of gas in his tank, can he complete his trip without buying more gas?

4. Muriel's mother begins her trip from San Fernando to Paso Robles on Route 5. Muriel's father drives from Ventura to Paso Robles. Does one of them drive farther? Who and by how much?

5. Naomi's car travels 25 miles per gallon. If gas costs her $1.05 per gallon, about how much will she have to spend on gas to make the longer trip described in Problem 4?

6. Lebec is halfway between Bakersfield and San Fernando. Mojave is directly east of Lebec. Armand wants to drive on the freeway from Mojave to Lebec. Would it be quicker for him to go through Bakersfield or through San Fernando?

Write each ratio in fraction form. Simplify where necessary.

1. 5 to 3

2. 1:14

3. 1.5 to 4.5

4. 6:6

5. 24.8:13.4

6. 101.9 to 98.6

7. 3:5

8. 1,295 to 1,187

9. 12:19

10. 10 to 100

11. 25 to 63

12. 3:20

13. 15 to 10

14. 13:80

15. 65 to 200

16. 2:1

17. 136 to 358

18. 746:746

19. 5:450

20. 28 to 29

21. 8 to 64

22. 100 to 200

23. 4.1:1.6

24. 10:15

25. 61:33

26. 4.2 to 1.4

27. 3:11

28. 5 motorcycles to 4 bicycles

29. 28 cars to 8 motorcycles

30. 2 bikers to 30 motorists

31. 400 miles in 5 hours

Write the unit rate.

32. $3,600 for 3 motorcycles

33. 16 riders for 16 motorcycles

34. 175 miles in 3.5 hours

35. 212.5 miles on 2.5 gallons of gas

Use with pages 200–201.

Write the value of x in each proportion.

1. $\frac{3}{1} = \frac{45}{x}$

2. $\frac{12}{7} = \frac{48}{x}$

3. $\frac{65}{x} = \frac{20}{4}$

4. $\frac{x}{63} = \frac{21}{49}$

5. $\frac{32}{96} = \frac{x}{12}$

6. $\frac{69}{57} = \frac{23}{x}$

7. $\frac{10}{1} = \frac{x}{19}$

8. $\frac{14}{x} = \frac{70}{85}$

9. $\frac{x}{68} = \frac{1}{17}$

10. $\frac{28}{12} = \frac{x}{21}$

11. $\frac{84}{18} = \frac{x}{12}$

12. $\frac{3}{10} = \frac{27}{x}$

13. $\frac{28}{6} = \frac{x}{15}$

14. $\frac{144}{24} = \frac{x}{14}$

15. $\frac{9}{x} = \frac{15}{70}$

16. $\frac{21}{11} = \frac{84}{x}$

17. $\frac{48}{16} = \frac{78}{x}$

18. $\frac{x}{42} = \frac{15}{18}$

19. $\frac{54}{81} = \frac{x}{36}$

20. $\frac{32}{100} = \frac{x}{25}$

21. $\frac{8}{10} = \frac{44}{x}$

22. $\frac{x}{28} = \frac{39}{12}$

23. $\frac{35}{x} = \frac{80}{32}$

24. $\frac{4}{27} = \frac{x}{81}$

25. $\frac{x}{16} = \frac{21}{84}$

26. $\frac{180}{70} = \frac{18}{x}$

27. $\frac{8}{36} = \frac{10}{x}$

28. $\frac{13}{28} = \frac{x}{56}$

29. $\frac{72}{x} = \frac{48}{36}$

30. $\frac{x}{48} = \frac{12}{64}$

Write the letter of the correct proportion.

1. Choan wants to change the engine in her car. The current engine is 250 cubic centimeters and has a 14-inch fan belt. The new engine is 350 cubic centimeters and has a proportionally larger fan belt. What size fan belt will Choan need for her new engine?

a. $\dfrac{14}{250} = \dfrac{n}{350}$ **b.** $\dfrac{350}{14} = \dfrac{n}{250}$ **c.** $\dfrac{350}{1} = \dfrac{250}{n}$

2. After Choan bought the new engine, she put a larger gas tank into her car. Her old gas tank held 15 gallons, and she could drive 360 miles on a full tank. Now she can drive 465 miles on a full tank of gas. What size gas tank did she install?

a. $\dfrac{1}{15} = \dfrac{n}{465}$ **b.** $\dfrac{360}{465} = \dfrac{n}{15}$ **c.** $\dfrac{15}{360} = \dfrac{n}{465}$

Solve.

3. A city is planning to build a parking lot for fans who drive to football games and hockey matches. For every 12 parking spaces reserved for hockey fans, football fans will have 30. How many spaces will football fans have if hockey fans have 2,000?

4. A group of 16 fans attending a football game brought along a number of jugs of apple juice. If they brought 10 quarts of juice, how many $2\frac{1}{2}$-quart jugs were needed to carry the juice?

5. For every 5 people who bought $9.75 tickets to the football game, 3 people bought $14.50 tickets. If each of 35 people bought a $9.75 ticket, how many people bought the more expensive ticket?

6. After entering the stadium, all the fans wanted souvenirs. For every 2 people who bought programs, 7 people bought football jerseys. If 42 people bought jerseys, how many people bought programs?

7. Lucy goes to the stands to buy snacks for her friends. She has been asked to buy peanuts for 11 people. A bag of peanuts costs $0.89, and 2 bags sell for $1.60. Lucy collected $8.50 to spend for peanuts. Will she be able to buy a bag for each person?

8. The average price of a ticket to a football game is $12.00. The stadium owners make an 8% profit on each ticket. By how much would they have to raise the average ticket price to make a profit of 11%?

Use after pages 204–205.

Use the diagram and scale of this modern metal sculpture to answer the questions.

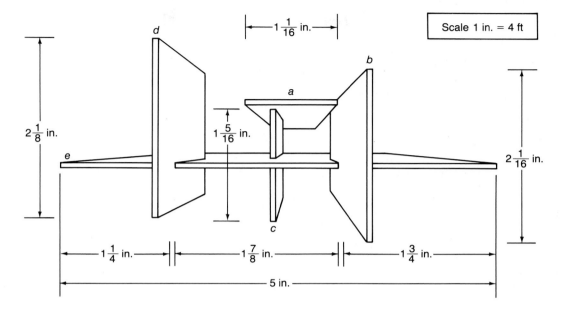

Scale 1 in. = 4 ft

1. How wide is *a*?

2. How long is *b*?

3. How far is *b* from the right edge of *e*?

4. How long is *c*?

Use a scale of 1 in.: $3\frac{1}{2}$ ft to find your answer.

5. How long is *d*?

6. How far is *d* from the left edge of *e*?

7. How wide is the entire sculpture?

Write each ratio as a percent.

1. 3 to 5

2. $\frac{14}{100}$

3. $\frac{6}{20}$

4. 1:4

5. 9 to 10

6. $\frac{35}{100}$

7. 7:25

8. 6 to 50

9. $\frac{17}{20}$

10. 38:50

11. 6 to 25

12. $\frac{98}{100}$

13. 9:25

14. 1 to 2

15. $\frac{3}{4}$

16. 8 to 10

17. 13:20

18. $\frac{66}{100}$

19. 49 to 50

20. 7 per 100

21. $\frac{8}{50}$

22. 1:25

23. 2:5

24. $\frac{38}{100}$

25. 3:20

26. 1 to 10

27. $\frac{4}{5}$

28. 17:20

29. $\frac{62}{100}$

30. 1:50

31. 3 to 100

32. 1 to 5

33. $\frac{3}{25}$

34. 47 per 50

35. 16 of 25

36. 8 tulips of 10 flowers

37. 53 daisies per 100 seeds

38. 1 rose of 5 flowers

39. 14 mums of 20 flowers

Write as a decimal.

1. 91%

2. 59.3%

3. 360%

4. 761%

5. 0.48%

6. 0.03%

7. 7%

8. 6%

9. 23.5%

10. 84%

11. 3,001%

12. 0.9%

13. 0.8%

14. 7,613%

15. 66.02%

16. 25.82%

17. 100%

18. 400%

Write as a percent.

19. 0.005

20. 0.872

21. 3.678

22. 9.2

23. 0.4

24. 4.30

25. 0.929

26. 0.15

27. 0.1258

28. 0.08

29. 0.125

30. 0.0003

31. 0.67

32. 0.0017

33. 0.4028

34. 0.6954

35. 0.03

36. 2.7833

Write as a fraction or as a mixed number in simplest form.

1. 125%

2. $66\frac{2}{3}\%$

3. 95%

4. $37\frac{1}{2}\%$

5. 240%

6. 90%

7. 84%

8. $133\frac{1}{3}\%$

9. $17\frac{1}{2}\%$

10. $6\frac{4}{5}\%$

11. $5\frac{2}{3}\%$

12. $9\frac{1}{5}\%$

13. $27\frac{1}{4}\%$

14. $28\frac{1}{4}\%$

15. $23\frac{1}{8}\%$

16. $55\frac{5}{9}\%$

Write as a percent.

17. $\frac{5}{12}$

18. $1\frac{7}{8}$

19. $\frac{5}{16}$

20. $2\frac{17}{40}$

21. $\frac{36}{8}$

22. $\frac{165}{100}$

23. $3\frac{8}{100}$

24. $\frac{2}{6}$

25. $\frac{7}{18}$

26. $\frac{3}{20}$

27. $\frac{3}{11}$

28. $\frac{9}{16}$

29. $\frac{14}{15}$

30. $\frac{1}{7}$

Solve by making an organized list.

1. At a cast party after a play, the leading actor wants to introduce her family to the director of the play. Her family includes her mother, father, husband, and daughter. How many possible ways can she introduce the family to the director if she always introduces her husband first?

2. The actor is starring in a play made up of 6 scenes that can be performed in any order. The scenes are entitled "Rebox," "Chromus," "Instant," "Chorale," "Allegro," and "Exit." This week the actors will begin each performance with "Chromus," followed by "Exit." From how many combinations can they choose the order of the remaining scenes?

3. The director holds auditions for a new play. Out of 200 actors, 6 have been chosen to perform in groups of 4 actors each. In how many combinations can the director use the 6 actors?

4. The producer has received manuscripts of new plays from playwrights. There is a stack of 6 plays to be read, and the producer has decided to read 5 of the plays during the next 2 days. The titles are *Quantity*, *The Next Bus*, *Walk North*, *Special*, *Concert Etude*, and *Pick a Number*. How many different combinations of 5 plays can the producer read?

5. The set designer is working on staging for a new play. He will use 3 panels of solid colors for each of 5 scenes. He can choose from 6 colors: orange, grey, calliope red, black, yellow, and pale blue. How many combinations of 3 colors are possible?

Solve by making an organized list.

6. Venezuela won 3 medals in the 1984 Summer Olympics. Each medal was either gold, silver, or bronze. How many possible combinations of the 3 medals could the Venezuelans have won?

7. The South Korean team won 19 medals in all, winning the same number of gold medals as silver medals. In how many different ways could it have won gold, silver and bronze medals?

8. The South Koreans won one more bronze medal than silver or gold medals. Which combination of those you counted for problem 2 is the one that the South Koreans actually won?

9. Ms. Casey has 3 forwards, 2 centers, and 3 guards on her basketball team. She sends 2 forwards, one center, and 2 guards to play at one time. How many different team combinations can she send into the game?

10. A relay team has 4 runners. How many ways can the order of the runners be arranged?

11. How many ways can a 4-person relay team be arranged if one runner must always run in the second or third position?

12. A round-robin format is often used in the Olympics. In this format, each team plays the other teams in the same division once. How many games would be played in a round robin with six teams?

13. Hans planned to watch Olympic games all day. In the morning he could have watched either wrestling or the high jump. In the afternoon he could have watched either the high jump, 100-meter run, or hurdles. In the evening, he could have watched wrestling, volley ball, or basketball. He did not want to watch any sport twice. How many ways could he have combined his sports viewing?

Write the percent of the number.

1. 6% of 900

2. 20% of 20.5

3. 30% of 70

4. 150% of 17

5. 325% of 4

6. 12% of 50

7. $133\frac{1}{3}$% of 330

8. 0.1% of 0.1

9. 0.5% of 98

10. 20% of 16

11. 75% of 4,004

12. 225% of 50

13. 22% of 100

14. 88% of 10

15. 17.5% of 20

16. $66\frac{2}{3}$% of 3

17. $8\frac{1}{2}$% of 80

18. $37\frac{1}{2}$% of 240

19. 3.5% of 600

20. 100% of 17

21. 15% of 120

22. 1% of 5

23. 1% of 1

24. 6% of 120

25. 0.3% of 400

26. 25% of 1,300

27. 60.7% of 5,000

28. 50% of 8

29. 8.25% of 200

30. 12.5% of 80

31. 90% of 2

32. 60% of $75

33. 350% of 16

34. 40% of $150.00

35. 25% of 212

36. $26\frac{1}{2}$% of $720

Write the percent.

1. What percent of 18 is 6?

2. 0.4 is what percent of 10?

3. 6.7 is what percent of 80?

4. What percent of 72 is 6?

5. What percent of 9 is 7.5?

6. 36 is what percent of 48?

7. 0.9 is what percent of 0.2?

8. What percent of 25 is 26?

9. What percent of 40 is 0.8?

10. 450 is what percent of 270?

11. 2.9 is what percent of 1.6?

12. What percent of 8 is 2.8?

13. What percent of 7.5 is 15?

14. 1.95 is what percent of 300?

15. 67 is what percent of 268?

16. What percent of 20 is 61?

17. What percent of 96 is 60?

18. 96.2 is what percent of 769.6?

19. 18 is what percent of 100?

20. What percent of 80.4 is 0.201?

21. What percent of 25 is 4.6?

22. 650 is what percent of 1,000?

23. 5.1 is what percent of 30?

24. What percent of 0.25 is 0.5?

25. What percent of 300 is 975?

26. 33 is what percent of 1?

27. 92 is what percent of 460?

28. What percent of 13.2 is 66?

29. What percent of 9,000 is 63?

30. 13.68 is what percent of 72?

31. 0.03 is what percent of 10?

32. What percent of 20 is 0.8?

33. What percent of 0.1 is 9.9?

34. 0.45 is what percent of 150?

35. 4.3 is what percent of 50?

36. What percent of 36 is 2.7?

Write the number.

1. 75% of what number is 21?

2. 8.99 is 29% of what number?

3. 42 is 12% of what number?

4. 6.2% of what number is 3.1?

5. 66 is $66\frac{2}{3}$% of what number?

6. 15.39 is 27% of what number?

7. 1.8 is 25% of what number?

8. $83\frac{1}{3}$% of what number is 30?

9. 4% of what number is 6?

10. 32 is 20% of what number?

11. 9.8 is 2% of what number?

12. 40% of what number is 16.6?

13. 72 is $37\frac{1}{2}$% of what number?

14. 68% of what number is 65.28?

15. 5.5 is 500% of what number?

16. 25% of what number is 0.88?

17. 20% of what number is 2.4?

18. 10.63 is 69% of what number?

19. 36% of what number is 64.8?

20. 34% of what number is 207.06?

21. $33\frac{1}{3}$% of what number is 75?

22. 9.43 is 85% of what number?

23. 28.47 is 3% of what number?

24. 97.5% of what number is 7.8?

25. 93.75 is $12\frac{1}{2}$% of what number?

26. 61.6 is 112% of what number?

27. 8.84 is 10% of what number?

28. 230% of what number is 2.3?

29. 25% of what number is 40?

30. 28% of what number is 7?

31. 87 is 116% of what number?

32. 45 is 75% of what number?

33. 68% of what number is 17?

34. 10.08 is 21% of what number?

35. 96.2% of what number is 211.64?

36. 332% of what number is 8.3?

Write the letter of the correct form of the interest formula.

1. Jo Ann Vance wants to deposit some of her $27,500 game-show winnings in a special bank account. She wants to earn $3,000 in interest in 3 years. How much of the $27,500 should she deposit in an account that pays 12.5% interest per year?

a. $I = prt$ **b.** $p = I \div rt$

c. $p = Irt$ **d.** $r = pt \div I$

2. Neil Green will borrow $2,800 to buy a trailer to carry the sailboat he won on *Shop Around*. The store will charge him interest at 17.5% per year for 3 years. How much interest will he have to pay?

a. $I = pr - t$ **b.** $I = prt$

c. $p = Irt$ **d.** $r = pt \div I$

Solve. Round to the nearest cent.

3. Al Lynch put the $6,575 he earned by playing *Name That Movie* in an account that pays $5\frac{3}{4}$% annual interest. He kept that amount in his account for $2\frac{1}{2}$ years. How much interest did he earn?

4. Marla Blanc Productions borrows $45,500 to make a pilot for a game show. The bank's rate is $16\frac{3}{4}$%, and the loan must be repaid in 1.5 years. What amount of money will the company pay the bank?

5. Alexandra Livi wants to use interest from her $15,842 winnings on *What's the Word* to pay for her room and board at college. She needs to receive $1,200 per year. The bank pays an annual interest rate of $7\frac{3}{4}$%. How much of the $15,842 does she have to put in the bank to earn the necessary interest?

6. Arnold Hooper charged $642.59 worth of clothes to wear as a contestant on *Fast Tracks*. Arnold won $750 on the show. The credit-card company charges an annual interest rate of 19.5%, and Arnold paid off the money after $1\frac{1}{2}$ years. Did his winnings pay for his clothing expenses?

7. Ellen Holmes needs a car to pull the trailer she won on *Guess Who*. She wants a car in the $7,500 to $9,000 price range, and she wants to be able to pay off the principal at the lowest possible interest rate. Look at the chart at the right. Which car should Ellen Holmes purchase?

	Tiger	Zephyr	Prairie
Price	$7,999	$8,325	$7,595
Down payment	$1,999	$1,250	$2,595
Principal	$6,000	$7,075	$5,000
Interest	$4,320	$4,245	$2,312.50
Payment period (years)	4	3	$2\frac{1}{2}$

Use a proportion to solve each problem.

1. 125 is 250% of what number?

2. 75.25 is what percent of 25?

3. What number is 4% of 0.5395?

4. What number is 1% of 62?

5. 4,541.6 is 5.6% of what number?

6. 0.0755 is what percent of 0.539?

7. What number is 24% of 886?

8. 18.92 is what percent of 22?

9. 217.25 is 79% of what number?

10. What number is 80% of 189.89?

Four people traveled across the Isthmus of Idic from west to east. Use the diagram of the isthmus to answer the questions.

11. Carole wanted to exercise as much as possible; so, she took no bridges or tunnels during her trip. How many meters did she climb altogether?

12. Michael traveled all the bridges, but no tunnels. His route involved climbing 1,500 meters. What percent of Carole's climb is this?

13. Dorothy wanted to walk as little as possible. Her climb was only 80% of Michael's climb. How many meters did she climb?

14. Dorothy's climb was 75% of Peter's climb. Peter took a scenic route. How many meters did Peter climb?

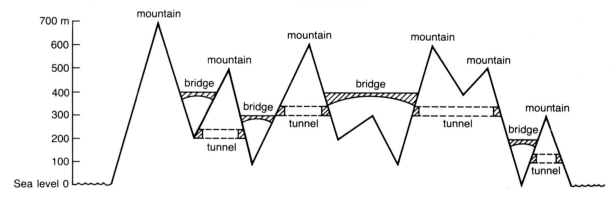

Isthmus of Idic

Write the percent of increase or decrease.

1. Original value: 400
   Decrease: 68

2. Decrease: 0.01
   Original value: 0.5

3. Original price: $24
   Decrease: $6

4. Original value: 50
   New value: 18.5

5. Increase: 157.5
   Original value: 1,500

6. Original value: 400
   Increase: 44

7. Original value: 36
   Increase: 4

8. Decrease: $9.90
   Original price: $36

9. Original value: 660
   Decrease: 220

10. Original value: 200
    New value: 30.4

11. Original value: 14
    New value: 35

12. Original value: 79
    Increase: 197.5

13. Original value: 2
    Increase: 0.4

14. Increase: $0.22
    Original price: $55

15. Original value: 19
    New value: 15.2

16. Original price: $4.00
    Increase: $7.00

17. Increase: 37
    Original value: 7.4

18. Original price: $136.00
    New price: $68.00

ADVERTISEMENT EXPENDITURES—1986
Bubble Soap, Inc.

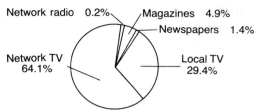

Network radio 0.2%   Magazines 4.9%
Newspapers 1.4%
Network TV 64.1%   Local TV 29.4%

Total Expenditures = $726,100,000

ADVERTISEMENT EXPENDITURES—1986
Yum-Yum Food, Inc.

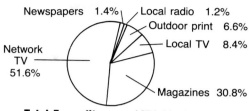

Newspapers 1.4%   Local radio 1.2%
Outdoor print 6.6%
Local TV 8.4%
Network TV 51.6%
Magazines 30.8%

Total Expenditures = $271,000,000

Copy each question that can be answered by using the circle graphs above. Then answer the questions.

1. How much money was spent by both companies on TV advertisements in 1986?

2. What percent of the two companies' earnings for 1986 was spent on advertising?

3. Which company spent more on magazine ads in 1986?

4. How much did producing a TV commercial cost in 1986?

Solve.

5. How much money did Bubble Soap, Inc., spend on newspaper and magazine ads?

6. How much money did Yum-Yum Food, Inc., spend on TV ads?

7. How much money did Yum-Yum Food, Inc., spend on print advertisements?

8. Which company spent more money on magazine ads?

9. After 1986, the managers of Bubble Soap, Inc., plan to spend the same proportion of the budget on newspaper ads and on magazine ads as they spent in 1986. They increase the percent spent on newspaper ads to 3.5% of the total advertising budget. What percent of their ad budget will they spend on magazines?

10. Which of the following conclusions can you draw from the circle graphs?

   a. Both companies spend the same amount of money on newspaper ads.

   b. Each company spends more than $\frac{3}{4}$ of its ad budget on TV ads.

   c. More people read magazines than newspapers.

   d. Each company spends at least $\frac{3}{5}$ of its ad budget on TV ads.

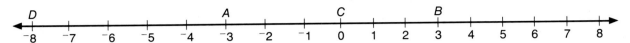

Use the number line to answer each problem.

1. What is the position of point A?

2. What is the position of point B?

3. If point E is added to the number line at $^-6$, between which two points is E located?

Write the opposite of each integer.

4. $^-21$

5. 618

6. 8

7. 0

Write the absolute value for each number.

8. $|9|$

9. $|^-39|$

10. $|^-94|$

11. $|189|$

Write the numbers from the least to the greatest.

12. 55, $^-64$, $^-54$, 64

13. 49, $^-101$, $^-5$, 17, $^-618$

Write the numbers from the greatest to the least.

14. $^-188$, $^-190$, $^-100$, 100

15. 12, $^-4$, $^-16$, 3, 9

Compare. Write $>$, $<$, or $=$.

16. $^-9 \bigcirc 0$

17. $5 \bigcirc ^-2$

18. $^-8 \bigcirc ^-4$

19. $250 \bigcirc ^-250$

20. $^-95 \bigcirc ^-103$

21. $39 \bigcirc ^-56$

Use the properties to find the missing integer.

1. 757 + 468 = 468 + ___?___

2. ⁻6 × ⁻2 = ⁻2 × ___?___

3. ⁻1(⁻3 × 5) = (⁻1 × ⁻3) × ___?___

4. 1 × 379 = ___?___

5. ⁻94 + (62 + 22) = (⁻94 + 62) + ___?___

6. ⁻105 + 0 = ___?___

7. 3(⁻9 + 1) = (3 × ⁻9) + (3 × ___?___)

8. 137 + (⁻16 + 8) = (137 + ⁻16) + ___?___

9. 26 × 0 = ___?___

10. 2(14 × 6) = (2 × 14) × ___?___

11. ⁻186 × 1 = ___?___

12. ⁻15 + ⁻13 = ⁻13 + ___?___

13. 96 + 0 = ___?___

14. ⁻66(2 + 49) = (⁻66 × 2) + (⁻66 × ___?___)

15. 4(⁻66 × 12) = (4 × ⁻66) × ___?___

16. 503 + (⁻1 + ⁻17) = (503 + ⁻1) + ___?___

17. 75(⁻2 + ⁻4) = (75 × ⁻2) + (75 × ___?___)

18. ⁻38 + 16 = 16 + ___?___

19. 367 × 12 = 12 × ___?___

20. ⁻942 × 0 = ___?___

21. 66 + (32 + 109) = (66 + 32) + ___?___

22. ⁻43 × 44 = 44 × ___?___

23. 16 + ⁻34 = ⁻34 + ___?___

24. ⁻7(⁻9 × ⁻6) = (⁻7 × ⁻9) × ___?___

25. ⁻632 × 471 = 471 × ___?___

26. 0 + ⁻55 = ___?___

27. 15 + (⁻6 + 4) = (15 + ⁻6) + ___?___

28. ⁻90 + ⁻80 = ⁻80 + ___?___

29. ⁻7(⁻3 + ⁻6) = (⁻7 × ⁻3) + (⁻7 × ___?___)

30. 6(9 + 5) = (6 × 9) + (6 × ___?___)

31. 300 + ⁻4 = ⁻4 + ___?___

32. ⁻7 × ⁻12 = ⁻12 × ___?___

Name the properties. Write *C* for Commutative, *A* for Associative, *D* for Distributive, *I* for Identity, and *Z* for Zero Property.

33. ⁻3(6 × ⁻9) = (⁻3 × 6) × ⁻9

34. ⁻25 × 0 = 0

35. ⁻19 + 0 = ⁻19

36. (18 + ⁻7) + 5 = 18 + (⁻7 + 5)

37. ⁻5 + 7 = 7 + ⁻5

38. 15(⁻3 + 17) = (15 × ⁻3) + (15 × 17)

Add.

1. $11 + 5$

2. $2,931 + {}^-685$

3. $458 + {}^-393$

4. ${}^-62 + {}^-71$

5. $674 + {}^-39 + 102$

6. ${}^-603 + 906$

7. $815 + 281$

8. $9 + {}^-12$

9. ${}^-763 + 54$

10. $(36 + {}^-27) + 446$

11. ${}^-698 + ({}^-32 + 250)$

12. ${}^-8,815 + {}^-9,776$

13. ${}^-310 + {}^-908$

14. $(358 + 1,024) + {}^-761$

15. $562 + {}^-593$

16. ${}^-176 + {}^-229$

17. $103 + {}^-702$

18. ${}^-894 + {}^-979$

19. ${}^-84 + {}^-22$

20. $94 + {}^-87$

21. $({}^-95 + 521) + {}^-299$

22. ${}^-838 + {}^-719$

23. ${}^-1,432 + 1,098$

24. $239 + {}^-184 + {}^-313$

25. ${}^-51 + {}^-98$

26. $952 + {}^-398$

27. ${}^-54 + 235$

28. ${}^-453 + {}^-198 + {}^-352$

29. ${}^-12 + {}^-15 + {}^-34$

30. $1,234 + {}^-5,309$

31. ${}^-17 + ({}^-12 + {}^-9)$

32. $(0 + {}^-5) + {}^-3$

33. ${}^-117 + (153 + {}^-321)$

34. $({}^-16 + 13) + {}^-20$

Solve.

35. The temperature at 4:00 A.M. was ${}^-6°C$. Since then it has risen 12 degrees. What is the temperature now?

36. The temperature at 7:00 P.M was $9°C$. Since then it has fallen 12 degrees. What is the temperature now?

Subtract.

1. ⁻98 − 51

2. 9,900 − 972

3. 94 − ⁻46

4. 663 − 248

5. ⁻6,731 − 3,003

6. ⁻18 − ⁻30

7. ⁻247 − ⁻338

8. ⁻715 − ⁻582

9. 262 − 243

10. ⁻80 − ⁻96

11. 5 − 9

12. ⁻665 − 99

13. 104 − ⁻243

14. 95 − ⁻35

15. ⁻679 − 308

16. 975 − 976

17. 29 − 100

18. ⁻71 − 490

19. ⁻26 − ⁻24

20. ⁻11 − 94

21. 208 − 724

22. ⁻24 − 21

23. ⁻466 − ⁻235

24. 67 − 3

25. ⁻7,272 − ⁻2,931

26. ⁻406 − ⁻790

27. ⁻3 − 17

28. 685 − 832

29. 6,827 − ⁻8,354

30. ⁻1,653 − ⁻9,679

31. 396 − ⁻2,021

32. ⁻29 − 201

33. ⁻777 − ⁻801

34. 366 − ⁻14

Solve.

35. In the morning, the temperature was 14°C. It is now 26°C. How much did the temperature change?

36. The temperature at 3:00 P.M. was 11°C. At 10:00 P.M., the temperature was ⁻2°C. How much did the temperature change?

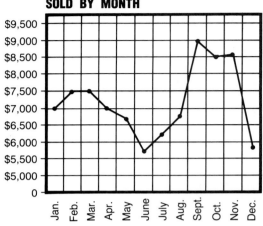

AMOUNT OF OFFICE FURNITURE SOLD BY MONTH

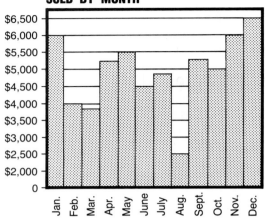

AMOUNT OF HOME FURNISHINGS SOLD BY MONTH

Can you use the line graph or the bar graph to answer each question? Write *yes* or *no*.

1. In which month did the office-furniture division sell the most?

2. How much did the home-furnishings division sell on Labor Day weekend?

3. Did the office-furniture division sell more in June than in October?

4. Did the company make a profit in August?

Use the line graph to answer each question.

5. In which three months is the most office furniture sold?

6. In which two months were sales the closest?

7. Which month shows the greatest increase in sales over the previous month?

8. Were sales higher or lower for the period from January to April than for the period from May to August?

Use the bar graph to answer each question.

9. Which month shows the greatest decrease from the previous month?

10. What is the difference in sales between the highest-selling and the lowest-selling months?

Use both graphs to answer each question.

11. Which division shows higher sales?

12. In which month did the home-furnishings division sell more than the office-furniture division?

Multiply.

1. ⁻823 · 5

2. (⁻17 · 15) · 3

3. ⁻10 · (⁻2 · 18)

4. ⁻988 · 30

5. (11 · ⁻4) · ⁻10

6. ⁻13 · ⁻12

7. 12 · ⁻15

8. ⁻13 · 63

9. ⁻40 · ⁻18

10. 13 · (⁻7 · ⁻9)

11. ⁻12 × ⁻18

12. 18 × 8

13. 36 × 297

14. (⁻17 × 17) × 5

15. 19 × 10

16. ⁻23 × ⁻14

17. 19 × ⁻15

18. ⁻792 × 12

19. ⁻5 × (6 × ⁻25)

20. 1,111 × ⁻6,962

21. ⁻147 × ⁻579

22. ⁻10 × ⁻16

23. 17 × 14

24. 92 × ⁻29

25. (⁻63 × 20) × 8

26. ⁻66 × ⁻88

27. ⁻16 × 11

28. ⁻94 × 20

29. 500 × 18

30. (⁻4 × 14) × ⁻11

31. ⁻72 × 66

31. 6 × ⁻323

33. ⁻13 × (⁻2 × 24)

34. 202 × 76

Solve.

35. Ricardo descended to a depth of 24 feet below sea level. His friend Martin descended 3 times as far. Write as an integer the depth of Martin's descent.

36. To finance their treasure hunt, the Diving Dolphins borrowed money from 5 friends. They now owe each friend $150. How much do the Dolphins owe in all?

Divide.

1. ⁻672 ÷ 96

2. 56 ÷ ⁻8

3. ⁻360 ÷ 60

4. ⁻1 ÷ ⁻1

5. ⁻2,772 ÷ ⁻63

6. 110 ÷ 2

7. ⁻222 ÷ 37

8. ⁻891 ÷ ⁻99

9. 3,600 ÷ 48

10. 132 ÷ ⁻12

11. ⁻656 ÷ ⁻82

12. 594 ÷ ⁻11

13. 4,620 ÷ ⁻60

14. ⁻6,144 ÷ ⁻768

15. ⁻195 ÷ ⁻5

16. ⁻1,328 ÷ ⁻83

17. ⁻1,034 ÷ ⁻22

18. ⁻7,221 ÷ 87

19. ⁻72 ÷ ⁻9

20. ⁻294 ÷ ⁻7

21. ⁻1,411 ÷ ⁻17

22. 18 ÷ 3

23. ⁻844 ÷ 4

24. ⁻592 ÷ 37

25. 4,081 ÷ 53

26. ⁻144 ÷ 2

27. ⁻444 ÷ ⁻74

28. ⁻183 ÷ ⁻61

Solve.

29. Wrectronics, Inc., manufactures household robots. Because of a newspaper story which reported that the robots' arms fell off after 6 months of normal use, Wrectronics stock dropped 20 points during a 5-day period. What was the average daily change in the stock price?

Write each number with a negative exponent.

1. $\dfrac{1}{5^2}$ **2.** $\dfrac{1}{2^4}$ **3.** $\dfrac{1}{125}$ **4.** $\dfrac{1}{64}$

5. $\dfrac{1}{10}$ **6.** $\dfrac{1}{8}$ **7.** $\dfrac{1}{17^2}$ **8.** $\dfrac{1}{6^5}$

Write each number in scientific notation.

9. 540.89 **10.** 1.3467

11. 0.00101 **12.** 10,000

Write each number in standard form.

13. 3.076×10^{-2} **14.** 1×10^5

15. 5.0154×10^2 **16.** 4.49×10^{-1}

Write the missing exponent for each problem below. Then use the exponents to find the first eight plays of the Mud Bowl. An exponent of 5 means the Muskrats moved forward 5 yards. An exponent of ⁻5 means the Muskrats moved back 5 yards. The Muskrats started from their own 40-yard line. Look at the field to help answer the last question.

17. $\dfrac{1}{6^3} = 6 \underline{\quad ? \quad}$

18. $0.000273 = 2.73 \times 10 \underline{\quad ? \quad}$

19. $5^{-2} \div 5^{-17} = 5 \underline{\quad ? \quad}$

20. $24{,}980 = 2.4980 \times 10 \underline{\quad ? \quad}$

21. $\dfrac{1}{12^5} = 12 \underline{\quad ? \quad}$

22. $31^{23} \times 31^{12} = 31 \underline{\quad ? \quad}$

23. $17^{10} \times 17^4 = 17 \underline{\quad ? \quad}$

24. $7^{-2} \times 7^{-8} = 7 \underline{\quad ? \quad}$

25. Did the Muskrats score a touchdown?

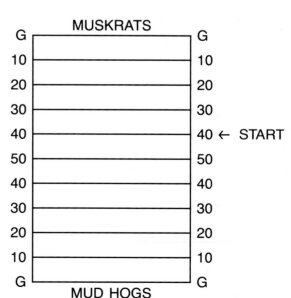

MUSKRATS

G		G
10		10
20		20
30		30
40		40 ← START
50		50
40		40
30		30
20		20
10		10
G		G

MUD HOGS

Estimation	Checking for a Reasonable Answer	Writing an Equation
Using a Graph	Writing an Equation	Using a Road Map
Choosing the Operation	Interpreting the Quotient and the	Making an Organized List
Solving Multi-step Problems	Remainder	Using a Formula

Write the strategy or method you choose. Then solve.

1. A company has 17 trucks that can carry 2,532 bricks each. It also has a truck that can carry 4,697 bricks. What is the average number of bricks per truck for all 18 trucks?

2. Ross borrowed $2,100 to buy a boat. He paid $504 interest over 2 years. What was the rate of interest?

3. Eduardo has $26.15 to buy nautical flags. He wants 3 flags that cost $5.88, $12.95, and $17.50. Does he have enough money for the flags?

4. The winning boat in a race across a lake $2\frac{3}{4}$ miles wide finished the course in $1\frac{1}{2}$ minutes. What was its average speed?

5. Patrick is buying life jackets. He can choose from seat cushions and wearable life jackets. He can also choose red, green, or gold. How many different combinations are available to Patrick?

6. Metrobuild constructed 1,200 houses in 1989. Of these, 84% sold for more than $100,000 and 12% sold for more than $225,000. The remaining houses were unsold. How many houses did Metrobuild sell in 1989?

7. Marian auctions used window frames in lots of 20. How many lots can she auction from a group of 956 frames?

Estimation	Checking for a Reasonable Answer	Using a Formula
Using a Graph	Writing an Equation	Using a Road Map
Choosing the Operation	Interpreting the Quotient and the	Making an Organized List
Solving Multi-step Problems	Remainder	

Write the strategy or method you choose. Then solve.

1. A powerboat was driven for 3 hours 45 minutes at an average speed of 44 miles per hour. How far did it travel?

2. Danielle wants to buy several boat models. The barge costs $8.69. The schooner costs $18.98. The clipper costs $12.25. Can Danielle buy one of each model with $40.00?

3. A supplier sells roofing shingles in boxes of 24. Martin needs 225 shingles for a repair job. How many boxes does he need to buy?

4. In 1989, a construction company used an average of $35\frac{1}{4}$ tons of cement each month. In January of 1990, it used $30\frac{3}{8}$ tons. What is the average weight of cement used per month for the 13 months?

5. Which two major routes would you travel from Austin to Owatonna, and how far would you travel?

6. If you used the direct route and cycled at an average speed of $10\frac{1}{3}$ miles per hour, how long would it take to travel

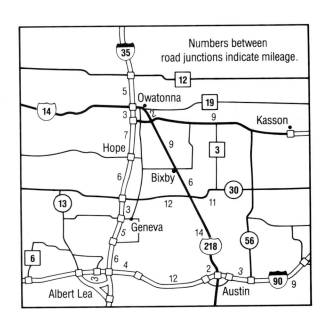

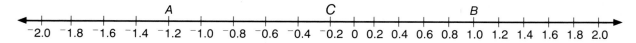

Use the number line to answer each problem.

1. What is the position of point A?

2. What is the position of point B?

3. If point E is added to the number line at 0.6, between which two points is E located?

Write $>$, $<$, or $=$.

4. $\frac{7}{9}$ ◯ $\frac{-1}{2}$

5. 0.1 ◯ -6

6. $^-0.73$ ◯ $^-0.69$

7. $^-0.05$ ◯ $^-0.05$

8. $\frac{-7}{8}$ ◯ $\frac{-2}{9}$

9. $\frac{3}{5}$ ◯ $^-0.07$

Write the numbers from the least to the greatest.

10. $^-9, \frac{5}{6}, ^-1\frac{1}{3}$

11. $0.03, 7.75, ^-0.03, ^-4.14$

12. $^-4.4, \frac{1}{2}, 0.62, ^-10\frac{1}{3}, \frac{3}{5}$

Write the numbers from the greatest to the least.

13. $0.05, ^-0.8, 0.82$

14. $\frac{2}{5}, 6\frac{2}{5}, ^-2\frac{1}{6}, ^-5\frac{1}{6}$

15. $^-5.82, ^-5\frac{1}{4}, 1\frac{1}{2}, 1.7, ^-1.6$

Add or subtract. Simplify where necessary.

1. $16 - \frac{^-4}{7}$

2. $^-0.07 + ^-9.42$

3. $^-2.3 - ^-0.9$

4. $\frac{1}{6} + ^-4\frac{3}{4}$

5. $5 - \frac{1}{2}$

6. $0.02 + ^-8$

7. $\frac{^-5}{6} - ^-10$

8. $^-5\frac{7}{10} + ^-14\frac{1}{6}$

9. $2.04 - ^-0.4$

10. $^-6.98 + 11.3$

11. $\frac{^-7}{10} - 12\frac{1}{3}$

12. $6\frac{1}{6} + \frac{7}{9}$

13. $^-0.6 - 0.4$

14. $14.55 + 3.9$

15. $\frac{1}{8} - ^-8$

16. $^-12\frac{1}{10} + ^-2\frac{8}{9}$

17. $6.6 - 9.16$

18. $^-0.1 + ^-0.03$

19. $^-3 - \frac{3}{10}$

20. $9\frac{3}{5} + ^-4\frac{7}{10}$

21. $^-0.21 - ^-2.5$

22. $0.61 + ^-0.94$

23. $20\frac{2}{3} - ^-16\frac{2}{3}$

24. $^-5\frac{3}{5} + \frac{7}{10}$

25. $0.16 - 0.5$

26. $^-8.98 + 9$

27. $^-6\frac{1}{6} - 6\frac{2}{9}$

28. $15\frac{1}{10} + 12\frac{3}{4}$

29. $^-6.7 - ^-9.1$

30. $0.02 + 19.8$

31. $15\frac{1}{2} - \frac{7}{10}$

32. $\frac{^-1}{7} + 2\frac{1}{6}$

33. $0.69 - 1$

34. $^-5.79 + ^-19.5$

Check That the Solution Answers the Question

Write the letter of the correct answer.

1. A mine shaft is ⁻730 feet deep. Every ⁻20 feet, a sample of the rock was taken. Were more than 35 samples taken from the mine shaft?

  a. one

  b. yes

  c. 36

2. One sample 6.8×10^{-1} meters long contains an average of one trace of gold every 1.6×10^{-2} meters. Are there at least 50 traces of gold in the sample?

  a. no

  b. ten fewer

  c. yes

Solve.

3. A geologist has 3 samples of gold, labeled *A, B,* and *C*. *A* measures 5.75×10^{-3} meters long, *B* measures 9.9×10^{-4} meters long, and *C* measures 1.86×10^{-2} meters long. Is the order from the smallest to the greatest *A, C, B*?

4. A miner is working in a shaft at a depth of ⁻981 feet. Every hour, he digs ⁻5 feet deeper. Will he reach the ⁻1,000-foot level if he digs for 4 hours?

5. A mechanical hoist is positioned 55 feet above a mine shaft, and a wire is run from the hoist to the ⁻465-foot level. Will 525 feet of wire be enough to reach that level?

6. In 1983, a geological exploration drilled to a depth of ⁻39,370 feet. If the drill hole was extended by 30 feet per day, would a depth of ⁻40,000 feet be reached in less than 3 weeks?

7. A team of miners runs a telephone cable from a station that is at a level of ⁻1,000 feet in a tunnel 250 feet from the mine shaft. The cable runs up the shaft and then to an office $\frac{1}{3}$ mile away. Did they use fewer than 3,000 feet of cable?

8. A bucket is lowered from the top of a 55-foot hoist. If it takes 3 minutes to reach ⁻890 feet, is it descending faster or slower than 3.5 miles per hour?

Use with pages 262–263.

Multiply or divide. Simplify when necessary.

1. $^-0.2 \cdot 0.81$

2. $^-6.16 \div 0.7$

3. $\frac{^-2}{9} \cdot \frac{^-3}{4}$

4. $1\frac{1}{3} \div 1\frac{1}{4}$

5. $^-0.8 \cdot ^-0.6$

6. $2.37 \div 0.1$

7. $9\frac{1}{10} \cdot 8\frac{3}{7}$

8. $\frac{^-1}{3} \div \frac{3}{7}$

9. $9.1 \cdot ^-0.45$

10. $0.99 \div 0.05$

11. $\frac{2}{3} \cdot ^-10\frac{1}{2}$

12. $\frac{2}{7} \div ^-1$

13. $1.34 \cdot 0.07$

14. $5.52 \div ^-6$

15. $\frac{^-2}{3} \cdot ^-3$

16. $^-16 \div \frac{5}{7}$

17. $^-0.13 \cdot ^-3.9$

18. $0.06 \div 0.3$

19. $\frac{3}{4} \cdot \frac{^-2}{9}$

20. $6\frac{1}{2} \div 1\frac{4}{9}$

21. $^-9.5 \cdot 12.7$

22. $^-8.4 \div ^-4.2$

23. $^-9 \cdot \frac{2}{7}$

24. $9\frac{3}{7} \div 1\frac{1}{3}$

25. $^-0.05 \cdot ^-16$

26. $1.4 \div ^-7$

27. $\frac{^-3}{4} \cdot 10\frac{2}{3}$

28. $\frac{^-1}{4} \div ^-1$

29. $^-0.05 \cdot 1.7$

30. $2.79 \div 3.1$

31. $9\frac{3}{4} \cdot 2\frac{2}{3}$

32. $9\frac{1}{10} \div \frac{^-7}{9}$

33. Ahmed has a summer job finishing tables for a furniture maker. He can finish $2\frac{1}{3}$ tables per week (7 days). The furniture maker received an order for 13 tables that must be done in five weeks and one day. Will Ahmed be able to finish them all on time? If not, how many will the furniture maker have to finish himself?

Write R if the number is rational and I if the number is irrational.

1. 41.373737 . . .

2. 6.246247248 . . .

3. 17.59086732 . . .

4. 8.21679

5. 6.21508462150846 . . .

6. 3.141592653 . . .

7. 56.3902064198

8. 7.23852385 . . .

9. 458.37928046

10. 38.221222223 . . .

11. 27.10429638 . . .

12. 12.240240240 . . .

13. 5.413709

14. 0.001001 . . .

15. 32.7333 . . .

16. 4.2358132134 . . .

Estimate the square root to the nearest tenth.

17. $\sqrt{15}$

18. $\sqrt{64}$

19. $\sqrt{45}$

20. $\sqrt{36}$

21. $\sqrt{121}$

22. $\sqrt{20}$

23. $\sqrt{2}$

24. $\sqrt{196}$

25. $\sqrt{49}$

26. $\sqrt{100}$

27. $\sqrt{44}$

28. $\sqrt{16}$

29. $\sqrt{33}$

30. $\sqrt{47}$

31. $\sqrt{81}$

32. $\sqrt{38}$

I.

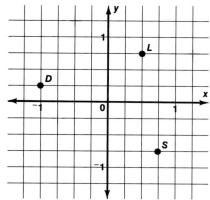

Copy graph I. Then use the graph to answer Problems 1 through 6.

1. What are the coordinates of point *D*?

2. What are the coordinates of point *S*?

3. What are the coordinates of point *L*?

4. Graph point *H* at (1.25,0.75).

5. Graph point *T* at (⁻0.75,⁻0.25).

6. Graph point *J* at (⁻0.5,1.25).

Draw a real-number plane for Problems 7 through 12.

7. Graph point *M* at (0.75,⁻0.5).

8. Graph point *N* at (⁻0.25,1).

9. Graph point *P* at (⁻0.75,⁻0.5).

10. Graph point *Q* at (1.25,1).

11. In which quadrant would (⁻4.5, 6.2) be?

12. In which quadrant would (3.1415,⁻4.6) be?

Each problem can be solved in four steps. Complete the plan for solving each problem by writing the three missing steps. Solve.

1. An antenna 20.6 meters high is erected at the top of a mine shaft. From the top of the antenna, 0.4 kilometers of wire are run down the shaft. The wire is 50 meters too short to reach the station level. How deep is the station level?

   Step 1: Convert 0.4 kilometers to meters.

   Step 2: ___?___

   Step 3: ___?___

   Step 4: ___?___

2. Samples are taken at regular distances in a mine. Sample 24 is taken at a depth of ⁻1.2 kilometers. How many meters below the sample 24 will the sample 30 be taken?

   Step 1: Convert ⁻1.2 kilometers to meters

   Step 2: ___?___

   Step 3: ___?___

   Step 4: ___?___

Make a plan, and solve.

3. A mine is 3^4 kilometers from a town. The road is marked so that there are 3^2 equal sections, and each section is divided into 90 subsections. How many meters long is each subsection?

4. A bucket is hoisted up from a depth of ⁻840 meters inside a mine. It moves at a rate of 125 centimeters per second. How many meters below the surface is the bucket after 3 minutes?

5. A mining company takes out a 2-year loan to buy a bulldozer that costs $125,000. The interest rate on the loan is 15%, and the company pays $30,000 down. What is the total price the company will pay?

6. A miner walked 550 yards from his car to a shaft that is ⁻1,490 feet deep. He descended to a point $\frac{4}{5}$ the depth of the shaft, took a sample, then traveled up the shaft, and returned to his car. How many feet did he travel?

7. An ore zone begins at a depth of ⁻214 meters and ends at a depth of ⁻307 meters. A silver vein running through the zone is $\frac{1}{150}$ of the width of the zone. How many centimeters wide is the vein?

8. A geologist labels samples according to the depth from which they were taken. Write these samples in order from the least to the greatest depth: (**A**) ⁻2.4 meters; (**B**) ⁻1.1 kilometers; (**C**) ⁻0.8 meters; (**D**) ⁻810 centimeters; (**E**) ⁻980 meters.

Use after pages 270–271.

Write each as an algebraic expression.

1. *b* increased by 14

2. the product of 7 and *c*

3. *g* divided by 2

4. *r* decreased by 10

5. the product of *a* and ⁻6

6. *z* divided by ⁻1

7. 12 subtracted from *q*

8. 16 times *p*

9. 8 more than *t*

10. 18 divided by *n*

11. the difference of *y* and 4

12. *s* increased by 11

13. 32 less than *k*

14. *j* added to 26

15. *h* divided by 9

16. the product of 18 and *b*

Evaluate each expression if the variable equals 1, 2, 3, 4, and 5.

17. $18 - s$

18. $5s$

19. $\frac{s}{4}$

20. $9 + s$

Evaluate each expression if the variable equals ⁻1, 0, 1, 2, and 3.

21. $k - 3$

22. $14 + k$

23. $5(k - 1)$

24. $k \div 3$

Write the letter of the correct algebraic expression.

25. Maria has many records. Fred has 5 times that amount.
    a. $5r$ b. $5 - r$ c. $r + 5$

26. Paul had some tapes. He divided them equally among 4 friends.
    a. $\frac{4}{t}$ b. $4t$ c. $\frac{t}{4}$

27. Setsuko had 12 record albums. She bought a few more.
    a. $12a$ b. $12 + a$ c. $a - 12$

Solve.

1. $n + 9\frac{1}{4} = 13\frac{3}{8}$

2. $r + 759 = 529$

3. $\frac{1}{7}c = 6$

4. $\frac{1}{23}w = 15$

5. $0.5w = 1.415$

6. $^-71.3n = 63.457$

7. $d + 0.069 = 0.139$

8. $0.004 - n = ^-0.636$

9. $4t = ^-28$

10. $n - \frac{5}{12} = \frac{7}{12}$

11. $z - \frac{1}{3} = \frac{4}{15}$

12. $4\frac{1}{2} + b = ^-1\frac{2}{5}$

13. $10\frac{1}{2}n = 6\frac{9}{16}$

14. $n - \frac{2}{7} = \frac{3}{14}$

15. $a - 733 = 129$

16. $^-0.55h = 4.40$

17. $n - 0.41 = 0.09$

18. $25 - p = 7$

19. $c + \frac{3}{10} = \frac{31}{70}$

20. $w + 6\frac{1}{2} = 10\frac{1}{6}$

21. $12.4d = 111.6$

22. $94.2 - w = 19.65$

23. $b - 93 = ^-12$

24. $\frac{3}{8}m = ^-\frac{27}{80}$

25. $211 + z = 657$

26. $^-203 - z = 420$

27. $^-16 - t = 40$

28. $6.174 + n = 5.324$

29. $^-\frac{1}{9}r = 9$

30. $6.4n = 352.64$

31. The state in which Melissa and Edward live requires a nickel deposit on all soft-drink containers. Edward and Melissa collect containers to cash in for the deposit. After one week, Melissa had 75 containers, which was $1\frac{1}{2}$ times as many as Edward had collected. The number of containers Melissa collected is given by the equation $1\frac{1}{2}n = 75$. How many bottles and cans did Edward collect?

Solve.

1. $2n + 17 = 47$

2. $\frac{1}{6}w + 76\frac{5}{8} = 54\frac{5}{8}$

3. $36.2 - 3b = 85.1$

4. $1.75y - 99.9 = 75.1$

5. $\frac{1}{2}m + 89 = 114$

6. $3e - 1 = {}^-2$

7. $1.25a + 13 = 38$

8. $7 - 0.6p = 6.88$

9. $100c + 16 = 46$

10. $\frac{1}{5}a - 42.3 = 105.1$

11. $3.875z + 1.25 = 40$

12. $19\frac{1}{8} + 3n = 22\frac{5}{16}$

13. $750 - \frac{1}{2}s = 700$

14. $26b + 14 = {}^-25$

15. $10r + 0.4 = 2$

16. $10.75 - 350z = 5.5$

17. $97 - 500t = 72$

18. $6v - 27\frac{3}{8} = {}^-34\frac{7}{8}$

19. ${}^-909 + 0.17b = {}^-926$

20. $24\frac{3}{8} - \frac{1}{5}c = 4\frac{3}{8}$

21. $3h + 75 = 150$

22. $3f - 15 = {}^-48$

23. $88\frac{1}{3} - 4s = {}^-88\frac{1}{3}$

24. $97.6 - 2.3q = 99.9$

25. ${}^-0.709t + 141.8 = 0$

26. $\frac{1}{16}j - 40 = 10$

Solve.

27. Fred gave his duplicate baseball cards to his cousin Karl. Duplicates were $\frac{1}{4}$ of Fred's collection. Karl already had 18 cards and now he has 34. The equation representing the size of Karl's collection is $\frac{1}{4}y + 18 = 34$. How many cards did Fred have to begin with?

Write the letter of the equation that describes the problem.

1. A number increased by 9 is $^-13$.

   a. $b + {}^-13 = 9$ **b.** $b - 9 = {}^-13$ **c.** $b + 9 = {}^-13$

2. The product of a number and 6, when increased by 8, is 16.

   a. $6y + 8 = 16$ **b.** $y(6 + 8) = 16$ **c.** $8(y + 6) = 16$

3. A number divided by $^-4$ and then decreased by 12 is 96.

   a. $^-4m - 12 = 96$ **b.** $\frac{1}{4}(m - 12) = 96$

   c. $\frac{m}{^-4} - 12 = 96$

4. Mike scored 38 points in one basketball game, four less than twice the school record.

   a. $\frac{x}{2} + 38 = 4$ **b.** $2x - 4 = 38$ **c.** $4 + 2x = 38$

5. The Gonzales family drove 750 miles during their vacation. They drove the same number of miles per day for 5 days, and 150 miles the sixth day.

   a. $\frac{7}{570}x = 150$ **b.** $5x - 150 = 750$

   c. $5x + 150 = 750$

6. Susan, Paul, and Eva ran the same distance together, and then Eva ran $1\frac{1}{2}$ miles more alone. The 3 ran a total of 12 miles.

   a. $3x + 1\frac{1}{2} = 12$ **b.** $1\frac{1}{2}x + 3 = 12$

   c. $12x - 3 = 1\frac{1}{2}$

Write a word problem for each equation and solve.

7. $^-2g + 9 = {}^-11$

8. $\frac{1}{3}n - 8 = 10$

9. $5y + 20 = 35$

Write the letter of the correct equation.

1. The Science Club arranged a trip to the Smithsonian. Only $\frac{2}{3}$ of the members were able to attend, which left one seat empty on the 25-passenger bus. How many members does the Science Club have?

   a. $1 + n = \frac{2}{3} \times 25$

   b. $\frac{2}{3} \times 25 = n + 1$

   c. $\frac{2}{3}n = 25 - 1$

2. This year, the Nature Club made 3 exhibits per month for its annual fair. This year's fair has twice as many exhibits as last year's. How many exhibits were there in last year's fair?

   a. $n = 2 \times 3$

   b. $2n = 12 \times 3$

   c. $12 \times 3n = 2$

Write an equation, and solve.

3. The Singing Club charged each of its 20 members $2.60 to hire a hall for a performance. The hall owner gave the club $4.50 change. How much did the club pay to hire the hall?

4. The Singing Club keeps sheet music in files. Each file holds 12 sheets. Of all the club's music, $\frac{2}{3}$ fit into 3 files. how many sheets of music does the club have?

5. The Tennis Club has 5 new members. Each buys a racket and a tube of balls. If 6 rackets cost $186.00 and 6 tubes of balls cost $27.00, how much do the 5 people pay for rackets and balls?

6. The Art Club visits a mansion that has 3 flights of stairs. The first flight is 29 steps long. The second flight is 4 steps longer than the third flight. There are 67 steps altogether. How many steps are there in the third flight?

7. The Art Club held a show for 2 days. A total of 269 people attended the show. On the second day, 15 more people attended than had come to the show the first day. How many people attended on the first day?

8. The Acting Club's two-act play begins at 3:20 P.M. The first act is twice as long as the second act, and there is a 15-minute break between acts. The play ends at 4:50 P.M. How long is Act I?

Use the guess-and-check method to solve.

1. Find a 2-digit number less than 20. When the product of its digits is squared, the square is 2 greater than the original number.

2. Find a 2-digit number for which the square root of the sum of the digits is the cube root of the original number.

3. The number *10* can be squared, and the sum of the digits of the square equals the sum of the digits of the original number (1 + 0 = 1 + 0 + 0). Find another 2-digit number between 10 and 20 that is like that.

4. If you double the number *117*, the sum of the digits will be the same as the sum of the digits of the original number. Find a number between 120 and 140 that is like that.

5. Find a 2-digit number less than 25 for which the sum of its digits is the same as the product of its digits.

6. Find a 2-digit number less than 20 for which the sum of its digits is half the original number.

7. Find a 2-digit number less than 50 for which the product of its digits is half the original number.

8. There are three numbers between 2 and 100 that, when squared, create numbers whose digits can be reversed without changing the squares. The highest of the three numbers is 26 ($26^2 = 676$), and the lowest is 11 ($11^2 = 121$). Find the third number.

Use the guess-and-check method to solve.

9. Find a 2-digit number less than 20 for which the product of the digits equals half the sum of the digits.

10. A 2-digit number between 20 and 30 has 5 factors less than the number itself. When added together, the factors equal the number. What is the number?

11. When a certain single-digit number is multiplied by 4, the sum of the digits of the product equals the original number. What is the single-digit number?

12. Find a number between 30 and 40 that is the product of two single-digit prime numbers. The sum of its digits is a cube.

13. Find a 2-digit number less than 20 for which the product of its digits is $\frac{1}{3}$ of the original number.

14. The sum of the digits of the number *180* equals the sum of the digits of half the number ($1 + 8 + 0 = 9 + 0$). Find a number between 190 and 200 that is like that.

15. If you double the number *306*, the sum of the digits equals the sum of the digits of the original number. ($3 + 0 + 6 = 6 + 1 + 2$). Find another number between 300 and 320 that is like that.

16. The square of the number *3* is equal to the sum of the digits of the cube of the number *3*. Find another single-digit number (other than the number *1*) that is like that.

Use the real numbers as the replacement set. Write the letter
of the solution set of the inequality.

1. $4y < 4$

2. $3 + y \geq 1$

3. $\dfrac{5}{y} = 5$

4. $y - 1 > 8$

5. $\dfrac{1}{2}y \leq {}^-3$

6. $2y > 8$

7. $y - 2 \geq 2$

8. $\dfrac{1}{8}y \geq 2$

9. $^-1 + y > 1$

10. $\dfrac{1}{3}y > 15$

11. $3y = 0$

12. $y + 2 > {}^-8$

13. $y - 4 \leq 5$

14. $y + 1 = {}^-4$

15. $y - 2 > {}^-96$

16. $\dfrac{1}{4}y \geq {}^-4$

17. $5y \geq 95$

18. $3y < {}^-9$

a. $y = \{19,20,21, \ldots\}$

b. $y = \{^-9,^-8,^-7, \ldots\}$

c. $y = \{4,5,6,7 \ldots\}$

d. $y = \{^-5\}$

e. $y = \{1\}$

f. $y = \{ \ldots {}^-2,^-1,0\}$

g. $y = \{16,17,18, \ldots\}$

h. $y = \{0\}$

i. $y = \{ \ldots 7,8,9\}$

j. $y = \{46,47,48, \ldots\}$

k. $y = \{5,6,7, \ldots\}$

l. $y = \{3,4,5, \ldots\}$

m. $y = \{^-2,^-1,0, \ldots\}$

n. $y = \{^-93,^-92,^-91, \ldots\}$

o. $y = \{ \ldots {}^-8,^-7,^-6\}$

p. $y = \{ \ldots {}^-6,^-5,^-4\}$

q. $y = \{^-16,^-15,^-14, \ldots\}$

r. $y = \{10, 11, 12, \ldots\}$

Solve.

1. $4y > 24$

2. $9\frac{1}{4} + b < \frac{1}{4}$

3. $p - 7 \leq {}^-1$

4. $s \div 8 \geq 0$

5. $\frac{r}{2} > \frac{{}^-3}{7}$

6. $c + 47.2 < 50$

7. ${}^-4 + m \leq 5$

8. $d + 0.51 > 0.39$

9. $0.9s \neq 90$

10. ${}^-83.2 + y > {}^-100$

11. $w - 14 > {}^-6$

12. $16z < 12$

13. $\frac{t}{5} \geq 17$

14. $m + 4 \leq 6$

Solve. Then find the group in which each answer appears to solve the riddle in Problem 19.

E

15. $4n + 7 > 23$ $n > $ ____?____

$18g \leq 36$ $g \leq $ ____?____

$\frac{1}{5}a < 1.2$ $a < $ ____?____

$3h - 2 \geq 7.6$ $h \geq $ ____?____

C

16. $f + 44.2 < 34.2$ $f < $ ____?____

$v - 37 > {}^-45$ $v > $ ____?____

$8x + 9 \leq {}^-63$ $x \leq $ ____?____

$\frac{1}{3}u > {}^-3$ $u > $ ____?____

F

17. $i - 22 > 33$ $i > $ ____?____

$3z - 161 \leq {}^-2$ $a \leq $ ____?____

$9r - 7 \leq 506$ $r \leq $ ____?____

$0.8 + \frac{1}{4}h < 14.8$ $h < $ ____?____

N

18. $a + 13.6 < 30.8$ $a < $ ____?____

$4b + 16 \geq 89$ $b \geq $ ____?____

$\frac{1}{5}c - 3 < 0$ $c < $ ____?____

$2z - 6\frac{3}{4} < 21\frac{1}{4}$ $z < $ ____?____

19. What goes all around and never moves?

A $\underset{\leq57}{\text{__?__}}$ $\underset{\geq3.2}{\text{__?__}}$ $\underset{<15}{\text{__?__}}$ $\underset{\leq^-7}{\text{__?__}}$ $\underset{\leq2}{\text{__?__}}$

Solve by making a table to find the pattern.

1. Jake is at a camera store. He has chosen a camera but is not sure how many rolls of film to buy. If he buys 1 roll of film, the total bill will be $64.95. If he buys 2 rolls of film, the total bill will be $67.40. How much will the total bill be if Jake buys the camera and 6 rolls of film?

2. If Jake has $74.00, how many rolls of film can he buy when he buys the camera?

3. A film-processing company has a special price rate for printing up to 6 copies from a negative. One print costs $0.45; 2 prints cost $0.85; 3 prints cost $1.20; and 4 prints cost $1.50. If the price rate is constant how much will 6 prints cost?

Copy and complete the table. Then solve.

4. Nina performed faster and faster as she carried out her summer project, taking photographs of animals in the park. Each day, she took 3 more photographs than she had taken on the previous day. On the first day of her project, she took 6 photographs. How many photographs had she taken by the end of the day 15?

Day	1	2	3										
Photos that day	6	9	12										
Total photos to date	6	15	27										

5. How many photographs did Nina take on the day 11 of her project?

6. If Nina needed only 300 photographs, on which day could she have finished her project?

Solve by making a table to find the pattern.

1. Blanca has joined a junior tennis club. She paid a membership fee and pays a set amount per hour each time she uses a tennis court. After her first visit, she had paid a total of $58.25; after her second visit, she had paid a total of $61.50. How much will Blanca have paid after she has gone to the tennis club 7 times?

2. How much does membership to the tennis club cost?

3. If Blanca introduces new members to the club, the amount she pays for using a court is reduced. If she introduces one new member, she will pay $2.85 per hour. If she introduces 2 new members, she will pay $2.45 per hour. What will be Blanca's cost for each visit if she introduces 5 new members?

Copy and complete the table. Then solve.

4. The Health Club closes at 8.55 P.M. One night, between 8.15 P.M. and 8.20 P.M., 3 people left the club. Every 5 minutes thereafter, twice as many people leave the club as had left during the previous 5 minutes. If there were 375 people in the club that night, when was the club empty?

Time	8:20 P.M.	8:25 P.M.	8:30 P.M.	8:35 P.M.	8:40 P.M.	8:45 P.M.	8:50 P.M.	8:55 P.M.
Members who left	3	6	12					
Total members who have left	3	9	21					

5. If there were 375 people in the club, at what time was the club about half-full?

6. If there had been 750 people in the club, would the club have been empty by 8:55 P.M.?

Solve.

1. $\frac{1}{8}y + 4 > 12$

2. $5t + 9 < {}^-31$

3. $5g - 10 \geq {}^-25$

4. $400d - 6 > 34$

5. $\frac{1}{2}s + 4 > {}^-6$

6. $\frac{1}{5}a + 11 > 21$

7. $83.2t + 10 > 51.6$

8. $2v + 4 \geq {}^-1$

9. $\frac{5}{6}w + 9 \leq 0$

10. $14c + 8 < 22$

11. $114u + 0.7 < 69.1$

12. $\frac{3}{7}s + 10 < {}^-20$

13. $\frac{1}{6}m - 4 \geq {}^-4$

14. $56r - 2 > 166$

15. $15r + 6 > {}^-24$

16. $0.8t + 0.2 \leq 16.2$

17. $\frac{11}{15}v - \frac{14}{15} > \frac{{}^-3}{10}$

18. $\frac{1}{9}a + 4 < 12$

19. $\frac{3}{4}p + 16.2 < {}^-58.8$

20. $150b + 3 < 63$

21. $700n - 500 < 200$

22. $\frac{4}{5}c - 5\frac{1}{3} \leq {}^-6\frac{14}{15}$

Write an inequality and solve. Use x for the variable.

23. Bruce has to collect at least 100 signatures to get his name on the ballot for student-body elections. He already has 25 signatures, but he must hurry; so, two friends agree to help him. How many signatures each must Bruce and his two friends collect for Bruce to get his name on the ballot?

24. Each candidate for student-body office gives a speech in a special assembly. This year there are 15 candidates. The assembly must be no longer than 55 minutes, and the school principal needs 10 minutes to speak. What is the longest that each speech can be?

Solve and graph the equation or inequality.

1. $x + 4 < {}^-2$

2. $2a + 3 = {}^-3$

3. $\frac{1}{2}h \le {}^-7$

4. $7m > {}^-14$

5. $\frac{1}{5}y - 3 = {}^-2$

6. $8b - 4 = {}^-4$

7. $\frac{1}{6}v - 1 \le 0$

8. $n + 6 > 8$

9. $14r - 20 < 22$

10. $z - 6 \ge 6$

Bethania travels frequently between Burlington, Boston, and Bangor. In order to fly between Burlington and Bangor, she has to change planes in Boston, which takes 15 minutes.

BURLINGTON		FLIGHT	FREQ
To Albany			
6:15 A.M.	8:55 A.M.	311	×167
6:20 A.M.	7:00 A.M.	351	1
7:40 A.M.	8:50 A.M.	660	6
11:10 A.M.	12:30 P.M.	314	×6
5:21 P.M.	6:40 P.M.	316	×6
To Binghamton			
6:20 A.M.	7:20 A.M.	100	×67
7:00 A.M.	9:35 A.M.	122	×67
2:20 P.M.	3:50 P.M.	392	7
2:55 P.M.	5:20 P.M.	374	×6
3:10 P.M.	4:10 P.M.	102	×6
To Boston			
6:05 A.M.	7:15 A.M.	220	×67
7:00 A.M.	8:00 A.M.	122	×67
7:00 A.M.	8:10 A.M.	270	7
8:00 A.M.	9:00 A.M.	722	6
8:15 A.M.	9:25 A.M.	224	×67
10:00 A.M.	11:00 A.M.	124	×67
1:00 P.M.	1:55 P.M.	363	×6
2:30 P.M.	3:40 P.M.	222	7
4:00 P.M.	4:55 P.M.	128	67
4:00 P.M.	4:55 P.M.	365	×67
5:30 P.M.	6:40 P.M.	226	×67
From Boston			
8:45 A.M.	9:40 A.M.	372	×67
8:45 A.M.	9:55 A.M.	272	7
9:30 A.M.	10:30 A.M.	723	6
10:00 A.M.	11:05 A.M.	225	×67
12:00 P.M.	1:00 P.M.	125	×67
2:15 P.M.	3:10 P.M.	364	×6
5:45 P.M.	6:45 P.M.	129	D
7:30 P.M.	8:40 P.M.	227	×67
9:30 P.M.	10:40 P.M.	230	×6

FREQUENCY SYMBOLS

X–Except	2–Tuesday	4–Thursday	6–Saturday
1–Monday	3–Wednesday	5–Friday	7–Sunday
D–Daily			

BOSTON

	To Bangor		Fl.	From Bangor		Fl.
	8:10 A.M.	10:00 A.M.	400	7:45 A.M.	9:50 A.M.	406
	9:00 A.M.	11:00 A.M.	391	9:30 A.M.	11:25 A.M.	408
Weekdays	10:15 A.M.	12:10 P.M.	407	11:00 A.M.	12:55 A.M.	392
	12:05 P.M.	2:00 P.M.	409	2:10 P.M.	4:15 P.M.	510
	3:40 P.M.	5:30 P.M.	505	4:25 P.M.	6:30 P.M.	519
	5:10 P.M.	7:05 P.M.	511			
Weekends	9:30 A.M.	11:25 A.M.	575	9:10 A.M.	11:00 A.M.	703
	2:15 P.M.	4:05 P.M.	580	3:25 P.M.	5:20 P.M.	584

Use the schedules to solve.

1. How many flights from Burlington to Binghamton are there on Saturday?

2. When is the earliest Saturday flight from Burlington to Albany?

3. If Bethania takes Flight 270 from Burlington, which flight will she take from Boston to Bangor?

4. Bethania takes Flight 222 to Boston from Burlington. How long will she have to wait for a flight to Bangor?

5. If Bethania leaves Bangor at 7:45 A.M. on a Tuesday and the flight lands 5 minutes early, what is the earliest flight she can take to Burlington?

6. From Burlington, Bethania needs to fly to Boston and back to drop a package at the airline terminal. Which weekday flight would involve the least amount of waiting before boarding the return flight?

7. Bethania leaves Burlington at 7:00 A.M. on a Friday. When will she arrive in Bangor if the flights are on schedule?

8. If Bethania wants to travel from Bangor to Burlington on a Saturday, which flights would carry her there the fastest?

The average scores for Masters Bowling Tournament champions from 1973 to 1984 were 218, 234, 213, 220, 218, 200, 202, 206, 218, 205, 212, 212.

1. Make a frequency table. Start with 200, and use intervals that have a width of 5. Complete the average score, tally, frequency, and relative frequency for each interval.

2. What is the range for the set of data?

3. In how many years was the average 205–209?

4. For what percent of the years was the average 215–219?

From 1969 to 1983, the amounts for the Professional Golf Association's leading money winners were as follows: $175,223; $157,037; $244,490; $320,542; $308,362; $353,201; $323,149; $266,438; $310,653; $362,429; $462,636; $530,808; $375,699; $446,462; $426,668.

5. Make a frequency table. Start with $100,000 and use intervals that have a width of $50,000. (The first is $100,000–$149,999.) Complete the average score, tally, frequency, and relative frequency for each interval.

6. What is the range for this set of data?

7. For what percent of the years were the winnings $100,000–$249,999?

8. For what percent of the years were the winnings $350,000 or more? Round to the nearest tens place value.

Write the median of each set of numbers.

1. 10, 11, 17, 14, 2

2. 8.9, 2.53, 11.04, 2.1, 3.57

3. $27, $54, $31, $57, $22

4. 32, 158, 143, 32

5. 9.3, 1.6, 8.2, 4.7

6. 0.2, 0.03, 0.15, 0.06, 0.21

Write the mode(s) of each set of numbers.

7. 18, 16.26, 16.26, 5, 10.35

8. 11.4, 14, 17, 14, 13

9. 6, 9, 5, 3, 6, 9, 1, 4

10. $2.50, $3.75, $2.25, $2.50

11. 2.9, 17, 2.9, 6.24, 9.89

12. 30, 90, 60, 40, 90

Write the mean of each set of numbers. Round to the nearest hundredths place value.

13. 8.5, 14, 13.8, 7.92, 13.63

14. 3.7, 11.2, 15

15. 19.5, 7, 20.5

16. 16, 41, 176, 14

17. 88, 56, 91, 77, 32

18. $1.25, $3.20, $5.40, $3.70

Write the missing number.

19. mean = 7.8   5, 8, ____?____, 12, 3

20. mean = 15.75   13.8, 14.2, 19.6, ____?____

21. mean = 12   9, 12, 15, 21, 4, ____?____

22. mean = 36   24.5, 28, 48, 37, ____?____

23. mean = 28.5 km   ____?____, 22 km, 45 km

24. mean = 69.25%   97%, 32%, ____?____, 84%

Solve.

25. Pat's scores on her last five mathematics tests were 89, 95, 78, 94, and 99. What was her average score? If Pat takes one more test this year, what is the highest average she can achieve?

26. An absentminded teacher lost a test paper from one of his students. He remembered that the mean score for the class of 25 was 83, and that the sum of the other 24 scores was 1,980. What was the grade on the lost paper?

The table shows the number of each dish served in a Chinese restaurant on two different days.

Dish	Monday	Tuesday
Beef with broccoli	43	40
Chow mein	59	41
Fried rice	62	45
Lo mein	51	42
Pepper steak	49	38
Daily special	44	72

1. Construct a horizontal double-bar graph to reflect these figures.

2. On which day was the greater number of meals served?

3. Which dish had the greatest change in popularity?

This histogram shows the range of lunch bills in the restaurant one day.

4. Into which price range did most of the bills fall?

5. Into which price range did the fewest bills fall?

6. How many customers paid between $8.01–$10?

7. What is the total number of bills shown?

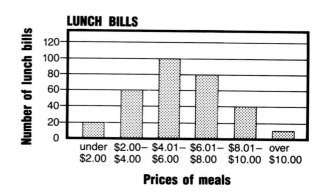

LUNCH BILLS

Number of lunch bills

Prices of meals

The Off-Center Art Center held a show of sculptures made by local artists. All the money made by selling the works was donated to the neighborhood Free Studio. The scattergram below shows the heights and the prices of the sculptures in the show.

Can you use the scattergram to answer each question? Write *yes* or *no*.

1. How many sculptures were sold?

2. How many sculptures were shown?

Use the scattergram to answer each question.

3. Were most sculptures priced at more than $150 or less than $150?

4. Was the tallest sculpture the highest priced?

5. How many of the sculptures were more than 4 feet 6 inches tall?

6. How many sculptures were priced at less than $80?

7. What percent of the sculptures were priced at more than $225?

8. Was any piece of sculpture less than 4 feet tall priced at more than $200?

Does the scattergram support each statement? Write *yes* or *no*.

9. In general, the larger sculptures were the most expensive.

10. Sculptures that were the same height were generally the same price.

11. The sculptures priced at less than $70 were not good work.

12. The cost of materials probably has something to do with the price.

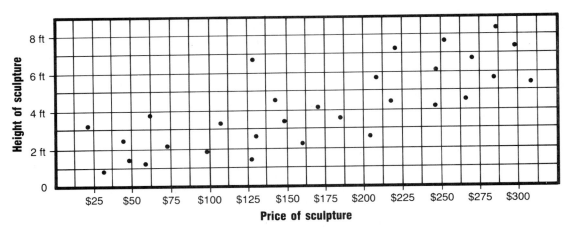

1. Make a broken-line graph to show the following statistics on silver production.

1925	66.16 million ounces
1930	50.75 million ounces
1935	45.92 million ounces
1940	69.59 million ounces
1945	29.06 million ounces
1950	42.31 million ounces
1955	36.47 million ounces
1960	36.00 million ounces

2. Which year had the greatest increase in silver production over the year before?

3. Make a double broken-line graph of the average temperatures each month in these two cities.

Month	Chicago	New Orleans
Jan.	26	55
Feb.	28	57
Mar.	36	61
Apr.	49	68
May	60	74
June	71	80
July	76	82
Aug.	74	82
Sept.	66	78
Oct.	55	70
Nov.	40	60
Dec.	29	55

4. For which city is the variation in temperature greater?

5. Which month shows the least difference between the two lines on the graph?

1. Use a compass and a protractor to construct a circle graph that shows the number of pages each person contributed to the Chess Club's newsletter. Use the first letter of each person's name to represent his or her contribution. Mark each part of the graph with the percent that it represents.

Andre	4	Eva	2
Beth	4	Franco	8
Carlos	4	Gordon	6
Dionne	2	Helga	2

2. What is the measure of the central angle of the part that represents Carlos's contribution?

3. What fraction of the total did Gordon contribute?

4. What fraction of the total did Andre contribute?

5. What fraction of the total did Andre, Dionne, and Beth contribute together?

6. What is the ratio of Gordon's contribution compared to Eva's?

Selecting an Appropriate Format • Tell which type of graph would best display the data.

7. the monthly temperatures of a city for a year

8. the lengths of the eight longest rivers in the world

9. the percent of space used for clothing, sporting goods, kitchen appliances, and furniture

10. the frequency of weights between 100–110 lbs, 110–120 lbs, 120–130 lbs, and 130–140 lbs

11. the percent of a garden used for azaleas, petunias, roses, and geraniums

12. the monthly precipitation in 2 different cities for 12 months

Tweed Polls, Inc., conducted a poll to ask residents of Ringford (population 16,000) their opinions about the choice of a raccoon as the new town mascot. Three groups of 250 people each were questioned. The table below shows their responses.

Age group		15–25	26–45	Older than 45
Percent of the town population		25%	40%	20%
	Approve	115	90	120
	Disapprove	100	105	80
	Undecided	35	55	50

Assume that the poll is representative of the opinions of all Ringford residents in the age groups sampled. Use the table to solve.

1. Which age group voiced the greatest difference of opinion between approval and disapproval?

2. What percent of the 26–45 age group was undecided?

3. In which age group did 40% of the people disapprove?

4. How many Ringford residents are more than 45 years old?

5. How many Ringford residents in the 15–25 age group disapproved?

6. How many Ringford residents in the 26–45 age group approved?

7. What percent of all Ringford residents 15 years of age and older disapproved?

8. How many residents of Ringford are less than 15 years of age?

9. If 80% of the undecideds in the older-than-45 age group had disapproved and 20% had approved, would the majority of the age group have disapproved?

10. Do the majority of residents of Ringford who are 15 years of age and older approve or disapprove?

To find out whether passengers would use a new service, Airways North conducted a poll. The results are shown below.

Age		20–40	20–40	Older than 40	Older than 40
Career		Self-employed	Executives	Self-employed	Executives
Percent of total first-class passengers		20%	28%	12%	24%
	Will use the service	150	210	175	270
	Will not use the service	200	240	215	170
	Undecided	150	50	110	60

A total of 8,260 passengers fly first class between New York and Rome each month. Based on the assumption that the passengers in the poll represent all of Airways North's first-class passengers, solve.

1. What percent of self-employed passengers questioned said they would use the new service?

2. Suppose that Airways North had questioned only executives older than 40, and the results showed that 60% of those polled would use the new service. Would this poll be a good indicator of the total population of passengers? Explain your answer.

3. To the nearest person, how many passengers are likely to use the service?

5. To make a profit, Airways North needs at least 2,750 passengers to use its new service each month. Using only the categories represented in the poll, should the new service be started?

4. If Airways North reduced the fare paid by executives by 10%, they expect that 75% of the undecided executives would use the new service. The airline, however, would have to book at least 3,100 passengers per month to make a profit. Can they obtain that number of passengers if they reduce the fare for executives?

6. How many passengers will the airline have if it reduces the fare?

You are going to toss a penny and spin the spinner at the right.

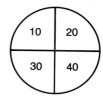

1. Draw a tree diagram to show the possible outcomes.

2. Write the possible outcomes.

3. How many possible outcomes are there?

4. Is the number of possible outcomes equal to 2 · 4?

Gym lockers are identified by the use of a letter (A, B, or C) and a number (1, 2, 3, 4, 5).

5. Draw a tree diagram to show the sample space.

6. Write the possible outcomes.

7. How many possible outcomes are there?

8. Write a multiplication sentence for the number of possible outcomes.

Solve.

9. Edgar is going to the sporting-goods store. He can take the bus, ride his bicycle, or walk. He can use Elm Street, Maple Boulevard, or Oak Avenue. How many different ways can Edgar get to the sporting-goods store?

10. A football stadium seats 25,000. Tickets are identified using a letter of the alphabet (A to Z) followed by a 3-digit number (0 to 9 in each place). Which is greater—the number of seats or the number of tickets? how much greater?

Write the number of permutations.

1. $_7P_2$

2. $_5P_4$

3. $_9P_6$

4. $_8P_3$

5. $_{10}P_2$

6. $_6P_3$

7. $_{12}P_5$

8. $_{20}P_4$

9. $_{15}P_6$

10. $_{17}P_3$

11. $_{100}P_2$

12. $_{40}P_5$

13. Evaluate 10!

Find the factorial.

14. $3! + 3!$

15. $8! \div 5!$

16. $4 \times 4!$

17. $2! \times 7!$

18. $9! + 6!$

19. $21! \div 18!$

20. $3 \times 5!$

21. $7! \div 4$

22. $10! \div 5!$

Write *true* or *false*.

23. $9 \times 8! = 9!$

24. $64! \div 63! = 64$

25. $3! + 5! = 8!$

26. $47! \div 47 = 46!$

27. $5! \times 4! = 20!$

28. $10! \div 7! = 720$

Solve.

29. Peter Possible has 25 different books on his shelf. In how many ways can he pick 3 books?

30. Mary Maybe has 16 different bottles of perfume. In how many ways can she arrange them 5 at a time?

31. In how many different ways can 8 people line up in front of a movie box office?

32. In how many ways can 7 photographs be hung in a horizontal line?

Write the number of combinations.

1. $_5C_2$

2. $_7C_4$

3. $_4C_3$

4. $_8C_5$

5. $_6C_3$

6. $_9C_5$

7. $_7C_3$

8. $_8C_7$

9. $_{10}C_5$

10. $_{11}C_8$

11. $_{12}C_7$

12. $_{14}C_{13}$

Write *permutation* or *combination*.

13. In how many ways can you arrange 5 letters 3 at a time?

14. How many committees of 4 students can be made from 16 students?

15. How many bunches of 5 flowers can be made from 14 flowers?

16. In how many ways can 5 students be seated in 5 chairs?

17. How many different 4-digit numbers can be made from the digits 1, 2, 6, 8, 9?

18. How many teams of 8 players can be formed from 20 players?

19. Write the $_5C_2$ combinations of the set *A, B, C, D, E*.

Solve.

20. Richard has a penny, a nickel, a dime, a quarter, and a half-dollar. How many different amounts can he leave as a tip if he wants to use exactly two coins?

21. Julie has 9 books. In how many different ways can she choose 3 books to read?

22. The Golden Happiness Store sells 7 different brands of persimmon juice. In how many different ways can Keiji buy 2 brands?

23. There are 10 people waiting to play tennis. How many different pairs can be selected for playing singles?

The following symbols are written on a set of cards.

The cards are shuffled and placed facedown in a stack. After a card is drawn from the stack at random, it is returned to the stack and the cards are shuffled and placed facedown again.

1. What is the probability of drawing a ≈ ? (Express as a fraction.

2. What is the probability of drawing a ◯ ? (Express as a percentage to the nearest tenth.)

3. What is the probability of drawing any of the following symbols: ☆ , ◯ , = ? (Express as a ratio.)

4. Drawing a Z has a probability of zero. What is the term for such an event?

5. Drawing a symbol has the probability of one. What term applies to this event?

Write the fraction for each probability.

6. P(△)

7. P(not ⌐)

8. P(= or ☆)

9. P(⦂)

10. P(◯ or not ◯)

11. P(☐ or ◠)

Solve.

12. You toss a number cube numbered 1 to 6. If it lands on a 1 or a 6, you win. What is the probability that you will win?

13. A spinner has 8 equal sections, numbered 1, 3, 4, 5, 5, 6, 7, 7. What is the probability that you will spin an even number?

14. Using the same spinner as above, what is the probability you will spin a prime number greater than 2?

A coin is tossed and the spinner at the right is spun. Write each probability as a fraction.

1. P(green, heads)

2. P(not red, tails)

3. P(blue, tails)

4. P(orange, heads)

5. P(yellow, heads)

6. P(not purple, heads)

A number cube with faces 1, 2, 3, 4, 5, 6 is rolled three times. Answer the following questions about these events and express your answers as fractions.

7. What is the probability an even number will come up each time?

8. What is the probability a number less than 5 will come up each time?

9. What is the probability that all three rolls will be different?

10. What is the probability that the sum of the three rolls will be 20?

Three coins are tossed. Answer the following questions about these events and express your answers as fractions.

11. What is the probability that all heads show?

12. What is the probability that no heads show?

13. What is the probability of getting heads only on the middle toss?

14. What is the probability of getting exactly two heads or exactly two tails? (HINT: Consider favorable outcomes and total number of outcomes.)

Write the letter of the correct answer.

1. There are 6 debating teams in a league. Each team has to debate 3 other teams. How many debates have to be held? Each dot represents a team, and each line segment represents a debate held.

a.

6 debates

b.
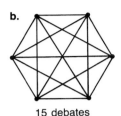
15 debates

c.
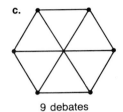
9 debates

d.
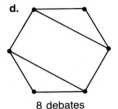
8 debates

2. How many combinations of quarts and pints can you use to make 2 gallons? The first number of the ordered pair represents the number of quarts, and the second number represents the number of pints.

   a. (1,6) (2,4) (3,2) (2,2)

   b. (6,4) (4,8) (2,12)

   c. (7,2) (6,4) (5,6) (4,8) (3,10) (2,12) (1,14)

Solve.

3. There are 5 members of a chess club. Can a tournament be arranged so that each member plays 3 other members one game each?

4. If there are 8 members of a chess club, how many games would be played if each member played 3 other members one game each?

5. Darlene has a container that holds 5 lb flour and a container that holds 2 lb flour. She needs 1 lb of flour for a recipe. How can she use the containers to measure out 1 lb? Use ordered pairs.

6. How many combinations of quarters and dimes can you use to equal $1.80?

Use with pages 338–339.

Pick a card. Do not replace it. Pick a second card. Write each probability as a fraction.

| B | A | S | E |

| B | A | L | L |

1. P(B, then A)

2. P(B, then E)

3. P(S, then E)

4. P(A, then A)

5. P(A, then not A)

6. P(S, then S)

The numbers 1 through 10 are written on pieces of paper. The papers are put into a hat and drawn out one by one. Answer the following questions about these events and express your answers as fractions.

7. What is the probability that the first two numbers are even?

8. What is the probability that the first two numbers are multiples of 3?

9. What is the probability that the first two numbers are 1 and 2, in that order?

10. What is the probability that the first three numbers are all different?

Five kittens and four puppies are in a kennel together. One animal at a time goes through the pet door. Answer the following questions about these events and express your answers as fractions.

11. What is the probability that the first pet through the door will be a puppy?

12. What is the probability that the first two will be puppies?

13. What is the probability that the first two will be kittens?

14. What is the probability that the first three will be puppies?

15. What is the probability that the first three animals will be different?

Mrs. Andersen's hens produced 630 white eggs and 210 brown eggs last week. Make your way from the front door of the chicken coop, around the nests and roosts, to the back door by answering the questions. Each answer will tell you which area of the coop to move to next. Copy the floor plan of the chicken coop. On your paper, draw a line from area to area to show your progress.

1. If 100 eggs are produced one day, how many would you predict will be brown?

2. If 104 eggs are produced, predict how many will be brown.

3. If 28 eggs are produced, predict how many will be white.

4. If 5 brown eggs are produced, predict how many white eggs will be produced.

5. If 12 eggs are produced, predict how many will be white.

6. How many white eggs are produced for every brown egg?

7. If 16 eggs are produced, predict how many will not be white.

8. If 33 white eggs are produced, how many brown eggs are likely to be produced?

9. How many eggs should be produced to get 9 that are white?

10. How many white eggs would you expect if 8 eggs are produced?

Chicken Coop

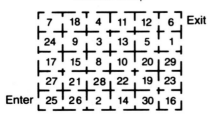

The graphs below show the steel production of the United States and Japan between the years 1945 and 1970.

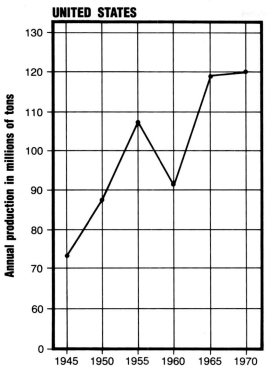

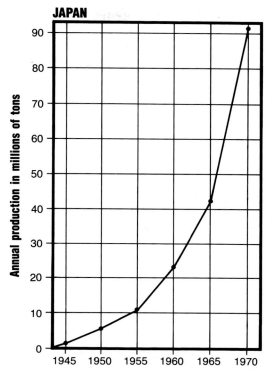

Use the graphs to solve.

1. Which country produced the most steel in 1970?

2. Which country increased its steel production by the greatest tonnage between 1960 and 1965?

3. Which country increased its steel production by the greatest tonnage between 1955 and 1965?

4. In which years did Japan's steel production drop?

5. By about how much did Japan's steel production increase in 1960 beyond its production in 1955?

6. Did the rate of steel production in the United States double between 1945 and 1970?

7. How did Japan's 1970 steel production compare with that of the United States in 1960?

8. Which country would you expect to have produced more steel in 1980 if both followed the trends plotted in the graphs?

Dobbs Industries started two new companies, Waveform, Inc., and Micromonitor, Inc. Dobbs invested the same amount of money in each company, but did not invest any further amounts after the two companies started operations in January 1979. The graphs below show the performance of each company from 1979 to 1984.

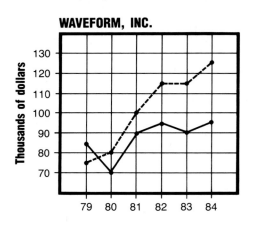

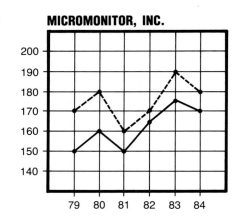

------ Total Income
——— Total Expenses

1. Which company made the most profit in 1983?

2. In which year did both companies make the same amount of profit?

3. Which company performed better between the years 1979 and 1981?

4. If Dobbs Industries had invested $50,000 in each company, in which year would the accumulated profits of Waveform, Inc., have been enough to repay Dobbs' investment in Waveform?

5. In which year could Micromonitor, Inc., repay Dobbs' investment in Micromonitor?

6. If Dobbs Industries expected yearly interest of 5% on its investment, in which year could Micromonitor repay Dobbs Industries?

Draw each of the following.

1. line *AB*

2. ray *DG*

3. line segment *SV*

4. point *R* on line *EF*

5. $\overline{AE}$ with midpoint *T*

6. $\overrightarrow{SU}$

7. $\overleftrightarrow{MN}$

8. $\overleftrightarrow{RT}$ and $\overleftrightarrow{CN}$ intersecting at *S*

9. parallel line segments *GK* and *QZ*

10. $\overline{HJ}$ congruent to $\overline{IL}$

Classify each angle by writing *acute, right, obtuse,* or *straight.*

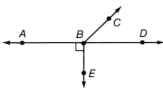

1. ∠ABC

2. an angle of 27°

3. ∠CBD

4. an angle of 180°

5. ∠ABD

6. an angle of 165°

7. ∠DBE

8. an angle of 42°

9. ∠CBE

10. an angle of 90°

11. ∠ABE

12. an angle of 98°

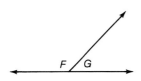

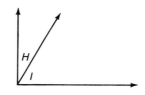

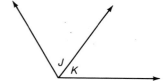

13. Which two angles are complementary?

14. Which two angles are supplementary?

Use a protractor to measure the angles.

15.

16.

17.

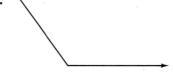

Use a compass and a straightedge to construct a line
segment that is congruent to each line segment below.

1. A •————————• B

2. C •——————————————• D

3. E •————————• F

4. G •————————————————————————————————• H

5. I •————————————————————————• J

Use a compass and a straightedge to construct an angle that
is congruent to each angle below.

6.

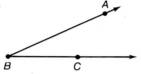

7.

8.

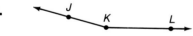

9.

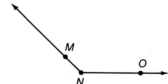

10.

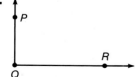

Copy each line segment. Then use a compass and a straightedge to construct the bisector of each line segment.

1.

_____

2.

_____

3.

_____

4.

_____

5.

_____

6.

_____

Copy each angle. Then construct the bisector of each angle.

7.

8.

9.

10.

11.

12.

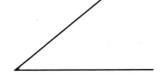

Work backward. Write the letter of the correct answer.

1. Alex is painting a house. He uses $\frac{1}{3}$ of the paint he bought on the dining room. He uses twice as much on the living room as on the kitchen, where he uses $1\frac{1}{2}$ gallons. He has $1\frac{1}{2}$ gallons of paint left. How much paint did Alex buy?

    a. 12 gallons

    b. 16 gallons

    c. 9 gallons

2. Naomi is cleaning out a storeroom at the paint shop. She puts $\frac{1}{2}$ the paint on display in the shop and takes $\frac{1}{2}$ of what is left to the basement. Although she takes $\frac{3}{4}$ of the remaining paint home, there are still 7 gallons left in the storeroom. How much paint was in the storeroom before she cleaned it?

    a. 168 gallons

    b. 112 gallons

    c. 56 gallons

Solve.

3. It took Nancy and Ramon 3 weeks to paint a house in their spare time. During the second week, they used $3\frac{1}{2}$ fewer gallons of paint than they used in the first week. In the third week, they used 13 gallons, which was twice as many as the number of gallons used in the second week. How much paint did they use?

4. Toku follows a budget to buy supplies to paint his room. He spends $\frac{1}{2}$ of his budget on a roller, a tray, and tape. He spends $12.27 on paint, and of the remaining money, he spends $\frac{2}{3}$ on a trim brush, which costs $3.82. How much money has he budgeted?

5. Susan wants to use blue, yellow, green, and pink paint to decorate her house. She needs 3 times as much blue paint as yellow paint and $\frac{1}{2}$ as much yellow paint as green paint. She needs $3\frac{1}{4}$ gallons of pink paint, which is $\frac{3}{4}$ of a gallon more than the green paint she needs. How much paint does Susan need in all?

6. Colleen's family plans to paint the windows of their house. Her father will paint twice as many windows as her mother, and Colleen and her 2 brothers will paint an equal number of the rest of the windows. Colleen decides to do her own share and her mother's share and paints 7 windows, which is one less than her father's share. How many windows are there?

Work backward. Write the letter of the correct answer.

1. In the first act of a play, all the actors were onstage. The second act opened with $\frac{1}{2}$ the actors onstage, and then 5 actors left. After that, $\frac{1}{2}$ the remaining actors left, and 4 actors remained onstage. How many actors were onstage in the first act?

   a. 36   b. 26   c. 28

2. Sam bought 8 of his friends tickets for a play. Each ticket cost $8.70. He also bought 2 books of plays, each costing $4.45. He spent exactly $\frac{1}{2}$ the money he had left for a record that cost $6.20. How much money did Sam originally have?

   a. $90.90   b. $84.70   c. $67.10

Solve.

3. In one scene of a play, 23 lines were spoken by the lead actor. The rest of the lines were spoken by Roger and Francis. Francis spoke twice as many lines as Roger, who had 9 lines. How many lines were spoken in the scene?

4. Rufus is in charge of lighting a play. Half the lights he uses are white. Of the remaining lights, $\frac{1}{3}$ have red filters, and 4 have blue filters. The 10 lights left have yellow filters. How many lights does Rufus use for the play?

5. Sally took money from her bank account to go out of town for an audition. She spent $54.00 for a round-trip bus ticket and $\frac{1}{2}$ of the remaining money for her hotel bill. She spent $7.90 for food and arrived home with $15.10. How much money did Sally take from her bank account?

6. Act I of a play lasts $\frac{2}{3}$ the time of the whole play. There is a 15-minute intermission. In Act II, Jack's speech takes up $\frac{1}{2}$ the time, and the rest is divided equally between speeches made by Rosa and Zoe. Zoe talks for 6 minutes, and the play ends at 8:17 P.M. When did the play begin?

7. At intermission, Xavier sold refreshments. Of the items he had, $\frac{1}{5}$ were granola bars and $\frac{1}{2}$ the remaining items were containers of popcorn. The rest were divided equally among apples, rice cakes, and containers of yogurt. Xavier sold the 8 apples he had. How many items did he originally have?

8. Information about a play took up $\frac{1}{3}$ of the pages in the program. Information about the actors took up $\frac{1}{4}$ of the remaining pages. Information about the director, the producer, and the designer took up 2 pages, the same number of pages devoted to the actors. How many pages were there in the program?

In the given figure, $\overleftrightarrow{a} \| \overleftrightarrow{b}$. Write *vertical, adjacent, corresponding,* or *alternate interior* to identify each pair of angles.

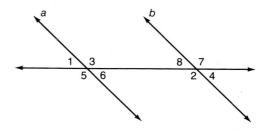

1. ∠2 and ∠7

2. ∠5 and ∠6

3. ∠1 and ∠8

4. ∠2 and ∠3

Using the same figure, write *congruent* or *supplementary* to name each pair of angles.

5. ∠2 and ∠3   6. ∠2 and ∠8

7. ∠5 and ∠8   8. ∠6 and ∠7

9. ∠2 and ∠7   10. ∠1 and ∠6

11. ∠3 and ∠4   12. ∠4 and ∠5

In the figure at right, $\overleftrightarrow{MN} \| \overleftrightarrow{OP}$. Write *true* if the angles are congruent and *false* if they are not congruent.

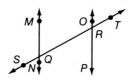

13. ∠QRP ≅ ∠MQR   14. ∠SQN ≅ ∠ORT

15. ∠MQS ≅ ∠ORT   16. ∠ORT ≅ ∠QRO

Use the figure at right to find the measure of each angle. In the figure, $\overleftrightarrow{c} \| \overleftrightarrow{d}$ and m∠5 = 155°.

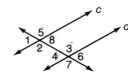

17. m∠1   18. m∠4

19. m∠7   20. m∠6

Solve.

21. Draw a line. Construct a line parallel to it. Then construct a line that is perpendicular to the parallel lines.

Write *acute, obtuse,* or *right;* and *equilateral, scalene,* or *isosceles* to classify each triangle.

1.

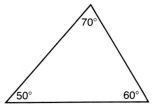

2.

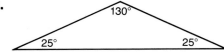

3.

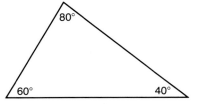

Write the measure of the third angle of each triangle.

4.

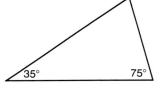

5.

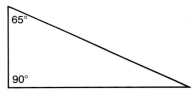

6.

7.

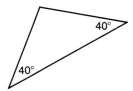

8. triangle with two angles of 42°

9. triangle with an angle of 60° and one of 110°

Write the name of the polygon. Then write *regular* or *irregular* for each.

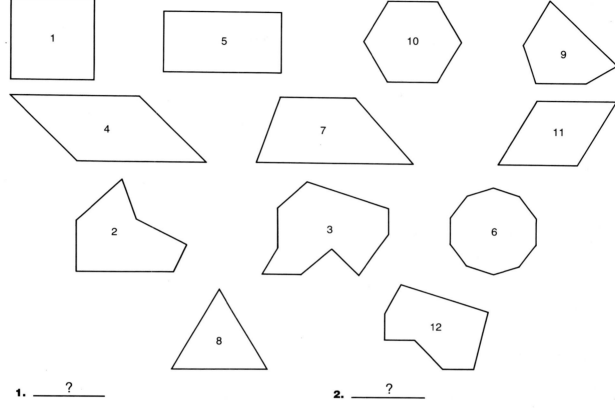

1. _____?_____

2. _____?_____

3. _____?_____

4. _____?_____

5. _____?_____

6. _____?_____

7. _____?_____

8. _____?_____

9. _____?_____

10. _____?_____

11. _____?_____

12. _____?_____

13. What is the sum of the interior angles of a polygon with six sides?

14. What is the sum of the interior angles of a polygon with nine sides?

Estimation	Making a Table to Find a Pattern	Using a Formula
Using a Graph	Writing an Equation	Making an Organized List
Choosing the Operation	Interpreting the Quotient and the	Using a Sample
Solving Multi-step Problems	Remainder	
Guessing and Checking		

Write the strategy or method you choose. Then solve.

1. Colin has a total of 700 coins in his collection. How many of them are Italian?

COLIN'S COIN COLLECTION

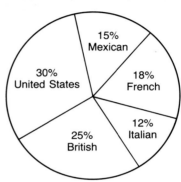

2. How many more coins are French than Mexican?

3. If Colin trades 20 United States coins for 16 British coins, will he have more or fewer British coins than United States coins in his collection?

4. There are 14 cars in a parking lot. When 5 cars leave, the lot is $\frac{1}{8}$ full. How many cars can the parking lot hold?

5. A boat travels across a lake at an average speed of $2\frac{1}{2}$ miles per hour. The lake is 440 yards wide. Does it take more than 5 minutes for the boat to cross the lake?

6. A boy is fishing with a 6-foot piece of string. If the boy stretches his arm 14 inches down a bank that is $2\frac{1}{2}$ feet above the water, could the string reach 5 feet underwater?

7. There are 13 elm trees and twice as many oak trees in a park. One third of the trees in the park are oak trees. How many trees are there in the park?

Estimation	Guessing and Checking	Using a Sample
Using a Graph	Writing an Equation	
Choosing the Operation	Using a Formula	

Write the strategy or method you choose. Then solve. For Exercises 1–3, refer to the graph.

1. How much money did Alicia earn during the summer vacation?

2. About how much money did all five students earn during the summer vacation?

3. About what was the average amount earned by the students during the summer vacation?

TOTAL EARNINGS OF STUDENTS DURING THE SUMMER VACATION

Paul Marian Jill Jorge Alicia

SCHOOL PLAY POLL RESULTS FOR 300 STUDENTS

Grade	Grade 6	Grade 7	Grade 8
Percent of total students in school	34%	36%	30%
Approve	40 students	45 students	42 students
Disapprove	35 students	40 students	48 students
Undecided	25 students	15 students	10 students

4. There are 2,000 students in the school. What percent of the students were questioned?

5. According to the poll, how many eighth-grade students in the total population approve of the play?

6. In the poll, do more students approve or disapprove of the play?

Use circle *A* to answer questions 1–6.

1. Name the center of the circle.

2. Name a radius of the circle.

3. Name a chord

4. Name a diameter of the circle.

5. Name a central angle.

6. Name an arc.

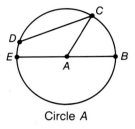

Circle *A*

Use circle *P* to answer questions 7–12.

7. Name a diameter of the circle.

8. Name two radii of the circle.

9. Name two arcs.

10. Name a chord.

11. Name two central angles.

12. Name the center of the circle.

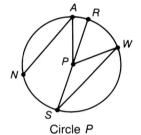

Circle *P*

13. If a circle has a radius of 4 inches, what is its diameter?

14. If a circle has a diameter of 19 cm, what is its radius?

$\triangle ABC \cong \triangle XYZ$. $\triangle DEF \cong \triangle WPQ$. Write the measure of the angle or the side.

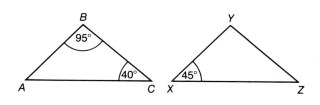
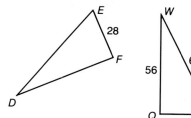

1. $\angle BAC$

2. $\angle XYZ$

3. $\overline{DE}$

4. $\overline{QP}$

5. $\overline{DF}$

6. $\angle YZX$

$LVBT \cong NJSR$. Write the measure of the angle or the side.

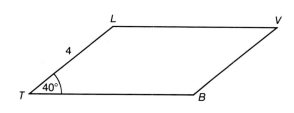

7. $\overline{LV}$

8. $\angle RNJ$

9. $\angle TLV$

10. $\angle SRN$

11. $\overline{RN}$

12. $\overline{SJ}$

13. $\angle SJN$

14. $\overline{RS}$

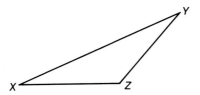
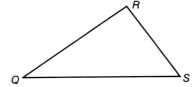

1. Use SAS congruence to construct a triangle congruent to △XYZ. (Copy sides $\overline{XZ}$, $\overline{YZ}$, and ∠Z.)

2. Use SSS congruence to construct a triangle congruent to △QRS.

3. Use ASA congruence to construct a triangle congruent to △XYZ. (Copy ∠X, ∠Z, and $\overline{XZ}$.)

4. Use SAS congruence to construct a triangle congruent to △QRS. (Copy sides $\overline{QR}$, $\overline{RS}$, and ∠R.)

Write the letter of the picture that can help you solve each problem.

1. A building has 3 identical floors. Each floor has a large window. The distance from the ground to the bottom of the lowest window is 3 feet, and the distance from the top of the building to the bottom of the highest window is 7 feet. How tall is the building?

2. A rectangular plot of land contains 3 square flower beds. Each flower bed is 7 feet long, and there is a border of 3 feet between each flower bed and the perimeter of the plot. There is also a border of 3 feet between the flower beds. How long is the plot of land?

Draw a picture on a separate piece of paper to help you find each solution.

a.

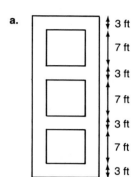

3 ft
7 ft
3 ft
7 ft
3 ft
7 ft
3 ft

3. The fence around a house measuring 30 feet by 22 feet was built a distance of 12 feet from the outside of the house. How long is the fence?

4. There are three volumes of an encyclopedia on a shelf. Each volume has 500 pages. The two covers of each volume are each 1.5 millimeters thick, and each section of 100 pages measures 18 millimeters. What is the distance between the center pages of the two outside volumes?

b.

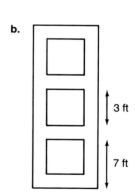

3 ft
7 ft

5. A floor is covered with square tiles of equal size. The fifth row of tiles from the north end of the room is also the seventh row from the south end of the room. A tile in the middle of the fifth row from the south end has 8 tiles on each side of it. How many tiles are there?

6. There are 4 boxes of equal height stacked in a room. The distance from the ceiling to the bottom of the top box is 3 feet 6 inches, and the distance from the ceiling to the bottom of the second-highest box is 5 feet. How high is the room?

c.

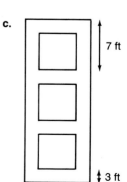

7 ft
3 ft

△LDR ~ △KCG. Write the measure of the angle or the side.

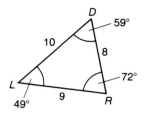

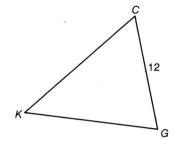

1. ∠CKG

2. $\overline{CK}$

3. ∠CGK

4. $\overline{KG}$

Polygon *AZETMHS* ~ polygon *JBFIPQN*. Write the measure
of the angle or the side.

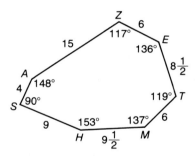

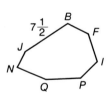

5. ∠JBF

6. $\overline{FI}$

7. $\overline{PI}$

8. ∠NJB

9. ∠FIP

10. $\overline{BF}$

11. ∠BFI

12. $\overline{QP}$

13. $\overline{NQ}$

14. ∠QNJ

15. ∠QPI

16. $\overline{NJ}$

Use the diagrams to answer the questions.

1. Is $\overline{DK}$ a line of symmetry of the hexagon?

2. Is $\overline{JL}$ a line of symmetry of the hexagon?

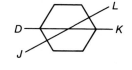

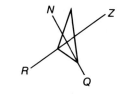

3. Is $\overline{RZ}$ a line of symmetry of the triangle?

4. Is $\overline{NQ}$ a line of symmetry of the triangle?

5. Is $\overline{GP}$ a line of symmetry of the polygon?

6. Is $\overline{UI}$ a line of symmetry of the polygon?

Copy the polygon on a real-number plane. Then draw a reflection of the polygon about the x-axis and about the y-axis.

7.

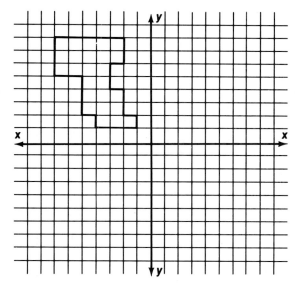

8. List the coordinates of the vertices of both reflections.

Copy the truck on a real-number plane. Then drive the truck along Route 66 by following the instructions and drawing a new truck for each.

1. Translate the figure 4 units to the right and 5 units down.

2. Rotate the figure around A so that B is at point ($^-$10,9).

3. Translate the figure 4 units to the right and 8 units down.

4. Rotate the figure around point ($^-$4,$^-$1) so that A is at point ($^-$10,$^-$3).

5. Translate the figure 11 units to the right and 5 units down.

6. Translate the figure 7 units to the right and 6 units down.

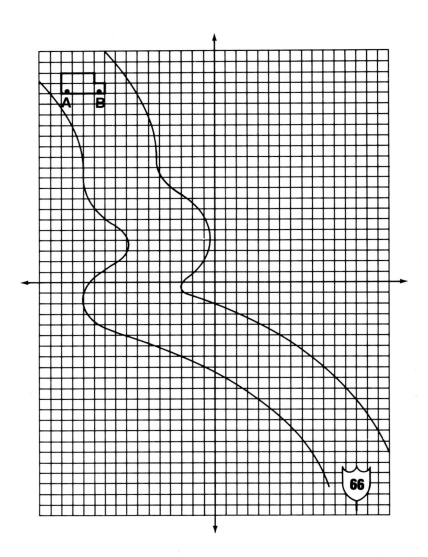

Holt, Rinehart and Winston, Publishers • 8

The chart below shows the area and the population of the region of Connacht in the Republic of Ireland and the area and population of the Republic of Ireland itself.

AREA AND POPULATION OF CONNACHT, REPUBLIC OF IRELAND

Counties	Area (square miles)	1966 population	1971 population
Galway	2,293	148,000	149,000
Leitrim	589	31,000	28,000
Mayo	2,084	116,000	110,000
Roscommon	951	56,000	54,000
Sligo	693	51,000	50,000

AREA AND POPULATION OF THE REPUBLIC OF IRELAND

27,137 square miles	2,884,000	2,978,000

Do you need the chart to answer each question? Write *yes* or *no*.

1. At the end of the nineteenth century, 25% of Ireland's population lived in urban areas. In 1971, 52% lived in urban areas. What was the percent of increase?

2. If 60% of the population of Sligo was younger than 45 in 1966, how many people in Sligo were older than 45 in 1966?

Solve. Use the chart to obtain additional information.

3. A farm in Leitrim covers 117.8 square miles. What percent of the county does the farm cover?

4. In which county was the percent of decrease in the population the greatest between 1966 and 1971?

5. What was the average population per square mile in Roscommon in 1971? Round to the nearest whole number.

6. What percent (to the nearest whole number) of the population of the Republic of Ireland lived in the Connacht region in 1971?

7. Between 1966 and 1971, was the percent of increase in the population of Galway greater or smaller than the percent of increase in the total population of the Republic of Ireland?

8. If a cartography company had mapped 80% of the Connacht region, how many square miles of the province would it still have to map to complete a map of Connacht?

Write the perimeter of each polygon.

1.

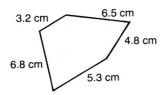

2.

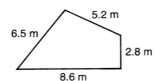

3.

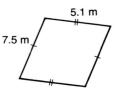

4.

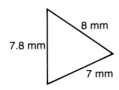

5.

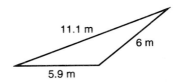

6.

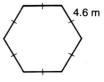

Write the perimeter of each rectangle.

7. $l = 19$ cm $w = 23$ cm

8. $l = 47.6$ m $w = 5.4$ m

9. $l = 31.2$ cm $w = 47.1$ cm

10. $l = 23.2$ cm $w = 8.6$ cm

11. $l = 14.5$ cm $w = 9.1$ cm

12. $l = 53.1$ cm $w = 46$ cm

Write the perimeter of each square.

13. $s = 19.6$ yd

14. $s = 27\frac{1}{4}$ ft

15. $s = 3.6$ mi

16. $s = 45$ in.

17. $s = 0.9$ mi

18. $s = 20\frac{1}{3}$ yd

Use with pages 398–399.

Write the measure of the missing side of each triangle.

1.

12 m

5 m

2.

29 in.

21 in.

3.

17 cm

15 cm

4.

60 ft

80 ft

5.

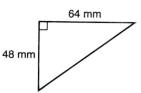

64 mm

48 mm

6.

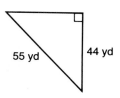

55 yd

44 yd

7. a right triangle with legs of 11 in. and 60 in.

8. a right triangle with a leg of 7 cm and a hypotenuse of 25 cm

Solve.

9. A string of buoys 100-m long stretches diagonally across a river. The distance from one end of the string to a point directly opposite the other end is 28 m. How wide is the river?

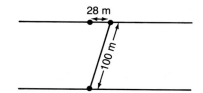

28 m

100 m

10. A ladder is leaning against a wall. Its bottom legs are 9 feet from the wall, and its top legs touch the wall 12 feet from the ground. How long is the ladder?

Use the table of trigonometric ratios on pages 402–403 of your text to find the value.

1. tan 44°

2. tan 32°

3. sin 19°

4. sin 24°

5. cos 31°

6. tan 36°

7. cos 20°

8. cos 37°

9. sin 31°

10. tan ∠A = 0.625   ∠A = __?__

11. sin ∠A = 0.454   ∠A = __?__

12. cos ∠A = 0.707   ∠A = __?__

13. cos ∠A = 0.940   ∠A = __?__

14. sin ∠A = 0.407   ∠A = __?__

15. tan ∠A = 0.675   ∠A = __?__

Write the measure of side *x*. Use the tables of trigonometric ratios on pages 402 and 403 of your text. Round to the nearest tenth.

16.

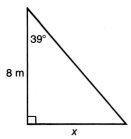

8 m   39°   *x*

17.

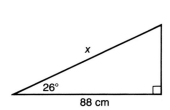

26°   *x*   88 cm

18.

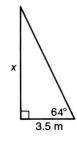

53°   7.5 ft   *x*

19.

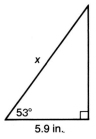

x   53°   5.9 in.

20.

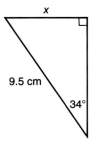

x   9.5 cm   34°

21.

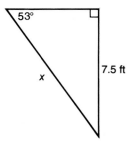

x   64°   3.5 m

Use with pages 402–403.

Write the circumference of each circle. Use 3.14 for π and round to the nearest tenth.

1.

$d = 27$ mm

2.

$r = 40$ cm

3.

$r = 8.6$ m

4.

$d = 15$ cm

5. $r = 9$ km

6. $d = 35$ cm

7. $r = 210$ m

8. $d = 50$ mm

Write the circumference of each circle. Use $\frac{22}{7}$ for π.

9.

$r = 20$ ft

10.

$d = 11\frac{1}{4}$ in.

11.

$d = 21$ mi

12.

$r = 1\frac{3}{4}$ yd

13. $r = 6$ yd

14. $r = 50$ in.

15. $d = 14$ ft

16. $d = 17$ mi

Complete. Use 3.14 for π. Round to the nearest tenth.

17. $C = 42.6$ cm
$d = \underline{\quad ? \quad}$

18. $C = 53.38$ m
$r = \underline{\quad ? \quad}$

19. $C = 62.8$ mm
$d = \underline{\quad ? \quad}$

20. $C = 69.08$ cm
$r = \underline{\quad ? \quad}$

Solve. Use 3.14 for π.

21. The radius of Sylvia's bicycle wheel is 31 centimeters. To the nearest tenth, how far does the wheel travel in 1 revolution?

22. If Sylvia rides 10 kilometers, how many revolutions will the wheel make? Round to the nearest whole number.

Write the missing steps. Then solve.

1. The author of a gardening book suggests that a gardener use $\frac{1}{3}$ lb of fertilizer per month for every 10-ft row of plants. Richard's garden has three 12-ft rows and eight 10-ft rows. Will a 5-lb bag of fertilizer be enough for one month?

   Step 1: Find the number of feet of rows in the garden.

   Step 2: ___?___

   Step 3: ___?___

2. Richard read that each foot of each row of snap-bean plants will produce $\frac{1}{2}$ lb of snap beans. Richard has room for 40 ft of bean plants. How much money can Richard expect to earn if he sells $\frac{1}{4}$ of his crop at $1.25 a pound?

   Step 1: ___?___

   Step 2: ___?___

   Step 3: ___?___

Solve.

3. Young parsnip plants should be thinned so that they grow 4.5 in. apart from one another. Richard will plant two 12-ft rows of parsnips. How many plants will fit in this space?

4. Richard is going to buy some young pepper plants at $2.29 per flat. (There are 4 plants to a flat.) He is going to plant the pepper plants $1\frac{1}{2}$ ft apart from one another in two 12-ft rows. How many flats will he need to buy, and how much will he pay for them?

5. When a blueberry bush is between three and five years old, it will yield from 6 to 16 pints of blueberries. Richard plants 2 one-year-old blueberry bushes. What is the greatest amount of money he can earn from selling blueberries the next season at $1.69 per pint?

6. A 10-ft row of cucumber plants yields 25 lb of cucumbers. A 15-ft row of turnip plants yields 15 lb. Cucumbers sell for $0.69/lb; turnips for $1.79/lb. Which crop will be more profitable when planted in two 12-ft rows?

Write the area of each square.

1. $s = 14\frac{1}{2}$ ft
2. $s = 6$ yd
3. $s = 19$ mi
4. $s = 32$ in.

5. $s = 25$ mi
6. $s = 6\frac{3}{4}$ in.
7. $s = 40$ yd
8. $s = 1$ ft

Write the area of each rectangle.

9. $l = 50$ m, $w = 35$ m
10. $l = 14.5$ cm, $w = 2.7$ cm

11. $l = 0.4$ m, $w = 5.2$ m
12. $l = 4$ mm, $w = 8$ mm

13. $l = 81$ cm, $w = 99$ cm
14. $l = 8$ cm, $w = 1$ cm

15. $l = 16.2$ m, $w = 2.8$ m
16. $l = 0.6$ m, $w = 10$ m

Write the area of each parallelogram.

17. $b = 74$ in., $h = 6$ in
18. $b = 46$ ft, $h = 33$ ft

19. $b = 43$ ft, $h = 8$ ft
20. $b = 18$ in., $h = 17\frac{1}{2}$ in.

21. $b = 5\frac{1}{2}$ mi, $h = \frac{3}{4}$ mi
22. $b = 7$ yd, $h = 33$ yd

23. $b = 200$ in., $h = 47\frac{1}{2}$ in.
24. $b = 22$ ft, $h = 15$ ft

Solve.

25. How many 1-cm^2 tiles will Joseph need to cover a rectangular tabletop that is 55 cm long and 33 cm wide?

26. Rosetta used 9 m^2 of carpeting in her foyer. The room is rectangular, with a length of 3.6 m. What is the width of the foyer?

Write the area of each triangle.

1.

42 yd

54 yd

2.

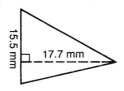

15.5 mm   17.7 mm

3.

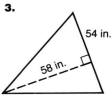

54 in.

58 in.

4. $b = 13.1$ m, $h = 5.5$ m

5. $b = 89$ km, $h = 29$ km

6. $b = 56$ ft, $h = 6$ ft

7. $b = 6.8$ cm, $h = 14.7$ cm

Write the area of each trapezoid.

8.

11 cm

9 cm

4 cm

9.

2 in.

3 in.   8 in.

10.

7.9 mm

17.9 mm

13.9 mm

11. $b_1 = 27$ ft, $b_2 = 4$ ft, $h = 64$ ft

12. $b_1 = 0.6$ mm, $b_2 = 0.2$ mm, $h = 0.4$ mm

Write the area of each polygon by adding the areas of the parts.

13.

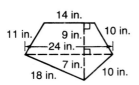

14 in.

11 in.   9 in.   10 in.

24 in.

7 in.

18 in.   10 in.

14.

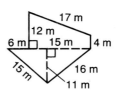

17 m

12 m

6 m   15 m   4 m

15 m   16 m

11 m

Write the area of each circle. Use 3.14 for π. Round to the nearest tenth.

1.

$r = 1.4$ m

2.

$d = 10$ cm

3.

$r = 4.5$ mm

4. $r = 7$ cm

5. $r = 6.7$ mm

6. $d = 0.4$ cm

7. $r = 15.2$ mm

8. $r = 29$ m

9. $d = 18$ mm

10. $r = 0.3$ cm

11. $d = 12.8$ mm

12. $r = 19.4$ m

Write the area of each circle. Use $\frac{22}{7}$ for π.

13. $r = 6$ ft

14. $d = 22$ in.

15. $r = 7$ yd

16. $r = 31$ in.

17. $r = 8$ ft

18. $d = 40$ yd

19. $d = 28$ in.

20. $r = 12$ yd

21. $d = 7$ ft

Write the area of each shaded region. Use 3.14 for π. Round to the nearest tenth.

22.

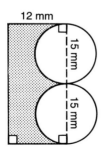

12 mm

15 mm

15 mm

23.

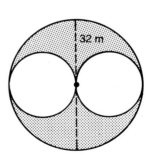

32 m

Read the paragraph. Then use the information in the
paragraph and the picture to help you answer each question.

Ramona makes models of buildings for
miniature railroad sets. There are 3 popular
scales to which models can be built.

Ramona is using this diagram of a freight
station to make 3 stations for customers—
one for each of the 3 scales described
above.

O scale is $\frac{1}{48}$ the size of actual objects.

HO scale is $\frac{1}{87}$ the size of actual objects.

N scale is $\frac{1}{160}$ the size of actual objects.

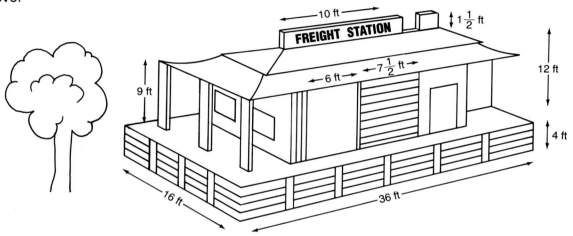

1. For each of the three scales, what is the
   perimeter in inches of the rectangular
   freight-station platform? Round to the
   nearest inch.

2. For the N-scale freight station, could a
   $\frac{3}{4}$-inch-square "freight carton" pass
   through the large freight entrance?

3. For the O-scale model, what is the
   height and the length in inches of the
   freight-station sign?

4. For the HO-scale freight station, would a
   $3\frac{3}{4}$-inch dowel be long enough to make
   the 3 columns at the left?

5. For the HO scale, what is the height in
   inches of a tree whose top leaves reach
   the top of the station sign? (Round to
   the nearest $\frac{1}{2}$ inch.)

6. For the O-scale freight station, would a
   7-inch dowel be long enough to make
   the 3 columns at the left?

Study the time line. Then, answer each question.

1. About how many years are represented on this time line?

2. About how many years separate the invention of ink and the invention of the newspaper? of ink and the ballpoint pen?

3. About how many years separate the invention of the first wheeled vehicles and the invention of the bicycle?

4. How many years separate the invention of vaccination and the invention of inoculation?

5. After which year were steam-powered locomotives invented?

6. About how many years separate the invention of paper and the invention of the newspaper?

7. Which conclusion can you draw from this time line?

   a. Without the invention of the hot-air balloon, the satellite could not have been invented.

   b. Without the invention of the piano, there would be no jukebox.

   c. Transistor radios could not have been in use before 1948.

   d. Without the invention of kites, the hot-air balloon could not have been invented.

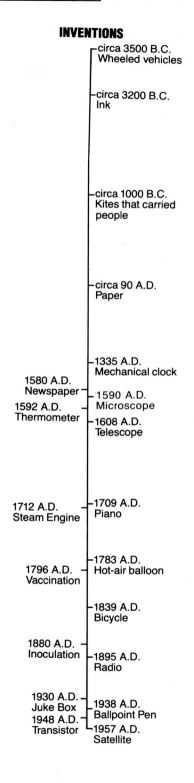

INVENTIONS

circa 3500 B.C.
Wheeled vehicles

circa 3200 B.C.
Ink

circa 1000 B.C.
Kites that carried people

circa 90 A.D.
Paper

1335 A.D.
Mechanical clock

1580 A.D. Newspaper

1590 A.D.
Microscope

1592 A.D. Thermometer

1608 A.D.
Telescope

1712 A.D. Steam Engine

1709 A.D.
Piano

1783 A.D.
Hot-air balloon

1796 A.D. Vaccination

1839 A.D.
Bicycle

1880 A.D. Inoculation

1895 A.D.
Radio

1930 A.D. Juke Box

1938 A.D.
Ballpoint Pen

1948 A.D. Transistor

1957 A.D.
Satellite

Write the name of each solid figure.

1.

2.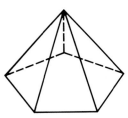

3.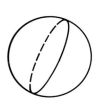

4.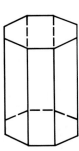

5.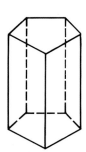

6.

7.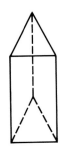

8.

Copy and complete the table.

	Polygon	Number of vertices	Number of faces	Number of edges	$V + F - E$
9.	Octagonal prism				
10.	Hexagonal pyramid				
11.	Pentagonal pyramid				
12.	Square pyramid				
13.	Pentagonal prism				

14. What is the relationship between the number of sides of a prism's base and the number of the prism's edges?

Write the total surface area of each prism. Round to the nearest tenth.

1.

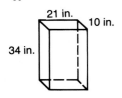

21 in.
10 in.
34 in.

2.

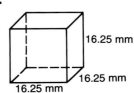

8.5 cm
7.5 cm
8.5 cm
12 cm
5 cm

3.

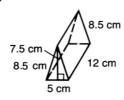

16.25 mm
16.25 mm
16.25 mm

4.

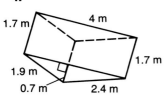

1.7 m
4 m
1.7 m
1.9 m
0.7 m
2.4 m

5.

4 ft
6 in.
6 in.

6.

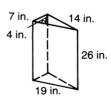

7 in.
14 in.
4 in.
26 in.
19 in.

Write the total surface area of each pyramid. Round to the nearest tenth.

7.

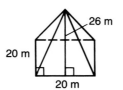

18 in.
12 in.
12 in.

8.

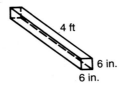

26 m
20 m
20 m

9.

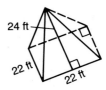

24 ft
22 ft
22 ft

10.

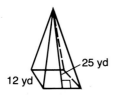

25 yd
12 yd

11.

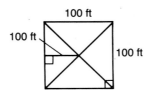

100 ft
100 ft
100 ft

12.

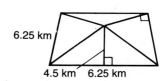

6.25 km
4.5 km   6.25 km

Write the total surface area of each figure. Use 3.14 for π.
Round to the nearest tenth.

1.

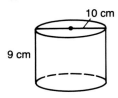

10 cm

9 cm

2.

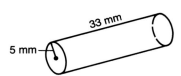

33 mm

5 mm

3.

4.5 m

12 m

4.

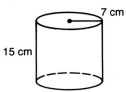

7 cm

15 cm

5.

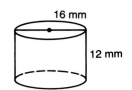

16 mm

12 mm

6.

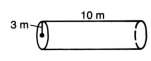

10 m

3 m

7.

30 cm

12 cm

8.

15.5 cm

42 cm

9.

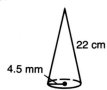

22 cm

4.5 mm

10.

40 cm

18 cm

11.

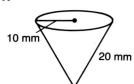

10 mm

20 mm

12.

16 mm

10 mm

Decide if each statement is *true* or *false*. If the statement is false, give an example in which the statement is not true.

1. $n - 1$ is always less than $n + 1$?

2. $1 - n$ is always less than $1 + n$.

3. For all positive numbers, $n \times n$ is always greater than n.

4. $\frac{b}{0}$ is always equal to 0.

5. $x + y$ is always equal to $y + x$.

6. $x \div y$ is always less than x.

7. For all positive integers, $3 \times n$ is always greater than $2 \times n$.

8. No even number greater than 2 is prime.

9. $x + y$ is never equal to $x - y$.

10. The sum of the measures of the angles of a triangle always equals $180°$.

11. If 2 hexagons have equal sides, their areas are the same.

Write the volume of each solid figure. Round to the nearest tenth.

1.

15 mm
12 mm
10.4 mm
12 mm

2.

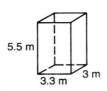

5.5 m
3.3 m
3 m

3.

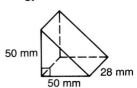

50 mm
28 mm
50 mm

4.

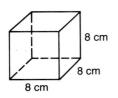

8 cm
8 cm
8 cm

5.

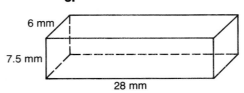

6 mm
7.5 mm
28 mm

6.

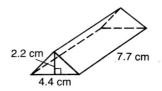

2.2 cm
7.7 cm
4.4 cm

7.

18 ft
10 ft
20 ft
14 ft

8.

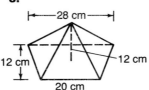

28 cm
12 cm
12 cm
20 cm

9.

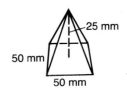

25 mm
50 mm
50 mm

Solve.

10. Which has the greater volume: a 6-cm cube or a prism with a 3-cm square base and height of 12 cm? How many times as great?

11. The Great Pyramid of Cheops has a square base 230 meters along each side, and a height of 150 meters. Find the volume.

Write the volume of each solid figure. Use 3.14 for π. Round to the nearest tenth.

1.

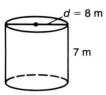

$d = 8$ m

7 m

2.

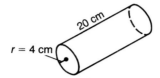

20 cm

$r = 4$ cm

3.

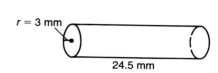

$r = 3$ mm

24.5 mm

4.

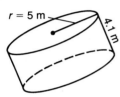

$r = 5$ m

4.1 m

5.

$r = 13$ cm

9 cm

6.

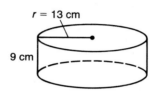

$d = 10$ mm

30 mm

7.

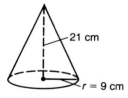

21 cm

$r = 9$ cm

8.

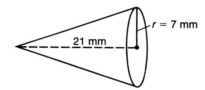

$r = 7$ mm

21 mm

9.

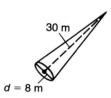

30 m

$d = 8$ m

10.

$r = 5$ cm

17 cm

11.

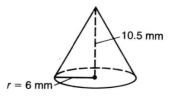

10.5 mm

$r = 6$ mm

12.

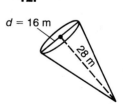

$d = 16$ m

28 m

Write the letter of the formula that you would use to solve each problem.

1. James is making a model of a spaceship. The bottom of the command and living areas is circular and measures 58.4 cm in diameter. James wants to put tape around the perimeter of this area. He has a 144 cm length of tape. Is it long enough?

  a. $C = \pi d$ **b.** $A = \pi r^2$

  c. $S = 2\pi rh + 2\pi r^2$ **d.** $A = s^2$

2. The command section of the ship is a cylinder with a radius of 14.3 cm and a height of 12.4 cm. How many square inches of foil does James need to cover the inside of the command section?

  a. $V = r^2 h$ **b.** $V = lwh$

  c. $S = 2\pi rh + 2\pi r^2$ **d.** $A = \frac{1}{2}bh$

Write the formula, then solve. Round to the nearest tenth of a centimeter.

1. The landing pad for the spaceship will be made of balsa wood. It is a rectangular prism 98.2 cm long, 88.6 cm wide, and 2.4 cm high. If Angie decides to fill it with sand, how many cubic centimeters of sand will she need?

2. The tail fins for the fuel tanks are each triangles with a base 1.8 cm wide and a height of 3.4 cm. How long is the slanted side of each fin?

3. Ramon is making conical caps for the fuel tanks. The radius of the tanks is 2.8 cm and the height of the caps is to be 3.5 cm. The main part of each tank is a cylinder 20.32 cm high. How much material will Ramon need in order to make both fuel tanks?

4. Angie will paint the curved walls of the living module. The diameter of the module's outside wall is 58.4 cm. The diameter of the module's inside wall is 32.4 cm. The height of the module is 12.4 cm. How many cm² is the area Angie will paint?

5. Is a sheet of tin 3.4 cm by 5.4 cm large enough to make 6 tail fins?

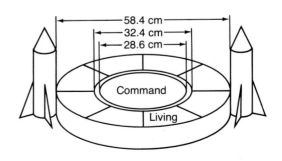

Write the letter of the ordered pair that satisfies the equation.

1. $y = 3x - 5$ **a.** (9,23)   **b.** (10,20)   **c.** (11,28)

2. $y = 4(x + 4)$ **a.** (7,40)   **b.** (4,32)   **c.** (12,34)

3. $y = 9x + 12$ **a.** ($^-$2,$^-$6)   **b.** (3,38)   **c.** (0,9)

4. $8y = 8x + 16$ **a.** (3,17)   **b.** (7,9)   **c.** (13,16)

5. $2y + 3x = 10$ **a.** ($^-$4,6)   **b.** (10,12)   **c.** (8,$^-$7)

6. $\frac{1}{6}y = x + 1$ **a.** (5,32)   **b.** (3,24)   **c.** (9,70)

7. $y = \frac{1}{2}x - 4$ **a.** (6,$^-$1)   **b.** (12,3)   **c.** (14,11)

8. $x + y = {}^-3$ **a.** (9,6)   **b.** (3,$^-$6)   **c.** (17,20)

9. $7y + x = 14$ **a.** (7,1)   **b.** (12,7)   **c.** (0,6)

10. $^-4y + 3x = {}^-7$ **a.** (1,$^-$1)   **b.** (4,2)   **c.** (3,4)

11. $x - \frac{1}{2}y = 15$ **a.** (27,26)   **b.** (28,27)   **c.** (29,28)

12. $7y - 0 = x$ **a.** (3,13)   **b.** (14,2)   **c.** ($^-$21,$^-$3)

13. $y = {}^-6x + 10$ **a.** (4,$^-$14)   **b.** ($^-$4,14)   **c.** (2,$^-$14)

14. $10(x - 2) = y$ **a.** (4,24)   **b.** (4,2)   **c.** (2,0)

15. $4y - 27 = x$ **a.** ($^-$11,4)   **b.** (7,5)   **c.** ($^-$11,$^-$4)

16. $x = 13 - \frac{1}{2}y$ **a.** ($^-$1,28)   **b.** (1,$^-$28)   **c.** ($^-$1,14)

17. $\frac{1}{2}y = 3x - 7$ **a.** ($^-$5,$^-$16)   **b.** (5,16)   **c.** (4,12)

Use $^-$2, 0, 1 as replacements for x. Write the solutions for each equation as ordered pairs.

18. $x + y = 5$ **19.** $2x + 3y = 8$ **20.** $2y - x = 10$

Copy and complete each table of values. Write the ordered pairs that are the solutions.

1. $y = 2x - 1$

x	$2x - 1$	y
$^-2$		
$^-1$		
0		
1		
2		

2. $y = 3x - 4$

x	$3x - 4$	y
0		
1		
2		
3		
4		

3. $y = x + 5$

x	$x + 5$	y
$^-4$		
$^-3$		
$^-2$		
$^-1$		
0		

4. $y = 2 - x$

x	$2 - x$	y
$^-10$		
$^-5$		
0		
5		
10		

5. $^-3x + y = 3$

x	$^-3x + y = 3$	y
$^-3$		
$^-1$		
0		
2		
4		

6. $2x + 3y = 1$

x	$2x + 3y = 1$	y
$^-7$		
$^-5$		
1		
8		
11		

On a separate sheet of paper, draw a diagram and solve.
Write your number in the space provided. Round to the
nearest whole number.

1. Here is a scavenger hunt clue: Enter the
24 ft by 36 ft rectangular plaza in the
Ashworth Park on the east border.
(There are two entrances directly in the
middle of the short sides of the plaza.)
Walk due west 18 ft, straight north 6 ft,
and then due west 6 ft where you will
find a piece of purple string. If you use
the shortest route, how far away is the
string from the western entrance?

2. A clue in a scavenger hunt is to Go 10
miles west, $2\frac{1}{2}$ miles due north, 10
miles due east, and $2\frac{1}{2}$ miles due south.
Take one red button from the pile hidden
in an opening in a large elm tree. Roger
wants to figure out how long it would
take him to get to the elm tree if he
drives 35 mph. How long would it take
him?

3. Roger was directed to go 3 blocks north
along 8th Road turn right and go 6
blocks due east along 6th Avenue to
14th Road. The blocks along 8th Road
are 276 ft long, which is 3 times as long
as the blocks along 6th Avenue. If a long
diagonal were drawn from Roger's
starting point to his stopping point, how
long would it be?

4. A scavenger hunt clue sends Chris to a
rectangular yard with a perimeter of
126 ft. Chris walks along the entire south
border due west, a distance of 25 ft. He
must find a marker on a bush in the
middle of the west border. How many
feet does he have to walk before he
should start looking for the bush?

5. Brian enters an *L*-shape hotel lobby to
search for a clue. The larger part of the
lobby is 120 ft square; the smaller part is
40 ft by 40 ft. Roger can walk in a
straight path from the northwest corner
of the larger part to the southeast corner
of the smaller part. How many feet long
is that path?

6. At the end of the scavenger hunt, all the
hunters must meet at the center of
circular park. From a point 400 yards
due west of the center of the park, Bruce
walks 300 yards north. From that point,
he walks diagonally toward the center of
the park for 300 yards. He is now at the
perimeter of the park. How many square
yards is the park?

On a separate sheet of paper, draw a diagram and solve.
Round decimal answers to the nearest tenth.

1. Candice Smythe, detective, is searching for buried treasure. Directions for finding the treasure say that it is in a rectangular area $2\frac{1}{2}$ mi by $5\frac{1}{2}$ mi. The treasure is in the middle of a straight path that runs northeast by southwest. About how many miles does Candice have to travel from the northeast corner before she starts digging?

2. A missing zebra was reported to be in the northwest corner of a rectangular area 65 ft by 65 ft. The runaway animal went on a straight path from the southeast corner to the southwest corner, from the southwest corner to the northeast corner, and then from the northeast corner to the northwest corner. How many feet did it travel?

3. Candice is 2 ft into a 201 ft² circular area when her assistant, Nedda Lovelace, calls her. Nedda says she is in the center of the area and is sinking in quicksand. About how many feet apart are they?

4. To find a missing circus elephant, Candice follows a trail of peanuts that starts at the elephant's cage. She follows the trail north 400 ft along Jones Street, then due east 800 ft on Claremont Avenue, and then due south 400 ft on Simmons Street. At that point, how far was Candice from the elephant's cage?

5. Candice must find a needle (a gold and emerald one) in a haystack. The haystack is in a square field with sides 3 mi long. Directions for finding the haystack are as follows: Start at the northeast corner. Travel south along the eastern border $1\frac{1}{2}$ mi. Then go due west 1 mi, and then go $\frac{3}{4}$ mi north. The haystack will be there. Candice wants to start at the northeast corner and take the shortest path to the haystack. How long is the shortest path?

6. Candice led the police to a counterfeiters' hideout even though she had been taken there blindfolded and in a roundabout way. She had memorized the following directions: Start at my office building. Walk 25 paces due west, 15 paces due south, 10 paces north, 17 paces east, 5 paces north, 8 paces east, then 20 paces north. How many paces from Candice's office building was the counterfeiters' hideout?

Copy and complete each table. Is the set of solutions a function? Write *yes* or *no*.

1. $y = {}^-4x + 10$

x	$^-4x + 10$	y
7		
4		
$^-1$		
0		
$\frac{1}{2}$		

2. $y = 12 - 3x$

x	$12 - 3x$	y
12		
$\frac{1}{3}$		
0		
7		
$^-5$		

Is the set of ordered pairs a function? Write *yes* or *no*.

3. $\left(1, \frac{1}{2}\right)$ $\left(3, \frac{3}{2}\right)$ (4,2) (0,0)

4. (17,16) (10,11) (10,15) (17,17)

5. (3,5) (4,7) $\left(13, \frac{1}{2}\right)$ (2,5)

6. (0,6) (4,7) (5,6) $\left(9, \frac{4}{10}\right)$

7. $(^-1,2)$ (3,5) $(^-1,4)$ (4,7)

8. (0,5) (3,5) (7,5) (9,5) (13,5)

9. $(^-1,6)$ $(^-2,4)$ (0,0) (1,0) (3,4)

10. (4,9) (5,15) (3,10) (4,8) (6,13)

Solve.

11. Bob Avis has been keeping track of the number of times his pet parakeet tweets per minute and of the room temperature. The table at the right shows his findings. Can you find the rule (let *t* represent temperatures and *w* represent tweets)?

Temperature (°F)	50	51	52	53	54
Tweets per minute	40	41	42	43	44

Write *yes* if the graph represents a function. Write *no* if it does not.

1.

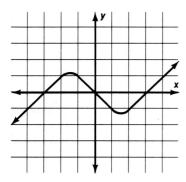

2.

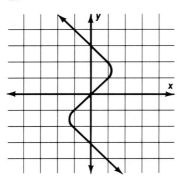

3.

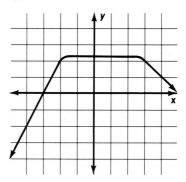

4.

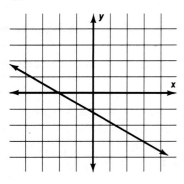

5.

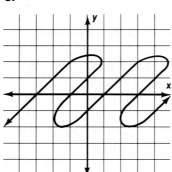

6.

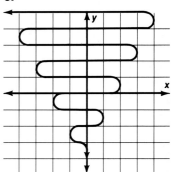

7.

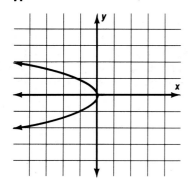

8.

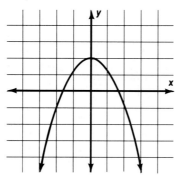

9.

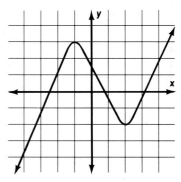

Choosing a Strategy or Method

Estimation	Choosing the Operation	Using a Formula
Using a Table	Guessing and Checking	Solving Multi-step
Using a Graph	Writing an Equation	Problems

Write the strategy or method you choose. Then solve.

1. On a map of the world, $2\frac{1}{2}$ inches equals 600 miles. How many miles would $5\frac{1}{4}$ inches represent?

Exploring Antarctica	$18.99
Australia—From A to Z	$ 5.29
Europe—The Renaissance	$14.49
South America and Democracy	$ 8.79
Africa—Its Ancient Kingdoms	$17.69
Asia in Photographs	$19.39

2. Diane has $60.29. Can she afford to buy *Exploring Antarctica, Australia—From A to Z,* and 2 copies of *Africa—Its Ancient Kingdoms?*

3. Gina has $44.25. Can she afford to purchase the four least expensive books?

THE SEVEN CONTINENTS

Name	Area (mi²)	Percent of world land	Highest point (ft)	Lowest point (ft below sea level)
Asia	17,400,000	30.1	Mt. Everest 29,028	Dead Sea 1312
Africa	11,700,000	20.2	Mt. Kilimanjaro 19,340	Lake Assal 512
North America	9,400,000	16.2	Mt. McKinley 20,320	Death Valley 282
South America	6,900,000	11.9	Mt. Aconcagua 22,834	Valdes Peninsula 131
Antarctica	5,400,000	9.1	Vinson Massif 16,864	unknown
Europe	3,800,000	6.6	Mt. Albrus 18,510	Caspian Sea 92
Australia	3,300,000	5.4	Mt. Kosciusko 7,310	Lake Eyre 52

4. About how many miles higher is the highest point on Earth than the lowest point? (Round to the nearest mile.)

5. Find the total percent of world land. Why is it not 100%?

Choosing a Strategy or Method

Estimation	Writing an Equation	Drawing a Picture
Using a Table	Solving Multi-step Problems	Using a Formula
Choosing the Operation	Working Backward	

Write the strategy or method you choose. Then solve.

1. The Kalahari Desert has an area of about 225,000 mi², which is 150,000 fewer square miles than $\frac{3}{4}$ of the area of the Gobi Desert. What is the area of the Gobi Desert?

2. Lake Michigan has an area of 22,300 mi², which is 14,372 mi² greater than $\frac{4}{5}$ of the area of Lake Erie. What is the area of Lake Erie?

3. Museum workers want to build a circular platform with a diameter of 12 feet. They will cover the platform edge with a strip of lace. How much lace will the workers need? Use 3.14 for π.

4. Artists want to use 6-in. square tiles to make a mosaic of famous volcanoes. The wall to be covered is 10 ft by 15 ft. How many tiles will they need?

5. The area of the Caspian Sea is 111,544 square miles greater than the area of Lake Superior. The area of Lake Superior is 9,400 square miles greater than Lake Michigan. The area of the Caspian Sea is 143,244 square miles. What is the area of Lake Michigan?

6. An exhibit will show a comparison between the height of the Sears Tower and the height of Mount Everest. Mount Everest is 29,028 ft tall. The Sears Tower is 1,454 ft tall. The scale of the exhibit is 10 in. = 1 mi. About how many inches taller than the model of the Sears Tower will the model of Mount Everest be?

Use after pages 448–449.

Copy and complete each table of values. Then graph the equation.

1.

x	$4y + 2x = {}^-16$	y
2		
0		
${}^-2$		
${}^-4$		

2.

x	$y = \frac{1}{3}x - 5$	y
${}^-3$		
0		
3		
6		

3.

x	$y = 2\left(x - \frac{1}{2}\right)$	y

Copy and complete the table of values for each equation.
Then solve the system of equations by graphing. Check
each solution.

1. $x + y = 5$
  $x - y = 1$

x	x + y = 5	y
⁻1		
0		
1		
2		

x	x − y = 1	y
0		
1		
2		
3		

2. $y = 2x - 1$
  $y = 3x$

x	y = 2x − 1	y
⁻1		
0		
1		
2		

x	y = 3x	y
⁻1		
0		
1		
2		

3. $4x + y = 3$
  $y - x = {}^-2$

x	4x + y = 3	y
⁻1		
0		
1		
2		

x	y − x = ⁻2	y
⁻3		
⁻2		
⁻1		
0		

Inequalities in Two Variables

Copy and complete each table of values. Then graph the inequality.

1. $x - y \geq 3$

x	$x - y = 3$	y
$^-2$		
$^-1$		
0		
1		
2		

2. $x + y \geq 4$

x	$x + y = 4$	y
$^-4$		
$^-2$		
0		
1		
3		

3. $3y - x < 0$

x	$3y - x = 0$	y
$^-9$		
$^-6$		
0		
3		
9		

Copy and complete each table of values. Graph the inequality.

1. $^-y > 4 + \frac{1}{2}x$

x	$^-y = 4 + \frac{1}{2}x$	y

2. $24 + 12y \leq 4x$

x	$24 + 12y = 4x$	y

3. $3x - y > 5$

x	$3x - y = 5$	y

Solve.

4. The citizens of Planesville are planning a park for their town. Two of the boundaries of the park will be portions of the positive x and y axes. The park will include all the points that are solutions to both the inequalities $x + 2y \leq 6$ and $3x + 2y \leq 10$. Graph the inequalities; then shade the area of the park.

Estimation	Guessing and Checking	Selecting Notation
Drawing a Picture	Making a Table to Find a Pattern	Making an Organized List
Choosing the Operation	Writing an Equation	Working Backward
Solving Multi-step Problems		

Write the strategy or method you choose. Then solve.

1. While hiking in the forest one day, Robert became lost. He came upon a marker that indicated that he was in the exact center of the forest. Robert knew that the forest was a square 60 km on a side, so he decided to walk out in a straight line. But the route he actually took went like this: 5 km north, then 10 km west, then 15 km south, 20 km east, 25 km north, and so on. How far did Robert walk before he got out of the forest?

2. A tour guide tells visitors to an adventure park that $\frac{1}{3}$ of the park consists of wildlife habitats. Hiking trails and picnic areas make up $\frac{1}{2}$ of the remaining park area. The guide also states that there are 2 mi^2 of buildings that house restaurants, movie theaters, and concert stages. The science buildings take up the remaining 1.75 mi^2. How many square miles does the adventure park contain?

3. At Poe Park, 1 food ticket costs $1.25, 5 cost $6.00, 10 cost $11.50, and 15 cost $16.50. How much do 25 food tickets cost?

4. If a group of 4 friends goes on the Volcano Train ride together, in how many different orders can they arrange themselves in a row of 4 seats?

Estimation	Guessing and Checking	Selecting Notation
Drawing a Picture	Making a Table to Find a Pattern	Making an Organized List
Choosing the Operation	Writing an Equation	Working Backward
Solving Multi-step Problems		

Write the strategy or method you choose. Then solve.

1. There are 3 students painting scenery. They have a can that contains 3 gallons of paint, an empty 2-gallon container, and an empty 1-gallon container. How can they divide the paint so that each one has the same amount?

2. Alicia gave her aunt the following directions for driving to the school play. Leave the highway at Exit 25. Go north 3 streets, and make a left turn at the Great States supermarket. Continue for 3 streets, and make a left turn at the traffic light. Continue for 5 streets to the library. Make another left, and go 3 streets to the school. What is a shorter route from Exit 25 to the school?

3. Advertisements in the school play program cost $7.50 for a small advertisement and $19.25 for a large advertisement. Kenzo sold twice as many small ads as large ads. He collected a total of $137 in advertising fees. How many small advertisements did he sell?

4. Andre won the drama-club raffle. His prize is a $99.99 shopping spree in a novelty store. He cannot spend a penny more or a penny less than $99.99. Find two groups of purchases that add up to $99.99.

Prices
Tiny teddy bear: $3.69
Board games: $12.99, $8.44, $4.58
Puzzles: $7.26, $6.35
Stickers: $0.27, $0.38, $0.57, $0.75
Posters: $1.19, $3.98, $5.69

MORE PRACTICE

Chapter 1, page 3

Write each in standard form.

1. 8 million, 300 thousand, 387

2. 42 million, 96 thousand, 400

3. 208 billion, 39 thousand, 18

4. 324 trillion, 82 million, 402

Write the short word name.

5. 8,450,000

6. 32,001,062

7. 49,000,000,483

8. 40,002,000

9. 526,000,800,400

10. 13,040,000,083

Write the place and the value of the underlined digit.

11. 9,724,8<u>6</u>2

12. 1<u>8</u>9,356,482

13. 9,068,<u>3</u>42,184

14. Write 8,400,560 in expanded form.

Chapter 1, page 5

Compare. Write >, <, or = for ●.

1. 74,286 ● 76,286

2. 121,845 ● 112,854

3. 29,684 ● 28,795

4. 412,777 ● 422,777

5. 54,012 ● 54,102

6. 40,465,100 ● 40,465,100

7. 84,533,334 ● 84,353,334

Order the numbers from the least to the greatest.

8. 965; 9,650; 960; 9,656

9. 332; 322; 3,323; 3,233

10. 6,895; 6,985; 6,859; 6,589; 6,588

Chapter 1, page 29

Add.

1. 0.73
   + 0.43

2. 3.84
   + 5.96

3. 82.473
   + 29.248

4. $19,801.46
   +   8,796.82

5. 0.492 + 8.978 + 4.527

6. 15,141.9 + 7.23 + 5,848.9 + 87.6

7. 45 + 856.9 + 833.86

8. $468.04 + $8.25 + $0.68 + $2.95

Chapter 1, page 31

Subtract.

1. 87.6
   − 26.2

2. 84.52
   − 32.38

3. 754.58
   − 237.96

4. 8.4391
   − 5.7846

5. 0.876
   − 0.59

6. 0.8071
   − 0.694

7. 0.87
   − 0.495

8. 0.8009
   − 0.437

9. 0.325
   − 0.253

10. 1.697
    − 0.379

11. 9.159
    − 7.395

12. 40.59
    − 3.599

13. 896.248 − 7.9063

14. $926 − $427.32

15. 5.0732 − 0.96438

Chapter 2, page 61

Multiply.

1. 4.5
   × 7

2. 18.76
   × 0.9

3. 407.26
   × 0.5

4. 0.2046
   × 7

5. 0.872
   × 0.48

6. 9.63
   × 82

7. 567.43
   × 8.2

8. 0.0025
   × 48

9. 5.12
   × 0.3

10. 9.25
    × 35.2

11. 35.12
    × 12.2

12. 465.32
    × 32.6

13. 0.899 × 863.04

14. 5,287.6 × 0.00487

15. 4.7 × 8 × 0.83 × 9.5

16. 0.187 × 63,412.1 × 7.2

Chapter 2, page 67

Divide.

1. 0.9)8.1

2. 0.8)0.00264

3. 7)1.68

4. 3.6)72.12

5. 2.7)91.8

6. 0.6)0.024

7. 0.008)0.048

8. 23)29.9

9. 2.8)169.12

10. 8.6)144.48

11. 0.72)169.20

12. 7)3.57

13. 8.5)49.98

14. 3.4 ÷ 0.84

15. 3.81 ÷ 0.104

16. 0.7)274.1

Chapter 3, page 93

List the factors to find the GCF.

1. 28, 88   **2.** 24, 72   **3.** 18, 90   **4.** 6, 15

5. 63, 18   **6.** 40, 56   **7.** 12, 21   **8.** 24, 42

9. 16, 24, 32   **10.** 6, 100, 48

Use the prime factorization to find the GCF.

11. 25, 41   **12.** 12, 48   **13.** 64, 46   **14.** 15, 54

15. 180, 45, 90   **16.** 4, 17, 97

Chapter 3, page 105

Solve each equation.

1. $y - 15 = 72$ **2.** $x - 34 = 89$ **3.** $j - 5.4 = 8.7$

4. $18 - x = 4$ **5.** $a - 10.3 = 17.9$ **6.** $7 + y = 32$

7. $x + 114 = 257$ **8.** $64 = 89 - b$ **9.** $x - 4.7 = 2.1$

10. $14 + m = 96$ **11.** $y - 11.2 = 83$ **12.** $z + 8.9 = 21$

13. $x + 24.7 = 32.1$ **14.** $10 + s = 16$ **15.** $r - 43.7 = 91.2$

Chapter 3, page 107

Solve each equation.

1. $3x = 27$ **2.** $4y = 120$ **3.** $3.5m = 182$

4. $9t = 423$ **5.** $2.8y = 8.4$ **6.** $0.6x = 84.6$

7. $24a = 312$ **8.** $8m = 192$ **9.** $16r = 304$

10. $\frac{x}{2.5} = 12$ **11.** $\frac{w}{7} = 15$ **12.** $\frac{x}{32} = 4$

13. $\frac{m}{19} = 38$ **14.** $\frac{x}{0.5} = 14$ **15.** $\frac{t}{4} = 197$

16. $\frac{x}{10} = 0.5$ **17.** $\frac{y}{6} = 3.2$ **18.** $\frac{a}{2.2} = 20$

19. $\frac{z}{28} = 4$ **20.** $\frac{p}{14} = 9$ **21.** $\frac{r}{54} = 6$

Chapter 3, page 109

Solve.

1. $8m - 15 = 9$

2. $8d - 32 = 16$

3. $\frac{x}{3} + 4 = 20$

4. $\frac{x}{5} - 9 = 15$

5. $\frac{y}{2} - 8 = 17$

6. $3x + 4 = 79$

7. $4x + 8 = 32$

8. $\frac{x}{8} + 12 = 16$

9. $\frac{y}{4} - 9 = 15$

10. $7x - 3 = 32$

11. $\frac{x}{5} - 4 = 7$

12. $9x - 4 = 50$

13. $0.5x + 4 = 9.5$

14. $26.1 + 6x = 40.5$

15. $2x - 46 = 80$

Chapter 4, page 133

Subtract. Write the answer in simplest form.

1. $\frac{7}{9} - \frac{4}{9}$

2. $\frac{9}{11} - \frac{5}{11}$

3. $\frac{2}{3} - \frac{1}{3}$

4. $\frac{14}{15} - \frac{8}{15}$

5. $\frac{3}{4} - \frac{5}{8}$

6. $\frac{4}{5} - \frac{3}{10}$

7. $\frac{21}{24} - \frac{4}{6}$

8. $\frac{1}{2} - \frac{1}{3}$

9. $\begin{array}{r} \frac{7}{9} \\ -\frac{2}{3} \\ \hline \end{array}$

10. $\begin{array}{r} \frac{2}{3} \\ -\frac{3}{11} \\ \hline \end{array}$

11. $\begin{array}{r} \frac{3}{4} \\ -\frac{1}{5} \\ \hline \end{array}$

12. $\begin{array}{r} \frac{3}{5} \\ -\frac{2}{7} \\ \hline \end{array}$

13. $4\frac{7}{10} - 2\frac{1}{8}$

14. $8\frac{19}{24} - 2\frac{8}{36}$

15. $18\frac{1}{2} - 8\frac{1}{4}$

Chapter 4, page 143

Multiply. Write the answer in simplest form.

1. $3\frac{4}{5} \times 2\frac{1}{3}$

2. $6\frac{3}{4} \times 4\frac{1}{3}$

3. $8\frac{5}{9} \times 7\frac{3}{7}$

4. $2\frac{1}{2} \times 3\frac{1}{3}$

5. $2\frac{1}{2} \times 4\frac{3}{8}$

6. $10\frac{3}{4} \times 7\frac{2}{3}$

7. $5\frac{7}{9} \times 13\frac{1}{2}$

8. $4\frac{4}{5} \times 3\frac{1}{8}$

9. $4\frac{1}{4} \times 3\frac{2}{3}$

10. $18 \times 7\frac{2}{3}$

11. $2\frac{5}{6} \times 12$

12. $48 \times 2\frac{1}{2}$

13. $1\frac{1}{3} \times \frac{3}{4} \times 4\frac{1}{2}$

14. $8\frac{2}{8} \times 4\frac{4}{5} \times 6\frac{1}{2}$

15. $3\frac{1}{2} \times 1\frac{1}{4} \times 2\frac{1}{3}$

16. $6\frac{1}{2} \times 4\frac{2}{3} \times 15$

Divide. Write the answer in simplest form.

1. $4\frac{2}{3} \div 1\frac{1}{3}$ **2.** $6\frac{1}{4} \div 2\frac{3}{4}$ **3.** $5\frac{7}{8} \div 3\frac{1}{8}$ **4.** $2\frac{1}{5} \div 1\frac{2}{5}$

5. $7 \div 3\frac{1}{2}$ **6.** $20 \div 3\frac{1}{3}$ **7.** $18 \div 2\frac{5}{9}$ **8.** $2 \div 1\frac{1}{4}$

9. $4 \div 1\frac{3}{4}$ **10.** $9 \div 2\frac{2}{3}$ **11.** $8 \div \frac{2}{3}$ **12.** $7\frac{5}{9} \div \frac{1}{2}$

13. $6\frac{2}{3} \div \frac{1}{6}$ **14.** $12\frac{1}{2} \div 2\frac{5}{9}$ **15.** $6 \div 3\frac{4}{7}$ **16.** $10\frac{1}{6} \div 2\frac{2}{3}$

Write a fraction or a mixed number in simplest form for each decimal.

1. 0.75 **2.** 0.6 **3.** 0.45 **4.** 4.25 **5.** 5.64

Write a decimal for each fraction or mixed number. Use a bar to show repeating decimals.

6. $\frac{3}{4}$ **7.** $\frac{7}{20}$ **8.** $\frac{11}{66}$ **9.** $\frac{15}{36}$ **10.** $\frac{1}{6}$

11. $\frac{13}{15}$ **12.** $\frac{5}{9}$ **13.** $1\frac{1}{2}$ **14.** $\frac{13}{5}$ **15.** $2\frac{1}{3}$

Copy and complete the chart for each container of water.

Length	Width	Height	Volume	Capacity	Mass
6 cm	5 cm	3 cm	**1.** ▆ cm³	**2.** ▆ mL	**3.** ▆ g
9 m	6 m	4 m	**4.** ▆ m³	**5.** ▆ kL	**6.** ▆ t
40 mm	50 mm	30 mm	**7.** ▆ cm³	**8.** ▆ mL	**9.** ▆ g
30 dm	8 dm	3 dm	**10.** ▆ m³	**11.** ▆ kL	**12.** ▆ t
120 cm	50 cm	60 cm	**13.** ▆ m³	**14.** ▆ kL	**15.** ▆ t
55 mm	21 mm	33 mm	**16.** ▆ mm³	**17.** ▆ mL	**18.** ▆ g

Chapter 5, page 175

Complete.

1. 12 ft = ■ in.
2. 5 mi = ■ yd
3. 14 yd = ■ ft
4. 96 in. = ■ ft
5. 57 ft = ■ yd
6. 21,120 ft = ■ mi
7. $8\frac{1}{2}$ ft = ■ in.
8. $8\frac{2}{3}$ yd = ■ ft
9. $2\frac{3}{5}$ mi = ■ ft
10. 90 in. = ■ ft
11. 30 in. = ■ yd
12. 14 ft = ■ yd
13. 63 in. = ■ ft
14. 1,320 yd = ■ mi
15. $3\frac{1}{2}$ mi = ■ ft
16. 4,224 yd = ■ mi
17. 9,240 ft = ■ mi
18. 414 in. = ■ yd
19. 66 in. = ■ yd
20. $1\frac{1}{6}$ mi = ■ ft
21. 306 in. = ■ yd

Chapter 5, page 177

Complete.

1. 5 qt = ■ pt
2. 15 gal = ■ qt
3. 7 lb = ■ oz
4. 64 fl oz = ■ c
5. 128 oz = ■ lb
6. 15 qt = ■ gal
7. $5\frac{1}{2}$ gal = ■ qt
8. $3\frac{1}{4}$ c = ■ fl oz
9. $7\frac{1}{2}$ lb = ■ oz
10. 15,000 lb = ■ T
11. 7 gal 2 qt = ■ qt
12. 94 oz = ■ lb ■ oz
13. 56 fl oz = ■ pt
14. $1\frac{1}{2}$ qt = ■ fl oz
15. 16 fl oz = ■ gal
16. 7 c = ■ qt
17. $7\frac{1}{2}$ gal = ■ pt
18. $3\frac{1}{2}$ qt = ■ fl oz

Chapter 5, page 181

Find the greatest possible error in measurement.

1. 13 m
2. 18 cm
3. 48 mm
4. 12 km
5. 300 cm
6. 40 mm
7. 325 cm
8. 875 km
9. 48.2 km
10. 76.4 mm
11. 9.6 m
12. 48.5 mm
13. 17.25 km
14. 18.75 m
15. 4.75 cm
16. 18.645 km

Chapter 6, page 213

Copy and write the missing fraction or percent.

1. $65\% = \blacksquare$

2. $\blacksquare\% = \frac{1}{9}$

3. $88\% = \blacksquare$

4. $\blacksquare\% = \frac{5}{6}$

5. $96\% = \blacksquare$

6. $\blacksquare\% = \frac{99}{22}$

7. $27\% = \blacksquare$

8. $\blacksquare\% = 18.2$

9. $49\% = \blacksquare$

10. $\blacksquare = 62\frac{1}{2}\%$

11. $\frac{15}{18} = \blacksquare\%$

12. $\blacksquare\% = 59.6$

13. $92\% = \blacksquare$

14. $\blacksquare = 40\%$

15. $37\frac{1}{2}\% = \blacksquare$

Chapter 6, page 225

Use a proportion to solve each problem.

1. Find 22% of 65.

2. What percent of 25 is 22?

3. 6.4 is what percent of 40?

4. Find 36% of 21.

5. What number is 13% of 250?

6. 225 is what percent of 500?

7. Find 12% of 91.

8. 13 is what percent of 52?

9. What is 125% of 40?

10. What is 25% of 116?

11. 35 is what percent of 700?

12. Find 9% of 429.

Chapter 7, pages 251 and 253

Find the product.

1. $5 \cdot {}^-5$

2. ${}^-5 \cdot 10$

3. ${}^-15 \cdot {}^-4$

4. ${}^-7 \cdot {}^-6$

5. ${}^-22 \cdot {}^-13$

6. ${}^-19 \cdot 27$

7. $36 \cdot {}^-14$

8. ${}^-52 \cdot {}^-4$

9. ${}^-4 \cdot (8 \cdot 9)$

10. $({}^-4 \cdot {}^-8) \cdot 9$

11. $({}^-15 \cdot {}^-7) \cdot {}^-15$

12. $16 \cdot (5 \cdot {}^-21)$

Divide.

13. ${}^-24 \div {}^-6$

14. ${}^-169 \div {}^-13$

15. ${}^-225 \div 45$

16. $625 \div {}^-125$

17. ${}^-82 \div 2$

18. $576 \div 24$

19. ${}^-488 \div {}^-8$

20. $1,024 \div {}^-32$

Evaluate.

21. $({}^-9 \cdot 21) + ({}^-8 \cdot {}^-7)$

22. $\dfrac{14 \cdot ({}^-2 - 30)}{{}^-7 + 14}$

Compute. Write the answer in simplest form.

1. $\frac{1}{4} + \frac{3}{4}$ 2. $\frac{3}{8} - \frac{1}{8}$ 3. $\frac{1}{2} - {}^-\frac{1}{2}$ 4. ${}^-\frac{2}{3} + {}^-\frac{1}{3}$

5. $\frac{2}{9} - \frac{2}{18}$ 6. $\frac{6}{7} + 4$ 7. ${}^-\frac{4}{5} + {}^-\frac{3}{7}$ 8. $\frac{9}{14} - 7$

9. ${}^-24 + {}^-4\frac{1}{3}$ 10. ${}^-\frac{4}{7} + {}^-\frac{2}{9}$ 11. $\frac{10}{15} - {}^-\frac{41}{45}$ 12. ${}^-1\frac{7}{8} - {}^-12$

13. $16.35 + {}^-16.35$ 14. $0.56 - {}^-1.48$ 15. ${}^-4.63 - {}^-4.63$

16. ${}^-12.1 + {}^-15.64$ 17. $31.3 + {}^-3.41$ 18. ${}^-264 - 8.65$

Compute. Write the answer in simplest form.

1. $\frac{1}{6} \div {}^-\frac{1}{12}$ 2. ${}^-\frac{2}{3} \cdot {}^-\frac{1}{6}$ 3. ${}^-\frac{1}{2} \div {}^-\frac{9}{24}$ 4. $\frac{3}{4} \cdot {}^-\frac{8}{9}$

5. ${}^-\frac{7}{8} \cdot {}^-4$ 6. $1\frac{2}{3} \div {}^-1\frac{2}{3}$ 7. ${}^-\frac{3}{5} \cdot \frac{9}{15}$ 8. ${}^-\frac{12}{13} \div {}^-\frac{1}{2}$

9. ${}^-\frac{7}{9} \cdot \frac{9}{11}$ 10. ${}^-1\frac{2}{3} \div {}^-3$ 11. $\frac{15}{19} \div {}^-\frac{2}{3}$ 12. ${}^-2\frac{6}{7} \cdot {}^-5$

13. ${}^-25 \div {}^-1.25$ 14. ${}^-6.7 \cdot 5.62$ 15. $12.9 \div {}^-12.9$

16. ${}^-4.16 \cdot 2.33$ 17. $229.9 \div {}^-22.99$ 18. ${}^-15.9 \cdot {}^-8.14$

If the number is rational, write it as a repeating or a terminating decimal. If it is irrational, estimate it to the nearest whole number.

1. $\sqrt{25}$ 2. ${}^-\frac{4}{5}$ 3. $\sqrt{10}$ 4. ${}^-\frac{10}{5}$ 5. $1\frac{2}{5}$

6. ${}^-\frac{6}{11}$ 7. $\sqrt{5}$ 8. $3\frac{2}{9}$ 9. $\sqrt{26}$ 10. ${}^-\frac{9}{2}$

11. $\sqrt{99}$ 12. ${}^-1\frac{1}{2}$ 13. ${}^-\frac{9}{17}$ 14. $2\frac{4}{9}$ 15. $\sqrt{45}$

16. ${}^-6\frac{8}{9}$ 17. $\sqrt{19}$ 18. $\frac{11}{4}$ 19. $\sqrt{81}$ 20. ${}^-\frac{21}{8}$

21. $\sqrt{144}$ 22. ${}^-\frac{3}{8}$ 23. $\sqrt{65}$ 24. ${}^-\frac{8}{23}$ 25. $\sqrt{1}$

Solve.

1. $2x + 6 = 28$
2. $9y - 15 = 21$
3. $4m + 6 = 34$
4. $9t - 9 = 36$

5. $\frac{1}{4}w + 5 = 25$
6. $7g - 13 = 29$
7. $\frac{c}{0.5} + 6 = 31$
8. $5c - \frac{1}{2} = 9\frac{1}{2}$

9. $\frac{p}{3} + 10 = 16$
10. $\frac{d}{2} + 13 = 25$
11. $\frac{z}{6} - 4 = 2$
12. $\frac{a}{9} - 4 = 4$

13. $0.25b - 11 = 4$
14. $0.05r + 5.75 = 10$
15. $\frac{r}{12} - 1.25 = 3$

16. $\frac{f}{-6} + 16 = 8$
17. $\frac{-h}{3} + 15 = 9$
18. $\frac{v}{-8} - 2 = {}^-9$

19. $\frac{1}{8}j + 5 = 10$
20. $1\frac{1}{4}l - 20 = 105$
21. $\frac{-d}{3} - 16 = {}^-24$

Solve and graph the inequality.

1. $m + 6 < 10$
2. $o + 10 > 19$
3. $x - 9 \le 4$
4. $z - 2 \ge 14$

5. $8d > 72$
6. $\frac{b}{7} > 3$
7. $\frac{a}{8} \ge 4$
8. $7q > 56$

9. $0.25g < 25$
10. $1.6s > 3.2$
11. $j + \frac{1}{4} \ne 2$
12. $\frac{y}{1.5} < 8$

13. $f - 9 \ne {}^-5$
14. $\frac{x}{\frac{1}{2}} \ge 4$
15. $p - 18 < {}^-9$
16. $\frac{n}{\frac{1}{3}} \le \frac{2}{3}$

17. $\frac{y}{8} < 4$
18. $\frac{-z}{-7} > 4$
19. $\frac{-r}{-11} \ne 2$
20. $\frac{1}{10}t < {}^-40$

Solve.

1. $3x + 2 < 5$
2. $7z - 4 \ge 2$
3. $8q + 12 \ne 19$
4. $14r - 70 \le 28$

5. $\frac{f}{10} - 8 > 12$
6. $\frac{d}{3} + 17 \ne 26$
7. $\frac{m}{12} - 42 \ne 6$
8. $\frac{k}{8} + 36 > 9$

9. $6.1n + 4 \ne 16.2$
10. $7.6c - 8.4 > 15.92$
11. $\frac{p}{9.1} - 7 < 16.8$

12. $\frac{j}{7.6} + 18.2 \ge 5.4$
13. $4e + \frac{3}{4} \ne 12\frac{1}{2}$
14. $\frac{2}{3}y - 8 \le 6$

15. $\frac{t}{14} - \frac{4}{7} > \frac{13}{14}$
16. $\frac{s}{5} + \frac{9}{11} > \frac{17}{33}$
17. $16u - {}^-4 > {}^-92$

18. $5v + 6 \le {}^-17$
19. $\frac{-q}{-2} - 10 \ne {}^-10$
20. $\frac{g}{7} + {}^-3 > {}^-14$

Chapter 9, page 317

For each set of data find the median, mode, and mean.

Set of data	Median	Mode	Mean
21, 23, 49, 18, 7, 21, 8	1. ■	2. ■	3. ■
37.2, 41.8, 29, 37.2, 46, 28.5	4. ■	5. ■	6. ■
$3\frac{1}{4}$, $1\frac{1}{2}$, $5\frac{2}{5}$, $3\frac{1}{8}$, $\frac{9}{10}$, $\frac{5}{8}$, $1\frac{3}{8}$	7. ■	8. ■	9. ■
2,192; 4,617; 3,147; 5,908	10. ■	11. ■	12. ■

Chapter 9, page 333

Find the number of permutations or combinations.

1. $_4P_2$ **2.** $_5P_2$ **3.** $_5P_3$ **4.** $_7P_3$

5. $_4P_3$ **6.** $_4C_3$ **7.** $_6C_3$ **8.** $_6P_4$

9. $_7C_3$ **10.** $_7C_5$ **11.** $_{12}P_5$ **12.** $_{10}C_5$

13. $_{14}C_6$ **14.** $_{20}P_5$ **15.** $_{11}C_9$ **16.** $_{15}C_{10}$

Solve.

17. How many numbers greater than 90,000 can be formed using each of the digits 5, 6, 7, 8, and 9 only once?

Chapter 11, page 401

For each right triangle, find the missing side, rounded to the nearest tenth. (HINT: Sketch the triangle.) $m\angle C = 90°$.

1. $a = 4$ cm, $b = 6.5$ cm   **2.** $a = 2.2$ m, $b = 3.5$ m

3. $a = 4$ km, $b = 4$ km   **4.** $a = 9.3$ mm, $b = 8.6$ mm

5. $a = 7$ cm, $c = 10.6$ cm   **6.** $b = 2$ m, $c = 7.2$ m

7. $a = 10$ in., $b = 12$ in.   **8.** $a = 5$ m, $c = 13$ m

9. $b = 2$ m, $c = \sqrt{5}$ m   **10.** $b = 2$ mm, $c = 3$ mm

Find the area of each square.

1. $s = 6$ cm   **2.** $s = 14$ m   **3.** $s = 7.5$ km   **4.** $s = 12.8$ dm

Find the area of each rectangle.

5. $l = 7$ m
$w = 5$ m

6. $l = 8.2$ cm
$w = 4.5$ cm

7. $l = 14.7$ mm
$w = 12.9$ mm

Find the area of each parallelogram.

8. $l = 9$ dm
$w = 4$ dm

9. $l = 22$ m
$w = 7.1$ m

10. $l = 23.2$ dam
$w = 5.7$ dam

Find the area of each triangle.

1. $b = 6$m
$h = 12$ m

2. $b = 7$ cm
$h = 6$ cm

3. $b = 11.9$ cm
$h = 3$ cm

4. $b = 14$ km
$h = 7.3$ km

5. $b = 6.9$ m
$h = 6.9$ m

6. $b = 31.8$ dm
$h = 28.4$ dm

Find the area of each trapezoid.

7. $b_1 = 9$ cm
$b_2 = 12$ cm
$h = 4$ cm

8. $b_1 = 15.6$ m
$b_2 = 7$ m
$h = 8$ m

9. $b_1 = 71$ mm
$b_2 = 42.8$ mm
$h = 66.9$ mm

Find the surface area of each cylinder. Use 3.14 for π, and round to the nearest tenth.

1. radius = 4 cm
height = 6 cm

2. radius = 12 m
height = 7 m

3. diameter = 28 mm
height = 106 mm

4. radius = 9.2 m
height = 17 m

5. diameter = 11.5 cm
height = 15.2 cm

6. diameter = 6.7 dm
height = 6.7 dm

Find the surface area of each cone. Use 3.14 for π, and round to the nearest tenth.

7. radius = 9 km
slant height = 2 km

8. radius = 7.5 m
slant height = 12 m

9. diameter = 37.8 mm
slant height = 105.2 mm

Find the volume of each rectangular prism. Round to the nearest tenth.

1. $\ell = 12$ cm, $w = 17$ cm, $h = 14$ cm

2. $\ell = 9.9$ m, $w = 21$ m, $h = 4.7$ m

Find the volume of each hexagonal prism. Round to the nearest tenth.

3. $B = 142$ km^2, $h = 7$ km

4. $B = 26.7$ m^2, $h = 31.4$ m

Find the volume of each pyramid. Round to the nearest tenth.

5. $B = 40$ cm^2, $h = 15$ cm

6. $h = 6.6$ mm, $B = 21.4$ mm^2

Solve for y, using $^-3$ and 4 as replacements for x.

1. $y = x - 5$

2. $y = 7 + x$

3. $y = 9x + 2$

4. $^-x + y = 17$

5. $y - 3x = 4$

6. $5x - 2y = 7$

Make a table of values for each equation. Use $^-2$, $^-1$, 0, and 3 as replacement values for x.

7. $y = 7x$

8. $y = 4x - 2$

9. $6x + 3y = 9$

For each equation, write the ordered pair that is *not* a solution.

10. $x + y = 8$ (0,8), (3,5), (2,9), (7,1)

11. $7x - 2y = 15$ $\left(2, \frac{-1}{2}\right)$, (5,10), $\left(4, 6\frac{1}{2}\right)$, $\left(0, 7\frac{1}{2}\right)$

Write *yes* if the relation is a function and *no* if it is not a function.

1. {(2,4), (3,5), (4,6), (5,7)}

2. {(7,13), (8,15), (9,17), (10,19)}

3. {(1,7), (1,8), (2,9), (3,10)}

4. {(1,11), (3,11), (5,11), (7,11)}

5. {(0,9), ($^-$1,18), (1,27), (0,36)}

6. {($^-$2, $^-$3), ($^-$4, $^-$5), ($^-$6, $^-$7), ($^-$8, $^-$9)}

MATH REASONING

Chapter 1

Logical Reasoning, pages 6–7

Using the Commutative and Associative Properties, regroup the numbers to find the sum by using mental math. Then find the sum.

1. $12 + 13 + 17 + 8$ **2.** $25 + 99 + 75 + 1$ **3.** $85 + 22 + 10 + 15$

Logical Reasoning, page 8

After more than two months of climbing, Sir Edmund Hillary and Tenzing Norgay became the first men to climb Mount Everest, the highest mountain in the world. The precise height of Mount Everest has been the subject of considerable debate. At various times in the past, it has been set at 29,002 ft by the British Government, 29,028 ft by the Indian Government, and 29,141 ft by wide, though unofficial, public usage. If you were reporting the approximate height of Mount Everest, what would you say it is?

Challenge, pages 22–23

Find the 4-digit number that satisfies all of these conditions.

- The number is less than 100 and greater than 90.
- If the number is rounded to the nearest whole number, the result is 94.
- The number's tenths digit is 2 less than its hundredths digit.
- If the number is rounded to the nearest tenth, the result is 93.6.

Chapter 1

Logical Reasoning, pages 26–27

Copy the star and the circled numbers on your paper. Write numbers in the blank circles so that each straight line has a sum of 4.0.

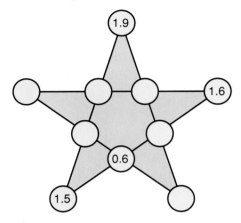

Logical Reasoning, pages 28–29

Suppose that the ⑥ key does not work on your calculator. Show how you might use the calculator to do these addition problems.

1. $355.9 + 34.6$

2. $1,624 + 126.4 + 821.64$

3. 36×37

4. $1,496 - 395$

Challenge, pages 30–31

Place plus or minus signs and decimal points between the digits, as necessary, to make the statements true.

Example: $4\ 2\ 1\ 7\ 6\ 3 = 21.83$

$$4.2 + 17.63 = 21.83$$

1. $7\ 5\ 8\ 4\ 9\ 3 = 3.54$

2. $2\ 1\ 5\ 0\ 7\ 5 = 17.2$

3. $6\ 3\ 8\ 2\ 7\ 9 = 50.3$

Chapter 2

Challenge, pages 52–53

"Messy Margie" created a puzzle square using operation signs that became unreadable inkblots. Can you help her fill in the correct signs? Copy the puzzle on your paper. Insert $+$, $-$, $\times$, or $\div$ in place of each inkblot to make the problems in each row and column correct.

8	•	3	•	2	=	12
•		•		•		•
5	•	2	•	9	=	12
•		•		•		•
9	•	2	•	6	=	12
=		=		=		=
12	•	12	•	12	=	36

Logical Reasoning, pages 56–57

During the first year that Brenda had her savings account, she received interest that equaled $0.0565 \times \$1,000$. The following year, the interest was $0.0548 \times \$1,100$. In which year did she receive more interest? What was the difference in the amounts of interest?

Logical Reasoning, pages 60–61

Look for a pattern as you complete Exercises 1–3. Use the pattern to complete Exercises 4–5.

1. $9 \times 8 = $ ■

2. $9 \times 8.8 = $ ■

3. $9 \times 88.8 = $ ■

4. $9 \times 888.8 = $ ■

5. $9 \times 8,888.8 = $ ■

Math Reasoning

Chapter 2

Logical Reasoning, pages 62–63

Bob wants to rent some camping equipment for a nine-day period. The equipment rental fee is $17.65 per day.

1. If Bob rents the equipment at this rate, how much will it cost for nine days?

2. Suppose he can pay a weekly rate of $110 and the daily rate for each additional day. Should he do this? Explain the reason for your answer.

Challenge, pages 64–65

Use the digits 1, 2, 3, 4, and 5 to complete the division problem.

$$\begin{array}{r} \blacksquare.\blacksquare\blacksquare \\ \blacksquare\blacksquare\overline{)51.68} \\ -\ \underline{\blacksquare\blacksquare} \\ 17 \end{array}$$

Challenge, pages 66–67

Place multiplication or division signs and decimal points between the digits to make the statement true. Exercise 1 is done for you.

1. 3 2 1 6 2 2 = 4.4   **2.** 3 8 0 5 2 = 3.8   **3.** 5 1 2 6 1 = 1
$32 \div 16 \times 2.2 = 4.4$

Math Reasoning

Chapter 3

Challenge, pages 82–83

Write the square roots and cube roots. Then use the code to discover
Jennifer's goal. Use the square root table on page 83 and the cube root
table on page 474.

$\sqrt{81}$ $\sqrt[3]{27}$

$\sqrt{49}$ $\sqrt[3]{64}$ $\sqrt[3]{512}$ $\sqrt{9}$ $\sqrt[3]{125}$ $\sqrt{16}$

$\sqrt{196}$ $\sqrt{121}$ $\sqrt[3]{27}$ $\sqrt{64}$ $\sqrt[3]{729}$ $\sqrt{9}$ $\sqrt[3]{216}$

3 = O	4 = E
5 = M	6 = R
7 = B	8 = C
9 = T	11 = D
14 = A	

Logical Reasoning, pages 88–89

The mathematician Christian Goldbach (1690–1764) stated that every
even number greater than 2 can be expressed as the sum of two prime
numbers.

$12 = 5 + 7$ $\qquad\qquad$ $8 = 5 + 3$

Show how each even number can be expressed as the sum of two prime
numbers.

1. 10 $\qquad$ **2.** 16 $\qquad$ **3.** 20 $\qquad$ **4.** 32 $\qquad$ **5.** 50

Logical Reasoning, pages 94–95

Solve.

1. Which is greater—the greatest
common factor of 16 and 55 or the
greatest common factor of 22 and
42?

2. The GCF of two numbers is 8. The
LCM of the numbers is 48. Both of
the numbers are less than 30. What
are the numbers?

Math Reasoning

Chapter 3

Logical Reasoning, pages 98–99

The number 4 can be expressed by $4 = 4 \times (4 - 4) + 4$ using four 4's and the rules for order of operations.

1. Express the number 1 using four 4's.

2. Express the number 2 using four 4's.

3. Express the number 5 using five 5's.

4. Express the number 6 using five 6's.

Visual Thinking, pages 106–107

The key to a code is at the right. Numbers are represented by the shapes of the lines they are within. For example, the number 3 is represented as ⌊.

1	2	3
4	5	6
7	8	9

Solve the following problems. Write each answer in code and as a number.

1. ⌈×☐=⌐☐

2. ⊓⌈⊔÷⌐=⊔⊔⌊

3. ⌋⌐⌐÷⌋⊔=⌋☐

4. ☐⌋⌋⌐⊓⌊⊓=☐⌐⌐⌐⌊

Visual Thinking, pages 110–111

Three small coin bags contain two coins each. One bag contains two dimes, another two nickels, and the third contains a nickel and a dime. Each bag is labeled 20¢, 10¢, or 15¢, but each is mislabeled. If you can remove only one coin, from which bag would you remove a coin to determine how all three bags should be labeled? Explain your answer.

15¢

10¢

20¢

Math Reasoning

Chapter 4

Visual Thinking, pages 120–121

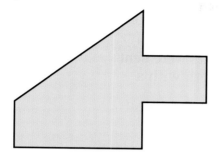

Copy this figure on your paper. Then divide the figure into two equal pieces by drawing two straight lines.

Challenge, pages 130–131

Eduardo needs to draw a line that is 6 in. long, but he does not have a ruler. He does have some sheets of notebook paper that are each $8\frac{1}{2}$ in. wide and 11 in. long. Describe how the notebook paper can be used to measure 6 in.

Challenge, pages 142–143

Copy the magic square on your paper. Complete the square so that the product of the numbers in each row, each column, and each diagonal is equal to 1.

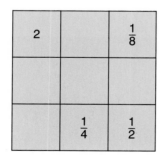

Chapter 4

Logical Reasoning, pages 148–149

Liechtenstein is the leading exporter of false teeth in the world. Assume that the manufacturers shipped out $36\frac{1}{2}$ million sets of teeth in a year. During that period, they averaged one defect in every 100 sets of teeth that were shipped. If shipments were sent out every day of the year, about how many sets of teeth with a defect would have been shipped on an average day?

Visual Thinking, pages 150–151

Trace or copy the points on your paper. Draw a horizontal or vertical straight line between the points that are equivalent quantities. You will end up spelling a good name for a European race car driver.

$\frac{4}{6}$ $0.\overline{6}$ 0.125 $\frac{1}{2}$ $\frac{1}{8}$ 0.25 0.375 $\frac{1}{4}$ $\frac{3}{4}$ $\frac{15}{20}$

•   •   •   •   •   •   •   •   •   •

•   •   •   •   •   •

$\frac{2}{3}$ $\frac{8}{12}$ 0.5 $\frac{3}{8}$ $\frac{6}{8}$ 0.75

Challenge, pages 152–153

On the small imaginary island of Nore, the residents were Bores and Snorers. Four-tenths of the Bores were Snorers. One-tenth of the Snorers were Bores. Six Bores were not Snorers. How many Snorers were there?

Math Reasoning

Chapter 5

Visual Thinking, pages 166–167

A treasure-hunting expedition will launch a robotic submersible at Point A. Its intended search pattern follows.

- travel east for 100 m
- travel south for 10 m
- travel west for 0.2 km
- travel east for $\frac{1}{100}$ km

Then it will surface. Ignoring any effects of ocean currents, how far should the submersible be from Point A when it surfaces?

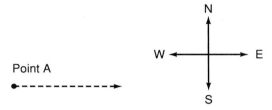

Challenge, pages 168–169

The Martin family has gone camping. In their provisions is a package of freeze-dried spaghetti that they want to prepare for dinner. It requires 200 mL of water. The problem is that the Martins forgot to bring their measuring utensils. They do, however, have a 1-L soft-drink bottle and an empty 400-mL soup can. How can they measure 200 mL of water by using these two items?

Challenge, pages 174–175

The tallest tree in the world is the Howard Libbey redwood in California. It is 362 feet tall. By comparison, the tallest human being in modern times was Robert Wadlow. He was 8 feet, 11 inches tall. How many "Wadlows" standing on top of one another would it take to reach the top of the Howard Libbey tree?

Chapter 5

Visual Thinking, pages 182–183

Use a clock to help you answer these questions.

1. What time is it when the number of hours after noon is 2 more than the number of hours before midnight?

2. What time is it when the number of hours after noon is 4 less than the number of hours before midnight?

Logical Reasoning, pages 186–187

Grace has 20 minutes to get to the airport before her plane departs. The airport is 20 miles away from her home. She drives at a speed of 30 miles per hour for the first 10 miles. Will she get to the airport before her plane leaves?

Challenge, pages 188–189

This table shows the relationship between temperatures in degrees Celsius (°C) and degrees Fahrenheit (°F).

°C	5	10	15	20	25	30	32.5
°F	41	50	59	68	■	■	■

1. Copy and complete the table.

2. This rule can be used to convert °C to °F.
   Use the table above to complete the rule.

$$°F = 1.8 \times °C + ■$$

Math Reasoning

Chapter 6

Challenge, pages 200–201

There are red, blue, and green marbles in a bag. The ratio of the number of blue marbles to the number of green marbles is $2:3$. The ratio of the number of red marbles to the number of blue marbles is $6:5$. The ratio of the number of red marbles to the number of green marbles is $4:5$. There are fewer than 40 marbles in the bag. Find the total number of marbles in the bag.

Challenge, pages 210–211

1. When the percent for the fraction $\frac{1}{5}$ is known, what is a shortcut for finding the percent for $\frac{3}{5}$? Show that your answer is correct.

2. When the fraction $\frac{a}{b}$ is expressed as a percent, the percent is greater than 100. How does the value of a compare with value of b?

Visual Thinking, pages 212–213

Use the figure to answer the questions.

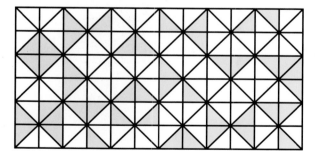

1. What percent of the figure is shaded?

2. How many more triangles would have to be shaded in order for 50% of the figure to be shaded?

3. How many triangles would have to have the shading removed in order for 25% of the figure to be shaded?

Chapter 6

Logical Reasoning, pages 216–217

Bob wants to borrow $250 from his brother Karl. Karl is willing to loan Bob the money if Bob repays the money in 5 equal monthly payments. Bob wants to repay the money by paying 20% of the outstanding balance each month until the debt is paid.

1. How much would Bob pay each month according to Karl's payment schedule?

2. How much would Bob pay the first month according to his own schedule?

3. At the end of 3 months, how much would Bob still owe if he uses his own payment schedule?

4. Using his own payment schedule, will Bob ever pay off the loan?

Challenge, pages 220–221

Jessica sold 40% of her baseball cards. Then she gave away 25% of the cards she had left. Now she has 18 cards. How many did she have before she began selling them and giving them away?

Visual Thinking, pages 226–227

Show how you can decrease the number of small, identical squares in the figure by 30% by removing 5 of the 24 sticks.

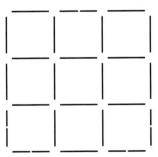

Math Reasoning

Chapter 7

Logical Reasoning, pages 240–241

Solve.

1. If t is a positive number, is ^-t positive or negative?

2. If ^-t is a positive number, is t positive or negative?

3. If t is a negative number, is ^-t positive or negative?

4. If ^-t is a negative number, is t positive or negative?

5. If ^-t is a positive number, is $^-(^-t)$ positive or negative?

6. If ^-t is a negative number, is $^-(^-t)$ positive or negative?

Challenge, pages 244–245

Find the values for the variables in the magic square. The sum of each row, each column, and each diagonal should be the same.

$^-3$	t	$^-5$
x	$^-2$	b
s	a	$^-1$

Challenge, pages 252–253

Solve.

1. $(^-4 \times 6 + 18 - {}^-11) \times (^-2 - {}^-13)$

2. $(^-9 \times {}^-8) \div (4 \times {}^-2)$

3. $12 - {}^-8 \times 2 + 20 \div {}^-4 + {}^-9$

Math Reasoning

Chapter 7

Challenge, pages 258–259

John, Penny, and Julian played a game. They each picked a rational number in the form of a fraction. The person who picked the number that was not the least and not the greatest was the winner. Here are the numbers they picked.

John: $^-\frac{73}{58}$ Penny: $^-\frac{50}{33}$ Julian: $^-\frac{91}{72}$

Use a calculator to determine the winner of the game.

Logical Reasoning, pages 264–265

Jean tells Mary that she has 2 rational numbers in mind. One of these, she says, is 5 times as large as the other, and their sum is $\frac{3}{4}$. What are the two rational numbers?

Challenge, pages 268–269

On graph paper, draw a real-number plane. Graph each pair of points and connect them with a straight line. When you finish, you will discover the names of Sue's best friends.

1. $(^-9,1), (^-9,5)$ **2.** $(^-9,3), (^-7,5)$ **3.** $(^-9,3), (^-7,1)$

4. $(^-5,1), (^-5,5)$ **5.** $(^-3,1), (^-3,5)$ **6.** $(^-3,5), (^-1,3)$

7. $(^-1,3), (1,5)$ **8.** $(1,5), (1,1)$ **9.** $(^-9,^-3), (^-7,^-3)$

10. $(^-8,^-3), (^-8,^-7)$ **11.** $(^-8,^-7), (^-10,^-7)$ **12.** $(^-10,^-7), (^-10,^-6)$

13. $(^-5,^-3), (^-5,^-7)$ **14.** $(^-5,^-3), (^-3,^-3)$ **15.** $(^-3,^-3), (^-3,^-7)$

16. $(^-1,^-3), (1,^-5)$ **17.** $(1,^-5), (3,^-3)$ **18.** $(1,^-5), (1,^-7)$

Chapter 8

Challenge, pages 280–281

Evaluate each expression for $n = 3$ in this magic square. What is the sum of each row, each column, and each diagonal?

$7 - n$	$6n$	$n + 5$
$n + 11$	$n + 7$	$2n$
$4n$	$n - 1$	$19 - n$

Logical Reasoning, pages 282–283

1. If $3x = 6$, then $6x = $ ■.

2. If $8t = 12$, then $4t = $ ■.

3. If $x + 5 = 9$, then $2x + 10 = $ ■.

4. If $b - 3 = 15$, then $3b - 9 = $ ■.

5. If $\frac{n}{3} = 10$, then $\frac{n}{6} = $ ■.

6. If $\frac{p}{4} = {}^-8$, then $\frac{p}{2} = $ ■.

Logical Reasoning, pages 284–285

Find a pattern. Use the pattern to find the value of each variable.

1. $1 \times 8 + n = 9$

2. $12 \times 8 + x = 98$

3. $123 \times 8 + p = 987$

4. $1{,}234 \times 8 + s = 9{,}876$

5. $12{,}345 \times 8 + t = 98{,}765$

6. $y \times 8 + w = 987{,}654$

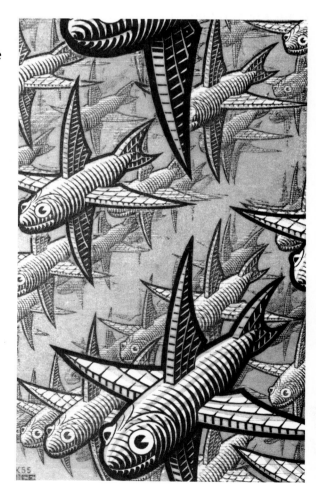

Math Reasoning

Chapter 8

Challenge, pages 292–293

Tim gave his friend this problem.

I am thinking of five different whole numbers that have a sum less than 16. The sum of the squares of these whole numbers is less than 56. Find

1. the numbers that solve the problem.
2. the sum of the numbers.
3. the sum of the squares of the numbers.

Logical Reasoning, pages 294–295

Complete. Write $<$ or $>$.

1. If $a < 5$, then $a + 6 \bullet 5 + 6$.

2. If $c > 10$, then $c - 6 \bullet 10 - 6$.

3. If $a < b$ and $b < c$, then $a \bullet c$.

4. If $r > s$ and $s > t$, then $r \bullet t$.

Visual Thinking, pages 300–301

The graph shows the solution of an inequality.

$$\xleftarrow{\quad\begin{array}{ccccccccccc} | & | & | & | & | & | & | & | & | & | & | \\ -5 & -4 & -3 & -2 & -1 & 0 & 1 & 2 & 3 & 4 & 5 \end{array}\quad}\rightarrow$$

1. What numbers are solutions of the inequality?

2. What numbers are not solutions of the inequality?

Math Reasoning

Chapter 9

Logical Reasoning, pages 316–317

The mean of 5 one-digit numbers is 4.8.

The median of the 5 numbers is 5.

The mode of the 5 numbers is 2.

What are the numbers?

Visual Thinking, pages 322–323

A driver is sitting in a car at a stoplight, waiting for the light to turn green. The light turns green and the driver accelerates the car. Which of the following graphs fits the situation?

a.

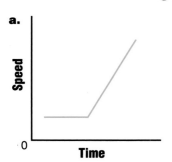

b.

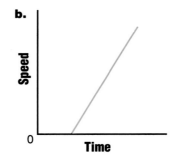

c.

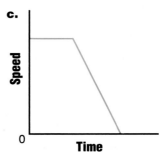

Challenge, pages 328–329

The license plates in a certain state have 2 letters and a 4-digit number.

1. How many different license plates can be made if any letter can be used and any of the digits 0 to 9 can be used?

2. How many different license plates can be made if the four-digit number has to be an odd number?

Chapter 9

Challenge, pages 332–333

You and 7 friends are at a restaurant. You are going to sit together at a table that seats 8.

1. In how many ways can your group be seated?

2. Suppose that it takes 10 seconds to change the seating order. How many seconds would it take to sit in all the possible seating arrangements?

3. How many days would it take to sit in all the possible seating arrangements?

Logical Reasoning, pages 334–335

Jason types 3 letters and addresses 3 envelopes. Before he places the letters in the envelopes, he accidentally drops all of them on the floor. He picks up the letters and envelopes and without looking, inserts each letter into an envelope. What is the probability that each letter was inserted into the correct envelope?

Challenge, pages 336–337

A cube with sides numbered 1 to 6 is tossed 6 times. The number 5 is rolled on the first toss. What is the probability of getting the number 5 on the next 5 tosses?

Math Reasoning

Chapter 10

Logical Reasoning, pages 356–357

A reflex angle is an angle with a measure between 180° and 360°.

1. What degree measure would you use on a protractor to draw a reflex angle of 200°?

2. Draw a reflex angle of 320°.

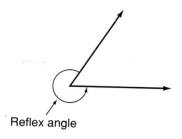

Reflex angle

Challenge, pages 360–361

Use a protractor to draw angles of 30° and 45°. Then use the angles you drew, a compass, and a straightedge to construct the following angles.

1. 60°   2. 90°   3. 75°   4. 120°

Visual Thinking, pages 366–367

How many triangles are in this figure?

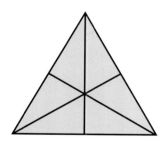

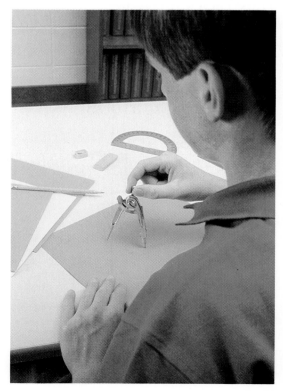

Math Reasoning

Chapter 10

Challenge, pages 368–369

Use polygons to solve the following problems.

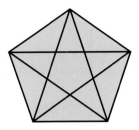

1. Each of 5 persons talked to the other 4 by telephone. How many calls were made?

2. Each of 8 persons talked to the other 7 by telephone. How many calls were made?

Visual Thinking, pages 380–381

Make four copies of this trapezoid. Then show how you can use the four congruent trapezoids to make a larger similar trapezoid.

Visual Thinking, pages 382–383

Trace each of the figures. Then write the word that results when the figure is reflected over the given line.

Math Reasoning

Chapter 11

Visual Thinking, pages 398–399

Use graph paper to draw six different polygons, each having a perimeter of 12 units. Make sure that the length of each side is a whole number. One polygon is drawn for you.

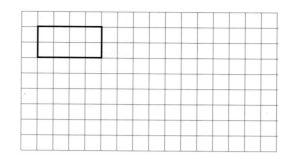

Challenge, pages 404–405

The diameter of each wheel on Robbie's bicycle is 28 inches.

1. How many feet will Robbie ride if each wheel makes 100 revolutions? Use $\frac{22}{7}$ for π.

2. How many revolutions will each wheel make if Robbie rides his bicycle 1 mile?

Visual Thinking, pages 410–411

You have seen that the area of a trapezoid can be $\frac{1}{2}$ the area of a certain parallelogram. Copy the trapezoid at the right. Show how the area of the trapezoid can be the sum of the areas of two triangles. Then find the area of the trapezoid.

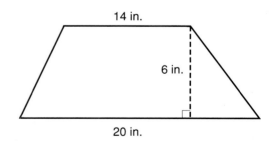

14 in.

6 in.

20 in.

Chapter 11

Challenge, pages 412–413

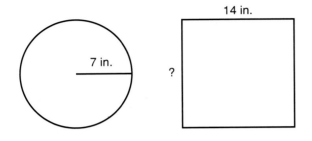

1. A circle has a radius of 7 in. The area of a rectangle that has a length of 14 in. is the same as the area of the circle. Find the width of the rectangle. Use $\frac{22}{7}$ for π.

2. Compare the area of a circle having a diameter of 14 in. with the area of a square with sides of 14 in. Use $\frac{22}{7}$ for π.

Visual Thinking, pages 426–427

Draw a picture of how this solid figure would look from

1. the top.

2. the side.

3. the front.

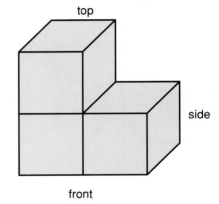

Logical Reasoning, pages 426–427

These two cans of peaches have the same unit price (price per ounce). The small can costs $1.28. What is the cost of the large can?

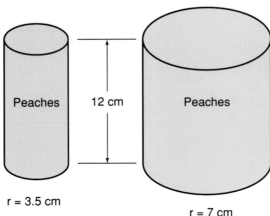

Math Reasoning

Chapter 12

Logical Reasoning, pages 440–441

Look for a pattern in the ordered pairs. Then complete the equation for the table of values.

1. $y = \blacksquare$

x	y
3	6
2	4
1	2
0	0
⁻1	⁻2
⁻2	⁻4

2. $y = \blacksquare + \blacksquare$

x	y
3	7
2	6
1	5
0	4
⁻1	3
⁻2	2

3. $y = \blacksquare - 3$

x	y
3	3
2	1
1	⁻1
0	⁻3
⁻1	⁻5
⁻2	⁻7

Visual Thinking, pages 446–447

Without graphing any points, describe the graph of each relation.

1. all the points that have the same x coordinate

2. all the points that have the same y coordinate

3. all the points that have 0 as the x coordinate

4. all the points that have 0 as the y coordinate

Challenge, pages 450–451

1. Graph the equation $x + y = 6$ using 6, 3, 0, and ⁻3 as replacements for x.

2. On the same set of axes, graph the equation $x - y = 6$. Use the same values for x that you used for $x + y = 6$.

3. How do the y values found for $x + y = 6$ compare to the y values found for $x - y = 6$?

4. Where do the equations $x + y = 6$ and $x - y = 6$ intersect? Describe the relationship between the graphs of the equations.

Chapter 12

Challenge, pages 452–453

Graph each system of equations. Tell how many solutions there are for each system.

1. $y = x + 2$
$2y = 2x + 4$

2. $y = x + 10$
$y = x - 1$

Logical Reasoning, pages 454–455

What two numbers are not on the graph described by these clues?

Clue 1: $|x| > 5$ **Clue 2:** $|x| < 5$

Challenge, pages 456–457

Graph the system of inequalities on the same coordinate axes to find the solution. Describe the solution of the system.

$y > x + 1$
$y > {}^{-}x - 1$

Math Reasoning

TABLE OF MEASURES

TIME

1 minute (min) = 60 seconds (s)
1 hour (h) = 60 minutes
1 day (d) = 24 hours
1 week (wk) = 7 days
1 year (y) = 12 months (mo)
1 year = 52 weeks
1 year = 365 days
1 century = 100 years

METRIC UNITS

LENGTH

1 millimeter (mm) = 0.001 meter (m)
1 centimeter (cm) = 0.01 meter
1 decimeter (dm) = 0.1 meter
1 dekameter (dam) = 10 meters
1 hectometer (hm) = 100 meters
1 kilometer (km) = 1,000 meters

MASS

1 milligram (mg) = 0.001 gram (g)
1 centigram (cg) = 0.01 gram
1 decigram (dg) = 0.1 gram
1 dekagram (dek) = 10 grams
1 hectogram (hg) = 100 grams
1 kilogram (kg) = 1,000 grams
1 metric ton (t) = 1,000 kilograms

CAPACITY

1 milliliter (mL) = 0.001 liter (L)
1 centiliter (cL) = 0.01 liter
1 deciliter (dL) = 0.1 liter
1 dekaliter (daL) = 10 liters
1 hectoliter (hL) = 100 liters
1 kiloliter (kL) = 1,000 liters

VOLUME/CAPACITY/ MASS FOR WATER

1 cubic centimeter (cm^3) $\rightarrow$ 1 milliliter $\rightarrow$ 1 gram
1,000 cubic centimeters $\rightarrow$ 1 liter $\rightarrow$ 1 kilogram

TEMPERATURE

0° Celsius (C) . . . . Water freezes
100° Celsius (C) . . . . Water boils

CUSTOMARY UNITS

LENGTH

1 foot (ft) = 12 inches (in.)
1 yard (yd) = 36 inches
1 yard = 3 feet
1 mile (mi) = 5,280 feet
1 mile = 1,760 yards

WEIGHT

1 pound (lb) = 16 ounces (oz)
1 ton (T) = 2,000 pounds

CAPACITY

1 cup (c) = 8 fluid ounces (fl oz)
1 pint (pt) = 2 cups
1 quart (qt) = 2 pints
1 quart = 4 cups
1 gallon (gal) = 4 quarts

TEMPERATURE

32° Fahrenheit (F) . . . . Water freezes
212° Fahrenheit (F) . . . . Water boils

FORMULAS

PERIMETER	Polygon	$P = $ sum of the sides
	Rectangle	$P = 2l + 2w$
	Square	$P = 4s$
CIRCUMFERENCE	Circle	$C = 2\pi r$, or $C = \pi d$
AREA	Circle	$A = \pi r^2$
	Parallelogram	$A = bh$
	Rectangle	$A = lw$
	Square	$A = s^2$
	Trapezoid	$A = \frac{1}{2}(b_1 + b_2)h$
	Triangle	$A = \frac{1}{2}bh$
SURFACE AREA	Cone	$S = \pi r^2 + \pi rl$
	Cylinder	$S = 2\pi rh + 2\pi r^2$
	Rectangular prism	$S = 2lw + 2lh + 2wh$
	Square pyramid	$S = s^2 + 4\left(\frac{1}{2}bh\right)$
VOLUME	Cone	$V = \frac{1}{3}Bh$, or $V = \frac{1}{3}\pi r^2 h$
	Cube	$V = e^3$
	Cylinder	$V = Bh$, or $V = \pi r^2 h$
	Rectangular prism	$V = lwh$
	Square pyramid	$V = \frac{1}{3}Bh$
	Triangular prism	$V = \frac{1}{2}Bh$
OTHER	Diameter	$d = 2r$
	Pythagorean rule	$c^2 = a^2 + b^2$
TRIGONOMETRIC RATIOS	sine of $\angle A$	$\sin A = \frac{a}{c}$
	cosine of $\angle A$	$\cos A = \frac{b}{c}$
	tangent of $\angle A$	$\tan A = \frac{a}{b}$
CONSUMER	Distance traveled	$d = rt$
	Interest (simple)	$I = prt$

SYMBOLS

$<$	is less than	$^-4$	negative 4	$m\angle A$	measure of $\angle A$
$>$	is greater than	$\lvert^-5\rvert$	absolute value of negative 5	$\triangle ABC$	triangle ABC
$\leq$	is less than or equal to			$\perp$	is perpendicular to
$\geq$	is greater than or equal to	5^{-4}	5 to the negative fourth power	$\parallel$	is parallel to
$\neq$	is not equal to			$\cong$	is congruent to
$\approx$	is approximately equal to	$\%$	percent	$\leftrightarrow$	corresponds to
$2 \cdot 3$	2 times 3	$3 : 5$	the ratio 3 to 5	$\sim$	is similar to
$4 \div 2$	4 divided by 2	\$4/h	the rate \$4 per hour	π	pi (about 3.14)
5^4	5 to the fourth power	@	at a certain amount each	$(5,3)$	the ordered pair 5,3
$0.\overline{36}$	0.363636 . . .	$^\circ$	degree	$P(5)$	the probability of the outcome 5
$\sqrt{}$	square root	$\cdot A$	point A		
$\sqrt[3]{}$	cube root	$\overleftrightarrow{AB}$	line AB	$3!$	$3 \cdot 2 \cdot 1$
		$\overrightarrow{AB}$	ray AB	$_7P_4$	$7 \cdot 6 \cdot 5 \cdot 4$
		$\overline{AB}$	line segment AB	$_5C_2$	$\frac{5 \cdot 4}{2 \cdot 1}$
		$\angle ABC$	angle ABC		

GLOSSARY

Absolute value of a number An integer's distance from zero. The distance is never negative.

Examples: $|^-4| = 4$

$\qquad |4| = 4$

Acute angle An angle whose measure is less than 90°.

Adjacent angles Two angles that have a common vertex, a common ray, and no common interior points.

Example: $\angle WXY$ and $\angle YXZ$ are adjacent angles.

Alternate interior angles In the figure below, $\angle j$ and $\angle m$ are alternate interior angles, and so are $\angle k$ and $\angle l$.

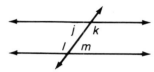

Angle Two rays that have a common endpoint. The endpoint is called the vertex of the angle.

Arc Part of a circle.

Associative Property of Addition The grouping of the addends does not change the sum. For any numbers a, b, and c, $a + (b + c) = (a + b) + c$.

Associative Property of Multiplication The grouping of the factors does not change the product. For all numbers a, b, and c, $(a \times b) \times c = a \times (b \times c)$.

BASIC A computer-programming language.

Basic counting principle If a first event has x outcomes and a second event has y outcomes, then the first event followed by the second event has $x \cdot y$ outcomes.

Binary A base-two system of numeration.

Bisect To divide into two congruent parts.

Bit Binary digit, 0 or 1.

Byte String of bits whose length is the smallest accessible unit in computer memory.

Central angle An angle whose vertex is at the center of a circle.

Chord A line segment whose endpoints are on a circle.

Circumference The perimeter of a circle.

Common factor A factor of two or more numbers. Example: 6 is a common factor of 12 and 18.

Common multiple A multiple of two or more numbers.

Example: 15 is a common multiple of 3 and 5.

Commutative Property of Addition The order of the addends does not change the sum. For any numbers a and b, $a + b = b + a$.

Commutative Property of Multiplication The order of the factors does not change the products. For any numbers a and b, $a \times b = b \times a$.

Complementary angles Two angles whose measures have a sum of 90°.

Complex fraction A fraction in which the numerator or denominator or both have a fraction or a mixed number as a term.

Example: $\dfrac{\frac{1}{4}}{3\frac{2}{3}}$

Composite number A number greater than 1 that has more than two factors.

Example: 12 is a composite number.
Factors: 1, 2, 3, 4, 6, 12

Congruent figures Figures that have the same size and shape.

Coordinates Numbers matched with points on a line. Number pairs matched with points on a plane.

Corresponding angles In the figure below, pairs of corresponding angles are $\angle p$ and $\angle t$, $\angle q$ and $\angle u$, $\angle r$ and $\angle v$, $\angle s$ and $\angle w$.

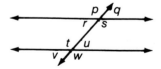

Corresponding parts In the triangles below, pairs of corresponding angles are $\angle U$ and $\angle X$, $\angle V$ and $\angle Z$, $\angle W$ and $\angle Y$. The corresponding sides are $\overline{ZY}$ and $\overline{VW}$, $\overline{VU}$ and $\overline{ZX}$, $\overline{UW}$ and $\overline{XY}$.

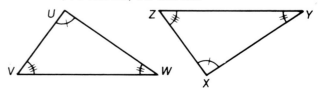

Cosine A trigonometric ratio, $\cos \angle A =$

$\dfrac{\text{length of side adjacent } \angle A}{\text{length of hypotenuse}}$, or $\dfrac{b}{c}$.

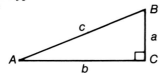

Cross products In the equation $\dfrac{w}{x} = \dfrac{y}{z}$, the products wz and xy are called cross products. Two ratios $\dfrac{w}{x}$ and $\dfrac{y}{z}$ are equal if, and only if, the product of the means $(x \cdot y)$ equals the product of the extremes $(w \cdot z)$.

Data A collection of facts that have not been processed into information.

Dependent events Events such that the outcome of the first event affects the probabilities of the outcome of the second event.

Diagonal A line segment other than a side that joins two vertices of a polygon.

Diameter A chord that passes through the center of a circle and has the length of two radii.

Discount Amount deducted from the marked price.

Distributive Property of Multiplication To multiply a sum by a number, you can multiply each addend by the number and then add the products. For any numbers a, b, and c, $a \times (b + c) = (a \times b) + (a \times c)$.

Endpoint A point at an end of a line segment or a ray.

Equally likely outcomes Outcomes that have the same chance of occurring.

Equation A number sentence that shows equality.

Examples: $5 + 6 = 11$, $4 + x = 31$

Equivalent fractions Fractions that name the same number, but use different terms.

Expanded form A representation of a number as a sum of multiples of powers of 10.

Exponent An exponent shows how many times a number or base is used as a factor.

Example: $8^4 = 8 \times 8 \times 8 \times 8$: 4 is the exponent.

Expression (algebraic) Symbols or the combination of symbols, such as numerals, letters, operation symbols, and parentheses, used to name a number.

Extremes In a proportion, the first and fourth terms are the extremes.

Example: $\dfrac{3}{4} = \dfrac{9}{12}$

3 and 12 are the extremes.

Factorial If $x > 0$, then x factorial is written $x!$ and means to multiply all the consecutive numbers from x to 1.

Example: $7! = 7 \times 6 \times 5 \times 4 \times 3 \times 2 \times 1 = 5{,}040$

FOR/NEXT A two-part BASIC command that makes a computer count and loop.

Fraction The quotient of two whole numbers; $x \div y = \dfrac{x}{y}$, $y \neq 0$. In the fraction $\dfrac{x}{y}$, x is called the *numerator* and y is called the *denominator*.

Frequency The number of times an item appears in a list of data.

GOTO A BASIC command that makes a computer go to the line number that follows.

Graph of an equation A picture of all solutions to an equation.

Greatest common factor The largest common factor of two or more numbers.

Example: For 12 and 20, 4 is the greatest common factor.

Greatest possible error One half the smallest unit of measurement used.

Histogram A bar graph that shows the frequencies of intervals of data.

HOME A BASIC command that tells a computer to move the cursor to the start of the first line on a CRT screen.

Hypotenuse In a right triangle, the side opposite the right angle.

IF/THEN A BASIC command that tells a computer to make a decision.

Example: IF N < 7 THEN 40 tells a computer to go to line 40 if the number in storage place N is less than 7; otherwise it is to go to the next line.

Independent events Events in which the outcome of the second event does not depend on the outcome of the first event.

Inequality A number sentence that uses a symbol such as $>$, $<$, $\leq$, $\geq$, or $\neq$.

Example: $x - 7 < 8$, $x + 14 > 21$, $6x \neq 18$

Infinite Continues without end; endless.

INPUT A BASIC command that tells a computer to wait for input and then to store the input in its memory.

INT In a BASIC computer program, INT(X) makes a computer cut off all the digits of the number X to the right of the decimal point.

Integers The whole-numbers and their opposites.

Examples: 0, 1, ⁻1, 2, ⁻2

Interest Payment for use of money.

Intersecting lines Lines that meet at one common point.

Inverse operations Operations that undo each other. Addition and subtraction as well as multiplication and division are inverse operations.

Example: $17 + 31 = 48$ and $48 - 31 = 17$
$36 \div 9 = 4$ and $4 \times 9 = 36$

Irrational number A number that cannot be written as a terminating or repeating decimal.

Examples: $0.161661666\ldots$

Least Common Denominator (LCD) The least common multiple of the denominators of two or more fractions.

Least Common Multiple The smallest nonzero common multiple of two or more numbers.

Example: For 8 and 12, 24 is the least common multiple.

Legs of a right triangle The perpendicular sides of a right triangle.

LET A BASIC command that tells a computer to store information in its memory.

Line A straight path of points that continues infinitely in two directions.

Line segment Part of a line with two endpoints.

Loop A command that causes a computer to go back to an earlier step in the program and repeat it.

Mean The sum of the numbers divided by the number of addends.

Example: The mean for 22, 33, 19, 8 is 20.5.

Means In a proportion, the second and third terms are the means.

Example: $\dfrac{2}{3} = \dfrac{8}{12}$
3 and 8 are the means.

Median When a set of numbers are arranged in order, the middle number or the average of the middle two numbers.

Examples: The median for 56, 73, 77, 84, 94 is 77.
The median for 38, 42, 48, 51 is 45.

Midpoint A point that separates a line segment into two congruent segments.

Mixed number The sum of a whole number and a fraction.

Mode The number occurring most often in a set of data.

Multiple Any product that has the number as a factor.

NEW A command that tells some computers to erase any programs or information stored in their memories.

Obtuse angle An angle whose measure is greater than 90° and less than 180°.

Opposite A number that is an equal distance from zero as another number, but in the opposite direction.

Example: $8 + {}^-8 = 0$
8 is the opposite of ⁻8.
⁻8 is the opposite of 8.

Ordered pair A pair of numbers (x,y) arranged in order so that x is first and y is second, usually used to describe a location in a coordinate plane.

Order of operations When there is more than one operation used; first multiply as indicated by exponents; second, multiply and divide from left to right in order; third, add and subtract from left to right in order, and; fourth, if parentheses are used, simplify within the parentheses first, using the first three rules.

Origin The point assigned to 0 on the number line or the point where the x- and y-axes intersect.

Outcome Any possible result in a probability experiment.

Parallel lines Two or more lines in a plane that do not intersect.

Parallelogram A quadrilateral in which each pair of opposite sides is parallel and congruent.

Percent Ratio of a number to 100, using the % sign.

Example: 13% means 13 of 100.

Permutation An ordered arrangement of some or all of the elements in a set. For example, there are 6 permutations of 2 letters from the 3 letters X, Y, and Z. The permutations are XY, XZ, YX, YZ, ZX, and ZY.

Perpendicular bisector A line that bisects a segment and is perpendicular to it.

Perpendicular lines Two lines that intersect to form right angles.

Pi (π) The number that is the ratio of the circumference of any circle to the length of a diameter of that circle. Approximations for π are 3.14 and $\dfrac{22}{7}$.

Plane A flat surface that continues infinitely in all directions.

Polygon A closed plane figure made up of three or more line segments joined at their endpoints.

Polyhedron A solid whose faces are polygons.

Power of a number A number found by multiplying another number by itself one or more times.

Example: 64 is a power of 4 because $64 = 4 \times 4 \times 4$.

Prime factorization A factorization in which all factors are prime numbers.

Example: $40 = 2 \times 2 \times 2 \times 5$

Prime number Any whole number greater than 1, whose only factors are itself and 1.

Principal The amount of money borrowed or saved on which interest is paid.

Prism A polyhedron that has two congruent bases in parallel planes and whose other faces are parallelograms.

Probability The number of favorable outcomes divided by the number of all possible outcomes. A number from 0 to 1.

Program Step-by-step instruction that directs the computer to perform operations.

Property of One The product of a number multiplied by 1, and the quotient of a number divided by 1 are the number itself. For any number a, $a \times 1 = a$, $a \div 1 = a$.

Proportion An equation that shows two equal ratios.

Example: $\frac{5}{10} = \frac{1}{2}$

Pythagorean Rule In any right triangle, the sum of the squares of the lengths of the legs is equal to the square of the length of the hypotenuse. $a^2 + b^2 = c^2$.

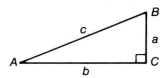

Quadrants The x-axis and y-axis divide the real-number plane into four parts called quadrants.

Quadrilateral A polygon that has four sides.

Radius A line segment from a point on a circle to the center of the circle.

RAM The part of the memory of a computer where the user can store information and programs. *RAM* stands for "Random Access Memory." This part of the memory is erased when NEW is entered.

Range The difference between the largest and the smallest number in a set of data.

Rate A ratio that compares different kinds of units.

Ratio Comparison of two numbers by division.

Rational number A number that can be written as the ratio of two integers, where the denominator is not zero.

Ray A part of a line that has one endpoint and continues infinitely in one direction.

Real numbers The set of rational and irrational numbers, whole numbers, and integers.

Reciprocals Two numbers whose product is 1.

Example: $\frac{7}{8}$ and $\frac{8}{7}$ are reciprocals of each other, because $\frac{7}{8} \times \frac{8}{7} = 1$.

Reflection A motion in which a geometric figure is flipped about a line.

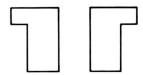

Regular polygon A polygon with congruent sides and congruent angles.

Relatively prime Two numbers whose only common factor is 1.

Example: 4 and 9 are relatively prime.

Repeating decimal A decimal in which one or more digits repeat endlessly.

Examples: $0.\overline{6}$ and $0.\overline{18}$

Right angle An angle that measures 90°.

Rotation A motion in which a geometric figure is turned about a fixed point.

Sample A segment of a population selected for study to predict characteristics of the whole.

Sample space A set of possible outcomes of an experiment.

Example: If a coin is flipped, the sample space is (H, T)

Scattergram A graph of ordered pairs of points showing positive, negative or no correlation between two sets of data.

Scientific notation Expressing a number as a product of two factors. One factor is a power of 10. The other factor is greater than or equal to 1 and less than 10.

Example: 4.72×10^5 is scientific notation for 472,000.

Significant digits The digits used in a measurement that tell the number of times the unit is contained in the measurement.

Similar polygons Two polygons that have the same shape, but not necessarily the same size.

Simplest form A fraction is in simplest form when its numerator and denominator are relatively prime.

Sine A trigonometric ratio. $\sin \angle A =$ $\dfrac{\text{length of side opposite } \angle A}{\text{length of hypotenuse}}$, or $\dfrac{a}{c}$.

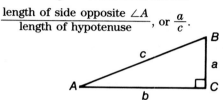

Skew lines Lines in space that are not parallel and do not intersect.

Slant height The distance along a face of a pyramid or a cone from the vertex to the base.

Solution A replacement of a variable that makes a number sentence true.

Example: $3x - 12 = 9$ 7 is the solution.
$x > 17$ 18, 19, 20, 21, . . . are solutions.

Square root A number when multiplied by itself gives the original number.

Example: 6 is the square root of 36.

Straight angle An angle whose measure is 180°.

String variables In BASIC, locations in a computer that store data of any kind. A letter and the $ symbol form string variables. $A\$$, $B\$$, etc.

Supplementary angles Two angles whose measures have a sum of 180°.

Symmetry The correspondence of parts on opposite sides of a point, line, or plane.

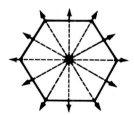

Tangent A trigonometric ratio. $\tan \angle A =$ $\dfrac{\text{length of side opposite } \angle A}{\text{length of side adjacent to } \angle A}$

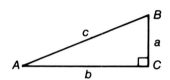

Terminating decimal A decimal that does not repeat.

Example: 0.25

Translation A translation moves a geometric figure along a line to a new position.

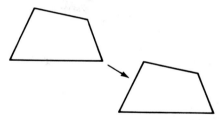

Transversal A line intersecting two or more lines at a different point on each line. $\overleftrightarrow{CD}$ is a transversal.

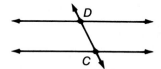

Tree diagram A diagram used to find the total number of outcomes in a probability experiment.

Unit price The ratio of the total price to the number of units.

Variable A letter or other symbol that may represent a number.

Vertex A point common to two rays of an angle, two sides of a polygon, or two edges of a solid figure.

Vertical angles Congruent angles formed by two intersecting lines. $\angle 3$ and $\angle 4$ form a pair of vertical angles.

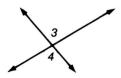

Whole number Any of these numbers: 0, 1, 2, 3, 4, 5, 6, . . .

Zero Property for Addition and Subtraction The sum or difference when zero is added to or subtracted from a number is the number. For any number a, $a + 0 = a$ and $a - 0 = a$.

Zero Property for Multiplication The product of a number and 0 is 0. For any number a, $a \times 0 = 0$.

Index

A 0
B 1
C 2
D 3
E 4
F 5
G 6
H 7
I 8
J 9